THE STUDY OF *Abnormal Behavior*

SELECTED READINGS

THE STUDY OF

Abnormal Behavior

SELECTED READINGS

MELVIN ZAX, Ph.D.
ASSOCIATE PROFESSOR OF PSYCHOLOGY
UNIVERSITY OF ROCHESTER

AND

GEORGE STRICKER, Ph.D.
ASSISTANT PROFESSOR OF PSYCHOLOGY
ADELPHI COLLEGE

The Macmillan Company, New York
Collier-Macmillan Limited, London

First Printing

Library of Congress catalog card number: 64-18423

THE MACMILLAN COMPANY, NEW YORK
COLLIER-MACMILLAN CANADA, LTD., TORONTO, ONTARIO

Printed in the United States of America

Preface

The instructive merits of primary source material and its motivating appeal to students is unchallenged. To place a reasonable selection of such material in a convenient, handy format begets a favored teaching aid, the book of readings. No single collection of source writing can satisfy all needs, obviously, but a book which supplies the kind of close view of empirical literature that is missing from most textbooks can prove at once useful and illuminating.

In selecting our content from the literature of abnormal behavior, we sought to compile articles which reflected the breadth of research in this area. Simultaneously, we attempted to avoid imbalance among the various theoretical positions. It was our further aim to balance the theoretical and the empirical, and thus our choices range from the very well-known to younger, less well-established researchers and pathfinders. The overriding criterion for every choice was that it represent a significant contribution to student understanding of its particular area. Regretfully, some important but overly sophisticated papers had to be eliminated.

The book is organized in three major units, each with an introductory section explaining chapter division. Each chapter is preceded by brief commentary which should place the individual articles in an appropriate context. The first unit covers significant theoretical problems of current concern in the study of abnormal behavior. It is hoped the student will derive from these discussions adequate background to fruitfully entertain the content of the field, and progress to the second unit with a working appreciation of the many problems involved. The next section offers a variety of approaches to psychopathology, the core of any consideration of abnormal psychology. The third and final section represents a separate and extensive treatment of psychotherapy, reinforcing its intimate relationship with psychopathology.

Acknowledgments are more directly appreciated in a book of readings than in any other work, and we wish to express our gratitude to the authors and publishers who were kind enough to allow us to reprint their works. Specific acknowledgements are included in the first page of each article. Special thanks are due Miss Carole Light and Mrs. Maythorne Winterkorn, who assisted in the assembly of the manuscript. Our wives, Joanne Zax and Joan Stricker, allowed this book to be completed, a measure of their charity. Praise and honor to them for sympathy and optimism.

Melvin Zax
George Stricker

Contents

SECTION I

GENERAL ISSUES IN ABNORMAL PSYCHOLOGY   1

1. Defining Normality and Abnormality   3

A CRITIQUE OF CULTURAL AND STATISTICAL CONCEPTS OF
ABNORMALITY
    HENRY J. WEGROCKI   3

TOWARD A CONCEPT OF THE NORMAL PERSONALITY
    EDWARD JOSEPH SHOBEN, JR.   12

2. Psychiatric Diagnosis   22

THE PROBLEM OF PSYCHIATRIC NOSOLOGY
    THOMAS S. SZASZ   22

PSYCHIATRIC DIAGNOSIS: A CRITIQUE
    EDWARD ZIGLER AND LESLIE PHILLIPS   32

3. Approaches to Diagnosis   46

WANTED—A GOOD COOKBOOK
    PAUL E. MEEHL   46

CLINICAL AND STATISTICAL PREDICTION: A REFORMULATION AND
SOME NEW DATA
    ROBERT R. HOLT   58

4. Social Psychiatry   73

SOCIAL STRUCTURE AND PSYCHIATRIC DISORDERS
    F. C. REDLICH, A. B. HOLLINGSHEAD, B. H. ROBERTS,
    H. A. ROBINSON, L. Z. FREEDMAN, AND J. K. MYERS   73

A REVIEW OF "MENTAL HEALTH IN THE METROPOLIS: MIDTOWN
MANHATTAN STUDY"
    ERNEST M. GRUENBERG   80

SECTION II

PSYCHOPATHOLOGY   93

5. Psychoneurosis   95

LEARNING THEORY AND THE NEUROTIC PARADOX
O. H. MOWRER   95

THE ASSESSMENT OF ANXIETY IN PSYCHOLOGICAL
EXPERIMENTATION
GEORGE C. ROSENWALD   128

EXPRESSIVE BEHAVIOR AND LANGUAGE PATTERNS
MARIA LORENZ   137

6. The Psychoses   153

THE PROCESS-REACTIVE CLASSIFICATIONS OF SCHIZOPHRENIA
WILLIAM G. HERRON   154

SPECIAL LOGIC OF SCHIZOPHRENIA AND OTHER TYPES OF AUTISTIC
THOUGHT
SILVANO ARIETI   167

AN INTERACTIONAL DESCRIPTION OF SCHIZOPHRENIA
JAY HALEY   183

CONTRADICTORY PARENTAL EXPECTATIONS IN SCHIZOPHRENIA
YI-CHUANG   196

AN INTENSIVE STUDY OF TWELVE CASES OF MANIC-DEPRESSIVE
PSYCHOSIS
MABEL BLAKE COHEN, GRACE BAKER, ROBERT A. COHEN,
FRIEDA FROMM-REICHMANN, AND EDITH V. WEIGERT   213

SCHIZOPHRENIA, PARANOID STATES, AND RELATED CONDITIONS
HARRY STACK SULLIVAN   232

7. Personality Disorders   243

ADULT CHARACTER STRUCTURE
GERALD S. BLUM   244

ANTISOCIAL PERSONALITIES
HERVEY CLECKLEY   249

PHASES OF ALCOHOL ADDICTION
E. M. JELLINEK   262

8. Psychosomatic Disorders   273

FUNDAMENTAL CONCEPTS OF PSYCHOSOMATIC RESEARCH
FRANZ ALEXANDER   273

ULCERS IN "EXECUTIVE" MONKEYS
JOSEPH V. BRADY   281

RELATIONSHIP OF SEPARATION AND DEPRESSION TO DISEASE
ARTHUR H. SCHMALE, JR.   286

9. Children's Disorders   304

EIGHT AGES OF MAN
ERIK H. ERIKSON   304

MATERNAL DEPRIVATION: TOWARD AN EMPIRICAL AND
CONCEPTUAL RE-EVALUATION
LEON J. YARROW   320

EARLY INFANTILE AUTISM, 1943–55
LEON EISENBERG AND LEO KANNER   350

10. Organic Syndromes   359

THE EFFECT OF BRAIN DAMAGE ON THE PERSONALITY
KURT GOLDSTEIN   359

FEEBLE-MINDEDNESS VERSUS INTELLECTUAL RETARDATION
EDGAR A. DOLL   376

SECTION III

PSYCHOTHERAPY   381

11. Approaches to Psychotherapy   383

A CRITIQUE OF THE PRESENT STATUS OF THE PSYCHOTHERAPIES
ROBERT P. KNIGHT   383

A PROCESS CONCEPTION OF PSYCHOTHERAPY
CARL R. ROGERS   393

A THEORETICAL APPROACH TO PSYCHOTHERAPY AS PERSONALITY
MODIFICATION
EDWARD JOSEPH SHOBEN, JR.   405

12. The Effects of Psychotherapy   417

THE EFFECTS OF PSYCHOTHERAPY: AN EVALUATION
H. J. EYSENCK   417

A Transvaluation of Psychotherapy: A Reply to Hans
Eysenck
   Saul Rosenzweig   424

The Effects of Psychotherapy: A Reply
   H. J. Eysenck   432

Calumet
   Saul Rosenzweig   434

Measurement of Personality and Behavior Changes
Following Psychotherapy
   Melvin Zax and Armin Klein   435

THE STUDY OF *Abnormal Behavior*

SELECTED READINGS

Section 1

GENERAL ISSUES IN

ABNORMAL PSYCHOLOGY

As IN ALL FIELDS there are numerous general issues of far-reaching consequence which workers in abnormal psychology have found reason to debate over the years. This section includes a sampling of these. Some have only become prominent in recent years, while others have been the cause of concern over a much longer period. It will be noted further that while in some cases the questions raised seem specifically relevant to the domain of abnormal psychology, in other cases their generality takes them well beyond the subject matter of this area. If the editors have made good choices, the reader should be left with many more questions than answers after a careful and thoughtful reading of the material in this section. Definitive answers are not easily provided in these speculative realms, and there was no intention to provide anything more than a sampling of a variety of representative views.

1. DEFINING NORMALITY AND ABNORMALITY

AN ISSUE with both long-range philosophical implications and shorter range practical ones is the question of how to define normality and abnormality. Various positions have been taken on this matter. One may hold that the striving for certain highly valued absolutes is the essence of what it is to be normal. On the other hand, cultural relativists argue that ideals are pertinent only to particular cultural groups and that there are no archetypical truths in the Platonist sense. Other students feel that the issue cannot be resolved by studying behavior, which varies widely, but instead by attending to underlying motivations. The papers which follow represent a sampling of the range to be found among the many approaches to this problem. Shoben views normality and good adjustment as a striving for certain specified goals which have value for him. Wegrocki recognizes that what is symptomatic behavior for one culture may be quite normal in another but stresses the importance of understanding the function served by a sample of behavior before labeling it as either pathological or normal.

A Critique of Cultural and Statistical Concepts of Abnormality

HENRY J. WEGROCKI
WORCESTER STATE HOSPITAL

One of the most significant contributions to a proper orientation and envisagement

Reprinted from the *Journal of Abnormal & Social Psychology*, 34(1939), 166–178, with the permission of the American Psychological Association and the author.

of human behavior has been the body of data coming in the past few decades from the field of ethnological research. Human behavior had so long been seen in terms of the categories of Western civilization that a critical evaluation of cultures other than our own could not help exercising a salutary effect on the ever-present tendency to view a situation in terms of familiar classifications. The achievement of a realization that the categories of social structure and function are ever plastic and dynamic, that they differ with varying cultures and that one culture cannot be interpreted or evaluated in terms of the categories of another, represents as tremendous an advance in the study of social behavior as did the brilliant insight of Freud in the field of depth psychology.

Wundt (20) to some extent, but especially Boas (3), have emphasized this approach continuously. One may say that most of the "mistakes" of earlier anthropologists have been due to the tendency of seeing the features of other cultures simply in terms of the categories of Western civilization and forming, consequently, a distorted impression of those features, whether they relate to religion, marriage, or some other aspect of social life.

In connection with this modern ethnological conception of the relativity of interpretations and standards, there has arisen the problem of whether the standard of what constitutes abnormality is a relative or an absolute one. Foley (10) infers from the ethnological material at hand that abnormality is a relative concept and criticizes Benedict (1), who seems to present evidence for the "statistical or relativity theory" yet "at times appears inconsistent in seeking for an absolute and universal criterion of abnormality." Briefly, the evidence from Benedict can be subsumed under three headings: (a) behavior considered abnormal in our culture but normal in other societal configurations; (b) types of abnormalities not occurring in Western civilization; and (c) behavior considered normal in our society but abnormal in others.

(a) Of "our" type of abnormal behavior considered normal in other cul-

tures, Benedict gives, as an example, that of the Northwest Coast Indians whom Boas has studied at first hand. "All existence is seen in this culture in terms of an insult-complex." This complex is not only condoned but culturally reënforced. When the self-esteem and prestige of the chief is injured, he either arranges a "potlatch" ceremony or goes headhunting. The injury to his prestige is a function of the prevalent insult-complex. Almost anything is an insult. It may be the victory of a rival chief in a potlatch competition; it may be the accidental death of a wife, or a score of other situations, all of which are interpreted as having a reference to the individual.

If, on the other hand, he has been bested in competition with a rival chief, he will arrange a potlatch ceremony in which he gives away property to his rival, at the same time declaiming a recitative in which there is "an uncensored self-glorification and ridicule of the opponent that is hard to equal outside of the monologue of the abnormal"; "either of the two mentioned above procedures are meaningless without the fundamental paranoid reading of bereavement."

Among other "abnormal" traits which are an integral part of some culture patterns, ethnological literature mentions the Dobuans (11), who exhibit an "unnatural" degree of fear and suspicion; the Polynesians, who regard their chief as tabu to touch, allegedly because of a prevalent "défense de toucher" neurosis; the Plains Indians with their religiously colored visual and auditory hallucinations; the Yogis with their trance states; and the frequent institutionalizations of homosexuality, whether in the religions of different cultures (e.g., shamans of North Siberia or Borneo) or in their social structures (e.g., the berdache of American Indian tribes or the homosexual youth of Grecian-Spartan antiquity).

(b) The second argument in favor of the cultural envisagement of abnormality is the existence of "styles" of abnormalities which presumably do not occur in our Western type of cultures. The "arctic hysteria" noted by Czaplicka (8) and its tropical correlative "lâttah" (Clifford, 6; 7) with their picture of echolalia, echopraxia and uncontrolled expression of obscenities, as well as the "amok" seizure of the Malayan world, are given as examples.

(c) Of normal behavior in our culture considered abnormal in others Benedict mentions as most conspicuous the role of personal initiative and drive in our own as compared with the Zuñi culture. Among the Zuñi Indians, for example, "the individual with undisguised initiative and greater drive than his fellows is apt to be branded a witch and hung up by his thumbs." Similarly, what seems to us a perfectly normal pattern of behavior—acquisitiveness, for example—would be looked upon by the potlatch celebrants as just a little "queer." For them, possession of property is secondary to the prestige they acquire when they distribute it.

These are then, briefly, the bases for the assertion that abnormality is a relative concept, differing from culture to culture, that no particular efficacy attaches to the expression and that it gains meaning only in terms of the social milieu in which it is considered.

The question of what are the differentia of normality and abnormality is of course the crux of the problem. Is the concept of abnormality culturally defined? Is that which is *regarded* as abnormal or normal in a particular culture the *only* criterion for calling a behavior pattern such? Foley, for whom abnormality is a purely statistical concept, would answer in a positive manner and points to Benedict's example of the Northwest Coast Indians who institutionalize "paranoia." Let us, however, consider this "institutionalization of paranoia," as well as some of the other bits of evidence, critically.

Is it not stretching the point to call the Indians' megalomaniac activities and beliefs delusions in the sense that the paranoiac in the psychopathic institution has his beliefs called delusions? Macfie Campbell (5) states that "the delusions of the ill-balanced and the beliefs of the orthodox are more closely akin than is usually recognized," and we cannot separate the two as sharply as we would wish to do. The abnormal delusion proper is, however, an attempt of the personality to deal with a conflict-producing situation, and the delusion "like fever, becomes an attempt by nature at cure." The patient's delusion is an internal resolution of a problem; it is his way of meeting the intolerable situation. That is why it is abnormal. It represents a spontaneous protective device of the personality, something which is not learned. It is a crystallization of something which hitherto had been prepotent. The individual's personality thereafter refracts and reflects in terms of a distorted slant.

The Haida chief, upon the death of a member of his family, also experiences a certain tension. He resolves this tension, however, in a way which is not only socially sanctioned but socially determined. His reaction is not something spontaneous arising out of the nuclear substrate of his instinctive life. It is not a crystallization in a certain direction of some previously unrealized protective potentialities of the psyche. His reaction is pre-determined socially. Since his milieu expects that reaction of him, he acts upon that expectation when the situation arises. Of course it is possible that historically the behavior may have had and must have had some spontaneous protective significance—most likely imbedded deeply in a web of primitive beliefs about magic practices. Yet the modern Alaskan chief, unlike his distant prototype, has no conflicts of doubt about the likelihood that malignant forces have caused the death of some member of his family; he *knows,* and he acts upon that knowledge by venting his emotions. There is no permanent change in his personality when a tension-producing situation arises. Emotions are aroused and appeased with no change in the personality profile.

In the personality of one who is labelled "abnormal" this change is, however, to be found. There is always "the way he was before" and "the way he is now," regardless of the fact that a present symptomatological picture had its roots in a prepotent substrate which would make for a particular personality outline. This is not true of the Haida chief, in whom the "delusions" of reference and grandeur are externally imposed patterns. A Northwest Coast Indian, if given the opportunity for a naturalistic investigation of the situations that provoke his "paranoid" reactions—as, for example, through an education—could unlearn his previous emotional habits or at the least modify them. He is capable of insight; the true paranoiac is usually beyond it. The latter, if he kills the person who he thinks is persecuting him, only temporarily resolves his difficulty; the Indian chief who kills another family "to avenge the insult of his wife's death" achieves a permanent affective equilibration with regard to that incident. His prestige restored, he once more enjoys his self-respect. The Haida defends imagined assaults against his personal integrity only when some violent extra-personal event occurs. The paranoid psychotic defends himself against imagined assaults even though there is no objective evidence of any.

The point that the writer would then emphasize is that the delusions of the psychotic and the delusions of the Northwest Coast Indian cannot by any means be equated. Mechanisms like the conviction of grandeur are abnormal not by virtue of unique, abnormal qualia but by virtue of their *function in the total economy of the personality.* The true paranoiac reaction represents a *choice of the abnormal;* the reaction of the Haida chief

represents no such choice—there is but one path for him to follow. If one of the chief's men showed paranoid symptoms by proclaiming that *he* really was the chief of the tribe and that his lawful place was being usurped, the institutionalization of paranoid symptoms within that culture would not, I am sure, prevent the rest of the tribe from thinking him abnormal.

Fundamentally the same criticism might be applied to the "défense de toucher" neurosis supposedly exemplified by the Polynesian tabu on touching the chief. Here, as in paranoia, we must consider whether the mechanism is a cultural habit reënforced by emotional associations or whether it is a true morbid reaction. Obviously it is the former. Thus by reason of that fact it *is not* abnormal. As in the paranoia of the Haida, there is no choice here and consequently no conflict. If a person is brought up with the idea that to touch the chief means death, his acting upon that idea in adulthood is not a neurosis but simply a habit. There is, in other words, the genetic aspect to true abnormality which cannot be evaded but which is overlooked when we speak of "abnormal" symptoms. The explanation of the delusion of persecution of the Dobu is of course subject to the same criticism, which would hold likewise for trances, visions, the hearing of voices and hysterical seizures. When these are simply culturally reënforced pattern-suggestions, they are not abnormal in the true sense of the word. When the Plains Indian by a rigid physical regimen of exhaustion and fatigue plus a liberal dose of suggestion achieves a vision, that achievement is not an abnormal reaction in the same sense that the visual hallucination of the psychotic is.

A similar example presented as an argument for the cultural definition of abnormality is the supposed institutionalization of homosexuality among different cultures. The difficulty with all discussions of this enormously complex topic is the lack of agreement among investigators as to the sense in which the homosexual is abnormal. Obviously, homosexuality is not the same type of morbid mental reaction as paranoia; in fact, it is not a morbid mental reaction at all. The abnormality of homosexuality exists at a different level; it is social and biological rather than psychological.* Homosexuality as an abnormal form of behavior cannot be spoken of in the same sense in which one speaks of visual and auditory hallucinations or grandiose delusions. Sex inversion is rather a statistical type of abnormality. It represents extreme deviations from the norm and makes for the non-conformity which engenders social antagonism and ostracism in certain societies. We are not justified, then, in saying that certain cultures institutionalize this abnormality; because when we call homosexuality an abnormality in the same sense in which we speak of a delusion as abnormal, we are misusing the term and being inconsistent about its application.

The second point of view from which the cultural definition is sometimes argued is that there occur among different cultures abnormalities which are peculiar to them, as, for example, "arctic hysteria," "amok," "lâttah" *et al*. The untenability of this hypothesis becomes evident when a little analytic insight is applied to the phenomena considered. In his masterly analysis of the lâttah reaction, Van Loon (19) has also, the writer thinks, given a good explanation of "arctic hysteria." "Lâttah," he writes, "is chiefly a woman's complaint. The symptoms appear in consequence of a fright or some other sudden emotion; the startled patient screams" and exhibits echola-

* By this it is meant that homosexuality is not a compromise symptom due to a conflict, as is the case with paranoid manifestations. Whatever abnormality attaches to it is a secondary function due to the conflicts it creates in a social milieu. In short, it creates conflicts; it is not created by them. Only in those cases where it is used as an escape mechanism can it truly be called abnormal.

lia, echopraxia, shouting of obscenities and a strong feeling of fear and timidity. "The immediate cause of becoming lâttah the patients report to be a dream of a highly sexual nature which ends in the waking up of the dreamer with a start. The waking up is here a substitute for the dream activity, protecting the dreamer's consciousness against the repressed complex." The same analysis might be applied to "arctic hysteria," which seems to show all the lâttah symptoms, although the occurrence of a sudden waking from sleep as the beginning of the complaint is nowhere reported.

The amok type of seizure, Van Loon explains, is due to hallucinations of being attacked by men or animals and seems to be confined to men. Clifford (7), on the other hand, considers amok from a genetic standpoint as having a background of anger, grudge, excitement and mental irritation, what the Malay calls "sâkit hâti" (sickness of the liver). "A Malay loses something he values, his father dies, he has a quarrel—any of these things cause him 'sickness of the liver.' The state of feeling which drives the European to suicide makes the Malay go amok." In the heat of the moment "he may strike his father, and the hatred of self which results, causes him to long for death and to seek it in the only way which occurs to a Malay, viz. by running amok." The psychoanalyst with his theories of the introjective process in melancholia would doubtless find "amok" a fertile field for interesting speculative analogies.

From the above discussion it is evident that the various "unique types of mental disorder" probably would yield readily to an analysis in terms of the categories of psychopathology. The mental disturbance can, to be sure, be understood only in terms of the cultural and social pattern within which it occurs, but the form that it does take is a secondary function of the abnormality. Only in this sense does culture condition abnormality.

The paranoid reaction can occur in almost any culture, but the form that it takes is culturally modifiable. Although the psychotic can feel himself persecuted in almost any culture, in the one the persecutor may be the sorcerer, in another a usurping chief, and in still another the President of the United States.

The third argument for the cultural definition of abnormality is one which infers that inasmuch as traits considered normal in our society are considered abnormal in other cultures, abnormality can be looked upon as simply that form of behavior which a group considers aberrant.

As previously mentioned with reference to homosexuality, the term "abnormality" cannot with exactitude be applied to *all* those forms of behavior which fail to meet with social sanction. That would be making the term meaningless. The same criticism might be applied to this third argument. There is no element of internal conflict in the Zuñi, for instance, who, feeling full of energy, gives vent to that energy. His behavior is aberrant because it conflicts with the prevailing pattern. That, however, *does not* constitute abnormality. Such a Zuñi is not abnormal; he is delinquent (13). He is maladjusted to the demands of his culture and comes into conflict with his group, not because he adheres to a different standard but because he violates the group standards which are also his own (to paraphrase Mead). Edwards (9) pointed out this very frequent confusion concerning abnormality when he differentiated four standard types of individuals: "The average individual is the fictitious individual who ranks at the midpoint in all distributions of test results. The normal individual is one who is integrated, healthy and without any great variation from the average. The adjusted individual is one who is reasonably well-fitted into his environment and to its demands. The effective individual is one who, whether he is adjusted or normal, accomplishes his purposes."

From the above criticisms we can readily see that a relativity or statistical theory of abnormality which argues from the ethnological material at hand cannot stand a close analysis. From Benedict's writings one might get the impression that she also, like Foley, believes that what is abnormal depends simply on whether or not it is regarded as such by the greater majority of individuals in a specific culture. In various parts of her book (2) though, as well as in her articles, there are statements which run counter to any such belief. That is what Foley had in mind when he stated that Benedict seemed "inconsistent in seeking for an absolute and universal criterion of abnormality." In a private communication, Benedict explains this seeming paradox as follows. "In 1930–1931 when I wrote the article you refer to and the bulk of the book, writers in abnormal psychology constantly confused adequate personal adjustment and certain fixed symptoms. I wanted to break down the confusion, to show that interculturally adequate functioning and fixed symptoms could not be equated." When Benedict showed that the Northwest Coast Indians exhibited paranoid-like symptoms, she did not wish to prove that what the psychopathologist would call abnormal has no universal validity, but rather that, in spite of the fact the Northwest Coast Indians acted *like* paranoids, they were actually well-adjusted and "adult" individuals. What she was really arguing against was the confusion between fixed symptoms and adequate personal adjustment.

There is, of course, one way in which culture *does* determine abnormality and that is in the number of possible conflicts it can present to its component individuals. (In this sense "determine" has, however, a different meaning from that used above.) In a civilization like that of Samoa, for example, there is a minimum of possible aberrant behavior because of the rarity of situations which can produce conflicts in individuals. Even there, however, as Mead points out (13), Christianity with its introduction of a different set of standards is bringing to the islands that choice which is the fore-runner of conflict and neurosis. A similar source of abnormality is the destruction of native culture and the production of new stresses. Profound depression and the absence of the will-to-live are among some of the abnormalities produced (15). McDougall (12) suggests that there may be temperamental differences in ability to adapt oneself to varying environments. He mentions, for example, the American Indian as being unadaptable because of his introverted disposition, as opposed to the care-free adaptable Negro with his extrovert temperament. Seligman (17) voices the same opinion when he speaks of the extroverted Papuan and the intro-verted Malayan.

Benedict speculates that possibly the aberrant may represent "that arc of hu-man capacities that is not capitalized in his culture" and that "the misfit is one whose disposition is not capitalized in his culture." She concludes that "the problem of understanding abnormal hu-man behavior in any absolute sense in-dependent of causal factors is still far in the future." "When data are available in psychiatry, this minimum definition of abnormal human tendencies will be prob-ably quite unlike our culturally condi-tioned, highly elaborated psychoses such as those described, e.g., under the terms schizophrenic and manic-depressive." Keeping away from any committal to a relativity theory of abnormality, she is criticized therefore by Foley (10) for whom, "it is obvious that deviation im-plies relative variability of behavior; the responses of the individual must be con-sidered in relation to the responses of other individuals." For Foley, therefore,

deviation from normative mean and ab-normality are synonymous. In that sense, then, abnormality is for him a statistical concept.

There are, however, many objections to this aspect of the statistico-relative for-mulation. The most important one is probably the fact that a statistical theory considers only the actual observable be-havior of an individual without delving into its meaning. Thus an erroneous iden-tification is established between behavior patterns which are similar but do not have the same causal background. For example, the paranoid behavior of the schizophrenic and the "paranoid" behav-ior of the Northwest Coast Indian are equated; because the latter does not repre-sent a deviation from the norm of that culture's behavior pattern while the for-mer does, they are accepted as substantiat-ing the statistical relativity theory. Of course we may arbitrarily define *abnor-mality* in such a way that it will mean the same as *deviation;* if, however, we proceed from an empirical point of view, it is obvious that we are not justified in equating such abnormalities as the psy-choneuroses, the psychoses, sex inversion and amentia, and in speaking of them as deviations from a norm.

A statistical norm implies a graduated scale in which the items can be ranged on the basis of the possession of a "more" or "less" of a certain property. In that sense we can see that only sex inversion and amentia can be spoken of as devia-tions from a norm, inasmuch as it would have some meaning to speak of a "more" or "less" of development of cortical neu-rones or a "more" or "less" of a sex-determining hormone. It would, how-ever, have only a qualitative significance if we spoke of one person's being "more" deluded than another or "less" paranoid. In this sense, therefore, we are not justi-fied in speaking of abnormality as a sta-tistical concept. There are rather certain abnormalities which, because of their nature, can be ranged on graduated scales and others which, because of a different substrate, cannot be similarly measured. A proximate graduation scale similar to one used in attitude testing can of course be utilized, but its use is bound up with all the prejudice that subjective judgments embody when topics of wide personal opinion-variance are considered. Besides, there is no real basis for comparative evaluation. Should, for example, a paranoid trait such as the conviction of persecution, be measured by judges with respect to the degree in which it inhibits the satisfactory functioning of the total personality and causes personal unhappiness, or with respect to the degree in which it interferes with an adequate adjustment to the social group and creates opposition within the environment? Should the frequency with which it manifests itself in life situations be the determining criterion, or the intensity with which it is adhered to? Finally, should the degree of insight a person has into it be the standard? The bases for judging the "more" or "less" of a paranoid trait are, as is obvious, very divergent. No single criterion is any more justifiable than any other. A "paranoid scale" would, therefore, be of slight operational significance.

Skaggs (18) was aware of this difficulty when he said: "It is the writer's view that abnormality is, of necessity, a qualitative and not a quantitative concept at the present time. While definitions of abnormality which involve statistical norms are commendable in their aim, the soundness of such definitions appears to be questionable."

Realizing further that only confusion results when we try to generalize about different abnormalities, he even suggests that "the terms sub-normal and super-normal be kept strictly apart from the term 'abnormality.'" Bridges (4) places all abnormalities not of a sub-normal or super-normal type in the category of the "para-normal," a group which, for

Skaggs, is really the only one deserving of the name "abnormal." Because this group cannot be quantitatively ranged it is small surprise that, for Skaggs, the normative definition of abnormality as a lack of integration and balance of the total personality seems the most logical one.

Of the three types of possible definitions of abnormality mentioned by Morgan—(1) the normative, (2) the pathological, and (3) the statistical (15)—we can see that when we take all those types of behavior which are referred to as abnormal, there will be some which will fall more readily into one category, others which will more easily fit into another.* Thus all the symptoms associated with the psychoneuroses seem best defined by a normative approach which arbitrarily postulates, on the basis of the best psychiatric opinion, a theoretical integrated balanced personality, wide deviations from which would be looked upon as "abnormal." The functional psychoses also fit into this group, shading, however, into the pathological where the organic psychoses, behavior disturbances due to cerebral lesions or malfunctionings, and extreme amentias belong; the statistical can really claim only the less decidedly pathological aments and those sex-inverts where the presumption of constitutional involvement is strong.

The confusion arises, of course, from subsuming different types of abnormalities under one heading "abnormality" and speaking of them as if they were homogeneous entities. Obviously abnormal behavior is *called* abnormal because it deviates from the behavior of the general group. It is not, however, the *fact* of deviation which makes it abnormal but its causal background. That is why the

* It might be remarked that these three types are not equivalent logically for the statistical and normative answer to the question: "What kind of behavior should we *call* abnormal?" while the pathological, in reality, says: "We grant that this bit of behavior is abnormal, but *why* is it abnormal?"

hallucinations of the Plains Indians are not abnormal, while those of the schizophrenic are. It is not the *fact* of social sanction in Plains Indian society which makes that bit of behavior normal, but the fact that it does not have the background of a symptomatic resolution of an inner conflict such as produces that phenomenon in the schizophrenic. The "abnormal" behavior of the Indian is analogous to the behavior of the psychotic *but not homologous*. Just because it is analogous, the confusion has arisen of identifying the two.

If, therefore, behavior anomalies which are at bottom constitutionally or pathologically conditioned be excluded or subsumed as a different group under the category of the non-normal, we could state the quintessence of abnormality (Bridges' "para-normality") as *the tendency to choose a type of reaction which represents an escape from a conflict-producing situation instead of a facing of the problem*.* An essential element in this type of problem-resolution is that the conflict does not seem to be on a conscious level, so that the strange bit of behavior resulting is looked upon as an abnormal intruder and, at least in its incipient stage, is felt as something which is not ego-determined.† Inasmuch as pathological and, above all, constitutional factors cannot be partialled out in the

* Sublimation would not fit into this category because, as Alexander states, "the process represents a legitimate activity directed outwards, with an aim lying outside of the personality, and, secondly, it has a social quality. It is a normal modification of impulses not adapted to reality." "In contrast, the neurotic supplants outwardly directed activity by bodily changes which have a purely subjective significance, or by commonplace activities which do not essentially get beyond the bounds of the personality, or by purely psychological quantities of imaginative activity." (Healy, Bronner and Bowers. *The structure and meaning of psychoanalysis,* 251.)

† In a letter commenting upon the above, Benedict writes: "I couldn't use this definition in 1931—I have always felt that the final answer must be in these terms."

aetiology of a behavior anomaly, however, the above definition has only an ideal value of slight practical significance.‡

It does clarify though, to some extent, the confusion which arises from labelling any bit of behavior "abnormal." It is obvious, for example, that masturbation *per se* is not abnormal and represents a quite normal, i.e., usual, growing-up phenomenon. In certain instances, however, its great frequency or its inappropriateness point to the use of it as an escape mechanism. What holds true for masturbation is true of all "abnormal mechanisms." *It is not the mechanism that is abnormal; it is its function which determines its abnormality.* It is precisely for this reason that the institutionalized "abnormal" traits in various cultures are not properly called "abnormal" entities. Because this distinction is not kept in mind and because a primarily statistico-relative conception of abnormality is adhered to, the unwarranted conclusion is drawn that standards of "abnormality" differ with cultures and are culturally determined.

References

1. Benedict, R. Anthropology and the abnormal. *J. Gen. Psychol.,* 10(1934), 59–82.
2. ——— *Patterns of culture.* Boston: Houghton Mifflin, 1934.
3. Boas, F. *Mind of primitive man.* New York: Macmillan, 1919.
4. Bridges, J. W. *Psychology—normal and abnormal.* New York: Appleton, Century, 1930.
5. Campbell, C. M. *Delusion and belief.* Cambridge: Harvard Univ. Press, 1926.
6. Clifford, H. *Studies in brown humanity.* London: G. Richards, 1898.

‡ In a monograph now in preparation, A. Angyal approaches the problem of abnormality from a different point of view and substitutes for the latter the concept of "bio-negativity." "A process is bio-negative if it is in, but directed against, the organism"—"the same factors may be bio-positive in certain types of personality organization and bio-negative in others." His conception neither opposes nor affirms the above formulation of abnormality, for it rests upon a different conceptual basis.

7. —— In court and kampong. London: G. Richards, 1897.

8. Czaplicka, M. A. Aboriginal Siberia: a study in social anthropology. Oxford: Clarendon Press, 1914.

9. Edwards, A. S. A theoretical and clinical study of so-called normality. J. Abnorm. Soc. Psychol., 28(1934), 366–376.

10. Foley, J. P., Jr. The criterion of abnormality. J. Abnorm. Soc. Psychol., 30(1935), 279–290.

11. Fortune, R. F. Sorcerers of Dobu. London: Routledge, 1932.

12. McDougall, W. Outline of abnormal psychology. New York: Scribners, 1926.

13. Mead, M. Coming of age in Samoa. New York: Morrow, 1928.

14. —— Growing up in New Guinea. New York: Morrow, 1930.

15. Morgan, J. J. B. The psychology of abnormal people. New York: Longmans, Green, 1928.

16. Pitt-Rivers, G. H. The contact of races and the clash of cultures. London: Routledge, 1927.

17. Seligman, C. G. Temperament, conflict and psychosis in a stone age population. Brit. J. Psychol., 9(1929), 187–202.

18. Skaggs, E. B. The meaning of the term "abnormality" in psychology. J. Abnorm. Soc. Psychol., 23(1933), 113–118.

19. Van Loon, F. H. G. Amok and lâttah. J. Abnorm. Soc. Psychol., 21(1926), 434–444.

20. Wundt, W. Völkerpsychologie. 10 vols. Leipzig: W. Engelmann, 1900–1920.

Toward a Concept of the Normal Personality *

EDWARD JOSEPH SHOBEN, JR.
TEACHERS COLLEGE, COLUMBIA UNIVERSITY

Clinical practice and the behavioral sciences alike have typically focused on the pathological in their studies of personality and behavior dynamics. While much of crucial importance remains to be learned, there is an abundant empirical knowledge and an impressive body of

Reprinted from the American Psychologist, 12(1957), 183–189, with the permission of the American Psychological Association and the author.

* This paper is revised from versions read on March 26, 1956, at the convention of the American Personnel and Guidance Association in Washington, D.C., and on November 16, 1956, at a conference on mental health research at Catholic University in Washington, D.C., under the joint sponsorship of Catholic University, the University of Maryland, and the U.S. Veterans Administration.

theory concerning the deviant and the diseased, the anxious and the neurotic, the disturbed and the maladjusted. In contrast, there is little information and even less conceptual clarity about the nature of psychological normality. Indeed, there are even those (5, 13) who argue that there is no such thing as a normal man; there are only those who manage their interpersonal relationships in such a way that others are strongly motivated to avoid them, even by committing them to a mental hospital or a prison, as opposed to those who do not incite such degrees of social ostracism.

This argument has two characteristics. First, it disposes of the issue by simply distributing people along a dimension of pathology. All men are a little queer, but some are much more so than others. Second, it has affinities with the two major ideas that have been brought to bear on the question of what constitutes normal or abnormal behavior: the statistical conception of the usual or the average and the notion of cultural relativism. If pathology is conceived as the extent to which one is tolerated by one's fellows, then any individual can theoretically be described in terms of some index number that reflects the degree of acceptability accorded him. The resulting distribution would effectively amount to an ordering of people from the least to the most pathological. Similarly, if the positions on such a continuum are thought of as functions of one's acceptance or avoidance by others, then they can only be defined by reference to some group. The implications here are twofold. First, the conception of pathology is necessarily relativistic, varying from group to group or culture to culture. Second, the degree of pathology is defined as the obverse of the degree of conformity to group norms. The more one's behavior conforms to the standards of the group, the less one is likely to be subject to social avoidance; whereas the more one's behavior deviates from the rules, the greater is the probability of ostracism to the point of institutional commitment.

Statistical and Relativistic Concepts of Normality

Yet it is doubtful that the issues are fully clarified by these statistical and culturally relativistic ideas. Is it most fruitful to regard normality or integrative behavior as merely reflecting a minimal degree of pathology, or may there be a certain merit in considering the asset side of personality, the positive aspects of human development? This question becomes particularly relevant when one is concerned with the socialization process

or with the goals and outcomes of psychotherapy or various rehabilitative efforts.

It seems most improbable that the family, the church, and the school, the main agents of socialization, exist for the minimizing of inevitable pathological traits in the developing members of the community. Rather, parents, priests, and educators are likely to insist that their function is that of facilitating some sort of positive growth, the progressive acquisition of those characteristics, including skills, knowledge, and attitudes, which permit more productive, contributory, and satisfying ways of life. Similarly, while psychotherapists may sometimes accept the limited goals of simply trying to inhibit pathological processes, there are certainly those (11, 16) who take the position that therapy is to be judged more in terms of how much it contributes to a patient's ability to achieve adult gratifications rather than its sheer efficiency in reducing symptoms or shoring up pathological defenses.

A general concern for such a point of view seems to be emerging in the field of public mental health (26). Beginning with an emphasis on treatment, the concept of community mental health swung to a preventive phase with the main interest focused on identifying the antecedents of mental disease and on reducing morbidity rates by attacking their determinants. The vogue of eugenics was one illustrative feature of this stage. More recently, there has been a considerable dissatisfaction with the whole notion of interpreting psychological states in terms of disease analogues (15, 23). Maladjustive behavior patterns, the neuroses, and —perhaps to a lesser extent—the psychoses may possibly be better understood as disordered, ineffective, and defensive styles of life than as forms of sickness. In consequence, there seems to be a growing tendency to conceive of the public mental health enterprise as emphasizing positive development with the prevention and treatment of pathology regarded as vital but secondary.

But in what does positive development consist? The statistical concept of the average is not very helpful. Tiegs and Katz (27), for example, reported a study of college students who had been rated for fourteen different evidences of "nervousness." By and large, these traits were normally distributed, suggesting that those subjects rated low must be considered just as "abnormal" (unusual) as those rated high. This conception seems to provide a superficial quantitative model only at the expense of hopeless self-contradiction and violence to the ordinary categories of communication. Even in a case that at first blush seems to cause no difficulty, the problem remains. Criminal behavior, for example, is distributed in a J-shaped fashion with most cases concentrated at the point of zero offenses, ranging to a relatively few instances of many-time offenders. Few would argue that the usual behavior here is not also the most "positive." But one suspects that the sheer frequency of law-abiding behavior has little to do with its acknowledged integrative character. If conformity to social rules is generally considered more desirable than criminality, it is not because of its rate of occurrence but because of its consequences for both society and the individual.

Thus, a statistical emphasis on the usual as the criterion of positive adjustment or normality shades into a socially relativistic concept with an implied criterion of conformity. The terms "usual" or "most frequent" or "average" are meaningless without reference to some group, and this state of affairs poses two problems. First, conformity in itself, as history abundantly demonstrates, is a dubious guide to conduct. Innovation is as necessary to a culture's survival as are tradition and conservation, and conformity has frequently meant acquiescence in conditions undermining the ma-

turity and positive development of human beings rather than their enhancement. On more personal levels, conformity sometimes seems related in some degree to personality processes that can quite properly be called pathological (2, 24). Second, relativistic conceptions of normality pose serious questions as to the reference group against which any individual is to be assessed. Benedict (3), for example, has made it quite clear that behavior which is considered abnormal in one culture is quite acceptable in others, that certain forms of abnormalities which occur in some societies are absent in others, and that conduct which is thought completely normal in one group may be regarded as intensely pathological in another. Such observations, while descriptively sound, can lead readily to two troublesome inferences. One is that the storm trooper must be considered as the prototype of integrative adjustment in Nazi culture, the members of the Politburo as best representing human normality Soviet-style, and the cruelest adolescent in a delinquent gang as its most positively developed member. The other is that any evaluative judgment of cultures and societies must be regarded as inappropriate. Since normality is conceived only in terms of conformity to group standards, the group itself must be beyond appraisal. Thus, the suspicion and mistrust of Dobu (10), the sense of resigned futility that permeates Alor (6), and the regimentation that characterizes totalitarian nations can logically only be taken as norms in terms of which individual behavior may be interpreted, not as indications of abnormal tendencies in the cultures themselves.

Wegrocki (28), in criticizing such relativistic notions, argues that it is not the form of behavior, the actual acts themselves, that defines its normal or pathological character. Rather, it is its function. What he calls the "quintessence of abnormality" lies in reactions which represent an escape from conflicts and problems rather than a facing of them. This formulation, implying that integrative adjustments are those which most directly confront conflicts and problems, seems essentially free of the difficulties inherent in statistical conceptions and the idea of cultural relativism. But it presents troubles of its own. For instance, what does it mean to "face" a problem or conflict? On what ground, other than the most arbitrarily moralistic one, can such confrontations be defended as more positive than escape? Finally, does this facing of one's problems have any relationship to the matter of conformity in the sense of helping to clarify decisions regarding the acceptance or rejection of group standards?

To deal with such questions requires coming to grips with certain problems of value. It is at this point that the behavioral sciences and ethics meet and merge, and it seems unlikely that any conception of normality can be developed apart from some general considerations that are fundamentally moral. Once the purely relativistic ideas of normality are swept away, it becomes difficult to avoid some concern for the issues of happiness and right conduct (*i.e.,* conduct leading to the greatest degree of human satisfaction) that are the traditional province of the literary interpreter of human experience, the theologian, and the moral philosopher. A primary challenge here is that of providing a rational and naturalistic basis for a concept of integrative adjustment that is at once consistent with the stance and contributions of empirical science and in harmony with whatever wisdom mankind has accumulated through its history.

Symbolic and Social Aspects of Human Nature

One way to meet this challenge is by frankly postulating a basic principle of value. The fundamental contention advanced here is that behavior is "positive" or "integrative" to the extent that it reflects the unique attributes of the human animal. There are undoubtedly other ways of approaching a fruitful concept of normality. Nevertheless, this assertion is consistent with the implications of organic evolution, escapes the fallacy of the survival-of-the-fittest doctrine in its various forms, and permits a derivation of more specific criteria of positive adjustment from the distinctive characteristics of man. No discontinuity within the phylogenetic scale need be assumed. It seems clear, however, that man, while certainly an animal, can hardly be described as "nothing but" an animal; and his normality or integration seems much more likely to consist in the fulfillment of his unique potentialities than in the development of those he shares with infrahuman organisms.

Foremost among these uniquely human potentialities, as Cassirer (4) and Langer (14) make clear, is the enormous capacity for symbolization. What is most characteristic of men is their pervasive employment of *propositional* language. While other organisms, especially dogs (22) and the higher apes (29), react to symbols, their faculty for doing so indicates only an ability to respond to mediate or representative as well as direct stimuli. Man, on the other hand, uses symbols designatively, as a vehicle for recollecting past events, for dealing with things which are not physically present, and for projecting experience into the future. Goldstein (12) makes the same point in his discussion of the "attitude toward the merely possible," the ability to deal with things that are only imagined or which are not part of an immediate, concrete situation. In patients whose speech has been impaired because of brain damage, this attitude toward the possible is disrupted. Thus, aphasics are typically unable to say such things as, "The snow is black" or "The moon shines in the daytime"; similarly, they are incapable of *pretending* to comb their hair or to take a drink of water, although they can actually *perform* these acts. Such patients appear to have lost the uniquely human capacity for thinking *about* things as well as directly "thinking things."

It is his symbolic ability, then, that makes man the only creature who can "look before and after and pine for what is not." Propositional speech makes it possible for him to learn from not only his own personal experience but from that of other men in other times and places, to forecast the consequences of his own behavior, and to have ideals. These three symbol-given attributes—the aptitude for capitalizing on experience, including the experience of others, over time, the capacity for foresight and the self-imposed control of behavior through the anticipation of its outcomes, and the ability to envision worlds closer than the present one to the heart's desire—constitute a basic set of distinctively human potentialities.

A second set of such potentialities seems related to the long period of helpless dependence that characterizes infancy and childhood. Made mandatory by the relative biological incompleteness of the human baby, this phase of development is likely to be lengthened as cultures become more complex. Thus, in such simpler societies as the Samoan (18), children can achieve a higher degree of independence at an earlier age than in the civilizations of the West, for example, where the necessity for learning complicated and specialized economic skills extends the period of dependence through adolescence and even into chronological young adulthood. The central point, however, is that unlike the young of any other species, human children in *all* cultural settings must spend a long time during which the gratification of their most basic needs is mediated by

somebody else and is dependent on their relationship to somebody else.

This state of affairs exposes youngsters during their earliest and most formative stages of development to two fundamental conditions of human life. The first is that one's survival, contentment, and need fulfillment involve an inevitable element of reliance on other people. The second is that the relative autonomy, authority, and power that characterize the parent figures and others on whom one relies in childhood are always perceived to a greater or lesser extent in association with responsibility and a kind of altruism. That is, the enjoyment of adult privileges and status tends to occur in conjunction with the acceptance, in some degree, of responsibility for mediating, in some way, the need gratifications of others. Mowrer and Kluckhohn (20) seem to be speaking of a similar pattern when they describe the socialization process as progressing from childhood *dependency* through *independence* to adult *dependability*.

Moreover, this reciprocal relationship between reliance and responsibility seems to obtain on adult levels as well as between children and parents, with the degree of reciprocity a partial function of the complexity of the culture. In simpler societies, a relatively small number of persons may assume primary responsibility for virtually all of the needs of the group in excess of its bare subsistence demands. Under civilized conditions, however, the specialization made necessary by technology and the pattern of urban living means that each adult is dependent on some other adult in some way and that, conversely, he is responsible in some fashion for the welfare of some other adult. The difference between the simpler and the more complex cultures, however, is only one of degree. The crucial point is that, throughout human society, men are in one way or another dependent on each other both in the familiar situation of parents and children and in the course of adult living. This pattern of interdependency gives to human life a social character to be found nowhere else in the animal kingdom. Even among the remarkable social insects, the patterns of symbiosis found there seem to be a result of a genetically determined division of labor rather than the fulfillment of a potentiality for the mutual sharing of responsibilities for each other.

It is in this notion of the fulfillment of distinctively human potentialities that a fruitful conception of positive adjustment may have its roots. From the symbolic and peculiarly social character of human life, it may be possible to derive a set of potential attributes the cultivation of which results in something different from the mere absence of pathology and which forms a standard against which to assess the degree of integration in individual persons. To accept this task is to attempt the construction of a normative or ideal model of a normal, positively developed, or integratively adjusted human being.

A Model of Integrative Adjustment

In the first place, it would seem that, as the symbolic capacity that endows man with foresight develops in an individual, there is a concomitant increase in his ability to control his own behavior by anticipating its probable long-range consequences. The normal person is, first of all, one who has learned that in many situations his greatest satisfaction is gained by foregoing the immediate opportunities for comfort and pleasure in the interest of more remote rewards. He lives according to what Paul Elmer More, the Anglican theologian, calls "the law of costingness":

. . . the simple and tyrannical fact that, whether in the world physical, or in the world intellectual, or in the world spiritual, we can get nothing without paying an exacted price. The fool is he who ignores, and the villain is he who thinks he can outwit, the vigilance of the nemesis guarding this law of costingness . . . all [one's] progress is dependent on surrendering one interest or value for a higher interest or value (19, p. 158).

Mowrer and Ullman (21) have made the same point in arguing, from the results of an ingenious experiment, that normality results in large part from the acquired ability to subject impulses to control through the symbolic cues one presents to oneself in the course of estimating the consequences of one's own behavior. Through symbolization, the future outcomes of one's actions are drawn into the psychological present; the strength of more remote rewards or punishments is consequently increased; and a long-range inhibitory or facilitating effect on incipient conduct is thereby exercised.

This increase in self-control means a lessened need for control by external authority, and conformity consequently becomes a relatively unimportant issue. The integratively adjusted person either conforms to the standards of his group because their acceptance leads to the most rewarding long-range consequences for him, or he rebels against authority, whether of persons or of law or custom, on *considered* grounds. This considered form of revolt implies two things. The first is an honest conviction that rules or the ruler are somehow unjust and that the implementation of his own values is likely to lead to a more broadly satisfying state of affairs. Such an attack on authority is very different from revolts that occur out of sheer needs for self-assertion or desires for power or as expressions of displaced hostility. The main dimension of difference is that of honesty as opposed to deception. The normal person is relatively well aware of his motives in either conforming or rebelling. The pathological rebel, on the other hand, tends to deceive himself and others about his goals. His reasons for nonconformity amount to rationalizations, and his justifications are typically projections. This kind of self-defeating and socially disruptive deceptiveness is seen daily in clinical practice.

The second characteristic of nonconformity in the normal person is that it is undertaken with an essential acceptance of the possible consequences. Having considered the risks beforehand, he is inclined neither to whine nor to ask that his rebellious conduct be overlooked if he runs afoul of trouble. In keeping with the "law of costingness," he is willing to pay the price for behaving in accordance with his own idiosyncratic values. "We have the right to lead our own lives," John Erskine (8) makes Helen of Troy say to her daughter Hermoine, "but that right implies another—to suffer the consequences. . . . Do your best, and if it's a mistake, hide nothing and be glad to suffer for it. That's morality." A psychological paraphrase of this bit of belletristic wisdom is not inappropriate: The assumption of responsibility * for one's actions is one of the attributes of personal integration.

But if personal responsibility and self-control through foresight can be derived as aspects of integrative adjustment from man's symbolic capacity, a third characteristic of interpersonal responsibility can be deduced from his social nature. If in-

* This conception of responsibility is by no means antideterministic. As Fingarette (8) points out, one can *understand* his own or another's behavior, in the sense of accounting for it or rationally explaining it, by the retrospective process of examining the past. Responsibility, on the other hand, is neither retrospective in orientation nor explanatory in function. It is future oriented and refers to the *act* of proclaiming oneself as answerable for one's own conduct and its consequences. Thus, "responsibility," in this context, is not a logical term, implying causation, but a behavioral and attitudinal one, descriptive of a class of human actions.

terdependency is an essential part of human social life, then the normal person becomes one who can act dependably in relation to others and at the same time acknowledge his need for others. The roots of the former probably lie, as McClelland (17) has pointed out, in the role perceptions which developing children form of parent figures and other agents of the socialization process. By conceiving of such people as at least in some degree the nurturant guides of others and through identification with them, the integratively adjusted individual "wants to be" himself trustworthy and altruistic in the sense of being dependable and acting out of a genuine concern for the welfare of others as he can best conceive it. Altruism in this context, therefore, means nothing sentimental. It certainly includes the making and enforcement of disciplinary rules and the imposition of behavioral limits, but only if these steps are motivated by an interest in helping others and express concern and affection rather than mere personal annoyance or the power conferred by a superior status.

Similarly, the acknowledgment of one's needs for others implies a learned capacity for forming and maintaining intimate interpersonal relationships. Erikson (7) refers to this aspect of the normal personality as the attitude of "basic trust," and it is not far from what can be meaningfully styled in plain language as the ability to love. One suspects that the origins of this ability lies in the long experience during childhood of having need gratifications frequently associated with the presence of another person, typically a parent figure. By this association and the process of generalization, one comes to attach a positive affect to others. But as the youngster develops, he gradually learns that the need-mediating behavior of others is maintained only by his reciprocating, by his entering into a relationship of mutuality with others. If this kind of mutuality is not required of him, he is likely to perpetuate his dependency beyond the period his biological level of development and the complexity of his culture define as appropriate; whereas if he is required to demonstrate this mutuality too soon, he is likely to form the schema that interpersonal relationships are essentially matters of traded favors, and that, instead of basic trust, the proper attitude is one of getting as much as possible while giving no more than necessary. The pursuit in research and thought of such hypotheses as these might shed a good deal of light on the determinants of friendship, marital happiness, and effective parenthood, the relational expressions of effective personal integration.

But there is still another interpersonal attitude relevant to a positive conception of adjustment that is somewhat different from that bound up with relationships of an intimate and personal kind. There is a sense in which each individual, even if he regards himself as unfortunate and unhappy, owes his essential humanity to the group which enabled him to survive his helpless infancy. As studies of feral children (25) have shown, even the humanly distinctive and enormously adaptive trait of propositional speech does not become usable without the stimulation and nurture of other people. A kind of obligation is therefore created for the person to be an asset rather than a burden to society. It is partly to the discharging of this obligation that Adler (1) referred in developing his concept of social interest as a mark of normality. While the notion certainly implies the learning of local loyalties and personal affections, it also transcends the provincial limits of group and era. Because man's symbolic capacity enables him to benefit from the record of human history and to anticipate the future, and because his pattern of social interdependency, especially in civilized societies, reaches across the boundaries of political units and parochial affiliations, it seems reasonable to expect the positively developed person to behave in such a fashion as to contribute, according to his own particular lights, to the general welfare of humanity, to take as his frame of reference mankind at large as best he understands it rather than his own group or clan.

Ideologies are at issue here, but there need be neither embarrassment nor a lack of room for debate regarding the specifics of policy and values in the hypothesis that democratic attitudes are closely bound up with personality integration. After all, democracy in psychological terms implies only a concern about others, a valuing of persons above things, and a willingness to participate in mutually gratifying relationships with many categories of persons, including those of which one has only vicarious knowledge. Departures from democratic attitudes in this psychological sense mean a restriction on the potentiality for friendship and imply both a fear of others and a valuation of such things as power over people, thus endangering the interpersonal rewards that come from acting on the attitude of basic trust. Democratic social interest, then, means simply the most direct route to the fulfillment of a distinctively human capacity derived from man's symbolic character and the inevitability of his social life.

Finally, man's ability to assume an attitude toward the "merely possible" suggests that the normal person has ideals and standards that he tries to live up to even though they often exceed his grasp. For an integrative adjustment does not consist in the attainment of perfection but in a striving to act in accordance with the best principles of conduct that one can conceive. Operationally, this notion implies that there is an optimum discrepancy between one's self concept and one's ego ideal. Those for whom this discrepancy is too large (in favor, of course, of the ideal) are likely to condemn themselves to the frustration of never approximating their goals and to an almost perpetually low self-esteem. Those whose discrepancies are too low, on the other hand, are probably less than integratively adjusted either because they are failing to fulfill their human capacity to envision themselves as they could be or because they are self-deceptively overestimating themselves.

This model of integrative adjustment as characterized by self-control, personal responsibility, social responsibility, democratic social interest, and ideals must be regarded only in the most tentative fashion. Nevertheless, it does seem to take into account some realistic considerations. It avoids the impossible conception of the normal person as one who is always happy, free from conflict, and without problems. Rather, it suggests that he may often fall short of his ideals; and because of ignorance, the limitations under which an individual lives in a complex world, or the strength of immediate pressures, he may sometimes behave in ways that prove to be shortsighted or self-defeating. Consequently, he knows something of the experience of guilt at times, and because he tries to be fully aware of the risks he takes, he can hardly be entirely free from fear and worry. On the other hand, a person who is congruent to the model is likely to be one who enjoys a relatively consistent and high degree of self-respect and who elicits a predominantly positive and warm reaction from others. Moreover, it is such a person who seems to learn wisdom rather than hostile bitterness or pathologically frightened withdrawal from whatever disappointments or suffering may be his lot. Guilt, for example, becomes a challenge to his honesty, especially with himself but also with others; and it signalizes for him the desirability of modifying his behavior, of greater effort to live up to his ideals, rather than the need to defend himself by such mechanisms as rationalization or projection. Finally, the model permits a wide variation in the actual behaviors in which normal people may engage and even makes allowance for a wide range of disagreements among them. Integrative adjustment does not consist in the individual's fitting a preconceived behavioral mold. It may well consist in the degree to which his efforts fulfill the symbolic and social potentialities that are distinctively human.

References

1. Adler, A. *Social interest: a challenge to mankind.* London: Faber & Faber, 1938.

2. Adorno, T. W.; Frenkel-Brunswik, Else; Levinson, D. J.; and Sanford, R. N. *The authoritarian personality.* New York: Harper, 1950.

3. Benedict, Ruth. Anthropology and the abnormal. *J. Gen. Psychol.,* 10(1934), 59–82.

4. Cassirer, E. *An essay on man.* New Haven: Yale Univ. Press, 1944.

5. Darrah, L. W. The difficulty of being normal. *J. Nerv. Ment. Dis.,* 90(1939), 730–739.

6. DuBois, Cora. *The people of Alor.* Minneapolis: Univ. Minnesota Press, 1944.

7. Erikson, E. H. *Childhood and society.* New York: Norton, 1950.

8. Erskine, J. *The private life of Helen of Troy.* New York: Bobbs-Merrill Co., 1925.

9. Fingarette, H. Psychoanalytic perspectives on moral guilt and responsibility: a re-evaluation. *Phil. Phenomenol. Res.,* 16(1955), 18–36.

10. Fortune, R. F. *Sorcerers of Dobu.* London: Routledge, 1932.

11. Fromm, E. *The sane society.* New York: Rinehart, 1955.

12. Goldstein, K. *Human nature in the light of psychopathology.* Cambridge, Mass.: Harvard Univ. Press, 1940.

13. Hacker, F. H. The concept of normality and its practical significance. *Am. J. Orthopsychiat.,* 15(1945), 47–64.

14. Langer, Susanne K. *Philosophy in a new key.* Cambridge, Mass.: Harvard Univ. Press, 1942.

15. Marzolf, S. S. The disease concept in psychology. *Psychol. Rev.,* 54(1947), 211–221.

16. May, R. *Man's search for himself.* New York: Norton, 1953.

17. McClelland, D. *Personality.* New York: William Sloane Associates, 1951.

18. Mead, Margaret. *Coming of age in Samoa.* New York: William Morrow, 1928.

19. More, P. E. *The Catholic faith.* Princeton: Princeton Univ. Press, 1931.

20. Mowrer, O. H., and Kluckhohn, C. A dynamic theory of personality. In J. McV. Hunt (ed.); *Personality and the behavior disorders.* New York: Ronald Press, 1944. Pages 69–135.

21. Mowrer, O. H., and Ullman, A. D. Time as a determinant in integrative learning. *Psychol. Rev.,* 52(1945), 61–90.

22. Pavlov, I. P. *Conditioned reflexes.* London: Oxford Univ. Press, 1927.

23. Riese, W. *The conception of disease.* New York: Philosophical Library, 1953.

24. Riesman, D. *The lonely crowd.* New Haven: Yale Univ. Press, 1950.

25. Singh, J. A. L., and Zingg, R. M. *Wolf-children and feral man.* New York: Harper, 1942.

26. Subcommittee on Evaluation of Mental Health Activities. *Evaluation in mental health.* Bethesda, Md.: Public Health Service, 1955.

27. Tiegs, E. W., and Katz, B. *Mental hygiene in education.* New York: Ronald Press, 1941.

28. Wegrocki, H. J. A critique of cultural and statistical concepts of abnormality. *J. Abnorm. Soc. Psychol.,* 34(1939), 166–178.

29. Yerkes, R. M. *Chimpanzees: a laboratory colony.* New Haven: Yale Univ. Press, 1943.

2. PSYCHIATRIC DIAGNOSIS

OVER THE YEARS various concerns have been raised about the value of diagnostic categories in general, and in particular the specific nosology which is used widely at present. The papers which follow by Szasz and by Zigler and Phillips present many of the criticisms and defenses of such categorization.

The Problem of Psychiatric Nosology: A Contribution to a Situational Analysis of Psychiatric Operations*

THOMAS S. SZASZ, M.D.
PROFESSOR, DEPARTMENT OF PSYCHIATRY,
STATE UNIVERSITY OF NEW YORK,
UPSTATE MEDICAL CENTER, SYRACUSE, N.Y.

The problem of psychiatric nosology has posed a persistent difficulty during the past half-century because, it seems to me, it is one of those problems that is insoluble in the form in which it is usually tackled. Certain fundamental concepts and technical aims must be clarified first. Only after this has been accomplished will we be in a position to return to the problem of psychiatric nosology and re-examine it in a new light.

Reprinted from the *American Journal of Psychiatry*, 1957, 114, 405–413, with the permission of the American Psychiatric Association and the author.

* This is an abbreviated version of a paper read with the title "Psychiatric Nosology: Clinical and Sociological Implications" in the theoretical symposium on "Psychiatric Nosology," at 113th annual meeting of The American Psychiatric Association, Chicago, Ill., May 13–17, 1957. The full length text will appear elsewhere.

What Does Psychiatric Nosology Classify?

I want to emphasize the need to scrutinize the very notion of "psychiatric nosology" and to divide it into workable fragments. The reason for this suggestion is that this problem encompasses, as far as I can see, the following, often mutually exclusive, methods and tasks. First, in relation to the word "psychiatric," there is ambiguity about the domain of this field. Is psychiatry a branch of medicine? And if so, do we mean by this that it is a therapeutic discipline based (as far as possible) on the methods of physics and chemistry? Or do we mean that it is the study of human behavior and human relationships? And if so, do we conceive of it as a branch of, or allied to, psychology and sociology? If this is what we mean, then we are committed to the psychological method and frame of reference. We cannot have both, or a combination of the two, either by simply wishing or by coining a word like "psychosomatic" (39). To illustrate this, let us consider the diagnosis of general paresis. Does this diagnosis refer to a physico-chemical or a psychological phenomenon? Clearly it refers to the former. It is not characteristic, or even descriptive, of any particular behavioral event. How then can we hope to bring it into a meaningful relationship with other "psychiatric diagnoses" such as hysteria, reactive depression or situational maladjustment? These, and many others, refer to behavioral events and are meaningless in a physico-chemical frame of reference. (They are, however, modeled after, and are not meaningless in, a medical framework of concepts.) Yet, such dissimilar concepts are now all subsumed under the heading of "psychiatric diagnosis." This is as though in the periodic table of elements, we would find coal, steel, and petroleum interspersed among items such as helium, sulfur and carbon. In my opinion, this is one of the reasons why the taxonomic system known as "psychiatric nosology" does not work and why attempts to improve it —which have not taken this factor into account—have failed to satisfy anyone but their authors.

A second source of difficulties arises as a result of the several implications of the word "nosology." Nosology means the classification of "diseases." This immediately casts psychiatry into the medical (and physico-chemical) mold into which it fits only according to the first definition of this discipline (36). In this view, psychiatry is the study of diseases of the brain, and psychiatric nosology is the classification of these diseases. Others, however, regard psychiatry as the study of diseases of the "mind"; "psychopathology" is the nosology based on this scheme (15). The trouble here stems from the concept "mind." Still others have attempted to overcome this difficulty by recourse to a system of "disorders of behavior" (8). Thus far we have enumerated three categories of concepts (brain, mind and behavior). To the taxonomy of each of these, the expression "psychiatric nosology" is applied. Not only do psychiatrists use different categories, usually without specifying their scheme, but often concepts from two or all three of these categories are combined within a single taxonomic scheme (*e.g.,* general paresis, latent schizophrenia and homosexuality).

Although the expression "psychiatric nosology" means principally the classification of psychiatric disorders (whatever these may be), modern developments in psychiatry have led to further taxonomic possibilities. This state of affairs has resulted from the fact that psychiatry consists of *both* a "basic science" and of a "clinical technique" (or several such techniques). It is only the latter that is oriented toward "diseases," "diagnosis" and "treatment." The former is oriented, like all sciences, toward an essentially non-judgmental (non-evaluative) under-standing of the phenomena which it studies. "Nosology" in this context be-comes akin to the taxonomic systems of the physical sciences in that it aims at a system of *ordering* phenomena that is useful not for "treatment" but for "scien-tific mastery" (whatever that may mean, depending upon the developmental stage in which the science finds itself and upon social factors). Some of the classificatory concepts of psychoanalysis (*e.g.,* repres-sion as a characteristic feature of "hys-teria") resemble most closely such nonevaluative concepts of classification. Unfortunately, however, most of these concepts have been re-introduced into a medically-modeled system of psycho-pathology (20).

An Operational Approach to Psychiatric Nosology

Classification is but a special case of the more general psychological phenomenon of category-formation. This process de-pends, as we know, upon the psychologi-cal characteristics of the person engaged in forming categories and upon the so-cial situation in which he participates. The dependence of the psychological variable upon brain function, for ex-ample, has been studied and demon-strated in an impressive fashion by Kurt Goldstein (16–18). The role of the latter factor, that is, the effect of the social situation on category-formation, is a matter of common knowledge and may escape attention precisely because it is so obvious. In other words, it would be banal to stress that from the point of view of the economist or of the jeweler there are no "similarities" between coal and diamond. In an economic situation, one may distinguish diamond, gold, platinum and money as members of the (same) category that pertains to *eco-nomic value*. The chemist, on the other hand, may classify diamond and coal as

"chemically similar" members of the category called *carbon*. Surely, there is no need to belabor this point. The ex-ample cited illustrates what I mean by an operational approach to nosology; the word "operational" is used in this con-text to denote not only the characteristic methods of observation but also the so-cial situation in which the observation is made and its purposes. This extension is inherent in the philosophy of opera-tionalism (14). Let us look at psychiatric nosology in this light.

It is apparent at once that the social situations in which so-called psychiatric observations are made are diverse, and yet it is generally assumed that one and the same system of classification should be useful for all of them. We may name but a few of the major "psychiatric situ-ations," without implying that our list is exhaustive: the mental hospital, private psychiatric practice (including the psy-choanalytic situation), the child guidance clinic, the psychoanalytic training system, military service, the court of law and jail. Psychiatric diagnoses are made and used in each of these settings (10, 13, 30, 34). *Yet the methods employed and the pur-poses for which diagnoses are made dif-fer.* I submit, therefore, that we can not expect to be able to take a system of psy-chiatric nosology developed in one situa-tion and expect it to be meaningful and serviceable in another.

Unfortunately space does not permit a detailed consideration of the charac-teristics of the various psychiatric situa-tions that have been listed. To do so would require, at the very least, a sep-arate treatise for each. I have offered fragments of such operational descrip-tions of specific psychiatric situations elsewhere (*e.g.,* for the psychoanalytic situation (37, 38), for the psychothera-peutic situation with the schizophrenic (32) and for the legal situation (40)).

Someone might ask, what is it that corresponds in these situations to the differences in the classificatory schemes of the jeweler and the chemist, in the example cited. My comments shall be restricted to answering this question. I hope that this will illustrate and clarify the general problem under discussion. For this purpose, we may consider three situations: that of the psychiatrist in a state mental hospital, the psychoanalytic situation and the situation in the court of law (psychiatric expert testimony). In the first of these, the relevant category into which the patient must be fitted is principally that of psychosis versus non-psychosis (4, 9). The former tends to justify forcible retention in the hospital, the latter does not. Also, the diagnosis of psychosis, in this context, legitimizes the use of various, sometimes drastic, therapies. In the psychoanalytic situation, the same term, that is "psychosis" (or "psychotic") refers *only* to certain mental mechanisms or patterns of human relationships; it does not refer to overt behavior or social judgment. This method of classification is somewhat analogous to that of the chemist, and consequently the concept "psychosis," as used here, will *not* point to any significant phenomenological similarities between the patient under study and others who may be either inside or outside of mental hospitals (32, 33). Finally, in the legal situation, psychiatric diagnostic terms must be categorized in terms of two mutually exclusive classes, those who are punishable and those who are not (35). This is inherent in the legal situation just as it is inherent in our present economic situation that diamond is more valuable than coal. A non-judgmental, purely descriptive system of classification—while it may be as accurate as it would be to state that both diamond and coal are forms of carbon—is no more appropriate to the legal situation, than would be its analogue for purposes of banking.

Let us now take a brief glimpse at the recent history of psychiatry, viewed in this light. We may restate our problem by recalling that the questions that we have asked were: *Whom do we study, where, and with what methods?* We have called attention to how various "psychiatric situations" on the current scene differ from one another. Let us ask the same questions now about the principal psychiatric figures since Kraepelin.

Kraepelin's chief objects of observation were inmates of mental hospitals (21). He studied them by direct common-sense observation. The underlying assumption was first that they suffered from diseases much the same as other diseases with which physicians were familiar, and second that society and the physicians who studied them were "normal" and constituted the standards with which their behavior was compared. Accordingly, patients were subsumed under categories ("diagnoses") based on the behavioral phenomena ("symptoms") that were judged to be dominant. The spirit of the inquiry precluded emphasis on specifically individualistic features and determinants. Kraepelin's approach, as Zilboorg (43) noted, was therefore at once humane and inhuman. He was interested in man, but was not interested in the patient as an individual.

The psychiatric situation that characterized Bleuler's work (2) was essentially similar to Kraepelin's. The main difference lay, I think, in the fact that Bleuler had a much greater interest in the patient as an individual. He, therefore, noted more personally unique phenomena and saw, for example, that patients with dementia praecox were not really "demented."

Now we come to Freud, who, most of us will agree, saw much more than his predecessors. I would like to suggest that he saw more partly because he was not fettered in making his observations in a single situation with limited techniques. Indeed, he enlarged the psychiatric situation to include almost anything that came across his horizon. Thus, he rapidly shifted from pure clinical observation with or without hypnosis, to observations of himself, of other socially normal individuals, so-called neurotics, as well as to observations of the biographies and autobiographies of artists, "psychotics" and others. On the whole, he too tended to use society and the observer as norms against which the patient and his conduct were measured. In contrast to his predecessors, however, he made this standard explicit. Prior to this time, it was not fully realized that such a standard was implicit in the then current schemes of psychiatric nosology. The nosological scheme that Freud used, as might be expected from what has just been said, was chaotic. He retained the Kraepelinian scheme as far as the diagnostic words were concerned but used them as he pleased. This has resulted, among other things, in repeated forays of re-labeling his cases by later authors (28). Once again, Zilboorg (42) clarified this matter by emphasizing that Freud cared little about the diagnostic labels he used. He concentrated, as we know, on accurate description, reconstruction and on the formulation of new abstractions to account for what he observed (e.g., transference, repression, reaction-formation, etc.).

There have been attempts to use psychoanalytic abstractions in the formation of new psychiatric nosologies. These have failed because they have mimicked the Kraepelinian and Bleulerian systems (e.g., by suggesting that hysteria be diagnosed by the presence of repression as the chief mechanism of defense). Such attempts could succeed, if at all, only by limiting their range of applicability and by adhering to operational criteria (e.g., the patient's reaction to the analytic situation (11)).

Adolf Meyer's approach was a great departure from the basic concepts of Kraepelin and Bleuler in that he did not subscribe to the notion that mental disorder is a phenomenon akin to physical disease (24, 25). Yet he remained more closely allied in his work to these

men than to psychoanalysis, probably chiefly because he continued to focus attention principally on so-called "clinical material" that is, on those who are mentally ill by social criteria. His method was, by his own statement, that of "common sense" (22), but in his thinking he combined biological, historical, psychological and social considerations. He developed a system of classification not of "diseases" but of "reaction types," meaning thereby that disorders of behavior may be classified according to their predominant symptoms. It is important to note that the technical terms—the "ergasias"—which Meyer suggested for these categories were never widely accepted in spite of his great influence on American psychiatry. Within a few decades his system of nosology became an historical relic.

Kurt Goldstein has become well-known for his observations in still another psychiatric situation: he studied the brain injured, combining in his approach the methods of neurology, clinical psychiatry and psychological testing (16). In addition, he introduced certain philosophical and linguistic considerations (17) in his studies which have also proved significant. While his name is not customarily associated with any nosological innovations, it should be noted that he did create two new categories— the concrete and the abstract attitudes (18)—and that these grew out of the particular situation in which his observations were made.

We may also note, at this point, that Bleuler's, Freud's and Goldstein's nosological categories continue to be used. All make good sense in the situations in which they originated. They have, however, since been removed, transplanted and combined with one another, and used in all manner of situations. Is it then surprising that our current psychiatric nosology is a modern Tower of Babel?

Considerations of some recent work

in psychoanalysis would throw further light on the interrelations of the social structure, the methods of, and the classificatory schemes appropriate to, various psychiatric situations. Suffice it to note that most of these developments have increasingly abandoned the traditional nosological concepts and have developed new concepts and terms of their own. Harry Stack Sullivan's contributions (31), for example, can not be fitted into our current official nosology without doing the utmost violence both to him and to our nosology. The same is true of other current contributions to the psychology of "schizophrenia" and of the entire trend toward an object-relationship type of approach (12). These considerations underscore the need to develop adequate systems of classification, rather than to continue paying lip service to an outmoded nosology, as we progress in our psychiatric knowledge.

Panchrestons in Psychiatry

In connection with the word "protoplasm," Hardin has recently called attention to the danger of words that "explain everything." He wrote:

Such enemies of thought, like all enemies, may be easier to spot if we label them. Such "explain-alls" need a name. As we borrow from the Greek to call a "cure-all" a *panacea,* so let us christen an "explain-all" a *panchreston.* The history of science is littered with the carcasses of discarded panchrestons: the Galenic *humours,* the Bergsonian *élan vital,* and the Drieschian *entelechy* are a few biological cases in point. A panchreston, which "explains-all," *explains* nothing (19, p. 113).

Clearly, panchrestons have played, and continue to play, an enormous role in psychiatry and psychoanalysis. Percival Bailey's address (1) last year to this Association may indeed be regarded as a discourse on the existence of panchrestons in psychiatry and on the uses to which they are put. He overlooked, however, all that we *do know,* and all that has been discovered during the past half century. By concentrating attention on panchrestons, one naturally limits himself to that which remains to be elucidated. I would like to emphasize this point, in order to make it clear that my subsequent comments are not intended as a wholesale criticism of psychiatry, or any of its branches, but are offered simply as additional considerations to be taken into account in connection with the problem of how to improve our nosology.

It is clear that many terms—some diagnostic, like schizophrenia, others nondiagnostic, like libido—function as panchrestons. In other words, "schizophrenia" is supposed to "explain" so-called insane behavior in much the same way as "protoplasm" explained the nature of life, and "ether" the manner in which energy travels through space. Not only do these words *not* explain the phenomena in question, but, as Hardin (19) rightly emphasized, they hinder understanding an explanation. If this is so, it means that just as "ether" and "protoplasm" obscured important problems in physics and biology, so "schizophrenia" (and many other psychiatric words) may obscure fundamental problems in psychiatry.

We touch here on an exceedingly important problem, but one that is in no way peculiar to psychiatry. Accordingly, we need not dwell on it and may assume that analogous developments in other sciences constitute a lesson that we must learn. From a point of view of psychiatric nosology this means that categories such as "schizophrenia" may be doubly harmful: first, such categories are unsatisfactory as readily validable concepts for purposes of classification, and secondly, they give rise to the misleading impression that there "exists" a more-or-less homogeneous group of phenomena which are designated by the word in question (*e.g.,* "schizophrenia," "hysteria," "malingering"). If this line of thought is correct—as I believe it is—it leads to the realization that the "problem of schizophrenia," which many consider to be the core-problem of psychiatry today, may be truly akin to the "problem of the ether." To put it simply: there is no such problem. The task is, rather, to redefine our questions so that they become manageable with the technical tools at our command. In the case of "schizophrenia" this will mean, first a conceptual clarification of the manifold meanings of the word, and then work along clearly defined methodological lines—whether biochemical or psychoanalytic—aimed at elucidating specific "facts" rather than "explaining" global concepts. Thus biochemical studies may throw light on disorders of brain function, much as the discovery of the histological lesions of general paresis threw light on the presence of a physically damaged brain in these patients. There is no reason to believe that this may not prove to be the case for *some* patients who by current criteria might be labeled "schizophrenic." Similarly, studies along psychological and social lines should prove enlightening about processes of object relationships, the use of language and symbol-formation and other features characteristic of the behavior, in certain situations, of so-called "schizophrenic" patients. It would be a mistake to believe—or so I submit—that such researches will "explain schizophrenia." *

* In last year's theoretical symposium Pauling stated: "I am sure that most mental disease is chemical in origin, and that the chemical abnormalities involved are usually the result of abnormalities in the genetic constitution of the individual" (27, p. 492). This is a sweeping claim that is buttressed, at present, by little more than the scientific prestige (derived from another field) of its distinguished author. It seems to me entirely plausible that investigations into what Pauling calls "molecular diseases" may prove exceedingly fruitful for our understanding of the physical basis of some aspects of human behavior. It is not in keeping with the spirit of the "scientific attitude," however, to hold out this (or for that matter any

Instead what may happen is that various behavioral processes will be better understood and the need for the word "schizophrenia" will disappear.

A Recapitulation and Some Further Conclusions

In the preceding pages, psychiatric situations and nosologies (more or less) appropriate to each were discussed in the light of the philosophy of operationalism. This word is used to designate that principle of scientific philosophy which emphasizes the over-riding importance of an explicit awareness of the particular methods of observation used in each study. I have extended its use, somewhat, to include in the concept of "method" the nature of the social setting in which the observation took place. This extension is implicit in the principles of operational philosophy and it has been explicitly developed by students of what is often referred to as the "sociology of science." The relevance of this extension to the study of psychiatry need not be belabored, since we are fully aware today of the immense significance of the interpersonal and social matrix in this area of knowledge.

The brief sketches of the various psychiatric situations that have been presented were offered to clearly identify these situations and to show that they differ in one or several parameters. Thus, there may be differences in the person and position of the observer and the observed, and there may be variations in the aims for which the classification ("diagnosis") is made, or in the principal action patterns inherent in the situation. It must be concluded that to hope that one and the same system of psychiatric nosology should be serviceable in all of

other) specific investigative technique as one that promises wholesale solution to a problem as poorly defined as that of "mental disease" (an expression that no doubt will also soon qualify for the title of panchreston).

these situations is to expect too much. Contrariwise, it is reasonable to assume that multiple nosological systems, each serviceable for one situation but not for others, may be developed without undue difficulties. Indeed, there are some in everyday use today, as for example, the categories of "sane-insane" as used in jurisprudence or "transference-reality" as used in the psychoanalytic situation. The notions of sane and insane pertain to the legal situation and can be correlated with the action-patterns of punishment and acquittal (40). The notion of transference pertains to the psychoanalytic situation and expresses the analyst's inference concerning some aspects of the patient's behavior: to the extent to which it is patterned upon past object relationships that are now re-experienced in relation to the analyst, it is "transference"; in so far as the behavior reflects the patient's current orientation to (external) objects, it is not "transference" but is considered to be "reality-oriented." None of these concepts can be readily applied in other situations, although our so called "common sense," and the needs of society, often press us, as psychiatrists, to use all available psychiatric notions in every conceivable situation. This sort of tendency has led the psychiatrist to be viewed—both by himself and by others—as a "universal social expert" who can offer "scientific" advice on all manner of problems ranging from how to raise children to how to pick men who will be "safe" political leaders. This "global" (not to say "megalomanic") view of psychiatry not only can not lay claim to being "scientific," but—and this may be even more damaging in the long run—it distracts attention from the truly worthwhile advances that have been made, and that are being made, in this field.

All of this, as I have said, runs counter to "common sense," and much of it runs counter to a currently prevalent tendency toward unbridled eclecticism (almost as if this were a "good"

thing in itself) as well as to a widespread predilection for a "global" type of psychiatric research (*e.g.,* attacks on the problem of "mental health" or "schizophrenia"). The need for science to deny (or more precisely, to transcend) "common sense" has been repeatedly emphasized, particularly by Bridgman (6). It was cogently re-emphasized recently by Hardin, when he stated,

> In the necessity of discarding 'protoplasm,' biology is now confronted with a painful decision of the sort that faced its older sister science, physics, more than half a century ago—the necessity of denying 'common sense' (19, p. 120).

Psychiatry, too, is confronted with the need to abandon "common sense." Thus "common sense" has assumed that insights gained from the psychoanalytic situation should be *directly* applicable to other situations, for instance to problems of child rearing or to the disposition of criminals in courts of law. Our experience shows that this is *not* possible. So we criticize, in turn, psychoanalysis, parents or lawyers, and refuse to draw the obvious conclusion which is that most psychoanalytic concepts make good sense in the psychoanalytic situation, but their relevance in other situations is a matter for careful and critical judgment. Psychoanalysis is here used for purposes of illustration only. Similar considerations hold true for concepts developed and used in other settings, such as in the state hospital ("manic-depressive psychosis"), in jail ("the Ganser syndrome") or in the military situation ("malingering").

Attention is also called to the role that words that purport to "explain"—when, in fact, they merely "name"—play in psychiatry and in psychiatric nosology. The word "schizophrenia" is singled out as probably the most important of these words. Its secure place in the taxonomy of our discipline, it is suggested, interferes with a better comprehension of the data for which this word allegedly accounts. The notion of "schizophrenia" further lends itself to the creation of a reified picture of this disorder, so that we imagine it to constitute a problem similar to others with which we are familiar in medicine, such as poliomyelitis or arteriosclerotic heart disease. It seems more likely that instead of "schizophrenia" being akin to such serviceable models of "disease," its common bonds are with such panchrestons as "protoplasm" in biology and "ether" in physics. If so, it is useless to search for the "cause" and "treatment" of the "entity" that will account for the observed phenomena now labeled "schizophrenia." Rather, a better comprehension of the "real facts"—if I may be excused for this expression—will probably lead to the gradual disappearance of this word, whose function, like that of all panchrestons, is to fill a scientific void.

In closing, I would like to mention a thought that has occurred to me in reflecting on this subject. It struck me as odd—however obvious it may seem —that our officially accepted nosological system is such that everyone pays lip service to it, but almost no one considers it satisfactory. Often one hears such statements as "Nosology is a necessary evil," or that "Nosology is the expression of the immaturity of psychiatry as a science." Such utterances are misleading. There is no science without classification. What matters is whether the taxonomic system used is appropriate for the endeavor at hand or not. The present situation with respect to psychiatric nosology may be compared to posting a blind policeman on a new superhighway and then expecting him to enforce the speed-laws. The rules of psychiatric nosology are not only being constantly violated, but they are violated gleefully. Nowadays, a contemptuous disregard for the rules of nosology has even become a part of the cloak of psychiatric authority.

An interpretation of this mode of social behavior would prompt one to assume that psychiatrists behave as if their system of nosology was created by "alien others" for no purpose other than to hinder them. Few feel sufficiently identified with this cause to do work along this line or to inspire their colleagues to change their ways. Yet, if one wants to work, all will agree that social order is better than anarchy. Similarly, nosological order would be better than the nosological anarchy which is our present state. Perhaps this symposium will prove to be the soil from which new nosological orders in psychiatry will grow.

Summary

The thesis of this essay is that most problems of psychiatric nosology, as currently formulated, are refractory to solution because of certain basic ambiguities in psychiatric concepts and operations. Scientific clarity and progress in this area depend upon clear agreement on the following issues: (1) The scope and subject matter that is to be designated as "psychiatry" (e.g., brain, mind, or behavior); (2) The scientific and technical methods that characterize this branch of knowledge (e.g., physics or psychology, physico-chemical techniques or psychotherapy); (3) The precise nature of the phenomena that we seek to classify (e.g., physical or chemical changes in the brain, social behavior, or behavior toward specific individuals). These are not three separate categories, but represent rather interlocking aspects of what must be, in the last analysis, operational descriptions of specific "psychiatric situations."

It is suggested that we distinguish sharply between the following principal psychiatric situations on the current American scene: the mental hospital, private psychiatric practice (including the psychoanalytic situation), the child guidance clinic, the psychoanalytic training system, military service, the court of law and jail. Illustrative samples of an operational analysis of a few of these situations are presented. A similar scrutiny of the psychiatric situations that characterized the work of each of the principal figures in the history of psychiatry since Kraepelin is suggested and briefly sketched. This mode of approach prompts one to take a more "relativistic" view of psychiatry, by which is meant the appreciation that different observational methods imply differences in the very nature of the observed "material." Thus, global approaches to psychiatry may have to be abandoned in favor of more limited, and socially and methodologically better defined, plans of attack on specific problems. It is further inherent in this line of thought that a nosological system developed in, and appropriate to, one type of psychiatric situation cannot be validly transferred to another, radically different psychiatric situation. This is a principle familiar to us from other branches of science and technology and the various systems of classification that they employ.

Considerations of nosology also prompt a scrutiny of the specific items that are classified. At present, probably the single most important diagnostic label in psychiatry is "schizophrenia." Some epistemological aspects of the problem of schizophrenia are briefly discussed, and it is suggested that this word may now function as a "panchreston" (or "explain-all") which, instead of illuminating, obscures the essential problems that face psychiatry today.

In conclusion, some observations are offered on the currently widespread disregard of nosological rules by psychiatrists and its inhibiting influence on progress in psychiatry.

References

1. Bailey, P. *Am. J. Psychiat.*, 113(1956), 387.

2. Bleuler, E. *Dementia praecox or the group of schizophrenia.* New York: International Univ. Press, 1950.

3. Blitzsten, N. L. *Am. J. Psychiat.*, **94** (1938), 1431.

4. Bowman, K. M., and Rose, M. *Am. J. Psychiat.*, 108(1951), 161.

5. Breuer, J., and Freud, S. *Studies in hysteria* (1895). New York: Nervous and Mental Disease Monographs, 1947.

6. Bridgman, P. W. *Scient. Monthly,* **79** (1954), 32.

7. Cameron, D. E. A theory of diagnosis. In Hoch, P. H., and Zubin, J., eds. *Current problems in psychiatric diagnosis.* New York: Grune & Stratton, 1953. Pages 33–45.

8. Cameron, N., and Magaret, A. *Behavior pathology.* New York: Houghton Mifflin Co., 1951.

9. Diethelm, O. The fallacy of the concept: psychosis. In Hoch, P. H., and Zubin, J. (eds.) *Current problems in psychiatric diagnosis.* New York: Grune & Stratton, 1953. Pages 24–32.

10. Ebaugh, F. G., Solomon, H. C., and Bamford, T. E. (eds.) *Military neuro-psychiatry.* Res. Publ. Ass. Nerv. Ment. Dis. Baltimore: The Williams and Wilkins Co., 1946. Volume XXV.

11. Eissler, K. R. *J. Amer. Psychoanal. Assoc.,* 1(1953), 104.

12. Fairbairn, W. R. D. *Psychoanalytic studies of the personality.* London: Tavistock Publications, Ltd., 1952.

13. Foxe, A. N. *Psychiat. Quart.,* 12(1938), 617.

14. Frank, P. *Modern science and its philosophy.* New York: George Braziller, 1955.

15. Glover, E. *J. Ment. Sc.,* 78(1932), 819.

16. Goldstein, K. *Aftereffects of brain injuries in war.* New York: Grune & Stratton, 1948.

17. ——— *Human nature in the light of psychopathology.* Cambridge, Mass.: Harvard Univ. Press, 1951.

18. ———, and Scheerer, M. Abstract and concrete behavior: An experimental study with special tests. *Psychol. Monographs,* 53(1941), No. 2 (Whole No. 239).

19. Hardin, G. *Scient. Monthly,* 82(1956), 112.

20. Hoch, P. H., and Zubin, J. (eds.) *Current problems in psychiatric diagnosis.* New York: Grune & Stratton, 1953.

21. Kraepelin, E. *Manic-depressive insanity and paranoia.* Edinburgh: E. and S. Livingstone, 1921.

22. Lief, A. *The commonsense psychiatry of Adolf Meyer.* New York: McGraw-Hill Book Co., 1948.

23. Macalpine, I. *Psychoanalyt. Quart.,* **19** (1950), 501.

24. Meyer, A. Genetic-dynamic psychology versus nosology (1926). In E. F. Winters (gen. ed.) *The collected papers of Adolph Meyer,*

Baltimore: The Johns Hopkins Press, 1951. Volume III.

25. ———— Preparation for psychiatry (1933). In E. F. Winters (gen. ed.) *The collected papers of Adolf Meyer*. Baltimore: The Johns Hopkins Press, 1951. Volume III.

26. Noyes, A. P. *Modern clinical psychiatry*, 4th ed. Philadelphia: W. B. Saunders Co., 1953.

27. Pauling, L. *Am. J. Psychiat.*, 113(1956), 492.

28. Reichard, S. *Psychoanalyt. Quart.*, 25 (1956), 155.

29. Solomon, H. C., and Yakovlev, P. I. *Manual of military neuropsychiatry*. Philadelphia: W. B. Saunders Co., 1945.

30. Stanton, A. H., and Schwartz, M. S. *The mental hospital*. New York: Basic Books, 1954.

31. Sullivan, H. S. *Conceptions of Modern Psychiatry*, 2nd ed. New York: W. W. Norton & Co., 1954.

32. Szasz, T. S. *Arch. Neurol. & Psychiat.*, 77(1957), 420.

33. ———— *J. Nerv. & Ment. Dis.*, in press.

34. ———— Malingering. *Arch. Neurol. & Psychiat.*, 76(1956), 432.

35. ———— *Arch. Neurol. & Psychiat.*, 75 (1956), 297.

36. ———— *Arch. Neurol. & Psychiat.*, 77 (1957), 86.

37. ———— *J. Amer. Psychoanal. Assoc.*, 4 (1956), 197.

38. ———— *Internat. J. Psychoanal.*, 38 (1957), 166.

39. ———— *Pain and pleasure. A study of bodily feelings*. New York: Basic Books, 1957.

40. ———— *Psychiatry*, in press.

41. ———— *Internat. J. Psychoanal.*, to be published.

42. Zilboorg, G. *Internat. J. Psychoanal.*, 35 (1954), 90.

43. ————, and Henry, G. W. *A history of medical psychology*. New York: W. W. Norton & Co., 1941.

Psychiatric Diagnosis: A Critique *

EDWARD ZIGLER AND LESLIE PHILLIPS
YALE UNIVERSITY, AND WORCESTER STATE HOSPITAL
AND CLARK UNIVERSITY, RESPECTIVELY

The inadequacies of conventional psychiatric diagnosis have frequently been noted (4, 10, 13, 18, 21, 23, 30, 34, 36, 42, 43, 45, 49, 52, 54, 55, 58, 62, 71, 72). The responses to this rather imposing body of criticism have ranged from the position that the present classificatory system is in need of further refinement (11, 18), through steps towards major revisions

Reprinted from the *Journal of Abnormal & Social Psychology*, 63(1961), 607–618, with the permission of the American Psychological Association and Dr. Zigler.

* This investigation was supported by the Dementia Praecox Reseach Project, Worcester State Hospital, and a research grant (M-896) from the National Institute of Mental Health, United States Public Health Service.

(10, 13, 36, 49, 62, 72), to a plea for the abolishment of all "labeling" (43, 45, 54). As other investigators have noted (11, 30), this last position suggests that the classificatory enterprise is valueless. This reaction against classification has gained considerable popularity in clinical circles. The alacrity with which many clinicians have accepted this view seems to represent more than a disillusionment with the specific current form of psychiatric diagnosis. These negative attitudes appear to reflect a belief that diagnostic classification is inherently antithetical to such clinically favored concepts as "dynamic," "idiographic," etc. Thus, a question is raised as to whether any diagnostic schema can be of value. Let us initially direct our attention to this question.

On Classification

The growth among clinicians of sentiment against categorization has coincided with a period of critical reappraisal within the behavioral sciences generally (5, 8, 12, 19, 20, 35, 37, 39, 50, 51, 57, 63, 64). This parallel development is more than coincidental. The reaction against "labeling" can be viewed as an extreme outgrowth of this critical self-evaluation, i.e., that psychology's conceptual schemata are artificial in their construction, sterile in terms of their practical predictions, and lead only to greater and greater precision about matters which are more and more irrelevant. It is little wonder that in this atmosphere, conceptualization has itself become suspect nor that Maslow's (41) exposition of the possible dangers of labeling or naming has been extended (55) as a blanket indictment of the categorizing process.

The error in this extension is the failure to realize that what has been criticized is not the conceptual process but only certain of its products. The criticisms mentioned above have not been in favor of the abolishment of conceptualization, but have rather been directed at the prematurity and rarifications of many of our conceptual schemata and our slavish adherence to them. Indeed, many of these criticisms have been accompanied by pleas for lower-order conceptualization based more firmly on observational data (35, 37, 63).

In the clinical area, the sentiment against classification has become sufficiently serious that several investigators (10, 11, 13, 30) have felt the need to champion the merits of psychiatric categorization. They have pointed out that diagnosis is a basic scientific classificatory enterprise to be viewed as essentially the practice of taxonomy, which is characteristic of all science. Eysenck (13) puts the matter quite succinctly in his statement, "Measurement is essential to science, but before we can measure, we must know what it is we want to measure. Qualitative or taxonomic discovery must precede quantitative measurement" (p. 34).

Reduced to its essentials, diagnostic classification involves the establishment of categories to which phenomena can be ordered. The number of class systems that potentially may be constructed is limited only by man's ability to abstract from his experience. The principles employed to construct such classes may be inductive, deductive, or a combination of both, and may vary on a continuum from the closely descriptive to the highly abstract.

Related to the nature of the classificatory principle are the implications to be derived from class membership. Class membership may involve nothing more than descriptive compartmentalization, its only utility being greater ease in the handling of data. Obversely, the attributes or correlates of class membership may be widespread and far-reaching in their consequences. The originators of a classificatory schema may assert that specified behavioral correlates accompany class membership. This assertion is open to test. If the hypothesized correlates represent the full heuristic value of the diagnostic schema and class membership is found not to be related to these correlates, then revision or discard is in order. A somewhat different type of problem may also arise. With the passage of time, correlates not originally related to the schema may erroneously be attributed to class membership. Nevertheless, the original taxonomy may still possess a degree of relevance to current objectives in a discipline. In these circumstances, its maintenance may be the rational choice, although a clarification and purification of categories is called for. The relationship of the two problems outlined here to the criticism of contemporary psychiatric diagnosis will be discussed later. What should be noted at this point is that the solution to neither problem implies the abolishment of the attempt at classification.

Another aspect of taxonomy is in need of clarification. When a phenomenon is assigned to a class, certain individual characteristics of that phenomenon are forever lost. No two class members are completely identical. Indeed, a single class member may be viewed as continuously differing from itself over time. It is this loss of uniqueness and an implied unconcern with process that have led many clinicians to reject classification in principle. While classificatory schemata inevitably involve losses of this type, it must be noted that they potentially offer a more than compensatory gain. This gain is represented in the significance of the class attributes and correlates. Class membership conveys information ranging from the descriptive similarity of two phenomena to a knowledge of the common operative processes underlying the phenomena.

A conceptual system minimizes the aforementioned loss to the extent that only irrelevant aspects of a phenomenon are deleted in the classificatory process. The implicit assumption is made that what is not class relevant is inconsequential. The dilemma, of course, lies in our lacking divine revelation as to what constitutes inconsequentiality. It is this issue which lies at the heart of the idiographic versus nomothetic controversy (1, 2, 6, 15, 16, 25, 26, 60, 61). The supporters of the idiographic position (1, 6) have criticized certain conceptual schemata for treating idiosyncratic aspects of behavior as inconsequential when they are in fact pertinent data which must be utilized if a comprehensive and adequate view of human behavior is to emerge. However, the idiographic position is not a movement toward the abolishment of classifi-

cation, a fact emphasized by Allport (1) and Falk (16). Rather, it represents a plea for broader and more meaningful classificatory schemata.

A conceptually different type of argument against the use of any diagnostic classification has been made by the adherents of nondirective psychotherapy (46, 53, 54). This position has advanced the specific contention that differential diagnosis is unnecessary for, and perhaps detrimental to, successful psychotherapy. This attitude of the nondirectivists has been interpreted (62) as an attack on the entire classificatory enterprise. To argue against diagnosis on the grounds that it affects therapeutic outcome is to confuse diagnosis as an act of scientific classification with the present clinical practice of diagnosis with its use of interviewing, psychological testing, etc. The error here lies in turning one's attention away from diagnosis as an act of classification, a basic scientific enterprise, and attending instead to the immediate and prognostic consequences of some specific diagnostic technique in a specific therapeutic situation, i.e., an applied aspect. To reject the former on the basis of the latter would appear to be an unsound decision.

Although the nondirectivists' opposition to diagnosis seems to be based on a confusion between the basic and applied aspects of classification, implicitly contained within their position is a more fundamental argument against the classificatory effort. Undoubtedly, diagnosis both articulates and restricts the range of assumptions which may be entertained about a client. However, the philosophy of the nondirectivist forces him to reject any theoretical position which violates a belief in the unlimited psychological growth of the client. It would appear that this position represents the rejection, in principle, of the view that any individual can be like another in his essential characteristics, or that any predictable relationship can be established between a client's current level of functioning and the ends which may be achieved. In the setting of this assumption, a transindividual classificatory schema is inappropriate. There is no appeal from such a judgment, but one should be cognizant that it rejects the essence of a scientific discipline. If one insists on operating within the context of a predictive psychology, one argues for the necessity of a classificatory system, even though particular diagnostic schemata may be rejected as irrelevant, futile, or obscure.

Let us now direct our discussion toward some of the specific criticisms of conventional psychiatric diagnosis—that the categories employed lack homogeneity, reliability, and validity.

Homogeneity

A criticism often leveled against the contemporary diagnostic system is that its categories encompass heterogeneous groups of individuals, i.e., individuals varying in respect to symptomatology, test scores, prognosis, etc. (34, 55, 67, 68, 71). Contrary to the view of one investigator (55), a lack of homogeneity does not necessarily imply a lack of reliability. King (34) has clearly noted the distinction between these two concepts. Reliability refers to the agreement in assigning individuals to different diagnostic categories, whereas homogeneity refers to the diversity of behavior subsumed within catogories. While the two concepts may be related, it is not difficult to conceptualize categories which, though quite reliable, subsume diverse phenomena.

King (34) has argued in favor of constructing a new diagnostic classification having more restrictive and homogeneous categories. He supports his argument by noting his own findings and those of Kantor, Wallner, and Winder (31), which have indicated that within the schizophrenic group subcategories may be formed which differ in test per-

formance. King found further support for the construction of new and more homogeneous diagnostic categories in a study by Windle and Hamwi (65). This study indicated that two subgroups could be constructed within a psychotic population which was composed of patients with diverse psychiatric diagnoses. Though matched on the distribution of these diagnostic types, the subgroups differed in the relationship obtained between test performance and prognosis. On the basis of these studies, King suggests that the type of homogeneous categories he would favor involves such classificatory dichotomies as reactive versus process schizophrenics and chronic versus nonchronic psychotics.

An analysis of King's (34) criticism of the present diagnostic system discloses certain difficulties. The first is that King's heterogeneity criticism does not fully take into consideration certain basic aspects of classification. A common feature of classificatory systems is that they utilize classes which contain subclasses. An example drawn from biology would be a genus embracing a number of species. If schizophrenia is conceptualized as a genus, it cannot be criticized on the grounds that all its members do not share a particular attribute. Such a criticism would involve a confusion between the more specific attributes of the species and the more general attributes of the genus. This is not to assert that schizophrenia does in fact possess the characteristics of a genus. It is, of course, possible that a careful analysis will reveal that it does not, and the class schizophrenia will have to be replaced by an aggregate of entities which does constitute a legitimate genus. However, when a genus is formulated, it cannot be attacked because of its heterogeneous nature since genera are characterized by such heterogeneity.

A more serious difficulty with King's (34) heterogeneity criticism lies in the inherent ambiguity of a homogeneity-heterogeneity parameter. To criticize a classificatory system because its categories subsume heterogeneous phenomena is to make the error of assuming that homogeneity is a quality which inheres in phenomena when in actuality it is a construction of the observer or classifier. In order to make this point clear, let us return to King's argument. What does it mean to assert that chronic psychosis is an example of an homogeneous class, while schizophrenia is an example of an heterogeneous one? In terms of the descriptively diverse phenomena encompassed, the latter would appear to have the greater homogeneity. The statement only has meaning insofar as a particular correlate—for instance, the relationship of test score to prognosis—is shared by all members of one class but not so shared by the members of the other class. Thus, the meaningfulness of the homogeneity concept is ultimately dependent on the correlates or attributes of class membership or to the classificatory principle related to these correlates or attributes. The intimacy of the relationship between the attributes of classes and the classificatory principle can best be exemplified by the extreme case in which a class has but a single attribute, and that attribute is defined by the classificatory principle, e.g., the classification of plants on the basis of the number of stamens they possess. Therefore, the heterogeneity criticism of a classificatory system is nothing more than a plea for the utilization of a new classificatory principle so that attention may be focused on particular class correlates or attributes not considered in the original schema. While this plea may be a justifiable one, depending on the significance of the new attributes, it has little to do with the homogeneity, in an absolute sense, of phenomena. Indeed, following the formulation of a new classificatory schema, the heterogeneity criticism could well be leveled against it by the adherents of the old system, since the phenomena encompassed by the new

categories would probably not be considered homogeneous when evaluated by the older classificatory principle.

Although differing in its formulation, the heterogeneity criticism of present psychiatric classification made by Wittenborn and his colleagues (67, 68, 71) suffers from the same difficulties as does King's (34) criticism. Wittenborn's findings indicated that individuals given a common diagnosis showed differences in their symptom cluster score profiles based on nine symptom clusters isolated earlier by means of factor analytic techniques (66, 69). It is upon the existence of these different profiles within a diagnostic category that Wittenborn bases his heterogeneity criticism. Here again the homogeneity-heterogeneity distinction is only meaningful in terms of an independent criterion, a particular symptom cluster score profile. Had it been discovered that all individuals placed into a particular diagnostic category shared a common symptom cluster score profile, then this category would be described as subsuming homogeneous phenomena. But the phenomena—the symptoms mirrored by the symptom profile—are not homogeneous in any absolute sense because the pattern of symptoms may involve the symptoms in descriptively diverse symptom clusters. Thus, the homogeneity ascribed to the category would refer only to the fact that individuals within the category homogeneously exhibited a particular pattern of descriptively diverse behaviors. However, the organization of symptoms mirrored by the symptom cluster profiles is not in any fundamental sense different from that observed in conventional diagnostic syndromes. Both methods of categorization systematize diverse behaviors because of an observed regularity in their concurrent appearance.

The difference between these two approaches, then, lies only in the pattern of deviant behaviors that define the categories. Indeed, Eysenck (14) has noted that both the clinician and the factor analyst derive syndromes in essentially the same manner, i.e., in terms of the observed intercorrelations of various symptoms. It is the difference in method, purely observational versus statistical, that explains why the final symptom structure may differ. The assumption must not be made that the advantage lies entirely with the factor analytic method. The merit accruing through the greater rigor of factor analysis may be outweighed by the limitations imposed in employing a restricted group of symptoms and a particular sample of patients. Thus, the factor analyst cannot claim that the class-defining symptom pattern he has derived is a standard of homogeneity against which classes within another schema can be evaluated. The plea that symptom cluster scores, derived from factor analytic techniques, substitute for the present method of psychiatric classification has little relevance to the heterogeneity issue.

In the light of this discussion we may conclude that the concept of homogeneity has little utility in evaluating classificatory schemata. Since the heterogeneity criticism invariably involves an implicit preference for one classificatory principle over another, it would perhaps be more fruitful to dispense entirely with the homogeneity-heterogeneity distinction, thus, allowing us to direct our attention to the underlying problem of the relative merits of different classificatory principles.

Reliability and Validity

A matter of continuing concern has been the degree of reliability of the present diagnostic system. Considerable energy has been expended by both those who criticize the present system for its lack of reliability (4, 7, 13, 42, 52, 55, 58) and those who defend it against this criticism (18, 29, 56, 59). Certain investigators (18, 56) who have offered evidence that the present system is reliable have also pointed out that the earlier studies emphasizing the unreliability of psychiatric diagnosis have suffered from serious conceptual and methodological difficulties.

In evaluating the body of studies concerned with the reliability of psychiatric diagnosis, one must conclude that so long as diagnosis is confined to broad diagnostic categories, it is reasonably reliable, but the reliability diminishes as one proceeds from broad, inclusive class categories to narrower, more specific ones. As finer discriminations are called for, accuracy in diagnosis becomes increasingly difficult. Since this latter characteristic appears to be common to the classificatory efforts in many areas of knowledge, it would appear to be inappropriate to criticize psychiatric diagnosis on the grounds that it is less than perfectly reliable. This should not lead to an underestimation of the importance of reliability. While certain extraclassificatory factors, e.g., proficiency of the clinicians, biases of the particular clinical settings, etc., may influence it, reliability is primarily related to the precision with which classes of a schema are defined. Since the defining characteristic of most classes in psychiatric diagnosis is the occurrence of symptoms in particular combinations, the reliability of the system mirrors the specificity with which the various combinations of symptoms (syndromes) have been spelled out. It is mandatory for a classificatory schema to be reliable since reliability refers to the definiteness with which phenomena can be ordered to classes. If a system does not allow for such a division of phenomena, it can make no pretense of being a classificatory schema.

While reliability is a prerequisite if the diagnostic system is to have any value, it must not be assumed that if human effort were to make the present system perfectly reliable, it could escape all the difficulties attributed to it. This perfect reliability would only mean that individuals within each class shared a particular commonality in relation to the classificatory principle of symptom manifestation. If one were interested in attributes unrelated or minimally related to the classificatory principle employed, the perfect reliability of the system would offer little cause for rejoicing. Perfect reliability of the present system can only be the goal of those who are interested in nothing more than the present classificatory principle and the particular attributes of the classes constructed on the basis of this principle.

When attention is shifted from characteristics which define a class to the correlates of class membership, this implies a shift in concern from the reliability of a system to its validity. The distinction between the reliability and validity of a classificatory system would appear to involve certain conceptual difficulties. It is perhaps this conceptual difficulty which explains why the rather imposing body of literature concerned with diagnosis has been virtually silent on the question of the validity of the present system of psychiatric diagnosis. Only one group of investigators (25, 27, 28, 29, 73) has specifically been concerned with the predictive efficacy of diagnoses and, thus, to the validity of psychiatric classifications; and even in this work, the distinction between validity and reliability is not clearly drawn.

In order to grasp the distinction between the reliability and the validity of a classificatory schema, one must differentiate the defining characteristics of the classes from the correlates of the classes. In the former case, we are interested in the principles upon which classes are formed; in the latter, in the predictions or valid statements that can be made about phenomena once they are classified. The difficulty lies in the overlap between the classifying principles and the class correlates. If a classificatory system is reliable, it is also valid to the extent that we can predict that the individuals

within a class will exhibit certain characteristics, namely, those behaviors or attributes which serve to define the class.

It is the rare class, however, that does not connote correlates beyond its defining characteristics. The predictions associated with class membership may vary from simple extensions of the classificatory principles to correlates which would appear to have little connection with these principles. Let us examine a simple illustration and see what follows from categorizing an individual. Once an individual has been classified as manifesting a manic-depressive reaction, depressed type, on the basis of the symptoms of depression of mood, motor retardation, and stupor (3), the prediction may be made that the individual will spend a great deal of time in bed, which represents an obvious extension of the symptom pattern. One may also hypothesize that the patient will show improvement if electroshock therapy is employed. This is a correlate which has little direct connection with the symptoms themselves. These predictions are open to test, and evidence may or may not be found to support them. Thus, measures of validity may be obtained which are independent of the reliability of the system of classification.

The problem of validity lies at the heart of the confusion which surrounds psychiatric diagnosis. When the present diagnostic schema is assailed, the common complaint is that class membership conveys little information beyond the gross symptomatology of the patient and contributes little to the solution of the pressing problems of etiology, treatment procedures, prognosis, etc. The criticism that class membership does not predict these important aspects of a disorder appears to be a legitimate one. This does not mean the present system has no validity. It simply indicates that the system may be valid in respect to certain correlates but invalid in respect to others. Much confusion would be dispelled if as much care were taken in noting the existing correlates of classes as is taken in noting the classificatory principles. A great deal of effort has gone into the formalization of the defining characteristics of classes (3), but one looks in vain for a formal delineation of the extraclassificatory attributes and correlates of class membership. As a result, the various diagnostic categories have been burdened with correlates not systematically derived from a classificatory principle but which were attributed to the classes because they were the focal points of clinical interest. A major question is just what correlates can justifiably be attributed to the class categories. To answer this question we must turn our attention to the purposes and philosophy underlying contemporary psychiatric diagnosis.

Philosophy and Purpose of Conventional Diagnosis

The validity of the conventional diagnostic system is least ambiguous and most free from potential criticism as a descriptive schema, a taxonomy of mental disorders analogous to the work of Ray and Linnaeus in biology. In this sense, class membership confirms that the inclusion of an individual within a class guarantees only that he exhibit the defining characteristics of that class. Only a modest extension of this system, in terms of a very limited number of well established correlates, makes for a system of impressive heuristic value, even though it falls considerably short of what would now be considered an optimal classificatory schema. As has been noted (11, 29), the present diagnostic system is quite useful when evaluated in terms of its administrative and, to a lesser extent, its preventive implications. Caveny et al. (11) and Wittenborn, Holzberg, and Simon (70) should be consulted for a comprehensive list of such uses, but examples would include legal determination of insanity,

declaration of incompetence, type of ward required for custodial care, census figures and statistical data upon which considerable planning is based, screening devices for the military services or other agencies, etc. In view of the extensive criticism of contemporary diagnosis, the surprising fact is not that so few valid predictions can be derived from class membership, but that so many can.

The value of the present psychiatric classification system would be further enhanced by its explicit divorcement from its Kraepelinian heritage by an emphasis on its descriptive aspect and, through careful empirical investigation, the cataloging of the reliable correlates of its categories. That this catalog of correlates would be an impressive one is expressed in Hoch's (22) view that the present system is superior to any system which has been evolved to replace it. It is an open question whether the system merits this amount of praise. In general, however, the defense of the present system—or, for that matter, diagnosis in general (11, 13, 29, 30)—tends to rest on the merits of its descriptive, empirical, and nondynamic aspects.

The present classificatory system, even as a purely descriptive device, is still open to a certain degree of criticism. Its classificatory principle is organized primarily about symptom manifestation. This would be adequate for a descriptive system if this principle were consistently applied to all classes of the schema and if the symptoms associated with each diagnostic category were clearly specified. There is some question, however, whether the system meets these requirements (49, 55). The criticism has been advanced that the present system is based on a number of diverse principles of classification. Most classes are indeed defined by symptom manifestation, but the organic disorders, for example, tend to be identified by etiology, while such other factors as prognosis, social conformity, etc. are also employed as classificatory principles. This does not appear, however, to be an insurmountable problem, for the system could be made a completely consistent one by explicitly defining each category by the symptoms encompassed. The system would appear to be eminently amenable to the unitary application of this descriptive classificatory principle, for there are actually few cases where classes are not so defined. Where reliable relations between the present categories and etiology and prognosis have been established, these also could be incorporated explicitly within the system. Etiology and prognosis would be treated not as inherent attributes of the various classifications, but rather as correlates of the particular classes to which their relationship is known. They would, thus, not be confounded with the classificatory principle of the system.

This course of action would satisfy the requirement of consistency in the application of the classificatory principle. A remaining area of ambiguity would be the lack of agreement in what constitutes a symptom. In physical medicine, a clear distinction has been made between a symptom, which is defined as a subjectively experienced abnormality, and a sign, which is considered an objective indication of abnormality (24). This differentiation has not, however, been extended to the sphere of mental disorders. A source of difficulty may lie in the definition of what is psychologically abnormal. In psychiatric terminology, symptoms include a wide range of phenomena from the grossest type of behavior deviation, through the complaints of the patient, to events almost completely inferential in nature. One suggestion (74) has been to eliminate the term "symptom" and direct attention to the manifest responses of the individual. This suggestion appears to be embodied in the work of Wittenborn and his colleagues (66, 67, 68, 69, 70, 71). Wittenborn's diagnostic system, in which symptoms are defined as currently discernible behaviors, repre-sents a standard of clarity for purely descriptive systems of psychiatric classification. This clarity was achieved by clearly noting and limiting the group of behaviors which would be employed in the system. But even here a certain amount of ambiguity remains. The number of responses or discernible behaviors which may be considered for inclusion within a diagnostic schema borders on the infinite. The question arises, then, as to how one goes about the selection of those behaviors to be incorporated in the classificatory system. Parsimony demands that only "meaningful" items of behavior be chosen for inclusion, and this selective principle has certainly been at work in the construction of all systems of diagnosis. In this sense, the present method of psychiatric classification is not a purely descriptive one, nor can any classification schema truly meet this criterion of purity. Meaning and utility inevitably appear among the determinants of classificatory systems.

Several investigators (9, 30, 38) have stressed the inappropriateness of discussing diagnosis in the abstract, pointing out that such a discussion should center around the question of "diagnosis for what?" Indeed, a diagnostic system cannot be described as "true" or "false," but only as being useful or not useful in attaining prescribed goals. Therefore, when a system is devised, its purposes should be explicitly stated so that the system can be evaluated in terms of its success or failure in attaining these objectives. Furthermore, these goals should be kept explicit throughout the period during which the system is being employed. The present diagnostic schema has not met this requirement. Instead, its goals have been carried along in an implicit manner and have been allowed to become vague. The result has been that some see the purpose of the schema as being an adequate description of mental disorders (29), others view it as being concerned with prognosis (22), and still others view the schemata goal as the discovery of etiology (9).

Typically, the present schema has been conceptualized as descriptive in nature, but a brief glance at its history indicates that the original purposes and goals in the construction of this schema went far beyond the desire for a descriptive taxonomy. As Zilboorg and Henry (76) clearly note, Kraepelin not only studied the individual while hospitalized, but also the patient's premorbid history and post-hospital course. His hope was to make our understanding of all mental disorders as precise as our knowledge of the course of general paresis. He insisted on the classification of mental disorders according to regularities in symptoms and course of illness, believing this would lead to a clearer discrimination among the different disease entities. He hoped for the subsequent discovery of a specific somatic malfunction responsible for each disease. For Kraepelin, then, classification was related to etiology, treatment, and prognosis. Had the system worked as envisaged, these variables would have become the extra-classificatory attributes of the schema. When matched against this aspiration, the present system must be considered a failure since the common complaint against it is that a diagnostic label tells us very little about etiology, treatment, or prognosis (44). However, it would be erroneous to conclude that the present system is valueless because its classes are only minimally related to etiology and prognosis.

What should be noted is that etiology and prognosis, though important, are but two of a multitude of variables of interest. The importance of these variables should not obscure the fact that their relationship to a classificatory system is exactly the same as that of any other variables. This relationship may take one of two forms. Etiology and prognosis may be the correlates of the classes of a diagnostic system which employs an independent classificatory principle like symptom manifestation. Optimally, we should prefer a classificatory schema in which the indices of etiology and preferred modes of treatment would be incorporated (29, 47). In essence, this was Kraepelin's approach, and it continues to underlie some promising work in the area of psychopathology. Although Kraepelin's disease concept is in disrepute (23, 40, 55), it is the opinion of several investigators (14, 49, 70) that further work employing the descriptive symptomatic approach could well lead to a greater understanding of the etiology underlying abnormal "processes."

Another manner in which etiology, treatment, or prognosis could be related to a classificatory schema is by utilizing each of these variables as the classificatory principle for a new diagnostic system. For instance, we might organize patients into groups which respond differentially to particular forms of treatment like electroshock, drugs, psychotherapy, etc. The new schemata which might be proposed could be of considerable value in respect to certain goals but useless in regard to others. Since we do not possess a diagnostic system based on all the variables of clinical interest, we might have to be satisfied with the construction of a variety of diagnostic systems, each based on a different principle of classification. These classificatory techniques would exist side by side, their use being determined by the specific objectives of the diagnostician.

Etiology versus Description in Diagnosis

The classical Kraepelinian classification schema shows two major characteristics: a commitment to a detailed description of the manifest symptomatic behaviors of the individual and an underlying assumption that such a descriptive classification would be transitory, eventually leading to and being replaced by a system whose classificatory principle was the etiology of the various mental disorders. Major criticism of this classificatory effort has been directed at the first of these. The reservations are that, in practice, such a descriptive effort allows no place for a process interpretation of psychopathology and that it has not encouraged the development of prevention and treatment programs in the mental disorders.

The authors do not feel that the failure of the Kraepelinian system has demonstrated the futility of employing symptoms as the basis for classification. It does suggest that if one approaches the problem of description with an assumption as to the necessary correlates of such descriptions, then the diagnostic system may well be in error. Kraepelin's empiricism is contaminated in just this way. For example, he refused to accept as cases of dementia praecox those individuals who recovered from the disorder, since he assumed irreversibility as a necessary concomitant of its hypothesized neurophysiological base. Bleuler, on the other hand, who was much less committed to any particular form of causality in this illness, readily recognized the possibility of its favorable outcome. It is not, then, the descriptive approach itself which is open to criticism, but description contaminated by preconception. An unfettered description of those schizophrenics with good prognosis in contrast to those with poor prognosis reveals clear differences in the symptom configuration between these kinds of patients (17, 48).

Kraepelin's basic concern with the problem of etiology has remained a focus of efforts in the clinical area. Although his postulate of central nervous system disease as the basis of mental disorder is in disrepute, and his systematic classificatory efforts are assailed, one nevertheless finds a striking congruence between Kraepelin's preconceptions and certain current attempts at the solution of the problem of psychopathology. There is an unwavering belief that some simple categorical system will quickly solve the mysteries of etiology. The exponents of these newer classificatory schemata have merely replaced symptoms by other phenomena like test scores (34), particular patterns of interpersonal relations (36), etc. It is the authors' conviction that these new efforts to find short-cut solutions to the question of etiology will similarly remain unsuccessful. The amount of descriptive effort required before etiological factors are likely to be discovered has been underestimated (32, 33), and the pursuit of etiology should represent an end point rather than a beginning for classificatory systems. The process of moving from an empirical orientation to an etiological one is, of necessity, inferential and therefore susceptible to the myriad dangers of premature inference. We propose that the greatest safeguard against such prematurity is not to be found in the scrapping of an empirical descriptive approach, but in an accelerated program of empirical research. What is needed at this time is a systematic, empirical attack on the problem of mental disorders. Inherent in this program is the employment of symptoms, broadly defined as meaningful and discernible behaviors, as the basis of a classificatory system. Rather than an abstract search for etiologies, it would appear more currently fruitful to investigate such empirical correlates of symptomatology as reactions to specific forms of treatment, outcome in the disorders, case history phenomena, etc.

The pervasive concern with etiology may derive from a belief that if this were known, prevention would shortly be forthcoming, thus, making the present complex problems of treatment and prognosis inconsequential. Unfortunately, efforts to short-circuit the drudgery involved in establishing an empirically founded psychiatry has not resulted in any major breakthroughs. Etiology is typically the last characteristic of a disorder to be discovered. Consequently, we would suggest the search for etiology be put aside and attempted only when a greater number of the correlates of symptomatic behaviors have been established.

The authors are impressed by the amount of energy that has been expended in both attacking and defending various contemporary systems of classification. We believe that a classificatory system should include any behavior or phenomenon that appears promising in terms of its significant correlates. At this stage of our investigations, the system employed should be an open and expanding one, not one which is closed and defended on conceptual grounds. Systems of classification must be treated as tools for further discovery, not as bases for polemic disputation.

As stated above, it is possible that a number of systems of classification may be needed to encompass the behaviors presently of clinical interest. It may appear that the espousal of this position, in conjunction with a plea for empirical exploration of the correlates of these behaviors, runs headlong into a desire for conceptual neatness and parsimony. It may be feared that the use of a number of classificatory systems concurrently, each with its own correlates, may lead to the creation of a gigantic actuarial table of unrelated elements. However, the authors do not feel that such a fear is well founded because it assumes that the correlates of these systems have no eventual relation one to the other.

We believe that this latter view is unnecessarily pessimistic. While in principle a multiplicity of classificatory systems might be called for, results from the authors' own research program suggests that a single, relatively restricted and coherent classification system can be derived from an empirical study of the correlates of symptomatic behaviors (49, 75). Such a system might serve a number of psychiatrically significant functions, including the optimum selection of patients for specific treatment programs and

the prediction of treatment outcomes. In conclusion, a descriptive classificatory system appears far from dead, and if properly employed, it can lead to a fuller as well as a more conceptually based understanding of the psychopathologies.

References

1. Allport, G. *Personality: A psychological interpretation.* New York: Holt, 1937.

2. ——— Personalistic psychology as science: A reply. *Psychol. Rev.,* 53(1946), 132–135.

3. American Psychiatric Association, Mental Hospital Service, Committee on Nomenclature and Statistics of the American Psychiatric Association. *Diagnostic and statistical manual: Mental disorders.* Washington, D.C.: APA, 1952.

4. Ash, P. The reliability of psychiatric diagnosis. *J. Abnorm. Soc. Psychol.,* 44(1949), 272–277.

5 Beach, F. The snark was a boojum. *Amer. Psychologist,* 5(1950), 115–124.

6. Beck, S. The science of personality: Nomothetic or idiographic? *Psychol. Rev.,* 60 (1953), 353–359.

7. Boisen, A. Types of dementia praecox: A study in psychiatric classification. *Psychiatry,* 1(1938), 233–236.

8. Brower, D. The problem of quantification in psychological science. *Psychol. Rev.,* 56 (1949), 325–333.

9. Cameron, D. A theory of diagnosis. *In* P. Hoch & J. Zubin, eds. *Current problems in psychiatric diagnosis.* New York: Grune & Stratton, 1953. Pages 33–45.

10. Cattell, R. *Personality and motivation structure and measurement.* New York: World Book, 1957.

11. Caveny, E., Wittson, C., Hunt, W., and Herman, R. Psychiatric diagnosis, its nature and function. *J. Nerv. Ment. Dis.,* 121(1955), 367–380.

12. Cronbach, L. The two disciplines of scientific psychology. *Amer. Psychologist,* 12(1957), 671–684.

13. Eysenck, H. *The scientific study of personality.* London: Routledge & Kegan Paul, 1952.

14. ——— The logical basis of factor analysis. *Amer. Psychologist,* 8(1953), 105–113.

15. ——— The science of personality: Nomothetic. *Psychol. Rev.,* 61(1954), 339–341.

16. Falk, J. Issues distinguishing idiographic from nomothetic approaches to personality theory. *Psychol. Rev.,* 63(1956), 53–62.

17. Farina, A., and Webb, W. Premorbid adjustment and subsequent discharge. *J. Nerv. Ment. Dis.,* 124(1956), 612–613.

18. Foulds, G. The reliability of psychiatric, and the validity of psychological diagnosis. *J. Ment. Sci.,* **101**(1955), 851–862.

19. Guthrie, E. The status of systematic psychology. *Amer. Psychologist,* **5**(1950), 97–101.

20. Harlow, H. Mice, monkeys, men, and motives. *Psychol. Rev.,* **60**(1953), 23–32.

21. Harrower, Molly, ed. *Diagnostic psychological testing.* Springfield, Ill.: Charles C. Thomas, 1950.

22. Hoch, P. Discussion. *In* P. Hoch & J. Zubin, eds. *Current problems in psychiatric diagnosis.* New York: Grune & Stratton, 1953. Pages 46–50.

23. ——, and Zubin, J., eds. *Current problems in psychiatric diagnosis.* New York: Grune & Stratton, 1953.

24. Holmes, G. *Introduction to clinical neurology.* Edinburgh: Livingstone, 1946.

25. Hunt, W. Clinical psychology—science or superstition. *Amer. Psychologist,* **6**(1951), 683–687. (a)

26. —— An investigation of naval neuropsychiatric screening procedures. *In* H. Gruetskaw, ed. *Groups, leadership, and men.* Pittsburgh, Pa.: Carnegie Press, 1951. Pages 245–256. (b)

27. ——, Wittson, C., and Barton, H. A further validation of naval neuropsychiatric screening. *J. Consult. Psychol.,* **14**(1950), 485–488. (a)

28. —— A validation study of naval neuropsychiatric screening. *J. Consult. Psychol.,* **14**(1950), 35–39. (b)

29. ——, Wittson, C., and Hunt, E. A theoretical and practical analysis of the diagnostic process. *In* P. Hoch & J. Zubin, eds. *Current problems in psychiatric diagnosis.* New York: Grune & Stratton, 1953. Pages 53–65.

30. Jellinek, E. Some principles of psychiatric classification. *Psychiatry,* **2**(1939), 161–165.

31. Kantor, R., Wallner, J., and Winder, C. Process and reactive schizophrenia. *J. Consult. Psychol.,* **17**(1953), 157–162.

32. Kety, S. Biochemical theories of schizophrenia. Part I. *Science,* **129**(1959), 1528–1532. (a)

33. —— Biochemical theories of schizophrenia. Part II. *Science,* **129**(1959), 1590–1596. (b)

34. King, G. Research with neuropsychiatric samples. *J. Psychol.,* **38**(1954), 383–387.

35. Koch, S. The current status of motivational psychology. *Psychol. Rev.,* **58**(1951), 147–154.

36. Leary, T., and Coffey, H. Interpersonal diagnosis: Some problems of methodology and validation. *J. Abnorm. Soc. Psychol.,* **50**(1955), 110–126.

37. MacKinnon, D. Fact and fancy in personality research. *Amer. Psychologist,* **8**(1953), 138–146.

38. Magaret, Ann. Clinical methods: Psychodiagnostics. *Annu. Rev. Psychol.,* **3**(1952), 283–320.

39. Marquis, D. Research planning at the frontiers of science. *Amer. Psychologist,* **3** (1948), 430–438.

40. Marzoff, S. S. The disease concept in psychology. *Psychol. Rev.,* **54**(1947), 211–221.

41. Maslow, A. Cognition of the particular and of the generic. *Psychol. Rev.,* **55**(1948), 22–40.

42. Mehlman, B. The reliability of psychiatric diagnosis. *J. Abnorm. Soc. Psychol.,* **47** (1952), 577–578.

43. Menninger, K. The practice of psychiatry. *Dig. Neurol. Psychiat.,* **23**(1955), 101.

44. Miles, H. Discussion. In P. Hoch & J. Zubin, eds. *Current problems in psychiatric diagnosis.* New York: Grune & Stratton, 1953. Pages 107–111.

45. Noyes, A. *Modern clinical psychiatry.* Philadelphia: Saunders, 1953.

46. Patterson, C. Is psychotherapy dependent on diagnosis? *Amer. Psychologist,* **3**(1948), 155–159.

47. Pepinsky, H. B. Diagnostic categories in clinical counseling. *Appl. Psychol. Monogr.* (1948), No. 15.

48. Phillips, L. Case history data and prognosis in schizophrenia. *J. Nerv. Ment. Dis.,* **117** (1953), 515–525.

49. ——, and Rabinovitch, M. Social role and patterns of symptomatic behaviors. *J. Abnorm. Soc. Psychol.,* **57**(1958), 181–186.

50. Rapaport, D. The future of research in clinical psychology and psychiatry. *Amer. Psychologist,* **2**(1947), 167–172.

51. Roby, T. An opinion on the construction of behavior theory. *Amer. Psychologist,* **14** (1959), 129–134.

52. Roe, Anne. Integration of personality theory and clinical practice. *J. Abnorm. Soc. Psychol.,* **44**(1949), 36–41.

53. Rogers, C. Significant aspects of client-centered therapy. *Amer. Psychologist,* **1**(1946), 415–422.

54. —— *Client-centered therapy.* Boston: Houghton Mifflin, 1951.

55. Rotter, J. *Social learning and clinical psychology.* New York: Prentice-Hall, 1954.

56. Schmidt, H., and Fonda, C. The reliability of psychiatric diagnosis: A new look. *J. Abnorm. Soc. Psychol.,* **52**(1956), 262–267.

57. Scott, J. The place of observation in biological and psychological science. *Amer. Psychologist,* **10**(1955), 61–63.

58. Scott, W. Research definitions of mental health and mental illness. *Psychol. Bull.,* **55** (1958), 1–45.

59. Seeman, W. Psychiatric diagnosis: An investigation of interperson-reliability after di-

dactic instruction. *J. Nerv. Ment. Dis.,* **118** (1953), 541–544.

60. Skaggs, E. Personalistic psychology as science. *Psychol. Rev.,* **52**(1945), 234–238.

61. ——— Ten basic postulates of personalistic psychology. *Psychol. Rev.,* **54**(1947), 255–262.

62. Thorne, F. Back to fundamentals. *J. Clin. Psychol.,* **9**(1953), 89–91.

63. Tolman, R. Virtue rewarded and vice punished. *Amer. Psychologist,* **8**(1953), 721–733.

64. Tyler, Leona. Toward a workable psychology of individuality. *Amer. Psychologist,* **14** (1959), 75–81.

65. Windle, C., and Hamwi, V. An exploratory study of the prognostic value of the complex reaction time tests in early and chronic psychotics. *J. Clin. Psychol.,* **9**(1953), 156–161.

66. Wittenborn, J. Symptom patterns in a group of mental hospital patients. *J. Consult. Psychol.,* **15**(1951), 290–302.

67. ——— The behavioral symptoms for certain organic psychoses. *J. Consult. Psychol.,* **16** (1952), 104–106.

68. ——— and Bailey, C. The symptoms of involutional psychosis. *J. Consult. Psychol.,* **16** (1952), 13–17.

69. ———, and Holzberg, J. The generality of psychiatric syndromes. *J. Consult. Psychol.,* **15** (1951), 372–380.

70. ———, Holzberg, J., and Simon, B. Symptom correlates for descriptive diagnosis. *Genet. Psychol. Monogr.,* **47**(1953), 237–301.

71. ———, and Weiss, W. Patients diagnosed manic-depressive psychosismanic state. *J. Consult. Psychol.,* **16**(1952), 193–198.

72. Whittman, P., and Sheldon, W. A proposed classification of psychotic behavior reactions. *Amer. J. Psychiat.,* **105**(1948), 124–128.

73. Wittson, C., and Hunt, W. The predictive value of the brief psychiatric interview. *Amer. J. Psychiat.,* **107**(1951), 582–585.

74. Yates, A. Symptoms and symptom substitution. *Psychol. Rev.,* **65**(1958), 371–374.

75. Zigler, E., and Phillips, L. Social effectiveness and symptomatic behaviors. *J. Abnorm. Soc. Psychol.,* **61**(1960), 231–238.

76. Zilboorg, G., and Henry, G. W. *History of medical psychology.* New York: Norton, 1941.

3. APPROACHES TO DIAGNOSIS

In 1954 Dr. Paul E. Meehl published a small but provocative volume contesting the operations of the clinician who uses his artistic or intuitive skills to predict the behavior of patients with what he termed a statistical approach to prediction. This latter might involve classifying the individual on the basis of a wide variety of objective data such as life history, psychometric tests, etc., and then entering a statistical or actuarial table giving the statistical frequencies of those behaviors among various diagnostic or behavioral classes. Predictions are then made on the basis of probability, or the statistical likelihood that an individual would be appropriately placed in any particular class. Obviously the statistical approach has the advantage that it may be carried out by relatively unskilled and inexperienced workers. However, more traditional clinicians would argue that something unique is lost by reducing predictions about behavior to statistical formulae. The article by Meehl which follows contains in effect a recipe for implementing his approach to cookbook prediction and evidence that more accurate prediction can be made through the statistical approach. Holt's paper is a response to Meehl's general argument.

Wanted—A Good Cookbook *

PAUL E. MEEHL
MINNESOTA CENTER FOR PHILOSOPHY OF SCIENCE

Once upon a time there was a young fellow who, as we say, was "vocationally

Reprinted from the *American Psychologist,* 11(1956), 263–272 with the permission of the American Psychological Association and the author.
* Presidential Address, Midwestern Psychological Association, Chicago, April 29, 1955.

maladjusted." He wasn't sure just what the trouble was, but he knew that he wasn't happy in his work. So, being a denizen of an urban, sophisticated, psychologically oriented culture, he concluded that what he needed was some professional guidance. He went to the counseling bureau of a large midwestern university (according to some versions of the tale, it was located on the banks of a great river), and there he was interviewed by a world-famous vocational psychologist. When the psychologist explained that it would first be necessary to take a 14-hour battery of tests, the young man hesitated a little; after all, he was still employed at his job and 14 hours seemed like quite a lot of time. "Oh, well," said the great psychologist reassuringly, "don't worry about *that*. If you're too busy, you can arrange to have my assistant take these tests *for* you. I don't care who takes them, just so long as they come out in quantitative form."

Lest I, a Minnesotan, do too great violence to your expectations by telling this story on the dustbowl empiricism with which we Minnesotans are traditionally associated, let me now tell you a true story having the opposite animus. Back in the days when we were teaching assistants, my colleague MacCorquodale was grading a young lady's elementary laboratory report on an experiment which involved a correlation problem. At the end of an otherwise flawless report, this particular bobbysoxer had written "The correlation was seventy-five, with a standard error of ten, which is significant. However, I do not think these variables are related." MacCorquodale wrote a large red "FAIL" and added a note: "Dear Miss Fisbee: The correlation coefficient was devised expressly to relieve you of all responsibility for deciding whether these two variables are related."

If you find one of these anecdotes quite funny, and the other one rather stupid (I don't care which), you are probably suffering from a slight case of bias. Although I have not done a factor analysis with these two stories in the matrix, my clinical judgment tells me that a person's spontaneous reactions to them reflect his position in the perennial conflict between the tough-minded and the tender-minded, between those for whom the proper prefix to the word "analysis" is "factor" and those for whom it is "psycho," between the groups that Lord Russell once characterized as the "simple-minded" and the "muddle-headed." In a recent book (10), I have explored one major facet of this conflict, namely the controversy over the relative merits of clinical and statistical methods of *prediction*. Theoretical considerations, together with introspections as to my own mental activities as a psychotherapist, led me to conclude that the clinician has certain unique, practically unduplicable powers by virtue of being himself an organism like his client; but that the domain of straight *prediction* would not be a favorable locus for displaying these powers. Survey of a score of empirical investigations in which the actual predictive efficiency of the two methods could be compared, gave strong confirmation to this latter theoretical expectation. After reading these studies, it almost looks as if the first rule to follow in trying to predict the subsequent course of a student's or patient's behavior is carefully to avoid talking to him, and that the second rule is to avoid thinking about him!

Statisticians (and rat men) with castrative intent toward clinicians should beware of any temptation to overextend these findings to a generalization that "clinicians don't actually add anything." Apart from the clinician's therapeutic efforts—the power of which is a separate issue and also a matter of current dispute—a glance at a sample of clinical diagnostic documents, such as routine psychological reports submitted in a VA installation, shows that a kind of mixed predictive-descriptive statement predominates which is different from the type of gross prediction considered in the aforementioned survey. (I hesitate to propose a basic distinction here, having learned that proposing a distinction between two classes of concepts is a sure road to infamy.) Nevertheless, I suggest that we distinguish between: (*a*) the clinician's predictions of such gross, outcome-type, "administrative" dimensions as recovery from psychosis, survival in a training program, persistence in therapy, and the like; and (*b*) a rather more detailed and ambitious enterprise roughly characterizable as "describing the person." It might be thought that *a* always presupposes *b*, but a moment's reflection shows this to be false; since there are empirical prediction systems in which the sole property ascribed to the person *is* the disposition to a predicted gross outcome. A very considerable fraction of the typical clinical psychologist's time seems to be spent in giving tests or semitests, the intention being to come out with some kind of characterization of the individual. In part this characterization is "phenotypic," attributing such behavior-dispositions as "hostile," "relates poorly," "loss in efficiency," "manifest anxiety," or "depression"; in part it is "genotypic," inferring as the causes of the phenotype certain inner events, states, or structures, e.g., "latent n Aggression," "oral-dependent attitudes," "severe castration anxiety," and the like. While the phenotypic-genotypic question is itself deserving of careful methodological analysis, in what follows I shall use the term "personality description" to cover both phenotypic and genotypic inferences, i.e., statements of all degrees of internality or theoreticalness. I shall also assume, while recognizing that at least one group of psychologists has made an impressive case to the contrary, that the description of a person is a worthwhile stage in the total clinical process. Granted, then, that we wish to use tests as a means to securing a description of the person, how shall we go about it? Here we sit, with our Rorschach and Multiphasic results spread out before us. From this mess of data we have to emerge with a characterization of the person from whose behavior these profiles are a highly abstracted, much-reduced distillation. How to proceed?

Some of you are no doubt wondering, "What is the fellow talking about? You look at the profiles, you call to mind what the various test dimensions mean for dynamics, you reflect on other patients you have seen with similar patterns, you think of the research literature; then you combine these considerations to make inferences. Where's the problem?" The problem is, *whether or not this is the most efficient way to do it.* We ordinarily do it this way; in fact, the practice is so universal that most clinicians find it shocking, if not somehow sinful, to imagine any other. We feed in the test data and let that rusty digital computer in our heads go to work until a paragraph of personality description emerges. It requires no systematic study, although some quantitative data have begun to appear in the literature (2, 3, 6, 7, 8, 9), to realize that there is a considerable element of vagueness, hit-or-miss, and personal judgment involved in this approach. Because explicit rules are largely lacking, and hence the clinician's personal experience, skill, and creative artistry play so great a role, I shall refer to this time-honored procedure for generating personality descriptions from tests as the *rule-of-thumb* method.

I wish now to contrast this rule-of-thumb method with what I shall call the *cookbook method.* In the cookbook method, any given configuration (holists please note—I said "configuration," not "sum"!) of psychometric data is associated with each facet (or configuration) of a personality description, and the closeness of this association is explicitly indicated by a number. This number need not be a correlation coefficient—its form will depend upon what is most appropriate to the circumstances. It may be a correlation, or merely an ordinary probability of attribution, or (as in the empirical study I shall report upon later) an average Q-sort placement. Whatever its form, the essential point is that the transition from psychometric pattern to personality description is an automatic, mechanical, "clerical" kind of task, proceeding by the use of explicit rules set forth in the cookbook. I am quite aware that the mere prospect of such a method will horrify some of you; in my weaker moments it horrifies me. All I can say is that many clinicians are also horrified by the cookbook method as applied in the crude prediction situation; whereas the studies reported to date indicate this horror to be quite groundless (10, Chap. 8). As Fred Skinner once said, some men are less curious about nature than about the accuracy of their guesses (15, p. 44). Our responsibility to our patients and to the taxpayer obliges us to decide between the rule-of-thumb and the cookbook methods on the basis of their empirically demonstrated efficiency, rather than upon which one is more exciting, more "dynamic," more like what psychiatrists do, or more harmonious with the clinical psychologist's self concept.

Let us sneak up the clinician's avoidance gradient gradually to prevent the negative therapeutic reaction. Consider a particular complex attribute, say, "strong dependency with reaction-formation." Under what conditions should we take time to give a test of moderate validity as a basis for inferring the presence or absence of this complex attribute? Putting it negatively, it appears to me pretty obvious that there are two circumstances under which we should *not* spend much skilled time on testing even with a moderately valid test, because we stand to lose if we let the test finding influence our judgments. First, when the attribute is found in almost all our patients; and second, when it is found in almost none of our patients. (A third situation, which I shall not consider here, is one in which the attribute makes no practical difference anyhow.) A disturbingly large frac-

tion of the assertions made in routine psychometric reports or uttered by psychologists in staff conferences fall in one of these classes.

It is not difficult to show that when a given personality attribute is almost always or almost never present in a specified clinical population, rather severe demands are made upon the test's validity if it is to contribute in a practical way to our clinical decision-making. A few simple manipulations of Bayes' Rule for calculating inverse probability lead to rather surprising, and depressing, results. Let me run through some of these briefly. In what follows,

$P =$ Incidence of a certain personality characteristic in a specified clinical population. ($Q = 1 - P$, $P > Q$)

$p_1 =$ Proportion of "valid positives," i.e., incidence of positive test finding among cases who actually have the characteristic. ($q_1 = 1 - p_1$)

$p_2 =$ Proportion of "false positives," i.e., incidence of positive test findings among cases who actually lack the characteristic. ($q_2 = 1 - p_2$)

1. When is a positive assertion (attribution of the characteristic) on the basis of a positive test finding more likely to be correct than incorrect?

$$\frac{P}{Q} > \frac{p_2}{p_1}.$$

Example: A test correctly identifies 80 per cent of brain-damaged patients at the expense of only 15 per cent false positives, in a neuropsychiatric population where one-tenth of all patients are damaged. The decision "brain damage present" on the basis of a positive test finding is more likely to be false than true, since the inequality is unsatisfied.

2. When does the use of a test improve over-all decision making?

$$P < \frac{q_2}{q_1 + q_2}.$$

If $P < Q$ this has the form $Q < \dfrac{p_1}{p_1 + p_2}.$

Example: A test sign identifies 85 per cent of "psychotics" at the expense of only 15 per cent of false positives among the "non-psychotic." It is desired to make a decision on each case, and both kinds of errors are serious.* Only 10 per cent of the population seen in the given setting are psychotic. Hence, the use of the test yields more erroneous classifications than would proceeding without the test.

3. When does improving a sign, strengthening a scale, or shifting a cut improve decision making?

$$\frac{\Delta p_1}{\Delta p_2} > \frac{Q}{P}.$$

Example: We improve the intrinsic validity of a "schizophrenic index" so that it now detects 20 per cent more schizophrenics than it formerly did, at the expense of only a 5 per cent rise in the false positive rate. This surely looks encouraging. However, we work with an outpatient clientele only one-tenth of whom are actually schizophrenic. Since these values violate the inequality, "improvement" of the index will result in an increase in the proportion of erroneous diagnoses. N.B.—*Sampling errors are not involved in the above.* The values are assumed to be parameter values, and the test sign is valid (i.e., $p_1 > p_2$ in the population).

Further inequalities and a more detailed drawing out of their pragmatic implications can be found in a recent paper by Albert Rosen and myself (12). The moral to be drawn from these considerations, which even we clinicians can follow because they involve only high-school algebra, is that a great deal of skilled psychological effort is probably being wasted in going through complex, skill-demanding, time-consuming test

* Inequalities (2) and (3) are conditions for improvement if there is no reason to see one kind of error as worse than the other. In trait attribution this is usually true; in prognostic and diagnostic decisions it may or may not be. If one is willing to say how many errors of one kind he is prepared to tolerate in order to avoid one of the other kind, these inequalities can be readily corrected by inserting this ratio. A more general development can be found in an unpublished paper by Ward Edwards.

procedures of moderate or low validity, in order to arrive at conclusions about the patient which could often be made with high confidence without the test, and which in other cases ought not to be made (because they still tend to be wrong) even with the test indications positive. Probably most surprising is the finding that there are certain quantitative relations between the base rates and test validity parameters such that the use of a "valid" test will produce a net rise in the frequency of clinical mistakes. The first task of a good clinical cookbook would be to make explicit quantitative use of the inverse probability formulas in constructing efficient "rules of attribution" when test data are to be used in describing the personalities of patients found in various clinical populations. For example, I know of an out-patient clinic which has treated, by a variety of psychotherapies, in the course of the past eight years, approximately 5000 patients, not one of whom has committed suicide. If the clinical psychologists in this clinic have been spending much of their time scoring suicide keys on the Multiphasic or counting suicide indicators in Rorschach content, either these test indicators are close to infallible (which is absurd), or else the base rate is so close to zero that the expenditure of skilled time is of doubtful value. Suicide is an extreme case, of course (14); but the point so dramatically reflected there is valid, with suitable quantitative modifications, over a wider range of base rates. To take some examples from the high end of the base-rate continuum, it is not very illuminating to say of a known psychiatric patient that he has difficulty in accepting his drives, experiences some trouble in relating emotionally to others, and may have problems with his sexuality! Many psychometric reports bear a disconcerting resemblance to what my colleague Donald G. Paterson calls "personality description after the manner of P. T. Barnum" (13). I suggest—and I am quite serious—that we adopt the phrase *Barnum effect* to stigmatize those pseudo-successful clinical procedures in which personality descriptions from tests are made to fit the patient largely or wholly by virtue of their triviality; and in which any nontrivial, but perhaps erroneous, inferences are hidden in a context of assertions or denials which carry high confidence simply because of the population base rates, regardless of the test's validity. I think this fallacy is at least as important and frequent as others for which we have familiar labels (halo effect, leniency error, contamination, etc.). One of the best ways to increase the general sensitivity to such fallacies is to give them a name. We ought to make our clinical students as acutely aware of the Barnum effect as they are of the dangers of countertransference or the standard error of *r*.

The preceding mathematical considerations, while they should serve as a check upon some widespread contemporary forms of tea-leaf reading, are unfortunately not very "positive" by way of writing a good cookbook. "Almost anything needs a little salt for flavor" or "It is rarely appropriate to put ketchup on the dessert" would be sound advice but largely negative and not very helpful to an average cook. I wish now to describe briefly a piece of empirical research, reported in a thesis just completed at Minnesota by Charles C. Halbower, which takes the cookbook method 100 per cent seriously; and which seems to show, at least in one clinical context, what can be done in a more constructive way by means of a cookbook of even moderate trustworthiness.* By some geographical coincidence, the psychometric device used in this research was a structured test consisting of a set of 550 items, commonly known as MMPI. Let me

*I am indebted to Dr. Halbower for permission to present this summary of his thesis data in advance of his own more complete publication.

emphasize that the MMPI is not here being compared with anything else, and that the research does not aim to investigate Multiphasic validity (although the general order of magnitude of the obtained correlations does give some incidental information in that respect). What Dr. Halbower asked was this: given a Multiphasic profile, how does one arrive at a personality description from it? Using the rule-of-thumb method, a clinician familiar with MMPI interpretation looks at the profile, thinks awhile, and proceeds to describe the patient he imagines would have produced such a pattern. Using the cookbook method, we don't need a clinician; instead, a $230-per-month clerk-typist in the outer office simply reads the numbers on the profile, enters the cookbook, locates the page on which is found some kind of "modal description" for patients with such a profile, and this description is then taken as the best available approximation to the patient. We know, of course, that every patient is unique—absolutely, unqualifiedly unique. Therefore, the application of a cookbook description will inevitably make errors, some of them perhaps serious ones. If we knew *which* facets of the cookbook sketch needed modification as applied to the present unique patient, we would, of course, depart from the cookbook at these points; but we don't know this. If we start monkeying with the cookbook recipe in the hope of avoiding or reducing these errors, we will in all likelihood improve on the cookbook in some respects but, unfortunately, will worsen our approximation in others. Given a finite body of information, such as the 13 two-digit numbers of a Multiphasic profile, there is obviously *in fact* (whether we have yet succeeded in *finding* it or not) a "most probable" value for any personality facet, and also for any configuration of facets, however complex or "patterned" (10, pp. 131–134). It is easy to prove that a method of characterization which departs from consistent adherence to this "best guess" stands to lose. Keep in mind, then, that the raw data from which a personality description was to be inferred consisted of an MMPI profile. In other words, the Halbower study was essentially a comparison of the rule-of-thumb versus the cookbook method where each method was, however, functioning upon the same information—an MMPI. We are in effect contrasting the validity of two methods of "reading" Multiphasics.

In order to standardize the domain to be covered, and to yield a reasonably sensitive quantification of the goodness of description, Dr. Halbower utilized Q sorts. From a variety of sources he constructed a Q pool of 154 items, the majority being phenotypic or intermediate and a minority being genotypic. Since these items were intended for clinically expert sorters employing an "external" frame of reference, many of them were in technical language. Some sample items from his pool are: "Reacts against his dependency needs with hostility"; "manifests reality distortions"; "takes a dominant, ascendant role in interactions with others"; "is rebellious toward authority figures, rules, and other constraints"; "is counteractive in the face of frustration"; "gets appreciable secondary gain from his symptoms"; "is experiencing pain"; "is naive"; "is impunitive"; "utilizes intellectualization as a defense mechanism"; "shows evidence of latent hostility"; "manifests inappropriate affect." The first step was to construct a cookbook based upon these 154 items as the ingredients; the recipes were to be in the form of directions as to the optimal Q-sort placement of each item.

How many distinguishable recipes will the cookbook contain? If we had infallible criterion Q sorts on millions of cases, there would be as many recipes as there are possible MMPI profiles. Since we don't have this ideal situation, and never will, we have to compromise by introducing coarser grouping. Fortunately, we know that the validity of our test is poor enough so that this coarseness will not result in the sacrifice of much, if any, information. How coarsely we group, i.e., how different two Multiphasic curves have to be before we refuse to call them "similar" enough to be coordinated with the same recipe, is a very complicated matter involving both theoretical and practical considerations. Operating within the limits of a doctoral dissertation, Halbower confined his study to four profile "types." These curve types were specified by the first two digits of the Hathaway code plus certain additional requirements based upon clinical experience. The four MMPI codes used were those beginning 123', 13', 27', and 87' (5). The first three of these codes are the most frequently occurring in the Minneapolis VA Mental Hygiene Clinic population, and the fourth code, which is actually fifth in frequency of occurrence, was chosen in order to have a quasipsychotic type in the study. It is worth noting that these four codes constitute 58 per cent of all MMPI curves seen in the given population; so that Halbower's gross recipe categories already cover the majority of such outpatients. The nature of the further stipulations, refining the curve criteria within each two-digit code class, is illustrated by the following specifications for code 13', the "hysteroid valley" or "conversion V" type:

1. Hs and $Hy \geqq 70$.
2. $D < (Hs$ and $Hy)$ by at least one sigma.
3. K or $L > ?$ and F.
4. $F \leqq 65$.
5. Scales 4,5,6,7,8,9,0 all $\leqq 70$.

For each of these MMPI curve types, the names of nine patients were then randomly chosen from the list of those meeting the curve specifications. If the patient was still in therapy, his therapist was asked to do a Q sort (11 steps, normal distribution) on him. The MMPI had been withheld from these therapists. If the patient had been terminated, a clinician (other than Halbower) did a Q sort based upon study of the case folder, including therapist's notes and any available psychometrics (except, of course, the Multiphasic). This yields Q sorts for nine patients of a given curve type. These nine sorts were then pairwise intercorrelated, and by inspection of the resulting 36 coefficients, a subset of five patients was chosen as most representative of the curve type. The Q sorts on these five "representative" patients were then averaged, and this average Q sort was taken as the cookbook recipe to be used in describing future cases having the given MMPI curve. Thus, this modal, crystallized, "distilled-essence" personality description was obtained by eliminating patients with atypical sortings and pooling sortings on the more typical, hoping to reduce both errors of patient sampling and of clinical judgment. This rather complicated sequence of procedures may be summarized thus:

Deriving cookbook recipe for a specified curve type, such as the "conversion V" above:

1. Sample of $N =$ nine patients currently or recently in therapy and meeting the MMPI specifications for conversion V curve.
2. 154-item Q sort done on each patient by therapist or from therapist notes and case folder. (These sorts MMPI-uncontaminated.)
3. Pairwise Q correlations of these nine patients yields 36 intercorrelations.
4. Selection of subset $N' =$ five "modal" patients from this matrix by inspectional cluster method.
5. Mean of Q sorts on these five "core" patients is the cookbook recipe for the MMPI curve type in question.

Having constructed one recipe, he started all over again with a random sample of nine patients whose Multiphasics met the second curve-type specifications, and carried out these cluster-and-pooling processes upon them. This was done for each of the four curve types which were to compose the cookbook. If you have reservations about any of the steps in constructing this miniature cookbook, let me remind you that this is all preliminary, i.e., *it is the means of arriving at the cookbook recipe.* The proof of the pudding will be in the eating, and any poor choices of tactics or patients up to this point should merely make the cookbook less trustworthy than it would otherwise be.

Having thus written a miniature cookbook consisting of only four recipes, Halbower then proceeded to cook some dishes to see how they would taste. For cross validation he chose at random four new Mental Hygiene Clinic patients meeting the four curve specifications and who had been seen in therapy for a minimum of ten hours. With an eye to validity generalization to a somewhat different clinical population, with different base rates, he also chose four patients who were being seen as inpatients at the Minneapolis VA Hospital. None of the therapists involved had knowledge of the patients' Multiphasics. For purposes of his study, Halbower took the therapist's Q sort, based upon all of the case folder data (minus MMPI) plus his therapeutic contacts, as the best available criterion; although this "criterion" is acceptable only in the sense of construct validity (1). An estimate of its absolute level of trustworthiness is not important since it is being used as the common reference basis for a comparison of two methods of test reading.

Given the eight criterion therapist Q sorts (2 patients for each MMPI curve type), the task of the cookbook is to predict these descriptions. Thus, for each of the two patients having MMPI code 123', we simply assign the Q-sort recipe found in the cookbook as the best available description. How accurate this description is can be estimated (in the sense of construct validity) by Q correlating it with the criterion therapist's description. These eight "validity" coefficients varied from .36 to .88 with a median of .69. As would be expected, the hospital inpatients yielded the lower correlations. The Mental Hygiene Clinic cases, for whom the cookbook was really intended, gave validities of .68, .69, .84, and .88 (see Table 1).

How does the rule-of-thumb method show up in competition with the cookbook? Here we run into the problem of differences in clinical skill, so Halbower had each MMPI profile read blind by more than one clinician. The task was to interpret the profile by doing a Q sort. From two to five clinicians thus "read" each of the eight individual profiles, and the resulting 25 sorts were Q correlated with the appropriate therapist criterion sorts. These validity coefficients run from .29 to .63 with a median of .46. The clinicians were all Minnesota trained and varied in their experience with MMPI from less than a year (first-year VA trainees) through all training levels to PhD staff psychologists with six years' experience. The more experienced clinicians had probably seen over two thousand MMPI profiles in relation to varying amounts of other clinical data, including intensive psychotherapy. Yet not one of the 25 rule-of-thumb readings was as valid as the cookbook reading. Of the 25 comparisons which can be made between the validity of a single clinician's rule-of-thumb reading and that of the corresponding cookbook reading of the same patient's profile, 18 are significant in favor of the cookbook at the .01 level of confidence and 4 at the .05 level. The remaining 3 are also in favor of the cookbook but not significantly so.

Confining our attention to the more appropriate outpatient population, for (and upon) which the cookbook was developed, the mean r (estimated through z transformation) is .78 for the cookbook method, as contrasted with a mean

TABLE 1

VALIDATION OF THE FOUR COOKBOOK DESCRIPTIONS ON NEW CASES, AND COMPARATIVE VALIDITIES OF THE COOKBOOK MMPI READINGS AND RULE-OF-THUMB READINGS BY CLINICIANS

1. Four patients currently in therapy Q-described by the therapist (10 hours or more therapy plus case folder minus MMPI). This is taken as best available criterion description of each patient.
2. MMPI cookbook recipe Q-correlated with this criterion description.
3. For each patient, 4 or 5 clinicians "read" his MMPI in usual rule-of-thumb way, doing Q-sorts.
4. These rule-of-thumb Q-sorts also Q-correlated with criterion description.
5. Cross-validation results in outpatient sample.

	MMPI Curve Type			
Validities	Code 123'	Code 27'	Code 13'	Code 87'
Cookbook	.88	.69	.84	.68
Rule-of-thumb (mean)	.75	.50	.50	.58

Range (4–5 readers) .55 to .63 .29 to .54 .37 to .52 .34 to .58

Mean of 4 cookbook validities, through $z_r = .78$

Mean of 17 rule-of-thumb validities, through $z_r = .48$

Cookbook's superiority in validly predicted variance = 38%

6. Validity generalization to inpatient (psychiatric hospital) sample with different base rates; hence, an "unfair" test of cookbook.

	MMPI Curve Type			
Validities	Code 123'	Code 27'	Code 13'	Code 87'
Cookbook	.63	.64	.36	.70
Rule-of-thumb (2 readers)	.37, .49	.29, .42	.30, .30	.50, .50

Mean of 4 cookbook validities, through $z_r = .60$

Mean of 8 rule-of-thumb validities, through $z_r = .41$

Cookbook's superiority in validly predicted variance = 19%

(for 17 rule-of-thumb descriptions) of only .48, a difference of 30 points of correlation, which in this region amounts to a difference of 38 per cent in the validly predicted variance! The cookbook seems to be superior to the rule-of-thumb not merely in the sense of statistical significance but by an amount which is of very practical importance. It is also remarkable that even when the cookbook recipes are applied to patients from a quite different kind of population, their validity still excels that of rule-of-thumb MMPI readers who are in daily clinical contact with that other population. The improvement in valid variance in the hospital sample averages 19 per cent (see item 6 in Table 1).

A shrewd critic may be thinking, "Perhaps this is because all kinds of psychiatric patients are more or less alike, and the cookbook has simply taken advantage of this rather trivial fact." In answer to this objection, let me say first that to the extent the cookbook's superiority did arise from its actuarially determined tendency to "follow the base rates," that would be a perfectly sound application of the inverse probability considerations I at first advanced. For example, most psychiatric patients are in some degree depressed. Let us suppose the mean Q-sort placement given by therapists to the item "depressed" is seven. "Hysteroid" patients, who characteristically exhibit the so-called "conversion V" on their MMPI profiles (Halbower's cookbook code 13), are less depressed than most neurotics. The clinician, seeing such a conversion valley on the Multiphasic, takes this relation into account by attributing "lack of depression" to the patient. But maybe he overinterprets, giving undue weight to the psychometric finding and understressing the base rate. So his rule-of-thumb placement is far down at the nondepressed end, say at position three. The cookbook, on the other hand, "knows" (actuarially) that the mean Q placement for the item "depressed" is at five in patients with such profiles—lower than the over-all mean seven but not displaced as much in the conversion subgroup as the clinician thinks. If patients are so homogeneous with respect to a certain characteristic that the psychometrics ought not to influence greatly our attribution or placement in defiance of the over-all actuarial trend, then the clinician's tendency to be unduly influenced is a source of erroneous clinical decisions and a valid argument in favor of the cookbook.

However, if this were the chief explanation of Halbower's findings, the obvious conclusion would be merely that MMPI was not differentiating, since any test-induced departure from a description of the "average patient" would tend to be more wrong than right. Our original question would then be rephrased, "What is the comparative efficiency of the cookbook and the rule-of-thumb method *when each is applied to psychometric information having some degree of intrinsic validity?*" Time permits me only brief mention of the several lines of evidence in Halbower's study which eliminate the Barnum effect as an explanation. First of all, Halbower had selected his 154 items from a much larger initial Q pool by a preliminary study of therapist sortings on a heterogeneous sample of patients in which items were eliminated if they showed low interpatient dispersal. Second, study of the placements given an item over the four cookbook recipes reveals little similarity (e.g., only two items recur in the top quartile of all four recipes; 60 per cent of the items occur in the top quartile of only one recipe). Third, several additional correlational findings combine to show that the cookbook was not succeeding merely by describing an "average patient" four times over. For example, the clinicians' Q description of their conception of the "average patient" gave very low validity for three of the four codes, and a "mean average patient" description constructed by pooling these clinicians' stereotypes was not much better (see Table 2). For Code 123' (interestingly enough, the

TABLE 2

VALIDITIES OF FOUR CLINICIANS' DESCRIPTION OF "AVERAGE PATIENT," OF THE MEAN OF THESE STEREOTYPES, AND OF THE COOKBOOK RECIPE (OUTPATIENT CASES ONLY)

MMPI Curve Type	Validities of "Average Patient" Descriptions by 4 Clinicians	Validity of Mean of These 4 "Average Patient" Stereotypes	Validity of Cookbook Recipe
Code 123'	.63 to .69	.74	.88
Code 27'	−.03 to .20	.09	.69
Code 13'	.25 to .37	.32	.84
Code 87'	.25 to .35	.31	.68

commonest code among therapy cases in this clinic) the pooled stereotype was actually more valid than rule-of-thumb Multiphasic readings. (This is Bayes' Theorem with a vengeance!) Nevertheless, I am happy to report that this "average patient" description was still inferior to the Multiphasic cookbook (significant at the .001 level).

In the little time remaining, let me ruminate about the implications of this study, supposing it should prove to be essentially generalizable to other populations and to other psychometric instruments. From a theoretical point of view, the trend is hardly surprising. It amounts to the obvious fact that the human brain is an inefficient recording and computing device. The cookbook method has an advantage over the rule-of-thumb method because it (a) samples more representatively, (b) records and stores information better, and (c) computes statistical weights which are closer to the optimal. We can perhaps learn more by putting the theoretical question negatively: when should we *expect* the cookbook to be

inferior to the brain? The answer to this question presumably lies in the highly technical field of computing machine theory, which I am not competent to discuss. As I understand it, the use of these machines requires that certain rules of data combination be fed initially into the machine, followed by the insertion of suitably selected and coded information. Putting it crudely, the machine can "remember" and can "think routinely," but it cannot "spontaneously notice what is relevant" nor can it "think" in the more high-powered, creative sense (e.g., it cannot invent theories). To be sure, noticing what is relevant must involve the exemplification of some rule, perhaps of a very complex form. But it is a truism of behavior science that organisms can *exemplify* rules without *formulating* them. To take a non-controversial example outside the clinical field, no one today knows how to state fully the rules of "similarity" or "stimulus equivalence" for patterned visual perception or verbal generalization; but of course we all exemplify daily these undiscovered rules. This suggests that as long as psychology cannot give a complete, explicit, quantitative account of the "dimensions of relevance" in behavior connections, the cookbook will not completely duplicate the clinician (11). The clinician *here* acts as an inefficient computer, but that is better than a computer with certain major rules completely left out (because we can't build them in until we have learned how to formulate them). The use of the therapist's own unconscious in perceiving verbal and imaginal relations during dream interpretation is, I think, the clearest example of this. But I believe the exemplification of currently unformulable rules is a widespread phenomenon in most clinical inference. However, you will note that these considerations apply chiefly (if not wholly) to matters of *content,* in which a rich, highly varied, hard-to-classify content (such as free associations) is the input information. The problem of "stimulus equivalence" or "noticing the relevant" does not arise when the input data are in the form of preclassified responses, such as a Multiphasic profile or a Rorschach psychogram. I have elsewhere (10, pp. 110–111) suggested that even in the case of such prequantified patterns there arises the possibility of causal-theory-mediated idiographic extrapolations into regions of the profile space in which we lack adequate statistical experience; but I am now inclined to view that suggestion as a mistake. The underlying theory must itself involve some hypothesized function, however crudely quantified; otherwise, how is the alleged "extrapolation" possible? I can think of no reason why the estimation of the parameters in this underlying theoretical function should constitute an exception to the cookbook's superiority. If I am right in this, my "extrapolation" argument applies strictly only when a clinician literally *invents new theoretical relations or variables* in thinking about the individual patient. In spite of some clinicians' claims along this line, I must say I think it very rarely happens in daily clinical practice. Furthermore, even when it does happen, Bayes' Rule still applies. The *joint* probability of the theory's correctness, and of the attribute's presence (granting the theory but remembering nuisance variables) must be high enough to satisfy the inequalities I have presented, otherwise use of the theory will not pay off.

What are the pragmatic implications of the preceding analysis? Putting it bluntly, it suggests that for a rather wide range of clinical problems involving personality description from tests, the clinical interpreter is a costly middleman who might better be eliminated. An initial layout of research time could result in a cookbook whose recipes would encompass the great majority of psychometric configurations seen in daily work. I am fully aware that the prospect of a "clinical clerk" simply looking up Rorschach pattern number 73 J 10–5 or Multiphasic curve "Halbower Verzeichnis 626" seems very odd and even dangerous. I reassure myself by recalling that the number of phenotypic and genotypic attributes is, after all, finite; and that the number which are ordinarily found attributed or denied even in an extensive sample of psychological reports on patients is actually very limited. A best estimate of a Q-sort placement is surely more informative than a crude "Yes-or-No" decision of low objective confidence. I honestly cannot see, in the case of a *determinate trait domain* and a *specified clinical population,* that there is a serious intellectual problem underlying one's uneasiness. I invite you to consider the possibility that the emotional block we all experience in connection with the cookbook approach could be dissolved simply by trying it out until our daily successes finally get us accustomed to the idea.

Admittedly this would take some of the "fun" out of psychodiagnostic activity. But I suspect that most of the clinicians who put a high value on this kind of fun would have even more fun doing intensive psychotherapy. The great personnel needs today, and for the next generation or more, are for psychotherapists and researchers. (If you don't believe much in the efficacy of therapy, this is the more reason for research.) If all the thousands of clinical hours currently being expended in concocting clever and flowery personality sketches from test data could be devoted instead to scientific investigation (assuming we are still selecting and training clinicians to be scientists), it would probably mean a marked improvement in our net social contribution. If a reasonably good cookbook could help bring about this result, the achievement would repay tenfold the expensive and tedious effort required in its construction.

References

1. Cronbach, L. J., and Meehl, P. E. Construct validity in psychological tests. *Psychol. Bull.,* 52(1955), 281–302.

2. Dailey, C. A. The practical utility of the clinical report. *J. Consult. Psychol.,* 17(1953), 297–302.

3. Davenport, Beverly F. The semantic validity of TAT interpretations. *J. Consult. Psychol.,* 16(1952), 171–175.

4. Halbower, C. C. A comparison of actuarial versus clinical prediction to classes discriminated by MMPI. Unpublished doctor's dissertation, Univ. of Minn., 1955.

5. Hathaway, S. R. A coding system for MMPI profiles. *J. Consult. Psychol.,* 11(1947), 334–337.

6. Holsopple, J. Q., and Phelan, J. G. The skills of clinicians in analysis of projective tests. *J. Clin. Psychol.,* 10(1954), 307–320.

7. Kostlan, A. A method for the empirical study of psychodiagnosis. *J. Consult. Psychol.,* 18 (1954), 83–88.

8. Little, K. B., and Shneidman, E. S. The validity of MMPI interpretations. *J. Consult. Psychol.,* 18(1954), 425–428.

9. —— The validity of thematic projective technique interpretations. *J. Pers.,* 23(1955), 285–294.

10. Meehl, P. E. *Clinical versus statistical prediction.* Minneapolis: Univ. of Minn. Press, 1954.

11. —— "Comment" on McArthur, C. Analyzing the clinical process. *J. Counsel. Psychol.,* 1(1954), 203–208.

12. —— and Rosen, A. Antecedent probability and the efficiency of psychometric signs, patterns, or cutting scores. *Psychol. Bull.,* 52 (1955), 194–216.

13. Paterson, D. G. Character reading at sight of Mr. X according to the system of Mr. P. T. Barnum. (Mimeographed, unpublished.)

14. Rosen, A. Detection of suicidal patients: an example of some limitations in the prediction of infrequent events. *J. Consult. Psychol.,* 18(1954), 397–403.

15. Skinner, B. F. *The behavior of organisms.* New York: Appleton-Century-Crofts, 1938.

Clinical and Statistical Prediction: A Reformulation and Some New Data *

ROBERT R. HOLT

RESEARCH CENTER FOR MENTAL HEALTH, NEW YORK UNIVERSITY

The controversial discussions started a few years ago by Meehl's tightly packed

Reprinted from the *Journal of Abnormal & Social Psychology,* 56(1958), 1–12, with the permission of the American Psychological Association and the author.

* The research reported in this paper was supported by the Veterans' Administration, the New York Foundation, and the Menninger Foundation, and was carried out jointly by Dr. Lester Luborsky and the author, with the collaboration of Drs. Wm. R. Morrow, David Rapaport, and S. K. Escalona.

little book, *Clinical vs. Statistical Prediction* (10), still continue—especially among graduate students in psychology, most of whom have to read it. Clinical students in particular complain of a vague feeling that a fast one has been put over on them, that under a great show of objectivity, or at least bipartisanship, Professor Meehl has actually sold the clinical approach up the river. The specific complaints they lodge against the book are, in my opinion, mostly based on misinterpretations, wishful thinking, or other errors, yet I have felt for some time that there was something valid in the irrational reaction without knowing why.

What I propose to show here is that clinicians do have a kind of justified grievance against Meehl, growing out of his formulation of the issues rather than his arguments, which are sound. Finally, I want to offer a slightly different approach to the underlying problems, illustrated by some data. It may not quite make the lion lie down with the lamb, but I hope that it will help us all get on with our business, which is the making of a good science and profession.

The Issues Restated

Meehl's book contains a review of the controversy, a logical analysis of the nature of clinical judgment, a survey of empirical studies, and some conclusions. I am not going to go into his treatment of the logical issues and his psychological reconstruction of clinical thinking; for the most part, I agree with this part of the book and consider it a useful contribution to methodology. I want to focus rather on his conception of what the issues are in the controversy, on his treatment of the evidence, and on some of his conclusions.

Many issues make better reading when formulated as battles, and the field of the assessment and prediction of human behavior has not lacked for controversy-loving gauntlet-flingers. The sane and thoughtful voices of Horst and his collaborators, urging compromise and collaboration (5), have been shouted down by the warcries of such partisans as Sarbin (14) on the actuarial side and Murray (12) on the clinical or (as he put it) organismic. Meehl approached the problem with a full awareness of the feelings on both sides, and apparently

with the hope that the therapeutic ploy of bringing them all out into the open at the beginning would enable him to discuss the issues objectively.

In a recent discussion of the stir his book has raised, Meehl has expressed surprise and dismay (11) that his effort to take a balanced and qualified position has led so many people to misunderstand him as claiming that clinical prediction has been proved worthless. Yet he is not blameless; by posing the question of clinical *vs.* statistical prediction, he has encouraged two warring camps to form. This in turn makes it appear all the more compellingly that there *are* two clear-cut types of prediction to be compared.

The root difficulty, I believe, lies in Meehl's acceptance of *clinical* and *actuarial* as concepts that can without further analysis be meaningfully applied to a variety of predictive endeavors of an experimental or practical sort. Accepting them as valid types, he can hardly do anything other than pit one against the other and try to decide what is the proper sphere of exercise for each. But the terms in this antithesis mean many things; they are constellations of parts that are not perfectly correlated and can be separated.

The issue cannot therefore be sharply drawn so long as we speak about anything as complex as "clinical prediction" or "the clinical method." Rather, I think the central issue is the *role of clinical judgment in predicting human behavior.* By clinical judgment here, I mean nothing more complicated than the problem-solving or decision-reaching behavior of a person who tries to reach conclusions on the basis of facts and theories already available to him by thinking them over.

Let us make a fresh start, therefore, by examining the logical structure of the predictive process with an eye to locating the points where clinical judgment may enter. The following five-step process is idealized, and in practice some of the steps are more or less elided, but that does not hurt this analysis.

First, if we are to predict some kind of behavior, it is presupposed that we acquaint ourselves with what we are trying to predict. This may be called job analysis or the study of the criterion. Perhaps those terms sound a little fancy when their referent is something that seems so obvious to common sense. Nevertheless, it is surprising how often people expend a great deal of time and effort trying to predict a kind of behavior about which they know very little and apparently without even thinking that it might help if they could find out more. Consider the job of predicting outcome of flight training, for example. Many attempts to predict passing or washing out have been made by clinicians without any direct experience in learning to fly, without any study of flight trainees to see what they have to *do* in order to learn how to fly a plane, or of the ways they can fail to make the grade (cf. 4).

There is a hidden trick in predicting something like success in flight training, because that is not itself a form of behavior. It is an outcome, a judgment passed by someone on a great deal of concrete behavior. The same is true for grades in college, success in any type of treatment, and a host of other criteria that are the targets in most predictive studies. Because it is hidden by the label, there is a temptation to forget that the behavior you should be trying to predict exists and must be studied if it is to be rationally forecast. In the highly effective pilot selection work carried out by psychologists during the war, careful job analyses were an important step in the total predictive process and undoubtedly contributed a good deal to the over-all success.

This first stage is hardly a good point at which to try to rely on clinical judgment. The result is most likely to be that guesses, easy and arbitrary assumptions, and speculative extrapolations will attempt to substitute for real information. And no matter how remarkable clinical judgment may sometimes be, it can never create information where there is none.

The *second* logical step is to decide what intervening variables need to be considered if the behavior is to be predicted. As soon as we get away from the simplest kind of prediction—that someone will continue to act the way he has been acting, or that test behavior A will continue to correlate (for an unknown reason) with criterion behavior B—we have to deal with the inner constructs that mediate behavior and the determining situational variables as well. You cannot make a rational choice of the kind of information you will need to have about a person to make predictions without some intervening variables, though they may remain entirely implicit. At this point, judgment enters— always, I think, though it may be assisted by empirical study. The best practice seems to be to give explicit consideration to this step, and to supply judgment with as many relevant facts as possible. This means studying known instances, comparing people who showed the behavior in question with others who in the same situation failed to.

All too often, when the problem of intervening variables is considered at all, it is handled by unaided clinical judgment. For example, in the Michigan project on the selection of clinical psychologists (7), a good many personality variables were rated, but there was no previous work highlighting the ones that might be related to success as a clinical psychologist. It was left up to each judge to form his own conception (from experience, theory, and guess) about what qualities mattered most. Again, this puts a greater burden on clinical judgment than it should reasonably be asked to bear. Yet some clinicians seem to have the mistaken notion that they are being false to their professional ideals if they stir from their armchairs at this point; nothing could be further from the best in clinical tradition, which is unashamedly empirical.

Third, it is necessary to find out what types of data afford measures or indications of the intervening variables, and can thus be used to predict the criterion behavior. If a good job has been done of the preceding step, it may be possible to rely entirely on judgment to make the preliminary selection of appropriate means of gathering predictive data. For example, if a job analysis and study of persons who have done well at the performance in question both suggest that verbal intelligence and information of a certain type are the main requisites, it would be easy to make good guesses about appropriate instruments to provide the predictive data. I use the word "guesses" deliberately, however, to emphasize the fact that judgment can do no more than supply hypotheses; it cannot substitute for an empirical trial to see whether in fact and under the conditions of this particular study the likely-looking instruments do yield data that predict the criterion.

Notice that almost any actuarial predictive system presupposes carrying through this step. If there is to be an actuarial table, one has to collect great numbers of cases to determine the success frequencies for each cell in the table; if a regression equation is to be used, there must be a preliminary study to fix the beta weights. Unfortunately, it is possible to work clinically *without* first getting an empirical check on one's hypotheses about likely-seeming instruments. At the risk of boring you, I repeat: there simply is no substitute for empirical study of the actual association between a type of predictive data and the criterion. Just as judgment is indispensable in forming hypotheses, it cannot be used to test them.

Perhaps this caution seems misplaced. Do I seem to be urging that you should first *do* a predictive study before embarking on one? I am. That is exactly what happens in actuarial prediction: the formula or table being pitted against judgmental prediction is typically being *cross*-validated, while in none of the studies Meehl cites were the clinical predictions under test being cross-validated. This alone is a major reason to expect superior performance from the actuarial predictions, and again it is a disadvantage under which the clinician by no means has to labor.

The next step, the *fourth* one, is to gather and process the data to give measures of the intervening variables. Meehl clearly recognizes that at this point clinical judgment either may play a large role or may be minimized. At one extreme, the data-yielding instrument may be a machine, a gadget like a complex coordination tester, which automatically counts errors and successes and makes a cumulative record of them. The resulting numbers may be directly usable in a regression equation without the intervention of anyone more skilled than a clerk. At an intermediate level, scoring most psychological tests requires a modicum of clinical judgment, though a high degree of reliability may be attained. At the other extreme is the interview; a great deal of clinical judgment is needed to convert the raw data into indices of the constructs the interviewer wants to assess.

It is easily overlooked that judgment needs the help of empirical study in this phase of the work too. The clinician's training supplies this empirical base in large part, but when he is using a familiar instrument to measure unusual intervening variables, or when he is working with an unfamiliar instrument, judgment grows fallible, and it is no more than prudent to piece it out by careful study of the same kind of predictive data on known subjects on whom the intervening variables have been well assessed independently.

The *fifth* and final step is the crucial one: at last the processed predictive data are *combined* so as to yield definite predictions in each case. The job can be done by clinical judgment, or it can be done by following a fixed rule (an actuarial table or regression equation) in a mechanical way. That much is clear; indeed, this is the locus of Meehl's main interest. I am taking it as granted that a clinician often integrates data in a different way than a statistician—as Meehl says, by performing a creative act, constructing a model of the person from the given facts put together with his theoretical understanding and thus generating perhaps a new type of prediction from a pattern he has never encountered before. We are all curious to know how well good clinicians can do it, and wonder if actuarial combination of data can do as well or better.

But it now seems plain that Meehl has been *too much* interested in this last stage, and as a result has neglected to pay enough attention to the way the earlier aspects of the predictive process were handled in the studies he has reviewed. Here I want to state my main critical point: *If two attempts to predict the same behavior differ significantly in the role played by clinical judgment as against actual study of the facts in one or more of the four earlier parts of the predictive process, a comparison of the successes of the two attempts can tell us nothing definite about the effectiveness of clinical judgment at the final, crucial stage.* For this reason, in none of the 20 studies Meehl cites were the comparisons pertinent to the point. Particularly at the vital third step, the predicting statisticians have had the advantage of having previously studied the way their predictive data are related to the criterion; the clinicians have not.

If your reaction is, "So much the worse for the clinicians; nobody stopped them," I am afraid you are thinking about a different question from the one Meehl has raised. If the issue were whether some clinicians have made themselves look foolish by claiming too much, then I should agree: these studies show that they have, and unhappily, they have brought discredit on clinical methods generally. But the studies cited by Meehl and more recently by Cronbach in the *Annual Review of Psychology* (2) unfortunately have too many flaws at other points to tell us what clinical judgment can or cannot do as a way of combining data to make predictions. It is as if two riflemen were having a target match, but one took a wrong turn on the way to the shoot, never showed up, and lost by default. He demonstrated himself to be a poor driver, perhaps, but we never found out how well he could shoot, which is what we really wanted to know.

The other point I want to make in connection with the five-step analysis of the predictive process is this: Since there are so many ways in which clinical judgment can enter, for better or for worse, it makes little sense to classify every attempt to predict behavior on one side or the other of a simple dichotomy, clinical vs. statistical. There can be many types of clinical and actuarial combinations, and many are in fact found in Meehl's mixed bag.

For purposes of exposition, I should like to suggest an only slightly extended typology. Extracting from the best actuarial studies those parts of their procedure during the first four steps that are simply the application of common sense and the scientific method, I propose that we make it quite plain that these can be separated from actuarial prediction at the final step by creating a third type. Thus we should have:

Type I. *Pure actuarial:* Only objective data are used to predict a clear-cut criterion by means of statistical processes. The role of judgment is held to a minimum, and maximal use is made of a sequence of steps exemplified in the most successful Air Force studies in selecting air crew personnel (job analysis, item analysis, cross-validation, etc.).

Type II. *Naive clinical:* The data used are primarily qualitative with no attempt at objectification; their processing is entirely a clinical and intuitive matter, and there is no prior study of the criterion or of the possible relation of the predictive data to it. Clinical judgment is at every step relied on not only as a way of integrating data to produce predictions, but also as an alternative to acquaintance with the facts.

Type III. *Sophisticated clinical:* Qualitative data from such sources as interviews, life histories, and projective techniques are used as well as objective facts and scores, but as much as possible of objectivity, organization, and scientific method are introduced into the planning, the gathering of the data, and their analysis. All the refinements of design that the actuarial tradition has furnished are employed, including job analysis, pilot studies, item analysis, and successive cross-validations. Quantification and statistics are used wherever helpful, but the clinician himself is retained as one of the prime instruments, with an effort to make him as reliable and valid a data-processor as possible; and he makes the final organization of the data to yield a set of predictions tailored to each individual case.

If we now re-examined the studies cited by Meehl and Cronbach, we see that most of them have pitted approximations to Type I actuarial predictive designs against essentially Type II naive clinical approaches. It seems hardly remarkable that Type I has generally given better results than Type II; indeed, the wonder should be that the naive clinical predictions have done as well as they have, in a number of instances approaching the predictive efficiency of actuarial systems.

Other studies cited have come closer to comparing Type II with Type III—naive vs. sophisticated clinical prediction instead of clinical vs. statistical. For example, the prognostic studies by Wittman (16) compared predictions of reaction to shock treatment made in a

global way at staff conference with a system she devised. But her system used highly judgmental predictive variables, as Meehl himself points out (ranging from *duration of psychosis* to *anal erotic vs. oral erotic*), and they were combined using a set of weights assigned on judgmental, not statistical grounds.* What she showed was that a systematic and comprehensive evaluation of the thirty items in her scale (all based on previous empirical work) made better predictions of the outcome of shock treatment than global clinical judgments not so organized and guided. A study of movement in family case work by Blenkner came to a very similar conclusion with somewhat different subject matter (1). When social workers rated an initial interview according to their general impressions, they were unable to predict the outcome of the case, whereas when their judgments were organized and guided by means of an outline calling for appraisals of five factors which had been shown in previous studies to be *meaningfully,* not statistically related to the criterion, then these judgmentally derived predictive variables, combined (like Wittman's) in an a priori formula, predicted the criterion quite well. Yet both studies are tallied as proving actuarial predictions superior to clinical.

Meehl's conclusion from his review of this "evidence" is that clinical prediction is an expensive and inefficient substitute for the actuarial method, and one that keeps clinicians from using their talents more constructively in psychotherapy or exploratory research.

The evidence available tells us hardly anything about the relative efficacy of clinical judgment in making predictions. The weight of numbers should not impress us; as long as the studies don't really bear on the issue, no matter how many are marshalled, they still have no

* It is true that the weights were applied in the same way for all cases; in this respect, the system deviates from the ideal Type III.

weight. Remember the *Literary Digest* poll: many times more straw votes than Gallup used, but a faulty sampling principle, so that piling up numbers made the conclusion less valid as it got more reliable. Moreover, the studies tallied are so different in method, involving varying amounts of clinical judgment at different points (in the "actuarial" instances as well as the "clinical" ones), that they cannot sensibly be added together.

What is fair to conclude, I think, is that many clinicians are wasting their time when they try to fall back on their clinical judgment in place of knowing what they are talking about. They have been guilty of over-extending themselves, trying to predict things they know nothing about, and learning nothing in the process of taking part in what Cronbach calls "horserace experimental designs," in which clinicians and statisticians merely try to outsmart each other. A multiplication of such studies will not advance clinical psychology.

One kind of comparative study might teach us something even though it would be hard to do properly: simultaneous attempts to predict the same criterion from the same data by clinicians and statisticians *who have gone through the same preliminary steps.* As the statistician studies the original group to determine the critical scores for his multiple cutting point formula (or whatever), the clinician will study the configurations of these scores in individuals of known performance. Then we will see how their respective predictive techniques work.

Does it really make sense, however, for both to use the same data and predict the same criterion? A second possibility would be for two otherwise equally sophisticated methods to predict the same criterion, each using the kind of data most appropriate to it. Or, third, the more clinical and the more statistical methods would not predict the same criterion, but each would undertake to predict the kind of behavior it is best

suited to, using the most appropriate kind of data.

Doesn't this third proposal abandon experimental controls necessary for intelligible results? To some extent, yes; but one may have to give up some control to avoid absurdity. As long as clinician and statistician are trying to predict the same criterion, the clinician is likely to be working under a severe, though concealed, handicap. The study will usually have been designed by the statistician; that is his business. He will naturally choose the kind of criterion for which *his* methods seem best adapted; indeed, the nature of his method makes it impossible for him to choose the kind of predictive task that would be most congenial to the clinician, such as drawing a multidimensional diagnostic picture of a total personality, or predicting what a patient will do next in psychotherapy. Thus, the statistician takes advantage of the foolish boast of the clinician, "Anything you can do, I can do better," and plans the contest on his own grounds. The clinician ends up trying to predict grade-point average in the freshman year by a "clinical synthesis" of high school grades and an intelligence test. This is a manifest absurdity; under the circumstances, how could the clinician do other than operate like a second-rate Hollerith machine? If clinical judgment is really to be tested, it must operate on data that are capable of yielding insights. Moreover, it makes hardly any more sense to expect it to grind out numerical averages of course grades than to expect an actuarial table to interpret dreams.

For reasons of this kind, McArthur (9) recently called for studies of the third type just listed, and maintained that there have as yet been no studies in which the clinician has been given a chance to show what he can do on his own terms. I want therefore to present briefly some results from one such attempt: a study in which clinicians tried to predict criteria of their own choosing, using clinical types of data—interviews and psychological tests (mainly projective techniques).* Since some preliminary reports of this work have already been quoted as showing the ineffectiveness of clinical predictions (cf. 2), I have a special desire to set the record straight.

Validating Naive and Sophisticated Clinical Predictions: Some New Data

The project was an effort to improve the methods by which medical men were selected for specialty training in the Menninger School of Psychiatry. It was begun by Dr. David Rapaport, together with Drs. Karl A. Menninger, Robert P. Knight, and other psychiatrists at the Menninger Foundation at the time the Menninger School of Psychiatry was founded 11 years ago. In the late summer of 1947, Dr. Lester Luborsky and I began work on it, and since then we have jointly carried major responsibility for the project although quite a number of other people have made important contributions.

Our work consisted of two predictive studies. Following the terminology suggested above, one used a naive clinical method, while the other was an attempt at a more sophisticated clinical method. The naive clinical design was simple: Psychiatrists and psychologists used their favorite means of assessing personality to forecast the level of future performance of psychiatric residents at the time when they applied to the School. The applicant came to Topeka after some preliminary correspondence, having survived a rough screening of credentials and application forms. He was seen by three psychiatrists, each of whom interviewed him for about an hour, rated his probable success as a resident on a 10-point scale, and made a recommendation: Take, Reject, or Doubtful. The

* This study is presented at length in a forthcoming book (3).

psychologist made similar ratings and recommendations after analyzing results of a Wechsler-Bellevue, Rorschach, and Word Association test. In addition, both psychologists and psychiatrists submitted brief qualitative reports of their appraisals of the man's positive and negative potentialities. All of the data and predictions were turned over to the Admissions Committee, which made the final decision to accept or reject each man.

During the years of the project, from 1946 through 1952, six successive classes of residents were chosen. The first 456 applicants who went through this procedure formed our experimental population (excluding small numbers of Negroes, women, and persons from Latin-American and non-European cultures, since these minorities offered special problems of assessment). A little over 62 per cent of these applicants were accepted by the Committee, but only 238 actually entered the School; 46 changed their minds and went elsewhere. Nevertheless, we kept in touch with them and the 172 rejectees by a mail follow-up questionnaire for several years, so that we have data on certain aspects of their subsequent careers.

The clinicians making the predictions had in some cases had considerable experience in training psychiatric residents, but there was no explicit job analysis or preliminary study of criterion groups. They simply fell to and made their predictions and their decisions.

To test the validity of these clinical decisions, let us use as a criterion, first, whether or not a man passed the certifying examination of the American Board of Psychiatry and Neurology—the criterion set up by the specialty itself. We have this information on all subjects from the lists published by the Board. The Admissions Committee's decisions had a good deal of validity as predictors of this criterion: 71 per cent of the men they voted to accept had passed the Board examination in psychiatry by the end of

1956, while only 36 per cent of the rejected candidates had done so. This difference is significant at better than the .001 point. The recommendations made by interviewers (taking them all as a group) and the recommendations of the psychological testers to accept or reject likewise were highly valid predictors of this criterion, significances in both cases also being beyond .001.

It is interesting that the Committee decisions were slightly *better* at predicting both staying in psychiatry and passing the certification examination of the American Board of Psychiatry and Neurology—better than either the psychiatric interviewers or the psychological testers. It is possible, however, that much or all of this apparent superiority is due to the fact that rejection by the committee did discourage a few applicants from seeking training elsewhere.

Data of this kind are encouraging to the people trying to run a school of psychiatry but hard to interpret in a larger context. Who knows but that an actuarial table based on objectively ascertainable facts like grades in medical school, marital status, age, etc. might not have done just as well? We never took such a possibility very seriously, but we did try out a few such objective predictors in our spare time, just out of curiosity. None of them showed any particular promise as a predictor of any criterion taken alone, though it is possible that patterns of them such as an actuarial table uses might have operated a little better than chance.

The criteria on which we spent most time and labor were measures of competence in psychiatric work during the last two years of the three-year residency. Whenever a resident completed a period of time on a particular service, we would interview the staff men, consultants, and others who had directly supervised his clinical work, and get them to rate it quantitatively. The resulting criterion measure had a coefficient of internal consistency above .9 * (for the last few classes), and we have every reason to think it has a great deal of intrinsic validity. We also got the residents to rate each other's work. The reliability of their pooled ratings of over-all competence is also .9, and this criterion (which we call "Peers' Evaluations") correlates from .66 to .78 with Supervisors' Evaluations.

These criterion judgments enable us to test the validity of the predictive *ratings*. The validity correlations are not exciting, though for the entire group of residents in the Menninger School of Psychiatry they are all significantly better than zero at the one percent point. Taking the *mean* of the ratings given by the psychiatrists who interviewed an applicant, this predictor correlates .24 with Supervisors' Evaluations. The predictions of the psychological testers were not significantly better: the validity coefficient is .27. There was some fluctuation from class to class, the interviewers' validities varying from exactly .00 to *.52*, the testers' validities from .12 to .47. Likewise, the validities of ratings made by individual clinicians vary over the same range: psychiatric interviewers from .01 to .27 ($N = 93$) or .47 (significant at only the 5 percent point because the N was only 13), and psychologists from .20 to .41 ($N = 40$). At the same time, those individual clinicians all did much better in making the basic discrimination: recommending acceptance of men who actually became psychiatrists.

These correlations are nothing to get excited about, and nothing to be ashamed of either, particularly in view of the restriction of range in this selected, accepted sample. They show that the naive clinical method depends a good deal on the ability of the particular clinician do-

* Correlations in bold type are significant at the one per cent point, those in italics, at the five per cent point. One-tailed tests are used throughout to test the null hypothesis that the predictor does not correlate *positively* with the criterion.

ing the predicting, and that—at least in this study—a pooling of judgment helped make up for the deficiencies of individuals.

Let us turn now to the second experimental design, which I have called a *sophisticated clinical* type of prediction. I shall have to skip lightly over many complicated details, and make things look a little more orderly than they actually were. The design included a job analysis of the work done by psychiatric residents, which was broken down into a few major functions (such as diagnosis, psychotherapy, administration of wards) and 14 more specific aspects of work. Then we attempted to specify attributes of personality that would facilitate or hinder a man in carrying out such work, first by collecting the opinions of persons who had had long experience in training psychiatrists, psychotherapists, or psychoanalysts. The second way we went about it was to make an intensive study of a dozen excellent residents and a dozen who were rated at the bottom by their supervisors. We went over all the original assessment data on them, interviewed them and tested them extensively, trying out many novel approaches and then seeing what discriminated these known extreme groups. Thus, we learned what personological constructs differentiated good from poor residents, and what tests and test indicators gave evidence of these constructs. Hoping to guide clinical judgment in the use of interviews and projective tests, we used the data from these small samples of extremes to help us write detailed manuals on the use of the interview, TAT, Rorschach, and other techniques in the selection of psychiatric residents. The manuals listed discriminating cues, both positive and negative, which were to be summed algebraically. We then made preliminary cross-validations of these manuals (as many as we could) with encouraging results (cf. 8) and revised them after studying predictive successes and failures.

As a last step, we set up another predictive study to submit our manuals to a final cross-validation on a group of 64 subjects and to accomplish several other purposes at the same time. Four psychologists served as judges; each of them scored tests or interviews according to our manuals and also made free clinical judgments based on increasing amounts of data. Two of the judges made such predictive ratings after going through an entire file of assessment data: credentials, intellectual and projective tests, and a recorded and transcribed interview.

How did we make out? Considering first the manuals, only indifferently well. Of the six, two proved worthless (TAT Content and a special projective test); the other four all showed more or less promise, but there was none that yielded consistently significant validities regardless of who used it. Reliability, in terms of scorer agreement, was on the whole not very good, for a good deal of clinical judgment was still demanded. Consider, for example, one TAT cue that worked well for one judge (validity of .26 against Supervisors' Evaluations of Overall Competence). This cue called for judgments of the *originality* of each TAT story, obviously a matter on which psychologists might fairly easily disagree: scores by Judges I and II correlated—.04. The validities attained by the manuals for the Interview, Rorschach, Formal Aspects of the TAT, and Self-Interpretation of the TAT were on about the same general level as those from our first, naive clinical design—mostly in the .20's.

Now for the free clinical predictive ratings. When the judge had only one test or an interview to go on he usually added little by going beyond the manual and drawing on his general experience and intuition. Some judges did slightly better with free ratings than with manual scores, some a little worse. At this point, you may wonder at all this exposition for so small a result: barely significant validity coefficients, about the same size as those from a naive clinical approach, despite the attempt to create a sophisticated clinical predictive system that involved many actuarial elements. I believe that the lesson of our findings up to this point is simple: *With an inadequate sample of information about a person, no matter how sophisticated the technique of prediction, there is a low ceiling on the predictive validity that can be attained.* In our experience, even a battery of two or three tests (if exclusively projective), or an interview and a couple of projective techniques, does not give an adequate informational sample to enable clinicians to make very accurate predictions of complex behavioral outcomes over a period of three years.

Look next at the results when experimental judges made their predictions from as complete a body of information about a man as could be assembled at the time he applied. The hard-headed statis-

tical expectation *should* be that validities would at best remain at the same level, and more likely would decline. The widely read preliminary report of the Michigan project on the selection of clinical psychologists (6) reported declining validities as increasing amounts of information were made available to judges (in a design which, for all its complexity, was essentially a naive clinical one). Not so many people have read the full final report (7), where this issue is not discussed; it is necessary to pore over many tables and tally numbers of significant correlations at various stages to find out for oneself that with the final criteria there was a slight *rising* trend in validities of clinical predictions as the amount of information available to the predicting judge was increased.

The same thing is true of our results, but in a dramatic and unmistakable way (see Table 1). Considering only the two

TABLE 1

SOME VALIDITIES FROM SYSTEMATIC CLINICAL ASSESSMENT OF APPLICANTS FOR RESIDENCIES IN THE MENNINGER SCHOOL OF PSYCHIATRY

Predictors:	Validities of Predictors Against Criterion Evalutions of:									
	Over-all Competence		Competence in Psychotherapy		Competence in Diagnosis		Competence in Management		Competence in Ad- ministration	
	Sup.[a]	Peer [a]	Sup.	Peer	Sup.	Peer	Sup.	Peer	Sup.	Peer
Predictive Ratings										
Judge I: PRT [b]	.26	.23	.12	.26	.13	.21	.31	.00	.20	.10
Judge II: TAT	—.10	—.02	—.16	—.01	—.05	.20	—.08	.01	.04	.11
Judge I: All data	.57	.52	.48	.55	.58	.42	.52	.36	.55	.42
Judge II: All data	.22	.48	.15	.36	.24	.42	.13	.24	.24	.27
Liking Ratings										
Judge I: PRT	.29	.34	.16	.35	.24	.36	.15	.17	.19	.16
Judge II: TAT	—.02	.13	—.08	.15	.00	.30	—.17	—.02	—.14	.10
Judge I: All data	.58	.64	.45	.58	.51	.52	.52	.52	.50	.46
Judge II: All data	.25	.49	.20	.47	.21	.56	.10	.30	.18	.30

[a] Sup. = Supervisors' Evaluations; Peer = Peers' (Sociometric) Evaluations.
[b] PRT = Picture Reaction Test, a specially devised projective test similar to TAT.
Numbers of cases: For Judge I—Supervisors' Evaluations, PRT: 63, all data: 37
Peers' Evaluations, PRT: 45, all data: 30
For Judge II—Supervisors' Evaluations, TAT: 63, all data: 64
Peers' Evaluations, TAT: 45, all data: 46

judges who went through the entire mass of material, their final free clinical ratings of Over-all Competence correlated .57 and .22 with Supervisors' Evaluations and .52 and .48 with the sociometric Peers' Evaluations. In considering these correlations, remember that they are attenuated by a significant restriction of range, since all subjects had successfully passed through an Admissions Committee screening which had considerable validity. They have not been corrected for less than perfect reliabilities, either.

An incidental finding is even more remarkable. The predictive analysis was made approximately a year after the assessment data had been gathered. The judges went right through the entire series of cases, making their ratings in a *blind* analysis; names and other identifying data were concealed, and there was no direct contact with the subjects. Nevertheless, judges formed rather vivid impressions from the material, including a feeling of how well they would like each candidate personally. For control purposes, they were required to rate this feeling of *liking*. When we undertook to correlate the liking rating with predictors and criteria so as to partial out this possible source of error, we found that it was the best predictor we had! These ratings of liking by Judges I and II correlated highly with their predictive ratings, but even more highly with Supervisors' Evaluations (.58 and .25) and especially with Peers' Evaluations (.64 and .49).* A study of these liking rat-

* One consequence of the delay between the gathering of the data and their analysis was that some of the Ss who entered the Menninger School of Psychiatry became known to the predictive judges, raising the possibility of contamination of their predictions by criterion-relevant knowledge. Despite the fact that the analysis of the assessment material was done "blind," identifying data having been removed or concealed, Judge I fairly often recognized the identity of Ss at the final stage of analysis. He therefore did not make predictive ratings, which is why his Ns are so low for this stage. There

ings suggests to us as the most plausible explanation that they differed from our intentional clinical predictions in being somewhat more irrational, affective—perhaps intuitive—reactions to the same data.

In all of the correlations I have been citing, you will perhaps have noticed that one judge consistently did slightly better than the other. This is certainly to be expected. When clinical judgment is the main technique of processing data, there are bound to be differences due to the skill of clinicians in doing this particular job.

Are we justified in citing these few high validities as evidence of what the sophisticated clinical method can do in a study where it is given a chance to prove itself on grounds of its own choosing? I believe that we are. The psychologists who were our Judges I and II were considered to be good but not extraordinary clinicians, certainly no better than the best of the psychologists and psychiatrists who made the "naive clinical" predictions. They differed principally in that they had an adequate sample of data and had been through all the preliminary stages of studying the criterion in relation to the predictors in earlier

were a few borderline instances of partial or questionable recognition, however, in which Judge I (four cases) or II (two cases) had some information or misinformation about the subject. If these cases are eliminated, Judge II's validities go up more often than they go down, the range being from a decrease of .16 to an increase of .15. Judge I's validities against Supervisors' Evaluations are negligibly affected, the range of effects extending from a loss of .08 to a gain of .20. Most of his validities against Peers' Evaluations were more seriously affected, however, especially at the final (all-data) stage of analysis, where losses of up to 28 correlation points occurred. On the whole, however, even a very conservative handling of the problem of possibly contaminated cases does not change the essential import of the results: It was still possible for Judge I to obtain four validities of .50 or higher, and for Judge II to obtain two validities of .36 or higher. (For a fuller discussion of the problem of contamination in these results, see [3].)

groups of subjects. Moreover, they used systematic methods of analyzing the data, attempting to record all inferences and working with a set of intervening variables—personality constructs which were directly inferred from the test and interview data, and from which in turn the behavioral predictions were made. In a true sense, their clinical ratings were not naively based on unguided and uncontrolled judgment; they constituted a cross-validation of a whole structure of hypotheses about the determinants of psychiatric performance based on intensive prior study. Even so, our study left a great deal to be desired as a model of the sophisticated clinical approach—particularly on the scores of (a) a better job analysis, (b) a more broadly based, configurational approach to the design of manuals, and (c) a better stabilized criterion (see 3).

By way of contrast, a few more data before a final summing up. You remember that the battery of tests used in the first naive clinical predictive design consisted of the Wechsler-Bellevue, Rorschach, and Word Association tests. (The Szondi was also given, but was usually ignored; and the Strong Vocational Interest Blank was also routinely given, but was never scored in time to be used in the actual assessment for the Admissions Committee). The Rorschachs we gave were of course scored in the conventional way as well as by our special manual, and we thought it might be fun to see how some of the usual Rorschach scores would be related to the criterion. So we tried 14 scores and simple indices (like A%) with one class, and were surprised to find some rather high correlations. We decided therefore to see how a straight statistical-actuarial method of using the Rorschach would perform. Scrutinizing the table of intercorrelations between the Rorschach scores, we chose five of them that promised the greatest chances of success: DR%, number of good M, new F+%, F% and Stereotype% (scored after Rapaport, 13)—the last two because

they looked as if they might be good "suppressor variables." A multiple regression equation was worked out to give the best linear combination of these variables to predict Over-all Competence; R for this Class was .43 ($N = 64$). We noticed, however, that in the regression equation only the first two scores seemed to be playing any appreciable part, and in fact the multiple correlation using only per cent of rare details and number of good M was also .43. The other three were dropped from the formula, which was then tested on the Rorschach scores and criterion ratings of the first three classes. As expected, the correlation dropped out of sight on being cross-validated; with the new group of 116 subjects, it was .04.

The Strong Vocational Interest Blank, which (with an intelligence test) gave the best validities in the Kelly-Fiske study, likewise failed to yield any good predictor of competence in psychiatry. Even the special key ("Psychiatrist A") produced by Strong from a statistical analysis of thousands of blanks filled out by diplomates in psychiatry (15) failed to predict any of our criteria at a statistically significant level: no r's as high as .2. This last finding deserves emphasis, because Strong's key was the product of a highly developed statistical technology, had an adequate numerical base, and had every opportunity to show what a pure actuarial method could achieve.

We made a further attempt to combine the best-predicting scores from the tests used in the standard battery into a regression equation. The R between Verbal IQ (Wechsler-Bellevue), Lawyer key (Strong VIB), DR% and No. Good M (Rorschach), and Overall Competence was .56 on the original group of 64; cross-validated on 100 cases, it dropped to .13.

Some Practical Implications

If we had concentrated on an actuarial rather than a clinical approach and had come up with a simple, objective procedure that had a high and stable level of validity in predicting psychiatric performance, it could have been misused. It might have tempted many psychiatric training centers to adopt a single mold from which would have been cast a generation of psychiatrists, who would have had to meet the problems of the future with a standard set of resources derived from the past. The more successful we are in finding objective, impersonal, and statistical methods of selecting members of a profession in the image of its past leaders, the more rigid will be the pattern into which it is frozen.

For a concrete example, consider Strong's Psychiatrist A key again for a moment. It expresses the pattern of interests held in common by men who were diplomates in psychiatry at the end of the war, most of whom must have trained fifteen to twenty years ago. It should hardly be surprising that residents whose interests most closely approached this pattern tended to have skills as administrators and diagnosticians rather than as psychotherapists. If they had happened to achieve a high correlation with our over-all criterion, it might have helped populate American psychiatry of the 1960's and 1970's with near-replicas of the old state hospital superintendent.

It might be argued, however, that a similar result could have been expected if we had succeeded in providing explicit methods of clinically analyzing other types of data to select psychiatric residents. They too would have been based on a study of men who were successful at one time in history, and would have suffered the same danger of getting out of date. The answer is that even sophisticated clinical prediction never gets quite that rigid. Changes creep in; the result may be that validities gradually regress, or the drift may be determined by valid appraisals of newly important variables. Clinical methods are more flexible than their actuarial counterparts; they *can* be more readily modified by new studies

based on observations of developing trends in the criterion. Moreover, valid clinical impressions can be obtained from an intensive study of a few known cases, while it takes large samples to set up or revise an actuarial system. There can be no guarantee that clinical methods *will* be kept up to date, of course, nor that the attempt to do so will not spoil their validities. Any predictive system needs constant overhaul and revalidation.

By sticking with the only capriciously accurate, sporadically reliable, and eminently flexible method of clinical judgment in selecting trainees, psychiatry will at least be able to keep in touch with developments in a growing and changing profession. Moreover, it will be able to maintain a healthy diversity within its ranks. There are many jobs to be done in psychiatry, requiring quite different kinds of men. There must be thoughtful men who like to sit in deep chairs and analyze patients all day long. There must be activists to organize new institutions and give inspirational leadership to groups of colleagues. Psychiatry needs many more men than it has whose main interest is in research and teaching, others to work with broad preventive programs in public health, group therapists, specialists in somatic treatments, and many more varieties of the general species. If the pure actuarial approach were to be seriously applied to psychiatry, it would be necessary to develop a formula for each of many different types of practice and to revise it constantly as new developments created needs for new types of practitioners. To do so would be impossibly expensive and laborious. Psychiatry is well off, therefore, sticking with a basically clinical approach to assessment and prediction in selecting its members, but trying constantly to make it more scientific.

The important issue, however, is not what method of selecting its members is best for any particular profession, but the relative inertia of actuarial predictive systems and the maneuverability introduced when the generating of predictions is done by clinical judgment. This freedom is a source of weakness as well as strength; it enables the clinician to fall into errors of many kinds (to which statistical predictions are less subject) and also to adapt himself sensitively to all kinds of changing circumstances. When clinical methods are given a chance—when skilled clinicians use methods with which they are familiar, predicting a performance about which they know something—and especially when the clinician has a rich body of data and has made the fullest use of the systematic procedures developed by actuarial workers, including a prior study of the bearing of the predictive data on the criterion performance, then sophisticated clinical prediction can achieve quite respectable successes. I hope that clinicians will take some heart from our results, but I urge them to refine their procedures by learning as much as possible about statistical prediction and adapting it to their own ends.

To summarize: Meehl failed in his aim to mediate the statistical-clinical quarrel because he defined the issues in a way that perpetuates competition and controversy. The real issue is not to find the proper sphere of activity for clinical predictive methods and for statistical ones, conceived in ideal-type terms as antithetical. Rather, we should try to find the optimal combination of actuarially controlled methods and sensitive clinical judgment for any particular predictive enterprise. To do so, we must strike the right balance between freedom and constraint, a balance which may shift a good deal in one direction or the other depending on the nature of the behavior being predicted. But we can find such balances only if clinically and statistically oriented workers give up contentious, competitive attitudes and seek to learn from each other.

References

1. Blenkner, M. Predictive factors in the initial interview in family casework. *Soc. Serv. Rev.*, 28(1954), 65–73.

2. Cronbach, L. J. Assessment of individual differences. In P. Farnsworth and Q. McNemar, eds., *Annual review of psychology*. Stanford, Calif.: Annual Reviews, 1956. Volume VII, pages 173–196.

3. Holt, R. R., and Luborsky, L. *Personality patterns of psychiatrists*. New York: Basic Books, 1958.

4. Holtzman, W. H., and Sells, S. B. Prediction of flying success by clinical analysis of test protocols. *J. Abnorm. Soc. Psychol.*, 49(1954), 485–490.

5. Horst, P. *et al. The prediction of personal adjustment*. New York: Soc. Sci. Res. Council Bull. 48(1941).

6. Kelly, E. L., and Fiske, D. W. The prediction of success in the VA training program in clinical psychology. *Amer. Psychologist*, 5(1950), 395–406.

7. ——— *The prediction of performance in clinical psychology*. Ann Arbor, Mich.: Univ. of Michigan Press, 1951.

8. Luborsky, L. L., Holt, R. R., and Morrow, W. R. Interim report of the research project on the selection of medical men for psychiatric training. *Bull. Menninger Clinic*, 14(1950), 92–101.

9. McArthur, C. Clinical versus actuarial prediction. In *Proceedings, 1955 invitational conference on testing problems*. Princeton, N.J.: Educational Testing Service, 1956. Pages 99–106.

10. Meehl, P. E. *Clinical vs. statistical prediction*. Minneapolis: Univ. of Minnesota Press, 1954.

11. ——— Clinical versus actuarial prediction. In *Proceedings, 1955 invitational conference on testing problems*. Princeton, N.J.: Educational Testing Service, 1956. Pages 136–141.

12. OSS Assessment Staff. *Assessment of men*. New York: Rinehart, 1948.

13. Rapaport, D., Gill, M. M., and Schafer, R. *Diagnostic psychological testing*. Chicago: Yearbook Publishers, 1946. Volume II.

14. Sarbin, T. R. A contribution to the study of actuarial and statistical methods of prediction. *Amer. J. Sociol.*, 48(1943), 593–603.

15. Strong, E. K., Jr., and Tucker, A. J. The use of vocational interest scores in planning a medical career. *Psychol. Monogr.*, 66(1952), (9), No. 341.

16. Wittman, M. P. A scale for measuring prognosis in schizophrenic patients. *Elgin Papers*, 4(1941). 20–33.

4. SOCIAL PSYCHIATRY

IN RECENT YEARS there has been a convergence of the fields of psychiatry, medical epidemiology, and social psychology resulting in a new branch of study—social psychiatry. The goal of workers in this relatively new and certainly burgeoning field has been to understand the effects that sociocultural conditions have on mental health. The article which follows by Redlich et al. is a preliminary report of findings of a social psychiatric study done in New Haven which culminated a few years later in the book *Social Class and Mental Illness* by Hollingshead and Redlich. The book review by Dr. Gruenberg is significant both because it presents some of the content and findings of the recent social psychiatric study carried out in midtown Manhattan and because, in the critique it offers, many of the complexities of this type of research are highlighted.

Social Structure and Psychiatric Disorders *

F. C. REDLICH, M.D., A. B. HOLLINGSHEAD, PhD.,
B. H. ROBERTS, M.D., H. A. ROBINSON, PhD.,
L. Z. FREEDMAN, M.D., J. K. MYERS, PhD.

NEW HAVEN, CONN.

This is a preliminary report of a research project † dealing with the relationship of social structure to psychiatric disorder.

The primary assumption was the ex-

Reprinted from the *American Journal of Psychiatry*, 109(1953), 729–734, with the permission of the American Psychiatric Association and Dr. Redlich.

* Read at the 108th annual meeting of the American Psychiatric Association, Atlantic City, N.J., May 12–16, 1952.

From the Yale University Departments of Psychiatry and Sociology, aided by USPHS Mental Health Act grant MH 263 (R), "Relationship of Psychiatric Disorders to Social Structure."

† In the spring of 1949, Redlich, Hollingshead, and Gruenberg made plans to investigate this problem. Gruenberg moved to another community and Hollingshead and Redlich then formulated the project. The following investigators were added to the research team: B. H. Roberts, L. Z. Freedman, psychiatrists; J. K. Myers, sociologist; H. A. Robinson, psychologist; and W. Caudill, anthropologist, who participated in the early phases of the investigation.

istence of a significant relationship between social status position and psychiatric disorders. More specifically, our main hypotheses were that (1) the prevalence of psychiatric disorders is significantly related to the social status position of the patients; (2) (diagnostic) types of disorders in psychiatric patients are significantly related to social status position; (3) types of psychiatric treatment are significantly related to social status position of the patients; (4) the psychodynamics of behavior disorders are related significantly to social status position; and (5) social mobility in the status structure is related to psychiatric disorder. These interlocking (and to some extent interdependent) hypotheses involve examinations of the relationship of psychiatric disorders and the social stratification of the community.

Our knowledge of social stratification rests on the investigations of Warner and associates (14), Hollingshead (6, 7), and others. No psychiatric literature on our topic exists, with the exception of Ruesch's (12, 13) contributions, Dollard and Miller's (2) recognition of the problem, and casual references, amongst others by S. Freud, of the importance of social class for psychiatric etiology and phenomenology. Also, various epidemiological studies by Faris and Dunham (4), Lemkau (10), Malzberg (11), Dayton (1), and Hyde (8, 9) relate single socioeconomic criteria to the incidence of psychiatric disorders. The scheme of social stratification used in our study is that of Hollingshead. His Index of Social Position utilizes 3 factors: (1) occupation, (2) education, and (3) ecological area of residence. Each factor is scaled and assigned a weight determined by a standard regression equation. The combined scores group themselves into 5 clusters (social strata or levels) and to each of these a numerical index is assigned. A brief and general descriptive characterization of each of these social levels follows:

LEVEL I—(the highest socio-economic position) comprises families of wealth, education, and top rank social prestige.

LEVEL II—consists of families in which the adults for the most part hold college or advanced degrees, and are in professional or high-level managerial positions.

LEVEL III—includes proprietors, the bulk of small business people, white-collar, and skilled workers; this group consists predominantly of high school graduates.

LEVEL IV—consists largely of semi-skilled workers and laborers, with an educational index below the secondary level.

LEVEL V—includes unskilled and semi-skilled workers, who have an elementary education or less, and who live in the poorest areas of the community.

The project is being carried out in the metropolitan area of New Haven, Connecticut. It consists of 4 successive studies: (1) a census of psychiatric patients herein referred to as the Psychiatric Census; (2) the social stratification of a 5 per cent random sample of families in the same area; (3) a case study consisting of the comparison of a group of neurotic and psychotic patients belonging to social levels III and V; and (4) an intensive study of the psychodynamics of a few cases belonging to different social levels. The current report deals with experiences and results obtained in the Psychiatric Census, and the 5 per cent sample of controls.

The Psychiatric Census was limited to residents of the New Haven metropolitan area with a population of about 250,000 in 1950. A systematic attempt was made to isolate and to acquire data for all individuals legally residing in this area who were psychiatric patients on December 1, 1950. A psychiatric patient is defined by us as a person in professional contact with a psychiatrist; i.e., a person who is seeing and/or obtaining help and care from a psychiatrist, regardless of whether this contact is for diagnostic or therapeutic purposes, whether it is voluntary or obligatory. The research team obtained the cooperation of all public and private psychiatric institutions and clinics in Connecticut and nearby states, and of all private psychiatric practitioners in Connecticut and in the metropolitan New York area. In addition, contact was made with well-known clinics throughout the country. The response was highly gratifying; all institutions and clinics cooperated, as did over 95 per cent of the private practitioners. It can reasonably be assumed, then, that a very high proportion of the total sample of psychiatric patients was obtained.

At this point we would like to emphasize strongly—to avoid any errors of interpretation—that this study is not dealing with psychiatric disorders prevailing in the population at large. It is merely a sample—and nearly a total sample—of the population of psychiatric patients *according to our definition*. In other words, we are primarily exploring the relationship of social structure to certain aspects of current psychiatric practice. In the general population, clearly, there are many persons with psychiatric problems who are seeking help in other ways and, unfortunately, many who are without the benefit of any therapeutic intervention. To date, the true prevalence and incidence of psychiatric disorders in the general population is unknown. As such knowledge would be of utmost importance for both psychiatry and public health, we strongly favor such a study. In light of the results from such a study, many data of our own study would become more meaningful.

For every patient in the New Haven area, the research team of psychiatrists and sociologists obtained information on 44 items relating to their social status and psychiatric condition—sociologists worked on sociological items, while psychiatrists independently gathered psychiatric data. These items had been carefully defined and organized into a schedule. Case records were relied upon for institutional and clinic patients; data on private patients were obtained by in-

terview with the psychiatrist. Records of 1,589 institutional and clinic patients were abstracted and 374 private practitioners' cases were obtained by interview, for a total sample of 1,963 cases. After the field work was completed, the schedules were edited, coded, and the data punched on I.B.M. cards for analysis.

The census data comprise psychiatric symptomatology and diagnosis; duration and onset of illness; referral to the practitioner and institution; nature and intensity of treatment; as well as sociological data, such as occupation, education, ethnicity of patient, religion, parents, siblings, children, and spouse. Our diagnostic classification is based on the Veterans Administration nomenclature; the number of categories in this scheme was somewhat reduced to eliminate classifications that were poorly defined, or in this population were not found in statistically significant numbers. The diagnoses were based on data from family and personal history, behavior status, and course of illness. By doing this a uniform diagnostic approach was ensured and the error of accepting diagnoses depending on the viewpoint of the individual institutions and practitioners was avoided. Ninety-five per cent of our own diagnoses were identical with the diagnosis of the psychiatric record. The reliability of our data-gathering technique was independently tested and found to be adequate.

Brief Survey of Findings

Before dealing with the principal hypotheses, a brief over-all survey of the census data is given. Of the 1,963 cases of the census study, 50.7 per cent were males, 49.3 per cent were females. The diagnostic distribution of the total group is presented in Table 1, and the age distribution in Table 2.

The low percentage of children and adolescents in contact with psychiatrists is remarkable. New Haven has 2 child

psychiatric clinics and a comparatively
high number of private practitioners of
psychiatry—a number of them working
with children, though none exclusively.
The low percentage of patients under 18
years of age may relate, among other
possible factors, (1) to the difficulties that
practitioners have in finding parents who
can afford psychiatric treatment for their
children, or to the unwillingness of parents to support long-term treatment, (2)

TABLE 1

PRINCIPAL DIAGNOSTIC GROUPS AND THE PER-
CENTAGE OF CASES IN EACH GROUP

Diagnosis	%
Psychoneurotic disorders	23.5
Intoxications and addictions	4.7
Schizophrenic and paranoid disorders	44.2
Affective disorders	8.0
Mental deficiency with psychotic disorder *	4.6
Arteriosclerotic and senile disorders	9.3
Convulsive disorders	1.9
Organic disorders other than arteriosclerotic and senile	3.6

* Mental deficiency without psychosis is not
considered in this study.

TABLE 2

PERCENTAGE DISTRIBUTION OF
PSYCHIATRIC CASES BY AGE
GROUP

Age	%
2–18	4.6
19–24	5.1
25–39	29.8
40–54	24.9
55–69	22.5
70 plus	12.8

to the general policy of child psychiatric
clinics to favor long-term intensive treatment by a therapeutic team (psychiatrist,
psychologist, and social worker) of a
relatively small number of cases, (3) to
the number of behavior disorders being
treated by pediatricians, family doctors,
and social agencies.

Table 3 presents the distribution of
these patients among the various types of
treatment agencies, and Table 4 lists the
various types of treatment used with this
population.

The "no treatment" classification refers almost exclusively to chronic hospitalized patients who receive care, medical attention, but no systematic, active,
or sustained treatment. The small percentage of patients either in psychoanalysis or intensive psychotherapy is of considerable interest, numbering but 5 per
cent of the total patient population.

TABLE 3

PERCENTAGE DISTRIBUTION OF PATIENTS BY
TREATMENT AGENCY

	%
State hospitals	66.8
Veterans' hospitals	4.2
Private hospitals	1.9
Clinics	8.1
Private practitioners' cases	19.0

TABLE 4

PERCENTAGE DISTRIBUTION OF PATIENTS BY
PRINCIPAL TYPE OF TREATMENT

Principal Type of Treatment		%
Psychotherapy		32.0
Psychoanalysis	1.1	
Analytic psychotherapy	3.8	
Eclectic methods	6.0	
Supportive methods	7.1	
Suggestive and directive methods	6.9	
Group psychotherapy	6.6	
Other types of psychotherapy	.5	
Organic		31.7
Electric convulsive treatment	18.7	
Insulin and other	1.5	
Drugs	4.3	
Lobotomy	6.2	
Other organic treatment	1.0	
No treatment		36.3

From the many data collected in this
study, we shall present here only a few
significant findings that bear upon hypotheses 1, 2, and 3, dealing with the relationship of prevalence, diagnosis, and
treatment to social levels. Our first hypothesis—stating that incidence of psychiatric disorders is significantly related
to the social status position of the patients—may be tested by comparing the
normal sample with the psychiatric sam-

ple in terms of social levels. Table 5 presents these data. It should be noted that in this and in the following comparisons, social levels I and II have been combined because of the paucity of cases ($N = 19$) in level I of the psychiatric sample.

These data show a very significant relation between social level and the prevalence of psychiatric patients according to our definition in the population of the New Haven community. With respect to the normal population, the relative

TABLE 5

DISTRIBUTION OF CONTROL AND PSYCHIATRIC POPULATIONS BY SOCIAL LEVEL

Social Level	Normal Population		Psychiatric Population	
	No.	%	No.	%
I and II	1,284	11.3	150	7.9
III	2,500	22.0	260	13.3
IV	5,256	46.0	758	38.6
V	2,037	17.8	723	36.8
Unknown *	345	3.0	72	3.7

$$\chi^2 = 281.0 \qquad p < .001$$

* The cases whose social level could not be determined, because of paucity of data, are not used in the calculation of χ^2.

number of psychiatric patients is found to be somewhat lower in the first 4 social levels, and considerably higher in level V. On the basis of these data, hypothesis 1 may be considered tenable.

Our second hypothesis postulates a significant relationship between the type of psychiatric disorder in the patient population and social level. In analyzing our data, we have employed 10 diagnostic groupings or categories; here, for the sake of brevity and to suggest a basic preliminary finding, we present a table that dichotomizes neurosis and psychosis by social level.

Table 6 reveals a marked inverse relationship between the incidence of neuroses and psychoses by social level. Neuroses show a relatively high incidence in the higher social levels and a remarkably low incidence in social levels IV and V.

The reverse is true for the psychoses. It may be assumed that the low percentage of neurotics in the lower levels of our patient population is due to socio-economic conditions of current psychiatric practice. The high number of psychotics cannot be explained at present. It actually may indicate an uneven distribution of psychotics in the total population.

The schizophrenics, who comprise 44.2 per cent of the patient population, and well over half (58.7 per cent) of the psychotic group, are the largest diagnostic group in our sample. The schizo-

TABLE 6

DISTRIBUTION OF NEUROSES AND PSYCHOSES BY SOCIAL LEVEL (PSYCHIATRIC CENSUS)

Social Level	Neuroses		Psychoses	
	No.	%	No.	%
I and II	98	65.3	52	34.7
III	115	44.2	145	55.8
IV	175	23.1	583	76.9
V	61	8.4	662	91.6
Total	449		1,442	

$$\chi^2 = 297.8 \qquad p < .001$$

phrenics are distributed among the social levels in a distorted fashion ($p < .001$); that is, there is a strong relationship between social level and the incidence of schizophrenia in our data. To indicate clearly the strength and direction of this distortion, Hollingshead constructed an Index of Prevalence, which at each social level represents differences between the potential (expected) number of schizophrenics in the normal population and the diagnosed schizophrenics in the Psychiatric Census. In this scheme, if a social level exhibits the same proportion of schizophrenia as it comprises of the general population, the Index will be 100. If the prevalence is disproportionately high, the Index is above 100. Table 7 presents these data.

The social level differences in the incidence of schizophrenia, with the systematic increases in the prevalence of this diagnosis as one progresses from level I to level V, are very striking, and strongly suggest the validity of our second hypothesis. The fact that the Index of Prevalence in social level V is 9 times as great as in combined social levels I and II is a remarkable finding. Its significance will be explored by detailed internal analysis of our data in later publications. It is possible, for example, that the higher marital and family instability at the lower social levels will relate to this finding. It is equally possible that this phenomenon may be, in part, a function of the larger proportional incidence of chronic cases in the lower social levels. It may be largely caused by existing conditions of psychiatric practice in which upper-level schizophrenics get cured and

TABLE 7

INDEX OF PREVALENCE FOR SCHIZOPHRENIA
BY SOCIAL LEVEL

Social Level	Normal Sample		Schizophrenia		Index of Prevalence
	No.	%	No.	%	
I and II ...	1,284	11.6	29	3.4	28
III	2,500	22.6	83	9.8	43
IV	5,256	47.4	352	41.6	88
V	2,037	18.4	383	45.2	253
Total ...	11,077		847		

discontinue contact with psychiatry; while the lower-level patients with "no home" to go to and less adequate treatment become "chronic" in public mental hospitals. Further analysis of our data and future research on incidence and prevalance of schizophrenia in the general population may answer these questions.

Summary data on our third hypothesis, that a significant relationship obtains between type of psychiatric treatment and social level, are demonstrated in Table 8.

The treatment differences between the social levels is striking and statistically significant ($p < .001$). There is a distinct progression in the percentage of cases who received no treatment (cases in custodial care) as one moves from the

higher to the lower levels. Likewise, the percentage of cases receiving some form of organic treatment as the principal form of therapy tends to increase as one descends from level I and II to the lower levels. In distinction to this, the percentage of patients who receive some form of psychotherapy systematically decreases as one moves from the higher to the lower social levels. Within this latter group (patients receiving some form of psychotherapy) we find marked differences between the types of psychotherapy administered to patients at the sev-

TABLE 8

PERCENTAGE DISTRIBUTION OF THE PRINCIPAL
FORM OF THERAPY BY SOCIAL LEVELS

Type of Treatment	Social Level			
	I & II	III	IV	V
Psychotherapy	79.1	52.7	31.1	16.1
Organic	11.8	28.7	37.1	32.7
No treatment	9.1	18.6	31.8	51.2

TABLE 9

PERCENTAGE DISTRIBUTION OF PATIENTS BY
SOCIAL LEVEL AND TREATMENT AGENCY

	Social Level			
	I & II	III	IV	V
State hospitals	14.0	41.9	68.5	84.5
Veterans' hospitals .	2.6	3.1	3.8	5.5
Private hospitals ..	14.7	3.1	.9	.0
Clinics	5.3	12.3	7.9	7.2
Private practitioners' cases	63.3	39.6	18.9	2.8

$$\chi^2 = 871.1 \qquad p < .001$$

eral social levels; psychoanalysis, for example, is limited to levels I and II.

Table 9 presents the social stratification of our psychiatric population in terms of the type of practice or treatment agency in which they are found.

These data demonstrate a highly significant and expected relationship between social level and type of practice. Some two-thirds of all upper-level patients are treated in private practice while patients of lower social levels are concentrated in state hospitals. This latter finding is undoubtedly related to the fact that a large proportion of the cases at level V are chronic psychotics requiring long-term care.

Summary

The relationship between social level and psychiatric disorders has been explored by a demographic study of patients (i.e., patients in professional contact with psychiatrists) in metropolitan New Haven, and by a background study of the stratification of a sample of the general population in the same community. Significant relationships have been found between social level and (1) prevalence of psychiatric patients according to our definition, (2) types of psychiatric disorders in the patient population, and (3) types of therapy. Our data throw some light on social stratification in current psychiatric practice; they suggest the existence of an uneven social class distribution of psychoses in the general population. The project will continue, by sociological, psychiatric, and psychological techniques, to gather facts and to explore the meaning of the preliminary findings reported in this paper. Only a study of incidence and prevalence of psychiatric disorders in the general population will solve some of the basic problems posed.

References

1. Dayton, Neil A. *New facts on mental disorder.* Springfield, Ill.: Charles C Thomas, 1940.

2. Dollard, John, and Miller, Neal. *Personality and psychotherapy.* New York: Mc-Graw-Hill, 1950.

3. Dollard, John. *Class and caste in a southern town.* New Haven: Yale Univ. Press, 1937.

4. Faris, R. E. L., and Dunham, H. W. *Mental disorders in urban areas.* Chicago: Univ. of Chicago Press, 1939.

5. Freud, S. *Introductory lectures on psychoanalysis,* Chapter XII. London: Allen and Unwin, 1929.

6. Hollingshead, August B. *Elmtown's youth.* New York: John Wiley and Sons, Inc., 1949.

7. ———. Class and kinship in a middle western community. *Amer. Sociol. Rev.,* 14(1949), 469.

8. Hyde, Robert W., and Chisholm, Roderick M. Studies in medical sociology: III—The relation of mental disorders to race and nationality. *New Eng. J. Med.,* 231(1944), 612.

9. Hyde, Robert W., and Kingsley, Lowell V. Studies in medical sociology: I—The relation of mental disorders to the community socioeconomic level. *New Eng. J. Med.,* 231(1944), 543.

10. Lemkau, Paul, et al. Mental hygiene problems in an urban district. *Ment. Hyg.,* 25(1941); 624, 26(1942); 100, 26(1942); 275, 27(1943); 279.

11. Malzberg, Benjamin. *Social and biological aspects of mental disease.* Utica, N.Y.: State Hospital Press, 1940.

12. Ruesch, J. Social technique, social status, and social change in illness. In Kluckhohn and Murray, eds., *Personality in nature, society and culture.* New York: Knopf, 1948.

13. Ruesch, J. et al. *Acculturation and illness,* Psychological Monographs; General and Applied, Wash., D.C., Vol. 62, No. 5, 1948.

14. Warner, W. Lloyd, and Lunt, Paul S. *Yankee city sons: Vol. I the social life of a modern community.* New Haven: Yale Univ. Press, 1941.

Discussion

DR. FREDERICK WEISS (New York, N.Y.).—Earlier studies of the problem, such as Niceforo's "Anthropology of the Non-Propertied Classes," Mosse's "Illness and Social Condition," Grotjahn's "Social Pathology," suffered from 2 deficiencies: from a lack of adequate statistical data, and from a very limited understanding of the specific dynamics of a social structure as well as of a psychiatric disorder. The relationship between these 2 factors is definitely not the same as, for example, the relationship between social structure and tuberculosis. I remember the strong impression I received when I saw the first time in the study of public health that a city map arranged according to social levels presented a practically exact negative of the same map showing the incidence of tuberculosis. In the case of mental illness, the relationship is not a merely quantitative one. Psychiatric disorders are not social disorders in this simple sense; but they are social disorders in the larger sense of the modern psychodynamic conception. Neuroses and functional psychoses develop in the unhealthy emotional climate of disturbed interpersonal relationships. The individual whose growing self is weakened by lack of love, affection, and genuine acceptance feels isolated in a potentially hostile world, develops basic anxiety, becomes more and more alienated from himself, and turns to neurotic or psychotic solutions to overcome his intrapsychic and interpersonal conflicts. Thus there exists a relationship between social structure and psychiatric disorders; but it is a qualitative one, determined not by the macroscopic factor of the social level—there are Harlem neuroses and Park Avenue neuroses—but by the microscopic factor of the earliest and closest environment. Adolf Meyer's concept of mental illness as a psychobiological reaction to life situations, Halliday's broad definition of psychosocial disorder, and Horney's view of neurosis as distorted human growth, might contribute to a better insight into the relationship between social structure and psychiatric disorders.

It is the threat to vital values, vital for the safety of the specific individual, that often sets in motion the neurotic or psychotic process. This vital value *may* be economic security, but it may also be the specific value of love, prestige, power, and, particularly, of the idealized image that the person has built of himself.

The figures in Table 6 of Dr. Redlich's paper, which dichotomizes neuroses and psychoses by social level, and which shows a relatively high incidence of neuroses in the higher levels, a remarkable low in levels IV and V, and the reverse for psychoses, have to be reevaluated in the light of the fact that only very few of the neurotic patients of lower levels reach the psychiatrist, while most of the psychotic patients of this group are institutionalized.

The fact that the index of prevalence of schizophrenia in level V is 9 times as great as in level I, corresponds to the findings of Ludwig Stern (1913), who studied the ratio of schizophrenia to manic-depressive psychosis. He found the ratio to be 2.6 in workers, but only 0.7 among business owners and public officials. Tietze, Lemkau, and Cooper (1939) also found this ratio to be 2.9 among laborers, but only 1.1 among proprietors, managers, and officials. This appears to be a rather significant finding, which should be analyzed, however, not only with focus on the general social level or relative predominance of Kretschmer's schizothymic or cyclothymic personality type, but with special attention to the psychodynamic aspects of the early emotional environment.

A Review of "Mental Health in the Metropolis: Midtown Manhattan Study"

ERNEST M. GRUENBERG, M.D.
COLLEGE OF PHYSICIANS AND SURGEONS,
COLUMBIA UNIVERSITY

Although the earliest morbidity surveys are less than 100 years old and no more than 100 such surveys have ever been

Reprinted from the *Milbank Memorial Fund Quarterly*, 42(1963), 77–94, with the permission of the publisher and the author.

done, it can be predicted that morbidity surveys will become more common because the conditions which are frequently fatal or are readily reportable are no longer our major health preoccupations. Interest in morbidity is supplanting interest in mortality as the grim reaper's effectiveness is postponed more and more until the later years of life.

Surveys of mental disorders are among the most common type of morbidity survey. At least two dozen such have been done and the most recently reported, Mental Health in the Metropolis: the midtown Manhattan study,* is in some ways the most sophisticated and in other ways the most cumbersome and awkward of the lot.

Investigators planning a morbidity survey must start by defining a population. Sometimes the population of a school system or of army draftees or members of a retirement system is selected. Members of these populations have their names written in lists of members and by picking a particular list the population to be surveyed is characterized, removing any ambiguity regarding who is and who is not a member of the population being studied. More commonly the population is defined in terms of residence in an area, as are the populations of the United States Census. This is a favorite way of specifying a population for political and certain other purposes. But as the Bureau of the Census knows and election boards can testify there is some ambiguity about the residence of a growing portion of our population. Some people have several homes and do not belong uniquely to any particular locale. This is true not only of those who "have a country and a town estate" but also of students away at college, Fulbright fellows, Guggenheim fellows and of bigamists. There are also some young men and some young women who have no real place of residence at all, having moved from a parental home into transient quarters and continue to move about in transient quarters until they ultimately get married and make a home or become confirmed bachelors and spin-

sters and set up single housekeeping. In addition, there are the elderly whose children have grown up and established their own homes—particularly the widows and widowers who circulate between married children, sometimes coming for "a visit" and staying for years, and sometimes "moving permanently" each time "it seems sensible under the circumstances." These people simply don't know, in fact, how stable their home placement is, and the enumerator cannot really tell either. Outside of the city limits, residence is further confused by the growing population in "mobile homes," some of which move quite frequently and others of which are mobile only in theory and stay for decades in one spot.

In the survey under review, an area with a population of some 174,000 was outlined on a map of Manhattan's East Side, blocks were randomly sampled, dwellings in the sampled blocks were randomly sampled, people in the sampled dwellings were randomly sampled, yielding a sample of 1,911 people. The people sampled were confined to the age level 20–59 and were limited to people who met certain rules regarding residence. For example, it excluded people in transient hotels and in clubs, but included boarders in other places. (This difference is one of many sources of possible bias which the careful reader may discover.) Of the 1,911 people drawn in the sample 1,660 answered a rather long, structured questionnaire which elicited much personal information about their past and present physical and mental symptoms of illness. A mere 251 (13 per cent) unknowns reflects a conscientious and competent field job.

This survey stemmed from a strong conviction that mental disorders have deep roots in community conditions. The late Dr. Thomas A. C. Rennie, the Cornell psychiatrist who conceived and initiated this survey was convinced that psychiatric patients required—in addition to what a psychiatrist can provide

* Srole, L.; Langner, T. S.; Michael, S. T.; Opler, M. K., and Rennie, T. A. C. Vol. I. New York, McGraw-Hill Book Co., Inc., 1962, 428 pp.

in the way of treatment—the help of social agencies, pastors, general practitioners, their families and their friends. This community orientation was demonstrated by his writings on community psychiatry, his multiple memberships on committees and boards, and by his appointment as the first chairman of New York City's Community Mental Health Board.

The breadth of Rennie's community interests (which was similar to that of Johns Hopkins' first Professor of Psychiatry, Adolph Meyer, Rennie's original psychiatric mentor) accounts for the breadth of the net which Rennie cast in the search for cases of illness in the population. He was interested in those conditions of mental malfunctioning which he had seen bring people in distress to psychiatrists seeking help. The survey looked for complaints or states of functioning which would be regarded as a basis for action by the clinician.

Because physicians (particularly good teachers of clinical subjects) traditionally hesitate to make diagnoses of patients they have not personally examined there was unwillingness to specify the exact nature of the disorders being counted. This unwillingness was strengthened by the fact that psychiatry has always been in an unsettled state regarding the diagnosis and nomenclature of mental disorders. The reasons for this unsettled state are complex and cannot be dealt with in this review, but there can be no doubt that diagnostic classification presents some problems for psychiatry which cannot be solved easily.

A person who is ill can be classified according to:

a. The disease which makes him ill (Diagnosis)
b. The extent to which his personal functioning is limited by his illness (Intensity)
c. The symptoms he is experiencing
d. The length of time he has had the disease (Past Duration)

e. The length of time he is likely to have it in the future (Future Probable Duration)
f. The type of course his illness has had (whether it is of chronic and stable intensity, progressive, remitting or recovering).

While a desire for neatness and simplicity may make us wish that illnesses had only one of these characteristics, the fact is that each case has all and experience has shown that these characteristics are "independent variables." I say they are "independent variables" because pairs of cases can be found alike on all variables but one, in which they differ. Thus a case of malaria may be identical to a case of tuberculosis on all variables but diagnosis; all fatal cases are equally limited in functioning; the symptoms of a case of schizophrenia and of a case of syphilis can be indistinguishable; many varieties of congenital conditions are lifelong; a new explosive totally disabling case of feverish pneumonia which will die within ten minutes of observation may not be distinguishable on the other variables from one which will drag on for weeks and recover.

In this morbidity survey, intensity of disorder was selected for investigation rather than types of disorder. The investigators classified the population according to the seriousness of psychiatric symptoms found and according to the extent of impairment in living experienced by each person. Symptoms were classified as *absent, mild, moderate, serious;* interference with life adjustment was classified as *none, some, great,* and *incapacitated.* This two-dimensional classification yields a sixteen-fold table from which a six-point scale was derived.

		Symptoms			
		None	Mild	Moderate	Serious
	None	0	1	2	
Inter-	Some			3	4
ference	Great				5
	Incapacity				6

While "severity of symptoms" are discussed as though they were phenomena quite independent of "interference with life adjustment," the blanks in this table show that either they are not independent in the minds of the investigators or that they are highly correlated in their data. I believe that the relationship between these two dimensions needs closer scrutiny both with respect to the concepts involved and with respect to the ways in which sick people vary in these two ways.

The prevalence of symptoms can be studied from several points of view. One approach might be to recognize that certain characteristics common in sick individuals may also be prevalent in people who are not sick. Criminality, for instance, has been observed in some people with psychotic conditions, but field studies have shown that it is even more common in individuals without psychotic conditions. (In the Midtown report the possibility that some of the symptoms enumerated occur in the absence of mental disorder is not investigated.) Moreover, the notion that certain physical illnesses are *ipso facto* evidence of psychosomatic conditions is very questionable. One might therefore try to determine to what extent certain "symptoms" are indeed symptoms of an illness. A second approach would be to assume that certain symptoms can be better understood if they are studied in all sorts of people without reference to the diseases present; this consideration would justify studies of suicide, alcoholism or insomnia, to give a few examples. Finally, one can simply take the presence of certain symptoms as a crude index of the presence of disorder. The Midtown study adopted this last viewpoint; it counted the number of people classified as having a specified severity of symptoms and a specified level of impairment in social functioning.

Case finding in morbidity surveys almost always involves a review of clinical records of the medical facilities which service the population. Sometimes they stop there. Redlich and Hollingshead's "Social Class and Mental Illness" was based entirely on clinical records of patients in psychiatric treatment. The survey of Baltimore's Eastern Health District conducted by Lemkau and his colleagues added to this method social agency record searches and independent appraisal of the significance of these records. The Onondaga County survey of the mentally retarded done by the New York State Mental Health Research Unit used a similar method.

For those who go further there are three additional steps which can be taken. One of the oldest is to ask all the professionals in contact with the population to nominate candidates for being counted as sick. One of the most extensive studies of this kind was the United States Census of 1880 which actually tried to count all the helpless people in the United States including the mentally ill and the mentally defective. Other surveyors have used such nominations as a first screen and then gone on to examine the candidates more intensively through direct contact. This method was used by Roth and Luton in their study of Williamson County, Tennessee and has been favored by many of the European investigators. This method of case finding has the appeal of a relatively inexpensive first stage (collecting nominations) and a relatively intense second stage. The investigators end up with a very discriminating set of conclusions about those identified as sick. This method was used with success by Strömgren, Brugger, Lin (in Formosa), Böök in Sweden and a number of other psychiatric surveyors.

This key informant plus clinical evaluation method has two major disadvantages. First, it is appropriate only in closely knit communities where it is reasonable to expect every ill person to be known to at least one key informant and the number of key informants is limited.

It is manifestly inappropriate in a metropolitan complex like New York. In Midtown Manhattan information about the sample of 1,911 persons might require interviews with several thousand key informants if one wished to contact their physicians, pastors, school teachers, policemen, their children's school teachers, etc. The second disadvantage is that the key informant screen does not require an explicit, equally intense scrutiny of each member of the population. The key informants do not review the whole membership but only that portion they are acquainted with. They do not give information about all members they are acquainted with but only those they know sufficiently well to nominate as possibly ill. Hence one is left uncertain as to the possibility that some members of any studied population are not sufficiently well known to any of the key informants to be properly screened at all. Roth and Luton found more cases in a subsample that they scrutinized carefully than had been found by following up on the suggestions of key informants.

The obvious way to avoid this danger is to skip the nominating process of the key informant and go directly to the whole sample population. In surveys of mental disorders this has actually been done only twice. Essen-Møller and two colleagues personally interviewed every adult in two Swedish parishes one summer and not only identified them in terms of clinical diagnoses but also classified each and every person regarding a series of personality traits which they wanted to study. (Unfortunately 'he classification, by Sjorbring, is one which is of interest to only a small clique of professionals.) Johannes Bremer, who has since completed his training in psychiatry, was assigned as a young government physician to a small fishing village in northern Norway and was unwillingly forced to extend his tour of duty by Hitler's occupation. He helped to while away the years by conducting a morbidity survey of the whole village, every member of which he knew personally as well as professionally, since he was the only physician available to any of them for any variety of medical care.

The alternative to a personal clinical contact by a trained psychiatrist with every member of the sample (of which Essen-Møller's is the only example), is a personal contact with every member of the population by some other person who conducts some sort of routine scrutiny. Nonpsychiatric interviewers have been used in a number of surveys to collect information about the sample population's health. They can ask if the respondent has had certain illnesses and record the answers. They can also ask whether other members of the household have had these illnesses or symptoms. This is the method used by the National Health Survey and was used in Hunterton County, New Jersey. Calibration studies have been done in both by more detailed examinations of random samples and there is currently considerable uneasiness about the validity and reliability of such data. However, validity and reliability of all scientific data are relative characteristics and it is important to recognize that sometimes the criteria being used for calibrating such data have only more prestige at the moment and have not themselves been shown to have great validity or reliability.

The Midtown Study used a specially created standard interview questionnaire administered by highly trained nonmedical professionals. The questionnaire was structured and included questions regarding specific symptoms experienced and attitude questions believed to be of clinical significance. Interview data can be taken by themselves and analyzed. This is done by the National Health Survey. It was done by Gurin, Veroff and Feld in a nationwide survey (*Americans View Their Mental Health*) and by several other studies.

Interview data can also be rated by clinicians. This is the method used in the Midtown Study. The data from these interviews were systematically reviewed by psychiatric clinicians who rated the respondents on the basis of these documents. In the Leighton Stirling County Study the interview data is supplemented by key informant data where available. In *A Mental Health Survey of Older People* in Syracuse, New York, the interview data were less structured than in the Midtown and Stirling County data, and relied heavily on trained observations of interviewers: the interviewers answered a semi-structured questionnaire in contrast to the Midtown, Stirling and Americans View Their Mental Health surveys, where the respondent answered a structured questionnaire. In both situations there are two sets of data: the record of responses to the questionnaire and the ratings of clinically-trained raters who have studied the filled-out questionnaire.

These two-stage methods involve problems of (1) interviewer variability, (2) rater variability and (3) rating validity. Interviewer variability can be estimated by two methods: first, a subsample can be repeatedly interviewed or, second, each interviewer can be assigned a random subsample of the whole population and the distribution of findings derived from different interviewers or groups of interviewers can be compared. The Midtown survey assigned interviewers in accordance with their presumed identification with and skill at achieving rapport with different classes of respondents (e.g., national or economic subsamples of the population) and thus sacrificed an opportunity to estimate interviewer variability by the second method. Nor was a subsample re-interviewed; but re-interviewing was planned and the report expresses hope that knowledge of this plan acted as a damper on interviewer bias. In the Syracuse survey of older people interviewer variability was encouraged and raters were expected to be unaffected by it. The effects were estimated by examining subsamples of the data, treating data from two classes of interviewers as separate sources of data.

Rater variability is dealt with in the Midtown report both by the social scientists who analyzed the data (Srole and Langner) and by the psychiatrists who developed the rating methods and did the rating. (Kirkpatrick and Michael). The variability is presented in terms of correlation coefficients and contingency probabilities for each rating.

From the contingency values in Table 1, it is clear that the psychiatrists who reported them were in close agreement in rating people well, totally incapaci-

TABLE 1

CONTINGENCY VALUES BETWEEN RATERS: (FACTOR EXPRESSING THE NUMBER OF "TIMES MORE OFTEN THAN WOULD BE PREDICTABLE BY PURE CHANCE" CONCORDANCE ON THE GIVEN RATING WAS ACHIEVED).

Severity of Symptoms	Difficulty in Functioning	"Contingency Value"	Final Category	Distribution (Per Cent)
0 None	None	4.3	Well	18.5
1 Mild	None	1.6	Mild Symptom Formation	36.3
2 Moderate	None	1.8	Moderate Symptom Formation	21.8
3 Moderate	Some	1.8	Marked Symptom Formation	13.2 ⎱
4 Serious	Some	3.9	Severe Symptom Formation	7.5 ⎰ Impaired
5 Serious	Great	9.5	⎱ Incapacitated	2.7
6 Serious	Incapacitated	45.0	⎰	

tated or severely impaired. But they were much less consistent in discriminating between the middle three categories and, I believe, that calculations based on these discriminations, judging from the limited data presented on their reliability, are not worthy of interpretation. However, the cutting point selected for analysis is where the raters themselves thought themselves weak, i.e., between *moderate* and *marked* symptom formations. Most of the published material depends on this discrimination. Those rated more serious than moderate were called *impaired* and the bulk of the data presentation relates to "per cent impaired."

Despite these criticisms this publication reflects a considerable advance in methods because available information on rater variability is presented. The Syracuse study of older people did not give data on rater variability.

The frequencies obtained from the home interviewing and rating process are shown in Table 1. A treatment census had been done for the *whole* Midtown population but had *not* been done for the surveyed sample. This resulted from the definition of the population to be sampled which excluded those living away in institutions. This is a disadvantage. It means that not only were those in mental hospitals excluded but also those in chronic disease hospitals, in nursing homes, in prisons, in the army and at colleges away from home. This is a common practice in both morbidity surveys and in sociological surveys. The Bureau of the Census moves in the same direction. I believe that particularly with respect to mental morbidity surveys these practices need to be re-examined. It might be useful in considering various rules for sampling defined populations to ask this question: *If every possible population were studied by this definition and this rule, would every person in existence be included in one or another of these populations?*

That is, if Midtown's rules for residence were applied to every geographical area in the country would everyone in the country be included in one area (and in only one)? I believe that long-stay prisoners and hospital patients would be left out. Our population sampling devices need further refinement in this direction. (The National Health Survey often ignores many persons not living in a familial household!)

The frequency of different varieties of symptom patterns is to be reported in subsequent volumes.

Morbidity and mortality data are conventionally first presented by age and sex. They are the standard way of dividing the population and they have much value even though there is no particular logic in selecting these two dimensions. In the Midtown study the prevalence of *impaired* conditions rises with age.

As indicated above, I place more credence on the bottom two lines than on the bottom three. If one assumes that the frequency of hospitalized people (less than six years continuously) is the same in the Midtown Sample as in Midtown, then one can add 0.5 per cent at each age level. *Incapacitated* is a criterion which was meant to be comparable to morbidity intensities found in hospitalized people. This criterion was also used on the older population studied in 1953 in Syracuse and it is interesting to put the two sets of data together.

These data showing a very marked rise with age in the prevalence of extremely sick people in American populations are a reliable finding comparable to data found elsewhere in similar types of morbidity surveys and cannot be over-emphasized.

In neither the Midtown nor the Syracuse studies was there a significant variation between the sexes in these rates. However, in other respects the sexes did vary in the Syracuse data and I predict that subsequent volumes of the Mid-

TABLE 2

PERCENTAGE DISTRIBUTIONS ACCORDING TO MENTAL HEALTH CLASSIFICATION
FOR DIFFERENT AGE GROUPS.

"Mental Health Categories"	Age Groups			
	20–29	30–39	40–49	50–59
Well	23.6	16.8	19.3	15.0
Mild Symptom Formation	37.5	37.6	37.0	33.1
Moderate Symptom Formation	23.6	22.4	20.5	21.1
Impaired	15.3	23.2	23.2	30.8
Marked Symptom Formation	(9.6)	(14.7)	(11.6)	(16.4)
Severe Symptom Formation	(4.1)	(7.5)	(7.7)	(10.5)
Incapacitated	(1.6)	(1.0)	(3.9)	(3.9)
N = 100 Per Cent	365	388	467	440

town data will likewise report variations by sex.

Socio-economic classifications of populations are popular and important. The Midtown Study depended on the use of the respondents' reply to the questions "When you were about 18 or 19 years old, what kind of work was your father doing for a living?" "At that time did he work for himself or for others?" and "About how many people did he have working for (under) him?" Information was also collected regarding the father's education. Replies were coded into a 27 category occupational code and then collapsed into skilled, semi-skilled and unskilled blue collar occupations and high,

middle and low-grade white collar occupations. The categories were picked so that the six categories were equal in size. (I cannot see any justification for this equalization of group size.)

Using this method of classifying respondents by socio-economic status (SES) of parents, the data in Table 4 were obtained.

These are very valuable data. The earlier morbidity surveys, which went beyond treatment censuses to examine untreated populations, did not make such classifications by parental occupational status.

It should be particularly stressed that the prevalence of cases does not change at

TABLE 3

PREVALENCE OF INCAPACITATING MENTAL ILLNESS IN MIDTOWN AND IN THE
SYRACUSE SURVEY. PER CENT IN SPECIFIED CATEGORY FOR
DIFFERENT AGE GROUPS.

Type of Case and Study	Age Group						
	20–29	30–39	40–49	50–59	65–74	75–84	85+
Incapacitated:							
Midtown Sample	1.6	1.0	3.9	3.9			
Certifiable—							
Syracuse					4.4	9.1	23.7
In Mental Hospital:							
Midtown	0.5	0.6	0.5	0.5	0.7	1.4	
Syracuse					1.2	1.4	1.0

TABLE 4

HOME SURVEY SAMPLE (AGE 20–59), PERCENTAGE DISTRIBUTIONS OF RESPONDENTS IN MENTAL HEALTH CLASSIFICATIONS BY PARENTAL-SES STRATA.

Mental Health Categories	Parental-SES Strata *					
	A	B	C	D	E	F
Well	24.4	23.3	19.9	18.8	13.6	9.7
Mild Symptom Formation	36.0	38.3	36.6	36.6	36.6	32.7
Moderate Symptom Formation	22.1	22.0	22.6	20.1	20.4	24.9
Impaired	17.5	16.4	20.9	24.5	29.4	32.7
Marked Symptom Formation	(11.8)	(8.6)	(11.8)	(13.3)	(16.2)	(18.0)
Severe Symptom Formation	(3.8)	(4.5)	(8.1)	(8.3)	(10.2)	(10.1)
Incapacitated	(1.9)	(3.3)	(1.0)	(2.9)	(3.0)	(4.6)
N = 100 Per Cent	262	245	287	384	265	217

* Socio-economic status A is highest white-collar group and F is lowest (unskilled) group.

every step. There actually appear to be three grades, roughly, rather than six and the lowest white collar occupational group is not much different from the highest blue collar group despite the change in shirt color at this point.

These data should all be standardized for the ages of the population but they are not. Instead, the study emphasizes that the per cent rated *well* declines with lower parental SES and the per cent rated *impaired* rises. They invent an easier-to-handle index by dividing the number "impaired" by the number "well" in each group which they call a "sick-well" ratio. This ratio is then compared for each age group separately and at each age it is higher for SES groups $E + F$ than for SES $A + B$ with $C + D$ at a more or less intermediate level.

This is a poor way to present the material and the authors should be urged to publish separately in greater extent a more conventional portrayal of their findings. The sick-well ratio is compounded of both a drop in proportion *well* and a rise in proportion *impaired*. There are good ways of looking at the effect of age on each line of their table without confining themselves to age-

specific rates. (They apparently know some techniques for adjusting data to take account of differing age distributions in different sub-populations, and use one in the chapter which follows the discussion of socio-economic status.)

Likewise they only assert that sex plays no part in these distributions and give no data in support but in view of their failure to handle age in a satisfactory manner and the fact that the sexes can be expected to be affected differently by parental SES, I can not be satisfied with the assertion unsupported by data. In the Syracuse survey of older people the two sexes showed very different patterns of morbidity rates when contrasted by socioeconomic groups.

Comparing those persons born outside the United States (generation I) with those born in the United States whose parents were born outside the United States (generation II and generation III and generation IV), no differences are found in the frequency rated *impaired* when appropriate sex and age standardization techniques are used. However, no data are given regarding the frequency of *severe* and *incapacitated* (although these data are given for the unstandardized populations, which is meaningless).

The investigators expected new immigrants to have a higher prevalence of impaired states. Because the findings did not confirm their assumptions they looked more closely at their data and decided that immigrants of a new kind were present: people who moved from urban setting to urban setting rather than from rural to urban setting. When the generation I group was classified into these two parts the expected differences (when standardized for age) were found.

In the effort to interpret the variations in the prevalence of morbidity in the subsections of the surveyed populations, investigators encounter several types of difficulties. The distribution of prevalence rates need first to be measured, then to be accounted for; each apparent observation of a variation in prevalence requires a separate search for a possible bias respecting that variation in case finding or case identifying procedures. Since no survey can really reach 100 per cent efficiency in case finding and a certain part of the defined population always remains unscreened, each type of variation in the findings requires its own examination of the "unknowns." (By "unknowns" I mean people included in the sample but not screened with respect to whether or not they are cases.) The present survey goes to some length to look for bias regarding SES in the raters and handles this in an ingenious manner. It has not been so successful regarding age and sex, and acknowledges this fact. Perhaps the Syracuse survey of older people has done better on age (which was a datum withheld from the raters as was SES information in the Midtown Study) but it too did not have a good way of looking for bias with respect to sex.

In looking at the unsurveyed, I believe the Midtown Study may have permitted bias to creep into their analysis

of SES differences. This is due to the fact that in excluding transients from the sample they used dwelling unit characteristics, excluding hotels and clubs. But lower SES transients do not live in hotels or clubs as much as wealthier people do and there is ample evidence that transient populations are high in prevalence of mental disorders. My guess is, however, that more care at this point would not have eliminated the observed differential between higher and lower SES groups.

Having found that the prevalence of mental morbidity rises with age, one has then to look for possible mechanism by which such a rise in prevalence could be produced. If, as the discussions in the Midtown Volume I frequently imply, a mental disorder once present in an individual always remains; then, of course, prevalence of such a disorder will inevitably rise with age unless it is associated with an excessive mortality rate or an excessive net emigration rate (the prevalence of sick persons among outmigrants from the population being studied is greater than the prevalence among in-migrants to it).

However, as some of the data reported here and much other evidence makes abundantly clear mental disorders do terminate. Michaels refers to this in one of the appendices. Hence, the rising prevalence rates must be accountable to at least one of three factors (1) More new cases arise each year than terminate (incidence more than terminations); (2) cases live longer than other people; (3) the proportion of emigrants who are sick is less than the proportion of immigrants who are sick. In practice, it is almost impossible to get direct estimates of these possibilities from a single cross-section picture of a population. Several modifications of the usual data-gathering patterns make it easier to know about these events. For example, if data are gathered regarding the duration of residence in the studied population, information can be obtained regarding the prevalence of morbidity among in-migrants. But even this leaves the out-migrants unknown. A follow-up in a year or two makes possible estimates of incidence and of terminations and of in-migrants and of out-migrants. Oddly enough no one ever seems to do this!

The appendix note on "incidence" and "prevalence" is poorly conceived. It treats these two measures of morbidity frequency as competitors in a popularity contest! It is as if geographers had debates on whether length or breadth were a better measure of size or as if those engaged in hydrodynamics debated as to whether rate of flow or duration of flow had a greater effect on the volume which moved.

Confusion on this issue is worse confounded because it is not clear as to the time dimension of the initial case identification procedure. Some items used are suggestive of current functional state, others of the "have you ever?" variety and still others refer clearly to childhood without reference to the present. Whether the raters made any explicit effort to distinguish present from past symptom patterns is not clear. As a result, they may be reporting something which could be called "lifetime prevalence," that is the proportion of the population studied who at any time has ever had any of the conditions being counted. This particular measure is an example of new gimmicks introduced into a field of mensuration which has enough real troubles without being further burdened by unhelpful tricks. Lifetime prevalence measures are of no visible usefulness. They depend not only on the limited reliability of present case finding and identifying techniques, but also on the distant memory of respondents. Even if the questions were explicit in distinguishing the past from the present (which they were not) the reliability of information regarding past symptoms

is even worse than that regarding the present. When data regarding past and present are fused it becomes almost impossible to handle the data in a productive fashion. The Midtown raters evidently had some related data not reported in their book which they used to judge the contemporary nature of the patient's condition. (*Scientific American,* December, 1962, p. 12.)

The issues regarding in-migrants as contrasted to out-migrants become even more complex and more urgent. The distinction between present prevalence and recent and past incidence become vital. The distinction between factors likely to produce illnesses and factors likely to perpetuate them may or may not be the same, but without separate data no one will ever find out.

Those who have been responsible for completing the analysis and publication of this study since Rennie's unfortunate death following the field work have been caught up in the temptation to make too much of the data they have. A morbidity survey can portray the distribution of disease prevalence in the population it studies within the limitations of its methods. This is the strength of the morbidity survey. There is really no substitute for it as a technique for measuring the distribution of disease prevalence in different populations. Sometimes it can give insight into the factors which determine the variations in prevalence, but it should not be expected to. The factors which produce variations in disease prevalence must be studied by other methods which include measures of incidence and duration and which deal with differential mobility and mortality of the sick and the well.

A few other findings on the distribution of *impairment* prevalence are incorporated in the present volume but without enough detail to justify the conclusion that they are well-established findings.

This particular publication is one of

Social Psychiatry 91

a growing group of studies of mental morbidity in the community. It contains many useful contributions for the specialist along with much speculation and digression. For some reason it, like a number of other recent studies, had not been presented as a technical monograph but as a hard-cover commercial book at high price meant to be both for the specialist and the interested reading public. If any research workers have been tempted to withhold their findings from the technical literature so as to provide meat for a general book, they should read this result and be discouraged from such a course. I believe that the two goals are incompatible in a single publication and that this volume is a good demonstration of that fact—the result is unsatisfactory for all.

References

1. Ødegaard, Ørunlv: Emigration and insanity. A study of mental disease among the Norwegianborn population of Minnesota. *Acta Psychiatrica et Neurologica,* Supplementum IV, (1932) 206 pages.
2. New York State Department of Mental Hygiene: Technical report of the Mental Health Research Unit. Syracuse: Syracuse University Press, 1955, 127 pages.
3. Hollingshead, A. B. and Redlich, F. C.: Social class and mental illness: a community study. New York: John Wiley & Sons, Inc. (1958), 442 pages.
4. Mental Health Research Unit, New York State Department of Mental Hygiene: a mental health survey of older people. Utica, New York: State Hospitals Press, (1961), 138 pages.
5. Bremer, Johannes: A social psychiatric investigation of a small community in northern Norway. *Acta Psychiatrica et Neurologica,* Supplementum LXII, (1951), 161 pages.
6. Böök, J. A. A genetic and neuropsychiatric investigation of a north Swedish population with special regard to schizophrenia and mental deficiency. *Acta Genetica et Statistica Medica,* 4(1953), 1–100.
7. Lemkau, Paul; Tietze, C. and Cooper, Marcia. Report of progress in developing a mental hygiene component of a city health district. *American Journal of Psychiatry,* 93(January, 1941), 805–811.
8. ———: Mental hygiene problems in an urban district. *Ment. Hyg.,* 25(October, 1941), 624–646.
9. ———: Mental hygiene problems in an urban district. *Ment. Hyg.,* 26(January, 1942), 1–20.
10. ———: Mental hygiene problems in an urban district. *Ment Hyg.,* 26(April, 1942), 275–288.
11. ———: Complaint of nervousness and the psychoneuroses. *Amer. J. of Orthopsychiat.,* 12(April, 1942), 214–223.
12. ———: Mental hygiene problems in an urban district. *Ment. Hyg.,* 27(April, 1943), 279–295.
13. ———: A survey of statistical studies on the prevalence and incidence of mental disorder in sample populations. *Pub. Health Rep.* 58(December, 31, 1943), 1909–1927.
14. Roth, William F. and Luton, F. H.: The mental health program in Tennessee. *Amer. J. of Psychiat.,* 99(March, 1943), 662–675.
15. Leighton, Alexander H. My name is legion: foundation for a theory of man in relation to culture. The Stirling County Study, I. New York: Basic Books, Inc. (1959), 452 pages.
16. Gurin, G.; Veroff, J. and Feld, S.: Americans view their mental health. [Joint commission on mental illness and health. Monograph series No. 4.] New York: Basic Books, Inc. (1960), 444 pages.
17. Leighton, Alexander H.: People of cove and woodlot, The Stirling County Study, II. New York: Basic Books, Inc., (1960), 574 pages.

(Portions of this review have already appeared in the *Scientific American* for October, 1962. A statement by certain of the authors in reply to some of the positions taken by this reviewer will be found in the *Scientific American* for December, 1962.)

Section 2

PSYCHOPATHOLOGY

THE HEART of the area of abnormal psychology is the study of psychopathology, or the study of the variety of mental and emotional disorders which occur. The general issues which were presented in the previous section derive a good deal of their importance from their implications for the understanding and treatment of psychopathology. Psychotherapy, which will be discussed in the following section, involves the treatment of the mentally ill, and this rests upon the understanding of the psychopathology involved.

There are a great variety of possible subdivisions into chapters with an area encompassing such a wide range of phenomena. The method chosen, despite the very cogent arguments to the contrary presented in the previous section, is by nosological categories. Despite the somewhat arbitrary nature of the divisions and the absence of real meaning for the borderline distinctions, the system has a very widespread usage, and thus, a good deal of communicative value. With the understanding that papers placed in one chapter may also have substantial implications for individuals classified in other groups, we will continue to use the standard diagnostic categories as a basis for chapter formation.

One of the most compelling alternatives which we found necessary to reject would divide the papers into descriptive, dynamic, and research-oriented. Treatment-oriented papers have been considered important enough for us to reserve an entire section for them. Descriptive papers attempt to present a picture of how psychopathology appears, while dynamic papers are more concerned with why it occurs. Research papers attempt to evaluate hypotheses about psychopathology in a rigorous, scientific manner. An application of this classificatory system was met by considerable overlap and ambiguity of decision, so that it seemed unwieldy to use it as a formal basis of division, but these terms will be used in describing some of the papers.

5. PSYCHONEUROSIS

HISTORICALLY, the initial recognition, treatment, and study of the psychoneuroses with the work of Sigmund Freud represents the beginning of the field of abnormal psychology. In the subsequent half-century this work has been accepted *in toto* by some theorists, accepted with either minor or radical modifications by many theorists, and rejected out of hand by another group of theorists. Mowrer is a learning theorist who has taken great exception to psychoanalytic formulation and, after a review of this approach and the evidence as he sees it, presents an alternative formulation. He objects to what he sees as the psychoanalytic demand that the neurotic be cured by making him more like the criminal, in that the neurotic has an excess of guilt, and the criminal little or no guilt. Anxiety is considered by many theorists to be at the heart of neurosis, either by being expressed directly or indirectly after defensive operations. Rosenwald presents a critique of the methodology of much anxiety research, a paradigm for research in keeping with a psychoanalytic conception of anxiety, and a laboratory application of this paradigm.

Finally, the paper by Lorenz discusses the language patterns which seem to typify certain neurotic and psychotic patients. Besides being descriptive, this approach has many implications for a dynamic understanding of the disorders that are taken up.

Learning Theory and the Neurotic Paradox

O. H. MOWRER, PH.D.

HARVARD UNIVERSITY, CAMBRIDGE, MASS.

Informed and forward-looking psycho-

Reprinted from the *American Journal of Orthopsychiatry*, 18(1948), 571–610, with the permission of the American Orthopsychiatric Association and the author.

clinicians today are generally agreed that the most important and exciting future advances in the understanding of personality and in psychotherapy will come from the mutual modification and blending of learning theory and psychoanalysis.* Notable steps have already been made toward such a synthesis † and one can foresee still greater activity and accomplishment in this area in the decades immediately ahead.

I invite you to consider what, in many respects, is the absolutely central problem in neurosis and therapy. Most simply formulated, it is a paradox—the paradox of behavior which is at one and the same time self-perpetuating and self-defeating! Ranging from common "bad habits" through vices and addictions to classical psychoneurotic and psychotic symptoms, there is a large array of strategies and dynamisms which readily fit such a description but defy any simple, common-sense explanation.

Common sense holds that a normal, sensible man, or even a beast, to the limits of his intelligence, will weigh and balance the consequences of his acts: if the net effect is favorable the action producing it will be perpetuated, and if the net effect is unfavorable the action producing it will be inhibited, abandoned. In neurosis, however, one sees actions which have predominantly unfavorable consequences, yet they persist over a period of months, years, or a lifetime. Small wonder, then, that common sense has abjured responsibility in such matters and has assigned them to the realm of the miraculous, the mystical, the uncommon, the preternatural.

Freud's Early Attempts to Resolve the Neurotic Paradox

In Western European culture, Sigmund Freud was the first man with requisite talent and courage to contend that the

neurotic paradox could be resolved in a completely naturalistic manner. One of his initial attempts to deal with it involved the concept of erotic fixation. He believed that because of early libidinal attachments either to another person (often of an incestuous nature) or to the self (as in narcissism), some individuals were arrested in development and, in consequence, persevered in abortive, self-defeating actions which a free, unfixated person would soon abandon.

Later, as a result of World War I, there came to Freud's attention individuals who were likewise fixated upon senselessly repetitive, self-defeating behavior. These people gave a history not of too powerful libidinal attachments, but of experiences which were so traumatic that they could not be fully assimilated.

Thus in *erotic fixation* on the one hand, and in *traumatic fixation* on the other, Freud offered two possible explanations of the basic feature of neurosis. Yet a question remained. Ordinarily, dangers, which are clearly past, however grave they may have been at the time, gradually lose their affective force, and pleasures which no longer please are similarly given up. This is the verdict of common sense, and it is also supported by results from the learning laboratory.‡ Why, then, do neurotics provide an apparent exception? Freud's emphasis upon fixation did not really solve the problem. He had posited that fixation was largely dependent upon the *quantitative* factor. In the course of development, everyone experiences trauma in some degree and is likewise more or less fixated libidinally. Freud suggested that it was perhaps the *intensity* of the trauma or the fixation which decided the issue. Yet some persons show them-

* To express my own views accurately, "learning theory" should be thought of as including "culture theory." Habits and attitudes are to an individual what culture is to a society. In common speech we recognize this perception when we say, "He is a learned man, a man of much culture." An adequate statement should also acknowledge the contributions, actual and potential, of social structure theory.

† See, for example, the recent paper by Shaffer (38).

‡ See Sections V–VIII.

selves capable of surviving equally severe traumata or of surmounting equally strong fixations without becoming neurotic. Confronted by these facts, Freud was sometimes reduced to positing constitutional factors as the determining ones, but he did not rest comfortably with such thinking.

As if recognizing the impasse to which these early formulations brought him, Freud remarks: "Here . . . we leave the path we have been following. At the moment it will take us no further, and we have much more to learn before we can find a satisfactory continuation of it" (11, p. 244). His next theoretical step was one which he made very confidently. It was to propose that psychic forces may be unconscious and still powerfully active in the economy of the total personality. "We challenge anyone in the world to give a more correct scientific explanation of the matter," he said, and then added that neurotic symptoms "show the way unmistakably to conviction on the question of the unconscious in the mind; and for that very reason clinical psychiatry, which only recognizes a psychology of consciousness, can do nothing with these symptoms except to stigmatize them as signs of a special kind of degeneration" (pp. 245-6).

There then follows a feat of intellectual penetration and conceptual analysis which has seldom been equaled in psychological literature. It will be my task to show, however, that Freud's theoretical scheme is correct only up to a point, and to maintain that the revision and correction of this scheme is one of the great scientific challenges and responsibilities of our time.

Let us begin with Freud's formulation of what I have called the neurotic paradox. He says (11):

When we undertake to cure a patient of his symptoms he opposes against us a vigorous and tenacious *resistance* throughout the entire course of the treatment. This is

such an extraordinary thing that we cannot expect much belief in it. . . . To think that the patient, whose symptoms cause him and those about him such suffering, who is willing to make such sacrifices in time, money, effort, and self-conquest to be freed from them—that he should, in the interests of his illness, resist the help offered him. How improbable this statement must sound! (p. 253).

Freud then comments upon the "highly varied and exceedingly subtle" forms which neurotic resistance may take. Even the first rule of analysis, that of free association, arouses opposition and reservation: "We do succeed in extracting from the patient a certain amount of obedience for the rule of the technique; and then the resistance takes another line altogether" (p. 255). The resistance may now assume the form of logical opposition to analytic theory. Or it may masquerade as a great thirst for knowledge and eagerness to be instructed and advised; or it may take the form of complete overt acceptance coupled with covert doubt.

But these resistances, serious as they may seem are relatively superficial; it is only with the emergence of the "transference" that the really "decisive battle begins." Here Freud remarks:

If the patient is a man, he usually takes his material from his relationship with his father in whose place he has now put the physician; and in so doing he erects resistances out of his struggles to attain to personal independence and independence of judgment, out of his ambition, the earliest aim of which was to equal or to excel the father, out of his disinclination to take the burden of gratitude upon himself for the second time in his life. There are periods in which one feels that the patient's desire to put the analyst in the wrong, to make him feel his impotence, to triumph over him, has completely ousted the worthier desire to bring the illness to an end. Women have a genius for exploiting in the interest of resistance a tender erotically tinged transference to the analyst; when this attraction reaches a certain intensity all interest in the actual situation of treatment fades away, together with every obligation incurred upon undertaking it (p. 256).

Nothing is empirically better founded than these observations of Freud concerning neurotic resistances. No clinician with even a modicum of awareness of what transpires in the therapeutic situation has failed to sense these strategies; indeed at times he feels all but overwhelmed by them. As data, as phenomena, they are among our most certain and most important. We can fully agree with Freud when he says that "the overcoming of these resistances is the essential work of the analysis, that part of the work which alone assures us that we have achieved something for the patient" (p. 257). The question is one of theoretical explanation and adequate conceptualization. To this end he continues:

I have given such a detailed consideration of this point because I am about to inform you that our dynamic conception of the neurosis is founded upon this experience of ours of the resistance that neurotic patients set up against the cure of their symptoms (p. 257).

In what way can we now account for this observed fact, that the patient struggles so energetically against the relief of his symptoms and the restoration of his mental processes to normal functioning? We say that we have come upon the traces of powerful forces at work here opposing any change in the condition; they must be the same forces that originally induced the condition. . . . As we already know from Breuer's observations, it follows from the existence of a symptom that some mental process has not been carried through to an end in a normal manner so that it could become conscious; the symptom is a substitute for that which has not come through. Now we know where to place the forces which we suspect to be at work. A vehement effort must have been exercised to prevent the mental process in question from penetrating into consciousness and as a result it has remained unconscious; being unconscious it had the power to construct a symptom. The

same vehement effort is again at work during analytic treatment, opposing the attempt to bring the unconscious into consciousness. This we perceive in the form of resistance. The pathogenic process which is demonstrated by the resistance we call *repression* (p. 259).

This quotation contains a theoretical insight which, in my judgment, has not been sufficiently appreciated. Even Freud did not fully exploit it. What it says, in effect, is that a neurotic is a person in whom there is a kind of inner debate, or conflict, which has been partially resolved by repression of one of the contending parties. When such a person comes into therapy, it is as if the therapist is invested by the patient slowly or quickly, with the attributes of the repressed part of his personality. The debate which has previously gone on between the two contending factions within the one individual *is now externalized as a struggle between the patient and the therapist.*

Freud called this phenomenon "transference" and he knew two very important things about it: (1) that the patient's neurotic suffering and symptoms are often dramatically alleviated by the development of transference (thus showing that symptoms and resistances are in some way equivalent); and (2) that it is through the handling or "working through" of the transference that permanent immunity to neurosis is achieved, if at all.

Again there can be only agreement with Freud.* Empirically his conten-

* Therapists of the so-called "nondirective" school will take issue with this statement. They maintain that the activation of transference represents a technical error, which they strive to avoid. In some instances, where the personality problem is not very deep-seated or where the therapeutic relationship remains a relatively casual one, it is perhaps correct to insist that transference does not take place. However, it seems probable that in more serious treatment situations, even the nondirective or, more accurately, the noninterpretative, approach arouses strong transference and that the chief

tions are well founded, but from the standpoint of theory much remains to be desired. It is surely obvious that the most pressing question is: whence comes this internal struggle which besets every neurotic and which is then converted into the interpersonal conflict which one sees in therapy? From the use of the term "transference" and from the statements made in the excerpts already quoted, one would suppose that the inherent logic of the situation would have driven Freud to assume that neurosis is but the internalization, or introjection, of the early conflicts which exist between the child and his principal socializers. Transference would thus be nothing more nor less than a social struggle between a relatively immature person and a more mature one, a struggle which initially existed in childhood, had been introjected, and then, in therapy, is again made external.

The next question would then be: What is it about the socialization of some children which leads to conflicts which are internalized and thus provide the basis of neurosis, whereas in other cases these conflicts are worked through in the child-parent relationship and the intrapsychic development of the child proceeds with relative harmony?

However, these were not the questions Freud asked. Possibly because of his preoccupation with dream interpretation, possibly because of deeply rooted forces within his own personality, he turned his theoretical analysis at this point into a direction which prevented his ever reaching the conclusions toward which his work otherwise so clearly points—a direction which has done much to mislead and retard both the conceptual and therapeutic endeavors of others.

The story of this fateful turn in Freud's reasoning is soon told. Freud

difference is in the method of handling it, though even this distinction may not prove to be as marked as is sometimes maintained.

pictured the mental anatomy of neurotics and normal persons alike, as follows:

The unconscious is a large ante-room, in which the various mental excitations are crowding one another, like individual beings. Adjoining this is a second, smaller apartment, a sort of reception-room, in which consciousness resides. But on the threshold between the two there stands a personage with the office of door-keeper, who examines the various mental excitations, censors them, and denies them admittance to the reception-room when he disapproves of them. . . . The door-keeper is what we have learnt to know as resistance in our attempts in analytic treatment to loosen the repressions.

Now I know very well that you will say that these conceptions are as crude as they are fantastic and not at all permissible in a scientific presentation. . . . Still, I should like to reassure you that these crude hypotheses, the two chambers, the door-keeper on the threshold between the two, and consciousness as a spectator at the end of the second room, must indicate an extensive approximation to the actual reality (pp. 260–1).

According to this conceptual scheme, impulses which are objectionable to the censor are kept imprisoned, as effectively as possible, in the antechamber; i.e., in the unconscious. They are, in short, repressed. To this Freud adds: "We know that the symptom is a substitute for some other process which was held back by repression" (p. 262). Like a dream or a Freudian error, the symptom represents a repressed impulse which, by means of the strategy of disguise, escapes into consciousness and finds a route, however devious, to gratification. What, then, are these imprisoned impulses most likely to be? To this Freud replied:

Every time we should be led by analysis to the sexual experiences and desires of the patient, and every time we should have to affirm that the symptom served the same purpose. This purpose shows itself to be the gratification of sexual wishes; the symptoms serve the purpose of sexual gratification for the patient; they are a substitute for satisfactions which he does not obtain in reality (p. 263).

All this, of course, is very familiar to the present audience. I again bring it to your attention only as a means of highlighting a point which may previously have escaped your scrutiny. You will recall that in the excerpts here quoted, Freud begins by posing what I have termed the neurotic paradox, the paradox inhering in the fact that neurotic symptoms are both self-defeating and yet self-perpetuating. We must now ask: Does Freud, in the work from which these quotations come, resolve this paradox? He certainly does not do it explicitly. It is as if he becomes so absorbed in discussing repression and symptom-formation that he loses sight of and never returns to this basic issue. However, by implication he may be assumed to say something like this: The reason neurotic symptoms cause suffering and are thus disadvantageous is that the censor objects to them; and the reason they are self-perpetuating is that to another part of the personality they are gratifying, relieving, pleasurable.

Superficially this may appear to be a very satisfactory resolution, but let us look deeper. If a person refrains from gratifying impulses which involve an objective danger, we need hardly refer to him as neurotic. A person would presumably be termed abnormal only if he inhibited sexual or other impulses when, in reality, the way was open for their gratification. Much effort on the part of Freudian analysts has always been directed toward trying to get their patients to "see the difference" between then and now—between childhood, when gratification of certain impulses was indeed hazardous, and adulthood, when the individual's status is realistically different.*

The essence then of neurosis would consist of the tendency on the part of the afflicted individual to continue to act as though the conditions of childhood, now past, still prevailed.

This formulation does not resolve our basic dilemma; it only restates it. The findings of laboratory experimentation, as well as common sense, lead us to believe that there is in all living organisms a tendency which pushes them in the direction of "reality testing." If an organism, out or fear, does something it would otherwise not do, or if it refrains from doing something which otherwise it would do, there is at least a recurrent disposition to "feel out" the situation, to see if the danger is "still there." But according to the earlier Freudian views, this tendency is for some reason lost by neurotic individuals —which is why they are neurotic—and it is presumed to be recoverable only through the process of psychoanalytic therapy.

Here the mystery is only pushed back a step, not removed. In Freudian terms one must say that in the normal person the censor is normally flexible, whereas in the abnormal person the censor is abnormally inflexible, rigid, severe. In other words, *a person is abnormal because his censor is abnormal.* This is an obvious piece of question-begging, particularly since no attempt was made in that period to explain how the censor "got that way." By implication one might infer belief in a traumatic explanation of such inflexibility, such unrealism, such severity on the part of the censor; but this would again be falling back on a concept which, as Freud himself remarked, "will take us no further." As of 1920, the date of publication of *A General Introduction to Psychoanalysis,* we must therefore conclude that the

---

* In the light of this logic, therapy then becomes essentially a matter of helping the patient correct overly extended generalizations by means of appropriate discriminations. This conception of neurosis and its treatment will be discussed more fully in Section IV.

basic neurotic paradox was still almost as far from a satisfactory resolution as ever.

Freud's Ill-fated Venture Beyond the Pleasure Principle

As if recognizing his earlier failure to resolve the central paradox of neurosis, in 1922 Freud published his highly speculative and controversial work, *Beyond the Pleasure Principle* (7). Taking the traumatic neuroses, anxiety dreams, certain monotonously repetitive games played by children, data drawn from the transference-neurosis, the apparent inability of some persons to escape from a kind of unrelenting "fate," and certain forms of masochism as a points of departure, Freud concluded:

In the light of such observations as these, . . . we may venture to make the assumption that there really exists in psychic life a repetition-compulsion, which goes beyond the pleasure principle . . . and this seems to us more primitive, more elementary, more instinctive than the pleasure-principle which is displaced by it (pp. 24–5).

Elsewhere (24) I have reviewed some of the principal arguments which have been advanced by others against this conception and have added some of my own. Here it need only be remarked that the repetition-compulsion was obviously an attempt—one might almost call it an act of desperation—to deal with the basic neurotic paradox. But that Freud himself was by no means satisfied with the result is indicated by the fact that with the publication of his *New Introductory Lectures* (9) in 1933, he reverted to a conceptual scheme only slightly different from the earlier one.

Freud's Second "Topography" and the Neurotic Paradox

Freud's first topographic, or spatial, conception of personality involved the un-

conscious, the concious, and the censor. His second system likewise involved a tripartite division of personality: the ego, super-ego, and id. Superficially, the id corresponds to the earlier conception of the unconscious, as "the various mental excitations . . . crowding one upon another, like individual beings"; the ego corresponds to the conscious part of personality; and the super-ego corresponds to the censor. But in his second formulation, Freud develops the second and third of these three conceptions so much further than in his first formulation that it is important, in any attempt to unravel the fundamental paradox of neurosis, to examine the second formulation in some detail.

Just as the best statement of his earlier views are contained in the two chapters on fixation and on resistance and repression in the *General Introduction,* so one finds the fullest elaboration of his later conceptions in Chapter 3, "The Anatomy of the Mental Personality," in the *New Introductory Lectures.* "Here," says Freud, "I am giving you a supplement to the introduction to psychoanalysis which I started fifteen years ago. . . ." He begins this chapter by announcing that psychoanalysis has advanced beyond the stage of being merely a psychology of the unconscious and now encompasses something new, which he calls "ego-psychology." "At last we had got so far that we could turn our attention from the repressed to the repressing forces, and we came face to face with the ego . . ." Almost at once he takes up the task of describing the super-ego, which he conceives as being a specialized portion of the ego.* It will be recalled

---

* It is not surprising to find Freud conceiving of the super-ego in this manner, for in the passage from his earlier writings already quoted the censor was "a personage with the office of door-keeper, who examines the various mental excitations, censors them, and denies them admittance to the reception-room" where consciousness resides. Clearly, such a door-keeper would be "in the employ" of conscious-

that one of the major weaknesses of Freud's earlier formulation was that in it he had little or nothing to say about the origin and developmental history of the censor, a weakness which left the neurotic paradox unresolved.* As if determined to make good this neglect—"psychoanalysis could not study every part of the field at once" he gives an account of the super-ego which contains some of the most penetrating insights shown in any of his writings.

After alluding to the tendency of psychotics to be preoccupied with violent self-criticism and delusions of observation and persecution, Freud says:

"Under the strong impression of this clinical picture, I formed the idea that the separating off of an observing function from the rest of the ego might be a normal feature of the ego's structure; this idea has never left me, and I was driven to investigate the further characteristics and relations of the function which had been separated off in this way. The next step was soon taken. The actual content of the delusion of observation makes it probable that the observation is only a first step towards conviction and punishment, so that we may guess that another activity of this function must be what we call conscience. . . . I will henceforward call this function in the ego the 'super-ego' " (pp. 85-6).

"The role, which the super-ego undertakes later in life, is at first played by an external power, by parental authority. The influence of the parents dominates the child by granting proofs of affection and by threats of punishment, which, to the child, mean loss of love, and which must also be feared on their own account. This objective anxiety is the forerunner of the later moral anxiety; † so long as the former is dominant one need not speak of super-ego or of conscience. It is only later that the secondary situation arises; the external restrictions are introjected, so that the super-ego takes the place of the parental function, and thenceforward observes, guides and threatens the ego in just the same way as the parents acted to the child before" (p. 89).

To this Freud adds that he cannot say as much as he would like about just how it is that the authority of parents becomes incorporated into the child as super-ego; but he gives to this process the appropriate term "identification." ‡ In summary he remarks: "For us the super-ego is the representative of all moral restrictions, the advocate of the impulse towards perfection, in short it is as much as we have been able to apprehend psychologically of what people call the 'higher' things in human life" (p. 95). Elsewhere (8) he refers to it as the "internalized voice of the community."

It is also important to note that in

---

ness. It is understandable, therefore, that in the later formulation the super-ego is seen as a specialized development of the ego.

* Freud answers those who had attacked his earlier theoretical system on the grounds that it neglected the "nobler" side of human personality, by saying sarcastically: ". . . psychoanalysis was met by illuminating criticisms to the effect that man is not merely a sexual being but has nobler and higher feelings. It might have been added that, supported by the consciousness of those higher feelings, he often allowed himself the right to think nonsense and to overlook facts" (p. 82). It is not that Freud ever overlooked the self-critical, moral forces; he acknowledged them from the beginning. Rather the problem comes from the way in which he evaluated them and the role he attributed to them in personality pathology. We shall return to this point later.

† For purposes of later discussion it is well to note Freud's use here of the terms "objective anxiety" and "moral anxiety." As he indicates in various other places, the first of these terms meant for him simply the reaction to objective danger, namely fear; and it is also clear that by the latter he meant what is commonly referred to as conscious guilt or "pangs of conscience" (p. 109). "Neurotic anxiety," by contrast, he thought of as something quite different. The question of the origin and ultimate nature of the latter is of crucial importance for the main thesis of this paper.

‡ The highly important question as to precisely how it is that the learning which underlies identification takes place, or fails to take place with ensuing character disturbances, is still unanswered. However, laboratory studies now in progress (28, 31) seem likely to throw light upon the problem.

this discussion Freud was taking issue with the traditional view that conscience is something innate, inborn—the "voice of God speaking within us." * "Conscience," said Freud, "is no doubt something within us, but it has not been there from the beginning. In this sense it is the opposite of sexuality, which is certainly present from the very beginning of life, and is not a thing that only comes in later. But small children are notoriously a-moral" (p. 89). Here he was certainly on solid ground, for those who contend most loudly for the innateness of conscience are usually among the strongest advocates of training calculated to produce conscience!

We have dwelt thus at length upon Freud's views concerning the super-ego for the reason that the resolution of the whole neurotic paradox hinges upon the way in which this part of the personality is perceived. We shall later revert to this topic, but for the moment will review Freud's characterization of the ego proper and its manifold functions as he conceived them.

One can hardly go wrong, says Freud, in regarding the ego as that part of the id which has been modified by its proximity to the external world and the influence that the latter has had on it, . . .† This relation

to the external world is decisive for the ego. The ego has taken over the task of representing the external world for the id, and so of saving it; for the id, blindly striving to gratify its instincts in complete disregard of the superior strength of outside forces, could not otherwise escape annihilation. . . . On behalf of the id, the ego controls the path of access to motility, but it interpolates between desire and action the procrastinating factor of thought, during which it makes use of the residues of experience stored up in memory.‡ In this way it dethrones the pleasure-principle, which exerts undisputed sway over the processes in the id, and substitutes for it the reality principle, which promises greater security and greater success (p. 106).

The ego advances from the function of perceiving instincts to that of controlling them, but the latter is only achieved through the mental representative of the instinct becoming subordinated to a larger organization, and finding its place in a coherent unity. In popular language, we may say that the ego stands for reason and circumspection, while the id stands for the untamed passions (p. 107).

The proverb tells us that one cannot serve two masters at once. The poor ego

---

* It is interesting to note how easily many theological statements containing the term "God" can be rendered into perfectly intelligible naturalistic statements if this term is translated as "mankind" or "the community." Such a rendition would leave Freud differing with traditional views about conscience mainly on the score of whether it is innate or learned.

† It may seem a self-contradiction that Freud should speak of the super-ego as a "split off" portion of the ego and then characterize the ego itself as a modified part of the id. The seeming contradiction is strengthened when one recalls that the id is for Freud that which is innately given in personality and the super-ego is acquired by the process of identification. We must remember that he is here attempting to deal with a very difficult problem of conceptualization. It would perhaps have been more exact to speak of the id as comprising what modern learning theorists call the *primary*

drives (and probably their attendant appetites) and of the super-ego as the socially acquired *secondary drives.* Since fear and love are believed to be the two principal ingredients of conscience, such a distinction seems particularly apt.

‡ It is virtually impossible to determine whether Freud meant the term "ego" to subsume the super-ego or to imply only the ego proper. There is no explicit reference to the super-ego function; but conscience, representing the culture (wisdom and virtue) of one's society, might well be thought of as "the residues of experience stored up in memory." The voice of community and conscience certainly restrains the pleasure-principle and "substitutes for it the reality principle" as a condition of the social, moral way of life as opposite to the solitary, a-moral type of existence. Here, as elsewhere in Freud's writings, one senses a tendency to glorify the 18th-Century conception of Reason. Freud refers approvingly to "the Logos," at the expense of that which has come down to us as mere tradition, however much human suffering and learning it may reflect (Section VIII).

has a still harder time of it; it has to serve three harsh masters, and has to do its best to reconcile the claims and demands of all three. . . . The three tyrants are the external world, the super-ego and the id (p. 108). . . . In this way, goaded on by the id, hemmed in by the super-ego, and rebuffed by reality, the ego struggles to cope with its economic task of reducing the forces and influences which work in it and [of imposing upon them] some kind of harmony; and we may well understand how it is that we so often cannot repress the cry: "Life is not easy." When the ego is forced to acknowledge its weakness, it breaks out into anxiety: reality anxiety in face of the external world, moral anxiety in face of the super-ego, and neurotic anxiety in face of the strength of the passions of the id (pp. 109–10).*

Little need be added here concerning the nature of the id, in part because it is not very different from Freud's earlier conception of the unconsciousness and in part because it is inherently uncomplicated. In summary, he remarks: "Naturally, the id knows no values, no good and evil, no morality. The economic, or, if you prefer, the quantitative factor, which is so closely bound up with the pleasure-principle, dominates all its processes. Instinctual cathexes seeking discharge—that, in our view, is all that the id contains" (p. 105; also pp. 103–4).

We are now finally in a position to return to our central task, that of understanding the dynamics of neurosis and, if possible, defining the logic of its treatment. Already a theory is implicit in the passages quoted from Freud; and it will now be our purpose to try to make this theory more explicit. However, we must be prepared to find here a structure which is far from complete and, in certain respects, manifestly unsatisfactory.

Briefly, Freud's theory is that human beings "fall ill," psychologically speaking, because they experience neurotic

* See footnote on p. 102.

anxiety. This, it will be recalled, is the anxiety which an individual feels when forces in the id, having been repressed, threaten to erupt into consciousness. He says:

From the very beginning our view was that men fall ill owing to the conflict between the demands of their instincts and the internal resistance which is set up against them; not for a moment did we forget this resisting, rejecting and repressing factor, which we believe to be furnished with its own special forces, the ego-instincts, and which corresponds to the ego of popular psychology (p. 83).

The resistance can only be a manifestation of the ego, which carried through the repression at one time or other and is now endeavoring to keep it up. And that too was our earlier view. Now that we have posited a special function within the ego to represent the demand for restriction and rejection, i.e., the super-ego, we can say that repression is the work of the super-ego—either that it does its work on its own account or else that the ego does it in obedience to its orders (pp. 97–8).

The objective of psychoanalytic therapy is easily inferred from these passages: it is to strengthen the "poor" ego so that it can ward off the restrictive demands of the super-ego and thus allow the forces of the id to find suitable outlets to gratification. Says Freud: "We must admit that the therapeutic efforts of psycho-analysis have chosen much the same method of approach. For their object is to strengthen the ego, to make it more independent of the super-ego, to widen its fields of vision, and so to extend its organization that it can take over new portions of the id. Where id was, there shall ego be."

On this platform psychoanalysis has done a prosperous business. It has attracted a world-wide following among those who purport to do psychotherapy; and its philosophy, expressed and implied, has permeated popular thought in almost every civilized country. To the social historian of the future will fall the task of determining why analytic therapy and philosophy have so caught the imagination of contemporary mankind. Our task is a simpler one: merely to ask if analytic theory has or has not succeeded in giving a rigorous explanatory account of the fundamental neurotic paradox.

In an earlier section we have seen that the only solution Freud proposed to this problem in terms of his first topographic system was to suggest that abnormal human beings have abnormal "censors," thus leaving unanswered the question as to what determines whether the censor itself will be normal or otherwise. So far we have found nothing in Freud's second topographic formulation which would carry us further; all it has said is that persons become abnormal or "fall ill" because their super-egos are unduly harsh, strict, demanding, and otherwise behave in a thoroughly unreasonable manner. And it is this unreasonableness which causes the impulse life of the individual to be unduly restricted, thereby predisposing him to anxiety and symptom formation.

Nor says Freud, can these "neurotic" super-egos be accounted for solely in terms of the harshness with which parents deal with their children:

If the parents have really ruled with a rod of iron, we can easily understand the child developing a severe super-ego, but, contrary to our expectations, experience shows that the super-ego may reflect the same relentless harshness even when the up-bringing has been gentle and kind, and avoided threats and punishments as far as possible. We shall return to this contradiction later, . . . (p. 90).

It follows from our account of its origin that it [the super-ego] is based upon an overwhelmingly important biological fact no less than upon a momentous psychological fact, namely the lengthy dependence of the human child on its parents and the Oedipus complex; these two facts, more-over, are closely bound up with each other. For us the super-ego is the representative of all moral restrictions, the advocate of the impulse towards perfection, in short is as much as we have been able to apprehend psychologically of what people call the "higher" things in human life. Since it itself can be traced back to the influence of parents, teachers, and so on, we shall learn more of its significance if we turn our attention to these sources. In general, parents and similar authorities follow the dictates of their own super-egos in the up-bringing of children. Whatever terms their ego may be on with their super-ego, in the education of the child they are severe and exacting. They have forgotten the difficulties of their own childhood and are glad to be able to identify themselves fully at last with their own parents, who in their day subjected them to such severe restraints. The result is that the super-ego of the child is not really built up on the model of the parents, but on that of the parents' super-ego; it takes over the same content, it becomes the vehicle of tradition and of all the age-long values which have been handed down in this way from generation to generation (pp. 94-5).

Mankind never lives completely in the present; the ideologies of the super-ego perpetuate the past, the traditions of the race and the people, which yield but slowly to the influence of the present and to new developments, and, so long as they work through the super-ego, play an important part in man's life, quite independently of economic conditions (p. 96).

What, more concretely, does all this come to? Everyone is now conversant with the concept of "culture lag." Like habits and attitudes in an individual, the traditions and values of a society tend to have momentum of their own which causes them to persist somewhat beyond the period of their actual usefulness.* But unrealistic habits and attitudes

* Both the cultural functionalists, such as Malinowski and Radcliffe-Brown, and anthropologists of the "historical" school, such as Smith and Boas, would admit this much. However, the former would maintain that "lag" is never very great, whereas the latter would

in an individual are ordinarily self-correcting. Why is this not also true of the habits and attitudes which constitute a neurosis? Far from being self-correcting, they tend to be self-exacerbating. What is the fateful differential? Freud, astute observer that he was, concluded that the answer is not a purely quantitative one, since the severity of the super-ego does not seem wholly or even mainly a function of the actual severity of the treatment which parents accord to their children.

Finally we extract an hypothesis on which Freud apparently pinned his last hope of accounting for the enigma of neurosis. This hypothesis, referred to as that of the "timelessness of the repressed," he sets forth as follows:

> Conative impulses which have never got beyond the id, and even impressions which have been pushed down into the id by repression, are virtually immortal and are preserved for whole decades as though they had only recently occurred. . . . It is constantly being borne in upon me that we have made far too little use of our theory of the indubitable fact that the repressed remains unaltered by the passage of time. This seems to offer us the possibility of an approach to some really profound truths. But I myself have made no further progress here (p. 105).*

But this suggestion obviously does not resolve the difficulty. The problems which Freud's theoretical system poses

maintain that it may last for hundreds or perhaps thousands of years. Present-day anthropologists are tending to agree that in those instances where there is what appears to be a protracted lag the apparent autonomy of the culture can be accounted for in terms of "secondary gains"; i.e., emotional satisfactions which have become dissociated from the economic or "practical" functions originally served.

* Here one is, of course, reminded of Jung's speculations concerning the "racial unconscious." But it is not easy to see how such a concept really advances our clinical understanding of or control over neurosis (cf. previous footnote). For further discussion of the relationship between time and the unconscious, see (12), pp. 94–6, 109, 123–4, and 128–9.

is now how to explain the durability of repressed impulses; it is rather the rigidity and immutability of the repressor —the super-ego—which calls for explanation. Although Freud came to believe that parts of the super-ego and even parts of the ego may be "unconscious," it would have made little sense for him to speak of the super-ego repressing itself, and thus producing the effect of "immortality." It is hardly remarkable that he admits to "no further progress here" and later refers to his attempt to resolve this paradox as "exhausting and perhaps not very illuminating" (p. 110).

If it appear an unduly harsh verdict, then, to say that Freud never succeeded in advancing a satisfactory answer to the most basic problem in neurosis theory, let him again speak for himself. In *The Problem of Anxiety* (12) Freud asks:

> Why are not all neuroses merely episodes in the individual's development which become a closed chapter when the next stage of development is reached? Whence comes the element of permanency in these reactions to danger? Whence springs the preference over all other effects which the affect of anxiety seems to enjoy in alone evoking reactions which we distinguish from others as abnormal and which in their inexpediency obstruct the stream of life? In other words, we find ourselves abruptly confronted once again by the oft-repeated riddle: What is the source of neurosis, what is its ultimate, its specific, underlying principle? After decades of analytic effort this problem rises up before us, as untouched as at the beginning (p. 120).

The Conditioned Reflex and Neurosis

The first great name among those who have attempted to resolve the enigma of neurosis on the basis of learning theory is that of Pavlov. His observations concerning disturbances in the behavior of the dogs which he and his co-workers used in studying the conditioned salivary reflex are now very widely known, and deservedly so. His books continue to offer challenging and instructive data for the serious student of dynamic psychology. But Pavlov himself was not such a student. He abhorred any concept so subjective as drive or motivation or satisfaction, and he was able to think only in terms of that particular conception of learning which stresses stimulus substitution, or, more familiarly, associative learning. Having observed behavior disturbances in his experimental subjects under a rather wide range of conditions, he concluded that there are two possible sources of such disturbances—conflict and trauma. Thus, "All these experiments clearly bring out the fact that a development of a chronic pathological state of the hemispheres can occur from one or other of two causes: first, a conflict between excitation and inhibition which the cortex finds itself unable to resolve; second, the action of extremely powerful and unusual stimuli" (34, p. 318).

In the one case the "chronic pathological state" was to be thought of then as due to a "clashing" of excitatory and inhibitory processes, while in the other it was regarded as a product of overexcitation. But in both instances Pavlov conceived of the resulting "disturbance of the higher nervous activity" as involving definite injury or damage to the brain cells. A neurosis was thus reduced to a "pathological" state (implying structural or at least "physiochemical" derangement) of cortical mechanisms, which stood in contrast to the "normal" or "physiological" state of these mechanisms. This same type of view was, of course, held by many psychiatrists who were Pavlov's contemporaries; but he seems to have found a special reason for accepting it in the fact that the "neurotic" behavior of his experimental animals was relatively permanent. He says: "From some of these disturbances the animal recovers gradu-

ally and spontaneously under the influence of rest alone, on discontinuance of the disturbing experiments; in other cases the disturbances are so persistent as to require special therapeutic measures" (p. 284).

Though Pavlov looked upon these disturbances as being "of a purely functional origin, and not due to surgical interferences or trauma" he did not believe that the disturbance itself was "purely functional." If such disturbances had been merely the products of learning, then he would have expected them to be temporary. All learned behavior, according to Pavlov, consisted of conditioned reflexes, and all conditioned reflexes are temporary, provisional; i.e., become "extinguished" unless they are periodically reinforced by the paired presentation of the "conditioned" and the "unconditioned" stimuli which were initially involved in the establishment of the new stimulus-response connection. Since behavior which he termed "neurotic" often appeared and persisted for a remarkably long time without any evident reinforcement of this kind, Pavlov inferred that such behavior could not have been learned and was therefore due to "pathological" brain changes.

This conclusion had two very important consequences. In the first place, it caused him to stress the constitutional factor in determining individual susceptibility to neurosis. He says: "The pathological state of the hemispheres in different individual animals from the action of injurious influences varies greatly. One and the same injurious influence causes severe and prolonged disorders in some dogs; in others the disorders are only slight and fleeting; while yet other dogs remain practically unaffected" (p. 284).

These observations led him to a rather elaborate classification of temperament-types in dogs, to the almost exclusive neglect of what may be termed life-history factors. He seems to have had little or no conception of the extent to which what is learned in one situation is often very powerfully influenced by what has been learned in *past* situations. Said otherwise, the *meanings* of situations differ as a function of prior experience. Although the constitutional factor cannot be arbitrarily excluded as a determinant of neurosis, the fact that Pavlov completely failed to control the surely equally potent factor of prior experience goes far to nullify the force of his conjectures in this connection. His second inference which is important here is: if neurosis is a matter of brain damage, however minute, then therapy might be expected to follow more or less traditional medical lines—sedation, rest, diet, and healthful living generally. In his last book (35) Pavlov elaborated his conceptions of diagnosis and treatment, but the results sounded strangely outmoded and futile. His fame will hardly rest upon this labor of his declining years.

Many other investigators sought to confirm and extend Pavlov's observations and theories. Prominent among these may be mentioned Anderson and Liddell. They believe that any of several experimental procedures may "strain an animal's nervous system to the breaking point" (5, p. 332). They believe that the conditioned-reflex type of training is especially trying for the reason that it involves a drastic restriction, both mechanical and psychic, of spontaneous movement and a resulting accumulation of nervous tension which would normally be kept dissipated in a situation permitting complete freedom of movement. The agitation of their "neurotic" sheep they interpret as representing a "neuromuscular outlet which has been closed through previous training [but which] now opens because of actual damage to the nervous system to prevent any further rise of tension. The nervous movements of the leg, and, in a more exaggerated form of the neurosis, the

tremors observed in the rest intervals between stimulations are to be regarded as the protective operation of the neuromuscular system to prevent the nerve cells of the higher centers from being subjected to further strain" (p. 352). Although differing in detail, this line of thought obviously follows the same main channels laid down by Pavlov.

Another rather different way of thinking about these problems which was inspired by Pavlov's work is that of Korzybski (21) and his associates. This writer believes that the original Russian words which Pavlov used for "conditioned" and "unconditioned" have been misinterpreted and mistranslated. He prefers to render them as "conditional" and "unconditional." Thus a conditional response is one that is flexible, shows discernment of circumstances, varies with conditions; whereas an unconditional response is one that is headlong, blundering, undiscriminating. The former are normal and serve to keep us out of trouble, whereas the latter are abnormal and get us constantly into trouble.

It is true that for Pavlov an unconditioned response was one with a kind of invariability about it; but he regarded such a response as invariable or reflexive because it is invariably or at least very generally useful. Thus, if a dog shows an "unconditioned" salivary reflex when food is placed in the mouth, this was hardly taken by Pavlov as defining a state of abnormality. Although Korzybski may be justified, on a strictly linguistic basis, in retranslating the Russian words used by Pavlov in this connection, he is clearly not justified otherwise, for such a reinterpretation radically alters the whole sense of Pavlov's experiments and theory.*

* Elsewhere (24) the writer has adduced evidence for believing that there are two basically different learning processes—problem-solving and conditioning. Pavlov's experiments with the salivary reflex give instances of con-

Even if Korzybski's claims were in this respect justified, he would still have to face the task of resolving the neurotic paradox. Specifically, in his terms, it is the problem of explaining what makes one individual characteristically behave conditionally (normally, rationally) and another behave unconditionally; or what makes one and the same individual sometimes behave in the former manner and at other times in the latter manner. With a grand sweep, Korzybski identifies the villain of the piece as something which he calls "Aristotelian logic." By this he seems to mean two things: (1) the tendency to look upon truth as absolute rather than relative, and (2) the tendency to continue to use, in a scientific age, language which was developed in a prescientific age.

There can be no question that Korzybski has been a pioneer in the kind of thinking which has recently attained its most precise expression in that form of statistical interpretation which holds that experimental or other evidence never *proves* or *disproves* the ultimate and final truth of a proposition; it only renders the proposition increasingly *probable* or *improbable*. It is also true that in certain types of persons seen clinically there is a tendency to think about their own and other's behavior in terms of categorical imperatives or absolutes, rather than functionally, genetically, causally. But we also find neurosis in persons who do not show this type of mentality; we cannot escape the conclusion that thinking of this kind is by no means a universal cause of neurotic difficulties, and suspect that even in specific cases it is probably not causal in any very basic sense.

---

ditioning in pure form, but one can meaningfully interpret Korzybski's "conditional" responses only if they are viewed as products of that type of learning here termed problem-solving. The shift in assumptions required by Korzybski's reinterpretation of Pavlovian conditioning will become clearer as the distinction between these two types of learning is elaborated in later sections.

Korzybski's concern about the misleading effects of prescientific language —such, for example, as speaking of the sun "rising" and "setting" when we know perfectly well that it doesn't do either—may be regarded even more lightly. I do not think my colleague, Professor I. A. Richards, will mind my quoting a recent apposite remark of his on this score to the effect that these ambiguities "never cause anyone any trouble. They are taken in a kind of Pickwickian sense, not seriously at all." * Certainly in my own clinical experience I have yet to find anyone who appeared to be seriously or even mildly neurotic because of confusions of this kind, although, to be sure, a neurotic person may *worry* about such things, along with almost anything and everything else.

A still different approach to the basic neurotic paradox which stems from Pavlovian thinking is suggested in a recent work by Hull (16). In his earlier writings, this author took a systematic position similar in most essential respects to that of the Russian investigator. But in the work cited, he shifted his conception of the reinforcement process from that posited by Pavlov to one much more nearly like that long advocated by Thorndike. For Pavlov, as we have seen, the essential conditions for learning, or reinforcement of new stimulus-response sequences, are provided when a stimulus which already has the power to evoke a given reaction is preceded by or combined with a stimulus which has formerly been neutral or ineffective in this respect. Thorndike, by contrast, has held that new "connections" are formed or old ones strengthened when, in the course of the random or variable behavior which an organism shows in a problem situation, the problem is resolved and the organism experiences relief, satisfaction, reward. The resulting learning consists then of a strengthening of the "connection" between problem or drive, and the

* Cf. (37).

response which solved this problem and so reduced the drive.

Taking this Thorndikian conception of reinforcement, which is particularly designed to explain problem-solving or so-called trial-and-error learning,* Hull has sought to extend it so as to account also for associative learning. Since drives are reduced and problems solved not in a vacuum but in concrete situations involving many other stimuli, Hull has proposed the hypothesis that the reinforcing effect provided by drive reduction will strengthen the connection not only between the drive and the particular response bringing about this fortunate state of affairs, but also between accompanying stimuli and this response. And, as Hull points out, one would expect this incidental form of learning to occur quite as readily with respect to irrelevant elements in the situation as to the relevant ones; that is:

Since organisms have no inner monitor or entelechy to tell them in advance which stimulus elements or aggregates are associated with the critical causal factor or factors of reactions situations [i.e., factors which determine whether a given response will or will not produce the desired result], the *law of reinforcement, other things equal, will mediate the connections of the non-critical stimulus elements to the reaction quite as readily as those of the critical ones* (16, p. 258).

As a result of the largely random flux of events in the world to which organisms must react, it inevitably comes about that they will often be stimulated by extensive groups of conditioned stimulus elements, *none* of which is causally related to the critical factor or factors in the reinforcement situation. In such cases, if the stimuli evoke the reaction it will not be followed by reinforcement. This, of course, is wasteful of energy and therefore unadaptive. The necessarily unadaptive nature of the appreciable portion of the habits set up by

* My colleague Richards has suggested to me that we might better call it "trial-and-triumph"!

virtue of the law of reinforcement naturally raises the question of how organisms are able to survive under such conditions. The answer is found in the behavioral principle known as *experimental extinction* (p. 259).

Following these remarks Hull proceeds to elaborate a theory from which it is an easy inference that "neurosis" is simply a loose way of referring to the fact that a human being or lower animal has a number of response tendencies which do not show an appropriate degree of discrimination. Simple-minded as such a thesis may sound, it is no more so than (a) the Freudian notion, previously discussed, that a neurotic is a person who fails to see the essential difference between conditions which existed in his childhood and those prevailing today (especially the castration complex) or (b) Korzybski's contention that a neurotic is a person who behaves "unconditionally," fails to distinguish between situations which *are* alike and those which *appear* to be.

Reduced to its lowest common denominator, we have here a conception of neurosis which appears perhaps more commonly than any other in the speculations of writers with very different backgrounds and preconceptions. What such a conception says, in effect, is that neurosis comes about as a result of overgeneralization, over-learning, which cause the affected individual to exhibit habits and attitudes which are no longer appropriate or are still appropriate in some circumstances, but not in others. In this way one can seemingly account for all the "parataxia of behavior" (Sullivan (40)) and all the "disproportionality of affect" which are so characteristic of persons whose behavior is said to be "neurotic," or, in more extreme cases, "crazy."

Certainly the learning requirements which are set for the human young are very great, and the zeal and determination manifested in this connection by the adult members of society are impressive.

What could seem sounder, simple as it is, than to suppose that a neurotic is simply a person in whom this socialization, or educative process has over-shot its mark. As a friend of the author once remarked, it looks as if the neurotic is a person in whom the culture has "taken all too well." Certainly the neurotic is a person manifesting striking inhibitions and incapacities; and there are still other observations which seem to justify the verdict that the basic difficulty of such a person is that his super-ego, or censor, is "too severe."

This perception of the situation, as we have seen, still leaves unanswered the fundamental problem as to why some individuals become neurotic; i.e., fail in their discriminative functions, whereas others do not. Freud considered but discarded the possibility that the difference lay in the severity with which children are actually dealt by their parents. Pavlov threw most of the burden of proof back upon biological heredity. Korzybski has posited as a purported explanation something which might be referred to as "social heredity," namely, that element of our culture which he terms "Aristotelian logic." Few of us will rest easy with either of these latter interpretations.

Nor do the results commonly obtained through would-be psychotherapy look as if we had thus isolated the active and specific virus of neurosis. Schisms and schools flourish with respect to therapeutic theory,* and the general public turns eagerly but vainly to those who are supposed to be experts in such matters for a meaningful philosophy of life and a guiding principle in practical affairs.

Does it seem too bold to suppose that the time has come for us to examine and,

if necessary, discard some of our most entrenched beliefs and interests? In the following sections, I shall indicate a mode of thought and action which may hold some promise of extricating us from our present plight.

An Experimentally Produced "Vicious Circle"

Laboratory findings provide very little support for the view that neurosis consists simply of over-learning of habits and attitudes which were acquired in circumstances wherein they were more or less appropriate but which now persist under altered circumstances in which they are no longer appropriate. Experimental studies (16, 29, 41) have shown over and over that habits which formerly produced desirable outcomes, but no longer do so, undergo the process of extinction.† There is equally impressive evidence for believing that attitudes, and emotions also, tend to disappear if the signal which arouses them is no longer really significant; that is, it is no longer followed by the event or situation with which they have previously been associated (16, 20, 34). In other words, it makes no difference whether we are working with the form of learning commonly known as problem-solving (habits) or with that form known as condi-

---

* In another connection the author has recently circularized thirty members of the American Orthopsychiatric Association concerning their perception of contemporary theory concerning psychotherapy. The most common evaluation was "chaotic."

† Allport (2) has suggested that habits and attitudes may sometimes continue to function even though the original circumstances which brought them into existence have long since ceased to exist. To this hypothetical phenomenon he has given the term "functional autonomy." However, in the light of ensuing criticism, Allport has been obliged to concede that in cases of apparent autonomy it is probable that although the original source of reinforcement no longer exists, the habit or emotion in question continues to be reinforced in some new or subsidiary manner (3). As Mowrer and Ullman (32) have pointed out, the concept of functional autonomy as originally formulated by Allport is not much different in principle from Freud's repetition compulsion.

tioning (attitudes, emotions): if the conditions of reinforcement—reward in the one case, and in the other, contiguous occurrence of the signal and the significate—no longer hold, there will be a disintegration, sometimes slow but ultimately certain, of the learned connection.

The assumption that a reinforced occurrence of a habit or attitude increases its likelihood of recurrence and that unreinforced occurrence decreases its likelihood of recurrence has recently been brought into question by a series of experiments initiated by Humphreys (17, 18, 19). This investigator found that learning, which has been established by means of alternately reinforced and unreinforced "trials," is more resistant to extinction than is learning that has been established under conditions of unfailing reinforcement. However, satisfactory explanations of this phenomenon are now available (16, 30), and it is to be noted that the procedure involving alternate reinforcement and non-reinforcement does not give rise to habits and attitudes which do not extinguish, but merely to habits and attitudes which are somewhat *slower* to extinguish.*

Employing the same general methods as those used by Pavlov to produce and

---

*In a personal communication, Dr. L. C. Wynne recently informed me of experimental results which indicate that if laboratory rats are sometimes punished and sometimes not for performing a "forbidden" act, the inhibition produced in this manner is more enduring than that established by consistent punishment. Superficially this finding may look like the Humphreys effect "in reverse," but actually it is a straightforward application thereof. Since the fear produced by intermittent punishment is more resistant to extinction than a fear produced by continuous reinforcement, the inhibitory effects in the one case will be expected to be more enduring than those observed in the other. Within the limits of Dr. Wynne's experiment, the inhibitions produced by discontinuous reinforcement did not, in fact, appreciably lessen under conditions of non-reinforcement. However, it can be confidently predicted that they, too, would ultimately disappear if the

study "experimental neuroses," a number of later investigators have likewise been able to produce in animal subjects disturbances of behavior and attitude of relatively permanent character. But the most plausible interpretation of these results is not that they represent either overlearning which fails to extinguish, or organic brain damage; instead they seem to involve *a rupture of the basic relationship between the subject and the experimenter.* The researches of Liddell and others (14, 16, 22) indicate that it is only by first gentling and "petting" an animal that one can later produce a "neurosis." And the latter condition apparently involves an impairment of the subject-experimenter relationship, produced by the way the experimenter subsequently treats the subject. If nothing is done to reestablish such a damaged relationship, it will hardly be surprising if the "neurosis" persists.

It is also worth noting that the criteria of "neurosis" used by animal investigators have not always been altogether satisfactory. Sometimes it has appeared that the capacity for self-mystification on the part of the experimenter was the principal desideratum. If as a result of a particular laboratory procedure animals behave in a manner which to the experimenter is unaccountable or "crazy" this behavior has often been dubbed "neurosis." We should, of course, insist upon a definition of neurosis that is a function of the subject's experience and personality, not of those of the experimenter.

The fact that much of the research which has thus been done with animals fails to throw any new light on the basic neurotic paradox does not mean that it is impossible to produce in such subjects behavior which is genuinely paradoxical. Here I want to speak of two such instances of behavior, which seem to take

---

extinction procedure were carried far enough. It therefore seems again unlikely that the Humphreys effect will provide a solution to the neurotic paradox.

us at least a little nearer to an understanding of the fundamental nature of neurosis.

Some years ago Dr. Judson S. Brown told me of a remarkable incidental observation he had once made. Later, on two separate occasions, students of mine reconstructed Dr. Brown's experimental conditions and reported the same observation. I am therefore highly confident of its reliability. The observation is this:

Let us imagine that a rat is put at the left-hand end of an alley about four feet long, with high sides and ends. The rat is allowed to explore for ten seconds, then an electric charge is put on the entire length of the grill constituting the floor of the alley. The rat is thrown into rather violent trial-and-error activity, in the course of which it discovers an opening at the extreme right-hand end of the alley, leading into a small compartment where there is no shock. There the animal is left for two or three minutes, and is then returned to the left-hand end. Again, after a period of ten seconds, shock is applied to the grill and the rat is driven, now much more quickly, into the safety compartment. On the third trial, the rat is likely to be sufficiently frightened to run immediately to the opposite end of the alley and into the safety compartment before the shock is applied. On subsequent trials the rat will gradually slow up in this behavior until, failing to get into the safety compartment within the period of grace, it again gets the shock and is thereby driven into the compartment. After a few "reminders" of this kind, the rat is likely to become highly reliable in its behavior, that is, it will continue for a great many trials, upon being put into the apparatus, to run directly to the safety compartment and in this fashion avoid receiving any electric shock. Although the number of runs which an animal will thus make between shocks tends to get greater and greater, yet there is an enduring tend-

ency to "reality test" which serves the function of keeping the animal informed as to whether the shock is "still there" thus enabling it to avoid making an endless series of responses which are not necessary.

By a very simple procedure, all this can be dramatically altered. After a rat has been well trained to avoid shock by running to the safety compartment within the ten-second period of grace, let us arrange the apparatus so that the right half of the grill is *permanently* charged. This will mean that in order for the rat to get from the left-hand end of the alleyway to the safety compartment, it must always cross a section of grill which is charged. On first thought, one might suppose that the shock thus received by the rat in the process of running from the left-hand end to the safety compartment would act as a punishment and would soon inhibit the running response. But nothing of the kind occurs. Instead, upon being introduced into the alleyway, the rat will run *even more promptly* to the safety compartment. And more remarkable still, this behavior goes on and on for hundreds of trials, although shock is never again administered in the part of the apparatus where the rat is introduced!

Here, surely, is crazy behavior. An observer viewing such a performance for the first time and without knowledge of the background of the experiment might well be moved to diagnose the rat's behavior as "masochistic." Now that the shock has been permanently withdrawn from the left-hand end of the grill, all the rat would have to do to avoid both the shock and the effort involved in running would be to sit still in that part of the apparatus where it is introduced. But instead the rat "prefers" to keep running across the charged grill, thus "punishing" itself hundreds and hundreds of times. In fact, the indications are that if the experimenter but had the patience to continue observing such a stereotyped, monotonously regular performance, this behavior would go on indefinitely.

Let us now ask how, if at all, this rather striking performance is related to the basic neurotic paradox. The behavior involved meets the requirement of being self-defeating and yet self-perpetuating. And it has the additional advantage—which carries us beyond anything which Freud proposed in this connection—of qualifying as a vicious circle, as Kunkel and Horney have used that expression. Horney describes this phenomenon as follows:

The formation of a vicious circle is typical not only in the context in which it has been discussed here; generally speaking it is one of the most important processes in neuroses. Any protective device may have, in addition to its reassuring quality, the quality of creating new anxiety. A person may take to drinking in order to allay his anxiety, and then get the fear that drinking, too, will harm him. Or he may masturbate in order to release his anxiety, and then become afraid that masturbation will make him ill. Or he may undergo some treatment for his anxiety, and soon grow apprehensive lest the treatment harm him. The formation of vicious circles is the main reason why severe neuroses are bound to become worse, even though there is no change in external conditions. Uncovering the vicious circles, with all their implications, is one of the important tasks of psychoanalysis. The neurotic himself cannot grasp them. He notices their results only in the form of a feeling that he is trapped in a hopeless situation. This feeling of being trapped is his response to entanglements which he cannot break through.* Any way that seems to lead out drags him again into new dangers (15).

Let us repeat the key sentence in the foregoing quotation: "Any protective device may have, in addition to its reassuring quality, the quality of creating new anxiety." Certain aspects of this mechanism are well illustrated in the experiment just described. The rat becomes

* Cf. (33), "An experimental analogue of fear from a sense of helplessness."

afraid of the experimental situation as soon as put into it; this fear drives it to the safety compartment where it is relatively fear-free; the running is thus powerfully reinforced as a form of problem-solving behavior; but in performing this act the animal also gets shocked; shock serves to reinforce the fear of the apparatus; and when the animal is again put into the apparatus, its fear prompts it to repeat the same cycle.

Implicit in this analysis and in much of what has been said previously is the assumption that there are two basic learning processes: problem-solving and conditioning. It is by the first of these that overt actions or habits are acquired; these serve to reduce drives, solve problems, provide pleasure. And it is by the second of these basic learning processes, that the emotions or secondary drives—as opposed to the primary drives which are biologically "given"—are themselves acquired. In the experiment under discussion, fear of the apparatus is reinforced every time the rat gets shocked therein; and the habit of running in response to this fear is reinforced by the fact that the running, though resulting in a momentary exposure to the shock, leads to a relatively enduring reduction in the secondary drive of fear. Only by positing these two basic, but basically different, learning processes does it seem possible to make a clear-cut analysis of a vicious circle of the kind just described and to resolve a number of other important dilemmas which have been discussed in detail elsewhere (24).

Some disturbing problems still remain. Horney speaks of a vicious circle as involving behavior which (a) serves more or less directly to reduce anxiety, but which (b) has the indirect or delayed effect of increasing it. In the paradigm just described we have spoken not in terms of anxiety, but in terms of fear. Although in the passage quoted Horney seems to be equating anxiety and fear, she indicates elsewhere (15, Chapter 3) that she agrees with Freud and most other clinicians that there is an important difference. However, in the experimental paradigm of a vicious circle we probably have no justification for speaking of anxiety, only of fear; and since there is general agreement that it is anxiety, not ordinary objective fear which is "the fundamental phenomenon and the central problem of neurosis" (12, p. 111), serious doubt is raised as to whether our paradigm is very illuminating so far as the neurotic paradox is concerned.

Moreover, assuming that such an experiment does provide a valid paradigm of neurosis, it would imply a conception of psychotherapy which experience shows is much too simple. In order to "cure" a rat of unnecessarily running away from a part of the apparatus which is no longer dangerous, all that is necessary is to block the entrance to the safety compartment, thus forcing the animal to retreat from the charged half of the grill back upon the uncharged half. Finding that this half of the grill is now permanently free of shock, the rat is perfectly willing to stop the unnecessary flight from it. If neurosis in human beings were due to a fundamentally similar mechanism, instruction in the changed realities of the situation or, in more extreme cases, spontaneous or forced "reality testing" might be expected to produce equally dramatic results. Clinical experience does not confirm such an inference.

Time and Integration Failure

Implicit in the passage previously quoted from Horney is another possible explanation of vicious circles. She speaks first of an activity which provides a means of reducing anxiety "and then" of increasing the individual's insecurity. In other words, she tacitly introduces the *time factor* as a variable in the vicious circle. In an experiment previously reported (32), this factor has been explicitly investigated and found to be a very potent one indeed.

Common sense teaches us and laboratory studies have confirmed that both rewards and punishments are more effective if they follow an action immediately than if they occur more remotely in time. This fact—subsumed under what is more technically referred to as the gradient of reinforcement for problem-solving and the gradient of reinforcement for conditioning—provides the basis for a paradox which, if not precisely the same as the neurotic paradox, carries us at least a step nearer its understanding. Actions which have exclusively rewarding consequences tend to be "stamped in," and actions which have exclusively punishing consequences naturally tend to get "stamped out." But more common are actions whose consequences are mixed, some rewarding and some punishing. If these consequences are equally distant in time from the action producing them, that action will be inhibited or reinforced roughly in proportion to the degree to which these consequences are predominantly punishing or rewarding. The net result is in no way paradoxical. But the instant that multiple consequences of an act become unevenly distributed in time, the possibility is opened for paradoxical outcomes.

In the experiment cited, hungry rats were taught to come to a little trough for a pellet of food whenever a buzzer was sounded. After all the subjects had stably acquired this behavior, an arbitrary "rule" was made by the experimenters to the effect that it was not "nice" or "proper" for a rat to take the pellet of food immediately upon its presentation. The "correct" behavior was to wait three seconds after the food had appeared and *then* take it. Since a full minute was allowed between successive trials, the rats did not have to take the pellet *precisely* at the end of the three-second delay; anytime after this lapse of time was all right. The point was that

PSYCHOPATHOLOGY

they were not to take the food *within* the tabu period. This rule was enforced by punishment in the form of electric shock.

All "offenders" received a shock of the same intensity and duration (two seconds), but the subjects were divided into different groups with respect to *how soon* the punishment was administered. In one group of subjects the punishment came immediately after the tabu period. Most of the rats in this group quickly learned to behave integratively; i.e., they learned to wait at least three seconds before taking the pellet of food, thus avoiding the shock and having the satisfaction of eating. But the groups in which the shock was delayed (3, 6, and 12 seconds, respectively) gave different results. The animals in these groups were inclined to behave non-integratively in one of two ways: they were inclined either to persist in taking the pellet of food within the forbidden period and thus get regularly shocked somewhat later, or to give up altogether the attempt to eat in the experimental situation. The first of these patterns involved getting the food but also getting the shock, and the second involved getting no shock but likewise getting no food.

In our original report of this experiment we labeled the rats which were more or less completely inhibited with respect to eating as "neurotic"; the animals that persisted in eating within the tabu period and being persistently shocked we labeled "delinquent" or "criminal." But this was probably because our conception of neurosis was then still largely dominated by Freud's view that a neurotic is an individual with an overly severe super-ego, one in whom attempts at control and restraint have been "all too effective," an individual in whom the problem is, in short, one of *over-learning*.

Presumably the rats that resolved the conflict between eating and getting shocked by not eating were not very

pleased about the situation, just as human beings are not pleased by the renunciations and disappointments they must endure. Freud's emphasis upon the thwarting of impulse and desire in the etiology of neurosis * now seems to have been a seriously misplaced one. As I have said elsewhere (27), I believe the indications are that human beings fall victims of neurosis, not because of what they would do but cannot, but because of what they have done and would that they had not. If this thesis, to which we shall return shortly, is valid, we should expect to find a more nearly valid paradigm of neurosis in those rats which persisted in taking food during the tabu period despite the continuing punishment.

It was not inappropriate that we should previously have referred to these animals as delinquent or criminal. Whatever else the criminal is or is not, he is surely a person who is not so much deterred as is the ordinary person by certain objective punishments or the prospect thereof. In the past we have had a tendency to contrast the criminal and the neurotic by saying that the criminal is under-socialized, under-trained, whereas the neurotic is supposedly over-socialized, over-trained. But for reasons which

* ". . . I will now add another piece of information which throws further light upon the significance of the symptoms. A comparative examination of the situations out of which the disease arose yields the following result, which may be reduced to the formula—namely, that these persons have fallen ill from *privation (frustration)* which they suffer when reality withholds from them gratification of their sexual wishes. . . . The symptoms can serve the purpose both of sexual gratification and of its opposite, namely, anxiety reduction. They are in fact, as we shall see, the effects of *compromises* between two opposed tendencies, acting on one another; they represent both that which is repressed, and also that which has effected the repression and has co-operated in bringing them about. . . . The symptom is then a double one and consists of two successive actions which cancel each other" (11, pp. 264–265).

I have advanced in another connection (25), I believe that the neurotic character lies much closer to the criminal character than we have commonly thought. The differential here would seem to consist mainly in the extent to which the function we call *conscience* has been developed in the two cases. Both the criminal and the neurotic have a tendency to behave immaturely, irresponsibly, antisocially. But unlike the pure criminal, the neurotic has a conscience which is strong enough to "bother" him. Like the normal person, the neurotic has a conscience, often a very powerful one; but the normal person "does business" with his conscience, whereas the neurotic distrusts, spurns, and represses conscience. However, this conscious repudiation of conscience does not mean that its forces are nullified. Instead they are merely muted, so that their signals to the ego become distorted and delayed. Instead of being experienced promptly and explicitly as conscience guilt, they appear in the form of depression, anxiety, and self-derogation. Since these states are thus dissociated from the circumstances and events that occasion them, they appear to be alien to the personality, unrealistic, irrational, abnormal, and it becomes exceedingly difficult if not impossible for the ego to make realistic, adequate adjustments to them.

Returning now for a moment to the experiment just described, let us ask if any of our subjects were truly neurotic. The answer is, probably not. The rats which persisted in taking food despite the delayed though inevitable punishment were presumably not as comfortable in the experimental situation as they would have been if they had worked out an integrative solution to this conflict. But we can hardly say they were neurotic. We must keep in mind that these rats had not been taught from earliest childhood to believe that this was a conflict which any proper, self-respecting rat would resolve integratively. They did

not, in other words, live in a society with a culture which demanded this kind of achievement. And they did not, therefore, have a conscience which condemned them for their failure. They suffered only from the objective discomfort and fear of the shock. To this was not added the forces of self-condemnation, and without this subjective increment to the objective realities we cannot appropriately speak of neurosis.*

However, by thus pursuing the logic of this and other animal studies, I believe we are led to a clearer perception of the nature of neurosis as we know it at the human level. We are brought to realize that Freud and many others have, indeed, erred precisely in the sense of trying to account for human neurosis in terms of what we may call, in the words of Allport (4), an "animal model," and that it is only by going beyond this predominantly biological type of preoccupation and facing man in terms of his spectacular uniqueness that we come to intimate grips with the essence of neurosis.

Negativism, Neurosis, and Resistance

In this paper we have followed a long and in certain respects disappointing historical course. We have traced the successive formulations of one of the most brilliant and original minds of modern times and found, in the end, no satisfactory resolution of the basic problem of neurosis. Then we turned to numerous other investigators who have approached the problem both from related and from radically different angles, but still there is no clear-cut answer. At this point we again might well exclaim with Freud, "After decades of scientific effort this

* At another time I shall further elaborate upon the implications of these remarks. They provide, I believe, an answer to the question as to why neurotics are said to be "unstable" and why the emotions of the neurotic are commonly characterized as "disproportionate" (26).

problem rises up before us, as untouched as at the beginning." But our labors have not been wholly unrewarding. They give us a perspective which earlier investigators lacked. They enable us to see more clearly the outline of the maze in which these gifted and intrepid explorers have struggled; they enable us to see what now appears to have been a fateful error, an early mistake in choice of paths which led to the discovery of much new territory but which has not led to the desired goal—a precise understanding of and a specific therapy for the psychoneuroses.

From Section I of this paper it will be recalled that one of Freud's first and most basic discoveries was that the neurotic is a person who has at some prior stage in his life cycle resolved a powerful psychic conflict by means of repression. Freud also saw with singular clarity that the forces behind the resistance which meets our therapeutic efforts are the same that have produced and subsequently maintain the original repression. And he saw that the struggle that ensues between therapist and patient is but an externalization of the inner struggle which is the heart of neurosis.

But to the end of his long career, Freud carried with him one highly doubtful assumption which thwarted his theoretical endeavors and blighted the therapeutic accomplishments of the school which he founded. For Freud the neurotic conflict originates in the fact that the great power and disciplinary efforts of parents are pitted against the biologically given drives of the small child. This may be said to have been his major premise, and one which we must reiterate and fully accept. But his minor premise, if we may continue this analogy from formal logic, was that because the child is so completely and protractedly dependent upon his parents, the latter's demands are relatively quickly and powerfully introjected. Freud believed that once this had happened there ensued a pitched battle between the super-ego and ego

on the one hand, and the id on the other. This battle he called the oedipus complex. He believed it was characteristically resolved by repressions—repressions which bring infantile sexuality and aggression under control during the so-called latency period but which, in the normal instance, are largely abrogated in adolescence. But, said Freud, if these repressions are initially too strong or overdone, they are not sufficiently undone in adolescence and may persist on into adult life, with the pathological consequences which we refer to collectively as neurosis.

What could be clearer, then, as the duty of the therapist than to set about undoing, belatedly, these too-strong repressions, weakening the severity of an over-severe super-ego, counteracting disciplinary efforts of parents which have "taken" only too well? The disturbing fact remains that this conception of neurosis and the therapeutic task has not led to very happy practical outcomes. It has not pointed the way to a more hygienic program for the early training of children, and it has not provided for human beings generally a more competent and satisfying life philosophy. The question which therefore presses in upon us is: What is it that is so tragically wrong with the system of thought which, on the whole, is so obviously right?

From our vantage point today we may see clearly what our predecessors discerned dimly or not at all. Standing on the shoulders of giants of the past, to borrow a phrase from Robert Burton, we may succeed where they failed. For Freud and innumerable followers neurosis was the consequence of repression which the ego and super-ego have turned against the forces of the id, but it is today increasingly evident that neurosis is rather the product of id and ego functioning in league *against the super-ego*. As Freud himself fully recognized, the human infant is in the beginning "all id," and as the ego evolves it is predominantly a pleasure-ego or id-ego. It is during the period of intensive socialization, between the years of two and six in European and American societies, that serious conflict first arises. However, it is at first mainly an external conflict, the conflict between the child and his would-be socializers. Characteristically, or at least recurrently, refractory, disobedient, and uncooperative, the child is commonly said to be in the *negativistic* stage. In the fortunate instance, as conscience is forged from an admixture of love and fear of parents, this early rebellion is replaced by a more or less harmonious synthesis of id, ego, and super-ego. But in the less fortunate case, conscience is formed but not accepted, and the unresolved struggle between the child and his socializers lives on as deep conflict between the id-ego of infancy and the now internalized but *unassimilated* psychic representative of parents and community; namely, the super-ego.

Sometimes small children may be observed stopping their ears with their fingers when their parents criticize or admonish them. The older child or adolescent cannot shut out the voice of his conscience by so simple an expedient, but by means of repression a similar result may be produced. The internalized criticisms and admonitions of parents and community are now muffled and no longer heard clearly and explicitly, but they are still capable of breaking through into consciousness as depression, anxiety, and inferiority-feeling. Symptoms are then formed as means of dealing with these distressing affects, and the afflicted individual is a full-fledged neurotic. Sooner or later, as one anxiety-reducing strategy after another is tried and found to be only partially effective, the individual may come to therapy, with the two great energy systems of his personality in a seemingly hopeless stalemate.*

* Since the above was written, a friend has given me the following quotation: "Let us note that in every one of us there are two guiding and ruling principles which lead us whither

At this point two options are open to the therapist, though in the past it has seemed to many that there was only one. The whole force of the Freudian tradition has disposed the therapist to assume that the patient's super-ego was too severe; if this were indeed the case, the therapist had no choice but to join forces with the (presumably repressed) id and thus attempt to woo the ego away from its allegiance to and domination by the tyrannical super-ego, to a more friendly accepting relationship with the id. As Alexander and French (1) recently observed, this strategy often results not in curing the patient, but in producing "a deep narcissistic regression" in which he luxuriates during the course of treatment, but from which he emerges with no fundamental change in his basic personality structure. The probable explanation of this untoward outcome is to be found in the mistaken belief that neurosis rests upon a conflict in which the ego and super-ego are aligned against the id. If we assume that this conflict is one in which the ego is far more powerfully allied with the id than with the super-ego, we see at once why orthodox Freudian treatment serves in many cases only to propitiate and prolong a neurosis rather than cure it.

If we proceed on the assumption that the neurotic's basic conflict is between an id-dominated ego and an unassimilated or repressed super-ego, we are fully prepared, both conceptually and practically, for the externalization of this conflict which occurs in therapy. Freud called this remarkable phenomenon "transference," and it is most aptly conceived as an action whereby the patient now "extrojects" his super-ego and invests the

they will; one is the natural desire of pleasure, the other is an acquired opinion which is in search of the best; and these two are sometimes in harmony and then again at war, and sometimes the one, sometimes the other conquers" (Plato, *Phaedrus,* p. 238). To this we need only add, "and sometimes they remain indefinitely deadlocked."

therapist with the mantle of parental authority and social sanctions. The ensuing resistance is thus nothing but the unresolved negativism of early childhood which has gone underground for a more or less extended period but is now once again brought out into the open.* So long as this conflict was internalized, there was little opportunity for it to be resolved, since the individual thus protects himself from the behests of conscience and from the continued learning that is involved in growing up. It is precisely the fortunate fact that neurotics tend in the therapeutic situation to resume the unresolved fight with their parents and with society that offers the greatest therapeutic opportunities. Freud correctly regarded "transference" as having highly important therapeutic potentialities. It now appears that greatest therapeutic progress is made not by assuming that parents produced too much learning in the childhood of the neurotic adult, but by making the opposite assumption—that the parents produced too

* The terms "symptom" and "defense" are commonly used as if referring to essentially the same phenomena. It may be an aid to greater explicitness and more exact conceptualization if the term "symptom" is used to refer to habits which an individual develops as means of dealing with the anxiety which results from inner neurotic conflict, and if "defense" is used to refer to habits which an individual uses as means of fending off the demands for change which the therapist (like the parent of an earlier era) makes of the patient. Defenses, thus defined, tend to be similar to—in some instances identical with—the tactics learned in childhood as means of resisting parental and other socializing pressures. We also see why it is that symptoms tend to disappear in therapy, long before the neurotic structure of the patient's personality is fundamentally modified. As the internal neurotic conflict is transformed back into a social conflict, symptoms are converted into defenses and the patient takes one of two courses: he either concludes that he doesn't need treatment—since his symptoms have disappeared—and breaks off the therapy, often in a "huff" with the therapist; or the patient enters into a relational struggle from which, if correctly handled, he will emerge a more mature and better integrated individual.

little learning. Therapy may then be conceived as an attempt not to reverse the earlier influences of parents, but to take up and resume the unfinished business of the parent-child relationship; namely, that of making the human animal into a normal, mature, morally and socially accountable human being. Neurosis is thus seen as a kind of ignorance rather than illness, and therapy becomes, explicitly and integrally, a part of the total educative enterprise, not an antidote for what is presumed to be too much education.

Learning theory again comes to our aid at this juncture and enables us to picture normal and neurotic development with special lucidity. Repeatedly in this paper there has been reference to the two basic learning processes—problem-solving and conditioning. I have elsewhere (24) pointed out a number of other dichotomies which more or less precisely parallel this two-fold division. We know that problem-solving behavior is mediated by the central nervous system and the skeletal musculature, and the conditioned reactions are mediated by the autonomic nervous system and by smooth muscle and visceral tissue. We know that the former is appropriately referred to as response-substitution (or trial-and-error learning), the latter as stimulus-substitution (or associative shifting), that the one is under direct voluntary control and that the other is not.

What is of special relevance here is that it is through our problem-solving behavior that we exert our *effects* upon the world about us, and it is through conditioning that the world *affects* us. The normal person is in more or less continuous interaction with his environment, modifying it, being *effective,* but being in turn modified by it, *affected.* "Give and take" is the maxim of the mature, well integrated, undefensive individual. In Figure 1, at the right, I have attempted to indicate diagrammatically the relationship of such an individual to his environment and something of his internal structure. The arrow extending from the individual across to the world represents his problem-solving behavior, his impact upon the world; and the arrow extending from the world back to the individual represents the conditioning process, the impact of the world upon the individual.

Examining the normal individual more closely, we find a differentiated

son is said to have "good character" and is characterized by *self-control,* which is to say that controlling agencies in the environment have been internalized, incorporated, and accepted as a part of the total self. Such a person has, in short, strongly *identified himself* with his society.

But such admirable and ideal personalities are not born, nor do they develop automatically. They are the hard-

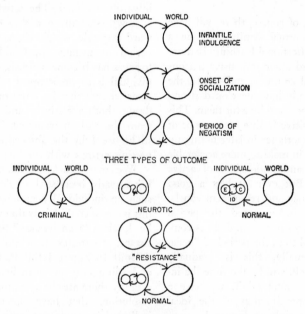

Diagrammatic representation OF THE VICISSITUDES OF HUMAN SOCIALIZATION.

area of the id labeled "E" for ego and another area labeled "C" for conscience or super-ego, which is the introjected form of the world, particularly the social world. Because of the harmonious relationship which the individual-as-a-whole has with his environment, the ego is on correspondingly good terms with the conscience. As common sense fully recognizes, such an individual's outward behavior is heavily influenced not only by prescriptions that are currently enforced by the external world, but also by the dictates of conscience. Such a per-

won products of successful socialization. Using the same mode of graphic representation, we may depict the situation genetically, beginning with the diagram at the top of Figure 1. During the period of "infantile omnipotence," to borrow Freud's apt phrase, the individual is indulged, waited on, "babied." His needs and wishes are gratified as fully as possible, and no demands are made of him other than that he be comfortable and thrive physiologically. But eventually a time must come—early in some societies, later in others—when this indulgence and irresponsibility must end. We begin to say "You are no longer a baby. You are a big boy (or girl) now," and we begin to enforce demands for the renunciation of infantile pleasures and for obedience and responsibility. This is the onset of socialization, and it marks the first serious attempt that is deliberately made to condition the child; i.e., to create in him social attitudes and emotions which we hope will lay the basis for good character.

Previously, of course, there will have been in the normal family situation a good deal of affectional learning. Because the mother and other responsive persons have mediated comforts and reliefs, the baby will already have developed strong dependence upon and love for them. This cushion of positive feeling seems to be of the utmost importance in later taking up the shock and in making more acceptable the demands and impositions of active socialization. But even at best a good deal of resistance and resentment can be expected. As already noted, the period between the ages of two and six is commonly referred to as the period of "negativism." Normally, this is gradually worked through, and by the time the individual is a young adult, we have a reasonable approximation of the ideal pictured at the right in Figure 1.

Unhappily the end results are not always of this type. Sometimes the opposition to authority and social sanctions which is aroused in the early attempts at socialization is continued, relatively unmodified, on into later life. When this occurs we encounter a criminal, an individual whose inner personality structure remains relatively little differentiated, whose ego is almost indistinguishable from the id and whose total energies are directed toward attacking, exploiting, and resisting the social order in which he finds himself. This conceptualization is admittedly greatly oversimplified and does not at all do justice to the complexities of criminal psychology, but it serves

to indicate the position in our schematization of the criminal personality-type and the extreme in socialization failure.

Between the criminal on the left, and the normal individual on the right, lies an intermediate type of personality, the neurotic.* Such an individual, as previously noted, has internalized many of the demands and obligations imposed by his socializers, but these demands—collectively known as conscience—are not inwardly accepted. The internal picture is now essentially a replica of the outward struggle which characterized the period of negativism. Childish refractoriness has become neurosis, and the individual is so preoccupied with this internal drama that he more or less withdraws, both effectively and affectively, from the real environment (symbolized in Figure 1 by the absence of interconnecting arrows with the "world").

We may quickly recapitulate what has already been said in detail. When such an individual comes into therapy, this internal conflict is again externalized; he develops "transference," becomes "resistant," regresses to childhood negativism.† In Figure 1 this stage is shown as leading only to normality, but theoretically there are the same three possible resolutions that have previously been indicated in connection with the period of childhood negativism: normality, criminality, and more neurosis. Actually, it seems that much would-be therapy leads, in practice, to all three types of result. Our task, clearly, is to discover why

* For a detailed defense of this way of conceptualizing these three major personality patterns, see (25).
† As Freud long ago pointed out, one of the distinguishing differences between neurosis and psychosis is in the capacity for relationship, in the ability to develop transference. The work of Sullivan (39), Fromm-Reichmann (13), and others shows that this capacity is not altogether absent in the psychotic but that it can be activated but slowly. Whether this is merely a quantitative difference or one involving a distinctive type of dynamism is one of our great unsolved problems.

this should be the case and to increase the incidence of the ideal outcome.

I believe that in general too little and technically improper attention has been given to the defensive interpersonal strategies which emerge in psychotherapy. I had originally planned to report some recent research findings and some illustrative excerpts from electronically recorded therapeutic interviews. This material will have to be reserved for a later presentation, at which time a number of matters pertaining both to practice and theory will be discussed. Since we are here primarily concerned with what I have called the neurotic paradox, I shall now try to bring together what has already been said and to show its bearing upon this formal theoretical issue.

A Proposed Resolution of the Neurotic Paradox

As defined at the outset of this paper, the neurotic paradox lies in the fact that human behavior is sometimes indefinitely perpetuated despite the fact that it is seriously self-defeating. Freud's major attempt to resolve this paradox involves the assumption that in neurosis there are acts and feelings which have been appropriate at one stage of the individual's life history, but are no longer so. More specifically, Freud believed that it was the super-ego which, as a result of too zealous childhood training, retained its over-severity into adult life despite altered circumstances, and in this way produced the distressing, hampering effects seen in neurosis. But this approach to the problem goes counter to one of the best established principles in the psychology of learning, which is, that all learning tends to undergo extinction unless it is at least periodically reinforced.

Recognizing this difficulty in Freud's formulations, Horney and others have sought to rectify it by positing that the wasteful self-defeating habits and attitudes which constitute neurosis do indeed become periodically reinforced through the operation of so-called vicious circles. But here again neurosis is conceived as a *learning excess,* and it is assumed that if one can but stop the cyclic sequence of events which keeps this learning reinforced, neurosis will be self-correcting.

Against these and similar attempts to resolve the neurotic paradox, we have posited the view that neurosis is not a learning excess but a *learning deficit.* Because of resistances which the infantile ego sets up against the socializing forces and because of the opposition which it later exerts against the internalized agent of these forces, namely, the super-ego, the ego remains immature, asocial, id-dominated.

That such an ego continues to experience anxiety is in no way surprising since it is still at war with the super-ego, which is constantly being kept alive and vigorous by the very nature of the social realities which it represents. We do not ask why the criminal continues to be a fearful individual. There is the ever-present danger that he will be apprehended and punished for his rebellious, antisocial behavior. And much the same is true of the neurotic. It is not that he is suffering from unreal or "childish," fears. He, too, faces a real danger, the danger of having his immaturities and "delinquencies" discovered—the danger, as one patient expressed it, of being "unmasked"—and of having to resume the painful task of renouncing the pleasure principle of infancy and accepting the reality principle of adulthood.

The problem, then, is not to explain why the neurotic does not *unlearn;* it is rather to account for the fact that he does not *learn*. We have already touched upon some of the reasons why small children resist primary socialization and why in later life the ego of the neurotic continues to fight with the super-ego. And we have also seen the way in which this intrapsychic struggle again becomes externalized in therapy and to what extent the transference behavior is essentially defensive, defensive in the sense of trying to avert the learning involved in further "growing up."

Having thus established the thesis that the neurotic is an underdone human being, in some respects not unlike the criminal, rather than an overdone, superhuman sort of creature, we must now turn and make an important modification of an earlier statement. We have repeatedly characterized the neurotic as a victim of underlearning, immaturity, ignorance; but this underlearning is of a special kind and is vouchsafed by what is, in one respect, "overlearning." Preston (36) has remarked that mental health is a matter of attitudes, and it is with respect to *attitudinal learning* that the neurotic is most deficient. To say that an individual is neurotic is not to say that there is anything deficient about his problem-solving learning ability. Indeed, it is the very fact that he has been so skillful in parrying the early attempts of his elders and, later, of his conscience, to socialize him that has kept him neurotic. The essence of the difficulty is precisely that, through problem-solving learning, or the primitive pleasure principle, he has learned how to keep from learning in the sense of being conditioned; i.e., changed emotionally and attitudinally. To put this matter somewhat paradoxically but succinctly, the neurotic is an individual *who has learned how not to learn*.

In therapy it is therefore true that there is a kind of unlearning that must occur—unlearning of the "skills" and strategies by which conditioning, whether by society or by conscience, has been warded off. These strategies must be activated in the therapy, but they must then be shown to be ineffective and, indeed, unnecessary. The way is then opened for the more basic kind of emotional learning against which past problem-solving behavior has served as a protection. Religious leaders are fond of saying that a sinner can be saved only if he "opens his heart to God." Perhaps we can appropriately paraphrase this statement by saying that a neurotic can be cured only if he "opens his heart" to the great moral teachings and emotional values of his society. Then and only then does it seem possible for the erstwhile neurotic to become a whole man or woman, at peace with himself and his fellow men.

There is a strange and basic contradiction in Freud's theoretical thinking. In 1911 he showed a penetrating grasp of the reason why human development is always difficult and uncertain in outcome (10). He pointed out that the infant is at first completely under the sway of the primitive pleasure principle, whereas the normal, mature adult follows what he designated as the reality principle. The progress from the one to the other he saw as dependent upon the slow and painful development of the capacity to forego immediate satisfactions and to submit to labor and other ordeals as means of achieving greater long-term gains and averting future suffering. Freud correctly insisted that the reality principle does not involve a repudiation of the pleasure principle but rather a refinement and "safeguarding" of it. The difficulty lies precisely in the fact that in making the transition from the one to the other, the individual has to learn to move at least temporarily away from satisfaction and comfort toward discomfort and pain, as a means of ultimately finding the route back to more assured, stable, long-term satisfactions. Human development is fraught with the repeated necessity for making *detours* of all kinds, and it is the individual's resistance or willingness in these paradoxical developmental steps that draws the fateful line between the neurotic and the normal personality.

All this Freud saw clearly. But a strange bias prevented him from assigning to it the real significance it appears to have in a total theory of personality. His bias was that he regarded the super-ego as a more or less archaic relic of childhood, and the traditions, values, and morality of the race as equally outmoded carry-overs from earlier stages in the history of the race. For Freud, human culture as transmitted from generation to generation was not in the least concerned with insuring and promoting human happiness; its sole function and objective was to insure the survival of the group. As he says in *Civilization and Its Discontents,* society provides man with greater security than he can achieve in a solitary mode of existence, and because of this, man barters "some part of his chances for happiness" for this security (8, p. 92). He does this very reluctantly and with a sense of the "cultural privation" which "dominates the whole field of social relations between human beings" (p. 63). We rightly find fault, said Freud, "with our present state of civilization for so inadequately providing us with what we require to make us happy in life, and for the amount of suffering of a probably avoidable nature it lays us open to . . ." (p. 92).

Because the super-ego is but the "internalized voice of the community," it is not surprising, therefore, that Freud expressed a low opinion of it:

In our investigations and our therapy of the neuroses we cannot avoid finding fault with the super-ego of the individual on two counts: in commanding and prohibiting with such severity it troubles too little about the happiness of the ego, and it fails to take into account sufficiently the difficulties in the way of obeying it—the strength of instinctual cravings in the id and the hardships of external environment. Consequently in our therapy we often find ourselves obliged to do battle with the super-ego and work to moderate its demands. Exactly the same objections can be made against the ethical standards of the cultural super-ego (139).

These highly dubious and arbitrary asseverations have, perhaps more than anything else, prevented a fruition of Freud's otherwise often profound and insightful theorizing. They drove him to a conception of normal personality as fantastic as it is pessimistic, according to which the ego stands alone, beleaguered on all sides by the contradictory, hazardous, and often unrealistic demands of the world, the id, and the super-ego. The goal of psychotherapy, stated most abstractly, was therefore to strengthen the ego in order that it might better endure and perhaps in some measure coordinate the devisive forces to which it is constantly exposed.

Clinical experience and other sources of evidence justify us in taking a radically different point of view. A less partisan examination of the facts suggests that human culture, far from being indifferent to human suffering and unhappiness, is eminently concerned with them, and that traditions and social values represent some of our soundest guides to psychological and social reality. In other words, it is increasingly evident that individual development from the primitive pleasure principle toward the reality principle, as Freud early conceived them, importantly involves the assimilation and acceptance of the great fundamental edicts of culture and conscience, not a distrust of and a standing apart from them as Freud was led to conclude.

Freud explicitly equated happiness to pleasure in the sense of instinctual pleasure. He was strangely blind and obdurate to the very apparent fact—apparent at least to individuals who have been able to take full advantage of developmental opportunities available within the established framework of their society—that there is such a thing as conscience pleasure, and that in the long run happiness is far more securely founded upon this than upon instinctual pleasure. Freud wrote voluminously about a highly questionable process which he termed *sublima-*

tion. Since man cannot, because of what Freud termed "cultural privation," find happiness in the free and complete gratification of his instinctual desires, his only hope of attaining even a modicum of happiness is achieved by eking out more limited and indirect gratifications of these impulses. A more felicitous conception is that of *substitution,* the process of replacing immediate, infantile, organic pleasures by the more enduring satisfactions which come from a sense of full and responsible observations of the rules and principles governing the activities of family, community, state, nation, and of the human enterprise generally. In so accepting these rules and principles, one wins back to a fuller and more assured satisfaction of even the instinctual needs than seems possible in any other pattern of existence.*

Briefly, let us see if we can more sharply focus the principal implications of this discussion. We have seen that a neurotic is a person who has proceeded quite a long way on the road toward becoming a mature, socially responsible adult but who at some point has gotten "stuck," "bogged down." By processes which we are only beginning to understand, the neurotic has earlier taken into himself the basic values and attitudes of his particular society and of his particular sub-group within that society. But what he has *not* done is fully to come to terms with and harmoniously assimilate these basic values and attitudes into the fabric of his total personality. Such a step the neurotic is unable (unwilling?) to make, and thereby hangs the mystery.

If the neurotic cannot go forward on life's pathway, neither can he go backward. To go backward is to become less human, more like an animal and it is constantly being borne in upon us that we cannot escape the fate of *being human beings.* The force that thus pushes us onward is not therefore some childish whimsey, a vagary of an eccentric up-

* For a somewhat similar view, see (23).

bringing, but one of the most powerful and pervasive of our total contemporary experiences.

With progress blocked and retreat cut off † the neurotic characteristically feels trapped, helpless, impotent. He cannot, in other words, either move forward, go back to where he came from, or stay where he is. The "road" seems hopelessly uphill in both directions, and yet he can find neither peace nor rest in pausing!

Growing up and becoming "normal," in the sense of measuring up to standard specifications for being a human being and fulfilling the expectations which are placed upon us, is something no one can do without help. Human socialization involves learning things, of both a technical and moral nature, which took the race millions of years to work out. Unaided, alone, isolated from other human contacts, no single individual would ever learn more than a tiny fragment, a minuscule beginning, of the totality which we call human culture. In the protective yet ever expectant atmosphere of the home and, later, the school, through a precious admixture of love and fear, the human animal is little by little prepared for and initiated into this great enterprise. But sometimes, for various reasons, individuals grow up physically and leave family and school,

† Perhaps the most basic difference between the neurotic and the psychotic is that, for the latter, the road back to childhood and infancy is less completely closed. This, presumably, is because parts of the prepsychotic's personality or "mind" are still very "primitive," as Fromm-Reichmann has suggested. But even here there are powerful pressures, within and without, pushing the individual toward adulthood and full humanity, as indicated by a remark, quoted by the same author, from a schizophrenic patient who had just come out of a long stupor and was found "sitting naked and masturbating on the floor of his room which was spotted with urine and sputum, . . ." When the therapist started to sit down on the floor near him, he reproved her, pulled a blanket around himself and said, "Even though I have sunk as low as an animal, I still know how to behave in the presence of a lady" (13, p. 420).

without having learned quite all that they should have learned in those settings. It is such persons who often find themselves confused, trapped, brought to a standstill. And it is only by the fortunate accident of their being able to resume, under more auspicious circumstances, a child-parent relationship with a second "father" or "mother" that some of the unlearned lessons are completed and the individual is able to move on and take his proper place among his fellows.

Thus it is that we come to see that neurosis involves, basically, a learning deficit rather than a learning excess, but one which the individual is often unable to correct, spontaneously and unaided.

When we see the development of human personality in this light, not only is the neurotic paradox formally resolved; we are also enabled to conceive the task of therapy as not that of attempting to stay or actually reverse the process whereby the human animal is converted into a full-fledged member of his society. Rather do we see therapy as the more promising venture of reinstituting and, if possible, in some measure completing the education of the laggard learner.

References

1. Alexander, F., and T. H. French. *Psycho-analytic therapy.* New York: Ronald, 1946.

2. Allport, G. W. *Personality—a psychological interpretation.* New York: Henry Holt, 1937.

3. ———. Motivation in personality: reply to Mr. Bertocci. *Psychological Review,* 47(1940), 533–554.

4. ———. *Animal models and human morals.* Ibid, 54(1947), 182–192.

5. Anderson, O. D., and H. S. Liddell. Observations on experimental neurosis in sheep. *Arch. Neurol. and Psychiatry,* 34(1935), 330–354.

6. Anderson, O. D., and R. Parmenter. A long-term study of the experimental neurosis in the sheep and dog, with nine case histories. *Psychosomatic Med. Monog. 2,* Nos. 3, 4, 1941.

7. Freud, S. *Beyond the pleasure principle.* New York: Boni and Liveright, 1922.

8. ———. *Civilization and its discontents.* London: Hogarth, 1930.

9. ———. *New introductory lectures on psychoanalysis.* New York: Norton, 1933.

10. ———. Formulations regarding the two principles in mental functioning. *Collected papers,* Vol. IV (1911); London: Hogarth, 1934.

11. ———. *A general introduction to psychoanalysis.* New York (1920): Liveright, 1935.

12. ———. *The problem of anxiety.* New York: Norton, 1936.

13. Fromm-Reichmann, Freida. Transference problems in schizophrenics. *Psychoan. Quart.,* 8(1939), 412–426.

14. Gantt, W. H. Experimental basis for neurotic behavior. *Psychosomatic Med. Monog.,* 3(1944), 203.

15. Horney, Karen. *The neurotic personality of our time.* New York: Norton, 1937.

16. Hull, C. L. *Principles of behavior.* New York: Appleton-Century, 1943.

17. Humphreys, L. G. Acquisition and extinction of verbal expectations in a situation analogous to conditioning. *J. Exper. Psychol.,* 25(1939), 294–301.

18. ———. The effect of random alternation of reinforcement on the acquisition and extinction of conditioned eyelid reactions. *Ibid,* 141–158.

19. ———. The strength of a Thorndikian response as a function of the number of practice trials. *Psychol. Bull.,* 37(1940), 571.

20. Kingsley, H. L. *The nature and conditions of learning.* New York: Prentice-Hall, 1946.

21. Korzybski, A. *Science and sanity.* Lancaster, Pa.: Science Press, 1941 (2nd ed.).

22. Liddell, H. S. Conditioned reflex method and experimental neurosis. In *Personality and the behavior disorders.* New York: Ronald (J. McV. Hunt, Ed.) Vol. 1, 389–412, 1944.

23. Maslow, A. H. "Higher" and "lower" needs. *J. Psychol.,* 25(1948), 433–436.

24. Mowrer, O. H. On the dual nature of learning—a reinterpretation of "conditioning" and "problem-solving." Harvard Ed. Rev., 17(1947), 102–148.

25. ———. What is normal behavior? in *An introduction to clinical psychology.* Ronald. (L. A. Pennington and I. A. Berg, Eds.), New York: 1948.

26. ———. *Anxiety* (S. S. Stevens, Ed.), in *Handbook of experimental psychology.* New York: John Wiley (1949).

27. ———. *The problem of anxiety—some conceptual difficulties* (in press).

28. ———. *The psychology of talking birds* (in press).

29. Mowrer, O. H., and Helen Jones. Ex-

tinction and behavior variability as functions of the effortfulness of task. *J. Exper. Psychol.,* **33**(1943), 369–386.

30. ———. Habit strength as a function of the pattern of reinforcement. *Ibid,* **35**(1945), 293–311.

31. Mowrer, O. H., and Dorothy Kunberger. *An experimental study of secondary reinforcement* (to be published).

32. Mowrer, O. H., and A. D. Ullman. Time as a determinant in integrative learning. *Psychol. Rev.,* **52**(1945), 61–90.

33. Mowrer, O. H., and P. Viek. An experimental analogue of fear from a sense of helplessness. *J. Abn. and Soc. Psychol.* (in press).

34. Pavlov, I. P. *Conditioned reflexes.* New York: Oxford, 1927.

35. ———. *Conditioned Reflexes and Psychiatry.* New York: Internat. Publishers, 1941.

36. Preston, G. H. *Psychiatry for the Curious.* New York: Farrar and Rinehart, 1940.

37. Richards, I. A. *Interpretation in Teaching.* New York: Harcourt, Brace, 1938.

38. Shaffer, L. F. The Problem of Psychotherapy. *Am. Psychol.,* **2**(1947), 459–467.

39. Sullivan, H. S. The Modified Psychoanalytic Treatment of Schizophrenia. *Am. J. Psychiatry,* **11**(1931), 519–540.

40. ———. *Conceptions of Modern Psychiatry.* Washington, D.C.: William Alanson White Psychiatric Foundation, 1945.

41. Youtz, R. E. P. Reinforcement, Extinction, and Spontaneous Recovery in a Non-Pavlovian Reaction. *J. Exper. Psychol.,* **23**(1938), 305–318.

The Assessment of Anxiety in Psychological Experimentation: A Theoretical Reformulation and Test *

GEORGE C. ROSENWALD

UNIVERSITY OF MICHIGAN

The effects of anxiety on performance have been subjected to fairly intensive

Reprinted from the *Journal of Abnormal and Social Psychology,* **62**(1961), 666–673, with the permission of the American Psychological Association and the author.

* An abbreviated version of this paper was prepared for presentation at the International Congress of Psychology in Bonn, Germany, 1960. It is based on a dissertation presented to the faculty of the Graduate School of Yale University in candidacy for the degree of Doctor of Philosophy.

The author is grateful to Irving L. Janis, William Kessen, and Roy Schafer for their advice and assistance throughout the conduct of this study, which was carried out while

experimental study in past years (1). A good deal of this research has shed light on the type of performance that is disrupted by anxiety. For instance, it has been shown that anxiety interferes with the accomplishment of complex tasks but facilitates the performance of simple tasks (3). Considerably less attention has been given to a theoretical analysis of

the author was a Public Health Trainee in Clinical Psychology.

Thanks go to Cynthia Dember for her assistance in the rating of story completions as well as to Carl Garvin, principal, and the students of the East Haven, Connecticut, High School for their helpful cooperation.

anxiety itself, the conditions of its arousal, and its defining properties. Experimenters do not always agree with each other or with theoreticians and clinicians as to the exact meaning of anxiety as a conceptual term. The first part of the present paper is a review of the psychoanalytic theory of anxiety. This framework is selected because many authors have operated within it. Following the presentation of the theoretical outline, some shortcomings of conventional experimental approaches to anxiety will be pointed out. Finally, an experiment will be reported, the procedures of which approximate the theoretical specifications more closely.

The first of the two conventional procedures to be discussed segregates the subjects with respect to anxiety level on the basis of a questionnaire to which the subject responds with an introspective report of his characteristic anxiety level and stress experiences (7, 15). The second procedure produces a stress in the subject through fictitious reports of his inadequate performance on tasks which are presented as tests of intelligence or as other measures of adequacy (6, 10). Sometimes these two procedures are employed jointly. They are subject to limitations which will become clear after the theoretical outline is presented.

The psychoanalytic theory of anxiety (4) begins with the observation that for some people the intensification of a particular drive constitutes a psychic danger. The nature and origin of this danger are to be sought in the individual histories of such persons. Unconsciously fantasied physical damage, helplessness, or loss of love are frequently encountered examples of such danger. In anticipation of this danger, such people characteristically distort the recognition and expression of the drive in question by means of defense mechanisms. These mechanisms avert the expected danger to the extent that they block or distort the drive successfully. Anxiety is defined as the psycho-

logical mechanism whereby the current intensification of a dangerous drive results in the elicitation of defenses. The term "signal anxiety" refers to this function specifically. Anxiety is therefore a theoretical construct which is anchored on the antecedent side to the intensification of a dangerous drive and on the consequent side to the rise of defensive behavior.* It should be noted that this strict definition of anxiety makes no phenomenological references to feelings of distress, heart palpitations, etc.

Defenses are therefore a central concept in the definition of anxiety. They are recognized when the individual behaves in ways which interfere with the experience or expression of his needs. For example, when it is observed that a person responds to extreme aggressive provocation with inexhaustible forbearance and forgiveness for the offender, it may be said that he is defending himself against aggression. In clinical practice and experimental studies (2) it has been found that people who are defensive characteristically distort their perception of stimuli which are associated with the arousal of dangerous drives. Moreover, it is found that the greater the danger, the greater is the distortion (11).

It is well known that anxiety is in certain instances further characterized by conscious experiences of distress and by physiological stress symptoms. However, these additional conditions are of secondary importance in the definition of anxiety and may be completely lacking. Thus the term anxiety may be applied regardless of whether subjective

---

* Anxiety as a mechanism should not be confused with anxiety as a character trait. To say "John is anxious about aggression," does not necessarily mean that John is aggressively stimulated at the present time and is counteracting this stimulation with defenses. Rather, it means that John would become defensive *if* he were aggressively stimulated. This is another way of saying that aggression is a dangerous drive for John or that John has conflicts about aggression.

experiential factors and physiological stress symptoms play a minimal role or assume spectacular importance, as they do, for instance, in anxiety attacks. Only its traceable origin in past experience, which has rendered the drive dangerous, and the automatic elicitation of defenses are central to the definition of anxiety. In fact, the concomitance of anxiety, whatever its experiential salience, and of defensiveness is so constant that it is difficult to distinguish conceptually or experimentally between the behavioral consequences of the one and the other. Under what conditions do the secondary experiential and physiological factors appear at all? The theory provides an explanation in terms of the effectiveness of the defense. If the defense mechanism does not sufficiently block or distort the dangerous drive, and the drive grows in intensity, then the experiential and physiological aspects of anxiety will gradually become more conspicuous. In other words, in the case of a person with ineffective defenses, these aspects will be added to signal anxiety when the drive is intensified. They subside as soon as the drive is sufficiently distorted.

It is an important part of the theory that anxiety operates automatically in many cases. That is to say, the elicitation of defenses does not depend on the experiential and physiological aspects of anxiety. This is especially characteristic of functioning normal adults. In fact, people who are frequently subject to anxiety *experiences* are often in need of treatment. Anxiety is not an ever-present condition or mood in well functioning individuals. Even in patients, the intensity and effects of anxiety and defensiveness vary with the intensity of the drive that gives rise to them. Only an acute intensification of dangerous drives will result in anxiety—experiential or otherwise. For instance, a person for whom aggressive stimulation is dangerous will try not to expose himself to social situations in which he may be aggressively

stimulated. Thus anxiety and defense arousing situations may only rarely occur in his life.

The view outlined here reserves the concepts of "anxiety" and "defense" for situations in which the danger has an internal source, specifically a drive, and the term "fear" for those in which the threat originates in the external world. Although borderline instances and cases of overlapping may be cited, the paradigm itself is clear in this respect.

In the light of this theory, both the questionnaire and the stress procedures mentioned initially have serious shortcomings. As for the questionnaire, its outstanding limitation is its reliance on the subject's introspective report of anxiety. By theory, subjects who rate themselves high on anxiety by reporting experiences of psychic distress and physiological stress are not only anxious in the primary sense of the word—they not only become defensive in the presence of the drive—but in addition, they utilize ineffective defenses which do not distort the drive sufficiently. Furthermore, they may not be successful in avoiding situations in which they are likely to be dangerously stimulated. While these individuals represent a challenging clinical problem, it is incorrect to designate others, who do not report experiences of anxiety, as not anxious in the strict sense. The only admissible distinction between subjects who report and subjects who do not report anxiety experiences is on the basis of the effectiveness of their defenses, not on the basis of whether or not defenses are being elicited. Subjects who do not report anxiety experiences are either not anxious about the drive, or they avoid anxiety arousing situations; or, if they do not avoid them, then anxiety never becomes more than a signal because their defenses are effective. It should be noted that people who resolve underlying conflict with relatively flexible defenses are not detectable by means of a questionnaire.

As for the stress procedure, it seems to approximate the specifications of fear arousal more than those of anxiety arousal. True, the prospects of failing an intelligence test or of showing up poorly on a measure of masculinity are dangerous both internally and externally; such failures would involve a compromise in the eyes of others as well as a drop in self-esteem. Yet it seems preferable to investigate these effects separately rather than under confounded conditions. If it were possible to bring about the intensification of a dangerous drive without simultaneously producing an immediate external threat, the conditions of anxiety arousal specified in the theory would seem to be most nearly met.

In view of these considerations, the following method was proposed. Aggression was selected as a drive about which people are anxious to varying degrees.* First, the degree of anxiety about aggression was to be determined for each subject by noting his extremity of defensive distortion in response to an aggressive assessment stimulus. Then, independently of this determination, subjects were to be exposed to an acute aggressive provocation. It was assumed that anxiety and defensiveness would automatically be aroused again, just as they were in response to the assessment stimulus, and that the effects of anxiety and defensiveness on behavior could then be measured. In other words, the subject's own "built-in" predisposition to become anxious as a result of drive arousal was to be utilized rather than a fictitious external threat. Nor was any use to be made of the subjects' awareness of their anxiety.

An anagram solving task was selected as a measure of the effects of anxiety on performance. Findings indicate that the

* The choice of aggression is not crucial to the theoretical formulation of this paper. Anxiety about dependency or sexuality could have been utilized as easily. This will be discussed later on.

effect of anxiety upon performance varies with the complexity of the task (3). A task is considered complex if the correct response is either weak in the initial response hierarchy or is in competition with other equally strong responses, whereas a simple task, like that in classical conditioning, is one in which the correct response is strong in the hierarchy. In the former tasks, anxiety has been found to have an impairing but in the latter a facilitating effect on performance. Anagram solution is a complex task which is known to be vulnerable to the effects of anxiety as measured by questionnaire (5).

The prediction tested by the present experiment is the following: In the case of subjects who are observed to become defensive in reaction to an aggressive assessment stimulus, an experimental intervention designed to arouse aggression results in impaired performance on a complex problem solving task. Subjects who do not become defensive in response to the assessment stimulus are not so affected by the experimental intervention.

Method

The experimental subjects were 62 high school students who were tested individually during two separate sessions. During the first session, a Story Completion test, an Anagrams test, and an abbreviated Intelligence test were administered (9). Thirty-nine of the subjects constituted the experimental group. At the beginning of their second session, they were subjected to an experimental intervention designed to arouse aggression. For the remaining 23 control subjects, this intervention was omitted. Following this, alternate forms of the three tests were administered to all subjects. Differences between the forms of the tests were controlled for by the use of a counterbalanced design.

The Story Completion test consisted of five incomplete stories which the subject was asked to complete. Each contained an aggressive provocation of the main figure.

This thematic test was selected as the assessment stimulus because projective devices are traditional for detecting anxiety and defensiveness in the sense defined, and because responses to such tests are ordinarily less subject to influence by socially conditioned attitudes. Such tests may identify individuals who characteristically respond to increases in drive in a defensive manner but are not necessarily aware of their anxiety or of the entailed defensive drive distortion. Because projective test responses reflect anxiety and defensiveness concerning which the subject has little or no control or awareness, they seem particularly suited to the present experimental paradigm.

The Anagrams test consisted of 10 scrambled four and five-letter words which the subject was asked to convert into meaningful words by rearranging the letters in his mind. Half the anagram solutions were "loaded"—that is, they had aggression related connotations; the other half was neutral. According to the conception of the present study and the findings of past research (5), the anagrams task should be subject to the effects of anxiety regardless of the content of the anagrams. The rationale of this prediction is entirely in terms of task complexity, and in this respect it differs from studies of perceptual defense. "Loaded" stimuli were included out of interest in the effects which content may perhaps have beyond those postulated. Just as incomplete stories with aggressive themes are more likely to point up a subject's anxiety about aggression than stories with other themes, so the aggressive content of the anagrams may add to the anxiety which a subject already experiences as a result of the experimental drive arousal.

The Information subtest of the Wechsler Adult Intelligence Scale was administered as a measure of intelligence (16).

The experimental intervention consisted of two parts. First, the subject was accused of and reprimanded for having discussed the experiment with his friends after having been asked at the end of the first session to refrain from doing so. He was told that this was childish, disobedient, and irresponsible. Second, he was asked to take a mirror tracing test as part of the study. His performance in this was characterized as inadequate, and the experimenter demanded that the subject return after school to continue practicing mirror tracing. The intervention was delivered in a sarcastic, belittling manner, and no replies were tolerated. (Mirror tracing, a measure external to the experiment proper, was chosen for the intervention because of possible changes in task set which might have affected performance on the Anagrams test had *it* been used for this purpose.) All of the subject's verbalizations at this time were recorded by the experimenter. The demand for after school practice was retracted at the end of the experiment, and the overall purpose of the study was explained.

Results

The five story completions obtained in the first session were used to obtain an index of defensiveness. Each completion was ranked with respect to defensiveness in relation to all others obtained in response to the same incomplete story. A completion was judged to be defensive in proportion to the extent to which aggression was *not* expressed, the extent to which the main figure of the story was *not* seen as active in bringing about a favorable solution to the presented conflict, the extent to which he was *not* seen as capable of acknowledging the discrepancy of interest between himself and the instigator of the aggressive provocation, and the extent to which he was *not* seen as blaming the instigator but rather as blaming himself. No attempt was made to categorize the completions according to specific defense mechanisms exemplified by them. Rather, the degree of defensiveness was determined by the magnitude of the distortion. By using an objective scoring manual (9), an alternate judge arrived at reliably similar rankings, with rho coefficients ranging from .71 to .92. The ranks obtained for each of the subject's five stories were summed, yielding his defensiveness score. The subjects were then divided at the median into a high defensive and a low defensive group.

In comparing the times required for solution on the first administration of the Anagrams test, it was found that high defensive and low defensive subjects performed comparably.

An analysis of performance changes from the first to the second administration of the Anagrams test is shown in Table 1. The breakdown of the chi square into the components attributable to Defensiveness, Treatment, and their interaction was undertaken, using Wilson's (1956) test. It was concluded that the performance changes of the high defensive and low defensive groups were significantly different, the former showing impairment and the latter improvement of performance when compared to the control subjects. Furthermore, these changes could be attributed to the effects of the experimental intervention since

TABLE 1

Extended Median Test (Siegel, 1956) and Wilson's Distribution Test (Wilson, 1956) for the Difference between Solution Times on the First and Second Administration of the Anagrams Test

(High scores indicate relative impairment)

	Experimental		Control	
	High-De-fensive	Low-De-fensive	High-De-fensive	Low-De-fensive
Above Overall Median	14	4	6	7
Below	5	16	5	5
χ^2 Total	11.90	$3df$	$p < .001$	
χ^2 Defensiveness	6.46	$1df$	$p < .02$	
χ^2 Treatment	0.62	$1df$	—	
χ^2 Defensiveness $\times$ Treatment	4.82	$1df$	$p < .05$	

Note.—A nonparametric test was employed to permit the pooling of difference scores obtained from two replications differing in the order of administration of parallel test forms and therefore not comparable in absolute values of solution time.

the interaction of Defensiveness and Treatment was found to be significant.

In addition, there is suggestive but statistically unreliable evidence that high defensive subjects required longer solution times for "loaded" than for neutral anagrams on the *first* administration of the test and that this was not so for the low defensive subjects. However, the reported effects of the experimental intervention were not limited to the loaded items. If anything, neutral items seemed to be affected somewhat more noticeably by the intervention than were loaded ones.

The high defensive and low defensive subjects did not differ in their performance on the intelligence scale either before or after the intervention.

Discussion

The above findings may be briefly summarized as follows: High defensive and low defensive subjects do not at the outset differ from each other in regard to their performance on the Anagrams test; they are differentially affected by the experimental intervention, with the high defensive subjects showing impairment and the low defensive subjects improvement as measured by solution times, and the content of the items does not seem to influence their susceptibility to the facilitating or impairing effects of the experimental intervention.

In connection with the first of these three findings, it should be noted that investigators assessing anxiety with questionnaires have found that subjects differ in performance even in the absence of any experimental arousal (3, 15). The failure of the present study to corroborate this observation may be taken as indirect evidence that Defensiveness rankings are not interchangeable with scores on an anxiety questionnaire, as indeed they were not intended to be. The present findings can be accounted for without assuming that any of the subjects ever became consciously distressed or experienced physiological stress symptoms, although such a contingency is certainly not ruled out. Since the effectiveness of defenses is theoretically related to the presence or absence of the experiential aspects of anxiety, it is possible that differences in performance which have been found in past studies between subjects high and low on an anxiety questionnaire are due to the degree of defense effectiveness rather than to the degree to which the subject becomes anxious in the theoretically strict sense. The present study is only a first attempt to elucidate experimentally the differences between the behavioral consequences of overt anxiety, introspectively observed by the subject and reported on a questionnaire, and of the disposition to become defensive, measured by projective devices and not necessarily accompanied by conscious experiences of distress.

An inspection of the items of the Taylor (14) scale suggests that a high score is likely to indicate a more or less permanent drive or affective state. The rationale and findings of the present study, however, explicitly provide for and give positive evidence of an acute rise in anxiety conditional on an acute rise in a dangerous drive. Once again, it appears that the present procedure for controlling anxiety could be applied to people who are not characteristically subject to the experiental accompaniments of anxiety, even though they may be judged anxious and defensive about a particular drive. The method described here might, therefore, facilitate the conceptual disentanglement of the effects of anxiety and defense.

The first and second findings, taken together, suggest strongly that the defensiveness rankings measure what it was hoped they would measure: not the person's usual or typical level of anxiety, but his disposition to become anxious

and to defend when dangerously aroused. In accordance with the rationale of this study, it should be possible to replicate the reported findings by raising the level of any other drive in subjects for whom that drive is known to be dangerous.

With regard to the second finding, the question arises as to what psychological mechanisms were responsible for the observed performance changes. It may be argued that a high defensive subject could so distort the meaning of the experimental intervention and of his reaction to it that he might ignore its provocative implications. After all, the intervention is a stimulus associated with drive arousal just as the incomplete stories were. In that case, should the intervention not fail to affect him? This is certainly possible, but it must be remembered that anxiety always occurs in combination with defensive efforts of varying kinds and degrees of success. At the present state of knowledge, the effects of anxiety and defense on cognitive behavior cannot yet be distinguished either • experimentally or even conceptually. In other words, the high defensive subjects' test performance was impaired by anxiety or the defensive distortion of the experimental intervention or both. Parallel with this, it is unclear whether investigators of anxiety who have not been systematically concerned with the effects of defense were justified in attributing their findings only to the effects of anxiety. Perhaps their data should be viewed in part from the standpoint of the defenses which are automatically aroused by the anxiety stimulus.

The separation of the effects of anxiety from those of defense would have more than semantic importance. It is conceivable that anxiety affects performance through the mediation of drive increments and irrelevant responses (1), whereas defense may exert its influence through the mediation of cognitive rigidity and the narrowing of attention and associative processes.* Whether or not a particular task performance is affected by anxiety and defensiveness would then depend on the effectiveness of an individual's defenses and on the vulnerability of the selected task to one or the other type of mediating mechanism. For instance, if performance of a task is most vulnerable to cognitive rigidity, then a subject who is only moderately defensive and experiences a good deal of distress will not be so severely penalized in his performance as another subject whose defenses are intensely and pervasively constricting and who is, therefore, free from experiences of overt distress and physiological stress. The analysis of intellectual functioning in different diagnostic groups tends to bear this out (8).

Little is known at the present time that would easily account for the improvement of the low defensive subjects. It is possible that unanxious, and therefore undistorted, experience of increased aggression provided them with greater energy, perhaps even with vindictive overtones. ("I'll show him who is immature!") Although the finding is not surprising in the light of clinical experience, there is little if any research support for the assumption that the aggressive drive can at times be utilized in this constructive way. Another possible explanation is that this added drive had merely a distracting effect on the low defensive subjects and that they overcame it by intensifying their efforts to attend only to the task. Whether or not *any* drive arousal will have such a facilitating effect on subjects who experience little anxiety about it is not known. It is quite possible that aggression, because of its nature, is more likely to have such energizing effects than is, say, an arousal of dependency needs. Furthermore, one of the criteria used for categorizing sub-

* The effect of rigid defenses and controls on one phase of creative and inventive behavior has been discussed by Schafer (12).

jects as high defensive or low defensive was whether or not they made reference to active problem solving behavior on the part of the main figure in their story completions. The low defensive subjects' superiority on the Anagrams test may be looked upon as another facet of their greater concern with or investment in problem solving. Just as these subjects involved their story figures in active problem solving attempts, so they became themselves involved in active attempts to restructure the anagram stimuli.

The findings of the experimental groups are interesting also in that they are consistent with economic considerations in psychoanalytic theory. It is assumed that the ego performs its adaptive functions, of which problem solving is one, with energy which is of instinctual origin but has undergone varying degrees of neutralization. The capacity to neutralize instinctual energy is thought to depend on the person's relative freedom from anxiety concerning the instinct in question. That is, defensiveness tends to preclude neutralization. The present findings can be explained as follows. The low defensive group had a greater quantity of neutralized, dischargeable energy available for problem solving and therefore showed an improvement, whereas the high defensive group had to block the aroused aggressive energy and therefore pre-empted it from adaptive utilization. These economic considerations seem the more applicable because the groups performed comparably in the absence of energic arousal and because the stimulus content was noncontributory to the observed effects.

An incidental observation needs to be mentioned in connection with the second finding. An analysis of the experimental subjects' verbal reactions to the experimental intervention revealed a tendency for high defensive subjects to object to the experimenter's accusation and arbitrariness more frequently than was true of low defensive subjects. Although this finding falls far short of statistical significance, failure to find a significant difference in the opposite direction serves as a reminder that one may not freely predict diffident and meek behavior from the presence of defensiveness in projective test responses. In many everyday situations, such defenses are overlaid with socially conditioned counterdefenses against passivity and timidity. In neurotic patients, considerable therapeutic work may often be required to bring to the surface the submissiveness which hides behind impressive swagger and assertiveness. However, this relationship between fantasy defensiveness and action assertiveness stands in need of further exploration.

The third finding suggests that theories derived from the phenomena of perceptual defense may not provide adequate explanations of the present observations. Apparently, psychological functions like those involved in the solution of anagrams can be subject to wholesale interference which transcends particular areas of tabu content. It is suggested that although anxiety is aroused by drives which have specifiable content, the effects, facilitating or inhibiting, of anxiety and defensiveness on performance may have a wider sphere of influence than the anxiety arousing content. There is no a priori reason to assume that anxiety will affect a given type of cognitive behavior differentially, depending on what drive gave rise to the anxiety. This too is borne out by the analysis of intellectual functions in patient groups (8).

Finally, it could be argued that the effect of the experimental intervention operated through a decrease in the cooperativeness or incentive of the high defensive subjects. The best reply to this and similar explanations is a question: Why should the experimental treatment have different effects on the

cooperativeness of people who have high and low defensiveness ratings? The advantage of combining predispositional and experimental controls is that the number of plausible explanations of the obtained effects can be greatly reduced.

Summary

The psychoanalytic theory of anxiety and defense was reviewed. Following this, weaknesses were pointed out in experimental methods which apply the term "anxiety" to overt experiences of subjective distress accompanied by physiological distress symptoms, or which seek to control the level of anxiety by means of external threats. A new procedure was proposed and tested, consisting in the experimental arousal of a motive known to be psychologically unacceptable or dangerous for the subject. Anxiety is thought of as the automatic accompaniment of such arousals, regardless of its experiential conspicuousness to the subject himself.

A thematic test was utilized to assess defensiveness about aggression. Subsequently, an experimental intervention, designed to arouse aggression, was administered to the subjects, and the effects of this intervention on the performance of a problem solving task were measured. Findings were as follows:

1. Under drive arousal, high defensive subjects showed impairment and low defensive subjects improvement in performance.

2. Subjects did not differ in level of performance before drive arousal.

3. The content of the stimulus material used to measure problem solving ability did not seem to contribute to the vulnerability of performance to the effects of anxiety and defensiveness.

This reformulation of anxiety appears to hold promise for the conceptual and experimental separation of the effects of anxiety and defense.

References

1. Child, I. L. Personality. *Annu. Rev. Psychol.*, 5(1954), 149–170.

2. Eriksen, C. W. The case for perceptual defense. *Psychol. Rev.*, 61(1954), 175–182.

3. Farber, I. E., & Spence, K. W. Complex learning and conditioning as a function of anxiety. *J. Exp. Psychol.*, 45(1953), 120–125.

4. Freud, S. *The problem of anxiety.* (Originally published 1926) New York: Norton, 1936.

5. Maltzman, I., Fox, J., & Morrisett, L., Jr. Some effects of manifest anxiety on mental set. *J. Exp. Psychol.*, 46(1953), 50–54.

6. Mandler, G., & Sarason, S. B. A study of anxiety and learning. *J. Abnorm. Soc. Psychol.*, 47(1952), 166–173.

7. Montague, E. K. The role of anxiety in serial rote learning. *J. Exp. Psychol.*, 45 (1953), 91–96.

8. Rapaport, D., Gill, M., & Schafer, R. *Diagnostic psychological testing.* Vol. I. New York: International Univ. Press, 1945.

9. Rosenwald, G. C. The effect of defensiveness on ideational mobility. Unpublished Ph.D. dissertation, Yale University, 1958.

10. Sarason, S. B., Mandler, G., & Craighill, P. G. The effect of differential instructions on anxiety and learning. *J. Abnorm. Soc. Psychol.*, 47(1952), 561–565.

11. Schafer, R. *Psychoanalytic interpretation in Rorschach testing.* New York: Grune & Stratton, 1954.

12. ———. Regression in the service of the ego: The relevance of a psychoanalytic concept for personality assessment. In G. Lindzey (Ed.), *The assessment of human motives.* New York: Rinehart, 1958. Pages 119–148.

13. Siegel, S. *Nonparametric statistics for the behavioral sciences.* New York: McGraw-Hill, 1956.

14. Taylor, Janet A. A personality scale of manifest anxiety. *J. Abnorm. Soc. Psychol.*, 48(1953), 285–290.

15. Taylor, Janet A., & Spence, K. W. The relationship of anxiety level to performance in serial learning. *J. Exp. Psychol.*, 44(1952), 61–64.

16. Wechsler, D. *Wechsler Adult Intelligence Scale.* New York: Psychological Corporation, 1955.

17. Wilson, K. V. A distribution-free test of analysis of variance hypotheses. *Psychol. Bull.*, 53(1956), 96–101.

Expressive Behavior and Language Patterns

MARIA LORENZ

HARVARD UNIVERSITY MEDICAL SCHOOL

Linguistic patterns, considered as a form of expressive behavior, seem to show certain consistencies with psychological patterns. This paper reports a study of the language of four groups of patients, consisting of ten patients each, clinically and psychologically evaluated as charac-

Reprinted from *Psychiatry*, 18(1955), 353–366, by special permission of The William Alanson White Psychiatric Foundation, Inc., holder of the copyright, and the author.

teristic reaction types—hysteric, obsessive-compulsive, manic, and paranoid schizophrenic.* Recorded interview ma-

* A previous paper (Lorenz, Language as expressive behavior, *A.M.A. Arch. Neurol. and Psychiat.*, 70(1953), 277–285) presented some observations of the language characteristics of particular patients and a discussion of the psychological implications of these characteristics in terms of expressive behavior; here the attempt is to generalize beyond the single patient, and to relate language categories to psychological categories.

terial from these patients, who were receiving individual therapy, was analyzed for recurrent and habitual language characteristics. Certain differentiating features were found to occur prominently in each group. The observations presented, however, are illustrative and descriptive, rather than quantitative. The purpose of this study is not to designate certain language characteristics as unique for certain clinical reaction types, but to serve as a preliminary survey of the joint occurrence of psychological traits and language traits. This study is limited by the fact that the sampling is small and is based on the observations of one person.

Language as Expressive Behavior

Since language is an integrated, complex activity by which form and expression are given to mental events, an approach is indicated which takes into account the Gestalt features of psychological phenomena. The methods of expressive behavior studies (1) appear to do so in their emphasis upon the emergence of configuration and pattern, and it is this approach which is here applied to language.

Expressive behavior is broadly defined as a reflection of the structure of personality in its relatively stable traits and dispositions, insofar as these are shown by external behavior such as movement (2, 3, 4). Certain aspects of movement have, in addition to an adaptive and purposeful function, the function of expressing characteristics of the agent (2). Reading these external signs and making valid inferences from them regarding personality make-up constitute the technique of expressive behavior studies. Habitual and unself-conscious activity, such as that exhibited in gait, posture, handwriting, speech, and facial expression, lends itself to this approach. An extension of expressive behavior techniques

is found in structured tests such as the Draw-a-Person Test and the Mosaic Test. Valuable psychological information has been obtained from more spontaneous sources such as the finger painting of children, the artistic productions of psychotic patients, the behavior of children in play therapy, and the behavior of adults in psychodrama. The expressive component of such activities is manifested in the spontaneous, unself-conscious tendency of the person to organize and integrate even his purposeful behavior along lines determined by his basic psychological nature. Language behavior, which has communication as its conscious purpose, also includes these components of spontaneity and unconsciously determined organization and integration.

The implied relationship between language and expression of the self rests upon philosophical and psychological tradition. Dilthey (5) claims that mental acts—cognitive, affective, and volitional —can be read off from the forms of language. He suggests that one important function of language is to express the mental attitudes which are adopted toward experience. Hartmann (6) also indicates that the fundamental notions of all thought lie as ready-made material to be read off in language. Stout (7) views language as an instrument by which the person examines the world about him and gives direction to his thought. Bühler (8) designates expression as a major function of language in that thoughts, as articulated, convey the psychological orientation of the speaker. Cassirer (9) has evolved a philosophical viewpoint based on the conception that language is the symbolic transformation of experience.

The close relationship of language to the expression of inner mental events is also confirmed by the developmental approach. Piaget (10), notably among others, indicates the close correspondence between the development of certain conceptual notions in the child and the forms of articulated expression as these successively appear in the child's language. There is also considerable anthropological and cultural evidence to suggest that the habits of thought of various peoples are reflected in the structure of their particular language.

The phenomenon of style in literature strongly asserts the relatedness of language characteristics to the personality of the writer. Interesting studies in literary psychology are those of Lee (11) and Spitzer (12). Psychological investigations of style through analysis of language characteristics have been made by Sherman (13), Newman (14, 15), and Sanford (16). These studies provide a number of helpful criteria for the objective scrutiny of language patterns, and show how psychological processes may be studied effectively in language. Glauber (17) indicates that character structure and speech pattern tend to develop in organic unity. Categories of verbal style and their significance receive recognition as diagnostic features in Rorschach testing by Phillips and Smith (18). Verbal communication as an integral and revealing aspect of the patient's thought processes in the Rorschach is also stressed by Piotrowski (19) and Rapaport (20).

The language of dreams, the language of phantasy, the language of the body, are familiar concepts in psychiatry —and it is not by accident that the word employed is *language*. The word carries the convergent meaning that all three activities are an *expression* of the person who dreams, elaborates phantasies, develops bodily symptoms.

The Hysteric Patient

The following are excerpts from the speech of four psychoneurotic patients, clinically and psychologically evaluated as hysteric:

Patient A: I was simply fascinated with them . . . it's pretty false . . . I always get into sort of jams . . . it's silly to look at it objectively . . . something dawned on me, sort of a great feeling of independence, like a chicken out of its egg . . . this is a mess.

Patient B: There's another thing that's a terrible worry . . . why can't I use my common sense . . . and the most frightening thought of all . . . the awful part of it . . . it hurts kind of a deep hurt . . . it's kind of hard to describe.

Patient C: It scared me pea green . . . I find myself thinking absolutely rigid, stiff as a board . . . let me cogitate, I'm afraid I'm projecting . . . that gibbering about myself is an imposition, silly. This business of being terribly conscious of your talking. Torturing myself with name calling . . . I was terrified, it horrified me . . . thinking in *non sequiturs,* such a queer situation anyway. I can't feel differences, messy gray area where you can't jell.

Patient D: I felt terrible . . . I felt isolated . . . I felt attracted on that basis . . . why do I block it, push it away, don't remember . . . I get out of this kind of tightness with people . . . I become aware of it in a negative sense, not intrigued any more, never enjoyed being a spectator, I wanted to be a participant . . . mystified by the fact that . . . he goaded me.

The language of this group as a whole is noteworthy for the vividness with which the temperament and personality of the speaker emerge. Content is subordinated to atmosphere and to feeling tone; subjective reactions are clearly brought into focus, while facts and the sequence of events are given secondary consideration. This is brought about in part by the use of subjectively descriptive adjectives which show the reaction of the patient to an experience more clearly than they show the experience itself. Thus situations, experiences, and descriptions of people are most commonly reported in terms of the effect they had upon the patient—of how he experienced them. For example, the content is colored by phrases such as "I was overawed," "I felt blue," "I was fascinated," "I was scared pea green," "I was intrigued." The hysteric uses many phrases drawing attention to the self, explicitly describing reaction and feeling.

This same characteristic appears in the recollection of past events. The material recalled is richer in the evocation of subjective reaction than it is in factual content. The past emerges with vivid recollection of sensation, feeling, attitude, and inner experience. The time orientation is anchored in the present, in the current situation, and events are *revived* as they are recalled. Emotional attitudes tend to fuse, and much that belongs to the past is indiscriminately re-experienced as part of the current emotional state. This can be verified by noting the tense of verbs; frequently the past progressive tense is used in preference to the simple past or past perfect tense. Thus the patient says, "He was scolding me," rather than "He scolded me," or "He had scolded me." This same device is employed by good storytellers, especially in tales of atmosphere or suspense, and for much the same purpose.

The intention of the speaker does much to shape the language he uses. The hysteric is concerned with evoking in the listener an appropriate appreciation of the intensity, uniqueness, or magnitude of an experience. For this purpose words of emphasis or exaggeration, such as superlatives, are used. The vocabulary may on first acquaintance seem novel and unique, but repeated interviews reveal the narrowness of its range, as expressions reappear and detract from the flexibility of language. The initial impression of vividness also decreases as one discovers the extent to which the hysteric makes use of the conventions and clichés of the language community in which he operates. The debutante speaks current debutante language, only more so; the bobby soxer employs the idioms of her set, only

more so. The language of the hysteric is particularly revealing of both origins and aspirations toward certain group identifications. A personality trait to which the patient aspires becomes incorporated in the language pattern, where it is overused and presents a caricature of his aim. One person, who was impressed by clarity and logic, prefaced many of her statements with *so, therefore, on account of,* and other phrases implying causal relationships. The tendency to absorb psychiatric jargon and employ it readily appears frequently in this group.

The emotive aspect of language is thoroughly exploited by the hysteric.* He is involved in a world of wanting, willing, liking, loving, hating. The verbs bear witness to this: He *goes, gets, wants, can have,* or *does.* He *likes, loves, hates.* He is *surprised, sorry, sad, mad.* The passive voice does not occur frequently. Projection into the future is more likely to be in terms of *I want, I wish, I will*

---

* Highly charged dramatic situations occur so frequently in the life history reported by hysterics that it is legitimate to assume that this flavor is to some extent imparted, evoked, or provoked by the hysteric himself. Despite, or because of, the hysteric's constant immersion in what appears to be strong feeling and emotion, one becomes guarded in ascribing to him the experience of the emotion; one may question whether it is not a *perception* of emotion that he deals with rather than the experiences of emotion. Incidentally, two specific details in life situations seem to recur quite frequently among these patients. Evidence is often brought of early competition or rivalry in the family constellation for the affection of a parental figure. More often than not, the bulk of affection appeared to go elsewhere, leaving the patient with a sense of deprivation. The second point is that these patients frequently identify, in a total rather than partial way, with some person to whom they were likened in the past. For example, a patient may say, "Everyone told me I looked like my grandmother. She was a very nervous person. Maybe that's why I'm so nervous now." Then it develops that the grandmother died of carcinoma and that the patient's present phobic state includes a conviction that she has carcinoma.

than in terms of *I ought, I should, I might,* or *I could.* Language is used to evoke, manipulate, appeal, display; and various devices are used to draw the auditor into relationship as a spectator and a supporter. The thematic material centers around affect—the presence or absence of affection is all-important—and around strivings.

The thematic material deals with experiences in which the person is an active participant, and rarely utilizes the role of observer. There is a lively interjection of comments, and a working-over of the material with use of emphasis, contrast, and negation.

The discursive function of language at times seems lacking, and volubility is substituted for articulateness. When the discursive function rather than description is needed in order to analyze or reason about something, the pattern of language may abruptly change. The communication may become conspicuous for its lack of devices for imparting movement, relationship, qualification, elaboration, or condensation. The theme emerges, but the supporting structure of articulate language that would give it coherence is lacking. It is then that repetitive speech automatisms invade the texture of language: *I don't know, I guess, I think, I mean, I feel.*

For example, a patient was trying to give her reason for beginning her visits to the psychiatrist:

Well, there's my complex no doubt. I do have a complex—uh, of course, it isn't completely—uh, I know in the Bible it says to be humble, I've always grown up on that, more or less that way. You can trace it back to my childhood, I suppose, and my mother —I mean, you know you can always say things, like if I was ever a mother, no doubt my daughter would say things, so it wouldn't ever happen to your daughter but on concentrating on that you overlook some other little thing, so that's the way it is—anyway, I guess—at least it's—I think it is.

One would say that this patient for some reason cannot properly conceptualize an aspect of the mother-daughter relationship which troubles her. The problem is pointed to; she talks about it; but she does not crystallize it. Instead she becomes overloaded with words that add nothing to the effectiveness of communication. One might guess that this phenomenon occurs when repression deprives the person of the actual content, but leaves as residue a disturbed, distressed, or puzzled feeling.

To sum up, the language of the hysteric subordinates objective content to subjective impression and reaction. The focus shifts fluidly from the percept to the perceiver; the attitudes of the speaker emerge more strongly than the content. The expressive and emotive use of language—to evoke, manipulate, appeal, display—is prominent. The speaker attempts to draw the listener into a relationship as a biased spectator and supporter. A sense of immediacy and involvement in the present is conspicuous. Thematic material centers about feelings and wishes. The discursive functions of language are frequently ignored, and volubility is substituted for articulateness. There is a ready absorption of current language habits from the social environment, and a great deal of exaggerated emphasis; but a static quality eventually arises from the cumulative effect of the latter.

The Obsessive-Compulsive Patient

The following excerpts are from the recorded speech of four obsessive-compulsive patients:

Patient E: I don't know if there's anything new or not . . . I don't feel capable of deciding such matters but . . . at first I didn't care because I figured eventually I'd get better . . . it always used to bother me . . . if I could interest myself in collecting stamps, for instance, I never did have a hobby I could stick to. I had just started when I came here. I decided . . . I seem to be worse here—there I felt better.

Patient F: Whichever it was I made a fool of myself. At first I didn't like him but later I began to. Anyway I talked to him as though . . . I began to think—I mean I felt . . . the next day was Monday and I had to buy some books, a few books and things for the classes, which started Tuesday . . . I realize that it was not very pleasant . . . at various times, on numerous occasions I experienced such a thing—possibly it is, but actually I doubt it.

Patient G: Well, they definitely don't, things don't bother me as much as they did—if then—maybe if something should happen for a few brief minutes, I'd forget about it . . . I can really see . . . I don't actually think . . . I don't particularly care . . . it's   pleasant . . . an   unpleasant thing. . . .

Patient H: He seems rather out of place . . . I rather enjoy talking to him . . . for example, I never would . . . one time it even seemed to me . . . I don't intend to mention names but . . . I will restrict myself to four or five little items.

While the hysteric may be said to describe his world in panoramic view, the obsessive-compulsive presents the miniature—the world of the circumscribed and particular. For example, the question, "Well, how have things been?" is likely to elicit from the hysteric such a response as, "Yesterday was the most dismal and gloomy day of my life," while the obsessive-compulsive is more likely to say, "I felt worse yesterday than I do today." This same example may serve to illustrate two other characteristics. First, the tone of the obsessive-compulsive person's remarks is flat and colorless in comparison with the vitality of the hysteric's. Second, the obsessive-compulsive, at the same time that he telescopes the dimension from *life* to *yesterday-today,* places his scrutiny more emphatically on a *relationship*—here one of contrast—rather than on the subject itself. Whether a thing is or is not, whether

it is better or worse, whether it differs from another, and the manner and degree in which it differs, become important concerns. The content is not built up by cumulative descriptive effect, by an elaboration of qualities. Focus shifts from the thing, act, or event to an analysis of the relationship that is asserted.

The following is an excerpt from an obsessive-compulsive patient's comments about his school life:

It was during high school, one person I remember. I had—I had never seen much of him, but I had at various times talked with people who—I don't know whether they didn't like him, but I—I don't think they did. Anyway, he was somebody who did very well around the school and in every way he was a good student and good socially, but he didn't do anything in sports.

In discussing a similar period in life, a hysteric patient said the following:

The dormitory atmosphere was geared to a sore point, to my whole psyche. The lunatic fringe—a whole slew of second-string people who were amateurs, an atrocious, half-baked performance.

These examples illustrate the more intellectualized approach of the obsessive-compulsive, in contrast to the impressionistic quality frequently found in the accounts of the hysteric. The speaker in the first example uses words which designate, specify, and limit, rather than describe. Even when the descriptive and differentiating capacity is better developed and the use of language is richer, the same quality emerges, as shown in the following example quoted from another obsessive-compulsive patient:

It is difficult to compare that period with any other, but on the whole, I wouldn't say it tended to be exceptionally productive. In addition, I had a lot of odd quirks at this time—simple things, like little nervous habits which I can visibly show you now.

The descriptive and qualifying words—*difficult, any, exceptionally, productive, odd, this, simple, little, nervous, visibly* —lie within a cool, objective evaluating range. Thus in the obsessive-compulsive one can detect a mental set toward judgment and evaluation, in contrast to the mental set of the hysteric toward the immediate subjective response. These attitudes of the obsessive-compulsive may be conveyed in a range from everyday simple words such as *all, most, better, worse, good,* and *bad,* to more highly differentiated, perhaps pedantic, words such as *differently, rather, merely, possibly, advisedly,* and so on. In any event, a characteristic device of the obsessive-compulsive is the use of terms of quantity, comparison, and degree.

The obsessive-compulsive's shift in focus from the object with its attributes to the assertion of relationship is conveyed by a recurrence in different modes on different levels of language; it emerges from the texture of a total interview rather than in a small segment of speech. In one quite rigid person whose recorded interviews were available for a period of many months, the following points were noted. There were frequent contrasts of *then* and *now,* of *here* and *there,* of *yesterday* and *today.* There was a frequent use of negation linked with subsequent positive statement: *It isn't . . . it's. . . .* Adjectives and adverbs were used in such a way that their antonyms were immediately suggested and sometimes explicitly stated: *good* and *bad, better* and *worse, always* and *never.* Disjunctives such as *but* and *or* were frequently introduced. In another patient, the system of *pleasant* and *unpleasant, comfortable* and *uncomfortable, major* and *minor* played a leading role. For example, the following excerpt, which was set in a whole pattern of recurrent contrasts in time, place, quantity, and degree, suggests the continuous awareness of tension between opposites:

Well, things don't bother me as much as they did, but I still think about them, some of them aren't pleasant and some of the unpleasant things are both major and minor things.

This mental set of judgment or evaluation is even more clearly brought out by the choice of verbs frequently used by many obsessive-compulsive patients. Verbs of a thinking, knowing, implying, meaning, recognizing, agreeing, or restricting order are common: *figure, suppose, decide, intend, would say.* In using these words, a distance of observation and evaluation is placed between the speaker and the content—a distance further increased by the introduction of words and phrases such as *apparently, possibly, perhaps, without a doubt, it seems.* These words imply an attitude of abstraction and of interposing an intellectual, rational perspective between the experience and the experiencing person. This attitude is also shown by the frequent use of substantives denoting concepts and abstractions rather than specific feelings or objects. Words such as *decisions, energies, agreements, thinking, ambitions, feelings, desires* often make up a large bulk of the subject content. It may be argued that these characteristics appear in the speech of any person who is in a ruminative or speculative frame of mind. The point made here is that this very mental set is a prevailing one in the obsessive-compulsive; thus it emerges in the texture of much of his spontaneous speech and is mirrored in his language habits.

The emergence of feeling is indirect, a scrutiny turned inward. *I feel* is a favored expression to preface the communication of an inward state. While the hysteric shows a richer play of directly labeled emotive states—he hates, loves, desires, he is irked, angry, irritable—the obsessive-compulsive turns toward his inner state and designates it: he feels bothered, comfortable, uncomfortable, worse, better, pleasant, unpleasant, or perhaps awful, and this is often the extent of his discrimination of feeling. It may be that the *scrutiny* of feelings is substituted for the active *experience* of feelings, and this may account for the lameness of the characterization of inner states. As I have indicated, the hysteric overemphasizes the emotions to such a degree that a doubt is raised as to the genuine nature of the felt experience. The obsessive-compulsive underplays the description of emotion. He seems less aware of the *quality* of an affect than of the comparative degree of comfort or discomfort. Hence, when the *I feel* is used or implied as a subjective state, it often points to 'feelings' that denote forces and tensions (can't-can, must, capable-not capable, better-worse, pleasant-unpleasant) rather than the more qualitatively differentiated levels of affect such as pain, pleasure, despair, anger, delight, and so on.

The following phrases occurred within a short paragraph taken from the speech of an obsessive-compulsive:

I feel it's up to people . . . I don't feel capable of deciding matters . . . I feel as though I've fallen down . . . I get so low . . . I don't seem to be able . . . I can't get help . . . I have to make . . . I can't do . . . I get . . . I don't get . . . I must. . . .

These may be contrasted with the following excerpts from the speech of two hysteric patients:

I'm apt to . . . I'm curious about . . . I become aware . . . why do I block . . . I feel isolated . . . I feel guarded . . . I have a strong desire . . . I never enjoyed . . . I keep on wondering . . . I'm receptive to . . . I feel in retrospect. . . .

I find myself thinking . . . I wasn't that naïve . . . I felt sort of lousy . . . afraid I'm projecting . . . I'm very conscious of . . . I feel itchy . . . I don't want to be pegged . . . I'm not worried.

In the obsessive, the spectrum of emotional awareness seems to shrink into a leading motive, and this motive often points toward tensions and forces rather than toward differentiated affective states. It is also of note that this awareness of feeling is concerned with the self and

that comments about the feelings and inner states of others are more rare than in the talk of hysterics.

There are a number of structural devices which emerge quite characteristically in the talk of the obsessive-compulsive. These are: the frequency of prefatory statements and introductory remarks, the frequency of modifying clauses introduced by *that* or *which,* the frequent use of the disjunctives *or, if,* and *but,* the frequency of localization in time and place, and the repetition of words and phrases. All of these detract from the easy progression of ideas and introduce a monotonous, repetitive quality.

Thus in the language of the obsessive-compulsive, the emphasis is on the specific and circumscribed, with an underplaying of subjectively qualifying attributes. There is a concern with relationship in terms of quantity, comparison, degree, and assertion and negation. The person works over the immediacy of awareness to create distance between himself and the mental event; and self-awareness emerges in terms of observation and scrutiny rather than in terms of the direct apprehension of inner states. Although the range of 'feeling' experiences varies in different obsessive-compulsive persons, there is a common denominator in that tensions between opposites are stated rather than differentiated affective states. From a structural viewpoint, the language pattern is replete with such stylistic devices as prefatory statements, repetitions, and modifying clauses.

The Manic Patient

The following are excerpts from the recorded speech of four patients diagnosed as manic:

Patient 1: I am at your disposal. I should never have come here at all or to any of these places. My brother Bob is to blame for the whole business. He has always been different from me. If our relations were reversed, and I knew that my brother wanted me to be a certain place at a given time, I should be there regardless of cost for myself. Bob is a creature of routine. I know on what days he will ask me to ride, and can guess pretty well what he's going to say. He will always be like that. Now when my father had rheumatism and it was decided that if he could use a wheel chair that my aunt had once used, it would give him relief, why I said to my aunt, "When you go home I'll go with you and get the chair." I did go and lugged that wheel chair down four stories, wheeled it up the street, and lugged it to my father's room to save him a few hours of needless suffering. And when my father saw what I had done, he said, "Tom, I didn't suppose there was any person on earth who loved me so much." Bob wouldn't have done that. He would have seen that it was done. About eight years ago I wanted to go into business, and he said. . . .

Patient J: What have I been doing? I've been for a walk, I've done exercises in the gym, knitted, crocheted, read, visited. I had a delightful time last night, I'm having a delightful time here. I'm perfectly happy. I can be happy wherever I am. I have enough to eat, I'm never starved. I have a roof over my head. I could be deprived of anything and still be happy. Are you a medical doctor, too? Any brothers or sisters? How many? Who is Dr. W? Dr. C doesn't know what to make of me. He said, "You seem better."

Patient K: I guess you do the best work when you are younger but Goethe was older. My genders are not too good, I only studied German for a year. French I studied for ten years but it isn't the French a Frenchman would understand, but they say they do. The southern Germans are very kindly. I have never been to Prussia but they are very rude. Dr. S had the students psychoanalyze me and said they wished they had my mind. Dr. P would stake his reputation that nine-tenths of my trouble was goiter. S used to say. . . .

Patient L: My God, can a man have a brain as quick as that, can a man act so quickly, can he be a psychio creature—he must be mad. You must have met Mr. T,

haven't you? When he walked into it the other day it was all planned by God, not by my lawyer. I said I didn't care. I still have a few dollars. I found six dollars hidden away in little bits. When I left here, I went to a sale of records and Connie bought a few. I bought the Shostakovitch. She's like a little Dresden China doll. How did she come out of that family? Her mother is so dull. Do you know her sister? The father is the sensitive one, of course, but he likes bad radio music.

When one compares the manic patient's language with that of other groups, certain characteristics emerge prominently.* The neurotic groups have been described as conveying mental content in such a way that the person emerges clearly. The hysteric personality emerges in the subjective coloring by which experiences are shaped in the process of communication. In the obsessive-compulsive a colorless and distant intellectual scrutiny shapes the mental content, weighing it with values, judgments, comparisons, and contrasts. But the manic patient's communication shows little personal qualification of either a descriptive or evaluating order. The content is a factual, anecdotal account of external events and circumstances; a play-by-play account is given of what happened and who said what. The orientation is toward the external world of situations, events, and people, but the speaker is more of a spectator and commentator than an actively involved participant. His language often has a quality of literal clarity and uncompromising objectivity in reflecting reality as he perceives it; his language may be termed representational or reproductive.

One of the outstanding characteristics of the manic patient's language pattern is the extent to which associations deter-

---

* In a previous paper (Lorenz, Language behavior in manic patients. *A.M.A. Arch. Neurol. and Psychiat.* 69(1953), 14–26) the language habits of manic patients were analyzed in some detail, and this analysis will not be repeated here.

mine the content. Each event, image, or idea immediately brings up some other event, image, or idea; it is as if a stimulus is immediately acted upon in terms of associative mechanisms. While associative mechanisms are always a part of mental activity, they do not usually assume the degree of dominance noted here; ordinarily there is a grading and shading of this response as other levels of mental activity are at the same time brought into play, and associations are refined by a process of scrutiny, selection, and rejection. Ordinarily a person exerts some command over the associated images brought to mind and expressed; but in the manic the expression of associations appears to be independent of goal direction—the touching off of connections seems to occur before receptiveness, selectivity, and adaptation for use become fully integrated.

A striking characteristic of the manic patient's associations is their one-dimensional aspect. They operate mainly along a linear perspective of recognition and recall of observable and reportable phenomena. The associations are frequently retrospective, introducing reference to experiences of the past, to facts and information previously acquired. But the recall of previous experience is not shaped by the present perspective in a way which would allow for the emergence of new ideas; that is, past events are recalled but are not integrated into the present mental set. Moreover, the associations seldom lead to any further illumination of appraisal, but are an enumeration of qualities implicit in the general subject, or are related by contiguity in place, by continuity in time, or by similarity or contrast. This leads to a serial expansion of a topic or theme, with nothing very new being added. Clusters of ideas around a topic are formed; a tendency to listing, naming, and enumerating also appears.

Although opinions, observations, and pronouncements are freely scattered through this language pattern, the *interpretative,* subjective coloring to which eye and ear are accustomed is lacking in one sense. That is, the *reactive* quality of the speaker is more apparent than the *responsive.* The language expresses the speaker's opinion and attitude *toward* persons and events, but very little of the effect of persons or events upon the speaker; the quotations given earlier from Patient L illustrate this. Perhaps this is the reason why manic patients are rarely described as being "sensitive" to the qualities of another person, despite their often quite astute and telling observations of personalities and personality traits.

There are two ways in which manic patients seem to reveal something of their inner world. In the use of denial, exaggeration, and emphasis, one not infrequently finds a clue to the quality of the affective needs and drives. Patient J is an example of transparent denial of loneliness and deprivation. The other way is the self-evaluation which appears in the repetitive anecdotes describing the person's role in various situations and in the frequent reference to comments made about the person by others. Patient I is an example of this.

The recorded speech of the manic patient often shows a strong sense of movement and rhythm. The style may be deliberate and oratorical, or rapid, peremptory, and staccato. This seems to be brought about by the balancing of phrases in sentences, the repetition of words, alliteration, and plays on the sound of words. Even in his spoken language, the manic patient is more concerned with the external and perceptual facets of words and sentences than with the meaning conveyed. In language, as in dress, a liking for the decorative or bedecked is often obvious. Stylistic devices frequently employed are repetition, listing, enumerating, itemizing, and the use of rhetorical questions and direct quotations.

To oversimplify, the figure that emerges in the language patterns of the manic is that of the realist, concerned with his status and role in life—the man of opinion and prejudice. This is brought about by the object-oriented quality of his speech, which reproduces rather than interprets objective reality. Common characteristics are the response to a stimulus in terms of associations that are retrospectively directed, and the tendency to serial expansion of a topic or theme in terms of qualities contained within the topic or theme. There is a prevalence of opinions and pronouncements, with considerable use of words of denial, exaggeration, and emphasis. The language shows a rhythmic pattern, and stylistic devices include rhetorical questions, direct quotations, naming, listing, and itemizing.

The Paranoid Schizophrenic Patient

The following are excerpts from the speech of six paranoid schizophrenic patients:

Patient M: To that extent I understand correctly but not completely. I don't think that any question has ever been raised on that score. There is a question concerning the fact of whether he is my father, concerning the question of being my father. I know that in some cases such a question does arise, but for me it never has. I know he is my father. He is the man who has begotten me. He is also a Jew. There is no question about any of those things, or do you think there is a question?

Patient N: And suddenly I had an idea that the way we were acting was probably —and the way we were feeling was probably—uh—extremely—uh—disturbing or amusing to somebody else, in other words, it—it was so unusual—uh—different I was just wondering whether—feelings and way of acting—made others feel I was just a little bit odd, peculiar or something like that. I—I felt for the first time that I see the thing externally rather than internally,

not following, not doing the right thing, not following the right footsteps, being too critical.

Patient O: Well, I mean that would be the reaction—be radical. Your attitude would be radical. You never show much reaction. It—it's within one, it's a strain with one, you can call it tension. I am a certain amount of flesh, a certain amount of feeling. Being human, one can only take so much. It's like being hit hard when you're tired.

Patient P: I think the persistence in interpreting such adjustments are themselves signs of the conquest of tuberculosis of the human species. I think the treatment of relaxations brings on a breathlessness which is an outward sign of something—the material world in which there can be the least controversy, the least idiosyncratic interpretation, in which there is no deceit and in which can be found diverse kinds of life ranging from intense activity to intense retrospection.

Patient Q: Take the situation such as the weather that has been here in Massachusetts. The situation is such that it's nip and tuck whether we're going to have precipitation or not. That—that same situation occurs elsewhere in the world as well as— uh—at different seasons of the year, in various parts of the world. So I think that it's possible for—uh—formation of precipitation by man on a scale that might possibly be useful in local areas. Certainly not extensively. Take trails, skywriting as an example. Producing any kind of weather conditions under controlled circumstances for the purposes of testing equipment.

Patient R: I didn't have anybody as such come up to me and say I was thinking about anything in particular, but the mood or emotions seem to be transferable. Notice that people become angry, two people start to argue, if one becomes angry the other one frequently follows suit. Or in a similar situation then the person has unpleasant thoughts and unpleasant mood is created and perhaps that is transferable too. Seems to me from my observations to be so.

If one asks oneself, after listening to a few minutes' spontaneous speech by a manic patient, what the person has said, it is not difficult to marshal quickly a number of facts, bits of information, and observations that have been communicated. If one applies the same test to a schizophrenic patient's talk, one is apt to begin with, "Well, I guess he was talking *about* . . . ," and then to have difficulty in abstracting the substance of his communication. An elusive and ambiguous *meaning* seems to be there, but is not readily reproduced. The thought which the paranoid schizophrenic expresses is not securely anchored in a recognizable world of time, place, and events. A preference is often given to observations beginning with impersonal constructions; a concept or idea is preceded by *there are* or some similar wording—for instance, *there are people who, there is a question of, there seems to be, there are doctors who.* Jespersen (21) calls this type of sentence "existential." The ambiguous beginning is reminiscent of the traditional beginning of the fairy tale, "Once upon a time, there was. . . ." This may offer a clue to interpretation. In ordinary usage, sentences of this existential order appear when the speaker is more concerned with the idea itself than with the external event. The fact that this sentence structure is frequent in schizophrenic language implies, perhaps, the contemplation of ideas rather than a focus upon actual happenings. A further extension of this mental set is noted in the frequent use of qualifications such as *the way in which, the manner in which,* and *certain* used in a nondefinitive way, as *certain other patients, in a certain way, a certain amount.* Many negations are employed, but not in the sense of denial as used by the manic and neurotic, who are apt to say *it is not* or *I don't think.* The paranoid schizophrenic uses negation more frequently in combination with verbs denoting understanding: *I don't know, I don't understand,* or *I don't believe, there is no indication.* References are frequently made to people or persons without specifying the particular group or person implied: *people say, people seem, they think, a person may.* Often the indefinite *one, you,* or *they* is used in preference to *I: One supposes, one may assume, you think and then you find it isn't so.* Sometimes sentences begin with a verb and omit the active agent entirely. The quotations from Patients Q and R are illustrative.

The ambiguous phrases used seem to imply that the speaker does not have in mind a particular or specific person, situation, or thing. References to something outside the speaker are left undefined. A thought *about* something occupies his attention and is presented as such. For example, Patient R says, "Notice that people become angry, two people start to argue, if one becomes angry the other one frequently follows suit . . . the person has unpleasant thoughts and unpleasant mood is created and perhaps that is transferable too." This statement gives the speaker's ideas about transference of moods and emotions; he uses as illustration a second idea of how this occurs, not an example of what actually has happened in some time and place to a particular person. While everyone at times appropriately makes statements which have no referent in a particular reality external to the speaker, the paranoid schizophrenic makes such statements frequently and inappropriately, suggesting that his frame of mind is oriented more toward his private world of thought than to the shared world. The distinction made by Russell (22) between content of thought and object of thought seems applicable, in that schizophrenic language appears to indicate a preoccupation with ideational content, rather than with the object about which ideas are expressed.

In the verbs used, much emphasis is placed upon the hypothetical, the possible, the contingent. Like the obsessive-compulsive, the paranoid schizophrenic uses such verbs as *seem, appear, suggests.* But the schizophrenic's use of this abstract, cognitive level of verbs extends further to imply a different mental set. Verbs in the area of *meaning, understanding, interpreting, intimating,* and *wondering* are frequently used—verbs which imply conjecture rather than established certainty. In addition, these patients use rather more frequently than do the other groups such words as *why, curious, interested, aware*—words which seem to imply uncertainty or questioning.

The schizophrenic's universe of discourse lies more in the ideational world than in the world of objective reality. The talk is apt to be about abstractions—*situations, effects, relationships, purposes, circumstances,* referring to ideas that have no specific or tangible counterpart in reality. For example, in a brief conversation one person used the following substantives: possibilities, limitations, persistence, assumption, guidance, diversity, happiness, interpretation, facts. Not only are terms such as these abstractions and conceptualizations, but many of them have the quality of being open rather than closed concepts, in the sense that the possibilities of interpretation are left open and are not specified or restricted.

A peculiarity that appears in the sicker patients is the use of compounded substantives in which ordinarily unrelated concepts are bound together and treated as a single unit. One patient speaks of "thought-emotions." Other patients repeatedly use phrases which serve as a subject unit, such as "difference in aggression and approach," "thought that is not positive in its total aspect," "circumstances of will power and ideas," "controlled circumstances," "human desires and possibilities," "insight and speculation," "emotions and thinking together," "transference of feelings."

When a paranoid schizophrenic patient seeks an analogy and creates a metaphor, words with emotional connotation suggestive of primitive feelings, aggression, violence, and the like, often make their appearance; the universe of discourse is disrupted by the appearance of such words—which are often quite concrete and specific—from an entirely different level of awareness. For example, the patient I have just mentioned, in a conversation primarily about moods, thoughts, and ideas, introduced the words *stampede of animals,* as his spontaneous analogy in discussing his ideas of thought transference: "I just assume that they [people] can feel the mood a person is in. . . . I suppose stampede of animals comes from some kind of transference." Another intellectualizing schizophrenic said: "I feel that it is even my duty to say them, to my father, and you are required to say them, then it would be necessary for me to have the courage or the *guts* to say them, and yet, to tell the truth, I do not know if they seem relevant." Thus the force of the unconscious in its undifferentiated, instinctual form appears as clearly in language habits as it does in other areas of behavior.

When one looks for evidence of the quality of object relationships in the language pattern of the paranoid schizophrenic, two features appear with some consistency. The question of whether one thing has a relationship to something else is a recurrent preoccupation that is explored in a variety of ways. While in the neurotic patient language attention is divided between content and the agent (11), in the paranoid schizophrenic, attention is divided between content and the third person. This third person may be a specific antagonist—*he,* or a system, or a scheme. The meaning of such words as symbols emerges more strongly than their use as referents. Thus the father, or brother, or friend who is referred to as *he* emerges as a figure or a role more than as a specific person existing in reality. Sometimes a name is coined for the antagonist; for one patient it was *the boss.* Originally there had been a particular boss in the patient's life history who had become the focal point for the patient's paranoid concern. During the patient's illness of many years, a gradual revision occurred in the meaning of *the boss*. Once it had had primarily a denotative meaning, with a peripheral connotation of a figure of power and authority. But as the original boss receded in time and place, a shift occurred in the balance of these two meanings, until the reference to the particular boss dropped out and the more peripheral meaning became central. Thus the word became a symbol for a constellation of boss-like qualities. Preoccupation with a system or scheme often emerges clothed in an extremely technical vocabulary. Despite the show of erudition, the patient's vocabulary of technical words has a 'pseudo' quality; it is impressive but not appropriate.

The passive orientation of the paranoid schizophrenic is shown by the frequent use of the passive voice and other verb constructions suggestive of passivity —for instance, *I am being bothered, was created in me, happens to me, things done to me, had to*. The reflexive use of pronouns, such as *myself*, is also frequent. Sometimes the kind of verbs used forms a distinct recurring pattern which emphasizes the passive attitude of the particular patient. One patient is being *forced*, another *controlled*, a third *selected* for a role, and other patients are *scorned* or *loved* or *hated*.

On the whole, the language of the schizophrenic group is more varied and richer in scope than that of other groups. During the earlier phases of illness this is most pronounced. Repetition of ideas, and eventually repetition of the same formulation of ideas, finally occurs in this illness, as it does in other groups; this may be more closely associated with chronicity than with the differential diagnosis of an illness. The impression of a richer scope of language may arise in part from the qualities of the words used. These are, as has been indicated, often terms of open meaning which imply and suggest a greater variety of ideas than those actually expressed.

To sum up what I have said of the paranoid schizophrenic patient, an important characteristic is the shift in focus from the object of thought to the inner content of thought. Some of the ways in which this is reflected are the use of existential sentences, beginning with *there are,* and the use of unidentified referents, such as *you, they* or *people*. Transitions in focus occur from the denotative to the connotative meaning of terms; a preference is shown for abstract terms capable of unlimited extension of meaning; and compound substantives are created. In the unconscious selection of metaphor and analogy, the paranoid schizophrenic sometimes expresses primitive feelings. Passivity is reflected in the use of verbs and the structure of sentences. The language pattern, in contrast to that of the neuroses, shows markedly less direct emphasis upon *I*. The signposts of language which provide orientation in dimensions of time, place, and circumstance, are less in evidence than in the language of the manic.

The language pattern of the psychotic patients shows to some degree many of the features demonstrated in the neuroses; but in the psychotic groups the person as an individual with specific traits and temperament emerges less clearly in the language pattern. The person, as expressed in his style and manner of speaking, is initially obscured by the expression of a *process* of thinking and experiencing. However, as one becomes familiar with the characteristics of the mental processes which appear in the language of these psychotic patients, the temperament and characteristics of the particular patient become more apparent.

Language expresses the person's selection and organization of the reality, inner and outer, which he perceives. It points to a mental set, a perceptual attitude or *Anschauung,* toward the world. The experimental psychology of perception already provides empirical demonstration for the existence of such preferences or dispositions. Klein (23) describes "leveling" and "sharpening" tendencies in perceptual organization. In language behavior, the hysteric's tendency to fuse impressions and the obsessive's tendency toward the particular and discrete, suggests parallel evidence on other levels of behavior.

How does the language pattern express a disposition or mental set? The use of verbs, as one element of the pattern, serves as an illustration. Suzanne Langer (24) states that "the present tense proves to be a far more subtle instrument than either grammarian or rhetorician generally realize, and has quite other uses than characterization of present acts and facts." She goes on to show how the present tense is used in daydreams, phantasy, and lyric style, the more formal past tense being used for the narrative, the story. It is of interest to note that the hysteric is at home in the present tense, and indeed often transposes the tense of verbs from past to present when deeply absorbed in his comments. Ryle (25) calls attention to the difference between dispositional verbs such as *know, believe,* and *aspire,* which signify ability, tendency, proneness-to, and modal verbs such as *can, must,* and *may* which imply an inference made. He contrasts a "capacity" verb such as *can* with a "tendency" verb such as *believe.* In the schizophrenic language here studied tendency verbs are prominent. The question can at least be raised whether the person who frequently uses dispositional verbs, who constantly *believes, wonders,* and *supposes,* is differently oriented toward reality from the person who disposes of reality in terms of what *does, can, could,* or *must* happen.

Spitzer (12), by a procedure of working from the peripheral detail toward the inner coherence or pattern of language, arrives at a psychological judgment about Racine, who by his language is characterized as "sifting reality through the intellect." Among the groups studied here, reality appears to be sifted through different media. The hysteric prefers to sift reality through emotional impression, the obsessive-compulsive sifts through evaluation and judgments, the manic represents literally, and the schizophrenic abandons representation of outward reality for a presentation of his inward reality.

Any of the language characteristics here described may be present in "normal" people. The consistent emergence of a particular habit in a particular person reflects some of the stable psychological attitudes of the person. People who have some psychological mechanisms in common also appear to have some habits of using language in common. These habits happen to stand out more sharply in the neuroses and psychoses in the sense indicated by James *—that pathology provides a crystallization and a better view in isolation of processes present in the "normal." The patients here discussed may be viewed as representatives of marked extremes in certain modes of mental and emotional adjustment, and their language habits as illustrative of these extreme tendencies.

References

1. Anderson, H. H., and Anderson, G. L. *An introduction to projective techniques.* New York: Prentice-Hall, 1951. See especially chapters 12 to 16.

2. Wolff, Werner. *The expression of personality.* New York: Harper, 1953.

3. Allport, Gordon W., and Vernon, Phillip E. *Studies in expressive movement.* New York: Macmillan, 1933.

4. Eysenck, H. J. *Dimensions of personality.* London: Routledge and Kegan Paul, 1947.

5. Hodges, Herbert A. *The philosophy of Wilhem Dilthey.* London: Routledge and Kegan Paul, 1952.

6. Von Hartmann, Eduard. *Philosophy of the unconscious.* New York: Macmillan, 1884.

7. Stout, G. F. *Analytic psychology.* Volume II. New York: Macmillan, 1902.

* For a discussion of James' point of view, see reference footnote on p. 145.

8. Bühler, Karl. *Sprach theorie.* Jena: Gustav Fisher, 1934.

9. Cassirer, Ernst. *The philosophy of symbolic forms: I, language.* New Haven: Yale University Press, 1953.

10. Piaget, Jean. *The language and thought of the child.* London: Routledge and Kegan Paul, 1952.

11. Lee, Vernon. *The handling of words.* New York: Dodd, Mead, 1923.

12. Spitzer, Leo. *Linguistics and literary history.* Princeton: Princeton University Press, 1948.

13. Sherman, Mandel. Verbalization and language symbols in personality adjustment. *Amer. J. Psychiatry,* **95**(1938), 621–640.

14. Newman, Stanley. Behavior patterns in linguistic structure. In *Language, culture and personality.* Menaska: Sapir Memorial Publication Fund, 1941.

15. Newman, Stanley, and Mather, Vera G. Analysis of spoken language of patients with affective disorders. *Amer. J. Psychiatry,* **94** (1938), 913–942.

16. Sanford, Filmore H. Speech and personality: a comparative case study. *Character and Personality,* **10**(1942), 169–198.

17. Glauber, I. P. Speech characteristics of psychoneurotic patients. *J. Speech Disorders,* **9**(1944), 18–30.

18. Phillips, Leslie, and Smith, Joseph G. *Rorschach interpretation: advanced technique.* New York: Grune & Stratton, 1953.

19. Piotrowski, Zigmund. The Rorschach method as a prognostic aid in the insulin treatment of schizophrenia. *Psychiatric Quart.,* **15**(1941), 807–822.

20. Rapaport, David. *Diagnostic psychological testing.* Volume II. Chicago: Year Book Publishers, 1946.

21. Jesperson, Otto. *The philosophy of grammar.* London: George Allen and Unwin, 1951.

22. Russell, Bertrand. *The analysis of mind.* London: George Allen and Unwin, 1951.

23. Klein, George S. The personal world through perception. In R. Blake and G. V. Ramsey (eds.), *Perception, an approach to personality.* New York: Ronald Press, 1954.

24. Langer, Suzanne K. *Feeling and form.* New York: Scribner's, 1953.

25. Ryle, Gilbert. *The concept of mind.* London: Hutchinson House, 1952.

6. THE PSYCHOSES

PSYCHOSIS IS THE MOST SEVERE mental illness and, as a result, very often requires hospitalization for the protection of both the psychotic individual and others around him. Being very severe, lay people find it difficult to think of disorders subsumed in this category as understandable entities and often dismiss it as "crazy" and beyond comprehension. Most psychologically oriented theorists prefer to think that psychotic behavior and thought represent an attempt to express something meaningful, albeit in a difficult and idiosyncratic manner. Several of the papers which follow focus on schizophrenia, the most widely studied of all psychotic disturbances. Schizophrenia has usually been thought of as including at least four major reaction patterns, and several minor ones, with very ambiguous shades of meaning between many categories. Recently a growing number of theorists have preferred to divide this disorder into two groups; those with process and reactive features. The term "process" refers to a long-term development with a poor prognosis, and reactive to a more situational development in an individual with a more adequate history and a better prognosis for recovery. Herron's paper provides a review of the research and theoretical material on schizophrenia viewed in this way. The paper by Arieti presents an attempt to further understand the thought processes in schizophrenia. Haley presents a viewpoint which focuses on the communicative experiences of the person who has developed schizophrenia and emphasizes the "double-bind" type of communication which he feels characterizes the schizophrenic. In the final paper on this disorder Lu reports an interesting study of the differences in the relationships between mothers and their schizophrenic and nonschizophrenic children. The paper by Cohen and her associates is an excerpt from a larger work based on the intensive study of a small group of manic-depressive patients. The selection by Harry Stack Sullivan reflects his thinking about the essential features and dynamic elements in the paranoid disorders.

The Process-Reactive Classifications of Schizophrenia

WILLIAM G. HERRON
SAINT BONAVENTURE UNIVERSITY

The heterogeneity of schizophrenic patients and the lack of success in relating variable schizophrenic functioning to diagnostic subtypes (28) have indicated the serious limitations of the current neuropsychiatric classification of schizophrenia. In response to these limitations interest has arisen in a two-dimensional frame of reference for schizophrenia. Such a conception is based on the patient's life history and/or prognosis. A number of terms—malignant-benign, dementia praecox-schizophrenia, chronic-episodic, chronic-acute, typical-atypical, evolutionary-reactive, true-schizophreniform, process-reactive—have appeared in the literature describing these two syndromes. Process schizophrenia involves a long-term progressive deterioration of the adjustment pattern with little chance of recovery, while reactive schizophrenia indicates a good prognosis based on a history of generally adequate social development with notable stress precipitating the psychosis.

In view of the current favorable interest in this approach to the understanding of schizophrenia (47) the present

Reprinted from *Psychological Bulletin,* **59**(1962), 329–343, with the permission of the American Psychological Association and the author.

investigation is designed as an evaluative review of the literature on the process-reactive classification.

Early Prognostic Studies

The process-reactive distinction had its implicit origin in the work of Bleuler (7). Prior to this the Kraepelinian influence had prevailed, with dementia praecox considered an incurable deteriorative disorder. Bleuler, while adhering to an organic etiology for schizophrenia, nonetheless observed that some cases recovered. This conclusion opened the field to a series of subsequent prognostic studies (5, 9, 20, 21, 22, 23, 30, 31, 32, 33, 36, 38, 42, 44, 51, 52, 53, 54) eventuating in formalized descriptions of the process and reactive syndromes in terms of specific criteria.

These early studies can be classified in three general categories: studies correlating the outcome of a specific type of therapy with certain prognostic variables, studies descriptively evaluating prognostic criteria, and studies validating a prognostic scale.

The first category is illustrated by the attempt of Chase and Silverman (9) to correlate the results of Metrazol and insulin shock therapy with prognosis, using 100 schizophrenic patients treated with Metrazol and 40 schizophrenic patients treated with insulin shock.

In the first part of this study the probable outcome of each of the 150 patients was estimated on the basis of prognostic criteria. The criteria considered of primary importance for a favorable prognosis were: short duration of illness, acute onset, obvious exogenic precipitating factors, early prominence of confusion, and atypical symptoms (marked by strong mixtures of manic-depressive, psychogenic, and symptomatic trends), and minimal process symptoms (absence of depersonalization, derealization, massive primary persecutory ideas, and sensations of influence, conscious realization of personality disintegration, bizarre delusions and hallucinations, marked apathy and dissociation of affect). When these conditions were reversed the prognosis was least favorable. The following factors were considered less important for a favorable prognosis: history of previous illness, pyknic body type, extrovert temperament and adequate prepsychotic life adjustment, catatonic and atypical subtypes. Asthenic body type, introversion, inadequacy of prepsychotic reactions to life situations, onset of illness after the age of 40, and hebephrenic and paranoid subtypes were considered indicative of unfavorable prognosis. Age of onset under 40, sex, education, and abilities, and hereditary background were not considered of prognostic importance. An analysis of the prognostically significant factors resulted in the evaluation of the prognosis for each case as good, fair, or poor.

Following termination of shock treatment all patients were followed-up for an average of 10 months and divided into three groups; much improved, improved, and unimproved. A comparison of the prognostic assessments with the results of shock indicated that of 43 cases in which the prognosis was considered good,

33 showed remissions, while of 74 cases with a poor prognosis, 63 did not improve. It was concluded that shock therapies were effective in cases of schizophrenia in which the prognosis was favorable, but were of little value when the prognosis was poor.

The second part of the research involved a reanalysis of the prognostic criteria in the light of the results of shock treatment. Short duration of illness and the absence of process symptoms were the most significant factors for favorable outcome, while long duration of illness (more than 2 years) and the presence of process symptoms were primary in determining poor prognosis.

A descriptive review of prognostic factors is seen in Kant's (23) description of the benign (reactive) syndrome as cases in which clouding and confusion prevail, or in which the schizophrenic symptoms centered around manic-depressive features or cases with alternating states of excitement and stupor with fragmentation of mental activity. Malignant (process) cases are characterized by direct process symptoms. These include changes in the behavior leading to disorganization, dulling and autism, preceding the outbreak of overt psychosis. The most subtle manifestation of this is the typical schizophrenic thought disturbance. The patient experiences the process as a loss of normal feeling of personality activity and the start of experiencing a foreign influence applied to mind or body.

The third category includes the Elgin Prognostic Scale, constructed by Wittman (51) to predict recovery in schizophrenia. It is comprised of 20 rating scales weighted according to prognostic importance: favorable factors are weighted negatively, and unfavorable factors are assigned positive weights. Initial validation involved 343 schizophrenic cases placed on shock treatment. Wittman and Steinberg (54) performed a follow-up study on 804 schizophrenics and 156 manic-depressive patients. The Elgin scale proved effective in predicting the outcome of therapy in 80–85% of the cases in both studies, and has been utilized in the work of Becker (3, 4), King (27), and McDonough (35) to distinguish the process-reactive syndrome. Included in the subscales of the Elgin scale are evaluations of pre-psychotic personality, nature of onset, and typicality of the psychosis relative to Kraepelin's definition.

Studies with Detailed Process-Reactive Criteria

The synthesis of early studies is found in the research of Kantor, Wallner, and Winder (24) establishing detailed criteria for distinguishing the two syndromes on the basis of case history material. A process patient would exhibit the following characteristics: early psychological trauma, severe or long physical illness, odd member of the family, school difficulties, family troubles paralleled by sudden changes in the patient's behavior, introverted behavior trends and interests, history of a breakdown of social, physical, and/or mental functioning, pathological siblings, overprotective or rejecting mother, rejecting father, lack of heterosexuality, insidious gradual onset of psychosis without pertinent stress, physical aggression, poor response to treatment, lengthy stay in the hospital, massive paranoia, little capacity for alcohol, no manic-depressive component, failure under adversity, discrepancy between ability and achievement, awareness of a change in the self, somatic delusions, a clash between the culture and the environment, and a loss of decency. In contrast, the reactive patient has these characteristics: good psychological history, good physical health, normal family member, well adjusted at school, domestic troubles unaccompanied by behavioral disruptions in the patient,

extroverted behavior trends and interests, history of adequate social physical, and/or mental functioning, normal siblings, normally protective accepting mother, accepting father, heterosexual behavior, sudden onset of psychosis with pertinent stress present, verbal aggression, good response to treatment, short stay in the hospital, minor paranoid trends, good capacity for alcohol, manic-depressive component present, success despite adversity, harmony between ability and achievement, no sensation of self-change, absence of somatic delusions, harmony between the culture and the environment, and retention of decency.

The first three criteria apply to the patient's behavior between birth and the fifth year; the next seven, between the fifth year and adolescence; the next five, from adolescence to adulthood; the last nine, during adulthood. Using these 24 points to distinguish the two syndromes they tried to answer three questions:

1. Do diagnoses based upon the Rorschach alone label as nonpsychotic a portion of the population of mental patients who are clinically diagnosed as schizophrenic?

2. Can case histories of clinically diagnosed schizophrenics be differentiated into two categories: process and reactive?

3. Are those cases rated psychotic from the Rorschach classed as process on the basis of case histories, and are those cases judged nonpsychotic from the Rorschach classified as reactive from the case histories?

Two samples of 108 and 95 patients clinically diagnosed as schizophrenic were given the Rorschach and rated according to the process-reactive criteria. In the first sample of 108 patients, 57 were classified as psychotic and 51 nonpsychotic on the basis of the Rorschach alone, while in the second sample, of 74 patients who could be rated as process or reactive, 36 were classified as psychotic, and 38 as non-psychotic from their Rorschach protocols. Those patients who were rated as reactive from their history were most often judged non-psychotic from the Rorschach, and those rated process from the case histories were most often judged as psychotic from the Rorschach.

Only one judge was used in the second sample to rate the patients as process or reactive, but two judges were used in the first sample. Of the 108 patients in this sample, both judges rated 86 cases, and were in agreement on 64 of these, which is greater than would be expected by chance.

However, the accuracy of the schizophrenic diagnosis is questionable in this study. If the Rorschach diagnosis is followed, then it appears that reactive schizophrenics are not psychotic. Furthermore, the psychiatric diagnosis appears to be somewhat contaminated because it was established on the basis of data collected by all appropriate services of the hospital, including psychological examinations. A similar type of contamination may have been present in classifying patients as process or reactive because one judge had reviewed each case previously and had seen psychological examination and history materials together prior to making his ratings. Three difficulties can be found with the criteria for process-reactive ratings. First, case histories are often incomplete and the patient is unable or unwilling to supply the necessary information. Second, it is difficult to precisely apply some of the criteria. For example, what is the precise dividing line between oddity and normality within the family? Third, in order to classify a patient it is necessary to set an arbitrary cut off point based on the number of process or reactive characteristics a patient has. Such a procedure needs validation.

Nonetheless, the results of this study support the view that schizophrenics can be classified as process or reactive, and that these syndromes differ in psychological functioning.

Another rating scale which has been used extensively to distinguish prognostically favorable and prognostically unfavorable schizophrenics was developed by Phillips (45). The scale was developed from the case histories of schizophrenic patients who were eventually given shock treatment. The scale evaluates each patient in three areas: premorbid history, possible precipitating factors, and signs of the disorder. Premorbid history includes seven items on the social aspects of sexual life during adolescence and immediately beyond, seven items on the social aspects of recent sexual life, six items on personal relations, and six items on recent premorbid adjustment in personal relations. The sections of the scale which reflect the recent sexual life and its social history are the most successful in predicting the outcome of treatment. The items in the scales are arranged in order of increasing significance for improvement and nonimprovement away from the score of three, which is the dividing point between improved and unimproved groups. The premorbid history sub-scale has been utilized as the ranking instrument in the studies described by Rodnick and Garmezy (49, 15).

Another approach to the separation of schizophrenics into prognostic groups uses the activity of the autonomic nervous system as the basis for division (39, 40, 41). Meadow and Funkenstein (39) worked with 58 schizophrenic patients tested for autonomic reactivity and for abstract thinking. Following therapy the patients were divided into two groups, good or poor, depending on the outcome of the treatment. The battery of psychological tests included the similarities and block design subtests of the Wechsler-Bellevue scale, the Benjamin Proverbs test, and the object sorting tests. The physiological test involved the systolic blood pressure reaction to adrenergic stimulation (intravenous Epinephrine) and cholinergic stimulation (intramuscular Mecholyl). On the basis of the physiological and psychological testing, schizophrenic cases were divided into three types: Type I, characterized by marked response to Epinephrine, low blood pressure, and failure of the blood pressure to rise under most stresses, loss of ability for abstract thinking, inappropriate affect, and a poor prognosis; Type II, characterized by an entirely different autonomic pattern, relatively intact abstract ability, anxiety or depression, and a good prognosis; Type III, showing no autonomic disturbance, relatively little loss of abstract ability, little anxiety, well organized paranoid delusions, and a fair prognosis.

However, as Meadow and Funkenstein (39) point out, there is considerable overlap of the measures defining these types so that the classification must be tentative. Also, of the psychological tests used, only Proverbs distinguished significantly between the patients when they were classified according to autonomic reactivity, while Block Design failed to distinguish significantly among any of the types. Further research using this method of division (40, 41) served as a basis for investigations of the process-reactive syndromes by King (27) and Zuckerman and Grosz (57).

King (27) hypothesized that predominantly reactive schizophrenics would exhibit a higher level of autonomic responsiveness after the injection of Mecholyl than predominantly process schizophrenics. The subjects were 60 schizophrenics who were classified as either process or reactive by the present investigator and an independent judge using the criteria of Kantor et al. (24). Only those subjects were used on which there was classificatory agreement. This resulted in 22 process and 24 reactive patients. In order to consider the process-reactive syndrome as a continuum, 16 subjects were randomly selected from these two groups and were ranked by two independent raters.

While the patient was lying in bed shortly after awaking in the morning the resting systolic blood pressure was determined. The patient then received 10 milligrams of Melcholyl intramuscularly, and the systolic blood pressure was recorded at intervals up to 20 minutes. Then the maximum fall in systolic blood pressure (MFBP) below the resting blood pressure following the injection of Mecholyl was computed for the different time intervals. There was a significant difference in the MFBP score for the reactives as compared with the normals. For the 16 subjects, the correlation between the sets of ranks on the process-reactive dimension and MFBP was —.58.

In a second part of the study 90 schizophrenics, none of whom had participated in the first part, were classified as either process, process-reactive, or reactive, using the criteria of Kantor et al. (24). On this basis the subjects were divided into three groups of 24. Also, scores for 22 subjects were obtained on the Elgin Prognostic Scale, and 12 of these were rated independently by two raters. The MFBP scores were 17.04 for the process group, 22.79 for the process-reactive group, and 26.62 for the reactive. Using an analysis of variance a significant F score occurs at the .01 level. The correlation between the Elgin Prognostic Scale and the MFBP scores for 22 patients was —.49.

Results of both parts of the study revealed that the patients classified as reactive exhibited a significantly greater fall in blood pressure after the administration of Mecholyl than the process patients. This evidence points to diminished physiological responsiveness in process, but not in reactive schizophrenia. However, Zuckerman and Grosz (57) found that process schizophrenics showed a significantly greater fall in blood pressure following the administration of Mecholyl than reactives. Since these results contradict King's findings the question of the direction of responsiveness to Mecholyl in these two groups requires further investigation before a conclusion can be reached.

Process-Organic Versus Reactive-Psychogenic

Brackbill and Fine (8) suggested that process schizophrenics suffer from an organic impairment not present in the reactive case. They hypothesized that there would be no significant differences in the incidence of "organic signs" on the Rorschach between a group of process schizophrenics and a group of known cases of central nervous system pathology, and that both organic and process groups would show significantly more signs of organic involvement than the reactive group.

The subjects consisted of 36 patients diagnosed as process schizophrenics and 24 reactive schizophrenics. The criteria of Kantor et al. (24) were used to describe the patients as process or reactive. Patients were included only when there was complete agreement between judges as to the category of schizophrenia. Also included in the sample were 28 cases of known organic involvement. All patients were given the Rorschach, and the protocols were scored using Piotrowski's (46) 10 signs of organicity.

Using the criterion of five or more signs as a definite indication of organic involvement there was no significant difference between the organic and process groups, but both groups were significantly different from the reactives. Considering individual signs, four distinguished between the reactive and organic group, while two distinguished between process and reactive groups. The authors concluded that the results supported the hypothesis that process schizophrenics react to a perceptual task in a similar manner to that of patients with central nervous system pathology. No specific hypothesis was made about individual Rorschach signs, but color naming, completely absent in the reactives, was indicated as an example of concrete thinking and inability to abstract, suggesting that one of the critical differences between process and reactive groups is in terms of a type of thought disturbance.

This study does not provide detailed information about the manner of establishing the diagnosis of schizophrenia or about the judges deciding the process and reactive syndromes. Also, a further difficulty is the admitted inadequacy of the organic signs, since 66 per cent of cases with organic pathology in this study were false negatives according to the Rorschach criteria. Thus while the existence of the process and reactive syndromes is supported by the results of this investigation, there is less evidence of an organic deficit in process schizophrenics.

Becker (3) pointed out that the consistency of the prognostic findings in schizophrenia has led to postulating two kinds of schizophrenia: process, with an organic basis, and reactive, with a psychological basis. He rejects this conclusion because research data in this area shows considerable group overlap, making it clinically difficult and arbitrary to force all schizophrenics into one group or the other. Also, if schizophrenia is a deficit reaction which may be brought about by any combination of 40 or more etiological factors, then the conception of two dichotomous types of schizophrenia is not useful. Finally, he maintains that 20 years of research have failed to find clear etiological differences between any subgroupings.

Instead, Becker stated that process and reactive syndromes should be conceived as end points on a continuum of levels of personality organization. Process reflects a very primitive undifferentiated personality structure, while reactive indicates a more highly organized one. He hypothesized that schizophrenics more nearly approximating the process syndrome would show more regressive and immature thinking processes than schizophrenics who more nearly approximate the reactive syndromes. His sample consisted of 51 schizophrenics, 24 males and 27 females, all under 41 years of age. Their thinking processes were evaluated by the Rorschach and the Benjamin Proverbs test. The 1937 Stanford-Binet vocabulary test was used to estimate verbal intelligence. A Rorschach scoring system was used which presumably reflected the subjects' level of perceptual development, while a scoring system was devised for the Proverbs which reflected levels of abstraction. Since there is a high relationship between intelligence and ability to interpret proverbs, a more sensitive index of a thinking disturbance was considered to be a discrepancy score based on the standard score difference between a vocabulary estimate of verbal intelligence and the proverbs score. Process and reactive ratings were made on the Elgin Prognostic Scale.

The Rorschach mean perceptual level score and the Elgin Prognostic Scale correlated $-.599$ for men and $-.679$ for women, indicating a significant relationship between the process-reactive dimension as evaluated from case history data and disturbances of thought processes as measured by the Rorschach scoring system. The proverbs-vocabulary discrepancy score was significantly related to the process-reactive dimension for men, but not for women. No adequate explanation was found for this sex difference, which mitigates the results. A further difficulty occurs because the case history and test evaluations were made by the same person. However, the results in part support the hypothesis, indicating evidence for a measurable dimension of regressive and immature thinking related to the process-reactive dimension.

McDonough (35), acting on the assumption that process schizophrenia involves central nervous system pathology

specifically cortical in nature, hypothesized that brain damaged patients and process schizophrenics would have significantly lower critical flicker frequency (CFF) thresholds and would be unable to perceive the spiral aftereffect significantly more often than reactive schizophrenics and normals. Four groups of 20 subjects each were tested. The organic group consisted of individuals with known brain damage. One hundred and sixty-one schizophrenic case histories were examined, and 76 were chosen from this group to be rated on the Elgin Prognostic Scale. The 20 patients receiving the lowest point totals were selected as being most reactive, while those with the 20 highest scores were considered most process.

Results of the experiment revealed that organic patients were significantly different from all other groups in CFF threshold and ability to perceive the spiral aftereffect. Process and reactive schizophrenics did not differ from each other on either task, but reactive schizophrenics had higher CFF thresholds than normals. These results do not indicate demonstrable cortical defect in either process or reactive schizophrenia.

Process-Poor Premorbid History Versus Reactive-Good Premorbid History

Rodnick and Garmezy (49), discussing the problem of motivation in schizophrenia, reviewed a number of studies in which the Phillips prognostic scale was used to classify schizophrenic patients into two groups, good and poor. For example, Bleke (6) hypothesized that patients whose prepsychotic life adjustment was markedly inadequate would have greater interferences and so show more reminiscence following censure than patients whose premorbid histories were more adequate.

The subjects were presented with a list of 14 neutrally toned nouns projected successively on a screen. Each subject was required to learn to these words a pattern of pull-push movements of a switch lever. For half the subjects in each group learning took place under a punishment condition, while the remaining subjects were tested under a reward condition. The subjects consisted of 40 normals, 20 poor premorbid schizophrenics, and 20 good premorbid schizophrenics. The results confirmed the hypothesis.

A reanalysis of Dunn's (11) data indicated that a poor premorbid group showed discrimination deficits when confronted with a scene depicting a mother and a young boy being scolded, but good premorbid and normal subjects did not show this deficit.

Mallet (37) found that poor premorbid subjects in a memory task for verbal materials showed significantly poorer retention of hostile and non-hostile thematic contents than did good premorbid and normal subjects. Harris (17) has found that in contrast to goods and normals poor premorbids have more highly deviant maternal attitudes. They attribute more rejective attitudes to their mothers, and are less able to critically evaluate their mothers. Harris (18) also found differences among the groups in the size estimation of mother-child pictures. The poors significantly overestimated, while the goods underestimated, and the normals made no size error.

Rodnick and Garmezy (49) reported a study using Osgood's (43) semantic differential techniques in which six goods and six poors rated 20 concepts on each of nine scales selected on the basis of high loadings on the evaluative, potency, and activity factors. Good and poor groups differed primarily on potency and activity factors. The poors described words with negative value, as more powerful and active. The goods could discriminate among concepts, but the poors tended to see most concepts as powerful and active.

Rodnick and Garmezy (49) also investigated differences in authority roles in the family during adolescence in good and poor premorbid patients. While results were tentative at that time, they suggested that the mothers of poor premorbid patients were perceived as having been more dominating, restrictive, and powerful, while the fathers appeared ineffectual. The pattern was reversed in the good premorbid patients.

Alvarez (1) found significantly greater preference decrements to censured stimuli by poor premorbid patients. This result was consistent with the results of Bleke's (6) and Zahn's (55) observations of reversal patterns of movement of a switch lever following censure. These experiments suggested an increased sensitivity of the poor premorbid schizophrenic patient to a threatening environment.

These studies reported by Rodnick and Garmezy (49) indicated that it was possible, using the Phillips scale, to effectively dichotomize schizophrenic patients. However, the Phillips scale had predictive validity only when applied to male patients. Within this form of reference it was also possible to demonstrate differences between goods and poors in response to censure, and in perception of familial figures. Variability in the results of schizophrenic performance was considerably reduced by dichotomizing the patients, but it was often impossible to detect significant differences between the performance of good premorbid schizophrenics and normals. Rodnick and Garmezy (49) suggest that the results be considered as preliminary findings pending further corroboration, though providing support for the concept of premorbid groups of schizophrenics differing in certain psychological dimensions.

Process-Reactive Empirical-Theoretical Formulations

Fine and Zimet (14, 56) used the same population employed by Kantor et al. (24) and the same criteria for distinguishing the process and reactive patients. For this study only those cases were included where there was complete agreement among the judges as to the category of schizophrenia. They studied the level of perceptual organization of the patients as shown on their Rorschach records. The process group was found to have significantly more immature, regressive perceptions, while the reactive group gave more mature and more highly organized responses. The findings indicated that archaic and impulse-ridden materials break through more freely in process schizophrenia, and that there is less ego control over the production of more regressive fantasies. Zimet and Fine (56) speculated that process schizophrenia mirrors oral deprivation of early ego impoverishment, so that either regression or fixation to an earlier developmental stage is reflected in his perceptual organization. In contrast, it is possible that the reactive schizophrenic's ego weakness occurs at a later stage in psychosexual development, and any one event may reactivate the early conflict.

An amplification of the process-reactive formation has been suggested by Kantor and Winder (25). They hypothesized that schizophrenia can be understood as a series of responses reflecting the stage of development in the patient's life at which emotional support was severely deficient. Schizophrenia can be quantitatively depicted in terms of the level in life to which the schizophrenic has regressed, and beyond which development was severely distorted because of disturbing life circumstances. The earlier in developmental history that severe stress occurs, the more damaging

the effect on subsequent interpersonal relationships. Sullivan (50) suggested five stages in the development of social maturity: empathic, prototaxic, parataxic, autistic, and syntaxic. The most malignant schizophrenics are those who were severely traumatized in the empathic stage of development when all experience is unconnected, there is no symbolism, and functioning is at an elementary biological level. The schizophrenic personality originating at this stage may show many signs of organic dysfunction. Prognosis will be most unfavorable, and delusional formation will tend to be profound.

In view of the primitive symbolic conduct and the lack of a self-concept in the prototaxic stage, the schizophrenic personality referable to this stage will be characterized by magical thinking and disturbed communication. The delusion of adoption often occurs. However, these patients are more coherent than those of the previous level.

The parataxic schizophrenic state involves the inability of the self-system to prevent dissociation. The autonomy of the dissociations result in the patient's fear of uncontrollable inward processes. Schizophrenic symptoms appear as regressive behavior attempting to protect the self and regain security in a threatening world. Delusional content usually involves world disaster coupled with bowel changes. Nihilistic delusions are common. While there is evidence of a self-system in these patients, prognosis remains unfavorable.

The patient who has regressed to the autistic stage, although more reality oriented than in the previous stages, is characterized by paranoid suspiciousness, hostility, and pathological defensiveness against inadequacy feelings. A consistent system of delusions will be articulated and may bring the patient into conflict with society. However, prognosis is more favorable at this stage than previously.

An individual at the syntaxic level

has reached consensus with society, so that if schizophrenia occurs it will be a relatively circumscribed reaction. Onset will be sudden with plausible environmental stresses, and prognosis is relatively good.

Becker (4) also elaborated on the lack of a dichotomy in schizophrenia. Individual cases spread out in such a way that the process syndrome moves into the reactive syndrome, so that the syndromes probably identify the end points of a dimension of severity. At the process end of the continuum the development of personality organization is very primitive, or involves severe regression. There is a narrowing of interests, rigidity of structure, and inability to establish normal heterosexual relationships and independence. In contrast, the reactive end of the continuum represents a higher level of personality differentiation. The prepsychotic personality is more normal, heterosexual relations are better established, and there is greater tolerance of environmental stresses. The remains of a higher developmental level are present in regression and provide strength for recovery.

Becker (4) factor analyzed some of the data from his previous study (3). The factored matrix included a number of background variables, the 20 Elgin Prognostic Scale subscores, and a Rorschach genetic level score (*GL*) based on the first response to each card. Seven centroid factors were extracted from the correlation matrix. Factors 4, 6, and 7 represented intelligence, cooperativeness, and marital status of parents, respectively. The highest loadings on Factor 5 were history of mental illness in the family, excellent health history, lack of precipitating factors, and clouded sensorium. The Rorschach *GL* score and the Elgin scales did not load significantly on Factors 4 through 7.

The remaining three factors parallel the factors Lorr, Wittman, and Schanberger (34) found with 17 of the 20 El-

gin scales using an oblique solution instead of the orthogonal solution used in this study. Factor 1 is called schizophrenic withdrawal, loading on defect of interest, insidious onset, shut-in personality, long duration of psychosis, and lack of precipitating factors. At one end this factor defines the typical process syndrome, while the other end describes the typical reactive syndrome. The Rorschach *GL* score loaded —.46 on Factor 1.

Factor 2, reality distortion, loads on hebephrenic symptoms, bizarre delusions, and inadequate affect. Rorschach *GL* score loaded —.64 on this factor. Factor 3 loaded on indifference and exclusiveness-stubbornness. The opposite pole of this factor involves insecurity, inferiority, self-consciousness, and anxiety. Rorschach *GL* score loaded .25 on this factor.

Further analysis indicated that when Factors 1 and 2 were plotted against each other an oblique rotation was required, introducing a correlation of from .60 to .70 between schizophrenic withdrawal and reality distortion factors. Similar obliqueness was found between Factors 2 and 3, suggesting the presence of a second-order factor.

However, the sampling of behavior manifestations in the Elgin scale overweights the withdrawal factor, which gives Factor 1 undue weight and biases the direction of a second-order factor toward the withdrawal factor. Also, it is not possible to accurately locate second-order factors with only seven first-order factors as reference points. In addition, sample size and related sampling errors limited inferences about a second-order factor. There is the suggestion, however, of the existence of a general severity factor, loading primarily schizophrenic withdrawal and reality distortion.

The author suggests utilizing the evidence from this study to form an index of severity of psychosis which could be used to make diagnoses with prognostic significance. This diagnostic procedure would include factor estimates of schizophrenic withdrawal and emotional rigidity, based on Elgin scale ratings, and reality distortion, based on the Rorschach *GL* score.

Garmezy and Rodnick (15) pointed out that despite failure to find support for a fundamental biological deviation associated with schizophrenia (26), the view of schizophrenia as a dichotomous typology influenced either by somatic or psychic factors has continuously been advanced. They maintain that on the basis of empirical evidence there is little support for a process-organic versus reactive-psychogenic formulation of schizophrenic etiology.

Reviewing a series of studies using the Phillips scale as a dichotomizing instrument (1, 6, 10, 11, 12, 13, 16, 18, 29, 49, 55), Garmezy and Rodnick concluded that the results indicate two groups of schizophrenic patients differing both in prognostic potential and sensitivity to experimental cues. There is an interrelationship among the variables of premorbid adequacy, differential sensitivity to censure, prognosis, and types of familial organization. This suggests a relationship between varying patterns of early experience and schizophrenia, though it does not embody the acceptance of a given position regarding psychological or biological antecedents in schizophrenia.

Reisman (48), in an attempt to explain the heterogeneous results of psychomotor performance in schizophrenics, suggested that there were two groups of schizophrenics, process and reactive, differing in motivation. The process group was seen as more withdrawn and indifferent to their performance, and consequently reflecting a psychomotor deficit not present in reactives. In order to test this hypothesis 36 reactives, 36 process patients, and 36 normals performed a card-sorting task. The groups were distinguished according to the criteria of Kantor, Wallner, and Winder

(24). On Trial 1 all subjects were requested to sort as rapidly as possible. Then the subjects were assigned to one of four experimental conditions, with an attempt made to equate across the experimental conditions for age, estimated IQ, length of hospitalization, and initial sorting time. Condition 1 (FP) involved sorting the cards seven more times and if the sort was fast the subjects were shown stress-arousing photographs. If they sorted slowly no photographs were shown. Condition 2 (SP) was the reverse of this. Condition 3 (FL) and Condition 4 (SL) were similar to the first two conditions except that a nonreinforcing light was used instead of the pictures. After Trial 8 all subjects were informed that there would be no more pictures or light, but were asked to sort rapidly for three more trials. With four conditions on Trials 2 through 8, 10 subjects from each of the three groups participated in each of the two picture conditions, while eight subjects from each group participated in each of the light conditions.

The results indicated that the normals performed about the same under all conditions. The process group under FP sorted as fast as normals, but performed slowly under the other three conditions, while the reactives were slowest under FP but were as fast as normals under the other three conditions. Within all three groups performance under FL did not differ significantly from performance under SL. Under FL and SL, however, reactives and normals sorted more rapidly than the process group. These results supported the hypothesis of a motivational deficit for process schizophrenics. The results also indicated that the pictures were negatively reinforcing for the reactives, while the process patients were motivated to see them. This suggested a withdrawal differential. The withdrawal of the process patients is of such duration that supposedly threatening photographs cause little anxiety. In contrast, reactive withdrawal is motivated by an environment that recently became unbearable. Confronted with pictures representing this environment the reactive patient experiences anxiety and avoidance. However, the results of this experiment are in contrast to the findings of Rodnick and Garmezy (49) that prolonged exposure to social censure will result in greater sensitivity to that stimulation.

Summary

This review of all the research on the process-reactive classification of schizophrenia strongly indicates that it is possible to divide schizophrenic patients into two groups differing in prognostic and life-history variables. Using such a division it is also possible to demonstrate differences between the two groups in physiological measures and psychological dimensions.

The result of such an approach has been to clarify many of the heterogeneous reactions found in schizophrenia. It also appears that the dichotomy is somewhat artificial and really represents end points on a continuum of personality organization. The most process patient represents the extreme form of personality disintegration, while the most reactive patient represents the extreme form of schizophrenic integration. The reactions of this type of patient are often difficult to distinguish from behavior patterns of normal subjects. There does not appear to be any significant evidence to support the contention of a process-organic versus a reactive-psychogenic formulation of schizophrenic etiology.

It is difficult to decide on the most appropriate criteria for selecting schizophrenic subjects so as to reduce their response variability. Preferences are generally found for one of three sets of criteria: Kantor, Wallner, and Winder's (24) items, the Elgin Prognostic Scale (52), or the Phillips Scale (45). The criteria of Kantor et al. (24) does not provide a quantitative ordering of the variables, and is descriptively vague in several dimensions as well as depending upon life history material which is not always available. While the Elgin Scale does provide a quantitative approach, it also has the disadvantages of descriptive vagueness and excessive dependence upon life history material. The Phillips Scale eliminates some of these difficulties, but its validity is limited to the adequacy or inadequacy of social-sexual premorbid adjustment. The need for more feasible criteria may be met by the factor analysis of pertinent variables to obtain a meaningful severity index (4), or by using rating scales in which the patient verbally supplies the necessary information. An example of the latter is the Ego Strength Scale (2), recently utilized in distinguishing two polar constellations of schizophrenia; a process type with poor prognosis and grossly impaired abstract ability, and a reactive type characterized by good prognosis and slight abstractive impairment (Herron, in press).

This need for more efficient differentiating criteria mitigates some of the significance of present findings using the process-reactive dimension. Nonetheless, the process-reactive research up to this time has succeeded in explaining schizophrenic heterogeneity in a more meaningful manner than previous interpretations adhering to various symptom pictures and diagnostic subtypes. Consequently, there appears to be definite value in utilizing the process-reactive classification of schizophrenia.

References

1. Alvarez, R. R. A comparison of the preferences of schizophrenic and normal subjects for rewarded and punished stimuli. Unpublished doctoral dissertation, Duke University, 1957.

2. Barron, F. An ego-strength scale which

predicts response to psychotherapy. *J. Consult. Psychol.,* **17**(1953), 327–333.

3. Becker, W. A genetic approach to the interpretation and evaluation of the process-reactive distinction in schizophrenia. *J. Abnorm. Soc. Psychol.,* **53**(1956), 229–236.

4. Becker, W. C. The process-reactive distinction: A key to the problem of schizophrenia? *J. Nerv. Ment. Dis.,* **129**(1959), 442–449.

5. Benjamin, J. D. A method for distinguishing and evaluating formal thinking disorders in schizophrenia. In J. S. Kasanin, Ed., *Language and thought in schizophrenia.* Berkeley: Univ. California Press, 1946. Pages 66–71.

6. Bleke, R. C. Reward and punishment as determiners of reminiscence effects in schizophrenics and normal subjects. *J. Pers.,* **23**(1955), 479–498.

7. Bleuler, E. *Dementia praecox.* New York: International Univ. Press, 1911.

8. Brackbill, G., and Fine, H. Schizophrenia and central nervous system pathology. *J. Abnorm. Soc. Psychol.,* **52**(1956), 310–313.

9. Chase, L. S., and Silverman, S. Prognosis in schizophrenia: An analysis of prognostic criteria in 150 schizophrenics treated with Metrazol or insulin. *J. Nerv. Ment. Dis.,* **98**(1943), 464–473.

10. Dunham, R. M. Sensitivity of schizophrenics to parental censure. Unpublished doctoral dissertation, Duke University, 1959.

11. Dunn, W. L. Visual discrimination of schizophrenic subjects as a function of stimulus meaning. *J. Pers.,* **23**(1954), 48–64.

12. Englehart, R. S. Semantic correlates of interpersonal concepts and parental attributes in schizophrenia. Unpublished doctoral dissertation, Duke University, 1959.

13. Farina, A. Patterns of role dominance and conflict in parents of schizophrenic patients. *J. Abnorm. Soc. Psychol.,* **61**(1960), 31–38.

14. Fine, H. J., and Zimet, C. N. Process-reactive schizophrenia and genetic levels of perception. *J. Abnorm. Soc. Psychol.,* **59**(1959), 83–86.

15. Garmezy, N., and Rodnick, E. H. Premorbid adjustment and performance in schizophrenia: Implications for interpreting heterogeneity in schizophrenia. *J. Nerv. Ment. Dis.,* **129**(1959), 450–466.

16. Garmezy, N., Stockner, C., and Clarke, A. R. Child-rearing attitudes of mothers and fathers as reported by schizophrenic and normal control patients. *Amer. Psychologist,* **14**(1959), 333 (Abstract).

17. Harris, J. G., Jr. A study of the mother-son relationship in schizophrenia. Unpublished doctoral dissertation, Duke University, 1955.

18. ———. Size estimation of pictures as a function of thematic content for schizophrenic and normal subjects. *J. Pers.,* **25**(1957), 651–672.

19. Herron, W. G. Abstract ability in the process-reactive classification of schizophrenia. *J. Gen. Psychol.,* **67**(1962), 147–154.

20. Hunt, R. C., and Appel, K. E. Prognosis in psychoses lying midway between schizophrenia and manic-depressive psychoses. *Amer. J. Psychiat.,* **93**(1936), 313–339.

21. Kant, O. Differential diagnosis of schizophrenia in light of concepts of personality stratification. *Amer. J. Psychiat.,* **97**(1940), 342–357.

22. ———. A comparative study of recovered and deteriorated schizophrenic patients. *J. Nerv. Ment. Dis.,* **93**(1941), 616–624.

23. ———. The evaluation of prognostic criteria in schizophrenia. *J. Nerv. Ment. Dis.,* **100**(1944), 598–605.

24. Kantor, R. E., Wallner, J., and Winder C. L. Process and reactive schizophrenia. *J. Consult. Psychol.,* **17**(1953), 157–162.

25. Kantor, R. E., and Winder, C. L. The process-reactive continuum: A theoretical proposal. *J. Nerv. Ment. Dis.,* **129**(1959), 429–434.

26. Kety, S. S. Biochemical theories of schizophrenia. *Science,* **129**(1959), 1528–1532, 1590–1596, 3362–3363.

27. King, G. Differential autonomic responsiveness in the process-reactive classification of schizophrenia. *J. Abnorm. Soc. Psychol.,* **56**(1958), 160–164.

28. ———. Research with neuropsychiatric samples. *J. Psychol.,* **38**(1954), 383–387.

29. Kreinik, P. S. Parent-child themas and concept attainment in schizophrenia. Unpublished doctoral dissertation, Duke University, 1959.

30. Kretschmer, E. *Physique and character.* New York: Harcourt, Brace, 1925.

31. Langfeldt, G. The diagnosis of schizophrenia. *Amer. J. Psychiat.,* **108**(1951), 123–125.

32. Lewis, N. D. C. *Research in dementia praecox.* New York: National Committee for Mental Hygiene, 1936.

33. ———. The prognostic significance of certain factors in schizophrenia. *J. Nerv. Ment. Dis.,* **100**(1944), 414–419.

34. Lorr, M., Wittman, P., and Schanberger, W. An analysis of the Elgin Prognostic scale. *J. Clin. Psychol.,* **7** (1951), 260–263.

35. McDonough, J. M. Critical flicker frequency and the spiral aftereffect with process and reactive schizophrenics. *J. Consult. Psychol.,* **24**(1960), 150–155.

36. Malamud, W., and Render, N. Course and prognosis in schizophrenia. *Amer. J. Psychiat.,* **95**(1939), 1039–1057.

37. Mallet, J. J. Verbal recall of hostile and neutral thematic contents by schizophrenic and normal subjects. Unpublished doctoral dissertation, Duke University, 1956.

38. Mauz, F. *Die Prognostik der endogen Psychosen.* Leipzig: G. Theime, 1930.

39. Meadow, A., and Funkenstein, D. H. The relationship of abstract thinking to the automatic nervous system in schizophrenia. In P. H. Hoch and J. Zubin, Eds. *Relation of psychological tests to psychiatry.* New York: Grune and Stratton, 1952. Pages 131–144.

40. Meadow, A., Greenblatt, M., Funkenstein, G. H., and Solomon, H. C. The relationship between the capacity for abstraction is schizophrenia and the physiologic response to autonomic drugs. *J. Nerv. Ment. Dis.,* **118** (1953), 332–338.

41. Meadow, A., Greenblatt, M., and Solomon, H. C. "Looseness of association" and impairment in abstraction in schizophrenia. *J. Nerv. Ment. Dis.,* **118**(1953), 27–35.

42. Milici, P. Postemotive schizophrenia. *Psychiat. Quart.,* **13**(1939), 278–293.

43. Osgood, C. E. The nature and measurement of meaning. *Psychol. Bull.,* **49**(1952), 197–237.

44. Paskind, J. A., and Brown, M. Psychosis resembling schizophrenia occurring with emotional stress and ending in recovery. *Amer. J. Psychiat.,* **96**(1940), 1379–1388.

45. Phillips, L. Case history data and prognosis in schizophrenia. *J. Nerv. Ment. Dis.,* **117**(1953), 515–525.

46. Piotrowski, Z. A. Positive and negative Rorschach organic reactions. *Rorschach Res. Exch.,* **4**(1940), 143–151.

47. Rabin, A. I., and King, G. F. Psychological studies. In L. Bellak, Ed. *Schizophrenia: A review of the syndrome.* New York: Logos, 1958. Pages 216–278.

48. Reisman, J. M. Motivational differences between process and reactive schizophrenics. *J. Pers.,* **28**(1960), 12–25.

49. Rodnick, E. H., and Garmezy, N. An experimental approach to the study of motivation in schizophrenia. In M. R. Jones, Ed. *Nebraska symposium on motivation: 1957.* Vol. V. Lincoln: Univ. Nebraska Press, 1957. Pages 109–184.

50. Sullivan, H. S. *Conceptions of modern psychiatry.* Washington: W. A. White Psychiatric Foundation, 1947.

51. Wittman, P. A scale for measuring prognosis in schizophrenic patients. *Elgin State Hosp. Pap.,* **4**(1941), 20–33.

52. ———. Follow-up on Elgin prognosis scale results. *Ill. psychiat. J.,* **4**(1944), 56–59.

53. Wittman, P., and Steinberg, L. Follow-up of an objective evaluation of prognosis in dementia praecox and manic-depressive psychoses. *Elgin State Hosp. Pap.,* **5**(1944), 216–227. (a)

54. Wittman, P., and Steinberg, D. L. Study of prodromal factors in mental illness with special references in schizophrenia. *Amer. J. Psychiat.,* **100**(1944), 811–816. (b)

55. Zahn, T. P. Acquired and symbolic affective value as determinant of size estimation in schizophrenic and normal subjects. *J. Abnorm. Soc. Psychol.,* **58**(1959), 39–47.

56. Zimet, C. N., and Fine, H. J. Perceptual differentiation and two dimensions of schizophrenia. *J. Nerv. Ment. Dis.,* **129**(1959), 435–441.

57. Zuckerman, M., and Grosz, H. J. Contradictory results using the mecholyl test to differentiate process and reactive schizophrenia. *J. Abnorm. Soc. Psychol.,* **59**(1959), 145–146.

Special Logic of Schizophrenic and Other Types of Autistic Thought

SILVANO ARIETI

NEW YORK CITY

In 1925 William Alanson White (1) complained that there was almost nothing in the literature on the mechanisms of thought processes in schizophrenia—

Reprinted from Psychiatry, **11**(1948), 325–338, by special permission of the William Alanson White Psychiatric Foundation, Inc., holder of the copyright, and the author.

a subject which he considered of paramount importance. With due regard to a few exceptions—outstanding among which are the contributions of Vigotsky (2) and those published in the monograph edited by Kasanin (3) with Sullivan, Goldstein, Von Domarus and other authors collaborating—the same complaint could be repeated today. The same complaint would be even more justified in regard to researches concerning a particular aspect of thought processes in schizophrenia and other psychopathological states—namely, the study of logic.

From the time of Aristotle, it has been known that the healthy human mind follows the so-called laws of thought. It is also known that the deranged mind does not always respect these laws of thought: that is, it may think "illogically." With an important exception, Von Domarus, to be mentioned later, science has not gone much beyond this point. The lack of research in this field is partially due to a consuetudinary aversion which physicians in particular and biologists in general have for any method which is not strictly empirical. On the other hand, philosophers and logicians themselves have to be blamed and for the opposite reason —that is, on account of a nonpsychological attitude which to physicians seems almost untenable. Since they are interested in thought itself and not in the thinker, they naturally have ignored the condition of health, illness, age, and the environmental situation in which the thinker happens to be.

It is my contention that the study of logic in mental illnesses may clarify several problems which have not yet been clarified by other methods of research. Furthermore, it is contended that it is not even necessary to be a logician in order to undertake such study. It will be shown in this paper that the application of a few elementary principles will open new avenues of research, the value of which cannot be properly estimated perhaps at the present time.

In the last half century, medical psychology has felt more and more the impact of psychoanalysis. The attention of an increasing number of workers has been concentrated upon the dynamics of emotional factors, conscious or unconscious, and has been more or less detracted from other aspects of psychological problems. Freudian psychoanalysis has made it possible to interpret the symptoms of the patient as a result of emotional forces or as attempts by the patient to fulfill psychologically what otherwise would be unfulfillable wishes. This interpretation and its derivatives have advanced tremendously knowledge and therapeutic means, especially in the field of psychoneuroses, but in the psychoses have led to a standstill. For instance, psychoanalysis may explain why a deluded patient wishes unconsciously that his delusion be reality, but has not explained how it is that he intellectually accepts his delusion as reality, in spite of contradictory evidence. An obsessive patient who has, let us say, the obsession that if he does not wear a special suit, his mother is going to die, recognizes fully the absurdity of such an idea. It is true that he will continue to wear that special suit, but he knows that the idea is illogical. He has retained sufficient logical power to recognize the unreal nature of such obsession. Psychoanalysis will help in explaining what unconscious emotional factors and dissociated ideas have determined this symptom. In the case of the deluded patient also, psychoanalysis may explain what unconscious emotional factors have determined the delusional idea but will not explain why such an idea is accepted as reality. It does not explain what change has occurred in the logic powers of the patient so that he is not able any longer to test reality. To say that the patient's ego is disintegrating is to satisfy oneself with obscure words.

In another publication, (4) I have suggested that the schizophrenic does not think with ordinary logic. His thought is not illogical or senseless, but follows a different system of logic which leads to deductions different from those usually reached by the healthy person. The schizophrenic is seen in a position similar to that of a man who would solve mathematical problems not with our decimal system but with another hypothetic system and would consequently reach different solutions. In other words, the schizophrenic seems to have a faculty of conception which is constituted differently from that of the normal man. It was further demonstrated that this different faculty of conception or different logic is similar to the one which is followed in dreams, in other forms of autistic thinking, and in primitive man. It was consequently called paleologic, to distinguish it from our usual logic which is generally called Aristotelian, since Aristotle was the first to enunciate its laws. It is not meant in this article that Aristotelian logic is correct in an absolute sense. The author is aware of the criticisms to which this logic has been subjected. Aristotelian logic is used only as a frame of reference, and only *relatively* to paleologic thinking.

In this paper the laws of paleologic, as they are deduced especially from the study of schizophrenic thought and dreams, will be examined in detail. I will then discuss in what situations and why a person may abandon a system of logic and adopt one which, as a rule, is repressed. This contribution should be considered preliminary in nature; further research is necessary to differentiate other laws of this archaic type of logic.

Von Domarus Principle

Paleologic is to a great extent based on a principle enunciated by Von Domarus.

(5, 6) This author, as a result of his studies on schizophrenia, formulated a principle which, in slightly modified form, is as follows: *Whereas the normal person accepts identity only upon the basis of identical subjects, the paleologician accepts identity based upon identical predicates.* For instance, the normal person is able to conclude "John Doe is an American citizen," if he is given the following information: "Those who are born in the United States are American citizens; John Doe was born in the United States." This normal person is able to reach this conclusion because the subject of the minor premise, "John Doe," is contained in the subject of the major premise, "those who are born in the United States."

On the other hand, suppose that the following information is given to a schizophrenic: "The President of the United States is a person who was born in the United States. John Doe is a person who was born in the United States." In certain circumstances, the schizophrenic may conclude: "John Doe is the President of the United States." This conclusion, which to a normal person appears as delusional, is reached because the identity of the predicate of the two premises, "a person who was born in the United States," makes the schizophrenic accept the identity of the two subjects, "the President of the United States" and "John Doe."

The mechanisms or successive steps of this type of thinking are not necessarily known to the schizophrenic who thinks in this way automatically, as the normal person applies automatically the Aristotelian laws of logic even without knowing them. For instance, a schizophrenic patient thinks without knowing why that the doctor in charge of the ward is her father and that the other patients are her sisters. A common predicate—a man in authority—leads to the identity between the father and the physician. Another common predicate—

females in the same position of dependency—leads the patient to consider herself and the other inmates as sisters.

At times the interpretation of this type of thinking requires more elaboration. For instance, a patient of Von Domarus' (5) thought that Jesus, cigar boxes, and sex were identical. Study of this delusion disclosed that the common predicate, which led to the identification, was the state of being encircled. According to the patient, the head of Jesus, as of a saint, is encircled by a halo, the package of cigars by the tax band, and the woman by the sex glance of the man.

At times paleologic thought is even more difficult to interpret because the principle of Von Domarus is applied only partially; that is, some partial identity among the subjects is based upon partial or total identity of the predicate. For instance, a person who is conceived by a schizophrenic as having a quality or characteristic of a horse may be thought of with a visual image consisting of part man and part horse. In this case one subject, the person, is partially identified with the other subject, the horse, because of a common characteristic—for instance, strength. It is well known how frequently similar distortions and condensations appear in hallucinations and drawings of schizophrenics. Similar conceptions appear in mythologies of ancient people and of primitives of today. As a matter of fact, anthropologic studies may disclose to the careful reader how often the principle of Von Domarus is applied in primitive thinking. Numerous studies, outstanding among which is the one by Storch, (7) have emphasized the similarities between primitive and schizophrenic thought, but the common underlying principles of logic which rule this thought have received no mention. Werner (8) writes: "It is one of the most important tasks of the developmental psychology to show that the advanced form of thinking characteristic of Western civilization is only one form among many, and that more primitive forms are not so much lacking in logic as based on logic of a different kind. The premise of Aristotelian logic that, when a thing is A it cannot at the same time be B, will not hold through for the primitive. . . ." Werner, however, does not attempt to enunciate the principles of a different logic. He does not add that for the primitive A may be B if A and B have only a quality (predicate) in common, although in his outstanding book, *Comparative Psychology of Mental Development,* he gives numerous examples proving this fundamental fact.

A step forward toward the interpretation of this way of thinking has been made by Max Levin (9) who compares schizophrenic thought to that of young children. Levin concludes that the patient as well as the young child "cannot distinguish adequately between a symbol and the object it symbolizes." For example, a middle-aged schizophrenic, speaking of an actor whom she admired, said, "He was smiling at me." The patient had seen on the cover of a magazine a picture of the actor in the act of smiling. Thus she had confused a picture of the actor with the actor himself. Levin reports that a 27-month-old child, drinking milk while looking at the picture of a horse, said "Give milk to the horse." At 25 months, the same child, looking at the picture of a car, tried to lift the car from the picture and said to his father, "Daddy, get car out." For the child the pictured objects were real. Levin is correct in his observations. However, he has not been able to see them in the light of Von Domarus' principle. What appears to us as a symbol of the object is not a symbol for the schizophrenic or for the child but a duplication of the object. The two objects have been identified on account of the similar appearance. Levin makes other exceptionally interesting observations which, however, do not receive complete interpretation, and he is led to the conclusion that infantile and schizophrenic concepts "are the result of amusing mixtures of relevant and irrelevant." For instance, he reports that "a child of two knew the word 'wheel' as applied, for example, to the wheel of a toy car. One day, at twenty-five months, as he sat on the toilet, the white rubber guard (supplied with little boys' toilet seats to deflect the urine) came loose and fell into the toilet bowl; pointing to it, he exclaimed, 'broke, wheel!' In explanation it is to be noted that he had many toy cars whose wheels, when of rubber, were always of white rubber. Thus he came to think that the word 'wheel' embraced not only wheels but also anything made of white rubber." Levin concludes that this example "shows how associations of the most ephemeral nature are permitted to enter into a concept when the child is too young to appreciate the non-essentiality." In view of what has been said before, it is obvious that an identification had occurred because of the same characteristic "white rubber."

The same principle of Von Domarus is applied in dreams. Freud (10) has demonstrated that a person or object *A* having a certain characteristic of *B* may appear in the dream as being *B* or a composite of *A* and *B*. In the first case there is identification; in the second, composition. The whole field of Freudian symbolism is based, from a formal point of view, on Von Domarus' principle. A symbol of *X* is something which stands for *X*, but also something which retains some similarity with *X*—common predicate or characteristic. For instance, penis may be identified with snake on account of the elongated shape of both, father with king on account of the position of authority they both enjoy, and so on. The reason why certain symbols are specific only for one person will be discussed later. It has to be pointed out again that what one, using

psychiatric terminology, calls a symbol is not a symbol for the schizophrenic or for the dreamer, but is, consciously or unconsciously, a duplication of the object symbolized.

The study of Von Domarus' principle in schizophrenia, in primitive thought, and in dreams requires that more consideration be paid to the predicate which determines the identification. In fact it is obvious that the predicate is the most important part in this type of thinking. Since the same subject may have numerous predicates, it is the choice of the predicate in the paleologic premises which will determine the great subjectivity, bizarreness, and often unpredictability of autistic thinking. For instance, in the quoted example of Von Domarus, the characteristic of being encircled was the identifying quality. Each of the three subjects which were identified—Jesus, cigar boxes, and sex—had a potentially large number of predicates, but the patient selected one which was completely unpredictable and bizarre. The predicate which is selected in the process of identification is called the "identifying link." Why a certain predicate should be selected out of numerous possible ones as the identifying link will be discussed shortly. A predicate is, by definition, something which concerns the subject. One is used to recognizing as predicates abstract or concrete qualities of the subject or something which in a certain way resides or is contained in the subject— for instance, being white, red, fluid, friendly, honest, suspicious, having a tail, and infinite other possibilities. These are called predicates of quality. There are, however, other characteristics which are paleologically conceived as pertaining to the subjects and, therefore, considered predicates, although they are not contained in the subject—for instance, the characteristic of occurring at a certain time or at a given place. For example, two completely different subjects may have as a common predicate the fact that they occur simultaneously or successively or in the same place. For instance, if a patient accidentally ate a certain exotic food on a day in which he had a pleasant experience, he may dream of eating again that special food because he wishes to revive the pleasant experience. Special food and pleasant experience are in the dream identified because they happen to be perceived at the same time. The identifying link in this case is a predicate of temporal contiguity. The predicate of contiguity may be not only temporal but also spatial. For instance, a patient may dream of being in her summer home in Connecticut. Nearby in Connecticut lives a man she loves. Home in Connecticut and loved man are identified because they both have the characteristic of residing in the same place. In this case the identifying link is a predicate of spatial contiguity. Two different subjects may be identified also because they originated from the same source or will give origin to the same event or to the same emotional reaction. For instance, a patient dreams of undressing a woman, with sexual intentions. In the dream he suddenly realizes that her vagina looks like an umbilicus. In his associations he remembers that when he was a child he thought that children were born from the umbilicus. In this dream vagina and umbilicus are identified because they both were thought of by the patient as organs which give birth to children. In this case the identifying link is a predicate of finality. In many cases the identifying link is a mixture of predicates of different types.

From the foregoing it appears that paleologic thinking is much less exact than Aristotelian. In the latter, only identical subjects may be identified. The subjects are immutable; therefore, only a few and the same deductions are possible. In paleologic thinking, on the other hand, the predicates lead to the identification. Since the predicates may be extremely numerous and one does not know which one may be chosen by the patient, this type of thought becomes unpredictable, individualistic, and often incomprehensible. If the identifying link is a predicate of quality, it will be relatively easy to understand the meaning of what the patient expresses. What are referred to in psychoanalytic literature as universal symbols are generally objects whose identifying link is a predicate of quality and, less frequently, of finality. If, however, the identifying link is an accidental predicate of contiguity, obviously the symbol is specific for the individual and many details concerning his life history are necessary in order to understand its meaning.

The unconscious choice of the predicate which is used as the identifying link, out of numerous possible ones, is often determined by emotional factors. In other words, emotional currents may determine which one of the predicates will be taken as the identifying characteristic. This extremely important point has been examined in detail in another of my publications (4) and will not be rediscussed here. It is obvious that if John Doe thinks that he is the President of the United States because he was born in the United States, he wishes to think so. His increased narcissistic requirements direct him toward the selection of that predicate—being born in the United States—out of many other possibilities. The same emotional factors described by Freud (11) in "Psychopathology of Everyday Life" and by Jung (12) in *Psychology of Dementia Praecox* are, of course, valid for paleologic thinking, also. However, these emotional factors do not explain the formal manifestations of this type of thinking. Conscious or unconscious emotions may be the directing motivation or the driving force of these thought processes, but the fact cannot be denied that these thoughts are molded according to a special pattern, which is conferred by the adoption of a different logic.

From the foregoing, the reader may have deduced the tremendous rôle played by Von Domarus' principle in non-Aristotelian thinking—a rôle whose importance escaped perhaps Von Domarus himself. For those interested in the problem mainly from a point of view of formal logic, I may add that of the four Aristotelian laws of thought—law of identity, law of contradiction, law of excluded middle, law of sufficient reason —the first three are annulled by Von Domarus' principle. In one of the following paragraphs, it will be shown how the fourth law also is altered.

Connotation, Denotation, Verbalization

Before proceeding with this examination of paleologic thinking, I have to remind the reader of what is traditionally meant in logic by different aspects of terms, that is, by connotation and denotation. Let us take, for instance, the term *table*. The connotation of this term is the meaning of the term, that is, the concept *article of furniture with flat horizontal top, set on legs*. The denotation of the term is the object meant, that is, the table as a physical entity. In other words, the term *table* may mean table in general or it may mean any or all particular tables. Every term has both these aspects. It means certain definite qualities or attributes and it also refers to certain objects or, in the case of a singular term, to one object which has those qualities. The connotation is in a certain way the definition of the object and includes the whole class of the object, without any reference to a concrete embodiment of the object.

I feel that, in addition to the two aspects of the terms which are traditionally considered in logic, one has to consider a third aspect, if he wants to understand better the problem from a psychological point of view. This is the verbal aspect of the term, the term as a

word or verbal symbol. I propose to call this aspect of the term *verbalization*. For instance, the term *table* may be considered from three aspects: its connotation, when one refers to its meaning; its denotation, when one refers to the object meant; its verbalization, when one considers the word as a word, that is, as a verbal representation or symbol of the object table or of the concept table.

Now it is possible to formulate a second important principle of paleologic. Whereas the healthy person in a wakened state is mainly concerned with the connotation and the denotation of a symbol but is capable of shifting his attention from one to another of the three aspects of a symbol, the autistic person is mainly concerned with the denotation and the verbalization, and experiences a total or partial impairment of his ability to connote. In view of this principle, two phenomena have to be studied in schizophrenia and other types of autistic thinking: first, the reduction of the connotation power; second, the emphasis on the verbalization.

REDUCTION OF CONNOTATION POWER

For the person who thinks paleologically, the verbal symbols cease to be representative of a group or of a class, but only of the specific objects under discussion. For instance, the word "cat" cannot be used as relating to any member of the feline genus, but a specific cat, like "the cat sitting on that chair." Oftener there is a gradual shifting from the connotation to the denotation level.*

* The statement made by many logicians that there is an inverse ratio between connotation and denotation does not hold true if the problem is considered from a psychological point of view. In other words, a decrease in the connotation power is not accompanied by an increase in the denotation power and vice versa. Many logicians, too, have criticized this concept of inverse ratio, because objects (denotation) can be enumerated, but qualities and meanings cannot be measured mathematically. I might add that the study of primitive thought

This gradual regression is apparent if we ask a not too deteriorated schizophrenic to define words. For instance, following are some words which a schizophrenic was asked to define and her replies:

Q. Book.
A. It depends what book you are referring to.
Q. Table.
A. What kind of a table? A wooden table, a porcelain table, a surgical table, or a a table you want to have a meal on?
Q. House.
A. There are all kinds of houses, nice houses, nice private houses.
Q. Life.
A. I have to know what life you happen to be referring to—*Life* magazine or to the sweetheart who can make another individual happy and gay.

From the examples it is obvious that the patient, a high school graduate, is unable to define usual words. She cannot cope with the task of defining the word as a symbol of a class or a symbol including all the members of the class, like all books, all tables, and so on. She tries first to decrease her task by limiting her definition to special subgroups or to particular members of the class. For instance, she is unable to define the word "table" and attempts to simplify her problem by asking whether she has to define various subgroups of tables—wooden tables, surgical tables, and so on. In the last example, she wants to know whether I am referring to two particular instances, *Life* magazine or to the life of the sweetheart. This reply, which reveals impairment of connotation power, is complicated also by the emphasis on the verbalization, as will be demonstrated in the following paragraph.

This tightness to the denotation prevents the schizophrenic from using figur-

_____
discloses that what would be called terms with great connotation (with meaning of specific objects) preceded terms with greater denotation, which originated at a higher level of development.

ate or metaphorical languages, contrary to what it may seem at first impression. It has already been stated by Benjamin (13) that the schizophrenic is unable to interpret proverbs correctly. He will give always a more or less literal interpretation of them. Figurate language increases the use of the term which acquires an unusual denotation and connotation. If one says, "When the cat's away, the mice will play," a normal listener will understand that by cat is meant a person in authority. A schizophrenic patient gave the following literal interpretation of that proverb: "There are all kinds of cats and all kinds of mice, but when the cat is away, the mice take advantage of the cat." In other words, for the schizophrenic the word "cat" could not acquire a special connotation.

The inability of the schizophrenic to use metaphorical language is revealed also by the following replies of a patient who was asked to explain what was meant when a person was called by the names of various animals, for instance:

Q. Wolf.
A. Wolf is a greedy animal.
Q. Fox.
A. A fox and a wolf are two different animals. One is more vicious than the other, more and more greedy than the other.
Q. Parrot.
A. It all depends what the parrot says.
Q. Peacock.
A. A woman with beautiful feathers. By the way, *Woman* is a magazine.

Many beginners in the field of psychiatry get the impression that schizophrenic language and thought are highly metaphorical and poetic. In reality it is not so. This impression is due to misinterpretation of the phenomena which were explained above in terms of Von Domarus' principle. For instance, a schizophrenic will be able to *identify* a man with a wolf on account of a common characteristic, greediness, but will not be able to accept the concept *wolf* as a symbol of greedy men. Two different mechanisms are employed. In the first instance, a very primitive paleologic mechanism is necessary; in the second instance a high process of abstraction is at play. If one understands fully this point, he understands also one of the fundamental differences between schizophrenic artistic productions and some manifestations of art of normal persons.

This restriction of the denotation power and decrease of the connotation power is very apparent in many instances reported by Goldstein. (14) In the color sorting test, one of Goldstein's patients picked out various shades of green, but in doing so he named them—peacock green, emerald green, taupe green, bright green, bell green, baby green. He could not say that all might be called green. Another patient of Goldstein's said in the same situation: "This is the color of the grass in Virginia, this is the color of the grass in Kentucky, this is the color of the bark of the tree, this is the color of the leaves." The words used by the patients in naming colors belonged to a definite situation. "The words," Goldstein writes, "have become individual words, i.e., words which fit only a specific object or situation." In other words, the meaning or the connotation of the word includes not a class but only a specific instance. There is therefore a definite restriction of the connotation power.* Goldstein calls these phenomena expressions of "concrete attitude."

EMPHASIS ON VERBALIZATION

Whereas the word is normally considered just as a symbol to convey a meaning, in the autistic person it acquires a greater significance. In many cases the attention of the schizophrenic is focused not on the connotation or denotation of the term, but just on its verbal expres-

---

* Many logicians, on the other hand, would say that the connotation is increased. This point of view is psychologically wrong. Reference footnote on p. 173.

sion—that is, on the word as a word, not as a symbol. Other paleologic processes may take place after the attention has been focused on the verbalization. For instance, a schizophrenic examined during the past war said that the next time the Japanese would attack the Americans it would be at Diamond Harbor or Gold Harbor. When she was asked why, she replied: "The first time, they attacked at Pearl Harbor; now they will attack at Diamond Harbor or at Sapphire Harbor." "Do you think that the Japanese attacked Pearl Harbor because of its name?" I asked. "No, no," she replied, "it was a *happy* coincidence." Note the inappropriateness of the adjective *happy*. It was a happy coincidence for her, because she could prove thereby the alleged validity of her paleophrenic thinking.

From this example, and from others which will follow, it is to be deduced that Von Domarus' principle is often applied when the emphasis is on the verbalization. Different objects are identified because they have names which have a common characteristic. The identification is very easily made if the terms are homonyms. Two otherwise different things are identified, or considered together, because they have the same verbalization, that is, the same phonetic or written symbol. In one of the examples mentioned above, the patient put together *Life* magazine and the life of the sweetheart. Another schizophrenic was noticed to have the habit of wetting her body with oil. Asked why she would do so she replied: "The human body is a machine and has to be lubricated." The word *machine,* applied in a figurative sense to the human body, had led to the identification with man-made machines. It is obvious that for the schizophrenic and, to a minor degree, for persons who are in other autistic conditions, the term is considered not as a symbol but as a characteristic, a quality or a predicate of the object which is symbolized. The identification, due to the similar or common verbal expression, is based not only on Von Domarus' principle but also on the second principle of paleologic, that is, the emphasis on the verbalization and the decreased importance of the connotation.

Werner (8) thinks that a name is not merely a sign for the primitive; it is part of the object itself. The verbalization thus is conceived as part of the denotation. The word does not have the same connotation for the primitive as for the civilized man; the meaning is often restricted to the specific instance which is denoted.

Children, too, experience names as fused in the object they denote. Piaget (15) has illustrated this phenomenon very well. When he asked children not older than six, "Where is the name of the sun?" he elicited the following responses: "Inside! Inside the sun" or "High up in the sky!"

The emphasis on the verbalization together with the application of Von Domarus' principle may also be found in normal adults in the technique of jokes and witticisms. Some of the examples mentioned above, such as the schizophrenic who was wetting her body with oil, have definite comical characteristics. The important point, however, is that what is comical for the healthy person is taken seriously by the schizophrenic. In a future publication the relation between wit and paleologic rules will be discussed. Freud (16) also, in his important monograph on wit, has described many mechanisms involved in the technique of witticisms but could not reduce them to the few principles of paleologic.

The emphasis on verbalization appears also in many dreams, as revealed first by Freud (10) in his monograph on dream interpretation. I report here one of the numerous examples he gives. C. dreams that on the road to X he sees a girl, bathed in a white light and wearing a white blouse. The dreamer began an affair with a Miss White on that road.

Causality

I mentioned before that the first three laws of thought of traditional logic were eliminated by Von Domarus' principle. On the other hand, there is retained in paleologic thinking the fourth law, the law of sufficient reason: "We must assume a reason for every event." The methods, however, by which a reason for, or a cause of, an event is searched are different from those used by the normal mind. The works of Piaget (17, 15) on the mentality of the child help in understanding this problem. The autistic person, as well as the child, confuses the physical world with the psychological. Instead of finding a physical explanation of an event, the child, as well as the primitive and the autistic, looks for a motivation or an intention as the cause of an event. Every event is interpreted as caused by the will of an animated being. Of course, similar explanations of incidents are justified many times. For instance, if one says "I read this book of geometry because I want to learn this subject," this psychological causality is justified. The child, however, invokes to a much larger extent motives and intentions as causes of phenomena. He is always in search for a motivation which leads to an action. Children, examined by Piaget in Switzerland, thought that God made the thunder in the sky, that the Negroes were made in that way because they were naughty when they were little and God punished them; that there were a great and a little Salève lakes, because some people wanted to go into the little one and some into the great one. Werner (8) reports other examples. A boy, five years of age, thought that in the evening it got dark because people were tired and wanted to sleep. The same child thought that the rain was due to the fact that the angels swept the heavens with their brooms and lots of water.

The intentions are ascribed first to other people, then to things. The moon follows the child, the sun goes up in the sky, the rivers run. The world becomes peopled in various degrees.

An animistic and anthropomorphic conception of the world thus originates. Many works of anthropology and comparative psychology fully illustrate how the same conception of psychological causality is present in the primitive of today and in the mythology of ancient peoples.

In dreams, too, events are engendered by wishes, intentions, or psychological motivations. Paranoiacs and paranoids interpret almost everything as manifesting a psychological intention or meaning related to their delusional complexes.

One may conclude therefore that whereas the normal person is inclined to explain phenomena by logical deductions, often implying concepts involving the physical world, the autistic person, as well as the primitive and the child, is inclined to give a psychological explanation to all phenomena.

Between causality by psychological explanation and causality by logical deduction there are many other intermediate types of explanation which are described by Piaget. For instance, moral causality, magical causality, and so on. In a future contribution I will deal with this difficult problem.

Conception of Time

This subject will be dealt with very briefly here, because it was elaborated in one of my previous publications. (18) Whereas the normal adult is able to think of the present, to revive the past, and to anticipate the future, or, in other words, is able to transport chronologically remote phenomena to the only possible subjective or psychologic tense—present —the autistic person thinks mostly about the present.

Animals are unable to prospect a distant future. Experiments with delayed reactions have disclosed that they cannot keep in mind future events for more than a few minutes. (19, 20) They can foresee only the very immediate future— that is, only the reaction to a stimulus as long as the stimulus is present or was present not longer than a few minutes before. Prehuman species may be called biologic entities without psychic tomorrow. Cattle go to the slaughterhouse without feelings of anxiety, being unable to foresee what is going to happen to them. In humans, ability to anticipate the future begins during the anal period. At that stage of development the child becomes able to postpone immediate pleasure for some future gratification. In other words it is when the ability to anticipate is developed that "the reality principle" originates.

Phylogenetically, anticipation appeared at the primordial eras of humanity when man became interested not only in cannibalism and hunting, which are related to immediate present necessities, but also in agriculture and in hoarding in order to provide for future needs. It is in this period that culture— that is, knowledge to be used in future times or to be transmitted to future generations—originated. A person who would be able to conceive mentally only the present time would aim only toward what Sullivan (21) calls "satisfaction." A person who is able to prospect the future as well would aim also toward what Sullivan calls "security."

Autistic phenomena always occur as present phenomena without any reference to the future, although they may be motivated by wishes for the future. As Freud has emphasized, in dreams the situation is always lived in the present. In schizophrenia too, there is what I have called a "restriction of the psycho-temporal field." The patient withdraws more or less to a narcissistic level, and his temporal orientation becomes also more and more similar to that of the narcissistic period, that is, related to the present time. Balken, (22) in her study with the Thematic Apperception Test, found that the schizophrenic does not distinguish between past, present, and future. According to her, the schizophrenic, in the attempt "to relieve the tension between the possible and the real" clings "desperately and without awareness to the present." In early schizophrenia, however, and especially in the paranoid type, the patient is still able to concern himself with past and future. Some delusions, especially with persecutory content, may involve the future rather than the present. The more the illness progresses, however, the more grandiose and related to the present time the delusions become. "I *am* the emperor of China; I *am* a millionaire."

To use Sullivan terminology, the schizophrenic, in a desperate attempt to *r*egain security, uses more and more autistic mechanisms.

Perceptualization of the Concept

From the foregoing the reader has certainly inferred that the autistic person has the tendency to live in a world of perception rather than in a world of conception. The more autistically a person thinks, the more deprived he becomes of concepts or of Plato's universals. His ideas become more and more related to specific instances, and not concerned with classes, groups, or categories. Naturally, all gradations are possible and could be retraced in primitives.

When the pathologic process progresses further, the ideational formations will contain more and more concrete elements, representing reality as it appears to the senses rather than to the intellect. Perceptual elements finally eliminate completely higher thought processes. Storch

(3) has demonstrated that the same process of perceptualization is found in the primitive as in the schizophrenic. Ideas are represented by sensory images. The wealth of vivid sensory images which are found in old myths was not the work of art but of necessity. The normal artist, too, uses perceptualization of concepts in his artistic productions but retains that ability to abstract which has not yet been acquired by the primitive and which has been lost by the schizophrenic. Perceptualization of the concept has its fullest expression in dreams and in hallucinations. As Freud and others have pointed out, the dream is just a translation of thoughts into visual images. Thoughts become visual perceptions. If the dreamer thinks about himself he sees himself in the dream. He sees himself as a physical entity or as a visual image, not as an abstract concept symbolized by the pronoun "I." These visual images use sensorial material. Since, for anatomical reasons, nobody can see his own face, the dreamer cannot recall the visual image of his face. This explains why the dreamer usually sees himself in the dream, but not his face. The sensorial material is revisualized and elaborated in accordance with paleologic and other archaic mechanisms. The same things could be repeated about hallucinations, except that in them auditory images are by far more common than visual.

This paragraph can therefore be summarized by stating that in autistic thought concepts have the tendency to disappear as concepts, inasmuch as their content tends to assume a perceptual expression. This process of perceptualization is completed in dreams and in hallucinations.

Further Application and Limitation of Paleologic Rules—Reference to More Primitive Mechanisms

The few principles of paleologic thought which were expounded above have a much vaster application than it may seem from the few examples given. The whole way of thinking may be entirely transformed as to become completely inaccessible.

Von Domarus' principle may lead to what may be called self-identification. Self-identification, or identification of the self with another person, may occur unconsciously in normal and in neurotic persons, or consciously as in the delusional psychotics. The formal mechanism is the following: "If X will be identified with Y, because they have a common quality, it will be sufficient for me to acquire a quality of the person I want to be identified with, in order to become that person."

The very common hysterical identifications follow this mechanism. Freud's patient, Dora, developed a cough like that of Mrs. K. with whom she wanted to identify. (23) A patient, mentioned by Fenichel, (24) felt an intense pain in one finger. She felt as if she had her finger cut with a knife. She identified herself with her loved cousin, a medical student, who, she imagined, might have cut himself while dissecting.

The deluded patient discovers in himself a quality possessed also by a hero, a saint, a general, and identifies himself with the person who has that given quality. Other deluded patients try to acquire or to confer on others identifying qualities. A paranoid schizophrenic wanted her child to become an angel. Since angels are nourished only "by spiritual food," she did not feed her child for a few days—that is, until her relatives became aware of her acutely developed condition.

Von Domarus' principle in reverse is also applied in paleologic thinking as well as in primitive and infantile thinking. If A has not a given quality of A', A cannot be A'. I shall resort again to one of the very interesting examples given by Levin, (25) although he has not fully interpreted it.

A bright six-year-old boy asked Levin whether twins are always boys. He replied that they may be either boys or girls, or a girl and a boy. When the child heard that twins may be a girl and a boy, he asked with surprise: "Then how could they wear the same clothes?" Levin concludes that the child had seen identical twins dressed alike, and his concepts of twins included an irrelevant detail, identity of raiment. If we apply Von Domarus' principle in reverse, the mental mechanism seems to be the following: "Twins have a common quality—identical raiment. If two people have not or cannot have identical raiment, they cannot be twins."

The five principles mentioned above —namely, (1) Von Domarus' principle, (2) the changed emphasis on the connotation, denotation, and verbalization of symbols, (3) psychological causality, (4) the narrower conception of time, and (5) the tendency to perceptualize concepts—obviously have a tremendous importance. These specific principles are representative of a power of perception and conception completely different from those usually possessed by the normal modern adult in waking status. These mechanisms offer to the thinker a completely different vision of the external universe as well as of his own inner experiences.

Throughout this paper the reader has probably been impressed by the continuous references to primitive and infantile thought. This has been done to convey the notion that the type of thought which uses a non-Aristotelian logic is representative of a certain stage of phylogenetic and ontogenetic development. Unfortunately, many modern studies of anthropology and of child psychology, influenced by orthodox Freudian psychoanalysis, have not gone at all into this type of research. The character structure of a primitive society is interpreted by some orthodox analysts as due to a reproduction at a phylogenetic level of an ontogenetic Freudian complex such as in Freud's "Totem and Taboo." (26)

Fromm (27) rightly calls this method the naive Freudian approach to anthropology. Other orthodox psychoanalysts, like Róheim (28) and Kardiner, (29) interpret the character structure and the whole primitive culture as the result of the special upbringing of children in that given culture. The fact that the primitive interprets the world paleologically and therefore has a completely different vision of the universe, and that this completely different vision of the universe, in its turn, has its influence upon the upbringing of children, is completely ignored by these orthodox authors. For instance, the projective mechanisms described by Kardiner have not been interpreted as at least partially due to a different type of causality—namely, to that psychological causality mentioned in a previous paragraph of this paper.

Since I have mentioned that this type of paleologic thinking is typical in autistic states and especially of schizophrenics, does it follow that the characteristics of schizophrenic thought can all be interpreted in view of the paleologic principles expounded above?

These principles explain a great deal but certainly cannot explain every characteristic of schizophrenia or even of schizophrenic thought. This limitation is due to two different reasons. The first one is that not all paleologic rules have yet been discovered. For instance, some of the paleologic laws, discussed above, may explain the formal mechanisms of delusions of misidentification or of grandeur, but cannot explain why the homosexually loved person is transformed into the persecutor. The emotional mechanism, which is at play in this transformation, is understood very well because of the contributions of Freud, and especially his work on the Schreiber case. (30) The concomitant paleologic mechanism is not yet clear, although some hypotheses are now under study.

The other reason is that schizophrenia involves the resurgence of archaic mechanisms, some of which are even more primitive than the paleologic. Paleologic thought is, by definition, thought that follows an archaic type of logic, which phylogenetically preceded the Aristotelian. However, not all thought is logical; primitive forms of thought follow no logic whatsoever, either Aristotelian or paleologic, but only associations. Associational thought, in contrast to logic thought, shows no signs of direction toward an end or conclusion. It consists generally of recollections which are at the mercy of the laws of association * and of primitive emotions.

Mrs. Nickleby, Dickens' character, is certainly remembered by the reader for her sparing use of logical processes in her conversational activities and for her conspicuous use of associational thought. In this type of thought ideas are expressed as they are recalled; they follow no logic rules but only the laws of associations—laws of contiguity and similarity—and

* Many readers may be surprised that I dare to mention the laws of association of ideas. Some psychological schools have tried to get rid of two fundamental characteristics of psychological phenomena: consciousness, denied by the behaviorists; and association of ideas, denied by those who are obsessively afraid of mental atomism. Nobody today would deny any longer that consciousness is a quality of some psychological processes. A two-minute observation can convince anyone of the fact that ideas do associate. I see my old high school and think of my adolescence; I hear somebody mention the name of Chopin, and I think immediately of an acquaintance of mine who is a pianist. The psychoanalytic treatment is based on free *associations* of ideas. In reality, associations in the analytic situation are free only from (Aristotelian) logic; they are not free from emotional currents, from paleologic mechanisms, and from the laws of association.

In a future contribution the transition will be studied from associational to paleologic thought. It will be demonstrated that the "associational link" becomes "the identifying link" in paleologic thought. In associational thought, if the associational link is a predicate of contiguity, the two ideas associate because of the law of contiguity. If the associational link is a predicate of quality, the ideas associate because of the law of similarity.

underlying emotional currents. In advanced schizophrenia, impairment is to be noted, not only in logic thought, but also in associational thought. Even the simplest ideas cannot associate properly, as pointed out by Bleuler. (31)

Paleologic and Psychopathological States

Now that the principal known laws of paleologic have been examined, it is appropriate to consider in what circumstances and why the normal adult abandons the Aristotelian way of thinking and adopts a more primitive type.

As mentioned before, logic (Aristotelian) thought is rigid and exact. In this type of thought only identical subjects can be identified. *A* is only *A* and cannot be *B*. The immutability of the subjects and the other characteristics described above make only few deductions possible. The person who thinks logically may find reality very unpleasant as long as he continues to think so. John Doe cannot think that he is the President of the United States just because he was born in the United States, but he may think so if he abandons this method of logic and embraces a new one. Once he sees things in a different way, with a new logic, no Aristotelian persuasion will convince him that he is wrong. He is right, according to his own logic.

The maiden may not dare to think that she wishes sexual relations, but if in the dream the penis assumes the form of a terrifying snake, her objections will be temporarily removed. These examples disclose that one has the tendency to resort to paleologic thinking when one's wishes cannot be sustained by normal logic. If reality cannot grant gratification of wishes, a new system of logic, which will transform reality into a more complacent form may be adopted.

This tendency, which each person has, to think paleologically, is, of course, usu-

ally corrected by Aristotelian thought. The laws of paleologic are unconsciously applied in neurotic manifestations and in dreams, but are rejected by the patient and by the waking person. This is possible because the neurotic and the waking person retain their normal Aristotelian logic. Only dissociated tendencies in the neurotic retain autistic mechanisms.

In schizophrenia, instead, the paleologic way of thinking has the upper hand and seems to the patient a sound interpreter of reality. Because of the above-described, individual, and often unpredictable characteristics of this type of thinking, the schizophrenic will not be able to obtain consensual validation, but will reach that inner security derived by the newly-established agreement between his logic and his emotions. He will have to withdraw more and more from this Aristotelian world, but will be finally at peace with himself.

The situation is not so clear-cut in the beginning of schizophrenia. The important contributions of Sullivan about the onset of schizophrenia will help one understand what is taking place at this stage of the illness.

After the state of panic which the new schizophrenic has undergone, the patient becomes aware of dissociated tendencies. He becomes aware not only of what was accepted and incorporated in his self-system but also of another and great part of his personality which was obscure to him.

It appears natural to Sullivan that the patient does not accept immediately this state of affairs, this new personality, and suffers terrifying experiences: "The structure of his world was torn apart and dreadful, previously scarcely conceivable, events injected themselves." (21) This description of Sullivan's is even better understood if one accepts the fact that the new schizophrenic realizes that his mind has started to think in a different way, obscure to him. He realizes that he is inclined to interpret the world in a different way, at variance from his previous way of thinking and from that of other people, and he is afraid that he will become insane. The schizophrenic fear of becoming insane is not just the phobic idea of insanity found in neurotics, but is a realization that some change in his way of thinking is actually taking place. At this stage the patient is able to think at the same time logically and paleologically, but his logic is not able any more to control the paleologic thoughts. Paleologic thinking will be first limited only to ideas connected with the patient's complexes, especially if the illness takes a paranoid course. The more progressed is the illness, however, the greater will be the percentage of paleologic thinking in the schizophrenic mixture of these two types of thoughts. Finally, when hebephrenic dilapidation approaches, there is a resurgence of thought mechanisms even more primitive than the paleologic.

References

1. White, W. A. The language of schizophrenia. In *Schizophrenia (dementia praecox)*. New York: Paul Hoeber, 1928. Pages 323–343.

2. Vigotsky, L. S. Thought in schizophrenia. *Arch. Neurol. and Psychiat.*, 31(1934), 1036.

3. Kasanin, J. S. (ed.). *Language and thought in schizophrenia: collected papers.* Univ. of California Press, 1944.

4. Arieti, S. Autistic thought: its formal mechanisms and its relations to schizophrenia. *J. Nerv. and Ment. Disease,* 111(1950), 288–303.

5. Von Domarus, E. Uber die Beziehung des normalen zum schizophrenen Denken. *Arch. Psychiat.,* 74(1925), 641. Berlin.

6. Kasanin, J. S. (ed.). The specific laws of logic in schizophrenia. *Language and thought in schizophrenia: collected papers.* Univ. of California Press, 1944.

7. Storch, A. *The primitive archaic forms of inner experiences and thought in schizophrenics.* New York and Washington: Nervous and Mental Disease Publishing Company, 1924.

8. Werner, H. *Comparative psychology of mental development.* New York: Harper & Brothers, 1940.

9. Levin, M. Misunderstanding of the pathogenesis of schizophrenia, arising from the concept of "splitting." *Amer. J. Psychiatry,* 94(1938), 877–889.

10. Freud, S. The interpretation of dreams. In S. Freud, *The basic writings of Sigmund Freud.* New York: Modern Library, 1938.

11. ――― Psychopathology of everyday life. *Ibid.*

12. Jung, C. G. *The psychology of dementia praecox.* New York: Nervous and Mental Disease Monograph Series No. 3, 1936.

13. Benjamin, J. D. A method for distinguishing and evaluating formal thinking disorders in schizophrenia. In Kasanin, S. J. (ed.). *Language and thought in schizophrenia: collected papers.* Univ. of California Press, 1944.

14. Goldstein, K. The significance of psychological research in schizophrenia. *J. Nerv. and Ment. Disease,* 97(1943), 261–279.

15. Piaget, J. *The child's conception of the world.* London: Routledge and Kegan Paul Ltd., 1929.

16. Freud, S. Wit and its relation to the unconscious. In S. Freud, *The basic writings of Sigmund Freud.* New York: Modern Library, 1938.

17. Piaget, J. *The language and thought of the child.* London: Routledge and Kegan Paul Ltd., 1948. Also, *The child's conception of physical causality.* London: Kegan, Trench, Trubner, 1930.

18. Arieti, S. The processes of expectation and anticipation. *J. Nerv. and Ment. Disease,* 100(1947), 471–481.

19. Hunter, W. S. The delayed reaction in animals and children. *Behavior monographs,* 2(1913), 86.

20. Harlow, H. F., Wehling, H., and Maslow, A. H. Comparative behavior of primates: delayed reaction tests on primates. *J. Comp. Psychol.,* 13(1932), 13.

21. Sullivan, H. S. *Conceptions of modern psychiatry.* Washington, D.C.: The William Alanson White Psychiatric Foundation, 1946.

22. Balken, E. R. A delineation of schizophrenic language and thought in a test of imagination. *J. Psychol.,* 16(1943), 239.

23. Freud, S. Fragment of an analysis of a case of hysteria (1905). In *Collected papers.* Volume III. London: Hogarth Press, 13(1946), 146.

24. Fenichel, O. *The psychoanalytic theory of neurosis.* New York: W. W. Norton & Co., 1945.

25. Levin, M. On the causation of mental symptoms. *J. Mental Science,* 82(1938), 1–27.

26. Freud, S. Totem and taboo. In S. Freud, *The basic writings of Sigmund Freud.* New York: Modern Library, 1938.

27. Fromm, E. Unpublished lectures given

at seminar on social psychology. New York: William Alanson White Institute of Psychiatry, 1948.

28. Róheim, G. *The riddle of the sphinx.* London: International Psycho-analytical Library, No. 25, 1934.

29. Kardiner, A. *The individual and his society.* New York: Columbia Press, 1939.

30. Freud, S. Psychoanalytic notes upon an autobiographical account of a case of paranoia (dementia paranoides) (1911). In S. Freud, *Collected papers.* Volume III. London, Hogarth Press, 1946. Pages 387–470.

31. Bleuler, E. *Dementia praecox, oder Gruppe der Schizophrennen.* Leipzig and Wien. Franz-Deutsche, 1911.

An Interactional Description of Schizophrenia *

JAY HALEY

VETERANS ADMINISTRATION HOSPITAL, PALO ALTO, CALIFORNIA

Despite all that is said about difficulties in interpersonal relations, psychiatric literature does not offer a systematic way of describing the interpersonal behavior of the schizophrenic so as to differentiate that behavior from the normal. The schizophrenic's internal processes are often described in terms of ego weakness, primitive logic, or dissociated thinking, but his interpersonal behavior is usually presented in the form of anecdotes. This paper will present a system for describing schizophrenic interactions with other persons, a system that is of necessity based on a theoretical framework describing all interpersonal relationships. To actually make a classification system of in-

terpersonal relations would require the herculean task of making natural history studies of all kinds of people interacting with each other. This paper will merely suggest an approach to such a classification system, first discussing the problems involved in classifying interpersonal relations, then presenting and analyzing a conversation between two schizophrenics, and finally indicating the significance of this kind of approach.

The following conversation between two hospitalized schizophrenics, a brief excerpt from the verbatim conversation that will be reproduced at greater length later in this article, is an example of the kind of interaction the paper attempts to classify.

Smith: Do you work at the air base? Hm?

Jones: You know what I think of work, I'm thirty-three in June, do you mind?

Smith: June?

Jones: Thirty-three years old in June. This stuff goes out the window after I live this, uh—leave this hospital. So I can't get my vocal chords back. So I lay off cigarettes. I'm a spatial condition, from outer space myself, no shit.

Reprinted from *Psychiatry,* 22(1959), 321–332, by special permission of The William Alanson White Psychiatric Foundation, Inc., holder of the copyright, and the author.

* The ideas in this paper are a product of the Communications Research Project. The staff consists of Gregory Bateson, Director; Jay Haley, Research Associate; John H. Weakland, Research Associate; Don D. Jackson, Consultant; and William F. Fry, Consultant. The project is financed by the Josiah Macy Jr. Foundation and administered by the Department of Anthropology, Stanford University, and functions at the Veterans Hospital, Palo Alto, California.

In this conversation no intrapsychic processes are immediately apparent. There is no dissociated thinking, autism, or withdrawal from reality. From what the men say one might conjecture the presence of such processes as dissociated thinking, but even without conjecture it should be possible to state what is present in this interpersonal behavior which differentiates these men from other men.

There are at least three possible psychiatric approaches to these data. The classical approach would determine whether or not the two young men are in contact with "reality." When one of them says he is from outer space and the other says the hospital is an air base, the classical theoretician would draw his conclusion of schizophrenia. He would analyze the data no further, because classical psychiatric theory assumes that these men are not responding to each other or to their environment but are behaving in an essentially random way because of some organic pathology.

Another approach, the intrapsychic, would center around the thought processes of the two patients. The analyst would conjecture about what the patients must have been thinking, or what kind of peculiar logic might have produced these odd associations. The intrapsychic point of view would presume that the conversation is meaningful, that it is based upon distorted thought processes, and that it contains so many associations unique to these men that it is necessary to know their life histories to understand why particular statements were made. From this point of view an analysis of the data is pointless, since insufficient information is provided by the conversation alone. The young men are "obviously" schizophrenic, and their statements are symbolic manifestations of deeply rooted fantasy ideas.

Finally, there is the interpersonal approach to these data, which emphasizes the ways in which the two men interact, or behave, with each other. This approach assumes that the two men are responding to each other rather than merely to their own thoughts, and that they respond in ways different from normal ways. What is potentially most scientific about the interpersonal approach is its emphasis upon observable data. The ways in which people interact with each other can be observed, whereas the identification of thought processes is inevitably based on conjecture. What is lacking in the interpersonal approach is a systematic descriptive system differentiating the deviant from the normal ways in which people interact with each other.

An ideal classification of interpersonal relations would indicate types of psychopathology, or differentiate people into classes, according to the presence or absence of certain readily observable sequences in their interaction with others. If such an ideal system could be developed, it would not only clarify diagnosis, currently based upon an antiquated system, but also clarify the etiology of psychopathology. If one says that a patient is withdrawn from reality, one says nothing about the processes which provoked this withdrawal. If one says that a patient interacts with people in certain deviant ways, then it is potentially possible to describe the learning situation which taught the person to behave in these ways.

Establishment of an Interpersonal Relationship

When two people meet for the first time and begin to establish a relationship, a wide range of behavior is potentially possible between them. They may exchange compliments, insults, sexual advances, statements that one is superior to the other, and so on. As the two people define their relationship with each other, they work out together what sort of communicative behavior is to take place in this relationship. From all the possible messages they select certain kinds and reach agreement that these rather than others shall be included. Their agreement on what is and what is not to take place can be called a mutual definition of the relationship. Every message they interchange either reinforces this definition or suggests a shift in it. If a young man puts his arm around a girl, he is indicating that amorous behavior is to be included in their relationship. If the girl says, "No, no," and withdraws from him, she is indicating that amorous behavior is to be excluded. The relationship they have together, whether amorous or platonic, is defined by the kind of messages they mutually agree shall be acceptable between them. This agreement is never permanently worked out but is constantly in process as one or the other proposes a new sort of message or as the environmental situation changes and provokes change in their behavior.

If human communication took place at only one level, the working out, or defining, of a relationship would be a simple matter of the presence or absence of messages. In that case there would probably be no difficulties in interpersonal relationships. However, human beings not only communicate, but they also communicate about that communication. They not only say something, but they also qualify or label what they say. In the example above, the young lady says, "No, no," and also withdraws from the young man. Her physical withdrawal qualifies, and is qualified by, her verbal statement. Since the qualification affirms her message, there is no particular difficulty. She is making it clear that amorous behavior does not belong in their relationship. But suppose she had said, "No, no," and moved closer to the young man. By snuggling up to him she would have qualified incongruently, or denied, her statement. When a message is qualified incongruently, then a relationship becomes more complex than when a message is simply present or absent. A classification of hu-

man behavior must take into account at least two *levels* of communication. To describe interpersonal behavior one must deal not only with communicative behavior but the qualifications of that behavior by the participants.

Any communicative behavior interchanged between two people does not exist separately from other behavior which accompanies and comments upon it. If one person says, "I'm glad to see you," his tone of voice qualifies his statement and is qualified in turn by it and by other qualifying messages that might also be present. Communication between people consists of (1) the context in which it takes place, (2) verbal messages, (3) vocal and linguistic patterns, and (4) bodily movement. As people communicate, their relationship is defined as much by the qualifications of their messages as by the presence or absence of messages. A person may make a criticism with a smile or a frown. The smile or frown as much as the criticism defines the relationship. An employee may tell his boss what to do, thus defining their relationship as one between equals, but he may qualify his statement with a self-effacing gesture or a weak tone of voice and thereby indicate that it is a relationship between unequals. If people always qualified what they said in a congruent way, relationships would be defined clearly and simply, even though two levels of communication were functioning. However, when a statement indicating one sort of relationship is qualified by a contradictory communication, difficulties in interpersonal relations become inevitable.

It is important to emphasize that one cannot *not* qualify a message. A person must speak a verbal message in a particular tone of voice, and if he says nothing, that, too, is qualified by the posture he presents and the context in which his muteness appears. Although the meanings of some qualifying messages are obvious, as when one pounds one's fists on the table when making a statement, subtle qualifications are always present. For example, the slightest upward inflection on a word may define a statement as a question rather than an assertion. A slight smile may classify a statement as ironical rather than serious. A minute body movement backwards qualifies an affectionate statement and indicates that it is made with some reservations. The absence of a message may also qualify another message. For example, if a person is silent when he is expected to speak, the silence becomes a qualifying message, and if a man neglects to kiss his wife good-bye when she expects it, the absence of this movement qualifies his other messages as much as, if not more than, the presence of it.

People tend to judge whether others are being sincere or deceitful, whether they are serious or joking, and so on, by whether they affirm what they say by congruent qualifications. And when one person responds to another with his own definition of the relationship between them, this response is to all levels of messages.

Control in a Relationship

When one person communicates a message to another, he is maneuvering to define the relationship. The other person is thereby posed the problem of accepting or rejecting the relationship offered. He can let the message stand, thereby accepting the other person's definition, or counter with a maneuver defining it differently. He may also accept the other person's maneuver but qualify his acceptance with a message indicating that he is *letting* the other person get by with the maneuver.

For example, if a young man spontaneously puts his arm around a young lady, she must either accept this message, thereby letting him define the relationship, or oppose it, thereby defining the

relationship herself. Or she might have controlled the definition by inviting this behavior. She may also accept it with the qualification that she is *letting* him put his arm around her. By labeling his message as one permitted by her, she is maintaining control of the relationship.

Any two people are posed these mutual problems: What messages, or what kinds of behavior, are to take place in this relationship? And who is to control what is to take place in the relationship and thereby control the definition of the relationship? It is hypothesized here that the nature of human communications requires people to deal with these problems, and interpersonal relations can be classified in terms of the different ways in which they do deal with them.

It must be emphasized that no one can avoid being involved in a struggle over the definition of his relationship with someone else. Everyone is constantly involved in defining his relationship or countering the other person's definition. If a person speaks, he is inevitably indicating what sort of relationship he has with the other person. By whatever he says, he is indicating, "This is the sort of relationship where this is said." If a person remains mute, he is also inevitably defining a relationship, because by not speaking he is circumscribing the other person's behavior. If a person wishes to avoid defining his relationship with another and therefore talks only about the weather, he is indicating that their communication should be neutral, and this defines the relationship.

A basic rule of communications theory proposed by Bateson (1) maintains that it is difficult for a person to avoid defining, or taking control of the definition of, his relationship with another. According to this rule all messages not only report but also influence or command. A statement such as, "I feel bad today," is not merely a description of the internal state of the speaker. It also expresses something like, "Do something about this," or "Think of me as a person who feels bad." Even if one remains silent, trying not to influence another person, the silence becomes an influencing factor in the interchange. It is impossible for a person to hand over to another the entire initiative regarding what behavior is to be allowed in the relationship. If he tries to do this, he is controlling the relationship by indicating that it is one in which the other person is to determine what behavior is to take place. For example, a patient may say to a therapist, "I can't decide anything for myself; I want you to tell me what to do." By saying this, he seems to be telling the therapist to control the relationship by directing the behavior in it. But when the patient requests that the therapist tell him what to do, he is telling the therapist what to do. This paradox can arise because two levels are always being communicated—for example: (1) "I am reporting that I need to be told what to do," and (2) "Obey my command to tell me what to do." Whenever a person tries to avoid controlling the definition of a relationship, at a different level he is defining the relationship as one in which he is not in control. A person who acts helpless controls the behavior in a relationship just as effectively as another who acts authoritarian and insists on a specific behavior. Helplessness will influence the other person's behavior as much as, if not more than, direct authoritarian demands. If one acts helpless, he may in one sense be controlled by the person caring for him, but by acting helpless he defines the relationship as one in which he is taken care of.

It should be emphasized here that "control" does not mean that one takes control of another person as one would a robot. The emphasis here is not on a struggle to control another person's specific behavior but rather on a struggle to control *what sort of* behavior is to take place in the relationship and therefore to define the relationship. Any two people must inevitably work out what sort of

relationship they have, not necessarily prescribing behavior, but at least circumscribing what behavior is to take place.

Avoiding Control in a Relationship

I have said that it is difficult for anyone to avoid working out what sort of relationship he has with another person. However, there is one way in which a person can avoid indicating what is to take place in a relationship, and thereby avoid defining it. He can negate what he says. Even though he will be defining the relationship by whatever he communicates, he can invalidate this definition by using qualifications that deny his communications.

The fact that people communicate on at least two levels makes it possible to indicate one relationship, and simultaneously deny it. For example, a man may say, "I think you should do that, but it's not my place to tell you so." In this way he defines the relationship as one in which he tells the other person what to do, but simultaneously denies that he is defining the relationship in this way. This is what is sometimes meant when a person is described as not being self-assertive. One man might respond to his wife's request to do the dishes by saying, "No, I won't," and sitting down with his newspaper. He has asserted himself in the sense that he has defined his relationship with his wife as one in which he is not to be told what to do. Another man might respond to a similar demand by saying, "I would like to do the dishes, but I can't. I have a headache." He also refuses to do the dishes, but by qualifying his message in an incongruent way. He indicates that *he* is not defining the relationship by this refusal. After all, it was the headache which prevented the dishwashing, not him. In the same way, if a man strikes his wife only when drunk, the act of striking her is qualified by the implication that *he* isn't responsible; the effect of the liquor is. By qualifying his messages with implications that *he* isn't responsible for his behavior, a person can avoid defining his relationship with another. These incongruent qualifying messages may be verbal, such as, "I didn't mean to do it," or they may be conveyed by a weak voice or a hesitant body movement. Even the context may negate a maneuver to define a relationship—for example, when one boy invites another to fight in church where a fight is not possible.

To clarify the ways in which a person might avoid defining his relationship with another, suppose that some hypothetical person decided to entirely follow through with such an avoidance. Since anything he said or did not say would define his relationship, he would need to qualify with a negation or a denial whatever he said or did not say. To illustrate the ways in which he could deny his messages, the formal characteristics of any message from one person to another can be broken down into these four elements:

1. I
2. am saying something
3. to you
4. in this situation

A person can avoid defining his relationship by negating any or all of these four elements. He can (1) deny that *he* communicated something, (2) deny that something was communicated, (3) deny that it was communicated *to* the other person, or (4) deny the context in which it was communicated.

The rich variety of ways in which a person can avoid defining a relationship can be summarized briefly.

1. To deny that *he* is communicating a message, a person may label himself as someone else. For example, he may introduce himself with an alias. Or he may indicate that he personally is not speaking, but his status position is, so that what he says is labeled as coming

from the boss or the professor, for example. He may indicate that he is only an instrument transmitting the message; he was told to say what he did, or God was speaking through him, and therefore he is not the one who is defining the relationship.

A person may also deny that *he* is communicating by labeling what he says as effected by some force outside himself. He may indicate that *he* is not really talking, because he is upset or deranged by liquor, or insanity, or drugs.

He may also label his messages as being the result of "involuntary" processes within himself, so that *he* isn't really the one communicating. He may say, "You aren't upsetting me; it's something I ate," and deny that his sick expression is a message from him about the relationship. He may even vomit or urinate and indicate that these things are organically caused and not messages from *him* which should be taken as comments on a relationship.

2. The simplest way in which a person can deny that he *said* something is to manifest amnesia. By saying, "I don't remember doing that," he is qualifying an activity with a statement negating it. He may also insist that what he says is being misunderstood, and that therefore the other person's interpretations do not coincide with what he really said.

Another way to deny that something is said is to immediately qualify a statement with one which contradicts it. This negates everything said as irrelevant nonsense that is therefore not a comment on the relationship. Or a person may make up a language, simultaneously communicating and negating that communication by the very fact that the language cannot be understood by the other person. In another variant, a person can indicate that his words are not means of communication but things in themselves. He may make a statement while discussing the spelling of the words in the statement, and so indicate that he has not communicated a message but has merely listed letters of words.

3. To deny that what he says is addressed *to* the other person, a person may simply indicate that he is talking to himself. He may also label the other person as someone else. For example, he can avoid talking to the other person by talking to the person's status position rather than to him personally. One can be sarcastic with a salesman at the door without defining one's relationship with that person, if the comments are about salesmen in general.

Or, if a person wishes to go to an extreme, he can say that the friend he is talking to is not really a friend but is secretly a policeman. Everything he says is then labeled as a statement to a policeman and therefore cannot define his relationship with his friend.

4. To deny that what he says is said in this situation, a person can label his statements as referring to some other time or place. He can say, "I used to be treated badly and I'll probably be treated badly in the future," and these temporal qualifications deny his implication that he is treated badly at the present moment. Similarly, he can say, "A person I used to know did such and such," and by making it a past relationship he denies that his statement is a comment on the present relationship.

To negate a situational statement about his relationship most effectively, he can qualify it with the statement that the place is some other place. He may label a psychiatrist's office as a prison and thereby deny that his statements are about his relationship with the psychiatrist.

In summary, these are ways of avoiding a definition of the relationship. When everything a person says to another person defines the relationship with that person, he can avoid indicating what sort of relationship he is in only by denying that he is speaking, denying that anything is said, denying that it is said to the other person, or denying that the interchange is occurring in this place at this time.

Interpersonal Relationships in Schizophrenics

It seems apparent that the list of ways to avoid defining a relationship is a list of schizophrenic symptoms. A psychiatrist makes a classical diagnosis of schizophrenia when he observes the most obvious manifestation of schizophrenia, an incongruity between what the patient communicates and the messages which qualify that communication. His movements negate or deny what he says, and his words negate or deny the context in which he speaks. The incongruities may be crude and obvious, like the remark, "My head was bashed in last night," made by a patient whose head is in good shape; or they may be subtle, like a slight smile or odd tone of voice. If the patient denies that *he* is speaking, either by referring to himself in the third person or calling himself by another name, the psychiatrist notes that he is suffering from a loss of identity. If the person indicates that "voices" are saying these things, he is described as hallucinating. If the patient denies that his message is a message, perhaps by busily spelling out his words, the psychiatrist considers this a manifestation of dissociated thinking. When the patient denies that his message is addressed *to* the other person, the psychiatrist considers him delusional. If the patient denies his presence in the hospital by saying that he is in a castle or a prison, the psychiatrist notes that he is withdrawn from reality. When the patient makes a statement in an incongruent tone of voice, he is manifesting inappropriate affect. If he responds to the psychiatrist's behavior with messages which qualify that behavior incongruently, he is autistic.*

* This description deals with the behavior of the schizophrenic and not with his subjective experiences, which, of course, may be terrifying.

The classic psychiatric symptoms of schizophrenia can be described interactionally as indicating a pathology centering around a disjunction between the person's messages and the qualifications of those messages. When a person manifests such a disjunction so that what he says is systematically negated by the ways he qualifies what he says, he is avoiding defining his relationship with other people. The various and seemingly unconnected and bizarre symptoms of schizophrenia can be seen to have a central and rather simple nucleus. If one is determined to avoid defining his relationship, or avoid indicating what sort of behavior is to take place in a relationship, he can do so only by behaving in those ways which are describable as symptoms of schizophrenia.

It was suggested earlier that non-schizophrenics may at times also avoid defining their relationships with others. Someone may deny he is doing something by qualifying his activity with the statement that a somatic influence or liquor is doing it and not him. These are patterns of other psychopathologies, and partial ways of avoiding defining a particular relationship at a particular time. At best they tend to be temporary, since headaches ease up and liquor wears off. If a person is more determined to avoid defining his relationship with anyone at any time, and if anything he says or does defines his relationship, then he must behave like a schizophrenic and fully and completely deny what he is saying or doing in his interaction with others. Different types of schizophrenics could be classified in terms of different patterns, and some of their patterns are observable in normal people. The differences from the normal lie in the consistency of the schizophrenic's behavior and the extremes to which he goes. He will not only deny that *he* is saying something, but he will also deny it in such a way that his denial is denied. He does not merely use a name other than his own, he uses one which is clearly not his,

such as Stalin, or in some other way negates his denial. Whereas more normal people will congruently negate something they say, the schizophrenic manifests incongruence even at this level.

To illustrate schizophrenic behavior let me cite a common occurrence. When a normal person takes out a cigarette and does not have a match he usually says to another person present, "May I have a light?" When he does this, he is qualifying a message concerning his unlighted cigarette with a congruent message about the need for a match, and he is defining his relationship with the other person by asking for a light. He is indicating, "This is the sort of relationship where I may request something." Under the same circumstances, a schizophrenic may take out a cigarette, look in his pockets for a match, and then hold the cigarette up in the air and stare at it silently. The person with the schizophrenic is faced with a rather peculiar sequence of communication. He is being appealed to for a match, and yet he is not. By merely staring at the cigarette, the schizophrenic is qualifying his message about an unlighted cigarette with an incongruent message. He is indicating that it is something to be stared at, not something to be lit. If he held up the cigarette as if it should be lit, he would be implicitly asking for a light and thereby defining his relationship with the other person. He can avoid indicating what sort of behavior is to take place, and therefore what sort of relationship he is in, only by looking at the cigarette in a detached way. A more obvious example is the behavior of a schizophrenic in a room with a stranger. He may not speak to the stranger, but since not speaking to him indicates what sort of relationship it is, the schizophrenic is likely to appear excessively preoccupied with something in the room, or with his thoughts. In this way he denies that he is defining his relationship with the other person by the way in which he qualifies his behavior.

By qualifying his messages to other people incongruently, the schizophrenic avoids indicating what behavior is to take place in his relationships and thereby avoids defining his relationships. The current trend in psychotherapy for schizophrenics takes into account this interpersonal behavior. The experienced therapist tends to take the schizophrenic's statements as statements about the relationship, and to ignore the denials of this. If the patient begins to talk in an odd language, such a therapist is less likely to interpret the symbolic content of that language and more likely to say something like, "I wonder why you're trying to confuse me," or, "Why do you speak to *me* in this way?"

Analysis of a Schizophrenic Conversation

To illustrate how the foregoing description of interpersonal relationships applies to schizophrenics, a recorded conversation between two young men will be presented here and subsequently analyzed. The numbers in brackets will be used in the analysis following the conversation to identify the passages analyzed. This conversation between two hospitalized schizophrenics took place when the men were left alone in adjoining offices where they could see each other through a connecting door. The men were presumably talking together for the first time, although they may have seen each other previously when entering the same building.

Jones [1]: [Laughs loudly, then pauses.] I'm McDougal, myself. [This actually is not his name.]

Smith [2]: What do you do for a living, little fellow? Work on a ranch or something?

Jones [3]: No, I'm a civilian seaman. Supposed to be high mucka-muck society.

Smith [4]: A singing recording machine, huh? I guess a recording machine sings sometimes. If they're adjusted right. Mh-hm. I thought that was it. My towel, mm-hm. We'll be going back to sea in about—eight or nine months though. Soon as we get our—destroyed parts repaired. [Pause.]

Jones [5]: I've got lovesickness, secret love.

Smith [6]: Secret love, huh? [Laughs.]

Jones: Yeah.

Smith [7]: I ain't got any secret love.

Jones [8]: I fell in love, but I don't feed any woo—that sits over—looks something like me—walking around over there.

Smith [9]: My, oh, my only one, my only love is the shark. Keep out of the way of him.

Jones [10]: Don't they know I have a life to live? [Long pause.]

Smith [11]: Do you work at the air base? Hm?

Jones [12]: You know what I think of work, I'm thirty-three in June, do you mind?

Smith [13]: June?

Jones [14]: Thirty-three years old in June. This stuff goes out the window after I live this, uh—leave this hospital. So I can't get my vocal chords back. So I lay off cigarettes. I'm a spatial condition, from outer space myself, no shit.

Smith [15]: [Laughs.] I'm a real space ship from across.

Jones [16]: A lot of people talk, uh—that way, like crazy, but Believe It or Not by Ripley, take it or leave it—alone—it's in the *Examiner,* it's in the comic section, Believe It or Not by Ripley, Robert E. Ripley, Believe It or Not, but we don't have to believe anything, unless I feel like it. [Pause.] Every little rosette—too much alone. [Pause.]

Smith [17]: Yeah, it could be possible. [Phrase inaudible because of airplane noise.]

Jones: I'm a civilian seaman.

Smith [18]: Could be possible. [Sighs.] I take my bath in the ocean.

Jones [19]: Bathing stinks. You know why? Cause you can't quit when you feel like it. You're in the service.

Smith: I can quit whenever I feel like quitting. I can get out when I feel like getting out.

Jones: [Talking at the same time.] Take me, I'm a civilian, I can quit.

Smith: Civilian?

Jones: Go my—my way.

Smith [20]: I guess we have, in port, civilian. [Long pause.]

Jones [21]: What do they want with us?

Smith: Hm?

Jones [22]: What do they want with you and me?

Smith [23]: What do they want with you and me? How do I know what they want with you? I know what they want with me. I broke the law, so I have to pay for it. [Silence.]

As Smith and Jones communicate and thereby inevitably maneuver to define their relationship, they obviously and consistently qualify their statements with negations. On the recording from which this transcript was taken, the qualifying inflections of voice make the incongruencies even more apparent.

The following brief examination of the verbal aspects of the conversation will indicate the ways that each of the two schizophrenics denies that he is defining a relationship: denial that *he* is communicating, denial that something is communicated, denial that it is communicated *to* the other person, or denial of the context in which it is communicated.

Jones [1]. The conversation begins when Jones gives a peculiarly loud and abrupt laugh followed by a pause. He then introduces himself in a friendly manner, but uses an alias, negating his move toward intimacy by the qualifying statement that *he,* Jones, is not making such a move.

Smith [2]. Smith replies with a friendly inquiry about the other person, but calls him a little fellow, qualifying his overture with an unfriendly comment on the other's size. (Jones is actually a little fellow who indicates that he is not too happy about this by speaking in an artificially deep bass voice.) Smith also poses the friendly question of whether Jones works "on a ranch or something," when it is obvious that Jones is a patient in a mental hospital and incapable of making a living; thus he denies that he is replying to Jones, a hospital patient.

Jones [3]. Jones denies that he is a patient by calling himself a civilian seaman, and then denies this by qualifying it with a statement that he is supposed to be high mucka-muck society. He has set up a situation in which no matter what he, Jones, says, it cannot be about his relationship with Smith because *he* isn't speaking.

Smith [4]. Smith mentions the recording machine (which is in the room but out of Jones' sight) and says that a recording machine can "sing," or inform. But this friendly warning, which would define their relationship as a sharing one, is qualified by a negation of it: he muses about the recording machine as if he were talking to himself and not the other person. He also denies that he is giving a warning by qualifying his statement with a quite incongruent one mentioning a towel. He next makes a possible statement about their relationship by saying, "We'll be going back to sea," but since they aren't seamen the statement negates itself.

Jones [5]. After a pause, Jones says he has lovesickness; a secret love. This is perhaps a comment on Smith's sharing statement about being seamen, yet he denies, or leaves ambiguous, the possibility that he is talking about Smith.

Smith [6 and 7]. Smith apparently accepts this as a possible statement about their relationship since he laughs uncomfortably and says he doesn't have a secret love.

Jones [8]. Jones then points out that he isn't talking about himself or Smith but about someone who looks like himself walking around over there. Since no one is walking around over there he qualifies his previous statement about love with a denial that *he* or Smith was the one talked about.

Smith [9]. Smith points out that his love is the shark and it's best to keep out of the way of him. He denies that he is defining his relationship with Jones by making it himself and a shark that is talked about.

Jones [10]. Jones subsides with a statement about being picked on or rejected, but he denies that he is referring to Smith by saying, "Don't *they* know I have a life to live?"

Smith [11]. After another pause, Smith makes a friendly overture but negates it as a statement about their relationship with an incongruence about the place. He calls the hospital an air base.

Jones [12]. Jones replies rather aggressively with a statement about his age, thereby denying his patient status by making his age the reason for his inability to work—as if he were saying, "It's not me, it's my age." However, he counters this denial by a statement contradicting it when he states his age as thirty-three. If he had said, "I am eighty-six," he would have been congruently stating age as a reason for not working. Thus he even denies his denial.*

Smith [13]. Smith chooses from his statement the least relevant part, the fact that in June the man will be thirty-three. How different such a reply is from a possible one qualifying Jones' statement, "Do you mind?" Rather than acknowledge "Do you mind?" as a statement about what sort of behavior is to take place in the relationship, and perhaps apologize for bringing up work, Smith comments on the month of June. In this way he denies that Jones' "Do you mind?" is a statement defining the relationship.

Jones [14]. Jones makes a congruent statement about the context, saying it is a hospital, but qualifies this with the statement that all he needs to do is give up cigarettes. He promptly negates this statement that implies there is nothing really wrong with him by saying he is a spatial condition from outer space.

Smith [15]. Smith joins him in this with a laugh and says he is also a space ship. Although they are mutually defining their relationship, they are negating this definition by the statement that they are not two persons sharing something but two creatures from outer space. This turns their statements about the relationship into statements about a fictional relationship.

Jones [16]. Jones again qualifies the context congruently by mentioning talking "like crazy," but he immediately qualifies this with a series of statements incongruent

* The incongruence of this third level of schizophrenic communication is one of the basic differences between the schizophrenic and the normal, as was mentioned earlier. Almost every statement in this recording consists not only of denials but of negations of those denials. When Jones introduces himself as "McDougal," he does so in a tone of voice which seems to indicate his name isn't really McDougal. An examination of this third level probably requires kinesic and linguistic analysis and is merely mentioned here.

with it and with each other as he talks about Ripley, and the comic section, and ends up saying "too much alone."

Smith [17 and 18]. Smith responds to these statements by talking to himself and not the other person.

Jones [19]. When Smith mentions bathing, Jones joins his monologue and once again makes a comment that has implications about sharing their situation. This is negated by his qualifying it with a statement that they are in the service.

Smith [20]. Smith joins him in a denial that this is a hospital by calling the place a port.

Jones [21 and 22]. After a pause, Jones makes a direct, congruent statement defining their relationship, "What do they want with us?," and he even repeats this when it is queried by Smith. This statement and the way it is qualified are congruent and in this sense it is a sane statement. He maneuvers to define the relationship without denying that he is doing so.

Smith [23]. Smith rejects this maneuver. He first says, "How do I know what they want with you? I know what they want with me." This statement is congruent with what Jones has said and defines his relationship with Jones even though he is rejecting Jones. In this sense it is a sane reply. However, Smith then qualifies his congruent statement with a thorough negation of it. By saying, "I broke the law, so I have to pay for it," he denies the place is a hospital, denies that he is talking about himself, since he hasn't broken the law, and denies that he and Jones are patients by making the place a prison. With one message he avoids defining his relationship with Jones and discards the attempt of Jones to work toward a mutual definition of their relationship. This denial ends the conversation and the relationship.

This brief analysis deals with only half the interaction between Smith and Jones. The ways in which they interpret, or respond to, the other person's statements have not been completely discussed. However, it seems apparent that they qualify each other's statements with messages which deny they are from that person, deny they are messages, deny they are addressed to the receiver, and deny the context in which they take place. The schizophrenic not only avoids defining his relationship with another person, he also can be exasperatingly skillful at preventing another person from defining his relationship with him. It is such responses which give one the feeling of not being able to "reach" a schizophrenic.

What makes it "obvious" that these two men behave differently from other men is the extreme incongruence between what they say and the ways they qualify what they say. Two normal men meeting for the first time would presumably introduce themselves and make some inquiry into each other's background as a way of seeking out some common interest. If the context was at all appropriate, they would work toward defining their relationship more clearly with each other. Should one say something that seemed out of place, the other would probably query it. They would not only be able to qualify what they said congruently, but they would be able to talk about their communications to clarify their understanding and therefore the relationship. Disagreements would tend to reach a resolution. However, when one of the participants in a conversation is determined to deny that what he says has anything to do with the relationship being worked out, then inevitably the conversation will have the disjunctive quality of schizophrenia.

If one should ascribe any goal or purpose to human relations, it would appear to be a highly abstract one. The wife who maneuvers to get her husband to do the dishes does not merely have as her goal his acquiescence in this act. Her larger goal seems to be related to an attempt to work out a definition of what sort of relationship they have with each other. Whereas more normal people work toward a mutual definition of a relationship and maneuver each other toward that end, the schizophrenic seems rather to desperately avoid that goal and work

toward the avoidance of any definition of his relationship with another person.

The Significance of the Analysis of Interpersonal Relationships

When schizophrenia is described as a disjunction between several levels of messages, questions can be posed about what sort of learning situation would induce such behavior. If one says the schizophrenic is withdrawn from reality or has delusions, such a description does not give any clues as to the etiology of the psychopathology. However, if one says the schizophrenic avoids defining his relationship with anyone by qualifying his statements incongruently, one can speculate about the kind of family interaction which encouraged this behavior. Not only can one speculate, but one can also observe the patient interacting with his family, to see if an interactional origin is apparent.

Preliminary investigations of schizophrenic patients interacting with their families suggest that the patient's way of qualifying his statements incongruently is a habitual response to incongruent messages from his parents. As an illustration, suppose that a mother said to her child, "Come and sit on my lap." Suppose also that she made this request in a tone of voice which indicated she wished the child would keep away from her. The child would be faced with the message, "Come near me," qualified incongruently by the message, "Get away from me." The child could not satisfy these incongruent demands by any congruent response. If he came near her, she would become uncomfortable because she had indicated by her tone of voice that he should keep away. If he kept away, she would become uncomfortable because after all she was inviting him to her. The only way the child could meet these incongruent demands would be to respond in an incongruent way; he would have to come near her and qualify that behavior with a statement that he was not coming near her. He might, for example, come toward her and sit on her lap while saying, "Oh, what a pretty button on your dress." In this way he would sit on her lap, but he would qualify this behavior with a statement that he was only coming to look at the button. Because human beings can communicate two levels of message, the child can come to his mother while simultaneously denying that he is coming to her—after all, it was the button he came to be near.

By saying, "Come sit on my lap," in a tone of voice which indicates, "Keep away from me," the mother is avoiding defining her relationship with the child. More than that, she is making it impossible for the child to define his relationship with her. He cannot define the relationship as one of closeness nor can he define it as one of distance if he is to satisfy her incongruent demands. He can only manifest incongruent messages himself and thereby avoid defining his relationship with her.

It seems possible that incongruent messages from a mother could impose on her child a response which avoids defining his relationship with her. It also seems possible that should the child define his relationship with her by communicating congruent messages, she could respond in an incongruent way and thereby compel him to avoid defining his relationship with her. In theory at least, it seems conceivable that a systematic incongruence between levels of messages could be manifested by someone if the communicative behavior within his family enforced such incongruence.* This

* Parental behavior consisting of incongruent messages has been defined elsewhere as a "double bind" situation (2).

would be particularly so if the child was largely confined to one relationship so that he did not learn to experience other kinds of behavior with other people. It is "socially acceptable" for a child to respond to his mother's incongruent request to sit on her lap by coming to her and saying, "Oh, what a pretty button." Yet this behavior is formally the same as that of the schizophrenic who becomes frightened and enters his doctor's office asking if this is Grand Central Station. He behaves as if he is seeking reassurance and simultaneously qualifies that behavior by a denial of it. The difference lies in the fact that his denial itself is qualified incongruently—he negates the denial by making it clearly fantastic.

A logical hypothesis about the origin of schizophrenic behavior, when the behavior is seen in communications terms, would involve the family interaction of the patient. (For a fuller discussion of the family of the schizophrenic, see reference 3.) If a child learned to relate to people in a relationship with parents who constantly induced him to respond to incongruent messages, he might learn to work out his relationships with all people in those terms. It would seem to follow that the control of the definition of relationships would be a central problem in the origin of schizophrenia.

References

1. Ruesch, J., and Bateson, G., *Communication, the social matrix of psychiatry*. New York: Norton, 1951.

2. Bateson, G., Jackson, D. D., Haley, J., and Weakland, J. Toward a theory of schizophrenia. *Behavioral Science*, 1(1956), 251–264.

3. Haley, J. The family of the schizophrenic; a model system. *J. Nerv. & Ment. Disease*, 129 (1959), 357–374.

Contradictory Parental Expectations in Schizophrenia: Dependence and Responsibility *

Yi-Chuang Lu, Ph.D.
MANTENO STATE HOSPITAL

This paper reports some preliminary findings of one aspect of a research on schizophrenic patients and their families. Previous investigations such as the works of Lidz (12–16), Hill (6), Wynne (21), Bowen (2, 3), Bateson (1), and Jackson (8), have indicated that parental pathology or pathological patterns of interpersonal relationships in the family are of etiological significance to the development of schizophrenia. Most of these studies have concentrated on the patients' families. In comparing parental or parent-child relations in the schizophrenics' families with those in the nonschizophrenics' families, other investigators use "normals" or "psychoneurotics" as controls. The pieces of research by Kohn

Reprinted from the *AMA Archives of General Psychiatry*, 6(1962), 219–234, with the permission of the American Medical Association and the author.

* This research is supported by a grant from the Psychiatric Training and Research Fund of the Department of Mental Health, State of Illinois.

Expanded version of a paper read at the 55th Annual Meeting of the American Sociological Association, Aug. 31, 1960, in New York City, as part of the program on "Sociology and Mental Health: Familial and Social Relationships and Schizophrenia."

(10), Clausen (4), and Myers and Roberts (18) are examples of this type. These latter researches have shown the prevalence of certain patterns of parental authority structure in the schizophrenics' families which are different from those in the nonschizophrenic families, at least among families in a certain socioeconomic class.

While the existing investigations on schizophrenia revealed the significance of parental or family pathology or parental authority structure (8), one question remains to be answered: "Why does one child in a family develop schizophrenia, while another child, presumably exposed to similar parental or family pathology or parental authority structure, does not?" This question suggests that merely studying parental or family pathology or parental authority structure in the family alone is not enough to explain the development of schizophrenia. To seek an answer, it is necessary to compare the parents' relationships with the preschizophrenics and the parents' relationships with the nonschizophrenic siblings of the patients. In the present research, therefore, the nonschizophrenic siblings are used as controls. The objective here is to discover the specific patterns, if any, of parent-child interactions that are related to the development of schizophrenia.* An attempt is also made to ascertain other significant life experiences of the preschizophrenics which are different from those of the nonschizophrenic siblings and which are related to the development of schizophrenia.

Method of Research

The sample of this research consisted of 50 schizophrenic patients who are part of the patient population in a male-female chronic schizophrenic research unit at the Manteno State Hospital, Illinois. Only those schizophrenic patients who had a nonschizophrenic sibling,† preferably of the same sex and near in age and whose parents, particularly the mothers, were available for interviews, were included in the sample. Other criteria for selection of cases included: no organic brain disease or mental deficiency, young (preferably under 35), white, with minimum grade school education, families from lower socioeconomic strata, preferably with parents who live in Chicago.

The data of this project were obtained by my interviewing the patients intensively and observing their behavior in the schizophrenic research unit of the hospital in the last 5 years. Intensive interviews were also conducted by me with the patients' fathers, mothers, siblings, and other significant persons in the patients' life. All these interviews were recorded verbatim and conducted for research purposes. The length of an interview with the schizophrenic patients varied. It ranged from half an hour to 2 hours or sometimes longer, depending on the mood, mental condition of the patients, or their desires to express themselves at the time of the interview. The first interview with a parent or sibling, particularly with

the mother, often lasted up to about 4 hours or more. Most of the family members spoke spontaneously and freely. The mothers in particular tended to confide their personal feelings and report the interpersonal relationships in the family. In addition to interviews by appointment, casual interviews with and observations of family members were also made during their visits with the patients on the hospital ground. The reliability and validity of the interview data were tested by comparing the patients' statements with those of their parents and siblings.‡ In addition to interviews, a schedule was constructed. Therefore, this project combines the use of both qualitative and quantitative data.§

The preliminary findings to be presented in this paper are based on analysis of the life histories of 24 out of the total of 50 cases in this sample. A detailed statistical presentation of all data will be deferred to the future when the schedule data of all 50 cases are completely analyzed. At the time of the investigation, most of the subjects reported in this paper were 35 years of age or under. They were white; 15 males and 9 females. The majority of them completed at least their grade school education; 10 of them attended college. Nine of the subjects are from families of lower-lower and 10 from upper-lower socioeconomic classes, 4 from lower-middle and 1 from upper-middle classes; ¶ immigrant backgrounds and diverse ethnic groups were predominant. The majority of the patients were Catholics, and some of the parents' marriages were of mixed religious faith.‖ The ages at the first schizophrenic break range from 16 to 30; the median age of the first break is 20.

‡ No attempt is made here in this paper to test the reliability and validity of the data. The reliability and validity will be presented when the final report of this research is made. The interview excerpts cited in this paper are for illustration only.

§ For other aspects of the research design, see my first paper on this research (17).

¶ The criteria for determining the socioeconomic class of a patient are based upon Lloyd Warner's Index of Status Characteristics (20).

‖ The precise description of the social characteristics of the patients in this sample and other findings will be presented in a future report when all the 50 cases are analyzed statistically.

* The parental relationships and other aspects of family life of the patients will be reported in the future.

† For a discussion on the decision as to whether a patient's sibling is nonschizophrenic, see my first report of this research (17).

Contradictory Parental Expectations of Dependence and Responsibility

A comparison between the parents' relationships with the preschizophrenic child and the parents' relationships with the nonschizophrenic sibling shows that they are quite different with respect to the parents' contradictory expectations for the child's dependence and responsibility and the child's efforts to fulfill these expectations. In this section, the terms "dependence" and "responsibility" will be defined; the differences between the role patterns of the preschizophrenic child and the nonschizophrenic sibling in relation to their parents will be presented and discussed; and case excerpts will be used to illustrate these differences. In the next section, an attempt will be made to show how later specific social situations acting on the previously developed relational role pattern of the preschizophrenic child precipitate the schizophrenic break. The third section will trace the different role patterns of the preschizophrenic child and the nonschizophrenic sibling to the different social, familial, and personal situations confronting them at their birth and infancy. Finally, the implications of these preliminary findings for a theory of schizophrenia will be discussed.

DEPENDENCE

The term dependence is used here to refer to one's reliance upon others for emotional support (response, recognition, security, appreciation, encouragement, and reassurance), for protection, and/or for care. In the preschizophrenic's relations with his parents, dependence also implies the former's sensitivity to the latter's feelings and expectations for obedience and submission—the parents' approval and acceptance being vital to his emotional survival. It also denotes the persistent efforts on the part of the off-

spring to please his parents and conform to their wishes and demands at the cost of his personal autonomy. Dependence is the opposite of independence or autonomy in decision-making or assuming responsibility.*

The data in this sample indicate that although the parents attempted to exercise authority over both the preschizophrenic child and his nonschizophrenic sibling since their childhood, the parents expected a higher degree of obedience, submission and dependence from the preschizophrenic than from the nonschizophrenic child. Twenty-two out of the 24 cases have reported such a difference. On his part, the preschizophrenic child was much more obedient, submissive to and dependent on the parents than the nonschizophrenic child, while the nonschizophrenic child got away from parental control and strove for independence. Of the 24 cases, 23 cases reported such a difference. The 22 patients whose parents had higher expectations for their dependence are also the patients who became more dependent on their parents.

The following excerpts show the differences between the preschizophrenic child and the nonschizophrenic sibling in regard to their dependent relationships with their parents.

A 19-year-old female patient with grade school education reported: "My parents are strict on their children. I think they are more strict on me and they punished me more (than other kids in the family). I always broke my arms since I was 2 years old. Both my mother and father took care of me on account of it. This made me more dependent on them. But other kids in the family had not been sick (physically). They were on their own. Both Sandra and Cathy (sisters) like to do things for themselves. But I like to depend on someone else to do things for me. I am much more dependent on my mother than Sandra and Cathy. I always told my mother everything.

* For a more detailed treatment of parent-child dominance-dependence role relations, see my article (17).

"Before I was mentally sick, I tried to please my parents by running errands for them, doing the things my mother asked me to do. But still they didn't appreciate it. I cared more about my parents' feelings than Sandra and Cathy.—At the age of 13, I went to work for a family to help take care of their children and their house. But it lasted only a couple of weeks because I was too tied to my mom and dad's apron strings. I was so used to my mom and dad that I couldn't be on my own. When I worked for this family, I lived in their house. But I called my mom every day. When I called her, she answered the phone right away. Apparently she was sitting there waiting for my call. She had protected me more than other kids at home. Sandra and Cathy were not tied to my mother's apron strings."

Another patient, aged 24, a male college student, said: "My mother babied me. Sometimes maybe she made me feel like a baby, like I was afraid to leave my home for the army, or something like that. I still feel I am dependent because I can't hold a job. I am dependent on my mother and father. Dependence means that they cook for me, they take care of the house, and they pay for my room and board. They just told me to cut the lawn, to go to the store, maybe to dust the furniture. I have never really taken care of myself. But Philip (brother) is very able to take care of himself than I of myself. He is able to hold a job. I was real close to my parents. I was closer to my father and mother than my brothers were. I confided in them about everything."

RESPONSIBILITY

While the parents expected the preschizophrenic child to be more dependent than they expected the nonschizophrenic sibling, they at the same time entertained a conflicting expectation that the preschizophrenic child assume *responsibility for achievement and perfection*. In this paper, the term "responsibility" is used to refer to 2 different categories of role demands. The first category is responsibility for the fulfillment of certain *generalized and often abstract demands,* such as high aspirations

for achievement, striving for social mobility, and striving for perfection. The second is responsibility for performing certain *concrete, specific, and immediate tasks* such as financial responsibility and household functions, particularly those relating to adult roles in the American society.

In this section, we are concerned only with the first category of responsibility— the more *generalized* expectations. In 19 out of 24 cases, the parents had, since the preschizophrenics' childhood, higher expectations for their achievements and for their striving for social mobility and perfection than for the patients' nonschizophrenic siblings. Although the parents who themselves were often perfectionists had great desires for the success of both the preschizophrenic and the nonschizophrenic sibling, it was the preschizophrenic in whom the parents constantly instilled such high expectations. The schizophrenics, their parents, and siblings often reported that the parents always expected and even insisted that their preschizophrenic children be perfect, be the best, and be on the top among their peers either educationally, occupationally, socially, or as a person.

The mother of a single, 24-year-old student who studied in a theological seminary to be a priest at the time of his schizophrenic break reported: "My husband, who was a foreman, was a perfectionist. I am also a perfectionist. I was a school teacher and I am a very ambitious person. Since Gordon (the patient) was a child and began to go to school, I expected him to be a scholar. I expected Fred (the nonschizophrenic sibling) to be successful, but I had never expected him as much as Gordon. When Gordon was at the eighth grade, his class prophecy of him was Professor Smith. I had always expected him to be a scholarly person. If he could be one, I would be satisfied. He always had good grades in school. If they could do it, of course you would expect them to. But I did not expect Fred as much, because he had not done so well in school. I wanted Gordon to go to the township high school because I wanted him to learn speech in order to study to be a priest. Gordon tried to please me much more than Fred. Since childhood, Gordon was much more dependent on me than Fred."

A 25-year-old college student whose father was a policeman said: "Before I was sick, my parents drove me very hard. My mother always told us to be better than we were and to do better. But she hasn't driven my brother so hard. My mother expected me to become a lawyer or some kind like that. It means that I will also be doubly important than I am. I mean, she could do it herself and do me no harm. What I do for myself is much better for myself than for anyone else. Mother always wanted me to do what she wanted. Even when I was a big boy at the age of twenty, she told me what to do. She always insisted on me to do what she wanted me to do. She would order me around while I wanted to do my own thinking."

On their part, the preschizophrenics had also attempted desperately to live up to the parental expectations, although some might complain about the parental drives for their success and perfection. In this sample, it was found that in 18 out of 24 cases the preschizophrenics had a much higher mobility aspiration and desire for achievement and perfection than the nonschizophrenic siblings. Seventeen cases in this group are the same cases among the 19 cases where the parents had higher expectations for the preschizophrenics' achievements and perfection than for the nonschizophrenic siblings. In other words, in almost all the cases where parents had higher expectations for the preschizophrenics' achievement and perfection than for the nonschizophrenic siblings, the preschizophrenics also tried harder to live up to that expectation than the nonschizophrenic siblings.

In many cases, the preschizophrenics' initial efforts and aspirations for achievement did actually result in their success as the best students in grade school, and,

for many, even in high school. The parents, siblings, and the schizophrenic patients themselves frequently reported that the preschizophrenics obtained the highest grades in their classes. Many were honor students, scholarship holders, and were valedictorians for their graduating class at grade school. Although many nonschizophrenic siblings had done well, they were seldom such top students at these early student periods. The preschizophrenics had not only striven for achievements; they also attempted to be perfect as defined by their parents, often vaguely, such as being "the best," "good," "nice," etc. Not infrequently they were extremely religious and obedient. In contrast, the nonschizophrenic siblings had not taken these parental expectations so seriously. They tried as much as possible to go out with their friends.

Take, for example, the case of Gordon, a student at a theological seminary who has been discussed in the first part of this section. The widowed mother gave the following description of her preschizophrenic and nonschizophrenic children:

"Gordon was too much of a perfectionist. He wanted everything in perfect order. But Fred is not a perfectionist at all. He is just the opposite of Gordon. Gordon was a very ambitious boy. But with Fred, I had to push him. Gordon's marks started falling down in the second year of theological seminary. He took too many courses in the second year, because he wanted to get into Novitiate. In one of the courses, he was in the class with younger students. They threw papers over him. He could do nothing about it, because he wanted to have 100 points in his conduct course. If he threw papers back to them, then he couldn't get it. He was too much of a perfectionist. He took things too seriously. Gordon was interested to work very much. You don't have to tell him to clean the basement, to mow the lawn, or to clean the house. He just kept everything beautifully at home. But Fred never did anything. Gordon worked so hard might be because he wanted to please me. He was so wonderful to me before he was sick. Naturally I praised him a lot for it. So he might want to please me even more. I never missed a birthday or a Mother's Day without a gift from Gordon. But Fred doesn't even know when my birthday is."

The patient, Gordon, also reported: "I think I am the favorite of my mother among all the boys in the family. You know, I have been the closest one to her. I had always tried to make her happy. But my brothers never cared about her like I did. My 2 older brothers graduated from high school and then went to work. I am the only one in the family who went to college; I think I was the smartest among my brothers at that time. I got the second honor in my class at the fourth grade and I got the first honor in my class at the sixth grade. As to high school, at first I also got good grades. But I didn't get good grades in the last 2 years. But they let me graduate anyway. I think I am the most ambitious one among my brothers. They wanted to do well too. But since they couldn't do it, they went to work. Now they are pretty successful in their work. My 2 older brothers are married now. My mother and I were the most religious persons in the family. I always wanted to be a priest and I still want to be one now. But my brothers never wanted to be priests and they never have been so religious. I always wanted to be good. My younger brother doesn't listen to my mother as I do."

The preschizophrenic's effort in conforming to parental expectations for success and perfection, together with its results, can also be seen in the following excerpt.

The parent of a single, 26-year-old ex-newspaper delivery boy said: "Graham (patient) used to like to jump on high things. But his brother did not care. Graham was extremely ambitious. He was the only one among my kids who always wanted to make something of himself. He always wanted to make the home better. He got a big citation and a medal from Mayor Kelly when he was 13 for collecting the largest amount of scrap paper during the wartime. He was also the one who made the speech

for the graduating class in grade school. He got so many medals but he never put them on. Other kids would be proud of this and put them on. But Graham never did. He wanted to be the best. But not my other kids."

The type of responsibility which the above interview excerpts bring out refers to the fulfillment of obligation or "duty" of a more generalized or abstract nature. This first category of responsibility is more or less a long-range goal to be achieved. It played a more prominent role in the preschizophrenic's life *long* before the appearance of schizophrenic symptoms. It is to be distinguished from the second category of responsibility which plays a definite role as a factor in *precipitating* the schizophrenic symptoms to be discussed later in this paper. This second category of responsibility is related to the performance of more specific, concrete, and immediate tasks.

So far, the data on parental expectations for dependence and for responsibility, and the data on their children's attempt to fulfill them, have been presented separately. Now it is necessary to see how many parents had entertained higher expectations for their preschizophrenic children than for their nonschizophrenic children to play *both* the role of dependence *and* the role of assuming responsibility for achievement and perfection, and how many preschizophrenics had made greater efforts than their nonschizophrenic siblings to play these contradictory roles. For the parents to expect the preschizophrenics to play the contradictory roles of dependence and responsibility is to involve the preschizophrenics in a dilemma. An examination of the data shows that in 19 out of 24 cases, the parents had expected their preschizophrenic children to play these contradictory roles of dependence and responsibility for achievement and perfection much more than they expected their nonschizophrenic children. Again, 17 out of the 24 preschizophrenics had persistently made greater efforts than their nonschizophrenic siblings to fulfill these contradictory parental expectations of dependence and responsibility for achievement and perfection. These 17 cases are among the 19 cases where there were higher contradictory parental expectations for the preschizophrenics than for the nonschizophrenics. Since these have been illustrated in the interview excerpts presented above, no more quotations will be given here.

Closely related to the contradictory parental expectations of responsibility and dependence is another set of contradictions in parental expectation and attitudes or behavior which merits a brief discussion here. This is the contradiction between parental expectation of the child's high achievement and perfection on one hand, and, on the other, the parents' competition with the preschizophrenic child for status, power, and possession.* It seems that whenever the child performed adequately according to the parental expectation of achievement, the parents would feel that their power and status were threatened. On the other hand, the preschizophrenic also competed with the parents while attempting desperately to fulfill parental expectations at the same time. Such parental expectations of the preschizophrenic's achievement and parent-child competition often began to occur when the preschizophrenic child was in high school. In comparison, the parents expected less from the nonschizophrenic sibling and were less competitive with him than with the preschizophrenic child. The preschizophrenic child also took them more seriously than the nonschizophrenic sibling. The following excerpt illustrates one aspect of such parental contradiction and the schizophrenic child's responses to them.

* There is an abundance of evidence in the interview data to show this contradiction. Due to limitation of space, the discussion and case illustration here are necessarily brief.

A 25-year-old single football player who won a football scholarship to a university reported: "My father and mother expected me to amount to something much more than they expected of my brother. I think I was more ambitious than my brother. My father especially expected me to do well in the football field, because all through his life he had wanted to be a football coach. But he had to support his family and so he had to give it up. Therefore he wanted me to be a coach. I feel I took what my parents said as real, and seriously, but my brother didn't. Whenever I played football with other kids in high school, my father used to come and insist on coaching me. My friends all laughed at me on account of it. But whenever I did play real well, my father would get mad at me. He wanted to feel he was better than me. I think he competes with me more than he with my brother."

DISCREPANCY BETWEEN ASPIRATION AND SELF-EVALUATION

In 14 out of the 24 cases in the data, the discrepancy between the preschizophrenic's aspiration for achievement, perfection, and his self-evaluation is greater than the discrepancy between those of the nonschizophrenic sibling.

As the preschizophrenics grew older, the fulfillment of contradictory parental expectations for dependence and responsibility of achievement and perfection became increasingly difficult for them, for the American culture deplores dependence and values increasing independence from parents as one enters adolescence and approaches adulthood. Moreover, competition during childhood among a small group of children was less keen than competition with peers on higher educational levels, who were a more selected group. In high school or college, the preschizophrenics' chance to remain at the top was decreased. Furthermore, there were some preschizophrenics who attended larger high schools and colleges than their nonschizophrenic siblings. The latter reported that it was much more difficult for the preschizophrenics to be on the top level than themselves, because of keener competition in larger schools. Consequently the preschizophrenics could not remain on the top as before. From the time they were in high schools or colleges, the preschizophrenics began to fall behind, but the nonschizophrenic siblings became much more successful than the preschizophrenics. Therefore it became increasingly difficult for the preschizophrenics to fulfill their parents' contradictory expectations for perfection and dependence. An adverse self-conception was thus formed when the preschizophrenics were not able to maintain their level of achievement and to obtain the same degree of parental approval and acceptance. While their self-evaluation became increasingly lower, their aspirations for achievement and perfection remained as high as before. Thus, there was great discrepancy between the preschizophrenics' aspiration for success and their self-evaluation. In contrast, the nonschizophrenic siblings became more insistent on independence from their parents as they grew older. And they were also much more realistic in setting the goals of their lives and were much more flexible in changing them. Since their goals were comparatively easier to reach than those of the preschizophrenics, and since their self-conceptions did not depend as much on parental approval, their self-evaluation was much higher than that of the preschizophrenics. Furthermore, as they became more successful in their endeavor, they gained more praise and approval from their parents which further lowered the preschizophrenics' self-evaluation. Thus the preschizophrenics felt they were incompetent. They lacked self-confidence. They had a sense of failure, especially after the parents' comparison of their "failure" with the nonschizophrenic siblings' "success." They were very jealous of their non-schizophrenic siblings, whom they greatly admired at the same time. They did not want to be themselves. They wanted to be like others, especially their siblings, while the nonschizophrenic siblings learned to accept themselves and not try to be somebody else. The following interview data illustrate the preschizophrenic's high aspirations for success and how his low self-evaluation was developed after he once lost out in the competition.

A 26-year-old unmarried high school student whose father had never been regularly employed and whose family had been on relief ever since the patient's childhood reported: "I was more ambitious than my brother because I was the valedictorian of my graduating class in grade school. I felt I was like Abraham Lincoln. But I wasn't proud of it; neither were my parents. When I spoke for my class, my girl was there. I felt I was somebody important. When I was about 12 years old, I thought I was in the brink of confidence and success.—As a child, I did want to be a drummer. I wanted to be successful in everything. My ambition was to be a doctor at that time. But then something went wrong. When I was 16, I competed and I was supposed to be the leader in the drum section in high school. Then one of my friends was made the drum section leader. I couldn't see how he was chosen, because he never had the training I had had. That was a great disappointment.—Well, my brother didn't have any ambition when he was a child. Now he goes to junior college, so he has ambition now. He is also married. But I am good at nothing."

The nonschizophrenic siblings' more realistic approach in setting the goals of their lives and their being more flexible to change them can be seen in the following statement.

A nonschizophrenic sibling whose widowed mother worked as an unskilled laborer to support both the patient and the nonschizophrenic sibling said: "I want very much to continue my college education. But judging from the financial condition of the family, I know it's impossible for me to do so. Now I realize I couldn't have it, so I don't insist on it. Now I just enjoy working."

The parent's comparison of the non-schizophrenic sibling's success with the preschizophrenic's failure and the preschizophrenic's jealousy over the former's success is shown in the following statements.

The father said: "Jerome (patient) always wanted to be better than others. But Carl and Francis (the nonschizophrenic siblings) don't care. My wife wanted Jerome to go to college in order to get better, so Jerome went to college. My wife also wanted the other 2 boys to go to college, but they didn't want to go. My wife always praised Carl and Francis, because they worked and made so much money. But Jerome didn't like it. He said, 'How come any time I get a new job, they always fire me?' What bothered Jerome most is that my wife always said the other two boys made so much money, nice money. She implied that Jerome didn't make so much money."

The patient, Jerome, also reported: "I am jealous of my younger brother, Francis, because he is able to hold a job."

The Social Situations Precipitating the Schizophrenic Break

So far, some background factors related to the development of schizophrenia have been discussed. Now it is time to turn to the question: "When or under what social situations did the schizophrenic symptoms first appear?" The data * tend

* The writer is aware of the fact that the data on the social situations precipitating the first schizophrenic breaks are reconstructive. There is a possibility that they are the after-the-event or selective perceptions of the informants. But until the time "observed stresses" precipitating the first schizophrenic breaks can be obtained, we have to rely on these reflections of "felt stresses" in the investigation. The situations under which the patients' schizophrenic symptoms appeared or subsided during hospitalization have been observed by the writer. But the treatment of this problem is not within the scope of this paper.

to indicate that schizophrenic symptoms first appeared after the preschizophrenic was confronted with the combination of 2 social situations which heightened to the critical point the dilemma between dependence and responsibility.†

The first of the 2 social situations is *sudden explicit expression* by the significant others (17) that the patient should assume *concrete* adult responsibility, or *sudden* pressure on the patient to assume *increased concrete* adult responsibility. This means that the preschizophrenic who had never been expected to bear financial, household, or other responsibility since childhood was now suddenly expected to take up this adult responsibility or to play the adult role. In other cases, the preschizophrenic who had taken up some such responsibility before was now subject to sudden pressure to assume an increased financial, household, or other responsibility.

The second social situation is the loss or lack of intimate relations with members of a peer group or persons on whom the patient could depend for emotional support. The group or persons are those the preschizophrenic looked up to and wished to identify himself with. Twenty-one out of 24 preschizophrenics were confronted with both of these social situations before their schizophrenic

† Ideally, it would be desirable to use, for purpose of comparison, a control group of preschizophrenics who had never been confronted with the social situations which critically heightened the dilemma between dependence and responsibility. But thus far it is not possible within the writer's resources to find such a control group. Therefore, the writer has to be content at this time to answer only the question of whether there were such social situations precipitating the onset of the symptoms of our schizophrenic patients. However, the fact that the schizophrenic patients in this sample had never been confronted with such combination of situations before their first schizophrenic breaks may suggest the role of such social situations in promoting the schizophrenic symptoms. Thus before a control group of preschizophrenics could be used, the patients' own experience during different periods of their lives is used as the control.

breaks. And among these 21, 15 are also the same patients who had, long before the schizophrenic breaks, persistently made greater efforts than their non-schizophrenic siblings to fulfill contradictory parental expectations of dependence and responsibility for achievement and perfection.

In general, when the situation suddenly called for someone in the family to take up responsibility, it was always the preschizophrenic who was expected to play that role. During adolescence and early adulthood most preschizophrenics had been struggling to meet the demands to accept concrete adult responsibilities. These responsibilities were particularly burdensome to them, for they had been extremely dependent all their lives. It was not uncommon that not long before the schizophrenic breaks, the preschizophrenics had attempted to work excessively hard. Besides going to school, they often took a full-time job plus a part-time job, or several part-time jobs. Such extreme compulsion to work was not found in the nonschizophrenic siblings. There are some cases where the onset of schizophrenic psychoses were followed by the death of the father which resulted in the sudden expectation or pressure for the preschizophrenics to take up the deceased father's role of providing for the family. In other cases, before the schizophrenic breaks, the preschizophrenics were suddenly expected to take up heavy household responsibilities or, in the case of some female patients, to assume the increased responsibility of bringing up or bearing children.

This sudden increase in parental pressure for the preschizophrenics to take up adult responsibility took place simultaneously with such events as the loss of friends who went into the services, or the moving of the families to new neighborhoods, or the preschizophrenics' change to a new or large school where it was difficult for them to establish peer relationships. Although many expecta-

tions for the preschizophrenics' assuming responsibility often came from the parents and close relatives, they may sometimes be reflections of the "generalized others" (17)—the expectations of the community or society in general. Or they may simply be a necessity because of the financial condition of the lower-class family.

The data on social participation indicate that although many preschizophrenics had been shy and passive in interpersonal relations, they managed all along to have friends and belong to some peer groups. At least there was someone besides their parents on whom they could depend. The schizophrenic breaks might be avoided as long as they were not expected to take up suddenly increased concrete responsibility, and as long as their dependence on their parents could be transferred to members of their peer, social, or occupational group, or to a sibling, or to the spouse. Some patients reported that just before they were mentally sick, they could no longer get the support of the members of their peer groups. They said that they needed encouragement from friends to give them self-confidence. But the parents of some patients increasingly insisted that they go to work instead of hanging around the street corners with their friends.

In contrast, the nonschizophrenic siblings were reported to be the ones who were not so dependent on their parents, who always had more friends. When the situation called for responsibility, they either shouldered it readily, or avoided it by leaving their parents and finding a life of their own.

The following excerpt will show how the onset of schizophrenic symptoms was preceded by the combination of these 2 factors: first, sudden pressure on the patient to assume increased concrete adult responsibility caused by the death of the father; and, second, the loss or lack of peer group or persons on whom the patient could depend for emotional support.

The elder sister of a patient reported: "Bob had the nervous breakdown after my father's death. Not soon after my father's death, my sister, brother and I all got married and left home. Bob was the only one left with my mother. He felt the responsibility to take care of her. As a matter of fact, he was the only one who was responsible for her financial support after my father's death. He felt he failed everybody. He is so dependent on my mother. He always needs someone. He needed young people. My mother was not enough. After my father's death, not only all of us left home and he had no one to hold on to, but all of his friends also went into the services. He had to take care of my mother."

Sometimes the sudden explicit expression of parental expectation for the patient to take up the adult role or responsibility might be prompted by the patient's sudden physical growth from boyhood to manhood.

The schizophrenic break of a 17-year-old student occurred after his widowed mother persistently insisted on his finding a job after the family moved to a new neighborhood where the patient could find no friends. The sibling reported: "After we moved to the Cermak Street address when Ernest was 17, my mother began to want him to get a job. That was just before he was mentally sick. At that time he was growing fast. He *suddenly* grew up to be real tall. Before that he was just a small boy and my mother never expected him to work before. But then my mother *suddenly* began to try to put more ambition in him. She said to him, 'You are such a big man now. You should go and find a job to help the family out.' But at the same time, my mother still continued to treat him like a little boy. She always did things for him, practically dressed for him. She got shoes for him and polished the shoes for him and did almost everything for him. Before we moved to the Cermak Street address and before he was transferred to the new school, everything was nice with him. But after we moved, it seems that he felt no one

was interested in him. He really didn't get any attention from us. I was busy with my outside activities. But before we moved, Ernest and I were real companions then. He was close to me."

The following case of a manual laborer illustrates the effect of the sudden pressure on the preschizophrenic to assume immediate increased financial responsibility in the family due to his parents' divorce, in combination with the preschizophrenic's separation from his peer group and elder sibling from whom he used to acquire emotional support.

The patient reported: "I had my first breakdown; I guess it's because I was overworked. It happened when I was about 16 or 17 after my father and mother were divorced. And my grandmother also died around this time. After my grandmother's death, my mother was ordered by the court to pay her sister some $2,000 to $3,000. My brother went into the service at about the same time. So I was the only one left to support my family. It was too much for me. After my parents' divorce, not only I had to support my mother, but also she needed a lot more money because she had to pay her sister. So I overworked. All I needed was to have a rest. Now I got my rest. So I am all right. Before my first breakdown at the age of 17, I used to run with a gang in the neighborhood. We grew up together. But just before my first breakdown, most of them went into the service. My brother also went into the service. I also passed both my physical and mental examinations. But I couldn't go because I had to support my mother. Then I got sick."

A 26-year-old young mother became schizophrenic when she was pregnant for her fifth child and after her husband on whom she had been extremely dependent began to spend both day and night outside of the home on business and paid no attention to her. The patient said: "The first time I was (mentally) sick was at a time I discovered I was 4 months pregnant with my fifth child. I worried a great deal. Because at that time *suddenly* there was too much work for me. I just couldn't take it. You see, besides taking care of the 4 kids and the housework, I had to redecorate the whole house over, from inside to outside of the house. I wanted to do a *perfect* job. I was very ambitious about it. And yet I had to do everything *alone*. Therefore when I learned I was pregnant again, I thought I couldn't take in any more responsibility. This also happened after 6 months my husband began to have a business of his own. And he became extremely busy. He had to go out at 4 o'clock in the morning and wouldn't finish his work until 9 or 10 in the evening. We could hardly talk to each other. That was too much for me. I needed to leave home and go somewhere else where I didn't have to take so much responsibility. But my husband wouldn't agree on this. Then I became sick."

The presentation of the above data shows that the kind of responsibility expected of the preschizophrenics which precipitated their schizophrenic symptoms differs from the relatively general, abstract, long-range expectation for achievement and perfection which the preschizophrenics had attempted to live up to since childhood. The former was a more specific, definite, immediate and sudden responsibility pressed on the preschizophrenics. Although they had attempted all their lives to fulfill contradictory parental expectations of dependence and responsibility for perfection and achievement, this more specific, immediate, and sudden increased responsibility became far more difficult for them to cope with. For one thing, this suddenly increased responsibility was naturally beyond the ability of the habitually dependent and inflexible persons to bear. Moreover, it consisted of specific tasks which had to be performed immediately. Therefore, to the preschizophrenics, success or failure would be determined within a relatively short time, and the "verdict" would be "pronounced" almost at once. Thus, the performance of concrete, specific and immediate tasks was in principle different from the previous effort in achieving those general, abstract, and long-range objectives. To the preschizophrenics, it served as an immediate test

of their adequacy and competence, and therefore affected their immediate self-conception and self-evaluation. Furthermore, the preschizophrenics were also aware of the cultural expectation for adults or persons approaching adulthood to assume increased specific responsibilities. At a time when there was the extra burden of assuming the suddenly increased responsibility, the deprivation of emotional support from peers further increased their anxieties because now they had to shoulder the heavy responsibility alone. Thus, the combination of the 2 social "pressures" heightened critically to a breaking point their dilemma between dependence and responsibility (independence) and precipitated the development of schizophrenic symptoms.*

The Social, Familial, and Personal Situations at Birth and Infancy

Now the question arises as to why the parents expected more from the preschizophrenic than from the nonschizophrenic child and why the preschizophrenic child tried much harder than his nonschizophrenic sibling to fulfill contradictory parental expectations. The process of such parents–preschizophrenic interaction and emotional entanglement seems to begin as early as the period of the patient's birth and infancy. It is necessary, therefore, to reconstruct the experiences of the parents and the infant at this period. It is expected that the social, familial, or personal situations confronting the preschizophrenic children at the time of their birth and infancy are different from those confronting the nonschizophrenic children.†

* Some of the schizophrenic symptoms and behavior of the patients observed in the hospital in relation to their dilemma will be presented in a future paper of the writer to be entitled: "Major Role Strains in Chronic Schizophrenia."

† Like the data on social situations precipitating the schizophrenic breaks and other data in this investigation, the data on social, familial

The parents, often the mothers, had paid more attention to the preschizophrenic child or given him more protection than the nonschizophrenic child because of one of the following 2 reasons: One consists of such unusual circumstances * as the preschizophrenic child's being sick as an infant, or an unusually big infant, or the only male child to carry the family name, or being the oldest or the youngest child, etc. The second reason is that the tension between father and mother or the parents' hardships and frustrations at the time of the birth or infancy of the preschizophrenic child was much more intense than at that of the birth or infancy of the nonschizophrenic sibling. These tensions and frustrations often arose out of the much more adverse financial condition at the time of the birth and infancy of the preschizophrenic child, or sexual difficulty between father and mother because of the fear of being pregnant again, or the mother's living and having difficulties with in-laws, or disappointment in the sex of the infant, or the mother's difficulty in the labor of the infant, etc. Out of the 24 cases there are 17 cases where the parents reporting either such unusual circumstances mentioned above or heightened tension between the parents at the time of the birth or infancy of the preschizophrenics, but not at the time of the birth or infancy of the nonschizophrenic siblings.

Another interesting fact about the difference between the preschizophrenic infant and the nonschizophrenic sibling is

and personal situations at birth and infancy are reconstructions of the informants. Until longitudinal studies are made beginning before the preschizophrenics' birth, this is probably the only way to obtain such data at this time.

* The role of the child who is a problem for his parents by reason of his atypicality in changing the structure of family relationships can be seen from Klebanoff's study of mothers of schizophrenics, mothers of brain-injured children, mothers of retarded children, and mothers of normal children (9).

the personal situation confronting them at the time of their birth. Out of the 14 cases where information is available, 10 cases have been reported by the mothers that the preschizophrenics were more passive or slower than the nonschizophrenic siblings after they were born. One may expect that the mother would give the child more protection or pay him more attention if he were more passive and needed more help from adults.

The following excerpt may serve to illustrate the differences in the social and familial situations confronting the preschizophrenic at birth and infancy and those confronting the nonschizophrenic sibling.

The mother said: "David (patient) was not a planned baby but Paul (nonschizophrenic sibling) was. David was born right after my husband was demoted in his work because of bad business conditions. Definitely among all my children David was born at a time where the financial condition of the family was the worst. There was too much tension between my husband and me. I definitely worried much more when David was born than at the birth of Paul and the other boys. After David was born, my sexual relations with my husband were not good, because I worried about having more babies. We did not use contraceptives. I am a Catholic and my husband was a Protestant. But after Paul was born, we didn't worry about it. Maybe it's because the financial condition was better. And when David was born, he was a big baby—9 lb. That was my hardest delivery among all. But Paul was a smaller baby than David. Another thing is that before David was born, both my husband and I wanted a girl so much, and therefore we were greatly disappointed. After we learned it was a boy, I didn't want to see David and my husband's face also turned white. But when Paul was born, I didn't care whether it was a boy or a girl. I took more care of David than Paul when they were babies. I stayed home more and I might have spent more time with David than Paul and made David dependent on me when they were young."

Comparison with Other Related Investigations

The preliminary findings presented in this paper raise some interesting questions in regard to some related studies in this area.

RELATION TO DOUBLE-BIND THEORY

The comparison between the preschizophrenics and their nonschizophrenic siblings in this paper shows how contradictory parental expectations of dependence and responsibility (independence) on the one hand, and the child's persistent efforts to fulfill these expectations, on the other, are related to the development of schizophrenia. These preliminary findings call attention to a closely related theory, the double-bind theory advanced by Bateson and his associates (1). In general, the double-bind theory is consistent with the preliminary findings presented in this paper. For in a sense this theory also implies that schizophrenic symptoms may develop if in an intense relationship a person is caught in a persistently unresolved contradictory or dilemma situation. The preliminary findings presented here, however, differ from the double-bind theory in several ways. First, while Bateson's theory emphasizes the mother's general ambivalence toward the preschizophrenic child as indicated by the incongruent messages of hostile (or withdrawing) and loving (or approaching) behavior that she communicates to him, the writer focuses on a more specific pair of contradictory expectations of the parent (or parents). The writer's data suggest that as far as the American families (from lower socioeconomic strata) are concerned, one of the most striking sets of contradictory expectations relates to the parents' expecting at the same time the child's dependence and independence (or

responsibility, decision-making, etc.). They tend to indicate that in the American culture which is dominated by the value orientation of independence, responsibility, achievement (work), and personal autonomy in adulthood, the persistently unresolved emotional conflict arising out of pressure to play the independent role and the dependent role at the same time is among the severest strains which seem to be related to the development of schizophrenic symptoms in this group of lower socioeconomic classes of families. In other words, those contradictory expectations which affect the preschizophrenic child's ability to fulfill the social expectations of his adult roles in his subculture are one of the most conspicuous sets of contradictory expectations experienced by preschizophrenics. Implicit in this analysis is the idea that not every pair of "double-bind" messages or expectations is of equal significance in the development of schizophrenic symptoms.

Second, while Bateson and associates stress the double-bind situation "created" by the mother's (and/or father's) simultaneously expressing 2 or multiple orders of messages to the child, or her one-way ambivalence as the most important etiological factor in the genesis of schizophrenia, the writer stresses the *2-way interaction* between the preschizophrenic child and the parent(s) as one of the factors related to the development of schizophrenic symptoms. To me, not only the contradictory *parental* expectations, but also the *extreme dependence* of the *preschizophrenic child* on his parent(s) or his persistent efforts to fulfill contradictory parental expectations play a significant role in promoting the "double-bind" relationships between the parent(s) and the child.

In other words, the double-bind theory seems to have emphasized the mother's active role and the preschizophrenic's passive role in such relationships. The data of the present research, however, show that the child also plays a role (17) in the promotion of such parent-child entanglement relationship. The possibility of a child avoiding "being caught" in a double-bind situation "created" by the mother is seen in the nonschizophrenic sibling's insistence to be independent from his parents and his refusal to take the contradictory parental expectations seriously. Therefore, without the preschizophrenic's part in promoting such a role pattern in the parent-child interaction, the mother's simultaneous expression of multiple levels of messages probably would not result in the double-bind relationship which is described by Bateson and his associates. Since the publication of Bateson's paper on double-bind theory, his position has been qualified by Weakland, one of Bateson's associates. Weakland acknowledged that potentially the child could "escape" the double-bind situation by establishing more satisfactory communication elsewhere and that the unavailability of such an escape is usually an outcome of the preschizophrenic's dependence on his parent (19). This qualification points to a direction which parallels the writer's preliminary findings. But the question remains whether the role of the preschizophrenic child in such parent-child relational formation can be considered so subordinate to the contradictory messages or expectations of the parents, especially as implied by the term "double-bind" and whether the child's dependence and "unavailability of avenue of escape" from the double-bind situation merely assist in forming such relational pattern. For in the parent-child reciprocal role relations such as those observed in the schizophrenic families, it is extremely difficult to determine which role, the parents' or the child's, is the independent variable. Stated positively, the question is whether the preschizophrenic child's extreme dependence on the parent is in itself also *a form of active participation* in the process of *promoting* such

mutual role formation. This significant question must be answered in any attempt to push forward the frontier of our knowledge. To raise this question poignantly and to direct empirical research in an endeavor to seek an answer, the writer proposes, in lieu of the double-bind theory, the concept of *"quadruple-bind"*: on the one hand, the parent(s) entertained contradictory expectations of dependence and independence (responsibility) and, on the other hand, the child attempts persistently to fulfill such contradictory expectations. This hypothesis of "quadruple-bind" then has the advantage of leaving open for future researchers to tackle the question of the relative importance of the child's role in promoting such parent-child role patterns.

Furthermore, while the writer agrees with Bateson and his associates on the extreme importance of the communication factor, she also takes into account the social-situational or milieu factor in precipitating the onset of schizophrenic behavior, which factor does not seem to have been sufficiently taken into consideration by Bateson. For it seems that communication alone does not explain how the preschizophrenics lose their ability to interpret and discriminate social reality validly, which many seem to have possessed before their schizophrenic breaks, and why the schizophrenic symptoms occur at that particular time.

RELATION TO SOCIAL CLASS
RESEARCH

The ecological research such as that by Faris and Dunham (5) and the social class research by Hollingshead and Redlich (7) suggest the inverse relationship between socioeconomic status and rates of schizophrenia. The social-psychological significance of low socioeconomic status for the development of schizophrenia in the American culture has also been somewhat reflected in the intensive studies presented in this paper. For the hardships and, thus, the tensions of the parents at the time of the birth or during the infancy of the preschizophrenic infant are, among other factors, related to the parents' ultimate emotional entanglement with the preschizophrenic which consequently gives rise to the special role assigned to the preschizophrenic infant in the family. Furthermore, the necessity for the children in the lower socioeconomic strata to assume heavier family responsibilities and the value of striving for upward social mobility is a reality in the daily struggle for existence in the American lower class families. Therefore it seems that certain conditions in the life of the lower socioeconomic strata are ultimately more conducive to the development of schizophrenia than those prevailing among the higher strata. However, one question which can be raised here is whether the contradictory parental expectations emerge from (a) a contradiction inherent in the value system prevalent among groups of lower socioeconomic status, or (b) the presence of a strong middle class orientation in these lower class families.* In the sample of this research, many mothers had married downward † either educationally, occupationally, or socioeconomically and had placed much emphasis on the achievement of the children. At the same time, facing the hard-

ships of life in the lower socioeconomic levels, the parents took over many values appropriate to such an existence. One of these values is the children's obedience and dependence (11). Some children in this sample may have faced a contradiction between middle class norms of achievement, responsibility, independence on the one hand; and on the other, lower class values of obedience and dependence.‡ Sometimes the contradiction confronting the preschizophrenic children may have been due to the mixed religious marriages or the immigrant backgrounds of the fathers and the mothers, or even due to contradictory values within a parent himself or herself.

Concluding Comments

The preliminary findings presented in this paper suggest that although the preschizophrenics and the nonschizophrenic siblings are reared in the same family, they may not be exposed to the same social and psychological conditions in different periods of their lives. First of all, the data tend to indicate that the social, familial, and personal situations confronting the preschizophrenics and the nonschizophrenic siblings at the time of their respective birth and infancy may not be the same. The special circumstances surrounding the preschizophrenic's birth or infancy define the special role which the infant is to occupy in the total family constellation, as well as the special role which he is to play in relation to his parents. This initial definition of the special role for the preschizophrenic infant may on the other hand assist the nonschizophrenic child to avoid playing that role in the family. Furthermore, the continuous reciprocal process

---

* Myers and Roberts in their investigation of "class III" and "class V" patients suggested that the schizophrenics whose anxieties centering on their failure to realize high goals were from class III rather than from class V, for striving for social mobility is a value of class III members (18). It is not yet certain, however, in the writer's sample, whether or not the high aspirations for achievement and perfection of the schizophrenics is due to the middle class orientation of the lower class families. More information on this will be provided when all statistical data are analyzed.

† For example, the mother of a patient is a high school graduate. But the patient's father is illiterate and has to depend on the patient's mother and their children to sign checks for him.

‡ The value of obedience and dependence in the patients' families can also be explained by the fact that the majority of families reported in this paper are Catholic.

of interaction between the parent and the preschizophrenic child throughout the latter's childhood and adolescence leads to a role pattern which is characterized by contradictory parental expectations coupled with the preschizophrenic's persistent efforts to fulfill them. This role relation differs from that between the parent and the nonschizophrenic sibling. In view of the possibility that the preschizophrenic child as well as the parent(s) participates in the formation of this specific relational pattern of contradictory parental expectations and the child's performance, the writer proposes the use of the concept "quadruple-bind" for future research. In addition to this basic difference between the preschizophrenic and the nonschizophrenic sibling, there might, due to contingencies, also be differences in other significant experiences later in life, such as those related to peer groups, schools, and occupations. The lack of support from these social groups may further reinforce the preschizophrenic's tendency to continue the original role pattern of complying with contradictory expectations of the parent(s), while the support the nonschizophrenic sibling gained from such groups may increase the latter's independence from the parent(s).

The presentation in this paper indicates that among other factors, the interplay of 3 conditions seems to be contributory to the development of schizophrenic symptoms in this sample of American lower-class families: (1) contradictory parental expectations regarding dependence and independence (responsibility, etc.), coupled with the preschizophrenic child's persistent efforts in compliance with both expectations; (2) certain experiences at birth or during infancy that incline both the parents and the preschizophrenic child to interact in the contradictory ways as described; and (3) certain sociocultural situations which heightened to the critical point the dilemma between dependence and inde-

pendence to which the schizophrenic symptoms may be considered as a response.

Finally, it must be pointed out that these preliminary findings which are based on part of the data in the sample are not conclusive. The hypotheses remain to be tested statistically when the schedule data of all the 50 cases are completely analyzed.

Acknowledgement is made to Nathaniel S. Apter, M.D., chief of the chronic schizophrenia research unit at the Manteno State Hospital, Illinois State Department of Mental Health, Richard Graff, M.D., Superintendent. I am indebted to Dr. Ernest W. Burgess of the University of Chicago, Dr. Robert Dentler of Dartmouth College, Dr. Bernard Farber of the University of Illinois, and Dr. Bingham Dai of Duke University for their criticisms and suggestions.

References

1. Bateson, G., et al. Toward a theory of schizophrenia. *Behav. Sci.,* 1(1956), 251–264.
2. Bowen, M. Family relationships in schizophrenia, in *Schizophrenia,* Alfred Auerback, ed. New York: The Ronald Press Company, 1959. Pages 147–178.
3. ———. A family concept of schizophrenia, in *The Etiology of Schizophrenia,* Don D. Jackson, ed. New York: Basic Books, Inc., 1960. Pages 346–372.
4. Clausen, J. A., and Kohn, M. L. Social Relations and schizophrenia: A research report and a perspective, in *The etiology of schizophrenia,* Don D. Jackson, ed. New York: Basic Books, Inc., 1960. Pages 295–320.
5. Faris, R. E. L., and Dunham, H. W. *Mental disorders in urban areas,* Chicago: Univ. of Chicago Press, 1939.
6. Hill, L. *Psychotherapeutic intervention in schizophrenia,* Chicago: Univ. of Chicago Press, 1955.
7. Hollingshead, A. B., and Redlich, F. C. *Social class and mental illness,* New York: John Wiley and Sons, Inc., 1958.
8. Jackson, D. D. Conjoint family therapy, some considerations on theory, technique and results. *Psychiatry* (Suppl.), 24(1961), 30–45.
9. Klebanoff, L. B. Parental attitudes of mothers of schizophrenic, brain-injured and retarded and normal children. *Amer. J. Orthopsychiat.,* 29(1959), 445–454.
10. Kohn, M. L., and Clausen, J. A. Parental authority behavior and schizophrenia. *Amer. J. Orthopsychiat.,* 26(1956), 297–313.

11. ———. Social class and parental values. *Amer. J. Sociol.*, 64(1959), 337–351.

12. Lidz, T., et al. The role of the father in the family environment of the schizophrenic patients. *Amer. J. Psychiat.*, 113(1956), 126–132.

13. ———, et al. The intrafamiliar environment of the schizophrenic patients: II. Marital schism and marital skew. *Amer. J. Psychiat.*, 114(1957), 241–248.

14. ———, et al. The intrafamilial environment of the schizophrenic patient: I. The father. *Psychiatry*, 20(1957), 329–342.

15. ———. Schizophrenia and the family. *Psychiatry*, 21(1958), 21–27.

16. ———, et al. Intrafamilial environment of the schizophrenic patients: VI. The transmission of irrationality. *A.M.A. Arch. Neurol. Psychiat.*, 79(1958), 305–316.

17. Lu, Y. C. Mother-child role relations in schizophrenia: A comparison of schizophrenic patients and nonschizophrenic siblings. *Psychiatry*, 24(1961), 133–142.

18. Myers, J. K., and Roberts, B. H. *Family and class dynamics in mental illness.* New York: John Wiley and Sons, Inc., 1959.

19. Weakland, J. H. "The double-bind" hypothesis of schizophrenia and three party interaction, in *The etiology of schizophrenia*, Don D. Jackson, ed. New York: Basic Books, Inc., 1961. Pages 373–388.

20. Warner, W. L., and associates. *Social class in America: A manual of procedure for the measurement of social status.* Chicago: Science Research Associates, Inc., 1949.

21. Wynne, L. C., et al. Pseudo-mutuality in the family relations of schizophrenics. *Psychiatry*, 21(1958), 205–220.

An Intensive Study of Twelve Cases of Manic-Depressive Psychosis*

MABEL BLAKE COHEN, GRACE BAKER,
ROBERT A. COHEN, FRIEDA FROMM-REICHMANN,
AND EDITH V. WEIGERT
WASHINGTON SCHOOL OF PSYCHIATRY

The purpose of this study is to examine the manic-depressive character by means of the intensive psychoanalytic psychotherapy of a number of patients. We feel

Abridged from an article appearing in *Psychiatry*, 17(1954), 103–137, with the special permission of The William Alanson White Psychiatric Foundation, Inc., holder of the copyright, and Dr. Mabel Blake Cohen.

* This article is a condensed and revised version of a report made to the Office of Naval Research under contract Nonr-751 (00), which was sponsored by the Washington School of Psychiatry and financed by the Navy during 1952 and 1953. The statements and opinions published here are the result of the authors' own study and do not necessarily reflect the opinion or policy of the Office of Naval Research.

The preliminary research for this project, which was begun as a seminar in the Washington School of Psychiatry, lasted from 1944 to 1947 and is reported on by Frieda Fromm-Reichmann in "Intensive Psychotherapy of Manic Depressives" [*Confinia Neurologica* (1949) 9:158–165]. The members of this original group were Drs. Grace Baker, Mabel Blake Cohen, Robert A. Cohen, Frieda Fromm-Reichmann, Robert Morse, David McK. Rioch, Olive Smith, Alfred H. Stanton, Herbert Staveren, Sarah S. Tower, Benjamin Weininger, and Mary Julian White.

The authors of the paper wish to express their appreciation to the other members of the original seminar for their contribution to this project. We wish also to express our gratitude to Mrs. Jane Burkhardt for her secretarial assistance throughout the project, and to Helen Swick Perry who acted as editorial consultant in the preparation of this paper.

this to be potentially useful, since the newer understanding of interpersonal processes and of problems of anxiety has not hitherto been brought to bear on this group of patients. The older psychoanalytic studies of the psychopathology of the manic depressive have largely described the intrapsychic state of the patient and left unexplained the question of how the particular pattern of maladjustive behavior has arisen. Thus, to use a simple example, the manic depressive is said to have an oral character. However, the question of how or why he developed an oral character is left unconsidered, except that such factors as a constitutional overintensity of oral drives, or overindulgence or frustration during the oral phase, are mentioned. Our purpose is to delineate as far as possible the experiences with significant people which made it necessary for the prospective manic depressive to develop the particular patterns of interaction which comprise his character and his illness. To this end, neither constitutional factors nor single traumata are stressed in this report, although we do not deny their significance. Rather, we have directed our attention to the interpersonal environment from birth on, assuming that it has interacted with the constitutional endowment in such a way as to eventuate in the development of a manic-depressive character in the child. In other words, the personality of the parents, the quality of their handling of the child, and the quality of the child's response to this handling have played an important part in the development of a characteristic pattern of relating to others and reacting to anxiety-arousing situations which we call typical of the manic-depressive character.

Such a study has many implications for the improvement of the therapeutic approach to the patient. We follow the basic premise of psychoanalytic theory —that in the transference relationship with the therapist the patient will repeat the patterns of behavior which he has developed with significant figures earlier in his life. By studying the transference, we can make inferences about earlier experiences; conversely, by understanding the patient historically, we can make inferences about the transference relationship. As our grasp of the patient's part of the pattern of interaction with his therapist improves, we can gain some concept of what goals of satisfaction he is pursuing, as well as of what sort of anxieties he is striving to cope with. We may then intervene through our part in the interaction to assist him more successfully to achieve his goals of satisfaction and to resolve some of the conflicts which are at the source of his anxiety.

In this research project, a total of twelve cases were studied. They were all treated by intensive psychoanalytic psychotherapy for periods ranging from one to five years. Nine of the cases were presented and discussed in the original research seminar from 1944 to 1947. During 1952 and 1953, the present research group studied three additional cases in great detail; the members of the group met in three-hour sessions twice monthly during that period. All twelve of the cases are referred to in brief throughout the report, and extracts are used from the last three cases (namely, Miss G, Mr. R, and Mr. H) to illustrate various points.

Family Background and Character Structure

FAMILY BACKGROUND

For all of the twelve patients studied, a consistent finding was made in regard to the family's position in its social environment. Each family was set apart from the surrounding milieu by some factor which singled it out as "different." This factor varied widely. In many instances it was membership in a minority group such as the Jews, as in the case of Mr. H. In others it was economic; for example, one patient's family had lost its money and was in a deteriorating social position, and in Mr. R's case, the father's illness and alcoholism had put the family in poor economic circumstances and in an anomalous social position. In another case, the difference resulted from the mother's being hospitalized for schizophrenia.

In every case, the patient's family had felt the social difference keenly and had reacted to it with intense concern and with an effort, first, to improve its acceptability in the community by fitting in with "what the neighbors think," and, second, to improve its social prestige by raising the economic level of the family, or by winning some position of honor or accomplishment. In both of these patterns of striving for a better social position, the children of the family played important roles; they were expected to conform to a high standard of good behavior, the standard being based largely on the parents' concept of what the neighbors expected. Thus Mr. R's mother was greatly overconcerned that he not walk in front of company in the living room, and Mr. H's mother threatened him with severe punishment when he misbehaved while out on the street with her. One mother described her early attitudes toward her child as follows:

I was always an independently minded person, not very demonstrative, so therefore most affection I may have had for anyone wasn't exactly worn on my sleeve. Kay I always loved and there was nothing I didn't try to get for her. My first thought, in most all my selfish material gains, was to get her things I had wanted or didn't have; to go places that I always longed to go to. Hasn't she ever told you of all the good times she has had? College proms, high school parties, dances, rides, silly girl incidents? I can remember so many she has had. Those were the things I had worked

for her to have, and believe me, I had to fight to get them. . . . If you could have just an inkling of the unhappiness I have had trying to give her the material things I thought she wanted, for she never showed any love to me, perhaps you would understand my part. I always tried to protect her from the hurts that I had. . . .

These attitudes on the part of the parents—chiefly the mother—inculcated in the child a strict and conventional concept of good behavior, and also one which was derived from an impersonal authority—"they." The concept seemed to carry with it the connotation of parents whose own standards were but feebly held and poorly conceptualized, but who would be very severe if the child offended "them."

In addition to the depersonalization of authority, the use of the child as an instrument for improving the family's social position again acted as a force devaluing the child as a person in his own right. Not "who you are" but "what you do" became important for parental approval. Getting good grades in school, winning the approval of teachers and other authorities, receiving medals of honor, winning competitions, and being spoken of as a credit to the parents were the values sought by the parents from the child. In a few cases the family's isolation seemed to stem from the fact that they were "too good" for the neighboring families, due to the fact that they had more money or greater prestige. But here, too, the child's role was seen as being in service of the family's reputation.

In a number of cases, the child who was later to develop a manic-depressive psychosis was selected as the chief carrier of the burden of winning prestige for the family. This could be because the child was the brightest, the best looking, or in some other way the most gifted, or because he was the oldest, the youngest, or the only son or only daughter.

The necessity for winning prestige was quite frequently inculcated most vigorously by the mother. She was usually the stronger and more determined parent, whereas the father was usually the weakling, the failure who was responsible for the family's poor fortunes. This was not invariably the case; thus one patient's mother had been hospitalized with schizophrenia from the patient's babyhood on. However, in the more typical cases, the mother was an intensely ambitious person, sometimes directly aggressive, at other times concealing her drive beneath a show of martyrdom. She tended to devalue the father and to blame his weakness, lack of ambition, or other fault for the family's ill fortune. The mother of the patient referred to as Kay wrote in the following terms:

About Kay's father, I'm afraid I can't tell you too much about him, because I was away a good deal, and didn't see too much of him. But as I remember him, I guess he was sort of a pathetic person, or at least I always had a feeling of pity. He had no real home; no immediate family; no decent jobs, at least in my opinion, and no real character.

This blaming of the father for the family's lack of position is in all likelihood due to the fact that in this culture the father is customarily the carrier of prestige, as well as being due to the peculiarities of the mother's relationship with him. The mother was usually thought of by the child as the moral authority in the family, and his attitude toward her was usually cold and unloving, but fearful and desirous of approval. Blame was also leveled at the mothers by the fathers for their coldness and contemptuousness. It seemed that the consistent use of blaming attitudes was of importance in establishing the child's patterns of self-evaluation.

The fathers in the cases studied were thought of by their children as weak but lovable. Two fathers were unsuccessful doctors, one an unsuccessful lawyer, one an unsuccessful tailor, another simply a ne'er-do-well, and so on. By and large they earned some kind of a living for their families and did not desert them but they were considered failures because of their *comparative* lack of success in relation to the standard the family *should* have achieved. The fathers usually were dependent on their wives, although they sometimes engaged in rather futile rebellious gestures against the pressures put on them—as when Mr. H's father spent the evenings playing pool and gambling with his men friends instead of at home listening to his wife's nagging. But, on the whole, they apparently accepted the blame visited upon them and thus implied to their children, "Do not be like me." Each patient, in general, loved his father much more warmly than his mother, and often attempted to defend and justify the father for his lack of success; but in the very defense of the father the patient demonstrated his acceptance of his mother's standards. This pattern was seen to occur regardless of the patient's sex.

Another important contrast in the child's attitude toward his parents was that in his eyes the mother was the reliable one. Thus the child faced the dilemma of finding the unreliable and more-or-less contemptible parent the lovable one, and the reliable, strong parent the disliked one. This pattern also was quite consistent in most of the families of these patients, whether the patient was a boy or a girl. The attitude of the mother toward the father served in addition as a dramatic example of what might happen to the child should he fail to achieve the high goals set by the mother.

EARLY DEVELOPMENT OF THE CHILD

Present-day concepts of the development of personality in infancy and early childhood no longer assume that the infant has no relationships with the people around him until he has reached the age of a year or so. Rather, it is believed that object relations develop from birth on, although it is obvious that early relationships must be quite different in quality from those experienced later on. Much evidence on infantile development in the early postnatal period * demonstrates that the infant reacts selectively to various attitudes in the mothering one. He thrives in an atmosphere of warmth, relaxation, and tenderness while he experiences digestive disorders, shows a variety of tension disorders, and even may die of marasmus in an atmosphere of tension, anxiety, and physical coldness. Under these circumstances, a vague, chaotic, and somewhat cosmic concept of another person—the mothering one—very soon begins to develop, and to this person the infant attributes his feelings of well-being or ill-being; this person is experienced as being extremely powerful.

We have compared the reports of the inner experiences of manic-depressives with those given by schizophrenic patients in regard to the times of greatest anxiety in each. While it is manifestly impossible to make specific constructions on the basis of such accounts, it is nevertheless our impression that they support the conception that the major unresolved anxiety-provoking experiences of the manic-depressive patient occur at a later stage in the development of interpersonal relationships than is the case with the schizophrenic. In the schizophrenic, a conception of self clearly differentiated from the surrounding world does not seem to have been developed, and the patient in panic believes that others are completely aware of his feelings, and that their actions are undertaken with this knowledge. The manic depressive

seems not to experience this breaking down of the distinction between himself and others in times of intense anxiety; rather, he mobilizes defenses which preserve the awareness of self as distinct from others. This formulation has much in common with that of Melanie Klein.

The common experience of therapists with the two disorders is to find the manic depressive much more irritating but much less frightening to work with than the schizophrenic. This may be related to the different concepts of self and others that the two groups of patients have.†

The Figure is intended to show pictorially the difference in interpersonal closeness and object relations between the schizophrenic and the manic-depressive characters.

Points *A*, *B*, and *C* represent successive stages in development. At and soon after birth (*A*), other persons— chiefly the mother—are hardly recognized as such; interpersonal closeness is great but is based upon the intense dependence of the infant upon his mother. As relationships develop, the primary closeness based upon identification diminishes (*B*). Later, a more mature closeness begins to develop (*C*), in which the self is at last perceived as distinct

---

* See particularly Margaret Ribble, *The rights of infants;* New York: Columbia Univ. Press, 1943. See also Spitz, R. Anaclitic Depression. In *The psychoanalytic study of the child,* Vol. II. New York: International Universities Press, 1946.

† For further discussion of this point see a later section of this paper on Differential Diagnosis of the Manic-Depressive.

and separate from other persons. It is evident that a critical phase in development (point *B* on the graph) occurs when the closeness with the mother based upon identification has begun to disappear, but the more mature type of relationship based on recognition of others as whole, separate persons has not as yet developed to any great degree.

We conceive of the major unresolved anxiety-provoking experiences of the schizophrenic patient as occurring at point *A*. At this phase of personality development, closeness is based upon identification, and relationships are partial in character. In the manic-depressive patient, these experiences would occur at point *B*, at a time when identification is less frequently used, but when the ability to relate to others as individuals distinct from one's self is in the earliest stage of development. Consequently, although relationships at point *B* are more mature than at point *A*, the individual in another sense is in a more isolated position, since he no longer employs the mechanism of identification to the degree that he did in earlier infancy but has yet to develop the capacity for a higher level of interpersonal relatedness. At this time, therefore, the developing child could be expected to feel peculiarly alone and consequently vulnerable to any threat of abandonment. We would conceive of the neurotic individual as having experienced his major unresolved anxiety experiences at point *C*, when interpersonal relatedness is more advanced than at *B*.

While reliable data about infancy are extremely difficult to gather, our series of manic-depressive patients show a preponderance of normal infancies, with one major exception, Mr. R, who was a feeding problem and was malnourished and fretful for the first several months of his life. The mothers of these patients appear to have found the child more acceptable and lovable as infants than as children, when the manifold problems of training and acculturation became important. Our impression is that it was the utter dependence of the infant which was pleasurable to the mother, and that the growing independence and rebelliousness of the early stage of childhood were threatening to her. Unconforming or unconventional behavior on the part of the child was labelled as "bad" by the mother, and she exerted great pressure to stamp it out. Thus, the heretofore loving and tender mother would rather abruptly change into a harsh and punishing figure, at about the end of the first year. The child, under the stress of anxiety, would have difficulty integrating the early good mother and the later bad mother into a whole human being, now good, now bad. While a similar difficulty in integration may face all children, this split in attitude toward authority, in the more fortunate, is eventually resolved as the personality matures; but it remains with the manic depressive for the rest of his life unless interrupted by life experience or therapy. An important authority is regarded as the source of all good things, provided he is pleased; but he is thought of as a tyrannical and punishing figure unless he is placated by good behavior. These early experiences probably lay the groundwork for the manic depressive's later ambivalence.

LATER DEVELOPMENT OF THE CHILD

In later childhood, when the child's personality traits and role in the family have begun to crystallize, the manic depressive may be likened to Joseph in the Bible story. Joseph was his father's favorite son. The envy of his eleven brothers was aroused by his father's giving him a multicolored coat, and was increased after they heard of two of Joseph's dreams. The first dream was about eleven sheaves bent down, and one standing upright; everybody knew that this represented Joseph with his eleven brothers bowing to him. In the other dream, eleven stars, the sun, and the moon were bowing to the twelfth star, and everybody agreed that this represented the mother, the father, and the eleven brothers bowing before Joseph. His envious brothers decided to kill him, but one of them, finding himself unable to agree to killing his own flesh and blood, influenced the others to throw him into a pit in the wilderness, and finally to sell him to a passing merchant from a foreign land. After his separation from his family, and his arrival in the foreign land, Joseph immediately grew in stature, and quickly rose to the position of the Pharaoh's first adviser. By his skill and foresight, he averted the evil effects of a threatening famine, not only in Egypt, but also in the neighboring countries.

This story can be used to illustrate some aspects of the manic depressive's relationship to his family. Many of these patients are the best-endowed members of their families, excelling in some cases in specific creative abilities over their siblings, and over one or both of their parents. Some of them have a special place in the family as a result of their own ambitious strivings as, for example, Mr. H. Others are the favorites of one or both parents for other reasons, sometimes because they are the only one of their sex among the siblings, as in one of our patients. All this makes for their enviously guarding their special position in the family group, despite their being burdened with great responsibilities in connection with their special position. It also subjects them to the envy of their siblings, and, quite often, to the competition of one or both parents. Neither the patients themselves nor the family members are, generally speaking, aware of their mutual envy and competition. Mr. H's difficulties with envy were particularly acute. His therapist reported as follows:

Mr. H suffers from extreme feelings of envy toward his male contemporaries who have been more successful than he. The envy is so acute and painful that it is for the most part kept out of awareness. It occasionally forces itself upon his attention, particularly at times when some one of his contemporaries has received a promotion or other sign of success. The patient always feels that he deserves the promotion more than the other person and believes that his illnesses are the stumbling block in the way of his receiving it, or, at times, that the lack of recognition is due to anti-Semitism. While he is an extremely intelligent and able person who does his work adequately, except in periods of emotional disturbance, he does not visualize himself as succeeding on the basis of his productivity, and he makes little effort to succeed on the basis of doing a better job than his competitors. His efforts toward success are directed toward getting to be the friend of the boss, becoming a companion of the boss in sports or games, or going to the races with the boss. By getting the boss to like him especially or find him pleasant and agreeable to be with, he hopes to interest the boss in promoting his future. During his psychotic episodes this pattern increases in its scope and becomes a grandiose fantasy in which he is being groomed for the Presidency of the United States or in which the eye of some mysterious person is watching over him. He once said, for instance, "There is an organization, the FBI, which is set up to find the bad people and put them where they can't do any harm. Why should there not be a similar organization which has been set up to find the good people and see to it that they are put in a position of importance?"

As mentioned previously, manic depressives usually come from families who are in minority groups because of their social, economic, ethnic, or religious status. The family members in these minority groups cling together in group-conscious mutual love and acceptance, and in the wish and need to maintain and raise their family prestige in their groups, and their group prestige before an adverse outer world. There is little room for, or concern with, problems of interpersonal relatedness. Under the all-important requirement of seeking and maintaining high prestige, it seldom occurs to any member of these groups to think in terms other than "we belong together." This, then, is a background in which neither the active nor the passive participants in developments of envy and competition are aware of these developments. Yet, without being aware of it, the best-endowed children will spend quite a bit of energy to counteract the envy of the siblings, of which they are unconsciously afraid. Often the children are brought up, not only by their parents, but also by the joint endeavor of several other important older members of the clan. In spite of all this supervision, there is rarely an individual on whom a child can rely with confidence in a one-to-one relationship. In fact, it is frequently the case that the family group has a number of authority figures in it—grandparents, uncles, aunts, and so on—so that the child's experiences of authority are with multiple parent figures. In this setting, the manic depressive in very early childhood is frequently burdened with the family's expectation that he will do better than his parents in the service of the prestige of the family and the clan; consequently, he may feel, or be made to feel, responsible for whatever hardship or failure occurs in the family. For example, one of our patients was held responsible by her sisters for her mother's death when the patient was eighteen months old—"Mother would still be here had you not been born"; for the failure of her father's second marriage, which had been made to provide a mother for the patient; and for her father's "ruined" feet, the result of tramping the streets as a salesman after his position of considerable prominence had ended in bankruptcy. Another patient at the age of three felt that he had to take over certain responsibilities toward the clan, sensing that his parents had failed in the fulfillment of these.

The special role in the family group which these patients hold is accentuated by the fact that they are, as a rule, pushed very early into unusual responsibility, or else themselves assume this role. As a result, their image of the significant people in the family usually differs considerably from that of the other siblings. With their different appraisal of one or both of their parents, from early childhood they are extremely lonely, in spite of growing up in the group-conscious atmosphere which we have described, where there is little feeling for privacy, and where the little-differentiated experiences of the various family members are considered in the light of the common good of the whole family, or the whole clan. In many cases these people are unaware of their loneliness, as long as they are well, because the sentiment of "we belong together" is fostered by their family.

As these people grow up, they remain extremely sensitive to envy and competition. They know what it is like to harbor it themselves and to be its target. One means of counteracting this envy, which early becomes an unconscious pattern, is to undersell themselves to hide the full extent of their qualifications. Another pattern which many of these patients develop to counteract feelings of envying and being envied is to be exceptionally helpful to their siblings, to other members of the early group, and, later on, to other people with whom they come in contact in various ways. They often use their talents for promoting other persons and their abilities. The price they unconsciously demand for this is complete acceptance and preference by the others. These traits are repeated in the transference situation during treatment.

For instance, a patient was brought to the hospital against her will, without any insight into her mental disturbance. Much to everybody's surprise, she most willingly entered treatment with one member of our group. Everything seemed to run in a smooth and promising way until suddenly, after about two weeks, the patient declared vehemently that she would continue treatment no longer. When she was asked for her reasons, she said that she had been under the impression that she might help her doctor, who was an immigrant, to establish herself professionally in the new country by allowing the doctor to treat her successfully. But during the two weeks she had been at the hospital, she had found that the doctor had already succeeded in establishing herself, and therefore the patient's incentive for treatment was gone.

THE ADULT CHARACTER

As adults, persons with cyclothymic personalities continue to manifest many of the same traits that they exhibited in childhood. During the "healthy" intervals between attacks, they appear from a superficial point of view to be relatively well adjusted and at ease with other people. A certain social facility is typical of the hypomanic, although it is not seen so clearly in the depressive person in his "healthy" intervals. For instance, the hypomanic typically has innumerable acquaintances with whom he appears to be on most cordial terms. On closer scrutiny of these relationships, however, it becomes apparent that they cannot be considered to be in any sense friendships or intimacies. The appearance of closeness is provided by the hypomanic's liveliness, talkativeness, wittiness, and social aggressiveness. Actually, there is little or no communicative exchange between the hypomanic and any one of his so-called friends. He is carrying out a relatively stereotyped social performance, which takes little or no account of the other person's traits and characteristics, while the other person, quite commonly, is allowing himself to be entertained and manipulated.

Both the hypomanic and the depressive share in their tendency to have one or a very few extremely dependent relationships. In the hypomanic this dependency is concealed under all his hearty good humor and apparent busyness, but it is quite clear in the depressive. The hypomanic or the depressive is extremely demanding toward the person with whom he has a dependent relationship, basing his claim for love and attention upon his need of the other, and making it a *quid pro quo* for his self-sacrifice. Demands are made for love, attention, service, and possessions. The concept of reciprocity is missing; the needs of the other for similar experiences are not recognized.* Yet the failure to recognize the needs of the other does elicit unconscious guilt which may be manifested by the manic depressive's consciously thinking of himself as having given a great deal. What the giving seems to amount to is a process of underselling himself. In the relationship the devaluation and underselling also indicate to the partner the person's great need of him, and serve to counteract the old, unconscious, fearful expectation of competition and envy from the important person. The cyclothymic person's own envy and competition, too, are hidden from his awareness, and take the form of feelings of inferiority and great need. The person conceives of himself as reaching success, satisfaction, or glory through the success of the other rather than by efforts of his own. Thus Mr. H made himself the stooge of the president of the class in high school, receiving as his reward the political plums that the president was able to hand out, and failing to recognize that what he actually wanted was to be class president himself. He continued this kind of relationship with some im-

* This formulation is similar to that made by O. Spurgeon English, who states, "Closely tied up with the matter of love is the patient's self-esteem or love of himself. The manic-depressive does not seem to have much feeling of love to give, and what he has he is afraid to give." English, Observation of trends in manic-depressive psychosis, *Psychiatry,* **12**(1949), 129.

portant figure—usually male—in every free period afterward, while in his psychotic attacks the wish to be president himself came to consciousness, and he made futile efforts to achieve it.

Thus, the process of underselling themselves, both for the sake of denying envy and in order to become the recipient of gifts from the other, often reaches the point where these persons actually paralyze the use of their own endowments and creative abilities. They themselves frequently believe that they have lost their assets or that they never had any. The process of underselling themselves, especially in depressives, also may convince other people in their environment of their lack of ability. At this point, they begin to hate these other people for being the cause of the vicious circle in which they are caught; and they hate themselves because they sense the fraudulence of their behavior in not having expressed openly all their inner feelings.

One patient said time and again during his depression, "I'm a fraud, I'm a fraud; I don't know why, but I'm a fraud." When he was asked why he felt fraudulent, he would produce any number of rationalizations, but at last it was found that the thing he felt to be fraudulent was his underselling of himself. This same patient got so far in his fraudulent attempt at denying his total endowment that he was on the verge of giving up a successful career—which, while he was well, held a good deal of security and satisfaction for him—in order to regain the love of an envious friend, which he felt he was in danger of losing because of his own greater success.

We see then, in the adult cyclothymic, a person who is apparently well adjusted between attacks, although he may show minor mood swings or be chronically overactive or chronically mildly depressed. He is conventionally well-behaved and frequently successful, and he is hard-working and conscientious; indeed, at times his overconscientiousness and scrupulousness lead to his being called obsessional. He is typically involved in one or more relationships of extreme dependence, in which, however, he does not show the obsessional's typical need to control the other person for the sake of power, but instead seeks to control the other person in the sense of swallowing him up. His inner feeling, when he allows himself to notice it, is one of emptiness and need. He is extremely stereotyped in his attitudes and opinions, tending to take over the opinions of the person in his environment whom he regards as an important authority. Again this contrasts with the outward conformity but subtle rebellion of the obsessional. It should be emphasized that the dependency feelings are largely out of awareness in states of well-being and also in the manic phase; in fact, these people frequently take pride in being independent.

His principal source of anxiety is the fear of abandonment. He is afraid to be alone, and seeks the presence of other people. Abandonment is such a great threat because his relationships with others are based upon utilizing them as possessions or pieces of property. If he offends them, by differing with them or outcompeting them, and they withdraw, he is left inwardly empty, having no conception of inner resources to fall back on. Also, if they offend him and he is compelled to withdraw, this leaves him similarly alone. In this situation of potential abandonment, the anxiety is handled by overlooking the emotional give-and-take between himself and others, so that he is unaware of the other person's feelings toward himself or of his feelings toward the other. This is clearly seen in the well-known difficulty which therapists have in terminating an hour with a depressive. Regardless of what has gone on during the hour, at the end of it the depressive stands in the doorway, plaintively seeking reassurance by some such question as "Am I making any progress,

Doctor?" An attempt to answer the question only leads to another or to a repetition of the same one, for the patient is not seeking an answer—or rather does not actually believe there is an answer—but instead is striving to prolong his contact with the doctor. In carrying out this piece of stereotyped behavior, he is unaware of the fact of the doctor's mounting impatience and irritation, and overlooks its consequence—namely, that, instead of there being increasing closeness between patient and doctor, a situation has now been set up in which the distance between them is rapidly increasing.

This character structure can be seen to have a clear-cut relationship to the infantile development which we have hypothesized for the manic depressive. According to this hypothesis, interpersonal relations have been arrested in their development at the point where the child recognizes himself as being separate from others, but does not yet see others as being full-sized human beings; rather he sees them as entities who are now good, now bad, and must be manipulated. If this is the case, then the adult's poorness of discrimination about others is understandable. His life and welfare depend upon the other's goodness, as he sees it, and he is unable to recognize that one and the same person may be accepting today, rejecting tomorrow, and then accepting again on the following day. Nor can he recognize that certain aspects of his behavior may be acceptable while others are not; instead, he sees relationships as all-or-none propositions. The lack of interest in and ability to deal with interpersonal subtleties is probably also due to the fact that the important persons in the child's environment themselves deal in conventional stereotypes. The child, therefore, has little opportunity at home to acquire skill in this form of communication.

We have said little in this report about the manic depressive's hostility. We feel that it has been considerably overstressed as a dynamic factor in the illness. Certainly, a great deal of the patient's behavior leaves a hostile impression upon those around him, but we feel that the driving motivation in the patient is the one we have stressed—the feeling of need and emptiness. The hostility we would relegate to a secondary position: we see hostile feelings arising in the patient as the result of frustration of his manipulative and exploitative needs. We conceive of such subsequent behavior, as demandingness toward the other or self-injury, as being an attempt to restore the previous dependent situation. Of course, the demandingness and exploitativeness are exceedingly annoying and anger-provoking to those around the patient—the more so because of the failure of the patient to recognize what sort of people he is dealing with. But we feel that much of the hostility that has been imputed to the patient has been the result of his annoying impact upon others, rather than of a primary motivation to do injury to them.

THE PSYCHOTIC ATTACK

The precipitation of the depressive attack by a loss is well known. However, there have been many cases in which attacks have occurred where there has been no loss. In some it has seemed that a depression occurred at the time of a promotion in job or some other improvement in circumstances. On scrutiny it can be seen that in those patients where a depression has occurred without an apparent change in circumstances of living, the change which has actually occurred has been in the patient's appraisal of the situation. The patient incessantly hopes for and strives for a dependency relationship in which all his needs are met by the other. This hope and the actions taken to achieve it are for the most part out of awareness since recognition of them would subject the person to feelings of guilt and anxiety. After every depressive attack, he sets forth upon this quest anew. In the course of time, it becomes apparent to him that his object is not fulfilling his needs. He then gets into a vicious circle: he uses depressive techniques—complaining or whining—to elicit the gratifications he requires. These become offensive to the other who becomes even less gratifying; therefore, the patient redoubles his efforts and receives still less. Finally, he loses hope and enters into the psychotic state where the pattern of emptiness and need is repeated over and over again in the absence of any specific object.

As to the person who becomes depressed after a gain rather than a loss, we interpret this as being experienced by the patient himself as a loss, regardless of how it is evaluated by the outside world. Thus a promotion may remove the patient from a relatively stable dependency relationship with his co-workers or with his boss, and may call upon him to function at a level of self-sufficiency which is impossible for him. Also, being promoted may involve him in a situation of severe anxiety because of the envious feelings which he feels it will elicit in others, the fear occurring as the result of his unresolved childhood pattern of envying those more successful than himself and, in return, expecting and fearing the envy of others at his success. Having made them envious, he may believe that he can no longer rely on them to meet his needs, whereupon he is again abandoned and alone. For example, an episode from Mr. R's life was described by his analyst as follows:

After about a year of treatment it was suggested to the patient by one of his fellow officers that he ought to apply for a medal for his part in the war and he found the idea very tempting. When this was discussed with me, I attempted to discourage it, without coming out directly with a strong effort to interfere, and the discouraging words I said were unheard by the patient. He went

ahead with a series of manipulative acts designed to win the medal, and it was awarded to him. No sooner had he received it than he became acutely anxious and tense. He began to suspect his compeers of envying him and plotting to injure him in order to punish him for having taken advantage of them by getting a medal for himself, and he thought that his superior officers were contemptuous of him for his greediness. His life became a nightmare of anxiety in which he misinterpreted the smiles, glances, gestures, hellos, and other superficial behavior of his fellow officers as signifying their hatred and disapproval of him.

The manic attack is similar to the depressive in following a precipitating incident which carries the meaning of a loss of love. It often happens that there is a transient depression before the outbreak of manic behavior. For instance, Mr. H was mildly depressed at Christmas time; his behavior from then on showed increasing evidence of irrationality which, however, was not striking enough to cause alarm until June, when he developed a full-blown manic attack. We believe, from our experience with patients who have had repeated attacks, that the presence of depressive feelings prior to the onset of the manic phase is very common, and perhaps the rule.

It is well known that many manic patients report feelings of depression during their manic phase. As one of our patients put it, while apparently manic:

I am crying underneath the laughter. . . . Blues all day long—feelings not properly expressed. Cover up for it, gay front while all the time I am crying. Laughing too much and loud hurts more. Not able to cry it complete and full of hell. All pinned up inside but the misery and hatred is greater than the need to cry. Praying for tears to feel human. Wishing for pain in hopes that there is something left. Fright is almost indescribable.

We agree with Freud, Lewin, and others that dynamically the manic behavior can best be understood as a defensive structure utilized by the patient to avoid recognizing and experiencing in awareness his feelings of depression. The timing of the manic behavior varies widely: it may either precede the depression, in which case it can be understood as a defense which has eventually failed to protect the patient from his depression; or it may follow the depressive attack, when it represents an escape from the unbearable depressive state into something more tolerable. Subjectively, the state of being depressed is one of more intolerable discomfort than the state of being manic, since the patient in effect is threatened with loss of identity of his self.

There are personalities who are able to lead a life of permanent hypomania, with no psychotic episodes. Of course, many chronic hypomanics do have psychotic episodes, but there are some who never have to be hospitalized. Such a patient was Mr. R, who had a very narrow escape from hospitalization when he became agitatedly depressed at a time when several severely anxiety-producing blows occurred in rapid succession. On the whole, however, he maintained what appeared to be an excellent reality adjustment. Subjectively, he was usually constrained to avoid thinking of himself and his feelings by keeping busy, but when he did turn his attention inward, then intense feelings of being in an isolated, unloved, and threatened position would arise.

We have noted in our private practices a trend in recent years for an increased number of persons who utilize rather typical hypomanic defense patterns to enter into analytic therapy. These people tend in general to be quite successful in a material sense and to conceal their sense of inward emptiness and isolation both from themselves and from others. Probably their entering analysis in increasing numbers has some correlation with the popular success achieved by psychoanalysis in recent years in this country. Once committed to treatment, these so-called extraverts rapidly reveal their extreme dependency needs, and, on the whole, our impression has been that psychoanalysis has proven decidedly beneficial to them.

In the light of the above discussion of the manic and depressive attacks, we have come to the conclusion that they need to be differentiated psychodynamically chiefly on the score of what makes the manic defense available to some patients while it is not so usable by others. Some investigators postulate a constitutional or metabolic factor here, but in our opinion adherence to this hypothesis is unjustified in the present state of our knowledge. We feel that further investigation of the manic defense is indicated before a reliable hypothesis can be set up.

We feel that the basic psychotic pattern is the depressive one. The onset of a depression seems understandable enough in the light of the patient's typical object-relation pattern described earlier. That is, becoming sick, grief-stricken, and helpless is only an exaggeration and intensification of the type of appeal which the manic depressive makes to the important figures in his life in the healthy intervals. When this type of appeal brings rejection, as it usually does when carried beyond a certain degree of intensity, then the vicious circle mentioned earlier can be supposed to set in, with each cycle representing a further descent on the spiral. At the end, the patient is left with his severely depressed feelings and with no feeling of support or relatedness from the people whom he formerly relied on. At this point, where the feelings of depression and emptiness are acute, the patient may follow one of three courses: he may remain depressed; he may commit suicide; or he may regress still further to a schizophrenic state.

If he remains depressed, he carries on

a chronic, largely fantastic acting-out of the pattern of dependency. There is no longer a suitable object. The members of the family who have hospitalized him are now only present in fantasy. The patient does, however, continue to address his complaints and appeals to them as though they were still present and powerful. In addition, he rather indiscriminately addresses the same appeal to all of those around him in the hospital. The appeal may be mute, acted out by his despair, sleeplessness, and inability to eat, or it may be highly vociferous and addressed verbally to all who come in contact with him, in the form of statements about his bowels being blocked up, his insides being empty, his family having been bankrupted or killed, and so on. The same pattern is developed with his therapist: instead of a therapeutic relationship in which he strives to make use of the doctor's skill with some confidence and notion of getting somewhere, the same empty pattern of mourning and hopelessness is set up, in which he strives to gain help by a display of his misery and to receive reassurance by repeatedly requesting it. It is notable and significant that his ability to work on or examine the nature of his relationships is nonexistent; that difficulties with others are denied and self-blame is substituted. The major therapeutic problem with the depressive is actually the establishment of a working relationship in which problems are examined and discussed. Conversely, the major system of defenses which have to be overcome in order to establish such a working relationship lie in the substitution of the stereotyped complaint or self-accusation for a more meaningful kind of self-awareness. There seems to be a sort of clinging to the hope that the repetition of the pattern will eventually bring fulfillment. Relinquishing the pattern seems to bring with it the danger of suicide on the one hand, or disintegration on the other. It is our opinion that, in the situation in

which the patient has given up his habitual depressive pattern of integration and has as yet not developed a substitute pattern which brings some security and satisfaction, he is in danger of suicide. The suicide, as has been well demonstrated by previous workers, has the meaning of a further, highly irrational attempt at relatedness. It can be thought of as the final appeal of helplessness. "When they see how unhappy I really am, they will do something." This fits in with the almost universal fantasy indulged in by most people in moments of frustration and depression of what "they" will say and do when I am dead. Along with this magical use of death to gain one's dependent ends, goes a fantasy of recapturing the early relationship by dying and being born again.

For instance, Miss G took an overdose of barbiturates as a last resort after her failure to persuade her father to accede to a request by other means. It appeared that in this case there was little intent to die, but that the action was resorted to because lesser means of convincing him had failed. Probably in this instance of a conscious suicidal gesture the manipulative goal is much more apparent and more clearly in awareness than with the majority of cases. On the other hand, self-destruction also has a more rational element; that is, it is the final expression of the feeling that all hope is lost, and the wish to get rid of the present pain. We are inclined to believe that the element of hopelessness in the act of suicide has not been given sufficient weight in previous studies.

Sullivan, at the end of a great many years of studying the obsessional neurotic, came to the conclusion that many of the more severely ill cases were potentially schizophrenic in situations where their habitual and trusted obsessional defenses proved inadequate to deal with anxiety. This statement also applies to the depressive: if the defensive aspects of the depression become ineffectual, then a collapse of the personality structure can occur with an ensuing reintegration on the basis of a schizophrenic way of life rather than a depressive one.

GUILT AND THE SUPEREGO

We have avoided using the term superego in this report, and have not involved the cruel, punishing superego in our attempted explanation of the depression. It is our opinion that utilization of the term superego in this way merely conceals the problem rather than explains it. There are several basic questions regarding the problems of conscience and guilt in the manic depressive. First, what influences account for the severe and hypermoral standards of these people? And second, what is the dynamic function of the self-punishing acts and attitudes which are engaged in during the periods of illness?

The overcritical standards of manic depressives are not explicable as a direct taking-over of the standards of the parents, since these patients in childhood have usually been treated with rather exceptional overindulgence. However, in the section on Family Background and Character Structure we have mentioned the peculiar combination of lack of conviction of worth and a standard of behavior in the family coupled with an intense devotion to conventional morality and to what other people think. It is logical that a child raised by an inconsistent mother who is at times grossly overindulgent and at others severely rejecting would be unable to build up a reasonable code of conduct for himself, and that his code—focussed around what an impersonal authority is supposed to expect of him and based on no concept of parental reliability or strength—would be both oversevere and frightening in its impersonality. In all probability, much of his moral code is based on the struggle to acquire those qualities of strength and virtue which he finds missing in his parents. Later in this report we will return to the problem of authority in the manic depressive. Suffice it to say here that in dealing with authority this type of patient shows a rigid preconception of what authority expects of him as well as a persistent conviction that he must fit in with these expectations which are beyond the reach of reason or experience. The authority appears, in our experience, at times as an incorporated superego and at other times as a projected, impersonal, but tyrannical force. Or rather, every significant person in the patient's social field is invested with the quality of authority.

In this relationship with authority, the self-punitive acts and experiencing of guilt can be understood as devices for placating the impersonal tyrant. The guilt expressed by the depressive does not carry on to any genuine feeling of regret or effort to change behavior. It is, rather, a means to an end. Merely suffering feelings of guilt is expected to suffice for regaining approval. On the other hand, it may also be seen that achieving a permanent, secure, human relationship with authority is regarded as hopeless. Therefore, no effort to change relationships or to integrate on a better level of behavior is undertaken, and the patient merely resorts to the magic of uttering guilty cries to placate authority.

Differential Diagnosis of the Manic Depressive

Some observers have stated that in the intervals between attacks, the manic depressive has a character structure similar to that of the obsessional neurotic. It has also been asserted that in the psychotic phase the manic-depressive illness is essentially schizophrenic. This latter statement is supported by the fact that many manic depressives do, in the course of time, evolve into chronic schizophrenic psychoses, usually paranoid in character, and that there are many persecutory ideas present both in the manic attack and in the depression. In general, there has always been much uncertainty as to who should be diagnosed manic depressive—an uncertainty which is reflected in the widely differing proportions of manic depressives and schizophrenics diagnosed in different mental hospitals.

What, then, is the point of singling out a diagnostic category called manic depressive? In our opinion, the manic-depressive syndrome does represent a fairly clear-cut system of defenses which are sufficiently unique and of sufficient theoretical interest to deserve special study. We feel that equating the manic-depressive character with the obsessional character overlooks the distinguishing differences between the two. The obsessional, while bearing many resemblances to the manic depressive, uses substitutive processes as his chief defense. The manic, on the other hand, uses the previously mentioned lack of interpersonal awareness as his chief defense, together with the defensive processes which are represented by the manic and the depressive symptoms themselves. The object relations of the obsessional are more stable and well developed than those of the manic depressive. While the obsessional's relations are usually integrations in which there is an intense degree of hostility, control, and envy, they do take into consideration the other person as a person. The manic depressive, on the other hand, develops an intensely dependent, demanding, oral type of relationship which overlooks the particular characteristics and qualities of the other.

According to Sullivan's conceptualization of the schizophrenic process, the psychosis is introduced typically by a state of panic, in which there is an acute break with reality resulting from the upsurge of dissociated drives and motivations which are absolutely unacceptable and invested with unbearable anxiety.

Following this acute break, a variety of unsuccessful recovery or defensive processes ensue, which we call paranoid, catatonic, or hebephrenic. These represent attempts of the personality to deal with the conflicts which brought about the panic: the paranoid by projection; the catatonic by rigid control; the hebephrenic by focussing on bodily impulses. According to this conception, the manic depressive can be differentiated from the schizophrenic by the fact that he does not exhibit the acute break with reality which is seen in the schizophrenic panic. On the other hand, his psychotic processes of depression, or of mania, can be thought of as serving a defensive function against the still greater personality disintegration which is represented by the schizophrenic state. Thus, in persons whose conflicts and anxiety are too severe to be handled by depressive or manic defenses, a schizophrenic breakdown may be the end result.

Contrasting the schizophrenic and the manic depressive from the point of view of their early relationships, we see that the schizophrenic has accepted the bad mother as his fate, and his relation to reality is therefore attenuated. He is inclined to withdraw into detachment. He is hypercritical of family and cultural values. He is sensitive and subtle in his criticisms, original but disillusioned. He is disinclined to rely on others and is capable of enduring considerable degrees of loneliness. His reluctance to make demands on the therapist makes the therapist feel more sympathetic, and therefore the therapist is frequently more effective. In addition, the schizophrenic patient is more effective in his aggression; he can take the risk of attacking, for he is less afraid of loneliness. He is more sensitively aware of the emotions of the therapist, since the boundaries between ego and environment are more fluid. The schizophrenic is not inclined to pretend, and is not easily fooled by other people's pretenses. Dream and fantasy life are nearer to awareness, and guilt feelings are also more conscious than unconscious.

The typical manic depressive, on the other hand, has not accepted the "bad mother" as his fate. He vacillates between phases in which he fights with the bad mother, and phases in which he feels reunited with the good mother. In the manic phase, his relationship with reality is more tenuous; he shows a lack of respect for other people, and all reality considerations are dismissed for the sake of magic manipulation to make the bad mother over into a good mother. The manic depressive is, therefore, mostly a good manipulator, a salesman, a bargaining personality. He is undercritical instead of being hypercritical. He easily sells out his convictions and his originality in order to force others to love him, deriving from this a borrowed esteem. In the depressive phase, he sacrifices himself to gain a good mother or to transform the bad mother into a good one. In order to do this, he calls himself bad, and suffers to expiate his sins. But these guilt feelings are, in a sense, artificial or expedient, utilized in order to manipulate the bad mother into becoming a good mother. The depressive does not come to terms with realistic guilt feelings. Instead, he uses his self-accusations, which frequently sound hypocritical, to convince the mother or a substitute that his need to be loved has absolute urgency. He denies his originality because he is terribly afraid of aloneness. He is more of a follower than a leader. He is dependent on prestige, and is quite unable to see through the pretense of his own or other people's conventionalities. He shows a high degree of anxiety when his manipulations fail. His denial of originality leads to feelings of emptiness and envy. His lack of subtlety in interpersonal relationships is due to his overruling preoccupation with exploiting the other person in order to fill his emptiness. This operates as a vicious circle: he has to maintain his claims for the good fulfilling mother, but his search for fullness via manipulation of another makes him feel helpless and empty. This incorporation of another person for the purpose of filling an inward emptiness, of acquiring a borrowed self-esteem, is very different from the lack of ego boundaries in the schizophrenic. The schizophrenic is in danger of losing his ego, and he expresses this danger in fantasies of world catastrophe. The manic depressive is threatened by object loss, since he habitually uses the object to patch up his ego weakness. Object relations in the manic depressive are, therefore, clouded by illusions, but even when he wails, demands, and blames the frustrating object, he is—by this very agitated activity in behalf of his own salvation, ineffective as it may be—defended against the loss of the ego. When the manic depressive becomes schizophrenic, this defense breaks down.

It should be noted that the infantile dependency and manipulative exploitativeness seen in the manic depressive are not unique to this type of disorder. They occur, in fact, in many forms of severe mental illness. The hysteric, for instance, exemplifies infantile dependency and exploitativeness as dramatically as the manic depressive, and in *la belle indifférence* one may see a resemblance to the euphoria of the manic or hypomanic. However, the combination of the dependent and exploitative traits with the other outstanding characteristics of the cyclothymic personality—particularly the communicative defect and the accompanying inability to recognize other persons as anything but good-bad stereotypes and the conventional but hypermoralistic values—does become sufficiently distinct and unique to distinguish these patients characterologically from other types.

Summary and Conclusions

An intensive study of twelve manic-depressive patients was made in order to reformulate and further develop the dynamics of the character structure of these patients in terms of their patterns of interpersonal relationships. In addition to further developing our knowledge of their psychodynamics, we hoped to arrive at therapeutic procedures which would prove more useful in interrupting the course of this kind of illness.

A comprehensive survey of the literature was made in order to determine the present state of development of psychopathological theory in regard to manic-depressive states.

The manic-depressive character was investigated from the point of view of (1) the patterns of interaction between parents and child and between family and community; (2) the ways in which these patterns influenced the character structure of the child and affected his experiencing of other people in his subsequent life; and (3) the way in which these patterns are repeated in therapy and can be altered by the processes of therapy.

PSYCHOPATHOLOGY

Among the significant parent-child interactions, we found that the family is usually in a low-prestige situation in the community or socially isolated in some other way and that the chief interest in the child is in his potential usefulness in improving the family's position or meeting the parents' prestige needs. A serious problem with envy also grows out of the importance of material success and high prestige. We also found that the child is usually caught between one parent who is thought of as a failure and blamed for the family's plight (frequently the father) and the other parent who is aggressively striving, largely through the

instrumentality of the child, to remedy the situation. And finally, the serious disturbance in the child's later value system (superego) is in part attributable to the lack of a secure and consistent authority in the home and to the tremendous overconcern of the parents about what "they" think.

A study of the major unresolved anxiety-provoking experiences of the manic depressive indicates that the crucial disturbance in his interpersonal relationship occurs at a time in his development when his closeness (identification) with his mother has diminished but his ability to recognize others as whole, separate persons has not yet developed. This accounts for the perpetuation of his response to important figures in his later life as either good or bad, black or white, and his inability to distinguish shades of grey.

THERAPY

As a result of our study of these patients, we found that our ability to intervene successfully in the psychosis improved. While all of the factors which contributed to successful therapy with these patients are by no means understood, we concluded that certain areas could be isolated, as follows:

Communication. The primary problem in therapy is establishing a communicative relationship, which is, of course, a reflection of the patient's basic life difficulty. The most characteristic aspect of the manic depressive's defenses is his ability to avoid anxiety by erecting conventional barriers to emotional interchange. We have learned to interpret this as a defense rather than a defect in the patient's experience, and we have found that when it is interpreted as a defense, he responds by developing a greater ability to communicate his feelings and to establish empathic relationships.

Dependency. A second major problem is that of handling the patient's dependency needs, which are largely gratified by successful manipulation of others. Since the manic depressive's relationships with others are chiefly integrated on the basis of dependency, the therapist is in a dilemma between the dangers of allowing himself to fit into the previous pattern of the dependency gratification patterns of the patient and of forbidding dependency *in toto*. Furthermore, the therapeutic relationship in itself is a dependent relationship. The therapist must be alert to the manipulative tendencies of the patient and must continually bring these into open discussion rather than permit them to go on out of awareness.

Transference-countertransference. The most significant part of treatment is, as always, the working through of the transference and countertransference problems. The patient's main difficulties with the therapist are those of dealing with him as a stereotype and as a highly conventionalized authority figure who is either to be placated or manipulated, and by whom all of his dependency needs are to be met. The main difficulties of the therapist are in the frustrations and helplessness of trying to communicate with the patient through his defensive barriers and the strain of constantly being the target for the manipulative tendencies. These problems inevitably involve the therapist in a variety of feelings of resentment and discouragement which must be worked through. We have found that a recognition of the ways in which transference-countertransference patterns manifest themselves and vary from the patterns found with other types of patients makes the working through of this problem possible.

Problem of Authority and Defining Limits. One of the great risks in therapy with the manic depressive is the danger of suicide when he is depressed or of the patient's damaging his economic and social security when he is in a manic phase. Much of the success in handling this destructive element must, of course, depend on successful therapy. However, we have found that a careful definition of limits and an appropriate expression of disapproval when the limits are violated is helpful.

FURTHER AREAS FOR STUDY

We feel that the conclusions derived from our intensive study of twelve patients require confirmation by further investigation of a larger series. A thorough statistical study of the families of manic depressives is desirable in order to confirm and elaborate the picture of the family patterns as we have developed it. And finally, a more intensive study of psychotherapeutic interviews with manic-depressive patients is needed in order to define more clearly the characteristic patterns of communication and interaction between patient and therapist, and to contrast these with the interactions in other conditions. This is a logical next step in advancing our knowledge of the psychopathology of all mental disorders.

Schizophrenia, Paranoid States, and Related Conditions

HARRY STACK SULLIVAN

Perhaps I should begin by saying why I lump schizophrenia, paranoid states, and related conditions. Conceptually, pure paranoia and pure schizophrenia may be pictured as two absolute—and, therefore, imaginary—poles. Yet the fact is that every person who gets lost in the schizophrenic morasses has paranoid feelings and can be led to express paranoid content at times; and, on the other hand, every paranoid person that I have encountered has in his history a period of schizophrenic content.

The person who approached pure paranoia would be one who, as an adequate way of handling his difficulties, transferred out of his awareness any feeling of blame in any connection. Since one cannot transfer blame into interstellar space, it is transferred onto the persons making up the environment. Anyone competent enough to accomplish this must necessarily also have some explanation of why the environment is so peculiarly vicious, and the net result is very highly systematized delusions of persecution and grandeur. And I may add that the nearer one gets to the pole of

pure paranoia, the more obviously the grandeur becomes an explanation for why one should be so persecuted. Despite suggestions to the contrary that occur here and there in the literature, the persecutory distortion comes first and the grandiose explanation second.

But how few people ever approach the absolute pole of pure paranoia may be suggested by the fact that out of, I suppose, fully three thousand veteran cases with which I had some contact in one of the hospitals where I have worked, only one even raised the diagnostic problem of whether he might be a pure paranoid. But it finally was discovered that even this patient's illness had begun with schizophrenic experience—a fact which emerged only in a subsequent hospitalization. At that time he was led to discuss the first of his allegedly recurring mental states, which actually was the beginning of his continued mental disorder, and it included definitely schizophrenic experience. This confirmed what I had long since decided—that it couldn't happen otherwise.

But why is it that one cannot make a blanket transfer of blame onto the environment without undergoing some of this use of the earlier types of referential process? I have a feeling that there is nothing profoundly obscure about it. Al-

Reprinted from *Clinical Studies in Psychiatry* by Harry Stack Sullivan, M.D. By permission of W. W. Norton and Company, Inc. Copyright © 1956 by The William Alanson White Psychiatric Foundation. (Chapter 14, abridged.)

232

though the self is primarily concerned with anxiety—with detecting the threat of anxiety and developing techniques for reducing anxiety and avoiding the recurrence of it—it also is intimately related in a great many ways to refined verbal thinking, to high-grade referential processes using verbal symbols. This is because the learning of language in childhood coincided with the development of the basic structure of the self, and because nonvalidated thinking—these earlier types of referential process—was something that had to be stamped out in the early stages of life as part of the very building of the self. Now the doctrine of pure paranoia would require that the person was wholly secure in his psychosis; there would literally, I think, from the standpoint of theory, be no necessity for the self, except as a device for keeping track of all the attacks upon one and so on. But so massive a maneuver as practically eliminating the necessity for the self would require something other than operations with the validated verbal symbols which are so intimately related to the self; in other words, the self must be subjected to processes which are not classically of it, and these processes are the early, nonvalidated types of thinking which appear in later life as schizophrenic processes. Thus I think it is safe to say that every paranoid person has at some time been schizophrenic for a little while, which means that the universe has been apprehended and dealt with by much more primitive and less refined referential processes than those which later make up the substance of the paranoid state.

The difficulty that we had in getting at the schizophrenic experience in the particular patient whom I have cited is, I think, suggestive of the difficulty encountered with all markedly paranoid-schizophrenic illnesses in getting at anything which can be used remedially. This patient approached pure paranoia in that he was not, from his point of view, in

any sense psychotic; there was only a conspiracy that caused him to be in the hospital again and again. He was litigious and he had, by means of lawsuits, made it extremely awkward for a number of people, including at least one very high government official. Counsel for the people against whom he had brought actions were not at all inclined to minimize the skill with which he could build up very impressive claims on the basis of what a psychiatrist could regard only as paranoid formulations, but which a jury might easily regard as an instance of an extraordinarily capable person's seeing how he was being gypped by corporations, government officials, and various other people. Now, to deal with any of this as possibly psychotic, one would have to get at material about which the patient could not immediately reason convincingly against one. And that material was the material that the patient himself could not understand—namely, the schizophrenic beginning of the thing. So, of course, one could get nowhere near any recollection of that; the patient had a perfect life-history that simply omitted it. But finally, by means of the persistence of a very capable psychiatrist, it was possible to document that such a thing had happened.

Thus, according to my way of thinking, there isn't very much use for the psychiatrist to assume that he is engaged in the cure of a markedly paranoid schizophrenic as long as that patient's history continues to reveal no markedly schizophrenic beginning of the illness. If the patient cannot be gotten to review a period when he was thoroughly schizophrenic, then I do not think the psychiatrist can do much with any of the later content. Only people who are quite gifted in referential operations, argument, and rationalization can sustain so complicated a distortion of reality as is the paranoid position. And so, when you encounter a person who can do so, there is no use in struggling with his interwoven blend of facts, misinterpretations, and slightly fraudulent distortions of events. You might just as well start arguing the validity of the value placed by somebody on the Republican or the Democratic political views, for you do not have the essential data, and so you can go on forever.

Delusions in Schizophrenia as Differentiated from Paranoia

Sometimes a remarkably good personal mythology, you might call it, appears as a result of the spread of meaning to a great many irrelevant events and the occurrence within awareness of the type of referential processes that characterize our thinking in our very early years of life before there is any very clear separation between one's self and all the rest that there is. This personal mythology has very close connection with myths that have been accepted by large groups of humanity over long historic periods, and it frequently appears in terms of great danger, attack, weakness and strength, and all such things. And so, to use the psychiatric jargon, the "paranoid coloring" appears—the idea that one is being poisoned, or being manipulated, or having this or that done to him by hostile people. Such ideas can always be found in the mental state of incipient schizophrenia and in early stuporous conditions.

Now the notion that people around one are dangerous and ill-disposed toward one and also the notion that there are transcendental superhuman powers that may be malignant or punitive are often thought of as being, in principle, paranoid ideas. But I think that the term *paranoid* must be restricted to those instances where there is this very conspicuous accompaniment of these ideas of malignant power: the person who entertains them becomes blameless, ennobled, and expanded in worth. This

is what we encounter in the paranoid states and in markedly paranoid schizophrenia.

But at the moment I am discussing the schizophrenic who incorrectly identifies—as all of us do occasionally—causal relationships, sometimes identifying a cause as being the malignancy of others, or the power of superhuman entities, or magical operations. The schizophrenic is not concerned with problems of blame. These things which sound like paranoid ideas are a part of the disturbance of his grasp of events, caused by the shifting types of referential process and the loss of boundaries of personality, along with, in many cases, extremely clever attempts to understand what has happened.

Now it is true, I suppose, that I have never dealt with a schizophrenic who had not been happy at some time in his life to find that someone else was to blame for something that he had been blamed for; yet I would say that few schizophrenics have come to their psychosis as a result of shame and chagrin for specific traits which they felt were blameworthy. Theirs is a more massive type of unhappiness. They have, perhaps, been excellent scapegoats for others, in that they were so bothered that they were not at all expert at returning the goat to the other person with thanks. They were people especially vulnerable to having blame transferred to them. And they have had the greatest difficulty finding scapegoats themselves; they just have not understood people, or how to deal with people, well enough to make others scapegoats. They are among the most handicapped at juggling blame around.

Take, for example, my patient who is a Yale graduate, but who cannot get started at anything and eventually becomes a night watchman. And then he begins to have curious attacks of somnolence and so on; things at times look different to him; and he falls upon the thought that poison is being put in the lunch that he brings to work at night.

Now what does this represent? By a lot of devious thinking one could say that he is washing his hands of his inadequacy and making somebody else responsible, in the shape of an enemy who is poisoning him. But when one talks with him, one does not find anything particularly like that reflected in any way. One finds that he has not hit upon an explanation for his inadequacies. Instead he is still looking for an explanation, and he is profoundly puzzled and very deeply disturbed. He has what somebody long since called the "insane mood"; the world is beginning to dissolve into a great many unstable things. And apropos possibly of some trifle of gustatory sensation or some hallucination or illusion, as he is drinking his coffee on a particular night, probably in quite an absent-minded condition, he notices perhaps nothing more than the flavor of the coffee. Then the thought of poison enters his mind; if he has been chronically poisoned, that would account for all this.

For the source of this type of explanation of things, we may look to a lot of more or less trivial fiction that all of us have been exposed to, as well as certain myths that appear both in this culture and in many other cultures. And it doesn't have much to do with blame; like a great many incipient schizophrenics, he has been very busy suffering from conflicts and a feeling of profound inadequacy, failure, and so on, but he has not really been blaming himself for it, and this mistaken explanation that he has hit upon has not particularly transferred blame from himself. Thus I do not call this paranoid, and in fact I do not think that it deserves a special name, for, although the explanation hit on by the night watchman is a little startling to a good many of us, it is of a piece with a vast amount of our own incorrect thinking.

In the course of schizophrenic stupor, however, a patient's primitive types of referential process may hit off in the general direction of his being Jesus Christ—the classic case—and the rest of the world, I suppose, then becomes the Jews who are intent on crucifying him. And here we do have a paranoid attitude, unlike the merely mistaken explanations. In other words, here the paranoid dynamism—the transfer of blame—has come into being through shifting the mythological and diffusely focused thinking in the direction of one's being the apotheosis of all that one has wished to be. If this suffices—that is, if the paranoid attitude gives enough feeling of security so that the schizophrenic disturbances of the level of awareness cease—then the person goes into a bitter, highly systematized paranoid state with remarkable speed. But this is quite uncommon. I am inclined to say that if the paranoid development would have sufficed, it would have come rather early. In other words, I think that those who have in the past had some success at occasionally making somebody else the scapegoat come most readily to the paranoid schizophrenic state—or rather, I should say, to the paranoid state, for they actually do not stay schizophrenic very long. They do a nice job of the transfer of blame and do not have to be very schizophrenic any more.

The fact that paranoid attitudes often do not suffice—that they frequently fail to solve the problems of schizophrenics—is demonstrated by a certain group of patients who show Christ identifications, yet remain catatonic. They grow whiskers, and put up great fights about being shaved, and sometimes they get to look singularly like the artists' conception of the Savior. But they continue to be catatonic; that is, they continue to have postural tension, interference with behavior, and so on—perhaps not as much as they had a while back, when they were just stuporous, but still they are by no means free and easy in their skeletal movements and so on. They do not preach the gospel, and they are not paranoid. They have done everything *but* solve their problem with a paranoid transformation of personality.

A Christ identification may, in the course of human events, progress to a paranoid state, so that the person becomes a more or less well-systematized paranoid schizophrenic. But quite as often, under therapeutic pressure—by which I mean that somebody who really wants the patient to get well pesters him in and out of season, by his presence at least—the Christ identification collapses, and the patient is again lost in the whole welter of universal patterns and is again definitely stuporous. I have had the dubious fortune, but at least theoretically important experience, of having a patient who not only had a Christ identification for a while, but who also was a pretty dangerously systematized paranoid schizophrenic for a while, and whose paranoid system collapsed under alleged therapeutic pressure from me, with the outcome that he was extremely assaultive for years. He is now, I suppose, in a state hospital if he isn't dead of tuberculosis— which is a well-known way out.

The fact that the paranoid schizophrenic can sometimes be thrown back into stupor, revert to simple or uncomplicated schizophrenia (by which I do not mean simple dementia praecox), and from that come out quite differently—as a social, if not a real recovery—indicates that the paranoid schizophrenic is by no means always successful in resolving his conflicts by transfer of blame. Such recovery is, I am sorry to say, not too frequent, but is well within the realm of possibility, and has several times been documented in my experience. Moreover, the failure of the transfer of blame to solve the problems of schizophrenics is shown by the shocking character of the persecutions, and so on, that many of them complain of; they are obviously having a very bad time. When the paranoid state becomes a durable maladjustment, it is plenty unpleasant; but it also has its very large returns in the way of security.

I shall not have a great deal to say about the delusions of paranoid schizophrenics. They have been plucked out of the total enigma that any schizophrenic mental state really is to any physician, in the sense that some things have been said which suited the psychiatrist's theoretic slant or personal interest. And so there is a welter of speculation that you can find hither and yon in the literature about the meaning of certain delusion formations. If you are very generous, you may assume that the writer was correct about the particular case he describes; but do not swallow it as an explanation of schizophrenic thinking. There is no explanation of schizophrenic thinking that can be transmitted by speech or in writing because schizophrenic thinking includes a great deal for which those modes of communication are not appropriate. So when you are told that one's homosexual craving leads to this or that, it may be so; you wouldn't know; and neither would the patient.

Pure paranoia, the imaginary state, means that one has become absolutely spotlessly blameless—one is perfect—and the many unpleasant things that one finds oneself engaged in are, of course, the work of the evil world in which one has to live. As a schizophrenic gets more and more to be the almost contented victim of the Masons, or something of the sort, you can assume that the schizophrenic process has probably passed over into the paranoid type of pretty stable maladjustment. It may interest you to try to figure out what signs show when this is to be regarded as irreversible. I know that there are, insofar as people are susceptible to generic classification, some paranoid schizophrenics that it is just perfectly stupid to think of changing. And I know that there are others whose paranoid maladjustment is essentially extremely unstable. I have, in the days when my recklessness was perhaps paving the way for a little sanity later, upset pretty elaborate paranoid systems by nothing more startling than a warm personal attitude toward the patient, combined with sundry attacks on the theories which were most blame-removing, and so on, and inquiries which were disastrous to any peace that the self had achieved. The patients became catatonic again, and we proceeded from there. Some of them, praise God, have been well enough to be out of the hospital for a good many years now, that being over twenty years ago.

Both the so-called paranoid coloring—which is more correctly, I think, identified as mistaken explanations for puzzling events—and the true paranoid attitude originate, I have no doubt, in the schizophrenic disturbance of awareness. But in the case of the paranoid attitude this device of the invention, the discovery, the false causal series, immensely relieves depressed self-esteem; it removes chronic and recurrent anxiety in a particularly neat way in that it makes *them,* not *me,* the source of these regrettable interests, activities, and so on. Now that could not happen—and does not happen, for a long time at least—in people who have been at a great loss as to what ailed them in relation to others—who have been at a loss as to why they could never be quite successfully human, and could not do the sorts of things that other people in their social position seem to have no difficulty in doing. In this case, the element of shame, chagrin, and contempt for oneself is of at least a different character, if not of an entirely different nature, from the feeling that the person has who knows he wants to do things which he regards as beneath contempt. The preschizophrenic wants to be human, and cannot find how to do it. The pre-paranoid schizophrenic wants, in addition to that, to be blameless, to be rid of things of which he is profoundly ashamed and which he regards as a part of his handicap in being human.

This may be in keeping with a thing said very emphatically by Kempf (1)—that it is the aggressive, successful people who move rapidly into paranoid development, and the ineffectual, submissive people who do not. I would put Kempf's formulation in these terms: People who are ashamed of certain traits which they are trying to conceal are, I suppose, very apt to make a lot of noise that sounds like aggressive attack on others; and people who are simply profoundly puzzled and who never do seem to make the successful experiment to find out what they want to know are much less offensively evident in their attack on others. The people who develop a schizophrenic episode have been very far from happy for a long time, but many of them do not feel vivid awareness of contemptible traits. They have nothing elaborate in the way of an explanation of their unhappiness; they have had so many hurts, so many rebuffs and frustrations, that they simply do not feel equal to generalizing their experience. They just drop it, one piece after another; you might say that they never have any past, because it is all too painful to look at. They do not blame themselves, and I think that in these people the paranoid development comes much later, if it comes at all. But those people who have a schizophrenic episode and who blame themselves—*really blame themselves*—for failing because of certain shameful things have a fine chance of paranoid development.

Environmental Factors in the Paranoid Process

The extent to which explanatory doctrines which make other people responsible for one's own shortcomings are utilized varies from family to family. That is, the products of one family will have great ingenuity at discovering how other people are to blame for their sins of omission and commission; and the products of another will be much less clever at discovering scapegoats. If a person always looks to other people as a basis for self-ennobling or self-relieving explanations of things in which these people actually have no genuine causal position, this is, I believe, invariably the work of those adults who gave this person his cultural components. That is, it is not an idea that occurs naturally in the higher animals that I have been fortunate enough to be able to observe. Moreover it seems to me to be beyond any cavil that there is a very important element of the scapegoat in the culture. It is so striking an element that the fear of becoming paranoid seems to me to be fairly close to the surface in people who have enough acquaintance with fairly sound psychiatric ideas in popular form to know something of the meaning of the paranoid states.

EARLY EXPERIENCES THAT
ENCOURAGE OR DISCOURAGE THE
PARANOID PROCESS

Yet in a culture which seems to encourage the feeling of the transfer of blame from out of one's awareness onto innocent bystanders—in a culture which predisposes its members to such a self-ennobling or self-justifying procedure—the question arises of why only some people go on from schizophrenic beginnings to chronically schizophrenic-paranoid states; and why the paranoid states as mental illnesses are only common, instead of extremely common. I think that this question is answered by the very agency that I have spoken of as determining the paranoid slant of a great many people—namely, the degree to which paranoid explanations, in the sense of explanations involving a transference of blame, have been *de rigueur* and satisfactory in the home environment. But if one parent has on many occasions quite pointedly objected to the other parent's washing his or her hands of blame by moving it over to the neighbors, for in-

stance, then the child who grows up in this home is, I believe, greatly impressed by the attitude of the person who opposes this blanket projection. The reason why this is so impressive to the child is, I think, that it is biological—in the realm of symbol operations—to use simple performances rather than complex ones, if one can—an observation I derive from my experience with dogs, horses, and so on. But in passing from the animal to the social human being, one encounters such a great discrepancy between the processes called out in the interest of feeling secure with one's fellows and the processes directed toward the achievement of more biologically conditioned satisfactions, that there is no one who does not have many complex processes in the sense of more or less conflicted collisions of goals. But in the earlier, formative years, any calm and uncruel questioning of a morbidity is apt to be deeply impressive upon the child—irrespective, I think, of emotional ties. I say this because in some of the material I have gotten from patients—obsessional patients, it is true—it has looked to me as if the parent who certainly did not contribute greatly to the child's feeling of security, who had not seemed warm or close to the child or optimistic about him, had nonetheless, by his sanity, if you please, left perduring impressions and had had beneficial, preventive effects on the absorption of morbidity from the sicker parent. Thus I am very much impressed with our tendency to catch on to anything that is really simple and workable, if we get a chance. So our families produce people with greater or less facility for washing their hands of blame by projection.

A second, and very important, factor which tends to prevent the development of the paranoid slant is that all but the first-born child have very valuable experience in observing the morbidities of the first-born or of the elder children. A sibling no more than a few years removed from one in age is much less terrifically complicated than a parent.

Things which would not be open to question in the recurrent behavior of the parent may, when they appear in a sibling, well continue to be open to question, and, in fact, lead to penetrating insight. Thus a paranoid elder brother in a family with a paranoid father would not be a probable source of paranoid tendencies in the third child, let us say, but, on the contrary, might actually act as a cautionary, preventive experience. During the period when this pattern of coming out lily-white because somebody else is to blame could simply become part of this third child, he would instead develop contempt for it in his elder brother, although such contempt could scarcely be felt for the significant father.

The third factor that enters into the thing is the gross character of interpersonal events outside the home. One may have thoroughly disastrous experiences in school or on the playground in trying to pass off blame for one's shortcomings onto somebody else. Since that constitutes a painful experience, it is apt to have some educative value and to appear as a tendency to be cautious, at least, in appraising the people to whom one addresses blame-washing movements. To the extent that this happens, it means that the self-system has developed critical aspects with respect to the free use of transference of blame; while the self-system is the source of the transfer of blame, it also has to protect security by using that device only under certain circumstances. But if, on the other hand, the post-family experience has included some distinguished successes in the use of transference of blame dynamics, to that extent this becomes a more dependable tool of the self-system.

A NOTE ON THE NATURE
OF BLAME

I think I have some thoughts about blame that probably are not universally accepted and certainly should be expressed. Blame is nothing inborn; it is not a fundamental characteristic of the human creature. It is definitely a term which applies to a type of experience that one had in childhood, or certainly well before maturity. The character of that experience is perhaps to be approached first by considering, Where does it hit?—that is, Where does the blame-event impinge? Quite clearly, it impinges generally in the region of insecurity. When we are to blame, that means we are unworthy. We have demonstrated an unworthiness that amounts either to an alleged shock to the person who has discovered that we are to blame for something or to distress to some significant person. For example, a more or less cruel parent may get a great kick out of piling blame on the child; or, perhaps more frequently, a teacher may get satisfaction out of making the child suffer for her embarrassments and at the same time conceal her own inadequacy as a teacher by making the child to blame for being stupid or something of the sort. All these blame-expressing statements are of a character which makes one unworthy—that is, which lowers one's self-esteem.

And so, when a person tells me with great solemnity, "I have always felt guilty about doing so-and-so," I prefer to switch into something which, it seems to me, should have an entirely identical meaning. I say, "In other words, you blame yourself for some inferiority or defect, or something of the sort, which led to that action. Is that right?" The person may accept this, or he may protest "No," saying that the reason why he feels guilty about it is that he just didn't have foresight enough to see what the consequences would be to the person who suffered. In which case I say, "Oh yes, you regret that you could not foresee pain for another," which is thoroughly estimable and is scarcely apt to lead to any serious mental disorder. If it is just that one regrets one's lack of foresight, one's inadequacy, either in energy or something else, then at least one is still among one's fellow men. But blame is something else, since it has the individuation which comes from the particular complex of cultural assimilation established by the home and by the pattern of the home and the siblings, and so on, that is less easily associated with the totality of human life. Recognition of defective foresight is the experience of everyone who has the least honesty in appraising life. The peculiar vicissitudes of blame processes, however, are by no means so universal. I think that these same considerations pretty well dispose of the question of guilt and guiltiness, except as a performance by a jury of one's peers, or something of the kind.

PARANOID OUTCOME OF REINFORCING BLAME PATTERN IN HOSPITAL SETTING

I now want to say something about the handling of the schizophrenic patient in the mental hospital—the environmental pressures placed on him and the extent to which this may have a marked effect in establishing the possibilities of paranoid outcome. I think very emphatically that the handling of the patient has such an influence when it places emphasis on blame and jugglings with blame, somewhat after the pattern that I mentioned of the school teacher. For example, I would expect an increase of paranoid outcomes per capita of schizophrenics in the practice of a psychiatrist who is content to abolish his own feelings of frustration and inadequacy about a given patient with the statement that the patient is not cooperative. The situation from the patient's standpoint is that he hasn't the faintest idea of what the doctor wants and that he can't get the doctor to tell him. And so, finding that he is a total loss, because he isn't doing this mysterious something that the doctor wants, why should he not avail himself of any opportunity to see how the doctor's performances are to blame?

A number of other things are also sometimes done which may encourage

paranoid developments in patients. For instance, the notion exists that conflict about homosexuality has some etiologic relationship to the occurrence of paranoia. So some psychiatrists are rather profoundly interested in the importance of this concept of homosexuality, and feel that a paranoid development is very likely in a patient who has homosexual inclinations. I would not be at all surprised if such a psychiatrist's investigation into the schizophrenic illness does not communicate to the patient some notion that he is almost certainly consigned to a life of degraded, perverse interest in members of his own sex, and that this is a risky and dangerous business—in addition to being, of course, awfully contemptible and so on. Of course, the patient does not get this only from the psychiatrist; he has picked up part of it, at least, previously. The tragedy is that schizophrenia does not occur in mature people, but in persons fixed either, I think, at the preadolescent or at the early adolescent level of development. And at those stages of development sex, lust, and the problems of intimacy with others are pressing problems which take on somewhat preternatural importance, and failure at dealing with them seems to constitute a great social liability. So the psychiatrist who feels that paranoid elaborations are a common outcome, and who is perhaps looking for evidences of paranoid attitudes, may actually offer what seems to the patient, in a more lucid moment, a good way out.

Among the most valuable therapeutic activities that I have ever engaged in is the process of dealing with a patient's problems by getting them located somewhere in the time-space pattern of the patient's life. And it is more or less the essential tool for disturbing the paranoid state, if it can be disturbed. For example, I may say to a patient who one day shows that he is particularly disturbed, "Well, this all seems very oppressive today; you were visited by your friend, the padre, this morning I believe." Let us say that the patient can keep track of things long enough to respond, "Yes, I think he got me to realizing how badly treated I was." I then say, "Well, let's not leave it in this uncertainty; do you recall anything he said that connected?" In other words, I am getting nearer and nearer to the context in which some process made its appearance. There is a profoundly sanifying effect in that; and I suppose that this is derived from the brute fact that if a person is oriented, he is usually adequate to deal with the momentary situation. But if, however, he has been brushed out of touch for a while by some emotional business, so that he is not very clear on where he is, or how he got there, then he can go on rapidly piling difficulty on difficulty; and there is no sense in attempting to cure the particular mélange of misinterpretations that appears, without first locating the simpler, earlier context.

THE PARANOID PROCESS IN THE
MYTHOLOGY OF A CULTURE

I would like to make here a distinction between processes which have the authority of being observed behavior of significant adults, in contrast to processes which have the much less immediate reality that comes to one in the shape of told folklore, read fairy tales, mythology, and so on. I have a theory of myths which is painfully simple. A myth originates with a dream which symbolizes, with peculiar clarity and in a rather vivid statement, a remedy for a vital problem in the culture—that is, something that is gravely problematic to practically everybody in a social area. The solution presented in the dream is likely to be something that is not authorized by the culture, but that is not a major crime—that does not represent a frontal attack on the whole culture complex. It represents a preverbal, or autistic verbal, attack on the problem. When a dream of that kind is told, it appeals very vividly

to the hearer, because it attacks a problem which he also is faced with; and so it is then told again, and again catches on. In the process, it becomes refined by the elimination of all the personal trimmings until only the great central action of the dream remains. Then it has become a myth of the people. Now the problems of human life have certain coincidences from one vast area to another—coincidences derived from certain incoherencies and imbecilities in the different cultures—and so there is an overlapping of some of the great fundamental mythological ideas. In the same way, it is not at all strange that in the process of our growing up, any of us may run off, at certain stages, crude imitations of some of these same mythological ideas. Some of us can remember dreams which are, in fact, a great improvement on any existing mythology for the current era. That type of process is primarily related to our sleeping state, for in the course of assimilating culture and learning how to live, we have specifically eliminated, in our conversation with our compeers, free access to that type of thinking. Thus it is of a different order of reality and implication from the type of process picked up from demonstrations in the home. That is, the distinction between *thee* and *me,* which is so of the essence of security operations by the self, is, I believe, not nearly so striking a characteristic of the rest of the personality. It may even be that my very little bid for fame will be that I was so lacking in self that I discovered that human personality exists only in interpersonal relations, except for the noisy self. Anyway, the schizophrenic is less handicapped, if you please, in coming to grips with life by these fantastically impractical mythological thoughts and so on, than he is by such things as the early observation that one can wash one's hands of a feeling of blame by finding that somebody else was responsible. Thus I think that contact with the paranoid attitudes expressed in the culture and represented in the prevailing myths and stories is less important than actual experience in the home. But, as I have pointed out, along with actual experience in the home with paranoid attitudes, there is sometimes also a corrective actual questioning of the validity of that type of defense.

Therapeutic and Prognostic Considerations of the Paranoid Process

By the time that the schizophrenic moves into paranoid elaborations, the travail of the self in attempting to patch up some kind of security with the persons of the environment—even if by now these persons are only psychiatrists and hospital attendants—has become almost cosmic. If, along with this immense insecurity, there has been a family background which makes paranoid elaborations acceptable—if there has been this historic success with them—then such elaborations are likely to appear. Perhaps they are encouraged by a great deal that can be interpreted in the same way in the mythology of the Western World, at least; the engrained descendant of such myths in the preverbal or autistic thinking of the child reappears in the schizophrenic processes. At any rate, the schizophrenic processes take on more and more the coloring of "This is terrible; it is not my fault; it is the work of so-and-so."

It is by disturbing such paranoid elaborations that one opens the way to recovery. Before such a patient can recover, I believe that one has to return him to the unhappy, boundless sort of cosmic existence which makes up severe schizophrenic stress—which in some cases, where I have succeeded at this maneuver, meant that the patient became stuporous. In other words, I find no instrumentality for attacking the paranoid processes *per se,* for this feeling of blameless perfection is a great improvement on anything else a person can expect in this world. The way by which I attempt to return such a pa-

tient to schizophrenic stress is by means of a frontal attack on the convenience of the projection—a frontal attack on the often transparently unjustified, grandiose explanatory ideas—the purpose of which is to cause anxiety, to disturb the self from what little complacency it has achieved in the paranoid illness. And along with this, and much more theoretically promising, is an insistence on finding out when, and under what circumstances, the paranoid convictions rise to the center of the stage, and when their influence over the patient's orientation becomes much less striking. All of this usually collides with some quite terrifying ideas in the patient, which in turn precipitate what I call the prognostic event. This event consists either of (1) the spread of schizophrenic uncertainties—a broadening of meaning, and so on, which makes it impossible for the patient to have anything as neat as even shifting paranoid delusions; or (2) an increase in the amount of time given over to vigorously paranoid ideas, an extension of these ideas, and a firm fixation of them on the physician. So far as I am concerned, this spells prognosis. If the former happens—that is, if the patient does move backward, in the sense of chronologically backward into the more schizophrenic state—then I have hopes, which are very guarded, of course, because I am dealing with a terribly risky, awfully handicapped personality. But if, on the other hand, the reaction to my frontal attack and my attempt to mark the timing of the most paranoid feelings consists of an intensification of those feelings and gets them pretty strongly attached to me, then clearly I am not going to be very successful in my maneuver, and the patient will probably persist in a paranoid schizophrenic condition.

Reference

1. Kempf, E. J. *Psychopathology.* St. Louis, Mo.: C. V. Mosby Co., 1920.

7. PERSONALITY DISORDERS

THE DIAGNOSIS of personality disorder is rapidly becoming the most popular available label in the out-patient situation, and by virtue of this is losing a good deal of meaning. Just as it was once popular to call any behavioral peculiarity "neurotic," more sophisticated individuals now point to these difficulties as personality or character problems. At one time this label was reserved for individuals with behavior problems that led them into difficulties with the law. The diagnostic category which is now used in such a case is *sociopathic personality disturbance*. Currently references to personality disorders are more widely used to describe individuals technically diagnosed as *personality trait disturbance* or *personality pattern disturbance*. The common feature that cuts across these categories is that the individuals have developed a way of life that creates disharmony in their personal relationships. Rather than placing emphasis on their symptoms, or on their subjective discomfort, the focus is on how they get along with others, and in this we usually find

some inadequacy, although the patient may not always recognize it as such and often does not recognize his role in disrupting his relationships. The paper by Blum is a selection from his excellent book, *Psychoanalytic Theories of Personality,* and presents a review of the orthodox psychoanalytic view of character as well as a variety of revisions and neo-analytic character types. It should be clear to the careful reader that the neoanalytic typologies are alternative descriptive schemes and are not mutually exclusive. Thus, it would be easy to recognize the essential similarities between Freud's oral character, Horney's compliant type, and Fromm's receptive type.

The remaining articles are essentially descriptive with some dynamic implications, and deal with subcategories of the sociopathic classification. Cleckley discusses the antisocial personality, previously labeled the constitutional psychopathic inferior, and more popularly, the psychopath, while in a classic paper Jellinek describes the stages along the road to alcohol addiction.

Adult Character Structure

GERALD S. BLUM
UNIVERSITY OF MICHIGAN

The experiences of the first two decades of life all contribute to the gradual emergence in the individual of characteristic ways of thinking, feeling, and behaving. Every adult man or woman comes to acquire a particular constellation of traits, a unique style of living. However, psychoanalytic theories of adult personality, apart from those dealing with pathology, tend to stress common patterns. The various theoretical views presented in this chapter, therefore, are concerned mainly with "types" of character structure.

Orthodox Position

DEFINITION AND CLASSIFICATION OF "CHARACTER"

Fenichel (3) describes character as "the ego's habitual modes of adjustment to the external world, the id and the superego, and the characteristic types of combining these modes with one another." This youngest branch of psychoanalysis, so-called "ego psychology," had its origins in two factors: first the growing awareness in psychotherapy of the necessity to analyze the patient's resistances and ego defenses; and second, the greater prominence of defenses in the clinical

picture of the neuroses. The historical development, remarks Fenichel, is easy to understand, since psychoanalysis began with the study of unconscious phenomena, alien to the ego, and proceeded only gradually to consider character or the customary mode of behavior.

Character, however, has a broader scope than the defense mechanisms, for it includes the positive, organizing functions of the ego. Through the defense mechanisms the ego protects the organism from external and internal stimuli by blocking reactions. But the ego also serves to sift and organize stimuli and impulses. Some are permitted direct expression, others indirect. Hartmann (6), enumerating ego functions, includes reality testing, the control of motility and perception, action and thinking, inhibition and delay of discharge, anticipatory signaling of danger, and a synthetic or organizing function.

Instinctual demands are always bound up in the character structure, according to Fenichel. The organization, direction, and sifting of impulses, which must be made consonant with demands of the external world, constitute the attitudes of the ego. Likewise the superego is decisive in forming character, for the individual sets up habitual patterns based on what he considers good or bad. In the latter connection the adoption and modification of ideals in later life are also of importance. The other source of influence, the external world, is crucial in the sense that man's character is said to be socially determined. In Fenichel's words: (3, p. 464):

The environment enforces specific frustrations, blocks certain modes of reaction to these frustrations, and facilitates others; it suggests certain ways of dealing with the conflicts between instinctual demands and fears of further frustrations; it even creates desires by setting up and forming specific ideals. Different societies, stressing different values and applying different educational measures, create different anomalies. Our present unstable society seems to be characterized by conflicts between ideas of individual independence (created during the rise of capitalism and still effective) and regressive longings for passive dependence (created by the helplessness of the individual with respect to security and gratifications as well as by active educational measures which are the outcome of the social necessity of authoritative influences).

The relative constancy of character is presumed to depend on three facets: partly on the hereditary constitution of the ego, partly on the nature of the instincts against which the defense is directed, and mainly on the special attitude forced on the individual by the external world.

Fenichel classifies character traits into two broad categories—sublimation and reactive. In the sublimation category the original instinctual energy is discharged freely as a result of an alteration in aim. The "genital character" belongs here. The conditions underlying the formation of sublimation traits are felt to be obscure. In general such traits are fostered by the absence of fixations, plus favorable environmental conditions for providing substitute channels of expression.

Instinctual energy in the case of the reactive category is constantly held in check by countercathexes. Attitudes are concerned with avoidance (phobic) or opposition (reaction formation). Fatigue, inhibition, rigidity, and inefficiency are

common. The flexibility of the person is limited, for he is capable neither of full satisfaction nor of sublimation. Some persons develop a defensive attitude only in certain situations; others have to protect themselves continually. The latter are said to employ "character defenses," which are unspecific and maintained indiscriminately toward everyone. For example, they may always be either impudent or polite, empty of emotions or ever ready to blame others. Reactions to conflict in the area of self-esteem manifest themselves in arrogant behavior to hide deep inferiority feelings; ambitious behavior to cover inadequacy; and so on. The development of reactive traits is said to be fostered by early psychosexual fixations.

Reich (8), a pioneer in the field of character analysis, describes reactive traits in terms of "character armor." A chronic alteration in the ego serves to protect against external and internal dangers. The armor, originally forged as a result of the conflict between instinctual demands and the frustrating outer world, gets its strength and reason for existence from continuing actual conflicts between these same opposing forces. Character grows out of the attempted solution of the Oedipus complex, with the subsequent hardening of the ego being accounted for by three processes: (1) identification with the main person who represents frustrating reality, (2) aggression turned inward as an inhibitory force, and (3) formation by the ego of reactive attitudes toward the sexual impulses. Thus, the armor serves to strengthen the ego by alleviating the pressure from repressed libidinal impulses. At the same time, though, it operates to insulate the person from external stimuli and renders him less susceptible to education.

CHARACTER TYPES

Orthodox psychoanalytic literature contains descriptions of a wide variety of types—oral, anal, urethral, phallic, genital, compulsive, hysterical, phobic, cyclic, schizoid, and others. However, organization of these types into a meaningful classification has remained elusive. Fenichel expresses his own discontent in the following words (3, p. 527):

The differentiation of individual character traits into those of the sublimation types and reactive ones is not of much value in judging personalities, since every person shows traits of both kinds. And still it seems the relatively most useful approach to distinguish personalities in whom the sublimation type of traits prevails from those that are predominantly reactive. It had become customary to distinguish genital from pregenital characters; however, although the traits of anal or oral characters consist of both sublimations and reaction formations, pregenital traits become predominant only in cases in which countercathexes suppress still operative pregenital impulses; in other words, pregenital characters, as a rule, are also reactive characters, whereas the attainment of genital primacy is the best basis for the successful sublimation of the remaining pregenital energies.

One source of confusion lies in the attempt to distinguish the more or less "normal" types from those which are primarily "neurotic." The problem becomes especially acute when, as in this text, the area of psychopathology has been excluded from consideration. A solution suggested by common practice is to designate arbitrarily the various pregenital types and the genital type as falling within the normal range and hence eligible for detailed discussion here. The psychoanalysts, in addition to Freud, who contributed heavily to the original formulation of these characterizations were Abraham, Jones, Glover, and Reich (1, 7, 5, 8).

The Oral Character. The oral character is one whose habitual mode of adjustment contains strong elements of oral fixations produced in early childhood. He is extremely dependent on others for the maintenance of his self-esteem. External supplies are all-important to him, and he yearns for them passively. The mouth serves an especially significant function. When he feels depressed, he eats to overcome the emotion. Oral preoccupations, in addition to food, frequently revolve around drinking, smoking, and kissing. As a consequence of the infantile association in the feeding situation, love is equated with food. Conflicted longings for love and narcissistic supplies may even generate physiological effects, such as the increased secretion of gastric juices observed in peptic ulcer cases.

Fenichel (3) links oral overindulgence in infancy to a later feeling of optimism and self-assurance, provided that the external environment does not threaten the individual's security. Early oral deprivation is said to determine a pessimistic or sadistic attitude. Persons in whom the oral-sadistic component is marked are aggressive and biting in their relationships. They continually demand supplies in a vampirelike fashion and affix themselves by "suction."

The passive-dependent, receptive orientation to life brings with it a number of other related personality characteristics. All positive or negative emphasis on taking and receiving is said to indicate an oral origin. Marked generosity and niggardliness both stem from oral eroticism. Generous persons sometimes betray their original stinginess, just as stingy ones occasionally resort to exceptional generosity. Gifts assume unusual importance. The particular form of behavior depends upon the ratio between sublimation and reaction formation in the handling of oral drives.

Some individuals manifest their dependent needs directly and insatiably by begging or even demanding to be cared for. According to Fenichel, the demanding tone prevails in persons who are incapable of getting sufficient reassurance, so that every real gift makes them long for more. The begging tone occurs in persons who actually are satisfied when taken care of, and who willingly sacrifice ambition and comfort in order to buy the necessary affection. Others tend to overcompensate for their unconscious passive longings by behaving in an extremely active and masculine fashion, under the pretense of being entirely independent. Alexander (2) describes the latter constellation as typical of the ulcer personality.

Another common form of behavior in oral characters is identification with the object by whom they want to be fed. Certain individuals always act like nursing mothers, showering everyone with presents and help. The attitude has the magical significance of "As I shower you with love, I want to be showered." Under favorable circumstances, this may serve a truly altruistic function. More often, it tends to be annoying. In contrast, some identify with a frustrating rather than a giving mother. Here the behavior is completely selfish and stingy, implying "Because I was not given what I wanted, I shall not give other people what they want." Additional oral traits described by Fenichel include curiosity (as a displacement of "hunger"), volubility, restlessness, haste, and a tendency toward obstinate silence.

The Anal Character. Traits associated with anal fixations were Freud's (4) first insights in the area of character structure. Personality features are said to grow out of the conflicts around toilet training, since the child, as we have seen earlier, has opportunities to please or defile his parents and also to gain physiological pleasure from elimination and retention. The predominant adult anal traits are known as the three "P's"—parsimony, petulance, and pedantry, or, as phrased more commonly, frugality, obstinacy, and orderliness. Fenichel (3) describes frugality as a continuation of the habit of anal retentiveness, sometimes motivated

by the fear of losing, sometimes more by erogenous pleasure. Based on the equating of feces with money, attitudes toward money become irrational, as were the original anal instinctual wishes. No longer viewed as an objectively useful thing, money is retained and hoarded or sometimes carelessly thrown away. Similar attitudes exist toward time, so that the anal character may be punctual to the fraction of a minute or grossly unreliable.

Obstinacy is a passive type of aggression, stemming from the child's refusal to produce when his parents were intent upon his doing so. After a while this "magical" superiority or feeling of power is replaced by a "moral" superiority in which the superego plays a decisive part. Stubbornness in the behavior of adults is explained as an attempt to use other persons as instruments in the struggle with the superego. By provoking people to be unjust, such individuals strive for a feeling of moral superiority which serves to increase self-esteem and to counterbalance pressure from the superego. The stubborn person considers himself to have been unfairly treated and often elicits affection forcibly by making his antagonist feel sorry afterward. Thus, says Fenichel, obstinacy, which originally is the combative method of the weak, later becomes a habitual method of struggle for maintaining or restoring self-esteem. Excessive orderliness arises from compliance and obedience to parental demands. Tidiness, punctuality, meticulousness, and propriety are all said to signify a displacement of compliance with the environmental requirements in regard to defecation.

The mechanism of reaction formation is frequently apparent in anal traits, for the scrupulously clean and orderly individual may at certain times be astonishingly messy and disorganized. Another example is painting, which in some cases represents a reaction formation to the unconscious desire for anal smearing. The artist who is not sublimating effectively often fails in his work or becomes inhibited in his ability to paint. Other anal characteristics manifest themselves as displacements to speech and thinking in the irrational modes of retaining or expelling words and thoughts. All anal traits are said to contain a sadistic element, in accordance with the original ambivalent object relations of the anal stage.

The Urethral Character. The outstanding personality features of the urethral character are ambition and competitiveness, both of which are presumed to be reactions against shame. The child who wets his pants is often made an object of ridicule and shame. In response to this feeling he later develops ambitious desires in order to prove that there is no longer any need for him to be ashamed. Another contributing element is the original competition with respect to urination, e.g., who can direct a longer stream.

Fenichel (3) also discusses the various displacements and secondary conflicts created by urethral ambition. The latter may be condensed with trends derived from earlier oral sources or, under the influence of the castration complex, may be displaced to the anal field. This is especially characteristic in girls because of the futility of urethral competition. Too, the reassurances which ambition and success provide against the idea of being castrated may be turned into prohibitions if they acquire, in connection with the Oedipus complex, the unconscious meaning of killing the father.

The Phallic Character. The phallic character behaves in a reckless, resolute, and self-assured fashion, mainly as a wish-fulfilling reaction to castration anxiety. The overvaluation of the penis and its confusion with the whole body, typical of the early phallic stage, are reflected by intense vanity, exhibitionism, and sensitiveness. These individuals usually anticipate an expected assault by attacking first. They appear aggressive and provocative, not so much from what they say or do, but rather in their manner of speaking and acting. Wounded pride, according to Reich (8), often results in either cold reserve, deep depression, or lively aggression. The resentment of subordination and the tendency to dominate others are both grounded in fear. Overtly courageous behavior, as exhibited by the motorcycle daredevil, is said to represent an overcompensation.

Basically the phallic character is extremely oral-dependent, and his narcissistic orientation precludes the establishment of mature relationships with others. The male, driven to attempts to demonstrate his masculinity, is nevertheless contemptuous and hostile toward women. The phallic female, motivated by strong penis envy, assumes the masculine role and strives for superiority over men. Narcissism is again a central characteristic.

The Genital Character. Fenichel (3) himself states that the normal "genital" character is an ideal concept. However, the achievement of genital primacy is presumed to bring a decisive advance in character formation. The ability to attain full satisfaction through genital orgasm makes the physiological regulation of sexuality possible and thus puts an end to the damming up of instinctual energies, with its unfortunate effects on the person's behavior. It also makes for the full development of love and the overcoming of ambivalence. Furthermore, the capacity to discharge great quantities of excitement means the end of reaction formations and an increase in the ability to sublimate. Emotions, instead of being warded off, are used constructively by the ego as part of the total personality. The formation of traits of the sublimation type thus becomes possible. Pregenital impulses are mostly sublimated, but some are also incorporated into the forepleasure mechanisms of the sexual act.

References

1. Abraham, K. *Selected papers on psychoanalysis.* London: Hogarth, 1927.
2. Alexander, F. Psychologic factors in gastrointestinal disturbances. *Psychoanal. Quart.,* 3(1934), 501–588.
3. Fenichel, O. *The psychoanalytic theory of neurosis.* New York: Norton, 1945.

4. Freud, S. Character and anal eroticism. In *Collected papers,* Vol. II. London: Hogarth, 1948. Pages 45–50.
5. Glover, E. Notes on character formation. *Int. J. Psychoanal.,* 6(1925), 131–154.
6. Hartmann, H. Comments on the psychoanalytic theory of neurosis. *Psychoanalytic Study of the Child,* 5(1950), 74–96.
7. Jones, E. *Papers on psychoanalysis.* New York: Wood, 1913.
8. Reich, W. *Character-analysis.* New York: Orgone Institute Press, 1945.

Antisocial Personalities

HERVEY CLECKLEY, M.D.

Antisocial behavior notoriously provokes interest. Crime, in the sense of an act that seriously harms another, catches the attention of the public and travels rapidly as news or gossip. So, too, does conduct that is unconventional or generally disapproved, though each person directly involved finds it agreeable. The story that a local debutante is promiscuous, that a young woman has had an abortion, or that a business executive was seen parked on a lonely road with his stenographer are stories that will be snatched up by each hearer and quickly repeated until few people in the community remain uninformed. Murder, rape, and kidnapping, as everyone knows, crowd other news from the headlines of the daily papers and are discussed (22) at length and in detail all over the nation. Though crime and misbehavior are popularly deplored, both attract eager attention and, as news,

Reprinted from *An Introduction to Clinical Psychology,* edited by L. A. Pennington and Irwin A. Berg. Copyright 1948, The Ronald Press Company.

seem to evoke excitement that might be called pleasurable.

Despite this widespread emotional susceptibility to antisocial behavior, reliable statistics (14) on the prevalence of crime and delinquency are difficult to obtain. According to official records (3), during the year 1944 some 1,356,655 major crimes occurred in the United States. Such a figure does not, of course, throw any light on minor antisocial activity and delinquency. Even sound definitions of what constitutes delinquency and other legally forbidden behavior are difficult to make.

So, too, the cost or the loss to society resulting from such behavior is impossible to estimate. The expense of maintaining prisons, courts, police forces, and other instrumentalities can be tabulated, but what the inmates of the prisons might have contributed if their abilities had been differently used, cannot. It is useless even to speculate about the percentage of citizens who avoid serious conflict with the law but whose lives are in general antisocial. In every community there are probably many men whose debts are never paid or have to be met year after year by other members of the family. Among both men and women it is not rare to find irresponsible sexual behavior that brings tragedy to marital partners and indirectly to children. It is impossible to estimate even roughly the proportion of people whose persistent illegal aggressions and delinquencies are of a sort for which their benefactors can make restitution and allow them to escape legal penalties. Quantitatively, the effort to survey antisocial behavior is not too profitable, though it will probably be granted by all that such behavior is common throughout the world and that it constitutes one of the greatest and most tragic problems of mankind.

Why does this socially destructive behavior occur? And why does it continue widespread in all communities and persist through the centuries, despite legal, religious, educational, and other agencies that seek to combat it? The motivation for many crimes, and perhaps for most minor acts discountenanced by the group, seems on the surface, obvious. The bank teller embezzles because he wants a new car. Two men quarrel and one, feeling himself outraged, gratifies his anger by shooting the other. Sexual desire is so readily comprehensible to the normal person that few honest observers would admit alienation from the impulses that lead to adultery and other generally disapproved amorous conduct. The burglar breaks into a house because, one might say, it seems an easier (or more exciting) way to get something of monetary value than by working for it. It might be argued that despite such motivation (which is probably shared by all of us) a mystery remains in that the consequences are not usually taken into consideration sufficiently to prevent such actions. It is hardly worthwhile to assume that the person misbehaving is merely stupid;

for, so often, his reasoning powers, when tested objectively, are excellent.

Until recent years it was customary to regard forbidden or "bad" behavior rather simply. The malefactor or delinquent was summarily condemned for his deeds and punishment assumed to be a fitting remedy. This attitude prevailed in regard to antisocial behavior throughout its entire range. The murderer, the adulteress, the burglar, the drunkard, the wastrel, and the disobedient child whose mischievous pranks outraged his elders were all judged as willfully and simply wicked in varying degrees. During recent decades attitudes less naive and less confidently absolute have emerged.

It is worthy of recollection that, two or three centuries ago, ordinary physical illness, such as pneumonia or a broken leg, was frequently interpreted as a chastisement from providence for evil-doing. Even today one hears such judgments, expressed a bit differently and lacking, perhaps, some of the old vivid certainty, but still as judgments that spring from the same assumption. Only the other day a strait-laced aunt of a man who had developed diabetes confidently explained to the writer that this condition was a consequence of her nephew's youthful "dissipation." While visiting a distant relative in a closed psychiatric hospital, the wife of an influential clergyman turned and asked, "It's true, isn't it, that all these deplorable people are here because the Devil got into them?" Her remark was not really a question but a firm announcement. This good lady, it must be admitted, scarcely thought of the Adversary as possessing these patients by the more concrete, medieval methods. She did not, in all probability, conceive of literal witchcraft or of familiar spirits entering the body in a physical sense; but even in her more metaphorical interpretation it is easy to sense an assumption of guilt and responsibility that can scarcely be taken for granted in such a complex proposition.

Long after it became unpopular to think of illness in general as punishment for wrongdoing, the tendency (23) prevailed to interpret serious mental disorders, as well as hysteria and other psychoneurotic manifestations, by a mixture of theology, magic, and sharp ethical judgment. Even today numerous physicians assume that seriously disabled patients without "organic" pathology merely lack "will power" or simply don't want to get well. Such physicians must assume, it would seem, that their psychoneurotic patients are not really ill but are choosing to conduct themselves reprehensibly and are doing so of their free volition.

Only in recent times has there been audible questioning of the motivation and causal forces that may lie behind crime, misdemeanor, and antisocial behavior in general. Most psychiatrists grant that the woman who steals unwanted articles from a department store under the pressure of a compulsive illness is different from the ordinary thief who, apparently, chooses to steal for gain. Social workers, seeing the background of a drunken father, an inconsistent mother whose righteous instructions differ obviously from her own actions, often find it hard to assume voluntary depravity in the delinquent child whose chief basis for formulating his conduct lies in the confusing background of such a home. If the subjectively painful and crippling effects of ordinary psychoneurosis arise from complex emotional forces, is it not possible that outwardly directed behavior also, that much delinquency and crime, may arise from similar sources? If the solution of the ordinary neurotic difficulties lies outside the range of simple voluntary effort, is it possible that the control of antisocial behavior may also lie beyond the subject's mere act of will? The work of Alexander (1, 2), particularly, should

give one cause to hesitate before dismissing such a question. Here and elsewhere (15, 17) evidence can be found that gives considerable support to the argument that persistent antisocial activity may, like the ordinary neurosis, be less voluntary, in the ordinary sense, than involuntary.

The theologically oriented critic might advance an argument that unconscious and involuntary mechanisms, and even cellular pathology, may be properly classified as "evil" in a broad biologic sense. Such an argument, however, can scarcely carry the burden of imputing blame so simply and absolutely to the victim as happened automatically with the older ideologies. If antisocial behavior, or even some antisocial behavior, is, like ordinary neurosis, something over which the subject does not have conscious control, those who attempt judicial or theological interpretations will have to grant that the Devil moves in more devious ways than was formerly assumed. It would also be more fair and more accurate for all of us to withhold moral censure and to ponder before we reach conclusions about suitable punitive measures.

The Delinquent

Delinquency is a term generally applied to behavior that is unacceptable socially and that is often damaging to others but in a degree less drastic than antisocial acts which are legally classified as felonies. The term is usually regarded as indicating a chronic scheme of life and is more often applied to children and adolescents than to adults. Into this category falls the schoolboy whose truancy is persistent, whose rowdy behavior does not yield to punishment or advice, whose minor thefts, unprovoked destructiveness, and lying are the despair of his parents. The teen-age girl whose sexual promiscuity is so impressive that the boys of the community joke among themselves about her would also qualify as a delinquent. Everyone, it will probably be granted, makes his mistakes, and most people probably can recall isolated acts in their own lives which, if they had become habitual, would have constituted delinquency. The average person, despite his mistakes, has or acquires the ability to learn by experience and to find acceptable goals. The bad consequences of his mistakes and the incentive of his goals enable him to avoid consistently inadequate and costly conduct, and to utilize his impulses in a satisfying and productive scheme of life.

The delinquent, usually because of complex factors that cannot readily be demonstrated, does not find his way to such a scheme. There often appears to be little relation between orthodox instruction in morality on the part of parents and the child's ability to avoid delinquency. The child of the slums whose parents steal and cheat is scarcely more often encountered than the incorrigible offspring of formally pious people who have laid down the rules of exemplary conduct, the rules apparently serving only to promote rebellion. Extremes in either direction, it would seem, might contribute to a child's difficulties in conforming to reasonable standards.

In considering true delinquency it is well not to forget how often rebellious and antisocial behavior occurs as a phase in the career of the well-adjusted citizen. These episodes often seem to be sporadic, fumbling attempts to find one's way. Few people, probably, will fail to discover examples in their own lives or in the lives of childhood friends. Stable businessmen, respected attorneys, deacons, civic leaders, physicians, vestrymen, and Sunday school superintendents, well known to the writer, are clearly recalled in earlier years as leaders or members of destructive gangs that, on certain holiday nights, marched in force down the chief residential street of their community, shouting profanity, hurling brickbats through plate-glass windows, smashing fences and gates, setting fire to small outbuildings, smearing monuments and fine houses with paint, puncturing automobile tires, and shooting recklessly with 22-caliber rifles.

An outstanding surgeon recently spoke, apparently with curiosity and sincerity, of his adventures while growing up in a strict rural community. With several other boys, most of whom are now well-behaved and successful members of society, he took particular delight in periodically startling young ladies, caught in response to Nature's call in outdoor toilets, by using long, leafy branches to scratch under the seats.

Another reliable informant gives in considerable detail a report of himself and a dozen other high-school boys, all from prominent families of the town. After pouring oil on car tracks where they descended a long, steep hill, they would pull the trolley from the wire, leaving the street car to race dangerously, and with little control, through a crowded street. This episode was repeated many times and only through good fortune were fatalities averted. Another group on several occasions broke into fine houses when the occupants were away on vacation, banged up valuable furniture with hammers, ripped curtains and linen to shreds, left the hot water running, and urinated on Persian carpets.

A former member of an exclusive fraternal group at a Southern college located in a rural setting recalls that the chief business at each meeting consisted in proud and highly realistic reports of current sexual adventures with Negro women, for whom these particular young men had unutterable contempt. The point of such behavior resides not, of course, in any argument that miscegenation is necessarily abnormal or that Negroes are inferior to white people, but in the boastful attitude towards such conduct in a social setting where no Negro, however distinguished or admirable, could be treated with any respectful intimacy. The attitude of the students was, apparently, more scatological than amorous. The partners in the sex act were, it would seem, not accepted as human partners at all but treated as passive objects of scorn, despised almost as if they served some eliminative function in which the male's immature concepts of virility were enhanced in direct proportion as the female was degraded.

An attractive and well-bred woman, now in the mid-thirties, who has for years been respected in her community and who is successfully raising her two children, once consulted the writer about behavior she feared was jeopardizing her security. She had recently been divorced after an extremely unhappy marriage. Despite the bitter relations which prevailed, she had never been sexually unfaithful until she and her husband separated. Soon afterwards, for reasons she could not explain, she began promiscuous and highly indiscreet activities with a number of men, giving herself to rude strangers who picked her up on the street, to a taxi driver, an itinerant salesman, and to several distant acquaintances for whom she entertained actual distaste. After several months of such behavior, most of which seemed not a result of ordinary sexual drive, she changed her ways and has been leading a conventional life.

These samples of human conduct in persons now well adjusted are cited not for censure, and certainly not for approval, but as illustrating the prevalence of episodic activity that would by most be considered delinquent. In contrast we see the numerous and better-known cases in which socially unacceptable, destructive, rebellious, and often apparently self-frustrating patterns of behavior continue consistently through the years. In many people, perhaps in most, faulty conduct occurs occasionally in the process of maturing. In the true delinquents such conduct is not readily abandoned, no better pattern of adjustment is discovered spontaneously, and a persistent scheme is followed that brings conflict with society and, usually, frustration to the subject.

A brief summary may make more concrete the usual concept of delinquency: *

This twelve-year-old boy was referred by the Juvenile Court to the local Child Guidance Clinic. Three years ago the truant officer found him selling papers at the railroad station during school hours, whereupon he was taken back to school and his mother notified. She came at once to the school and whipped her son violently in the principal's office. A few months later he was brought before the court for stealing bicycles and it was revealed that he had stolen perhaps a dozen, averaging one or more per week. Within the next year he was detected as one of a small gang who had over a long period been stealing skates, watches, electric razors, and other small articles from local stores. These takings were surreptitiously sold to a man at a filling station who seldom gave the boys more than a dollar for any article.

The mother reports that this boy is impossible to control. Sometimes in open defiance, sometimes by stealth, he leaves home and does not return until nearly midnight. Once he stayed away until morning and investigation revealed that he and several other boys had a secret meeting place in a large opening on the river bank where a sewer emerged. Here they gathered and smoked cigarettes and occasionally drank a bottle of beer. At school he was described as often truant and as a troublemaker. Despite good ability, according to a psychometric test, he was failing in several of his studies.

This boy and his mother occupy one room in a large unprepossessing house, which several other families share, located in a dismal section of town. The mother and son take their meals with some of these people. The mother nags the boy repeatedly, but, except when she loses her temper, she usually lets him have his way and

* The author's permission to publish this case report is extended to The Ronald Press Company.

fails to back up her threats of punishment. She habitually announces before the other people in the house that she can do nothing with her son, that it is impossible to control him.

The boy's father deserted him and his mother after being discharged from the army and without even returning to see them. He sends a very small allowance which is all these two people have to live on. The mother does not know where her husband is, and apparently has given no thought to the question of whether or not she will get a divorce. She appears to have little real concern for her son, seeming content that she has offered him good verbal rules for the conduct of his life. It is reported that she devotes very little attention to him and that she frequently goes out at night with men.

Through an officer of the Salvation Army and through other agencies, recreational outlets were arranged for this boy. He was interviewed a number of times at the Child Guidance Clinic, and efforts were made to instruct his mother in better methods of management. The question of placing him in a foster home has been considered, but in recent months his conduct has shown distinct improvement and the court has not been willing to take this step against his mother's objections.

The Criminal

The antisocial pattern of maladjustment may persist as ordinary delinquency, or it may extend to acts classed as felonies and constitute what is ordinarily regarded as a criminal career. If, on the other hand, the antisocial or unconforming scheme of behavior is relatively free from major crime but consistent and without a readily understandable purpose, we approach what is called *psychopathic personality*.

Persons who fit best under the term *criminal* seem in general to be more purposive than the typical delinquent and to work for goals more appealing to the ordinary man, however much the ordinary man may disapprove of the methods chosen to attain these goals. In general, too, the criminal seems more often to be careful in his efforts to avoid detection and punishment. Usually he is more capable of explaining his motivation than the delinquent, and it is easier to appreciate the temptation which lay behind his deed. Perpetrators of major crimes available for study consist almost entirely of those who have been discovered and caught. This fact contributes, perhaps, to the impression that the felon, though he may repeat his antisocial deeds, seldom persists so inveterately as the delinquent.

The ordinary criminal, then, the man who, torn with jealous rage, murders his successful rival, the master racketeer who defies the law and reaps great wealth, or the bank robber who, after careful planning, risks his life for big stakes, seems, at least superficially, easier to account for than many delinquents by the old and once scarcely challenged assumption that the wrongdoer deliberately chooses to be wicked and harmful. If one inquires more closely into the background of persons who commit such crimes, the question will probably arise as to what confusions and conflicts may have shaped these persons so as to make them react in such a manner. What now seems coolly deliberate, might, if we could follow it to its roots, be found also to spring from conflict and from outer distorting forces now misunderstood or unconscious. But from a simple cross-section view of his life, the ordinary felon can be fitted more easily into the concepts of guilt and culpability than can the delinquent. It is probably from these examples that such confident interpretations of antisocial behavior, in all its range, as uncomplicated and freely chosen "evil" were originally formulated.

The criminal, then, as distinguished from the delinquent and even more sharply from the psychopathic personality group, may be regarded as one who works consistently and with good use of his rational powers and other endowments toward his own ends. He is better able to take advantage of his gains and to consolidate them than either of the other types. He impresses the observer, both in his career and his explanation of himself, as more consistently purposive. Lindner (14), making use of psychoanalytic terminology, writes of the criminal as a person whose ego does not succeed in resisting his primitive *id* impulses but accepts them with relatively little modification and, serving as an accomplice, allows them to gain direct expression in action. In contrast, the patient with psychoneurotic symptoms is described as a person with a strong ego which successfully resists the socially and personally unacceptable impulses. These, finding inadequate satisfaction, cause painful conflict which may be experienced as anxiety or expressed symbolically in the symptoms. Similarly the victim of a psychosis is interpreted as a person whose ego, instead of giving itself over to the *id* impulses or successfully denying them, is broken in the conflict or forced to withdraw from its ordinary functioning. In these terms one might speak of the delinquent as a person whose ego allows, or is forced to allow, the antisocial impulses from the *id* to work through it, but with less active and purposive cooperation, with more confusion at ego levels. One might also say that in the typical delinquent we do not see evidence of such effective ego activity as in the criminal. The outer world is not dealt with as shrewdly. Unpleasant consequences are less skillfully avoided. Perhaps the ego is less wholeheartedly cooperative, or perhaps its functioning is impeded because it is still in part resisting the *id*.

The Psychopathic Personality

Under this term many types of personality disorder and maladjustment are listed. According to established medical usage, we find in this classification all persons affected to some degree by the psychopathology which if further advanced would constitute the well-known psychoses. These schizoid, cycloid, and paranoid personalities are numerous and their disabilities are real. It is not, however, with such conditions that we are here concerned. These could better be treated along with schizophrenia, manic-depressive psychosis, and paranoia, since they are essentially similar illnesses, although in a milder form and in a less extreme degree.

We also find some writers who include all forms of sexual deviation under this heading. Sexual disorders are, of course, serious, but they too constitute a different subject from the one that now concerns us. It is true that some sexual deviates show also the type of maladjustment we mean to discuss, but the writer feels that nothing would be gained and much would be lost by attempting to identify sexual deviation as a whole with psychopathic personality or to treat it under the same heading. After all, schizophrenics, paretics, and other psychotic patients often show deviations in their sexual drives and practices. It would scarcely be profitable, however, to classify these psychoses with ordinary sexual deviation, or vice versa. It should also be remembered that many sexually deviated persons conduct themselves without the asocial or antisocial activity which is always characteristic of the particular group we are concerned with and which has so confusingly been placed in this wastebasket category through established usage. Homosexuals and persons suffering from other erotic aberrations are unlikely to be seen by physicians or to reach the attention of legal authorities unless they show some additional maladjustment. It would seem reasonable, therefore, to assume that all available statistics probably overemphasize the presence of general social disorder in deviates.

It is rather difficult, so long as one uses currently accepted terminology, to disentangle our subject from the numerous and not too relevant conditions with which it is classified. Most psychiatrists in ordinary conversation about patients tend to use not the formal term *psychopathic personality* but the abbreviation *psychopath* and this word is almost always taken to mean a specific kind of patient rather than all the diverse kinds listed officially in this category.

What most psychiatrists mean by the term *psychopath* and what we mean to discuss as psychopathic personality is a well-known and a distinct reaction-type. It would, perhaps, be worthwhile to outline a few characteristic points in an effort to define and briefly portray this type.

1. The psychopath, not always but usually, is attractive and impressive. Whether encountered in a business interview, in a psychiatric examination, or in a social group he is likely to be adjudged intelligent, alert and, often, a person of force and character.

2. He is free from delusions, hallucinations, and all other signs of psychosis. Psychometric tests indicate that he has at least average, and often excellent, reasoning power. He is also usually free from anxiety, feelings of insecurity, and all other manifestations of psychoneurosis. Direct examination, in fact, shows nothing that would suggest him to be other than a competent and, perhaps, a superior person.

3. He demonstrates his good reasoning ability in discussing plans for his future and in accounting for his past mistakes. Verbally, he shows evidence of excellent judgment. From his ability to discuss himself and the complexities of human life, one would assume that he could make a happy and successful adjustment.

4. Despite these points, when the full story of his career is available, one finds a remarkably consistent pattern of failure and folly. Much of his faulty conduct is similar to what is characteristic of the delinquent, but far more regular and with far less apparent purpose or incentive. In looking over his record it is difficult to escape the thought

that such a man seems, perhaps unconsciously or involuntarily, to be seeking failure and frustration for himself.

5. Though he describes such excellent plans of conduct, he does not act upon them in his living. No matter how many hardships, punishments, and losses overtake him, he does not learn by his experience to modify his ways. In words he *knows* what should be done or not done, but this information and his apparent foresight enter (5) little or not at all into his actual behavior.

6. Though he often appears to be a candid and reliable person, he shows no regard at all for his commitments. After breaking his word many times in important matters, he still looks anyone straight in the eye and gives his pledge as if he felt it should be taken seriously.

7. He expresses normal and proper affective attitudes when such matters are discussed. It is not unusual for him to give the impression of being a particularly devoted and sincere husband, lover, friend, or parent. In his conduct, however, he shows no evidence of being moved or constrained by any of the emotions he describes so convincingly. After some experience with him, the observer is driven to conclude that his loves, ambitions, regrets, and shames exist only at a verbal level, or at least that they lack sufficient substance to influence his conduct.

8. The psychopath, though he may admit that something is wrong with him and even diagnose himself and discuss psychiatric interpretations of the disorder, always lacks an important element in what would constitute real insight. Just as he may *know* in words how to modify his behavior, so he uses to describe his situation the same words that would be chosen by another to express a genuine understanding. Just as something is lacking in his experiencing of what he talks about when planning to modify his behavior, there seems to be in his apparent insight only a verbal mimicry. What is left out seems to be not a mere quality but an absent dimension. The thoughts by which he expresses an apparent insight seem not to enter into his emotional experience, not to have meaning for him.

9. His sexual life invariably shows abnormality. This may be in the form of homosexuality or some other well-known

deviation, but such distinct and well-formulated trends are by no means common in the typical psychopath. When present it would seem more reasonable to consider them as additional disorders rather than typical expressions of the fundamental psychopathology. The regular deviation in the sexual experience of these patients is an incapacity to form any lasting attachment or any strong, vivid personality relation. Though described by some as moved by strong sexual drives, psychopaths, on thoughtful observation, seem rather to be lacking in ordinary considerations that make for restraint in acting on sexual impulses. The writer is doubtful if the typical psychopath has, even in the simplest sense, as strong a sex drive as the conventional person. Though he does not hesitate to satisfy his sexual inclinations despite conditions that would make an ordinary person decide to refrain, the psychopath, apparently, finds only a shallow and transient satisfaction and does not give the impression that such experience means as much to him as to others.

Though distinct and consistent homosexuality is not typical, many psychopaths show a tendency to enter into deviated relations occasionally or for some secondary purpose. This tendency impresses the writer as a manifestation of poorly formulated or immature sexuality, an expression of the fact that erotic experience is deficient in its meaning to the subject, rather than of true homosexuality.

10. Unlike the serious criminal, most psychopaths seldom commit murder or other grave felonies. They defraud, cheat, often steal, and regularly ignore the loss or suffering their activity brings to others, whether the victims are strangers, friends, or members of the family. They frequently bully and threaten, often indulge in minor fights or beat their wives and children, but their physical violence seldom leads them to kill. Callous to a remarkable degree about the effect of their conduct on others, whether in terms of physical pain, shame, disgrace, or financial hardship, and little less restrained by losses and punishments to themselves, it is difficult to account for the fact that these people do not more often commit major crimes that would bring about their permanent removal from the social group.

A case studied by the writer * and referred to previously (4) illustrates a typical career:

This young man in the early twenties comes from a respected and prominent family in a small Southern town. Three siblings are well adjusted. During his school years he became a serious problem because of continual truancy, disorderly activity in the classroom, and what appeared to be rebellious conduct in general. Unlike many other difficult boys, he never seemed to be rebelling against anything that could be named, or in accordance with any imaginable principle. Even in early life his conduct suggested what Lindner has emphasized about this type of maladjustment in his phrase, *rebel without a cause* (15).

When truant he seemed to be led away by little that would seem adventurous or be judged stimulating or tempting by most boys. He wandered about street corners or the fringes of town, sometimes carrying out minor destructive acts, but often appearing bored and dejected. Even his unruly behavior in the classroom lacked that comic or prankish quality that usually appeals to the other children, and even to them it soon became tedious. He often stole small change, pocketknives, or other possessions from his school fellows, and occasionally spoke or wrote in notes to girls the four-letter words generally regarded as obscene. Before he was twelve years old it had become a common practice for him to steal things from his home and sell them in the town. Usually these were petty thefts, a chicken from the back yard, a package of bacon from the pantry, or a pair of book ends. Occasionally he took a watch or a piece of his mother's jewelry, and for these relatively valuable objects he was content to accept a dollar or even fifty cents. Sometimes he exercised true ingenuity in concealing his guilt, but again he did not trouble to hide acts that would obviously lead to detection. When accused, he lied not only with skill but with remarkable equanimity and with what appeared to be a candor impossible to anyone but the innocent.

In school, despite his truancy and mis-

* The author's permission to publish this case report is extended to The Ronald Press Company.

conduct, he was regarded as a bright boy by the teachers, and during periods when he gave even slight attention to lessons he learned well. He was a fine-looking lad, easy in manner, usually polite, and often successfully flattering in casual contacts with his elders. His teachers and the school principal, affected by his ability, his fine bearing, and his apparent sincerity, were inclined to feel that essentially he must be a sound character, and they took pains over a long period to work with him and with his family to bring about a better adjustment.

Soon after his thievery began, his father, thinking he might particularly want money, raised his allowance to a generous amount. Efforts were made to have him take part in games and sports, and the Boy Scout leader tried to interest him in outdoor activities. Superficially he seemed agreeable and there was a brief show of enthusiasm, but none of these pursuits engaged him for long. He stole as regularly with a large allowance as before, and did not use what he stole for any apparent purpose. While in the teens he began to steal automobiles, and his father, seeking to satisfy what one might presume to be the impulse behind this conduct, bought him an automobile of his own. This did not deter him. On one occasion he actually stopped while riding in his personal car, parked it, and drove off in another. He soon abandoned the stolen car without having achieved any financial or other discernible gain from it.

From fifteen years of age onward, he frequently left home, sometimes staying out all night and sometimes not returning for several days. Once he got permission to take the family car, saying he wanted to go to a movie with another boy. He was careful to ask his mother about the supper hour, promising specifically to return in good time for this meal. Nothing further was heard from him until nearly two A.M. when he called from a town eighty miles away, insisting that his father come for him. The night had grown stormy and his parents had been extremely uneasy about his safety. The town had been searched and the local police had been called on for help. He greeted his parents nonchalantly after their trip through the rain and wind of a bitter night, and explained that he had planned to drive to New York but, having run out of gasoline and finding himself short of funds, he and his companion had changed their minds.

For years this young man has forged his father's name to checks. After leaving home without giving his parents notice or any news that would let them know whether or not he was alive or dead, he would sometimes stay a week in a near-by city, charging hundreds of dollars' worth of merchandise to the family. He often obtained several new suits in this fashion, but much of what he bought he never found use for. As he grew older he frequently forged the names of others to checks and signed his own for large sums without having any account in the banks. He readily obtained employment but soon lost each position, sometimes because he merely stayed away from work, sometimes through stealing money or merchandise from his employers, sometimes through cheating the customers. He often gave convincing excuses when absent from work, telling in detail about some accident or illness in his family. The dramatic reality of these tales was so vivid that employers did not at first feel it necessary to check the facts. On other occasions when he stayed off a few hours or a day without giving notice, he merely informed the boss that he didn't feel like working and seemed indignant when this explanation was not accepted as a good reason for his absence.

At the time of this man's first interview he had been in jail scores of times. Reliable information indicates he would have had to serve sentences on more than a hundred occasions had it not been for the intervention of his family. By paying costs and damages, and by their influence, they had usually obtained his release after arrest. He always made an excellent impression on the authorities, and usually on his victims, expressing contrition and outlining his resolutions and plans for the future with such wise and convincing words that it seemed almost a tragic error not to give him a fresh opportunity.

His relations with women have been indiscriminate and apparently without any serious attachment on his part. His outer charm and what resembles a deep earnestness have enabled him to seduce a number of women regarded as respectable, including the wife of a friend who at the time was fighting overseas. He has consorted freely with cheap prostitutes, and a few years ago married one whom he had previously shared in a single night with drinking acquaintances. He left her as abruptly and with as little sense of obligation as he did the women of good reputation whom he seduced.

People who talked with him after disasters overtook him, or when he was seeking leniency from the courts, were invariably impressed with him. Several of these advisers, including judges, physicians, and clergymen, not only felt that he was a man of remarkable ability who had at last found himself and who would now conduct himself admirably, but even confessed that he was able to give them new points of view and make them hope to improve their own lives. After every incident of this sort he immediately returned to the familiar pattern.

Despite the intervention of his family this young man has not escaped unpleasant penalties. During the short prison sentences he served he always seemed extremely chagrined and unhappy and spoke eloquently of how carefully he would avoid any deed that would result in further confinement. Once while serving a term of two years in a penitentiary, he so favorably impressed the authorities that parole was granted. While on parole he stole an automobile which he put to no important use and was returned to confinement.

During examination this young man was poised, alert, and seemed to be a person not only of intelligence but of sincerity. He denied everything he felt the examiner probably did not know, and in such a way that one would not be inclined to question the truth of his statements. In discussing what he realized was known, he expressed regret with such apparent dignity and conviction that any observer would find it hard not to believe this was a man who had learned deep and inexpressible things from his experience.

The case outlined briefly above represents what we believe is typical of the *psychopath*. Many additional features are seen in such personalities and sometimes

the maladjustment is much less extreme, the active drive toward unprepossessing folly and its consequent disasters less consistent. In some, alcoholism is a feature, though *never,* we maintain, *a fundamentally causative one*. In others a violent or sadistic drive emerges and murder results. Many persons who commit brutal and perverse sex acts on women and children are psychopaths who have also more specific deviations of impulse. Always the psychopath is callous and remarkably free from true remorse, whether he has carved a murdered woman's thighs in careful slices while smoking a cigarette, or he has dismembered and thrown into a public park the body of an eight-year-old girl, without or after, raping her.

In the writer's experience male psychopaths have been more common than females. It should be emphasized, however, that women are seen who show the disorder in its classic form. The same total disregard for consequences to oneself, the same inability to be moved by the shame and hardship brought to others for whom love is eloquently but superficially expressed, characterize psychopathic personality in the female.

Summary

The varied forms of antisocial behavior impress the observer as having important common characteristics. Here, as contrasted with ordinary neurosis, malfunctioning of the personality is expressed chiefly at a social level and as aggression or other conduct unacceptable to others. In ordinary neurosis, generally speaking, malfunctioning is expressed subjectively as suffering and disability.

Ordinary criminal behavior lends itself less readily to interpretation as a kind of neurosis than many other types of delinquency. The typical psychopathic personality, however, presents a life scheme so difficult to account for by voluntary

motivation and in terms of social and biologic goals that it is difficult not to assume a serious mental illness.

Considerable evidence can often be
gained by psychiatric study which suggests that a delinquent boy's persistent
stealing may be the indirect expression
of his blocked sexual impulses. Sometimes an adolescent girl's sexual promiscuity can be found to represent her
blundering search for emotional security
and the sort of love she did not obtain
from parents who subtly rejected her.
Such manifestations constitute displacement, somewhat differently but as truly,
as the obsessive-compulsive patient's incessant handwashing that arises not from
a fear of germs but of his erotic drive.
In the true psychopath we find a career
in which antisocial and asocial conduct
predominate. When we survey a long
section of this career it is difficult not to
be impressed by the fact that the psychopath's actions sum up regularly into
a pattern of self-defeat. Considering all
objectives that he claims and all that are
comprehensible to man, it looks as if he
were, unconsciously, working to fail, to
achieve frustration. Unlike the ordinary
criminal, he seems, in his deeper strategy if not in his immediate conscious tactics, to be moving in a self-destructive
scheme rather than in one that is simply
antisocial. The writer believes that in the
extreme psychopath we are dealing with
a personality not simply but dynamically
motivated, and with a personality whose
disorder is so deep and so disabling that
it often constitutes incompetency, and
for practical purposes should be classed
as psychosis.

Unlike patients with other psychoses,
these people do not show in verbal tests
the traditional signs of major personality
disorder. In verbal tests they are rational,
free from delusions, manifest good judgment and every indication of competency.
In the more practical test of living they
show less adequacy, less "sanity," than
many patients with schizophrenia. Their

excellent rational ability, as estimated by
psychometric tests and otherwise, is
proved to be an abstraction of what such
performances are usually considered to
imply. Their well-preserved and often
impressive personality structure, contrasting so sharply with schizophrenic dilapidation, is, perhaps, less real than it
seems. Though superficially intact, the
ego in these patients seems to lack a
necessary dimension, to be largely façade.
Some element essential to sane or effective evaluation, as contrasted to reasoning verbally, an element essential for
competent behavior, is left out of the psychopath's human functioning. Though
not rationally disordered, he is *semantically disordered* (5).

As in all medical matters the question
arises: What can be done? Psychiatry
and psychology are still far from being
able to offer a ready cure for the forms
of human dysfunction that constitute
antisocial behavior.

Delinquency, and particularly juvenile delinquency, deserve all the psychiatric and psychological attention that the
resources of the community can afford.
Treatment often results in improvement.
A better general understanding of psy-
chopathologic forces would probably result in many cases that could be helped
by treatment instead of being handled
from a strictly punitive point of view.

Psychiatry is not at present prepared
to advise society that, with the ordinary
felon, therapy should take precedence
over the protection of others. Work is
being done in this field, and some reports (15) give encouragement to the
hope that treatment may play an increasingly effective part in penal institutions.

When we consider the psychopath, it
seems to the writer that steps of practical
importance should be taken at once. At
present these people, no matter how great
their disability, are usually pronounced
sane and competent by the courts. Psychiatrists, following theoretical and tra-

ditional criteria, support and often determine these rulings. This makes it impossible, under ordinary conditions, for the patient to be committed and placed in a psychiatric hospital, no matter how severe his disorder may be. If, as occasionally happens, the jury is more impressed by the man's demonstrated disability than by expert testimony, and if it commits him to a psychiatric hospital, he is there promptly declared sane and competent and discharged. On the other hand, when the psychopath is tried for his deeds against others and wishes to avoid penal confinement by being sent to a hospital, he can often assist his attorneys in presenting a picture of mental disorder that enables him to escape jail.

In actuality such people, as thousands of medical histories demonstrate, pass rapidly through courts, jails, and hospitals, only to be sent back scores of times, hundreds of times, to renew their damaging and often tragic careers. If psychiatry could reopen the question of the psychopath and find itself willing to call incompetent all such patients whose behavior clearly and unanswerably indicates incompetency, it would be possible to control their activities and perhaps eventually to work out methods for improving their adjustment.

With psychopaths inclined also to major crime, an unequivocal recognition of the fundamental disorder would do much to prevent the peculiarly dreadful offenses which so often are headlined in the news. This very day the front pages of newspapers all over the nation carry an account of what is described as the "bestial sex-slaying" of an eleven-year-old girl. It is pointed out that the seventeen-year-old boy who committed this crime had a record of previous offenses, that his parents protested against his release from reform school. The school authorities correctly maintain that, since the boy had served his sentence, they had "no alternative but to release him."

If the serious nature of the psycho-path's disorder could be officially and legally recognized, it would be less difficult to hold such patients where they could be prevented from carrying out such crimes. Any psychiatrist familiar with this disorder would realize that the basic disability of the person, rather than merely an arbitrary penal term, must be given chief consideration in determining whether or not he is safe to release.

To the clinical psychologist, as well as to the psychiatrist, the psychopath offers a challenging problem. In the study of this deviation, as in the study of the delinquent and the criminal, ordinary psychometric tests are of importance. Through other methods designed to evaluate more recondite personality features, such as the *Rorschach* and the *Thematic Apperception Tests,* the clinical psychologist should play a part not only in diagnosis but in the common effort to interpret and understand these deviations and the biologic and sociological factors that may contribute to their development. In community clinics particularly, the clinical psychologist can function to greatest advantage in working on a preventive basis. He, further, can provide liaison between the general body of people in need of guidance and the psychiatrist whose attention is called to many serious medical problems that might otherwise progress unobserved. Complete cooperation between the psychologist and the psychiatrist is essential, each supplementing the other in the common effort to combat deviation and maladjustment, to promote healthy personality development.

References

1. Alexander, F. The neurotic character. *Int. J. Psychoanal.,* 2(1930), 292–311.

2. ———, and Healy, W. *Roots of crime.* New York: Knopf, 1935.

3. Banay, R. S. Wanted: An institute for criminal science. In Seliger, R. V., Lukas, E. J., and Lindner, R. M., eds., *Contemporary criminal hygiene.* Baltimore: Oakridge Press, 1946.

4. Cleckley, H. The psychopath viewed practically. In Seliger, R. V., Lukas, E. J., and Lindner, R. M., eds., *Contemporary criminal hygiene*. Baltimore: Oakridge Press, 1946.

5. ———. *The mask of sanity*. St. Louis: C. V. Mosby, 1941.

6. Glueck, S., and Glueck, E. T. *Five hundred criminal careers*. New York: Knopf, 1930.

7. ———. *Preventing crime: A symposium*. New York: McGraw-Hill, 1936.

8. Healy, W., and Blonner, A. *Delinquents and criminals, their making and unmaking*. New York: Macmillan, 1926.

9. ———. *New light on delinquency and its treatment*. New Haven: Yale Univ. Press, 1936.

10. Henderson, D. K. *Psychopathic states*. New York: Norton, 1939.

11. Hooton, E. A. *Crime and the man*. Cambridge: Harvard Univ. Press, 1939.

12. Kahn, E. *Psychopathic personalities*. New Haven: Yale Univ. Press, 1931.

13. Korzybski, A. *Science and sanity: an introduction to non-Aristotelian systems and general semantics,* 2nd ed. Lancaster, Pa.: Science Press, 1941.

14. Lindner, R. M. *Stone walls and men*. New York: Odyssey Press, 1946.

15. ———. *Rebel without a cause*. New York: Grune & Stratton, 1944. See also Lindner, R. M., and Seliger, R. V., eds., *Handbook of correctional psychology*. New York: Philosophical Library, 1947.

16. Lowrey, L. G. Delinquent and criminal personalities. In Hunt, J. McV., ed., *Personality and the behavior disorders*. New York: The Ronald Press Co., 1944.

17. Menninger, K. A. *Man against himself*. New York: Harcourt Brace, 1938.

18. Peru, P. W. The concept of psychopathic personality. In Hunt, J. McV., ed., *Personality and the behavior disorders*. New York: The Ronald Press Co., 1944.

19. Reckless, W. C. *Criminal behavior*. New York: McGraw-Hill, 1940.

20. Stevenson, G. S. The prevention of personality disorders. In Hunt, J. McV., ed., *Personality and the behavior disorders*. New York: The Ronald Press Co., 1944.

21. Taft, D. R. *Criminology*. New York: Macmillan, 1943.

22. Teeters, N. D. Fundamentals of crime prevention. In Seliger, R. V., Lukas, E. J., and Lindner, R. M., eds., *Contemporary criminal hygiene*. Baltimore: Oakridge Press, 1946.

23. Zilboorg, G. *The medical man and the witch during the Renaissance*. Baltimore: Johns Hopkins Univ. Press, 1935.

Phases of Alcohol Addiction

E. M. JELLINEK

In 1946 E. M. Jellinek, on the basis of a questionnaire study of members of Alcoholics Anonymous, first formulated his concept of phases in the drinking history of alcoholics. With the original publi-

Reprinted from the *Quarterly Journal of Studies on Alcohol,* 13(1952), 673–684, with the permission of the Publications Division, Rutgers Center of Alcohol Studies and the author.

cation * of this concept Jellinek outlined a more detailed questionnaire, which in

* Jellinek, E. M. Phases in the drinking history of alcoholics. Analysis of a survey conducted by the official organ of Alcoholics Anonymous. (Memoirs of the Section of Studies on Alcohol, Yale University, No. 5.) *Quart. J. Stud. Alc.,* 7(1946), 1–88. Published also as a monograph (Hillhouse Press, New Haven, 1946) under the same title; the monograph is now out of print.

the intervening years has been administered to some 2,000 alcoholics. The elaboration of the phases concept resulting from analysis of these additional materials has been presented by Jellinek in lectures at the Yale Summer School of Alcohol Studies (July 1951 and July 1952) and at the European Seminar on Alcoholism (Copenhagen, October 1951). The summary of these lectures, as published under the auspices of the Alcoholism Subcommittee of the World Health Organization,* is reproduced here in full.

Introduction

Only certain forms of excessive drinking —those which in the present report are designated as alcoholism—are accessible to medical-psychiatric treatment. The other forms of excessive drinking, too, present more or less serious problems, but they can be managed only on the level of applied sociology, including law enforcement. Nevertheless, the medical profession may have an advisory role in the handling of these latter problems and must take an interest in them from the viewpoint of preventive medicine.

The conditions which have been briefly defined by the Subcommittee as alcoholism are described in the following pages in greater detail, in order to delimit more definitely those excessive drinkers whose rehabilitation primarily requires medical-psychiatric treatment.

Furthermore, such detailed description may serve to forestall a certain potential danger which attaches to the disease conception of alcoholism, or more precisely of addictive drinking.

With the exception of specialists in alcoholism, the broader medical profession and representatives of the biological

---

* Expert Committee on Mental Health, Alcoholism Subcommittee, Second Report. Annex 2, The Phases of Alcohol Addiction. World Hlth. Org. Techn. Rep. Ser., No. 48, Aug. 1952.

---

and social sciences and the lay public use the term "alcoholism" as a designation for any form of excessive drinking instead of as a label for a limited and well-defined area of excessive drinking behaviors. Automatically, the disease conception of alcoholism becomes extended to all excessive drinking irrespective of whether or not there is any physical or psychological pathology involved in the drinking behavior.

Such an unwarranted extension of the disease conception can only be harmful, because sooner or later the misapplication will reflect on the legitimate use too and, more importantly, will tend to weaken the ethical basis of social sanctions against drunkenness.

THE DISEASE CONCEPTION OF
ALCOHOL ADDICTION

The Subcommittee has distinguished two categories of alcoholics, namely, "alcohol addicts" and "habitual symptomatic excessive drinkers." For brevity's sake the latter will be referred to as nonaddictive alcoholics. Strictly speaking, the disease conception attaches to the alcohol addicts only, but not to the habitual symptomatic excessive drinkers.

In both groups the excessive drinking is symptomatic of underlying psychological or social pathology, but in one group after several years of excessive drinking "loss of control" over the alcohol intake occurs, while in the other group this phenomenon never develops. The group with the "loss of control" is designated as "alcohol addicts." (There are other differences between these two groups and these will be seen in the course of the description of the "phases.")

The disease conception of alcohol addiction does not apply to the excessive drinking, but solely to the "loss of control" which occurs in only one group of alcoholics and then only after many years of excessive drinking. There is no intention to deny that the nonaddictive alcoholic is a sick person; but his ailment is not the excessive drinking, but rather the psychological or social difficulties from which alcohol intoxication gives temporary surcease.

The "loss of control" is a disease condition per se which results from a process that superimposes itself upon those abnormal psychological conditions of which excessive drinking is a symptom. The fact that many excessive drinkers drink as much as or more than the addict for 30 or 40 years without developing loss of control indicates that in the group of "alcohol addicts" a superimposed process must occur.

Whether this superimposed process is of a psychopathological nature or whether some physical pathology is involved cannot be stated as yet with any degree of assurance, the claims of various investigators notwithstanding. Nor is it possible to go beyond conjecture concerning the question whether the "loss of control" originates in a predisposing factor (psychological or physical), or whether it is a factor acquired in the course of prolonged excessive drinking.

The fact that this "loss of control" does not occur in a large group of excessive drinkers would point towards a predisposing X factor in the addictive alcoholics. On the other hand this explanation is not indispensable as the difference between addictive and nonaddictive alcoholics could be a matter of acquired modes of living—for instance, a difference in acquired nutritional habits.

THE MEANING OF SYMPTOMATIC DRINKING

The use of alcoholic beverages by society has primarily a symbolic meaning, and secondarily it achieves "function." Cultures which accept this custom differ in the nature and degree of the "functions" which they regard as legitimate. The differences in these "func-

tions" are determined by the general pattern of the culture, e.g., the need for the release and for the special control of aggression, the need and the ways and means of achieving identification, the nature and intensity of anxieties and the modus for their relief, and so forth. The more the original symbolic character of the custom is preserved, the less room will be granted by the culture to the "functions" of drinking.

Any drinking within the accepted ways is symptomatic of the culture of which the drinker is a member. Within that frame of cultural symptomatology there may be in addition individual symptoms expressed in the act of drinking. The fact that a given individual drinks a glass of beer with his meal may be the symptom of the culture which accepts such a use as a refreshment, or as a "nutritional supplement." That this individual drinks at this given moment may be a symptom of his fatigue, or his elation or some other mood, and thus an individual symptom, but if his culture accepts the use for these purposes it is at the same time a cultural symptom.

In this sense even the small or moderate use of alcoholic beverages is symptomatic, and it may be said that all drinkers are culturally symptomatic drinkers or, at least, started as such.

The vast majority of the users of alcoholic beverages stay within the limits of the culturally accepted drinking behaviors and drink predominantly as an expression of their culture, and while an individual expression may be present in these behaviors its role remains insignificant.

For the purpose of the present discussion the expression "symptomatic drinking" will be limited to the predominant use of alcoholic beverages for the relief of major individual stresses.

A certain unknown proportion of these users of alcoholic beverages, perhaps 20 per cent, are occasionally inclined to take advantage of the "functions" of alcohol which they have experienced in the course of its "cultural use." At least at times, the individual motivation becomes predominant and on those occasions alcohol loses its character as an ingredient of a beverage and is used as a drug.

The "occasional symptomatic excessive drinker" tends to take care of the stresses and strains of living in socially accepted—i.e., "normal"—ways, and his drinking is most of the time within the cultural pattern. After a long accumulation of stresses, however, or because of some particularly heavy stress, his tolerance for tension is lowered and he takes recourse to heroic relief of his symptoms through alcoholic intoxication.* Under these circumstances the "relief" may take

to a constant alcoholic relief, and drinking becomes with them a "mode of living." These are the "alcoholics" of whom again a certain proportion suffer "loss of control," i.e., become "addictive alcoholics."

The proportion of alcoholics (addictive and nonaddictive) varies from country to country, but does not seem to exceed in any country 5 per cent or 6 per cent of all users of alcoholic beverages. The ratio of addictive to nonaddictive alcoholics is unknown.

The Chart of Alcohol Addiction

The course of alcohol addiction is represented graphically in Figure 1. The

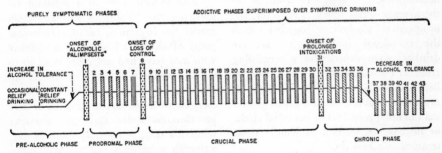

The phases of alcohol addiction. THE LARGE BARS DENOTE THE ONSET OF MAJOR SYMPTOMS WHICH INITIATE PHASES. THE SHORT BARS DENOTE THE ONSET OF SYMPTOMS WITHIN A PHASE. REFERENCE TO THE NUMBERING OF THE SYMPTOMS IS MADE IN THE TEXT.

on an explosive character, and thus the occasional symptomatic excessive drinker may create serious problems. No psychological abnormality can be claimed for this type of drinker, although he does not represent a well-integrated personality.

Nevertheless, within the group of apparent "occasional symptomatic excessive drinkers" there is a certain proportion of definitely deviating personalities who after a shorter or longer period of occasional symptomatic relief take recourse

* This group does not include the regular "periodic alcoholics."

diagram is based on an analysis of more than two thousand drinking histories of male alcohol addicts. Not all symptoms shown in the diagram occur necessarily in all alcohol addicts, nor do they occur in every addict in the same sequence. The "phases" and the sequences of symptoms within the phases are characteristic, however, of the great majority of alcohol addicts and represent what may be called the average trend.

For alcoholic women the "phases" are not as clear-cut as in men and the development is frequently more rapid.

The "phases" vary in their duration

according to individual characteristics and environmental factors. The "lengths" of the different phases on the diagram do not indicate differences in duration, but are determined by the number of symptoms which have to be shown in any given phase.

The chart of the phases of alcohol addiction serves as the basis of description, and the differences between addictive and nonaddictive alcoholics are indicated in the text.

THE PREALCOHOLIC SYMPTOMATIC PHASE

The very beginning of the use of alcoholic beverages is always socially motivated in the prospective addictive and nonaddictive alcoholic. In contrast to the average social drinker, however, the prospective alcoholic (together with the occasional symptomatic excessive drinker) soon experiences a rewarding relief in the drinking situation. The relief is strongly marked in his case because either his tensions are much greater than in other members of his social circle, or he has not learned to handle those tensions as others do.

Initially this drinker ascribes his relief to the situation rather than to the drinking and he seeks therefore those situations in which incidental drinking will occur. Sooner or later, of course, he becomes aware of the contingency between relief and drinking.

In the beginning he seeks this relief occasionally only, but in the course of 6 months to 2 years his tolerance for tension decreases to such a degree that he takes recourse to alcoholic relief practically daily.

Nevertheless his drinking does not result in overt intoxication, but he reaches toward the evening a stage of surcease from emotional stress. Even in the absence of intoxication this involves fairly heavy drinking, particularly in comparison to the use of alcoholic beverages by other members of his circle. The drinking is, nevertheless, not conspicuous either to his associates or to himself.

After a certain time an increase in alcohol tolerance may be noticed, i.e., the drinker requires a somewhat larger amount of alcohol than formerly in order to reach the desired stage of sedation.

This type of drinking behavior may last from several months to two years according to circumstances and may be designated as the prealcoholic phase, which is divided into stages of occasional relief-drinking and constant relief-drinking.

THE PRODROMAL PHASE

The sudden onset of a behavior resembling the "blackouts" in anoxemia marks the beginning of the prodromal phase of alcohol addiction. The drinker who may have had not more than 50 to 60 g. of absolute alcohol and who is not showing any signs of intoxication may carry on a reasonable conversation or may go through quite elaborate activities without a trace of memory the next day, although sometimes one or two minor details may be hazily remembered. This amnesia, which is not connected with loss of consciousness, has been called by Bonhoeffer the "alcoholic palimpsests," with reference to old Roman manuscripts superimposed over an incompletely erased manuscript.

"Alcoholic palimpsests" (1) * may occur on rare occasions in an average drinker when he drinks intoxicating amounts in a state of physical or emotional exhaustion. Nonaddictive alcoholics, of course, also may experience "palimpsests," but infrequently and only following rather marked intoxication. Thus, the frequency of "palimpsests" and their

* The italicized figures in parentheses following the designations of the individual symptoms represent their order as given in Figure 1.

occurrence after medium alcohol intake are characteristic of the prospective alcohol addict.

This would suggest heightened susceptibility to alcohol in the prospective addict. Such a susceptibility may be psychologically or physiologically determined. The analogy with the "blackouts" of anoxemia is tempting. Of course, an insufficient oxygen supply cannot be assumed, but a malutilization of oxygen may be involved. The present status of the knowledge of alcoholism does not permit of more than vague conjectures which, nevertheless, may constitute bases for experimental hypotheses.

The onset of "alcoholic palimpsests" is followed (in some instances preceded) by the onset of drinking behaviors which indicate that, for this drinker, beer, wine, and spirits have practically ceased to be beverages and have become sources of a drug which he "needs." Some of these behaviors imply that this drinker has some vague realization that he drinks differently from others.

Surreptitious drinking (2) is one of these behaviors. At social gatherings the drinker seeks occasions for having a few drinks unknown to others, as he fears that if it were known that he drinks more than the others he would be misjudged: those to whom drinking is only a custom or a small pleasure would not understand that because he is different from them alcohol is for him a necessity, although he is not a drunkard.

Preoccupation with alcohol (3) is further evidence of this "need." When he prepares to go to a social gathering his first thought is whether there will be sufficient alcohol for his requirements, and he has several drinks in anticipation of a possible shortage.

Because of this increasing dependence upon alcohol, the onset of *avid drinking* (4) (gulping of the first or first two drinks) occurs at this time.

As the drinker realizes, at least vaguely, that his drinking is outside of the ordinary, he develops *guilt feelings about his drinking behavior* (5) and because of this he begins to *avoid reference to alcohol* (6) in conversation.

These behaviors, together with an *increasing frequency of "alcoholic palimpsests"* (7), foreshadow the development of alcohol addiction; they are premonitory signs, and this period may be called the prodromal phase of alcohol addiction.

The consumption of alcoholic beverages in the prodromal phase is "heavy," but not conspicuous, as it does not lead to marked, overt intoxications. The effect is that the prospective addict reaches towards evening a state which may be designated as emotional anesthesia. Nevertheless, this condition requires drinking well beyond the ordinary usage. The drinking is on a level which may begin to interfere with metabolic and nervous processes as evidenced by the frequent "alcoholic palimpsests."

The "covering-up" which is shown by the drinker in this stage is the first sign that his drinking might separate him from society, although initially the drinking may have served as a technique to overcome some lack of social integration.

As in the prodromal phase rationalizations of the drinking behavior are not strong and there is some insight as well as fear of possible consequences, it is feasible to intercept incipient alcohol addiction at this stage. In the United States of America, the publicity given to the prodromal symptoms begins to bring prospective alcoholics to clinics as well as to groups of Alcoholics Anonymous.

It goes without saying that even at this stage the only possible modus for this type of drinker is total abstinence.

The prodromal period may last anywhere from 6 months to 4 or 5 years according to the physical and psychological make-up of the drinker, his family ties, vocational relations, general interests, and so forth. The prodromal phase ends and the crucial or acute phase begins with the onset of loss of control, which is the critical symptom of alcohol addiction.

THE CRUCIAL PHASE

Loss of control (8) means that any drinking of alcohol starts a chain reaction which is felt by the drinker as a physical demand for alcohol. This state, possibly a conversion phenomenon, may take hours or weeks for its full development; it lasts until the drinker is too intoxicated or too sick to ingest more alcohol. The physical discomfort following this drinking behavior is contrary to the object of the drinker, which is merely to feel "different." As a matter of fact, the bout may not even be started by any individual need of the moment, but by a "social drink."

After recovery from the intoxication, it is not the "loss of control"—i.e., the physical demand, apparent or real—which leads to a new bout after several days or several weeks; the renewal of drinking is set off by the original psychological conflicts or by a simple social situation which involves drinking.

The "loss of control" is effective after the individual has started drinking, but it does not give rise to the beginning of a new drinking bout. The drinker has lost the ability to control the quantity once he has started, but he still can control whether he will drink on any given occasion or not. This is evidenced in the fact that after the onset of "loss of control" the drinker can go through a period of voluntary abstinence ("going on the water wagon").

The question of why the drinker returns to drinking after repeated disastrous experiences is often raised. Although he will not admit it, the alcohol addict believes that he has lost his will power and that he can and must regain it. He is not aware that he has undergone a process which makes it impossible for him to control his alcohol intake. To

"master his will" becomes a matter of the greatest importance to him. When tensions rise, "a drink" is the natural remedy for him and he is convinced that this time it will be one or two drinks only.

Practically simultaneously with the onset of "loss of control" the alcohol addict begins to *rationalize his drinking behavior* (9): he produces the well-known alcoholic "alibis." He finds explanations which convince him that he did not lose control, but that he had a good reason to get intoxicated and that in the absence of such reasons he is able to handle alcohol as well as anybody else. These rationalizations are needed primarily for himself and only secondarily for his family and associates. The rationalizations make it possible for him to continue with his drinking, and this is of the greatest importance to him as he knows no alternative for handling his problems.

This is the beginning of an entire "system of rationalizations" which progressively spreads to every aspect of his life. While this system largely originates in inner needs, it also serves to counter *social pressures* (10) which arise at the time of the "loss of control." At this time, of course, the drinking behavior becomes conspicuous, and the parents, wife, friends, and employer may begin to reprove and warn the drinker.

In spite of all the rationalizations there is a marked loss of self-esteem, and this of course demands compensations which in a certain sense are also rationalizations. One way of compensation is the *grandiose behavior* (11) which the addict begins to display at this time. Extravagant expenditures and grandiloquence convince him that he is not as bad as he had thought at times.

The rationalization system gives rise to another system, namely, the "system of isolation." The rationalizations quite naturally lead to the idea that the fault lies not within himself but in others, and this results in a progressive withdrawal from the social environment. The first sign of this attitude is a *marked aggressive behavior* (12).

Inevitably, this latter behavior generates guilt. While even in the prodromal period remorse about the drinking arose from time to time, now *persistent remorse* (13) arises, and this added tension is a further source of drinking.

In compliance with social pressures the addict now goes on *periods of total abstinence* (14). There is, however, another modus of control of drinking which arises out of the rationalizations of the addict. He believes that his trouble arises from his not drinking the right kind of beverages or not in the right way. He now attempts to control his troubles by *changing the pattern of his drinking* (15), by setting up rules about not drinking before a certain hour of the day, in certain places only, and so forth.

The strain of the struggle increases his hostility towards his environment and he begins to *drop friends* (16) and *quit jobs* (17). It goes without saying that some associates drop him and that he loses some jobs, but more frequently he takes the initiative as an anticipatory defense.

The isolation becomes more pronounced as his entire *behavior becomes alcohol-centered* (18), i.e., he begins to be concerned about how activities might interfere with his drinking instead of how his drinking may affect his activities. This, of course, involves a more marked egocentric outlook which leads to more rationalizations and more isolation. There ensue a *loss of outside interests* (19) and a *reinterpretation of interpersonal relations* (20) coupled with *marked self-pity* (21). The isolation and rationalizations have increased by this time in intensity and find their expression either in contemplated or actual *geographic escape* (22).

Under the impact of these events, a *change in family habits* (23) occurs. The wife and children, who may have had

good social activities, may withdraw for fear of embarrassment or, quite contrarily, they may suddenly begin intensive outside activities in order to escape from the home environment. This and other events lead to the onset of *unreasonable resentments* (24) in the alcohol addict.

The predominance of concern with alcohol induces the addict to *protect his supply* (25), i.e., to lay in a large stock of alcoholic beverages, hidden in the most unthought-of places. A fear of being deprived of the most necessary substance for his living is expressed in this behavior.

Neglect of proper nutrition (26) aggravates the beginnings of the effects of heavy drinking on the organism, and frequently the *first hospitalization* (27) for some alcoholic complaint occurs at this time.

One of the frequent organic effects is a *decrease of the sexual drive* (28) which increases hostility towards the wife and is rationalized into her extramarital sex activities, which gives rise to the well-known *alcoholic jealousy* (29).

By this time remorse, resentment, struggle between alcoholic needs and duties, loss of self-esteem, and doubts and false reassurance have so disorganized the addict that he cannot start the day without steadying himself with alcohol immediately after arising or even before getting out of bed. This is the beginning of *regular matutinal drinking* (30), which previously had occurred on rare occasions only.

This behavior terminates the crucial phase and foreshadows the beginnings of the chronic phase.

During the crucial phase intoxication is the rule, but it is limited to the evening hours. For the most part of this phase drinking begins sometime in the afternoon and by the evening intoxication is reached. It should be noted that the "physical demand" involved in the "loss of control" results in continual rather than continuous drinking. Particularly the "matutinal drink" which occurs toward the end of the crucial phase shows the continual pattern. The first drink at rising, let us say at 7 A.M., is followed by another drink at 10 or 11 A.M., and another drink around 1 P.M., while the more intensive drinking hardly starts before 5 P.M.

Throughout, the crucial phase presents a great struggle of the addict against the complete loss of social footing. Occasionally the aftereffects of the evening's intoxication cause some loss of time, but generally the addict succeeds in looking after his job, although he neglects his family. He makes a particularly strong effort to avoid intoxication during the day. Progressively, however, his social motivations weaken more and more, and the "morning drink" jeopardizes his effort to comply with his vocational duties as this effort involves a conscious resistance against the apparent or real "physical demand" for alcohol.

The onset of the "loss of control" is the beginning of the "disease process" of alcohol addiction which is superimposed over the excessive symptomatic drinking. Progressively, this disease process undermines the morale and the physical resistance of the addict.

THE CHRONIC PHASE

The increasingly dominating role of alcohol, and the struggle against the "demand" set up by matutinal drinking, at last break down the resistance of the addict and he finds himself for the first time intoxicated in the daytime and on a weekday and continues in that state for several days until he is entirely incapacitated. This is the onset of *prolonged intoxications* (31), referred to in the vernacular as "benders."

This latter drinking behavior meets with such unanimous social rejection that it involves a grave social risk. Only an originally psychopathic personality or a person who has later in life undergone a psychopathological process would expose himself to that risk.

These long-drawn-out bouts commonly bring about *marked ethical deterioration* (32) and *impairment of thinking* (33) which, however, are not irreversible. True *alcoholic psychoses* (34) may occur at this time, but in not more than 10 per cent of all alcoholics.

The loss of morale is so heightened that the addict *drinks with persons far below his social level* (35) in preference to his usual associates—perhaps as an opportunity to appear superior—and, if nothing else is available, he will *take recourse to "technical products"* (36) such as bay rum or rubbing alcohol.

A *loss of alcohol tolerance* (37) is commonly noted at this time. Half of the previously required amount of alcohol may be sufficient to bring about a stuporous state.

Indefinable fears (38) and *tremors* (39) become persistent. Sporadically these symptoms occur also during the crucial phase, but in the chronic phase they are present as soon as alcohol disappears from the organism. In consequence the addict "controls" the symptoms through alcohol. The same is true of *psychomotor inhibition* (40), the inability to initiate a simple mechanical act—such as winding a watch—in the absence of alcohol.

The need to control these symptoms of drinking exceeds the need of relieving the original underlying symptoms of the personality conflict, and the *drinking takes on an obsessive character* (41).

In many addicts, approximately 60 per cent, some *vague religious desires develop* (42) as the rationalizations become weaker. Finally, in the course of the frequently prolonged intoxications, the rationalizations become so frequently and so mercilessly tested against reality that the entire *rationalization system fails* (43) and the addict admits defeat. He now becomes spontaneously accessible to treatment. Nevertheless, his obsessive drinking continues as he does not see a way out.

Formerly it was thought that the addict must reach this stage of utter defeat in order to be treated successfully. Clinical experience has shown, however, that this "defeat" can be induced long before it would occur of itself and that even incipient alcoholism can be intercepted. As the latter can be easily recognized it is possible to tackle the problem from the preventive angle.

The "Alcoholic Personality"

The aggressions, feelings of guilt, remorse, resentments, withdrawal, etc., which develop in the phases of alcohol addiction, are largely consequences of the excessive drinking, but at the same time they constitute sources of more excessive drinking.

In addition to relieving, through alcohol, symptoms of an underlying personality conflict, the addict now tends to relieve, through further drinking, the stresses created by his drinking behavior.

By and large, these reactions to excessive drinking—which have quite a neurotic appearance—give the impression of an "alcoholic personality," although they are secondary behaviors superimposed over a large variety of personality types which have a few traits in common, in particular a low capacity for coping with tensions. There does not emerge, however, any specific personality trait or physical characteristic which inevitably would lead to excessive symptomatic drinking. Apart from psychological and possibly physical liabilities, there must be a constellation of social and economic factors which facilitate the development of addictive and nonaddictive alcoholism in a susceptible terrain.

The Nonaddictive Alcoholic

Some differences between the nonaddictive alcoholic and the alcohol addict have been stated passim. These differences may

be recapitulated and elaborated, and additional differential features may be considered.

The main difference may be readily visualized by erasing the large bars of the diagram (see Figure 1). This results in a diagram which suggests a progressive exacerbation of the use of alcohol for symptom relief and of the social and health consequences incumbent upon such use, but without any clear-cut phases.

The prealcoholic phase is the same for the nonaddictive alcoholic as for the alcohol addict, i.e, he progresses from occasional to constant relief of individual symptoms through alcohol.

The behaviors which denote that alcohol has become a drug rather than an ingredient of a beverage (symptoms 2 to 6) occur also in the nonaddictive drinker, but, as mentioned before, the "alcoholic palimpsests" occur rarely and only after overt intoxication.

"Loss of control" is not experienced by the nonaddictive alcoholic, and this is the main differentiating criterion between the two categories of alcoholics. Initially, of course, it could not be said whether the drinker had yet reached the crucial phase, but after 10 or 12 years of heavy drinking without "loss of control," while symptoms 2 to 6 were persistent and "palimpsests" were rare and did not occur after medium alcohol intake, the differential diagnosis is rather safe.

The absence of "loss of control" has many involvements. First of all, as there is no inability to stop drinking within a given situation there is no need to rationalize the inability. Nevertheless, rationalizations are developed for justifying the excessive use of alcohol and some neglect of the family attendant upon such use. Likewise, there is no need to change the pattern of drinking, which in the addict is an attempt to overcome the "loss of control." Periods of total abstinence, however, occur as a response to social pressure.

On the other hand, there is the same tendency toward isolation as in the addict, but the social repercussions are much less marked as the nonaddictive alcoholic can avoid drunken behavior whenever the social situation requires it.

The effects of prolonged heavy drinking on the organism may occur in the nonaddictive alcoholic too; even delirium tremens may develop. The libido may be diminished and "alcoholic jealousy" may result.

Generally, there is a tendency toward a progressive dominance of alcohol resulting in greater psychological and bodily effects. In the absence of any grave initial psychopathy, however, the symptoms of the chronic phase as seen in addicts do not develop in the nonaddictive alcoholic. In the presence of grave underlying psychopathies a deteriorative process is speeded up by habitual alcoholic excess, and such a nonaddictive drinker may slide to the bottom of society.

8. PSYCHOSOMATIC DISORDERS

THE CONCEPT of psychosomatic disorders, or more correctly, *psychophysiological reaction,* is a very difficult one for many lay people. It does *not* involve diseases which are all in the mind, which is a crude and inaccurate description of a conversion reaction, and it is *not* an exaggeration of multiple complaints, as is true of hypochondriasis. Rather it is a real physical illness, with medically identifiable physiological loci, but one of the causes is seen as being psychic. Thus it may be correct to think of an ulcer as psychosomatic because there is a real lesion whose severity is linked to psychological events, but it would be quite wrong to dismiss it as "only psychosomatic." Alexander presents some of the fundamental concepts of research in this area, and the other two authors describe research studies. Brady's study was with monkeys but carries many implications for the development of ulcers in humans. Schmale presents a very interesting hypothesis which has intrigued many workers in this area, and which could serve to broaden the range of psychosomatic medicine well beyond its current limits.

Fundamental Concepts of Psychosomatic Research: Psychogenesis, Conversion, Specificity[*]

FRANZ ALEXANDER
CHICAGO PSYCHOANALYTIC INSTITUTE

Although psychosomatic research is of recent origin, it deals with one of the oldest, if not *the* oldest, problems of scientific thought—with the mind-body prob-

Reprinted from *Psychosomatic Medicine,* 5 (1943), 205–210, with the permission of the Hoeber Medical Division, Harper & Row Publishers, Inc., and the author.

* Paper presented at the Conference on Psychiatry, held at Ann Arbor, Michigan, October 22–24, 1942, under the auspices of the University of Michigan and the McGregor Fund.

lem. This may explain the heavy load of traditional concepts and assumptions which hamper its development. At first I shall take up the concept of *psychogenesis* in general, then that of *hysterical conversion* in particular, and finally the question of the *specificity* of emotional factors involved in somatic dysfunctions.

Psychogenesis

The question of psychogenesis is linked up with the ancient dichotomy: psyche versus soma. When the *Journal of Psychosomatic Medicine* was started, our editorial staff felt that in the first issue some clear statement should be made about this confusing philosophical issue to discourage authors from writing endless discussions on this point. I quote from this introductory statement of the editors:

> Emphasis is put on the thesis that there is no logical distinction between 'mind and body,' mental and physical. It is assumed that the complex neurophysiology of mood, instinct and intellect differs from other physiology in degree of complexity, but not in quality. Hence again divisions of medical disciplines into physiology, neurology, internal medicine, psychiatry and psychology may be convenient for academic administration, but biologically and philosophically these divisions have no validity. It takes for granted that psychic and somatic phenomena take place in the same biological system and are probably two aspects of the same process, that psychological phenomena should be studied in their psychological causality with intrinsically psychological methods and physiological phenomena in their physical causality with the methods of physics and chemistry (1).

In spite of this statement, we still receive manuscripts in which the authors involve themselves in a hopeless struggle with this age-worn problem. For example, an author gives an excellent description of the effect of psychological factors upon some clinical condition, then becomes apologetic and tries to dodge the whole issue of psychogenesis by saying that one should not speak of psychogenesis but of the coexistence of certain psychological factors with certain physical symptoms.

It is important that the question of psychogenesis should be clarified, stating explicitly what is meant by it. First let us examine an example. In the case of emotionally caused elevation of the blood pressure, psychogenesis does not mean that the contraction of the blood vessels is effected by some non-somatic mechanism. Rage consists in physiological processes which take place somewhere in the central nervous system. The physiological effect of rage consists of a chain of events —among them the elevation of blood pressure—in which every link can be described at least theoretically in physiological terms. The distinctive feature of psychogenic factors such as emotions or ideas and fantasies is that they *can* be studied also psychologically through introspection or by verbal communication from those in whom these physiological processes take place. An automobile climbing a hill has no sensation of effort, tiredness, or of a goal to reach. In contrast to a man-built machine the organism climbing a mountain has an awareness of certain of its internal physiological processes in the form of effort, tiredness, discouragement, renewed effort, and so on. Moreover, man in contrast to the animal organisms is able to convey these internal sensations to others by verbal communication. Verbal communication is therefore one of the most potent instruments of psychology and consequently also of psychosomatic research. When we speak of psychogenesis we refer to physiological processes consisting of central excitations in the nervous system which can be studied by psychological methods because they are perceived subjectively in the form of emotions, ideas, or wishes. Psychosomatic research deals with such processes in which certain links in the causal chain of events lend themselves, at the present state of our knowledge, more readily to a study by psychological methods than by physiological methods since the detailed investigation of emotions as brain processes is not far enough advanced. My expectation is, however, that even when the physiological basis of psychological phenomena is better known we will not be able to dispense with their psychological study. It is hardly conceivable that the different moves of two chess players can ever be more clearly understood in biochemical or neuro-physiological than in psychological and logical terms.

Conversion

The concept of hysterical conversion too is closely related to the philosophical question of mind and body. The expression itself carries the connotation that a psychological process is transmuted into a bodily manifestation. Freud formulated the concept of conversion in the following way: "In hysteria the unbearable idea is rendered innocuous by the quantity of excitation attached to it being transmuted into some bodily form of expression, a process for which I should like to propose the name of conversion" (20). Essentially an hysterical conversion symptom is nothing but an unusual innervation; it does not differ in principle from any other voluntary innervation or from such expressive movements as speech, laughter, or weeping. When we want to hit someone our arms are brought into movement; when we speak our ideas are converted into movements of the laryngeal muscles and of the lips and tongue. In laughter or weeping also, an emotion finds bodily expression. It was unfortunate that Freud spoke, referring to hysterical conversion, of a "mysterious leap" from the psychic to the physiologic (19). In a conversion symptom like hysterical contracture, the "leap from the psychic into the somatic"

is not more mysterious than in any of the common motor innervations, such as voluntary movements or expressive movements as laughter or weeping. The meaning of conversion symptom was originally very definite: a conversion symptom was a symbolic substitute for an unbearable emotion. It was assumed that the symptom relieved, at least to some degree, the tension produced by the repression of the unbearable emotion. It was considered a kind of physical abreaction or equivalent of an unconscious emotional tension. From the beginning Freud insisted that the repressed emotion ultimately can be always retraced to a sexual tension. Ferenczi made this even more explicit by postulating that a physical conversion symptom is always a kind of genitalization of that part of the body (15). I shall not enter into the discussion of the validity of the exclusively sexual origin of conversion symptoms at the present moment.

Repeated attempts have been made to extend the original concept of hysterical conversion to all forms of psychogenic disturbances of the body, even to those of the visceral vegetative organs. It was claimed that the essence of psychogenic disturbances is always the same. A repressed emotional tension finds expression through bodily channels. Whether it takes place in vegetative organs controlled by the autonomic nervous system or in the voluntary neuro-muscular and sensory perceptive systems is a secondary matter. According to this concept emotional hypertension is the conversion of repressed rage or some other emotion into a physical symptom—the elevation of blood pressure. The adherents to this concept even went so far as to say that a peptic ulcer might be considered a conversion symptom. Some repressed emotion, let us say some biting fantasies, find somatic expression in tissue changes of the stomach. In previous writings I have tried to demonstrate the grave error inherent in such superficial generalizations

(2, 3, 7). I pointed out that the original concept of hysterical conversion is still an excellent and valid one if it is restricted to those phenomena on which it was originally based by Freud. At the same time I introduced the concept of another form of psychogenic process which is observed in vegetative disturbances such as emotional hypertension or in psychogenic organic conditions such as peptic ulcers. Since these publications I have arrived at still more precise formulations which I should like to present on this occasion.

I still uphold my original suggestion that we restrict hysterical conversion phenomena to symptoms of the voluntary neuro-muscular and the sensory perceptive systems and differentiate them from psychogenic symptoms which occur in vegetative organ systems, the functions of which are under the control of the autonomic nervous system. The rationale of this distinction is about as follows: Hysterical conversion symptoms are substitute expressions—abreactions—or emotional tensions which cannot find adequate outlet through full-fledged motor behavior. For example, sexual excitation, which normally is gratified by intercourse, if repressed may find expression in some other motor innervation such as convulsions imitating the muscular movements of intercourse. Or, anger which cannot find expression through yelling, shouting, accusing, hitting, might lead to conversion symptoms in organs which are used for the legitimate expression of rage—the larynx or the extremities in the form of hysterical aphasia or paralysis. As Freud originally stressed it, these substitutive innervations never bring full relief; they are only attempts at relief; the symptoms express at the same time both the repressed emotion and its rejection. Just because they do not relieve the tension fully we have a pathological condition. The important issue, however, is that the emotional tension is at least partially relieved by the symptom itself. We deal with a different psychodynamic and

physiological situation in the field of vegetative neuroses although there are some similarities to the conversion symptoms. Here the somatic symptoms are not substitute expressions of repressed emotions but they are normal physiological accompaniments of the symptom. For example, the emotional states of rage and fear are connected with a physiological syndrome consisting of such diversified vegetative processes as the stimulation of the adrenal system, mobilization of sugar, elevation of the blood pressure, changes in the distribution of blood which is squeezed out from the splanchnic area into the muscles, to the lungs and the brain. These physiological processes are normal corollaries of rage and fear; they do not relieve suppressed rage but they accompany rage. They are the adjustment of the organism to definite tasks which it has to face in a dangerous situation, to fight or to flee. They are a utilitarian preparation and adaptation of the internal vegetative processes to a specific type of behavior which is requested from the organism. The elevated blood pressure or mobilization of sugar does not relieve the anger in the least; these symptoms do not appear in place of the emotional tension; they simply accompany the emotion of rage; they are an inseparable part of the total phenomenon which we call rage. They are the systemic reaction of the body to rage. The chronicity of an emotional tension alone is what makes such a condition morbid. The non-neurotic individual is able to get rid of his rage by some legitimate expression. Some psychoneurotics can drain off the suppressed hostile feelings in compulsion symptoms. The hypertensive patient's pathology consists in the fact that he is under a constant or frequent, not repressed, but unexpressed, emotional tension which is not drained either by psychoneurotic symptoms or by legitimate expression such as verbal or physical combat. He has not the relief that the angry man has of beating up his adversary or at least telling him what he has on his mind. The difference between conversion symptom and vegetative neurosis is now obvious. A conversion symptom is a symbolic expression of a well-defined emotional content—an attempt at relief. It is expressed by the voluntary neuromuscular or sensory perceptive systems whose original function is to express and relieve emotional tension. A vegetative neurosis like emotional hypertension is not an attempt to express an emotion but is the physiological accompaniment of constant or periodically recurring emotional states.

The same conditions described in emotional hypertension can be applied readily to all other vegetative systems. Similarly a gastric neurosis consisting of a chronic disturbance of the secretory and motor functions of the stomach is not the expression or drainage of an emotional tension but the physiological accompaniment of it. These patients want to be loved, to be taken care of, a wish to which they cannot give legitimate expression because of a neurotically exaggerated sense of shame or guilt; therefore they are under constant influence of these emotional tensions. The wish to be loved is deeply associated with the wish to be fed since the nursing situation is the first one in which the child enjoys parental love and care. Because of early emotional associations the chronic longing to be loved and taken care of is apt to stimulate the stomach functions. The stomach symptoms are the physiological corollaries of the passive state of expectation of receiving food. The disturbance of the secretory and motor functions of the stomach is not the substitute expression of an emotion but the physiological counterpart of an emotion, namely, of the desire to be taken care of. The wish to be taken care of may be repressed and transformed into the wish to be nursed. This is not a conversion, however, but the substitution of one desire for another. Corresponding to this wish to be nursed are certain vegetative innervations which are not substitutes for the wish to be nursed but are the inseparable physiological sequelae. If the desire to be taken care of is satisfied for example through sanitorium treatment, the constant pressure of this wish may cease and with it the stomach symptoms may fully disappear. Neurotic stomach symptoms, however, are not conversions of a repressed longing for love into stomach symptoms; they do not appear in place of the emotions, but are the physiological concomitants of a chronic or periodic emotional tension. Bulimia, in contradistinction to a stomach neurosis, may be considered as a conversion symptom. Here the wish to be loved, to be given things or to take things is drained, that is to say satisfied, at least to some extent by incorporating food. Eating becomes both a satisfaction and a symbolic substitute for being loved or being impregnated or for a biting aggressive attack. It fulfills all the requirements of a conversion symptom. Asthma also has components of a hysterical conversion symptom since it can serve as the direct expression and partial substitute for a suppressed emotion such as the wish to cry. Breathing—although an automatic function—is also under the control of voluntary innervations. Acid secretion of the stomach, however, is not. Breathing is used in such expressive functions as speech and crying; stomach secretion may be a concomitant of an emotional state but is never used for its symbolic expression as is speech or crying. Possibly there are mixed conditions in which both types of mechanism coexist. The psychodynamic background of most psychogenic skin disturbances is still very unclear, but it appears that in the skin both conversion mechanisms and vegetative neurotic symptoms may occur. The skin is partially a sensory perceptive but also a vegetative organ. Blushing is obviously a conversion symptom. On the other hand it is probable that the physiological mechanism in psychogenic urticaria follows the pattern of vegetative neuroses. Psychosomatic disturbances involving sphincter functions both under autonomic and voluntary control, such as constipation, diarrhea, pollakuria, urine retention, etc., represent a combination of hysterical conversion symptoms and vegetative nuroses.

Finally, peptic ulcer is neither a conversion symptom nor a vegetative neurosis. In some cases it is the somatic end result of a long-standing neurotic stomach dysfunction but in itself has nothing whatever directly to do with any emotion. It is not the symbolic expression of a wish or a self-punishment. It is a secondary physiological end-effect of a long-standing dysfunction. It is an organic disturbance which in many cases is the end result of a psychogenic functional disturbance, a vegetative neurosis of the stomach.

To summarize: it seems advisable to differentiate between hysterical conversion and vegetative neurosis. Their similarities are rather superficial: both conditions are psychogenic, that is to say, they are caused ultimately by a chronic repressed or at least unrelieved emotional tension. The mechanisms involved, however, are fundamentally different both psychodynamically and physiologically. The hysterical conversion symptom is an attempt to relieve an emotional tension in a symbolic way; it is a symbolic expression of a definite emotional content. This mechanism is restricted to the voluntary neuro-muscular or sensory perceptive systems whose function is to express and relieve emotions. A vegetative neurosis consists of a psychogenic dysfunction of a vegetative organ which is not under control of the voluntary neuro-muscular system. The vegetative symptom is not a substitute expression of the emotion, but its normal physiological concomitant. We assume that corresponding to every emotional state there is a certain distribution of vegetative innervations. When we have to fight or undergo physi-

cal exertion the vegetative organs of digestion are relaxed whereas the muscular system and the lungs are in a state of preparation. The emotional attitude accompanying and preceding food intake and digestion again is accompanied by a different distribution of vegetative tonus. In this instance the visceral organs become hyperemic whereas the skeletal muscle tonus decreases and the concomitant drowsiness is the indication of a transitory anemia of the cortex. If these emotional states are chronically sustained the corresponding vegetative innervations also become chronic. The circulatory system of the hypertensive behaves as if this person were ready to attack somebody at any moment. On the other hand, when the stomach neurotic breaks down under an excessive load of responsibility he recoils from his habitual overactivity and assumes the vegetative mood of the state that accompanies digestion, to which his alimentary tract reacts with a continuous hyperactivity. This recoiling from exaggerated outward activity and strain we may call "vegetative retreat." It is a counter-coup phenomenon, a kind of exhaustion following sustained effort. According to all indications an outward directed active aggressive state is connected with a sustained excess of tonus of the sympathetic-adrenal system from which the individual when exhausted may retreat into the opposite attitude in which the tonus of the vagal-insular system is increased. This increased tonus of the parasympathetic system possibly connected with a simultaneous relaxation of sympathetic-adrenal tonus is what I denote by the expression "vegetative retreat." This may assume different forms consisting in some hyperactivity of visceral organs resulting from parasympathetic excitation such as hypersecretion and hypermotility of the stomach, diarrhea, or psychogenic hyperinsulinism (psychogenic hypoglycemia).* Possibly

* In a number of patients with a so-called psychogenetic fatigue, Sidney A. Portis suggested that a possible physiological mechanism involved

the condition described by Gowers as vagal attacks which he considered as related to the epileptic seizure is the most extreme example of a vegetative retreat (21).

Specificity

This brings us to the last crucial problem of psychosomatic research, the question of specificity, which I shall only briefly touch upon on this occasion. According to one school of thought there is no specific correlation; any emotional tension may influence any vegetative system. The choice of the symptoms may depend upon the history of the patient and on his constitution; if he has a weak stomach, he has a stomach upset when he gets angry; if he has a labile vasomotor system he might become a hypertensive under the influence of aggressions. Perhaps an early respiratory infection has made his lungs susceptible; then he will react to every emotional upset with an asthma attack. The other heuristic assumption, which has guided our investigative work in the Chicago Psychoanalytic Institute, is that the physiological responses to different emotional tensions are varied; that consequently vegetative dysfunctions result from specific emotional constellations. As I have emphasized, we know from human and animal experiment that different emotional states have their specific vegetative tonus. The vegetative syndrome which corresponds to rage and fear is definitely different from that of passive relaxation during digestion; a state of impatience or of tense attentiveness has bodily concomitants in vegetative and skeletal innervations different from those in a paralyzing state of panic. The vegetative concomitants of various emotional states are as different from each other as laughter from weeping—the physical expression of merriment from that of sorrow. It is therefore to be expected that just as the nature of the chronic unrelieved emotional state varies, so also will the corresponding vegetative disturbance vary. The results of current investigations are all in favor of the theory of specificity (4–7, 9–11, 13–14, 16–18, 22–32, 34).* Gastric neurotic symptoms have a different psychology from those of emotional diarrhea or constipation; cardiac cases differ in their emotional background from asthmatics. The emotional component in functional glycosuria has its own peculiarities and there is good evidence that the emotional factor in glaucoma has again its specific features. This emotional specificity can only be ascertained, of course, by careful, minute observation for which the best method available is the prolonged interview technique of psychoanalysis. However, briefer but careful psychiatric anamnestic studies conducted by well-trained observers often reveal the specific personality factors involved in different types of cases. To what extent constitutional factors influence the picture, and to what extent a pre-existing organic pathology or sensitivity are responsible are questions to be decided by further careful clinical studies.

Summary

1. An attempt is made to clarify the concept of psychogenesis.
2. The fundamental psychological and physiological differences between *conversion symptoms, vegetative neuroses,* and *psychogenic organic disease* are elaborated.

was that of hyper-insulinism. This resulted from a temporary or prolonged parasympathetic stimulation. Daily physiological doses of atropine by mouth brought about a cessation of the fatigue symptom. See Sidney A. Portis and Irving H. Zitman, A mechanism of fatigue in neuropsychiatric patients, *J.A.M.A.*, Vol. 121, 1943.

* For a more complete literature concerning specific emotional factors, I refer to Dr. H. F. Dunbar's book, *Emotions and bodily changes* (12) and different reviews published in the *Journal of Psychosomatic Medicine* (8, 33, 35, 36). See also Weiss and English, *Psychosomatic medicine*, Saunders Co., 1943.

3. The problem of specificity of emotional factors in different vegetative neuroses is discussed. Evidence for the specificity of emotional factors is offered.

References

1. Introductory Statement. *Psychosom. Med.*, 1(1939), 1.

2. Alexander, F. Functional disturbances of psychogenic origin. *J.A.M.A.*, 100 (1933), 469.

3. ——— Critical discussion of the extension of the theory of conversion hysteria to the field of organic diseases. In *Medical value of psychoanalysis*, 2nd ed. New York: Norton, 1936.

4. ——— Emotional factors in essential hypertension. *Psychosom. Med.*, 1(1939), 173.

5. ——— Psychoanalytic study of a case of essential hypertension. *Psychosom. Med.*, 1 (1939), 139.

6. ——— Gastrointestinal neuroses. In Portis, S. A.: Diseases of the Digestive System. Philadelphia: Lea & Febiger, 1941.

7. ——— and Co-workers. The influence of psychologic factors upon gastrointestinal disturbances: a symposium. *Psychoanal. Quart.*, 3 (1934), 501.

8. Brush, L. Recent literature relative to the psychiatric aspects of gastrointestinal disorders. *Psychosom. Med.*, 1(1939), 423.

9. Daniels, G. E. Psychiatric aspects of ulcerative colitis. *New Eng. J. Med.*, 226(1942), 178.

10. Deutsch, F. Emotional factors in asthma and other allergic conditions. Paper read before the Ass. Med. Social Workers, Feb. 1938.

11. Dunbar, H. F. Psychoanalytic notes relating to syndromes of asthma and hayfever. *Psychoanal. Quart.*, 7(1938), 25.

12. ——— Emotions and bodily changes. 2nd ed. New York: Columbia Univ. Press, 1938.

13. ——— Character and symptoms formation. *Psychoanal. Quart.*, 8(1939), 18.

14. ——— Wolfe, T., and Rioch, N. The psychic component of the disease process in cardiac, diabetic and fracture patients. *Am. J. Psychiat.*, 93(1936), 649.

15. Ferenczi, S. The phenomena of hysterical materialization. In *Further contributions to the theory and technique of psychoanalysis*. London: Hogarth Press, 1926. Page 89.

16. French, Th. M. Psychogenic factors in asthma. *Am. J. Psychiat.*, 96(1939), 67.

17. ——— Physiology of behavior and choice of neurosis. *Psychoanal. Quart.*, 10(1941), 561.

18. ——— Alexander, F., and Co-workers. Psychogenic factors in bronchial asthma. Part I.

Psychosom. Med. Mon., 1(1941), #4. Part II. *Psychosom. Med. Mon.*, 2(1941), #1, 2. Washington: National Research Council.

19. Freud, S. *A general introduction to psychoanalysis*. New York: Boni & Liveright, 1920.

20. ——— The defence neuro-psychosis. (1894.) In *Collected Papers*, 1:59. London: Hogarth Press, 1924.

21. Gowers, Sir Wm. Vagal and vaso-vagal attacks. In *The Border-Land of Epilepsy*. Philadelphia: Blakiston, 1907.

22. Hill, L. B. Psychoanalytic observations on essential hypertension. *Psychoanal. Rev.*, 22 (1935), 60.

23. Menninger, K. A., and Menninger, Wm. C. Psychoanalytic observations in cardiac disorders. *Am. Heart J.*, 11(1936), #1.

24. Miller, M. L. Bloodpressure findings in relation to inhibited aggressions in psychotics. *Psychosom. Med.*, 1(1939), 162.

25. ——— A psychological study of eczema and neurodermatitis. *Psychosom. Med.*, 4(1942), 82.

26. ——— and McLean, H. V. The status of the emotions in palpitation and extrasystoles with a note on the effort syndrome. *Psychoanal. Quart.*, 10(1941), 545.

27. Mittelman, B., Wolf, H. G., and Scharf, M. Emotions and gastroduodenal functions. Experimental studies on patients with gastritis, duodenitis and peptic ulcer. *Psychosom. Med.*, 4(1942), 5.

28. Saul, L. J. A note on the psychogenesis of organic symptoms. *Psychoanal. Quart.*, 4 (1935), 476.

29. ——— Psychogenic factors in the etiology of the common cold and related symptoms. *Int. J. Psychoanal.*, 19(1938), 451.

30. ——— Hostility in cases of essential hypertention. *Psychosom. Med.*, 1(1939), 153.

31. ——— Some observations on the relations of emotions and allergy. *Psychosom. Med.*, 3(1941), 66.

32. ——— The emotional settings of some attacks of urticaria. *Psychosom. Med.*, 3(1941), 349.

33. Stokes, J. H., and Berman, H. Psychosomatic correlations in allergic conditions: a review of problems and literature. *Psychosom. Med.*, 2 (1940), 438.

34. Vander Heide, C. A study of mechanisms in two cases of peptic ulcer. *Psychosom. Med.*, 2 (1940), 398.

35. Weiss, E. Recent advances in pathogenesis and treatment of hypertension. A review. *Psychosom. Med.*, 1(1939), 180

36. White, B. V., Cobb, Stanley, and Jones, Ch. M. Mucous colitis. A psychological medical study of 60 cases. *Psychosom. Med. Mon.*, 1 (1939), #1. Washington: National Research Council.

Ulcers in "Executive" Monkeys

Joseph V. Brady
WALTER REED ARMY INSTITUTE OF RESEARCH

Physicians and laymen alike have long recognized that emotional stress can produce bodily disease. Psychic disturbances can induce certain skin and respiratory disorders, can set off attacks of allergic asthma and may even play a part in some forms of heart disease. Of all the body's systems, however, the gastrointestinal tract is perhaps the most vulnerable to emotional stress. The worries, fears, conflicts and anxieties of daily life can produce gastrointestinal disorders ranging from the "nervous stomach," which most of us know at first hand, to the painful and often disabling ulcers which are the traditional occupational disease of business executives.

Emotional stress appears to produce ulcers by increasing the flow of the stomach's acid juices. The connection between emotional disturbance, stomach secretion and ulcers is well documented. A recent study of 2,000 Army draftees, for example, found that those who showed emotional disturbance and excessive gastric secretion during their initial physical examination developed ulcers later on under the strains of military life.

But not every kind of emotional stress produces ulcers, and the same kind of stress will do so in one person and not

in another. Experimental investigation of the problem is difficult. Animals obviously cannot provide wholly satisfactory experimental models of human mind-body interactions. They can, however, be studied under controlled conditions, and it is through animal experiments that we are finding leads to the cause of ulcers as well as to the effect of emotional stress on the organism in general.

Various investigators have succeeded in inducing ulcers in experimental animals by subjecting them to physical stress. But the role of the emotional processes in such experiments has been uncertain. Experiments on dogs by George F. Mahl of Yale University Medical School indicate that a "fear producing" situation lasting many hours increases the animals' gastric secretions, but these animals do not develop ulcers. William L. Sawrey and John D. Weisz of the University of Colorado produced ulcers in rats by subjecting them to a conflict situation: keeping them in a box where they could obtain food and water only by standing on a grid which gave them a mild electric shock. But this experiment, as Sawrey and Weisz themselves pointed out, did not prove conclusively that emotional stress was the crucial factor in producing the ulcers.

Our studies of ulcers in monkeys at the Walter Reed Army Institute of Re-

search developed somewhat fortuitously.
For several years we had been investigating the emotional behavior of these
animals. In some of our experiments we
had been keeping monkeys in "restraining chairs" (in which they could move
their heads and limbs but not their
bodies) while we conditioned them in
various ways. Since these procedures
seemed to impose considerable emotional stress on the animals, we decided that
we ought to know something about their
physiological reactions. Preliminary investigation showed that stress brought
about dramatic alterations in the hormone content of the animals' blood, but
a more extensive study of 19 monkeys
was brought to a halt when many of
them died.

At first we considered this merely a
stroke of bad luck, but the post-mortem

findings showed that more than bad
luck was involved. Many of the dead
monkeys had developed ulcers as well as
other extensive gastrointestinal damage.
Such pathological conditions are normally rare in laboratory animals, and previous experiments with monkeys kept in
restraining chairs up to six months convinced us that restraint alone did not
produce the ulcers. Evidently the conditioning procedures were to blame.

One of the procedures which showed
a high correlation with ulcers involved
training the monkey to avoid an electric
shock by pressing a lever. The animal
received a brief shock on the feet at
regular intervals, say, every 20 seconds.
It could avoid the shock if it learned to
press the lever at least once in every 20-
second interval. It does not take a monkey very long to master this problem;

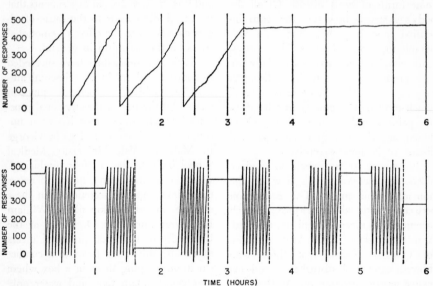

Responses of monkeys WERE RECORDED AUTOMATICALLY. SLOPE OF THE LINES SHOWS
THE RATE OF LEVER-PRESSING (*vertical lines indicate resetting of stylus*). UPPER CHART
SHOWS RESPONSES OF AN EXECUTIVE MONKEY DURING THE LAST HALF OF A SIX-HOUR
AVOIDANCE SESSION (*left side*) AND THE FIRST HALF OF A SIX-HOUR REST PERIOD; SHOCKS
WERE PROGRAMMED EVERY 20 SECONDS. MONKEYS KEPT ON THIS SCHEDULE DEVELOPED
ULCERS. LOWER CHART SHOWS RESPONSES DURING A 30-MINUTES-ON, 30-MINUTES-OFF
SCHEDULE WITH SHOCKS PROGRAMMED EVERY TWO SECONDS. MONKEYS ON THIS SCHEDULE
FAILED TO DEVELOP ULCERS, DESPITE MORE INTENSE ACTIVITY AND PRESUMABLY GREATER
PSYCHIC STRESS.

within a short time it is pressing the lever far oftener than once in 20 seconds. Only occasionally does it slow down enough to receive a shock as a reminder.

One possibility, of course, was that the monkeys which had developed ulcers under this procedure had done so not because of the psychological stress involved but rather as a cumulative result of the shocks. To test this possibility we set up a controlled experiment, using two monkeys in "yoked chairs" in which both monkeys received shocks but only one monkey could prevent them. The experimental or "executive" monkey could prevent shocks to himself and his partner by pressing the lever; the con-

lever at a rate averaging between 15 and 20 times a minute during the avoidance periods, and to stop pressing the lever when the red light was turned off. These responses showed no change throughout the experiment. The control monkey at first pressed the lever sporadically during both the avoidance and rest sessions, but lost interest in the lever within a few days.

After 23 days of a continuous six-hours-on, six-hours-off schedule the executive monkey died during one of the avoidance sessions. Our only advance warning had been the animal's failure to eat on the preceding day. It had lost no weight during the experiment, and it

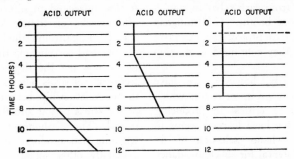

Stomach acidity OF EXECUTIVE MONKEYS, AS SHOWN IN THESE HIGHLY SIMPLIFIED CHARTS, DID NOT INCREASE DURING AVOIDANCE SESSIONS BUT RATHER DURING THE SUBSEQUENT REST PERIODS. THE GREATEST INCREASE FOLLOWED A SIX-HOUR SESSION; NO RISE FOLLOWED A ONE-HOUR SESSION.

trol monkey's lever was a dummy. Thus both animals were subjected to the same physical stress (i.e., both received the same number of shocks at the same time), but only the "executive" monkey was under the psychological stress of having to press the lever.

We placed the monkeys on a continuous schedule of alternate periods of shock-avoidance and rest, arbitrarily choosing an interval of six hours for each period. As a cue for the executive monkey we provided a red light which was turned on during the avoidance periods and turned off during the "off" hours. The animal soon learned to press its

pressed the lever at an unflagging rate through the first two hours of its last avoidance session. Then it suddenly collapsed and had to be sacrificed. An autopsy revealed a large perforation in the wall of the duodenum—the upper part of the small intestine near its junction with the stomach, and a common site of ulcers in man. Microscopic analysis revealed both acute and chronic inflammation around this lesion. The control monkey, sacrificed in good health a few hours later, showed no gastrointestinal abnormalities. A second experiment using precisely the same procedure produced much the same results. This time the executive monkey developed ulcers in both the stomach and the duodenum; the control animal was again unaffected.

In a series of follow-up experiments which is still in progress we have tried to isolate the physiological and psychological factors which produce the "laboratory ulcers." For example, one of our groups suggested that the "social" interaction between the two monkeys might be important. Certainly the most casual observation showed that considerable "communication" was going on between the two animals, who were seated within easy chattering distance of each other. We therefore studied several pairs of animals isolated from each other in soundproof "telephone booths." Unfortunately isolation failed to protect the executive monkeys, for they continued to develop ulcers.

More recently, however, we have found a factor or group of factors which does seem to be critical in producing ulcers. What we have learned seems to pivot on our chance selection of six hours as the interval for shock-avoidance and for rest in the conditioning procedure. We made this discovery when we sought to improve on the results of our experiments. Though laboratory animals can rarely be made to develop ulcers, we had come upon a procedure that seemed to produce ulcers "to order." The only uncertainty was the length of exposure required. This varied greatly among individual monkeys; some came down with ulcers in 18 days, others took as long as six weeks. If we could develop a technique guaranteed to produce ulcers in, say, 10 days, we could stop the shock-avoidance sessions on the eighth or ninth day, apply various therapeutic measures and study the monkey's response to them.

It seemed reasonable to assume that we might induce ulcers more rapidly and dependably by simply increasing the stress on the animals. We therefore put several monkeys on an 18-hours-on, six-hours-off schedule. After a few weeks one of the animals died, but of tuberculosis, not ulcers. The rest continued to press their levers week after week with no apparent ill effects. Finally, when it began to seem as if we might have to wait for the animals to die of old age, we sacrificed them—and found no gastrointestinal abnormalities whatever!

We put another group on an even more strenuous schedule: 30 minutes on and 30 minutes off, with the shocks programmed for every two seconds rather than every 20. Again one of the animals died, this time of a generalized virus infection unrelated to ulcers. The others, after weeks of frantic lever pressing, showed no gastrointestinal changes.

We had to conclude that the crucial factor was not the degree or even the frequency of stress but was to be sought in the relationship between the length of the stress period and that of the rest period. The six-hours-on, six-hours-off schedule had produced ulcers (and occasionally other somatic disorders) despite individual differences in monkeys, variations in diet and maintenance routines and gross alterations in preliminary physiological tests. No other schedule we had tried produced ulcers at all.

This unexpected finding suggested that we should investigate what was going on in the monkeys' stomachs during the conditioning procedure. A standard technique for investigating gastric processes in experimental animals makes use of an artificial opening, or fistula, in the animal's abdominal and stomach walls through which the contents of its stomach can be sampled. Such fistulas have played an important role in expanding our knowledge of the gastrointestinal system. In the early 19th century the famous U. S. Army surgeon William Beaumont made the first systematic study of the digestive process with the cooperation of a young Canadian who had a fistula due to an imperfectly healed gunshot wound. More than a century later Stewart G. Wolf, Jr., and Harold G. Wolff at the Cornell University Medical College, with the help of a man who had a similar injury, conducted a pioneer investigation of the relationship between emotional stress and ulcers. They found that situations which produced feelings of anxiety or aggression in their subject stepped up his gastric secretions and engorged his stomach wall with blood. Physiological changes of this sort, they believed, are the precursors of ulcers.

Edwin Polish of our department of neuroendocrinology has been studying the stomach acidity of some of our executive monkeys by means of artificial fistulas. His measurements, though far from complete, seem to provide one possible explanation of the results of our experiments.

The stomach secretions of the executive monkeys do indeed become considerably more acid, but not (as one might expect) during the avoidance periods. When the animals are actually pressing the levers the acidity of their stomachs rises little. The significant increase in acidity begins at the end of the avoidance session and reaches a peak several hours later, while the animal is presumably resting. This finding suggests a close relationship between the formation of ulcers and the cyclic character of the six-hours-on, six-hours-off procedure. Emotional stress, it appears, must be intermittent—turning the animal's system on and off, so to speak—if it is to cause ulcers. Continuous emotional stress seems to permit a stable adjustment (at least for a while) under which ulcers do not develop. It is tempting to consider the analogy of the vacuum tube or light bulb which seems to last much longer under conditions of continuous current than

when it is subjected to frequent heating and cooling.

Like most analogies, this one limps badly and has its limitations. For example, our experiments show that periodic stress does not always bring on ulcers, and Polish's findings are consistent with this. His measurements indicate that the greatest increase in acidity occurs after a six-hour avoidance session. After a three-hour session acidity rises, but less sharply; after a one-hour session it does not rise at all. (*See Figure page 283.*) Periodic emotional stress apparently causes ulcers only if its period coincides with that of some natural rhythm of the gastrointestinal system.

Obviously our knowledge of the physiological and psychological processes which produce ulcers is far from complete. Our understanding of even the relatively well-controlled experiments I have described is just beginning to progress beyond the primitive level. We have yet to discover why emotional stress steps up the stomach's acidity later rather than immediately. We are still looking for a method of producing ulcers at will, in days rather than weeks. Eventually we hope to learn to detect an incipient ulcer before the animal collapses, by examining the subject's blood, urine and other secretions, thus making postmortem examinations unnecessary.

There are many other questons about the effects of emotional stress which we have not yet begun to investigate. Really thorough examination of the experimental animals might well show other types of damage of which we are at present unaware. The two monkeys which died of causes unrelated to ulcers, for example, may have succumbed because their resistance had been lowered in some way by psychological stress. It would be surprising to find physical processes wholly unimpaired in monkeys who have been on a 30-minutes-on, 30-minutes-off schedule for several weeks. The opportunity to bring psychosomatic relationships under experimental scrutiny in the laboratory seems to open broad horizons for research into the causes and alleviation of this poorly understood class of ills.

Relationship of Separation and Depression to Disease: A Report on a Hospitalized Medical Population*

ARTHUR H. SCHMALE, JR.†
DEPARTMENTS OF PSYCHIATRY AND MEDICINE,
UNIVERSITY OF ROCHESTER SCHOOL OF MEDICINE AND DENTISTRY

From everyday experiences we are familiar with such expressions as "he died of a broken heart," "he just gave in to being sick," "there was nothing to live for," to explain a change in the health of some individuals following the loss of a loved one. These ideas come from many sources, including personal experiences, folklore, literature, drama, and religious teachings. In medicine, during the eighteenth and nineteenth centuries, it was common to ascribe illness to grief, disappointment, bereavement, despair, and mental depression (30). With the development of "scientific" medicine, in-

Reprinted from *Psychosomatic Medicine*, 20 (1958), 259–277, with the permission of the Hoeber Medical Division, Harper & Row, Publishers, Inc., and the author.
* Presented in part at the Annual Meeting of the American Psychosomatic Society, Atlantic City, N.J., May 4, 1957. This investigation was supported in part by a grant from the Foundations Fund for Research in Psychiatry.
† United States Public Health Service Research Fellow in Medicine and Psychiatry, 1955–57, and Markle Scholar in Medical Science, 1957.

terest in the pathophysiology of disease took precedence. Then it was thought people died not of grief, but of heart disease, cancer, etc.

Within recent medical times psychologic investigations have reawakened interest in the psychological settings in which illness developed. Reports in the literature have singled out real or threatened loss as a precipitating factor in a variety of disorders. These include cancer (1, 13, 30), thyrotoxicosis (8, 29, 33, 37), asthma (16), tuberculosis (9, 26, 27, 48), ulcerative colitis (10, 32), obesity (22), leukemia and lymphoma (18–20), rheumatoid arthritis (34), congestive heart failure (7), disseminated lupus erythematosus (35), Raynaud's disease (36), diabetes mellitus (24), infectious hepatitis (40), and functional uterine bleeding (23). [Reports of the disease- and death-producing effects of ostracism, spells, and sorcery in primitive societies (6) as well as the diseases and deaths occurring in the inmates of concentration camps (46) and the prisoners of war (39, 45) who were said to have felt they were in an impossible or insolvable situation and gave up may also be examples of this phenomenon.]

Patients with a variety of medical disorders have been observed at the University of Rochester during the past ten years by a group of psychologically trained internists. These observations have led to an increasing interest in the history of object loss and depressive-like reactions which have been reported by patients to have occurred prior to the onset of the disease for which they have been hospitalized. These observations have been reported on by Greene in his studies of leukemia and lymphoma (18–20), by Engel in his study and review of ulcerative colitis (10) and by Engel and Reichman in their gastric-secretion studies in an infant with a gastric fistula (11).

The present study is one of a series attempting to delineate in an unselected medical population the incidence of such phenomenon and to establish more specific criteria for what is being called "separation and depression." It also represents an attempt to further an understanding of health and disease in terms of ego and object relationships.

Material

The present study was preceded by two pilot studies. The first study included 97 unselected women patients all admitted to one hospital medical division during January, 1955. The second included 17 patients, both men and women, admitted to the medical service during July and August, 1956. These initial studies indicated the difficulties in evaluating object relationships in the aged, the adolescent, and the indigent. Consequently only semiprivate patients between the ages of 18 and 45 were included in the current study.

The material for this report was pro-

vided by 42 patients between the ages of 18 and 45, admitted to the men's and women's semiprivate divisions of Strong Memorial Hospital during 23 days in September and October, 1956. (During this time period a total of 129 patients were admitted and 54 of the patients were between the ages of 18 and 45. Twelve of this group of 54 could not be studied because of the seriousness of their condition or because they were discharged, transferred, or died before they could be interviewed. Therefore the 42 patients represent all the patients who could be studied, and as such constitute a group unselected except for age.) The vital statistics, medical history, and medical discharge diagnoses of these patients can be seen in Tables 1, 2, and 3, respectively. In all

TABLE 1

VITAL STATISTICS

	Women	Men	Total
No. patients	23	19	42
Mean age	30	31	..
Marital status			
Single	5	6	11
Married	17	11	28
(1 pt. married 3 times)			
Widowed	1	..	1
Separated	..	2	2
No. with children	13	9	22
Mean no. children	2.3	1.5	..
Religion			
Protestant	13	7	20
Catholic	10	12	22
Sibling status			
Only child	..	..	1
One sibling	..	..	10
Two siblings	..	..	4
Three siblings	..	..	10
Four or more siblings	..	..	17
Patient oldest	..	..	7 ..
Patient youngest	..	..	6 ..
Education			
College grad.	2	5	7
1–3 years college	4	3	7
High school grad.	8	2	10
1–3 years high school	6	7	13
Grade school	3	1	4
No record	..	1	1

TABLE 1 (Continued)

	Women	Men	Total
Occupation			
Housewife (9 spouses semi-skilled workers)	11	..	11
Semiskilled labor	1(1) *	8(3) *	9
Managerial	1(1) *	4(2) *	5
Skilled labor	1	3(3) *	4
Student	2	2	4
Secretarial	4(2) *	..	4
Teacher	3(2) *	..	3
Engineer	..	2	2

* Spouse also employed.

TABLE 2

MEDICAL HISTORY

	Women	Men	Total
No. patients	23	19	42
No. previously hospitalized	16 *	18	34
Mean no. hospitalizations	2.5	2.9	..
Chronic disease	9	11	20
Current hospitalization			
Acute process	17	7	24
Acute exacerbation of chronic disease	7	11	18
Mean no. days hospitalized	9.5	9.6	..

* Not including hospitalization for childbirth.

TABLE 3

DIAGNOSIS ON MEDICAL DISCHARGE

Patient no.	Psychic
2	Hysterical conversion, headache
22	Hysterical conversion, hemiplegia and hemianesthesia, left
39	Delusional pain, psychotic reaction, acute

	Skin
5	Dermatitis herpetiformis, chronic, recurring
10	Moniliasis
12	Neurodermatitis, chronic, recurrent
16	Neurodermatitis, chronic, with nephritis, subacute

	Musculoskeletal
30	*Herniation of nucleus pulposus ($L_2 — L_3$)
14	*Low back pain, chronic, intermittent of several years' duration and congenital anomaly of 5th lumbar vertebra

	Respiratory
7	Bronchitis, acute
38	Bronchitis, acute and diabetes, controlled
42	Bronchitis, acute
28	*Bronchopneumonia, unresolved, with recurrent symptoms
25	*Bronchiectasis, left lower lobe

	Cardiovascular
33	Congenital patent ductus arteriosus with beginning heart failure
19	Congenital patent ductus arteriosus with pulmonary artery stenosis, cardiac insufficiency with paroxysmal ventricular fibrillation and death
6	Rheumatic heart disease, inactive, with auricular fibrillation, cerebral embolism, hemeplegia, rt., and dysarthria
13	Rheumatic heart disease, inactive, with post mitral commissurotomy chest pain and thrombophlebitis
21	*Hypertensive cardiovascular disease, symptomatic
40	Hypertensive cardiovascular disease with cardiac insufficiency, acute
32	Hemorrhoids, internal, acute bleeding

	Hemic and lymphatic
3	Infectious mononucleosis
4	*Infectious mononucleosis

	Digestive
8	Laennec's cirrhosis with anemia and massive edema due to nutritional deficiency
9	Regional ileitis with exacerbation of symptoms
15	Constipation, chronic, with dilatation of the colon
20	Duodenal ulcer, chronic, with bleeding, acute
23	Cholecystitis, chronic
27	Ulcerative colitis, 1st attack

	Urogenital
18	Hyperplasia of endometrium with menometrorrhagia, and diabetes, controlled
24	Ovarian cyst, ruptured

Patient no.	Psychic
29	*Low back pain with urethral stricture, nonspecific, and prostatic hypertrophy

Endocrine

11	Hyperthyroidism
36	Hypothyroidism secondary to goitrogenic drug and nontoxic goiter

Nervous

35	Meningitis, aseptic
1	Simple migraine
34	Multiple sclerosis, symptomatic
41	Papillary ependymoma—cerebellar-pontine angle left, postexploration bleeding and death
31	*Brain tumor, type unspecified, grand mal and petit mal convulsions
37	Paroxysmal disorder of the nervous system due to unknown cause, grand mal convulsions
17	Subarachnoid hemorrhage of the brain

Undiagnosed

39	*Undiagnosed disease with hepatomegaly and splenomegaly

* Asterisk indicates presumptive diagnosis.

cases the discharge diagnosis was a composite of the opinions and judgments of the house staff, consultants, and ward attending staff. In those cases where the investigator felt the evidence for the diagnosis was unconfirmed or was inadequate in explaining the patient's major complaints, the diagnosis was considered presumptive and is marked with an asterisk.

Thirty-three of this group of 42 patients were referred and were attended by a private physician as well as the house staff while in the hospital. Nine of the patients did not have a private physician and were attended by the house staff and their attending physicians.

Method

The interview data were obtained with an open-ended, minimal-activity, tape-recorded interview of up to 90 minutes. At least one member of the family of 25 patients was interviewed, and in 22 instances the patients were seen for a brief follow-up interview.

Patients were seen as soon after admission as possible, generally within 24 hours. (From the previous studies it became evident that interviewing the patient soon after admission greatly increased the spontaneity of the communications about interpersonal activities.) Whenever possible, the patient was taken to a private room for interviewing and was told that this was a part of a study not directly related to his immediate care but was of interest to the medical staff in general and concerned the setting in which people became ill. The patient was also told that this interview was confidential and, with his consent, would be recorded. (All patients consented to be recorded initially and only one patient refused on a follow-up interview.)

During the interview the investigator followed the patient in his associations, descriptions, and reactions pertinent to any recent changes in object relationships relating to family, friends, work, ideals, and health.

The approximate time period between the recent changes in object relationships and/or emotional reactions and the onset of symptoms of the disease were established as clearly as possible. The first signs or symptoms as reported by the patient and/or family members which were considered by the investigator as evidence for the process leading to hospitalization were taken as the time of disease onset. [For example, when bleeding was reported as the first symptom in such disease processes as hyperplasia of the endometrium, duodenal ulcer, and internal hemorrhoids (patients #18, #20, and #32, respectively), or pain in such disease processes as ruptured ovarian cyst, herniation of nucleus pulposus and subarachnoid hemorrhage of the brain (patients #24, #30, and #17, respectively), there was no difficulty in determining what represented the first symptom of disease and what was the preceding psychic reaction. However, when symptoms such as weakness, fatigue, and dizziness occurred as the first symptom with such diseases as heart failure, infectious mononucleosis, and hyperthyroidism (patients #23, #3, #11, respectively), it was a difficult if not arbitrary choice to distinguish between what was psychological and what is more usually considered somatic activity. Thus there were 7 patients in this study where an arbitrary choice as to time of disease onset had to be made. In all 7 patients the choice was made on the basis of the independent medical opinions expressed in the patients' written histories.]

References to past health and significant object changes or losses in the past were also explored. Special attention was paid to communications about early family relationships, prolonged or serious illness, and separations and deaths within the patient's significant object group.

Such verbal and nonverbal activity as sudden shifts in content, crying, inappropriate laughter, anger toward the investigator, changes in significant dates, slips, and obvious omissions were considered to be clues and indications of current and past psychic conflict. Whenever it seemed helpful in establishing the degree of reaction to changes in interpersonal relations and health, these clues were explored.

Thus predisease changes in relationship were based on (1) what the patient and/or family reported as recent object loss or threat of loss, which occurred prior to the onset of symptoms; (2) what the patient and/or family member reported as major feeling or affective states which had been perceived and observed prior to the onset of the disease (whether or not related to reported losses), and finally (3) on the investigator's interpretations of the patient's verbal and nonverbal communications related to cur-

rent as well as past object losses and their reactions to such losses.

Results

CHANGES IN RELATIONSHIPS REPORTED

Operationally four categories were delineated according to a reported change in relationship with a highly valued object. These categories included actual loss, threat of loss, symbolic loss, and no perceived loss of any object, as reported by the patient and/or family member.

Actual loss of an object occurred as a loss due to death of a significant family member or a loss related to a change which involved a complete severance of the relationship with the highly valued person. These actual losses included marital separation, broken engagement, parental disownment, the death of a favorite sibling, and a son's desertion. Five patients were in this category. (See Case Example 1 in the Appendix, p. 298.)

Actual threat of loss of an object included an actual change in an object which constituted a threat or anticipation of loss. These threats for the patient included major changes in health, and/or behavior of parents, siblings, children, and lifelong friends. Nine patients were in this category. (See Case Example 2.)

Symbolic loss of an object was evidenced by a reported feeling of loss related to an event which although insignificant in itself initiated or reawakened conscious conflict over actual or fantasied past losses. These symbolic losses related to such events as a failing grade on a report card; patient finding daughter dating boy her husband forbade her to see; friend forgetting dinner engagement with patient; and another teacher criticizing patient's pupils. Sixteen patients were in this category. (See Case Example 3.)

No loss of object, actual, threatened,

or symbolic, was reported. There were 12 patients who reported no apparent loss. [For 11 of the 12 patients, however, the investigator was able to make an interpretation of actual, threatened, or symbolic loss. This interpretation was based on the affects reported and observed as well as on the activities which were reported to have occurred following changes in relationships (see Case Example 4). These changes in relationship included the delayed arrival of a friend, death of a stepfather, anniversary of mother's death, leaving home, being forced to move, son's starting school.]

AFFECTS REPORTED

The patients' reactions to events immediately preceding the onset of disease were taken as the second variable for categorizing the separation and depression responses of these patients.

Seven different categories of affects or feeling states of displeasure were described according to the reported major reactions to relationship activities prior to the onset of diseases (Fig. 1). (These feelings were described as disturbing and preoccupying by most of the patients. Many also indicated they had no acceptable means of expressing these feelings in their relationship activities.) These included anxiety, anger, fear, guilt, shame, helplessness, and hopelessness. To these seven categories was added a no-affect category which arbitrarily included all other affects. Only those affects which were reported and considered by the patient and/or family member as difficult to control and more than fleeting in nature were included.

Anxiety. A feeling of "uneasiness" and "restlessness" perceived as excitement or tension, with no conscious awareness of change in relationship to an object or of loss for the self. Nearly all the patients experienced such feelings fleetingly. Three patients, however, reported such feelings which persisted for days

without conscious awareness of the source or possible means of relief. (See Case Example 5.)

Anger. A feeling of "irritation" and "annoyance" due to a change in a rela-

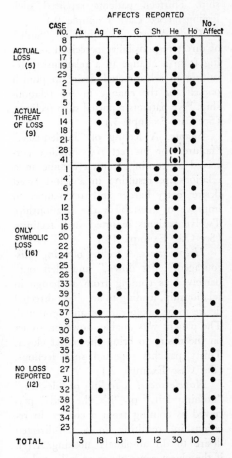

Figure 1. *Affects reported* AS REACTION TO RELATIONSHIP ACTIVITIES PRIOR TO THE ONSET OF DISEASE. *Ax*, ANXIETY; *Ag*, ANGER; *Fe*, FEAR; *G*, GUILT; *Sh*, SHAME; *He*, HELPLESSNESS; *Ho*, HOPELESSNESS. PARENTHESES SHOW AFFECT REPORTED BY FAMILY MEMBER ONLY.

tionship leading to an object-directed desire to force the object to relate as the patient wished. Eighteen patients reported such feelings. (See Case Example 3.)

Fear. A feeling of being "afraid," "scared," "terrified" perceived as coming from a change in a relationship, leading to the object directed desire to flee, run away, or avoid the change in relationship. Thirteen patients reported such feelings. (See Case Example 9.)

Guilt. A feeling of "blame," "fault," or direct responsibility perceived as coming from a change in a relationship resulting in self-directed desire to punish oneself for the change in the relationship. Five patients reported such feelings. (See Case Example 3.)

Shame. A feeling of "inadequacy," "failure," or indirect responsibility perceived as coming from a change in a relationship, resulting in a self-directed desire to try harder and to do more to improve or reestablish the relationship. Twelve patients reported such feelings. (See Case Example 10.)

Helplessness. A feeling of being "discouraged," "let down," and "left out" perceived as coming from a change in relationship, leading to an object-directed desire to be taken care of and protected. The patient was unable, however, to act on the desire to bring the object closer. Thirty patients reported such feelings. (See Case Example 2.)

Hopelessness. A feeling of "despair," "nothing left," or "it's the end," perceived as coming from a change in relationship, resulting in a self-directed desire to do absolutely nothing. Even if the object came closer or indicated an interest in a relationship, the patient was unable to relate. Ten patients reported such feelings. (See Case Example 1.)

No Affect. Feelings not significantly altered as the result of recent events or the feelings reported did not fall within the specific categories defined above. There were 9 patients whose verbalizations fell into this category. (Again, as with the reported-object-loss category it was possible for the investigator to interpret significant affect in eight of these

nine patients. This was done on the basis of observed affects and ego defense patterns. See Case Example 5 for a reported loss but no reported reaction to the loss, and Case Examples 6 and 7 where neither loss nor affect was reported.)

As can be seen from Figure 1, most patients experienced a number of different affects as they reacted to and tried to deal with recent changes in relations. (See Case Example 8.)

There were 24 patients and/or family members who reported feelings of helplessness as the last predominant affect prior to the onset of disease and another 10 patients who had given up completely and reported feelings of hopelessness. (These affects of helplessness and hopelessness were viewed as being indicative of depression, as will be discussed later.) Of the 8 remaining patients there were 7 in whom an interpretation of helplessness or hopelessness was based on reported events and activities which were seen as ineffective attempts at warding off these feelings (Case Example 6) or activities symbolic of depression based on past unresolved conflicts over loss (Case Examples 4 and 7). In general, the responses to such relationship changes as spouse going back to work, temporary forced separation from fiancé, parents taking vacation, anniversary of mother's death, visiting family home for first time since marriage and failing of business beyond deadline set were those of denial, with a projection of the feelings of being lost or helpless onto spouse, parent, child, or friend along with a loss in interest and a sudden loss of effectiveness in their previous roles. Such responses were interpreted by the investigator as signs of helplessness and/or hopelessness.

In 1 of the 42 patients the investigator was unable to find evidence for an interpretation of either object loss or a recent feeling of helplessness or hopelessness prior to the onset of the symptoms which led to the patient's hospitalization.

THE RELATIONSHIP OF OBJECT LOSS
TO TIME OF ONSET OF DISEASE

In 16 patients of the 42, either they reported and/or it was interpreted from their communications, as shown in Figure 2, that the final or only recent sig-

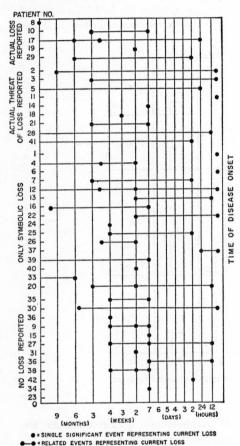

PATIENT NO.

● = SINGLE SIGNIFICANT EVENT REPRESENTING CURRENT LOSS
●—● = RELATED EVENTS REPRESENTING CURRENT LOSS

Figure 2. *Relationship of object* LOSS TO
TIME OF DISEASE ONSET.

nificant change in object relationship preceded the onset of the symptoms of disease by 24 hours. (See Case Example 9.)

In another 15 patients the recent significant change in object relationship occurred within the week prior to the onset of illness (see Case Example 10).

Thus 31 of the 42 patients experienced the onset of disease within a week after the final significant change in relationship.

Another 8 patients reported that the final object relationship change occurred within a month, and of the three remaining patients two reported that the significant change representing a loss occurred between six to twelve months prior to the onset of the symptoms.

PAST OBJECT LOSSES AND
PAST HEALTH

Loss or threat of loss through the first 16 years of life was selected as including the most formative years for establishing object relations, ego processes, and physiological functioning. The losses or threats of losses during these years most commonly reported were those of death and separation from a parent, parent surrogate, or sibling, and/or hospitalization, prolonged illness or disability of patient, parent or sibling. Table 4 depicts the breakdown of the losses or threats of losses reported by 35 of the 42 patients to have occurred within the first 16 years of life.

TABLE 4

INCIDENCE OF LOSS OR THREAT OF LOSS
THROUGH AGE 16

		No. Patients Reporting
Death		5
Separation		6
Hospitalization		3
Prolonged illness or disability		6
Combinations of above		15
Death	8	
Separation	5	
Hospitalization	8	
Prolonged illness	10	
Total no. patients reporting loss or threat of loss		35

Many of the patients revealed unresolved past conflicts verbally and non-verbally. These communications were interpreted to represent either continuing unresolved object loss or threat of loss or changes in object relationships which reactivated past unresolved conflicts. Unresolved conflicts were grouped under three headings: overprotection, rejection, and death in Figure 3.

Eight patients included under "over-

rent symptoms. Thus 33 out of 42 patients were preoccupied or, because of the nature of the current changes in object relations, became preoccupied with past conflicts never completely resolved.

Twenty-nine patients reported that one or more previous significant changes in object relationship had been followed by a significant change in health. These

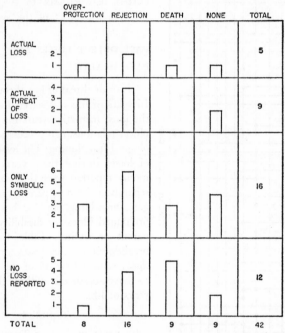

Figure 3. *Reported and observed* UNRESOLVED PAST CONFLICTS.

protection" were unable to accept not having what they wanted when they wanted it, and as it had been provided by one or more parent-type objects in some earlier period in life. The 16 patients listed under "rejection" had lost one or both parents through separation, not including that by death, or had one or more demanding and controlling parents or had many siblings so that the patient felt unaccepted, unwanted, and at a distance from the parents. Nine patients were still or again grieving over a significant loss which had occurred 3 to 32 years prior to the onset of the cur-

48 combinations of circumstances are indicated in Figure 4.

Discussion

Several problems present themselves in evaluating these results.

First, a consideration must be given to the possible chance or coincidental relationship between object loss and changes in health. Although this has not been specifically investigated the evidence from this retrospective study of medically sick individuals, as well as the studies of others mentioned previously, make such a consideration seem unlikely. Further investigations are planned which will include a longitudinal study of ambulatory or healthy groups of people.

Secondly, a consideration is given to the possibility that the feelings of helplessness or hopelessness may be an expression of disease or a reaction to disease occurred as a part of or as a response to disease were always in addition to the predisease feelings of helplessness and hopelessness and here, too, specific studies are being designed to clarify these issues. [The change in an individual's psychological perspective as the result of illness is well established (15). Here, however, another parameter or an earlier point on

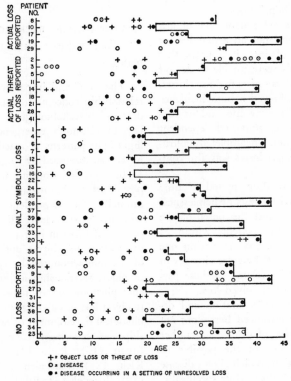

Figure 4. *The life incidence* OF OBJECT LOSS OR THREAT OF LOSS AND DISEASE.

which may color the patient's communications about predisease object relationships. In many patients the feelings of helplessness and hopelessness clearly antedated any evidence of disease. Here the time relationships were well established and confirmed by family members and other observers. In other patients, where the disease onset was insidious or difficult to determine, the evidence was more presumptive. Finally, such feelings which the spectrum of time in relationship to changes in health is revealed. The indication is that feelings of helplessness or hopelessness may actually set the stage for illness to occur when it does. Thus illness may be an adaptive attempt or a non-adaptive consequence of unsolved object loss.]

There was a consistent pattern to the psychological setting in which this group of medical patients experienced a change in health which led to hospitalization. Such a setting included a recent change in object relationships, actual or fantasied, which the patients felt represented a loss or threat of loss for their psychic selves. These losses or threats of losses were reported and interpreted to have been unresolved at the time of the disease onset on the basis of the patients' reported and interpreted feelings of helplessness and/or hopelessness.

Since the most frequent type of loss was symbolic and not an actual loss or current threat of loss, it appears that these individuals were unable to defend against reminders of previous losses. These patients showed a high incidence of object loss in early life and/or lifelong feelings of unsupported dependent needs and rejection. Uncompleted mourning over past object losses was also common.

The relatively short period of time between the final feelings of helplessness and hopelessness and the onset of the medical disease (16 patients within 24 hours and an additional 15 within one week) suggests that there are changes in biological activities related to these psychic reactions to unresolved loss.

The concept of "separation and depression" to be advanced here does not establish the cause of disease but rather the setting, or one of the possible or necessary conditions which allows disease to appear when it does. More specifically, this study suggests that the psychic states of helplessness or hopelessness may be related to increased biological vulnerability. Such effects on the somatic system may have important implications for studies of disease prevention as well as for the further understanding of disease onset and treatment. It is hoped that such a concept will also have predictive value when used in conjunction with biological indicators of organ system thresholds as such became known. [An example of this kind of predictive study based on biological indicators as demonstrated by

Mirsky (38) has been reported by Weiner et al. (47).] Theoretically, by knowing the patient's patterns of object relationships, including the kinds of object conflicts which threaten the patient's concept of himself, and the ego processes available to handle such conflicts, it may be possible to predict the specific kinds of circumstances under which the patient will become sick.

PSYCHODYNAMIC BACKGROUND OF THE "SEPARATION AND DEPRESSION" PROCESS

The need and importance of object-relationship concepts to explain and understand psychobiological relationships beyond Cannon's emergency theory of flight-fight patterns of reactions to stress have been discussed by Engel (12).

In object-relationship terms man is postulated to be in an ever-changing, mutually interdependent relationship with his environment. His psychic perception of this can be represented as self in relation to objects and the process of the interaction can be viewed as ego or object relationship activity. The psychic phenomenon of depression related to object loss has its roots in early psychobiological development of object relationships as has been conceptualized by Freud (17), Rado (41), Balint (2), Klein (28), Fairbairn (14), Jacobson (25), Benedek (3), Bibring (5), Greene (21), and others and has been demonstrated by Spitz and Wolf (44), as well as by Engel and Reichsman (11) and others. A developmental concept of the manifestations of depression based on theoretical object relationship models has been worked out by the investigator (43). In this developmental concept it is postulated that psychobiological depression can occur at any time after there is a beginning psychic representation of the mother-child symbiosis. This representation is derived, theoretically, from the introjected mother-type object which acquires psychic representation through successful interreaction with the infant, as postulated by Benedek (3). The psychic processes one goes through to acquire relationships in the external world are felt to be prototypes of all subsequent ego processes necessary to acquire a new object as well as psychically to give up an old object in order to acquire the new. Along with these ego processes go various affect states which are thought to represent a signal system which warns of the failure of current activities and the need for a shift to new or different ego functioning. [Blau (4) conceives of these affect signals as evolving out of anxiety as the ego matures. He considers rage, fear, and depression as secondary emotions of displeasure, and guilt, shame and disgust as tertiary emotions.] These ego processes and their warning affects are thought to be part of a continuum, which at the time of a loss of an object, real or symbolic, conscious or unconscious, is set into motion psychically to enable the person to relinquish real or symbolic dependence on the object whose loss threatens the psychic self.

The use of the reported and interpreted feelings of helplessness and hopelessness to represent evidences of depression is based in part on Bibring's concept of depression. He stated: "the ego's shocking awareness of its helplessness in regard to its aspirations, is assumed to represent the core of normal, neurotic and probably also psychotic depression" (5).

FORMULATIONS

The following formulations have evolved from the systematic observations of these unselected medical patients, from the insights gained by the studies of other members of the research group, and from general psychoanalytic concepts.

"Separation," is defined as the loss or threat of loss of an object of gratification —real or symbolic, internal or external, conscious or unconscious. This object must have had an intrapsychic representation based on the patient's past relationships with this object or other symbolically similar objects.

"Depression," as used here, refers to the psychobiological reactions related to the threat of loss for the psychic self which results from an inability to resolve the real or fantasied loss.*

"Separation and depression" are thus aspects of a psychic reaction pattern. Starting with a change in relationship, this process involves the actual or fantasied loss of an object upon which the self has real or symbolic dependence, and includes the attempts and final failure to maintain the self during the period of giving up the object with resulting feelings of helplessness or hopelessness.

The affects of helplessness and hopelessness which seem to prevail at the time of disease onset were used as evidence for giving up the fight or flight, in an external object direction (helplessness), and/or giving up of the self-directed, internally oriented fight or flight (hopelessness). The exact influence of such psychic giving-up on resistance, immunity, organ dysfunction, and cell growth and multiplication awaits further study.

Yet to be studied and understood is why these patients became medically sick and not just psychologically depressed. Currently, disease is being seen as one possible manifestation of depression. However, just as easily one could envision disease and depression as distinct and separate consequences or attempts at

* Depression is viewed as more than an affective state, a basic ego mechanism or what is usually included in the diagnostic categories of neurotic or psychotic depression. As represented here, depression involves the objectless, almost closed energy system state of psychobiological isolation which results from an inability to maintain and reachieve need gratification through relationship activity.

adaptation to feelings of helplessness or hopelessness.

Summary

This is one of a series of studies being made to investigate the relationship of "separation and depression" to the onset of medical disease.

In this report a group of 42 semi-private hospitalized medical patients between the ages of 18 and 45 was studied for predisease setting based on reported object-relationship changes and reported and observed major affective reactions to such changes.

Twenty-nine patients and/or family members reported loss of an object and feelings of helplessness and hopelessness immediately preceding the onset of the symptoms of the illness which led to hospitalization.

Five patients reported feelings of helplessness or hopelessness prior to the onset of symptoms but reported no loss of an object.

In 41 of the 42 patients the investigator felt that there was verbal and/or nonverbal evidence for the interpretation of actual, threatened, or symbolic object loss as well as evidence for feelings of helplessness or hopelessness prior to the onset of disease.

Thirty-one patients developed the onset of their disease within one week after what was considered the final or only change in relationship to which the patient experienced a feeling of helplessness or hopelessness.

Early life losses or threats of loss, past conflicts reawakened or still unresolved, and the incidence of past separations preceding changes in past health of this group of patients were also reported.

"Separation and depression" as defined refers to the psychic pattern of unsuccessful resolution of object loss. Starting with a change in a relationship, this concept involves the actual or fantasied loss of an object upon which the self has real or symbolic dependence and includes the attempts and final failures to reestablish or give up the lost or threatened relationship, as evidenced by feelings of helplessness or hopelessness.

Case Examples are appended to illustrate how the setting of the current disease onset was reported and how the investigator made his interpretations of this material.

Appendix

CASE EXAMPLE 1

Patient #19 was of Italian descent, a 43-year-old father of three, who had a congenital patent ductus arteriosus and pulmonary artery stenosis. For the past 23 years he had been on continuous therapy for heart failure which began shortly after his marriage. His most recent change in health occurred when his oldest son suddenly announced he was joining the Navy, and left home within a few days. The patient, when asked about his feelings, said, "I felt, what's the use . . . nothing matters anymore. . . . Thought he knew my condition and assumed he would stay home and always take care of us." Following this the patient sobbed though no tears were visible. The patient's symptoms began sometime during the two-week period following the son's announcement and his departure. Some six weeks later at the time he received his first letter from his son, the patient experienced an increase in symptoms, characterized by an irregular, fast heartbeat and dizzy spells. The letter indicated that his son did not plan to visit home during his forthcoming furlough. The patient was admitted to the hospital two weeks later for evaluation of his cardiac status, and he died suddenly of ventricular fibrillation on the second hospital day.

Interpretation: His son's departure led to a feeling of hopelessness because the son was expected to be a source of future personal and family support. His son's letter intensified his feelings of loss.

CASE EXAMPLE 2

Patient #7 was a 31-year-old self-employed appliance salesman, hospitalized with infectious mononucleosis. His first symptoms appeared within eight hours after his wife returned to work against his wishes. She had stopped work three months earlier because of a sudden perforation of a silent unknown (at least to my patient) duodenal ulcer. The patient's eyes were glassy when he related how close to death his wife had been. "She was as sick as anybody can be and live . . . another two to three hours and it would have been too late." [How did this make you feel inside?] "Pretty well torn apart, like I had been through the mill." [Any experiences like this before in your life?] "No, never had come close to losing anyone close to me before . . . have had frustrations. . . ." When he was asked for specific examples of frustrations the patient was unable to recall any. The patient then indicated that his wife had made remarkable progress; in fact, she had gone back to work some two or three weeks ago even though she wasn't completely herself yet. [What were your feelings about this?] "Don't like it one bit. I don't think she's capable yet. She insisted and the doctor said she could . . . would rather she stop working altogether, but I know she won't. Guess I should be glad she is working now that I'm here." The patient chuckled, paused and was then asked what he meant by "not liking it one bit." "A little frustrated, shall we say [*laugh*] yes, one of those frustrating cases." [Frustrated?] "I think the thing that engendered it the most was I felt I was perfectly able to take care of her, financially included . . . it's not that I want her to be *dependable* [*sic*] on me, it's just I want her to get back on her feet again. I came pretty close to losing her and I don't want to lose her."

When he first noticed symptoms, he was engaged in making a cabinet for his wife. He felt dizzy and weak, "Like I had lost a little of the acute perspective of what was going on . . . just a sense of inertia."

Interpretation: Consciously the patient wanted to be the self-sufficient good provider, but unconsciously there were conflicting, ungratified dependent needs. His wife's recent illness and her decision to return to work stirred up the conflict which he could not resolve and he became "frustrated." The investigator interpreted "frustrated" to mean an affect of helplessness which stemmed from the patient's inability to change his wife's mind about what he considered a danger to her health. Thus her return to work served as an actual threat of loss of an object and his symptoms began in a setting of feeling there was no solution to the threat (helplessness).

CASE EXAMPLE 3

Patient #6 was a 42-year-old white Catholic widow and mother of six children. The patient, her mother, and five of the six children were living together at the time of the onset of the illness. The patient's illness began with a period of unconsciousness followed by double vision, slurred speech, and hemiplegia. The patient did report an "ordinary" bifrontal headache for a week prior to losing consciousness and expressed the opinion that her headache and the ensuing illness were due to the strain of painting which she had done the previous week in addition to her usual work.

The morning the patient became ill she arose late and went into the bathroom to prepare for church. She found a wet towel in the bathtub, and the bathtub faucet dripping. "I get so mad that they let it drop in . . . went to pick it up . . . and must have fallen into the tub . . . just felt like I just wanted to sleep there." [You got mad?] "Was raving . . . all I ever do, doesn't do any good. Don't think they ever hear me. Just holler to try and get rid of the feeling. They probably heard me—sure, but don't do no good." [Your reaction?] "Got used to it." [How does it make you feel, talking about it?] The patient shook her left fist. [You're shaking your fist?] "Yes, I've broken up a number of fights and even got it in the mouth once. They are so big though, fight a lot, they get it from their father—he was Irish." [He was a fighter?] "No, but he was Irish, I'm German . . . get so worried over kids

. . . worry about them and how they are going to be. Hate to hear people say 'if only their father was living' as if I hadn't done as good as if their father was living." [What was the reason for his death?] "He was diabetic . . . sick for five years, wouldn't take care of himself. Think he got discouraged having children so fast [six children in five years of marriage]. Think he blamed me but it takes two to make a bargain, I always say. Isn't that right, Doctor?"

Interpretation: The patient's anger toward her children's increasing indifference to her needs and demands for control of their behavior was verbalized, but she felt it was futile. These feelings toward her children were thought to be symbolic of those directed towards her dead husband who did not take care of himself and left her to raise six children. The affect of anger was expressed verbally and by gesture. The affect of guilt was interpreted from her reaction toward people who expressed feelings of regret about her husband's absence and from her need for reassurance that she was only partially responsible for having so many children.

The final affect, before the patient lost consciousness, was thought to be one of giving up (hopelessness).

CASE EXAMPLE 4

Patient #30, a healthy, single, college graduate, had left his mother's home to seek employment about five months before hospitalization. This move was made after much hesitation and indecision. In the five months of separation the patient and his mother exchanged four visits, traveling some 400 miles each time. The only things the patient perceived as missing in his new setting was his daily exercise, and the good food he got at home. However, he felt that the absence of these only partially explained his feelings of being "slowed down" and "uneasy" in his new surroundings. However in an attempt to overcome these feelings he finally arranged to go bowling with a friend, but the friend was an hour late. As he was waiting the patient recalled feeling angry, and saying to himself, "Isn't this the way things always work out!" In this setting while bowling alone

he began to feel pain in the lower back.

The patient's past history revealed that when he was eight years old his father died and his mother had to seek employment. The patient reported that he had felt "alone" and "on his own" since that time.

Interpretation: The delayed arrival of the patient's friend constituted a loss symbolic of the patient's earlier actual loss of father and relative loss of mother because of her change in roles following his father's death and more recently his loss of mother by his moving away from home. His reaction to the move away from mother and home was one of defensive denial and projective focusing onto bodily needs. These defenses were not completely effective and he experienced an objectless restlessness (anxiety). The patient's anger toward his friend which was followed by a feeling of helplessness (expressed by "Isn't this the way things always work out!"), indicated the undefended, unresolved, or reawakened feelings of loss for the self.

CASE EXAMPLE 5

Patient #40, a 38-year-old hypertensive, obese man related that a business which he vowed to have on a paying basis within a certain period of time continued to fail. When questioned about his feelings he said, "Didn't bother me much but I don't know how much longer my wife can stand it." This statement was followed by a paroxysm of coughing and then by audible rales with marked dyspnea. (His first symptoms of heart failure began some two months before admission, two weeks following the deadline date he had set for having his business on a paying basis.)

Interpretation: The patient was thought to be denying and projecting his feelings of threat of loss and helplessness onto his wife. (His pattern of denial, projection, and somatization was a life-long one beginning at age nine with the death of his mother. This he reported was difficult on his brother because they both were sent to live with an uncle. It was within that same time while living at his uncle's he first became obese and was taken to a doctor for attempts at medical control. Throughout his life he had had many social and business reverses which were all attributed to his misplaced faith and trust in others, and all the reverses were seen as losses for others but not for himself.)

CASE EXAMPLE 6

Patient #35, a 24-year-old man whose stepfather had died four weeks before the onset of symptoms, reported no significant loss or affect of loss. However, in the period of one month before the onset of his meningitis he did reveal a change in behavior which included starting on a diet of soft foods, expressing a desire to move back home to mother (this his wife related), buying a car which up to that time he felt he could not afford, and then selling a piece of property on which he planned to build a home, in order to pay for the car. His symptoms began in the setting of selling his property.

Interpretation: Increased dependency and signs of helplessness were thought related to the actual loss of his stepfather, which was also symbolic of a number of significant past losses. (His father died when he was eight years old. His mother remarried when he was 11 and he didn't feel accepted by his stepfather until after he joined the Navy and left home at age 17. His having chosen to be a Navy hospital corpsman, and his interest in helping in the autopsy room in his spare time were taken as evidences of his conflict over loss of objects. Of confirmatory significance was his statement about his mother which was made to illustrate his not being bothered by object losses. "It wouldn't bother me if my mother died tomorrow—just one of those things—happens to everyone.")

CASE EXAMPLE 7

Patient #15, a 43-year-old childless housewife with chronic constipation and many intermittent digestive complaints, reported that her mother died 19 years ago, at age 43. The patient's symptoms, leading to the present hospitalization, occurred during the week of her own forty-third birthday, which coincided with the anniversary of her mother's death at age 43.

When the patient was confronted with the coincidence of mother's death at age 43 and her recent increase in symptoms beginning the week of the forty-third birthday, she repeated something she had already mentioned in another context this time, however, with tears in her eyes. She said, "Really should have done more for her but I just *don't* know what to do."

Interpretation: The patient's age reaching that of her mother's at time of death reawakened unresolved feelings of guilt and helplessness. Thus the patient's own forty-third birthday served as a symbolic threat of loss for the patient's psychic self.

CASE EXAMPLE 8

Patient #1, a young schoolteacher, in response to misbehavior of several of her pupils reported: "I felt lost as to what to do." She could appreciate the fun her pupils had in playing the prank, yet she felt the need to punish them in some way. After attempting several courses of action she recalled a feeling of being afraid which she related to the anticipated reaction of a fellow teacher. However, she felt she then temporarily forgot the situation by going on with her class work. Four hours later, when discussing the students' misbehavior with the other teacher, the teacher called her pupils "brats." The patient felt angry but refrained from answering because she felt her colleague would not understand. "No use discussing it." Several minutes later after the other teacher left, the patient noted she felt immobilized and disinterested as she attempted to finish her work, and it was then she experienced her first symptoms of migraine headache.

Interpretation: The affects of helplessness, fear, anger, shame, and helplessness appeared in the sequence of working through the anticipated symbolic threat of object loss. The affect of helplessness was the affect experienced at the time of the onset of symptoms.

CASE EXAMPLE 9

Patient #2, a 45-year-old mother of ten children, was informed while at the wedding reception of a daughter that her third husband, who had almost died of hepatic failure some nine months before, was seen taking a drink—the first since his illness. The patient felt "upset," "thought I had drink all out of him . . . I've been working twice as hard and nothing pleases him." Patient went to husband and said, "Drink is going to kill you." He replied, "That's what I want—to get away from you," and walked away. The patient reported she then had a strange feeling in her head "like everything was crashing inside me." Then thought, "things are too much for me, want to get away from them—want to run but no place to run. Don't want to go on—everything inside dead." She then was aware of an "awful headache" and doesn't remember anything preceding the doctor's visit the following morning. Later that same day on admission to the hospital the patient was found to have weakness and hypesthesias of the right side of her body, right arm, and right leg.

Interpretation: The patient, an hysterical masochistic woman was actually threatened with object loss by her husband's poor health which would be made worse by drinking. His drinking produced feelings of anger, fear, and finally, when he directly rejected her, hopelessness. Within a matter of minutes following her rejection she developed her first symptoms which led to hospitalization.

CASE EXAMPLE 10

Patient #16, an 18-year-old high school student with chronic eczema since childhood and nephritis which began nine months before this admission, learned at midsemester he was failing a course and was very much afraid of his father's reaction to this news. (He felt he had never been accepted by his father because he was not intellectually inclined.) His father's only comment, however, was "do better next time." However the boy reported he now felt "lousy" and "worried" because of what the teacher must have thought of him to give him a failing grade; however, he was unable to discuss it with her. Within the week he had a flareup of his chronic dermatitis, which included skin burning and itching, erythyma, vesiculation, and excoriation with secondary infection beginning in the antecubital fossa and spreading to the entire arms, neck, face, and finally, chest.

Interpretation: An adolescent boy, who has had difficulty relating to his father because of his father's past demands for his achievement, is symbolically threatened by a failing grade. The unexpected failure reawakened his feeling of inferiority (shame), which led to a feeling of helplessness in not meeting the expectations of his parental figures even though he had tried. With reassurance from his father he focused his feelings of helplessness onto the relationships with his teacher. This all occurred within the week following the unexpected failing grade.

References

1. Bacon, C. L., Renneker, R., and Cutler, M. A psychosomatic survey of cancer of the breast. *Psychosom. Med.,* 14(1952), 453.
2. Balint, A. Love for the mother and mother love (1939). *Internat. J. Psycho-Analysis,* 30(1949), 251.
3. Benedek, T. F. Toward the biology of the depressive constellation. *J. Am. Psychoanalyt. A.,* 4(1956), 389.
4. Blau, A. A unitary hypothesis of emotions: Anxiety, emotions of displeasure and affective disorders. *Psychoanalyt. Quart.,* 24(1955), 75.
5. Bibring, E. The Mechanism of Depression. In P. Greenacre, ed., *Affective disorders.* New York: Internat. Univ. Press, 1953.
6. Cannon, W. B. Voodoo death. *Am. Anthropol.,* 44(1942), 169.
7. Chambers, W. N., and Reiser, M. F. Congestive heart failure. *Psychosom. Med.,* 15 (1953), 38.
8. Conrad, A. The psychiatric study of hyperthyroid patients. *J. Nerv. & Ment. Dis.,* 79 (1934), 505, 656.
9. Day, G. P.P.S.: Pneuma, psyche and soma. *Lancet,* 2(1952), 691.
10. Engel, G. L. Studies of ulcerative colitis: III. The nature of the psychologic processes. *Am. J. Med.,* 19(1955), 231.
11. ——— and Reichsman, F. Spontaneous and experimentally induced depressions in an infant with a gastric fistula: A contribution to the problem of depression. *J. Am. Psychoanalyt. A.,* 4(1956), 428.
12. Engel, G. L. Selection of clinical material in psychosomatic medicine: The need for a new physiology. *Psychosom. Med.,* 26(1954), 368.
13. Evans, E. *A psychological study of cancer.* New York: Dodd Mead, 1926.
14. Fairbairn, W. R. D. A synopsis of the development of the author's views regarding the structure of the personality. In *An object-rela-*

tions theory of the personality. New York: Basic Books, 1952. Chapter VII.

15. Fenichel, O. *The psychoanalytic theory of neurosis.* New York: Norton, 1945. Page 257.

16. French, T. M. Psychogenic factors in asthma. *Am. J. Psychiat.,* 96(1939), 87.

17. Freud, S. Morning and melancholia (1917). In *Collected Papers.* London: Hogarth, 1946. Volume 4, page 152.

18. Greene, W. A., Jr. Psychological factors and reticuloendothelial disease: I. Preliminary observations on a group of males with lymphomas and leukemias. *Psychosom. Med.,* 16(1954), 220.

19. —— Young, L. F., and Swisher, S. N. Psychological factors and reticuloendothelial disease: II. Observations on a group of women with lymphomas and leukemias. *Psychosom. Med.,* 18(1956), 284.

20. Greene, W. A., Jr., and Miller, G. Psychological factors and reticuloendothelial disease: IV. Observations on a group of children and adolescents with leukemia: An interpretation of etiopathogenesis in terms of the mother-child unit. *Psychosom. Med.,* 20(1958), 124.

21. Greene, W. A., Jr. Early object relations, somatic, affective and personal: An inquiry into the physiology of the mother-child unit. *J. Nerv. & Ment. Dis.* (in press.)

22. Hamburger, W. W. Emotional aspects of obesity. *M. Clin. North America,* 35(1951), 483.

23. Heiman, M. The role of stress situations and psychological factors in functional uterine bleeding. *J. Mt. Sinai Hosp.,* 23(1956), 775.

24. Hinkle, L. E., and Wolf, S. A summary of experimental evidence relating life stress to diabetes mellitus. *J. Mt. Sinai Hosp.,* 19(1952), 537.

25. Jacobson, E. Contribution to the metapsychology of cyclothymic depression. In P. Greenacre, ed., *Affective Disorders.* New York: Internat. Univ. Press, 1953.

26. Kissen, D. M. *Specific psychological factors in pulmonary tuberculosis. Health bulletin* Vol. 14, issued by the Chief Medical Officer of the Department of Health for Scotland, 1956.

27. —— *The relapse in pulmonary tuberculosis due to specific psychological causes. Health bulletin* Vol. 15, issued by the Chief Medical Officer of the Department of Health for Scotland, 1957.

28. Klein, M. A contribution to the psychogenesis of manic-depressive states (1935). *Contributions to psychoanalysis 1921–45.* London: Hogarth Press, 1948.

29. Kleinschmidt, H. J., and Waxenberg, S. E. Psychophysiology and psychiatric management of thyrotoxicosis: A two-year follow-up study. *J. Mt. Sinai Hosp.,* 23(1956), 131.

30. Kowal, S. J. Emotions as a cause of cancer. *Psychoanalyt. Rev.,* 42(1955), 217.

31. LeShan, L., and Worthington, R. E.

Some psychologic correlates of neoplastic disease: A preliminary report. *Quart. Rev. Psychiat. & Neurol.,* 16(1955), 281.

32. Lindemann, E. Psychiatric problems in conservative treatment of ulcerative colitis. *Arch. Neurol. & Psychiat.,* 53(1945), 322.

33. Litz, T. Emotional factors in etiology of hyperthyroidism. *Psychosom. Med.,* 11(1949), 2.

34. Ludwig, A. O. Psychogenic factors in rheumatoid arthritis. *Bull. Rheumatic Dis.,* 2 (1952), 33.

35. McClary, A. R., Meyer, E., and Weitzman, E. L. Observations on the role of the mechanism of depression in some patients with disseminated lupus erythematosus. *Psychosom. Med.,* 17(1955), 311.

36. Millet, J. A. P., Lief, H., and Mittelmann, B. Raynaud's disease: Psychogenic factors and psychotherapy. *Psychosom. Med.,* 15(1953), 61.

37. Mittelmann, B. Psychogenic factors and psychotherapy in hyperthyreosis and rapid heart imbalance. *J. Nerv. & Ment. Dis.,* 77(1933), 465.

38. Mirsky, I. A., Futterman, P., and Kaplan, S. Blood plasma pepsinogen: II. The activity of the plasma from "normal" subjects, patients with duodenal ulcers and patients with pernicious anemia. *J. Lab. & Clin. Med.,* 40(1952), 188.

39. Nardini, J. E. Survival factors in American prisoners of war of the Japanese. *Am. J. Psychiat.,* 109(1952), 241.

40. Papper, S., and Handy, J. Observations in a "control" group of patients in psychosomatic investigation. *New England J. Med.,* 255 (1956), 1067.

41. Rado, S. The problem of melancholia. *Internat. J. Psycho-Analysis,* 9(1928), 219.

42. Rapaport, D. On the psychoanalytic theory of affects. *Internat. J. Psycho-Analysis,* 34 (1953), 177.

43. Schmale, A. H., Jr. A developmental concept of depression based on object relationship models (to be published).

44. Spitz, R. A., and Wolf, R. M. Analytic depression: An inquiry into the genesis of psychiatric conditions in early childhood, II. *Psychoanalyt. Study Child,* 2(1946), 313.

45. Strassman, H. D., Thaler, M. B., and Schein, E. H. A prisoner of war syndrome: Apathy as a reaction to severe stress. *Am. J. Psychiat.,* 1122(1956), 998.

46. Tas, J. Psychical disorders among inmates of concentration camps and repatriates. *Psychiat. Quart.,* 25(1951), 679.

47. Weiner, H., *et al.* Etiology of duodenal ulcer: I. Relationship of specific psychological characteristics to rate of gastric secretion. *Psychosom. Med.,* 19(1957), 1.

48. Wittkower, E. *A psychiatrist looks at tuberculosis.* London: National Association for the Prevention of Tuberculosis, 1949.

9. CHILDREN'S DISORDERS

THERE ARE many reasons why it is important to study the disorders of children apart from their adult counterparts. First of all, many workers feel that at least some disorders of childhood are unique to that period of life and could not appear at a later time. Furthermore, many events in childhood potentially can be expressed in adult behavior patterns. Lastly, those theorists who subscribe to a developmental personality theory feel that an understanding of childhood is essential to a full understanding of the adult. Erikson presents such a conceptual scheme of childhood development in this selection from his major work, *Childhood and Society*. He may be classed as a neo-Freudian in that his theory owes a good deal to Freud, but in many places, particularly in the detailed attention to later childhood, goes considerably beyond Freud. Yarrow's review paper deals with maternal deprivation and attempts to understand some of the reasons for the grave implications of early deprivation for the adult. Previously many workers were willing to accept the romantic notion that absence of mother love was the culprit. Without denigrating the importance of the mother-child relationship, Yarrow attempts to understand why it should be so crucial. Eisenberg and Kanner describe infantile autism, a profound pathological syndrome unique to childhood.

Eight Ages of Man

ERIK H. ERIKSON
HARVARD UNIVERSITY

Basic Trust vs. Basic Mistrust

The first demonstration of social trust in the baby is the ease of his feeding, the depth of his sleep, the relaxation of his bowels. The experience of a mutual regulation of his increasingly receptive capacities with the maternal techniques of provision gradually helps him to

Reprinted from *Childhood and Society*, Second Edition, Revised and Enlarged, by Erik H. Erikson. By permission of W. W. Norton & Company, Inc., New York, N.Y. Copyright 1950 & © 1963 by W. W. Norton & Company, Inc.

balance the discomfort caused by the immaturity of homeostasis with which he was born. In his gradually increasing waking hours he finds that more and more adventures of the senses arouse a feeling of familiarity, of having coincided with a feeling of inner goodness. Forms of comfort, and people associated with them, become as familiar as the gnawing discomfort of the bowels. The infant's first social achievement, then, is his willingness to let the mother out of sight without undue anxiety or rage, because she has become an inner certainty as well as an outer predictability. Such consistency, continuity, and sameness of experience provide a rudimentary sense of ego identity which depends, I think, on the recognition that there is an inner population of remembered and anticipated sensations and images which are firmly correlated with the outer population of familiar and predictable things and people.

What we here call trust coincides with what Therese Benedek has called confidence. If I prefer the word "trust," it is because there is more naïveté and more mutuality in it: an infant can be said to be trusting where it would go too far to say that he has confidence. The general state of trust, furthermore, implies not only that one has learned to rely on the sameness and continuity of the outer providers, but also that one may trust oneself and the capacity of one's own organs to cope with urges; and that one is able to consider oneself trustworthy enough so that the providers will not need to be on guard lest they be nipped.

The constant tasting and testing of the relationship between inside and outside meets its crucial test during the rages of the biting stage, when the teeth cause pain from within and when outer friends either prove of no avail or withdraw from the only action which promises relief: biting. Not that teething itself seems to cause all the dire consequences sometimes ascribed to it. As outlined earlier, the infant now is driven to "grasp" more, but he is apt to find desired presences elusive: nipple and breast, and the mother's focused attention and care. Teething seems to have a prototypal significance and may well be the model for the masochistic tendency to assure cruel comfort by enjoying one's hurt whenever one is unable to prevent a significant loss.

In psychopathology the absence of basic trust can best be studied in infantile schizophrenia, while lifelong underlying weakness of such trust is apparent in adult personalities in whom withdrawal into schizoid and depressive states is habitual. The re-establishment of a state of trust has been found to be the basic requirement for therapy in these cases. For no matter what conditions may have caused a psychotic break, the bizarreness and withdrawal in the behavior of many very sick individuals hides an attempt to recover social mutuality by a testing of the borderlines between senses and physical reality, between words and social meanings.

Psychoanalysis assumes the early process of differentiation between inside and outside to be the origin of projection and introjection which remain some of our deepest and most dangerous defense mechanisms. In introjection we feel and act as if an outer goodness had become an inner certainty. In projection, we experience an inner harm as an outer one: we endow significant people with the evil which actually is in us. These two mechanisms, then, projection and introjection, are assumed to be modeled after whatever goes on in infants when they would like to externalize pain and internalize pleasure, an intent which must yield to the testimony of the maturing senses and ultimately of reason. These mechanisms are, more or less normally, reinstated in acute crises of love, trust, and faith in adulthood and can characterize irrational attitudes toward adversaries and enemies in masses of "mature" individuals.

The firm establishment of enduring patterns for the solution of the nuclear conflict of basic trust versus basic mistrust in mere existence is the first task of the ego, and thus first of all a task for maternal care. But let it be said here that the amount of trust derived from earliest infantile experience does not seem to depend on absolute quantities of food or demonstrations of love, but rather on the quality of the maternal relationship. Mothers create a sense of trust in their children by that kind of administration which in its quality combines sensitive care of the baby's individual needs and a firm sense of personal trustworthiness within the trusted framework of their culture's life style. This forms the basis in the child for a sense of identity which will later combine a sense of being "all right," of being oneself, and of becoming what other people trust one will become. There are, therefore (within certain limits previously defined as the "musts" of child care), few frustrations in either this or the following stages which the growing child cannot endure if the frustration leads to the ever-renewed experience of greater sameness and stronger continuity of development, toward a final integration of the individual life cycle with some meaningful wider belongingness. Parents must not only have certain ways of guiding by prohibition and permission; they must also be able to represent to the child a deep, an almost somatic conviction that there is a meaning to what they are doing. Ultimately, children become neurotic not from frustrations, but from the lack or loss of societal meaning in these frustrations.

But even under the most favorable circumstances, this stage seems to introduce into psychic life (and become prototypical for) a sense of inner division and universal nostalgia for a paradise forfeited. It is against this powerful combination of a sense of having been deprived, of having been divided, and of having been abandoned—that basic trust must maintain itself throughout life.

Each successive stage and crisis has a special relation to one of the basic elements of society, and this for the simple reason that the human life cycle and man's institutions have evolved together. In this chapter we can do little more than mention, after the description of each stage, what basic element of social organization is related to it. This relation is twofold: man brings to these institutions the remnants of his infantile mentality and his youthful fervor, and he receives from them—as long as they manage to maintain their actuality—a reinforcement of his infantile gains.

The parental faith which supports the trust emerging in the newborn, has throughout history sought its institutional safeguard (and, on occasion, found its greatest enemy) in organized religion. Trust born of care is, in fact, the touchstone of the *actuality* of a given religion. All religions have in common the periodical childlike surrender to a Provider or providers who dispense earthly fortune as well as spiritual health; some demonstration of man's smallness by way of reduced posture and humble gesture; the admission in prayer and song of misdeeds, of misthoughts, and of evil intentions; fervent appeal for inner unification by divine guidance; and finally, the insight that individual trust must become a common faith, individual mistrust a commonly formulated evil, while the individual's restoration must become part of the ritual practice of many, and must become a sign of trustworthiness in the community.* We have illustrated how tribes dealing with one segment of nature develop a collective magic which

---

* This is the communal and psychosocial side of religion. Its often paradoxical relation to the spirituality of the individual is a matter not to be treated briefly and in passing (see *Young Man Luther*). (E.H.E.)

seems to treat the Supernatural Providers of food and fortune as if they were angry and must be appeased by prayer and self-torture. Primitive religions, the most primitive layer in all religions, and the religious layer in each individual, abound with efforts at atonement which try to make up for vague deeds against a maternal matrix and try to restore faith in the goodness of one's strivings and in the kindness of the powers of the universe.

Each society and each age must find the institutionalized form of reverence which derives vitality from its world-image—from predestination to indeterminacy. The clinician can only observe that many are proud to be without religion whose children cannot afford their being without it. On the other hand, there are many who seem to derive a vital faith from social action or scientific pursuit. And again, there are many who profess faith, yet in practice breathe mistrust both of life and man.

Autonomy vs. Shame and Doubt

In describing the growth and the crises of the human person as a series of alternative basic attitudes such as trust vs. mistrust, we take recourse to the term a "sense of," although, like a "sense of health," or a "sense of being unwell," such "senses" pervade surface and depth, consciousness and the unconscious. They are, then, at the same time, ways of *experiencing* accessible to introspection; ways of *behaving,* observable by others; and unconscious *inner states* determinable by test and analysis. It is important to keep these three dimensions in mind, as we proceed.

Muscular maturation sets the stage for experimentation with two simultaneous sets of social modalities: holding on and letting go. As is the case with all of these modalities, their basic conflicts can lead in the end to either hostile or

benign expectations and attitudes. Thus, to hold can become a destructive and cruel retaining or restraining, and it can become a pattern of care: to have and to hold. To let go, too, can turn into an inimical letting loose of destructive forces, or it can become a relaxed "to let pass" and "to let be."

Outer control at this stage, therefore, must be firmly reassuring. The infant must come to feel that the basic faith in existence, which is the lasting treasure saved from the rages of the oral stage, will not be jeopardized by this about-face of his, this sudden violent wish to have a choice, to appropriate demandingly, and to eliminate stubbornly. Firmness must protect him against the potential anarchy of his as yet untrained sense of discrimination, his inability to hold on and to let go with discretion. As his environment encourages him to "stand on his own feet," it must protect him against meaningless and arbitrary experiences of shame and of early doubt.

The latter danger is the one best known to us. For if denied the gradual and well-guided experience of the autonomy of free choice (or if, indeed, weakened by an initial loss of trust) the child will turn against himself all his urge to discriminate and to manipulate. He will overmanipulate himself, he will develop a precocious conscience. Instead of taking possession of things in order to test them by purposeful repetition, he will become obsessed by his own repetitiveness. By such obsessiveness, of course, he then learns to repossess the environment and to gain power by stubborn and minute control, where he could not find large-scale mutual regulation. Such hollow victory is the infantile model for a compulsion neurosis. It is also the infantile source of later attempts in adult life to govern by the letter, rather than by the spirit.

Shame is an emotion insufficiently studied, because in our civilization it is so early and easily absorbed by guilt.

Shame supposes that one is completely exposed and conscious of being looked at: in one word, self-conscious. One is visible and not ready to be visible; which is why we dream of shame as a situation in which we are stared at in a condition of incomplete dress, in night attire, "with one's pants down." Shame is early expressed in an impulse to bury one's face, or to sink, right then and there, into the ground. But this, I think, is essentially rage turned against the self. He who is ashamed would like to force the world not to look at him, not to notice his exposure. He would like to destroy the eyes of the world. Instead he must wish for his own invisibility. This potentiality is abundantly used in the educational method of "shaming" used so exclusively by some primitive peoples. Visual shame precedes auditory guilt, which is a sense of badness to be had all by oneself when nobody watches and when everything is quiet—except the voice of the superego. Such shaming exploits an increasing sense of being small, which can develop only as the child stands up and as his awareness permits him to note the relative measures of size and power.

Too much shaming does not lead to genuine propriety but to a secret determination to try to get away with things, unseen—if, indeed, it does not result in defiant shamelessness. There is an impressive American ballad in which a murderer to be hanged on the gallows before the eyes of the community, instead of feeling duly chastened, begins to berate the onlookers, ending every salvo of defiance with the words, "God damn your eyes." Many a small child, shamed beyond endurance, may be in a chronic mood (although not in possession of either the courage or the words) to express defiance in similar terms. What I mean by this sinister reference is that there is a limit to a child's and an adult's endurance in the face of demands to consider himself, his body, and his wishes as evil and dirty, and to his belief in the infallibility of those who pass such judgment. He may be apt to turn things around, and to consider as evil only the fact that they exist: his chance will come when they are gone, or when he will go from them.

Doubt is the brother of shame. Where shame is dependent on the consciousness of being upright and exposed, doubt, so clinical observation leads me to believe, has much to do with a consciousness of having a front and a back —and especially a "behind." For this reverse area of the body, with its aggressive and libidinal focus in the sphincters and in the buttocks, cannot be seen by the child, and yet it can be dominated by the will of others. The "behind" is the small being's dark continent, an area of the body which can be magically dominated and effectively invaded by those who would attack one's power of autonomy and who would designate as evil those products of the bowels which were felt to be all right when they were being passed. This basic sense of doubt in whatever one has left behind forms a substratum for later and more verbal forms of compulsive doubting; this finds its adult expression in paranoiac fears concerning hidden persecutors and secret persecutions threatening from behind (and from within the behind).

This stage, therefore, becomes decisive for the ratio of love and hate, cooperation and willfulness, freedom of self-expression and its suppression. From a sense of self-control without loss of self-esteem comes a lasting sense of good will and pride; from a sense of loss of self-control and of foreign overcontrol comes a lasting propensity for doubt and shame.

If, to some reader, the "negative" potentialities of our stages seem overstated throughout, we must remind him that this is not only the result of a preoccupation with clinical data. Adults, and seemingly mature and unneurotic ones, display a sensitivity concerning a possible shameful "loss of face" and fear of being attacked "from behind" which is not only highly irrational and in contrast to the knowledge available to them, but can be of fateful import if related sentiments influence, for example, interracial and international policies.

We have related basic trust to the institution of religion. The lasting need of the individual to have his will reaffirmed and delineated within an adult order of things which at the same time reaffirms and delineates the will of others has an institutional safeguard in the _principle of law and order_. In daily life as well as in the high courts of law—domestic and international—this principle apportions to each his privileges and his limitations, his obligations and his rights. A sense of rightful dignity and lawful independence on the part of adults around him gives to the child of good will the confident expectation that the kind of autonomy fostered in childhood will not lead to undue doubt or shame in later life. Thus the sense of autonomy fostered in the child and modified as life progresses, serves (and is served by) the preservation in economic and political life of a sense of justice.

Initiative vs. Guilt

There is in every child at every stage a new miracle of vigorous unfolding, which constitutes a new hope and a new responsibility for all. Such is the sense and the pervading quality of initiative. The criteria for all these senses and qualities are the same: a crisis, more or less beset with fumbling and fear, is resolved, in that the child suddenly seems to "grow together" both in his person and in his body. He appears "more himself," more loving, relaxed and brighter in his judgment, more activated and activating. He is in free possession of a surplus of energy which permits him to forget failures quickly and to ap-

proach what seems desirable (even if it also seems uncertain and even dangerous) with undiminished and more accurate direction. Initiative adds to autonomy the quality of undertaking, planning and "attacking" a task for the sake of being active and on the move, where before self-will, more often than not, inspired acts of defiance or, at any rate, protested independence.

I know that the very word "initiative" to many, has an American, and industrial connotation. Yet, initiative is a necessary part of every act, and man needs a sense of initiative for whatever he learns and does, from fruit-gathering to a system of enterprise.

The ambulatory stage and that of infantile genitality add to the inventory of basic social modalities that of "making," first in the sense of "being on the make." There is no simpler, stronger word for it; it suggests pleasure in attack and conquest. In the boy, the emphasis remains on phallic-intrusive modes; in the girl it turns to modes of "catching" in more aggressive forms of snatching or in the milder form of making oneself attractive and endearing.

The danger of this stage is a sense of guilt over the goals contemplated and the acts initiated in one's exuberant enjoyment of new locomotor and mental power: acts of aggressive manipulation and coercion which soon go far beyond the executive capacity of organism and mind and therefore call for an energetic halt on one's contemplated initiative. While autonomy concentrates on keeping potential rivals out, and therefore can lead to jealous rage most often directed against encroachments by younger siblings, initiative brings with it anticipatory rivalry with those who have been there first and may, therefore, occupy with their superior equipment the field toward which one's initiative is directed. Infantile jealousy and rivalry, those often embittered and yet essentially futile attempts at demarcating a sphere of unquestioned

privilege, now come to a climax in a final
contest for a favored position with the
mother; the usual failure leads to resigna-
tion, guilt, and anxiety. The child in-
dulges in fantasies of being a giant and
a tiger, but in his dreams he runs in ter-
ror for dear life. This, then, is the stage
of the "castration complex," the fear of
having the (now energetically eroticized)
genitals harmed as a punishment for the
fantasies attached to their excitement becomes intensified.

Infantile sexuality and incest taboo,
castration complex and superego all unite
here to bring about that specifically human crisis during which the child must
turn from an exclusive, pre-genital attachment to his parents to the slow process of becoming a parent, a carrier of
tradition. Here the most fateful split and
transformation in the emotional powerhouse occurs, a split between potential
human glory and potential total destruction. For here the child becomes forever
divided in himself. The instinct fragments which before had enhanced the
growth of his infantile body and mind
now become divided into an infantile
set which perpetuates the exuberance of
growth potentials, and a parental set
which supports and increases self-observa-
tion, self-guidance, and self-punishment.

The problem, again, is one of mutual
regulation. Where the child, now so
ready to overmanipulate himself, can
gradually develop a sense of moral responsibility, where he can gain some insight into the institutions, functions, and
roles which will permit his responsible
participation, he will find pleasurable accomplishment in wielding tools and
weapons, in manipulating meaningful
toys—and in caring for younger children.

Naturally, the parental set is at first
infantile in nature: the fact that human
conscience remains partially infantile
throughout life is the core of human
tragedy. For the superego of the child
can be primitive, cruel, and uncompromising, as may be observed in instances

where children overcontrol and overcon-
strict themselves to the point of self-
obliteration; where they develop an over-
obedience more literal than the one the
parent has wished to exact; or where
they develop deep regressions and lasting
resentments because the parents themselves do not seem to live up to the new
conscience. One of the deepest conflicts
in life is the hate for a parent who
served as the model and the executor of
the superego, but who (in some form)
was found trying to get away with the
very transgressions which the child can
no longer tolerate in himself. The suspiciousness and evasiveness which is thus
mixed in with the all-or-nothing quality
of the superego, this organ of moral
tradition, makes moral (in the sense of
moralistic) man a great potential danger
to his own ego—and to that of his fellow
men.

In adult pathology, the residual conflict over initiative is expressed either in
hysterical denial, which causes the repression of the wish or the abrogation of
its executive organ by paralysis, inhibition, or impotence; or in overcompensa-
tory showing off, in which the scared individual, so eager to "duck," instead
"sticks his neck out." Then also a plunge
into psychosomatic disease is now common. It is as if the culture had made a
man over-advertise himself and so identify with his own advertisement that only
disease can offer him escape.

But here, again, we must not think
only of individual psychopathology, but
of the inner powerhouse of rage which
must be submerged at this stage, as some
of the fondest hopes and the wildest
phantasies are repressed and inhibited.
The resulting self-righteousness—often
the principal reward for goodness—can
later be most intolerantly turned against
others in the form of persistent moralistic
surveillance, so that the prohibition rather
than the guidance of initiative becomes
the dominant endeavor. On the other
hand, even moral man's initiative is apt to

burst the boundaries of self-restriction, permitting him to do to others, in his or in other lands, what he would neither do nor tolerate being done in his own home.

In view of the dangerous potentials of man's long childhood, it is well to look back at the blueprint of the life-stages and to the possibilities of guiding the young of the race while they are young. And here we note that according to the wisdom of the ground plan the child is at no time more ready to learn quickly and avidly, to become bigger in the sense of sharing obligation and performance than during this period of his development. He is eager and able to make things cooperatively, to combine with other children for the purpose of constructing and planning, and he is willing to profit from teachers and to emulate ideal prototypes. He remains, of course, identified with the parent of the same sex, but for the present he looks for opportunities where work-identification seems to promise a field of initiative without too much infantile conflict or oedipal guilt and a more realistic identification based on a spirit of equality experienced in doing things together. At any rate, the "oedipal" stage results not only in the oppressive establishment of a moral sense restricting the horizon of the permissible; it also sets the direction toward the possible and the tangible which permits the dreams of early childhood to be attached to the goals of an active adult life. Social institutions, therefore, offer children of this age an *economic ethos,* in the form of ideal adults recognizable by their uniforms and their functions, and fascinating enough to replace the heroes of picture book and fairy tale.

Industry vs. Inferiority

Thus the inner stage seems all set for "entrance into life," except that life must first be school life, whether school is field or jungle or classroom. The child must forget past hopes and wishes, while his exuberant imagination is tamed and harnessed to the laws of impersonal things—even the three R's. For before the child, psychologically already a rudimentary parent, can become a biological parent, he must begin to be a worker and potential provider. With the oncoming latency period, the normally advanced child forgets, or rather sublimates, the necessity to "make" people by direct attack or to become papa and mama in a hurry: he now learns to win recognition by producing things. He has mastered the ambulatory field and the organ modes. He has experienced a sense of finality regarding the fact that there is no workable future within the womb of his family, and thus becomes ready to apply himself to given skills and tasks, which go far beyond the mere playful expression of his organ modes or the pleasure in the function of his limbs. He develops a sense of industry—i.e., he adjusts himself to the inorganic laws of the tool world. He can become an eager and absorbed unit of a productive situation. To bring a productive situation to completion is an aim which gradually supersedes the whims and wishes of play. His ego boundaries include his tools and skills: the work principle (Ives Hendrick) teaches him the pleasure of work completion by steady attention and persevering diligence. In all cultures, at this stage, children receive some *systematic instruction,* although, as we saw in the chapter on American Indians, it is by no means always in the kind of school which literate people must organize around special teachers who have learned how to teach literacy. In preliterate people and in non-literate pursuits much is learned from adults who become teachers by dint of gift and inclination rather than by appointment, and perhaps the greatest amount is learned from older children. Thus the *fundamentals of technology* are developed, as the child becomes ready to handle the utensils, the tools, and the weapons used by the big people. Literate people, with more specialized careers, must prepare the child by teaching him things which first of all make him literate, the widest possible basic education for the greatest number of possible careers. The more confusing specialization becomes, however, the more indistinct are the eventual goals of initiative; and the more complicated social reality, the vaguer are the father's and mother's role in it. School seems to be a culture all by itself, with its own goals and limits, its achievements and disappointment.

The child's danger, at this stage, lies in a sense of inadequacy and inferiority. If he despairs of his tools and skills or of his status among his tool partners, he may be discouraged from identification with them and with a section of the tool world. To lose the hope of such "industrial" association may pull him back to the more isolated, less tool-conscious familial rivalry of the oedipal time. The child despairs of his equipment in the tool world and in anatomy, and considers himself doomed to mediocrity or inadequacy. It is at this point that wider society becomes significant in its ways of admitting the child to an understanding of meaningful roles in its technology and economy. Many a child's development is disrupted when family life has failed to prepare him for school life, or when school life fails to sustain the promises of earlier stages.

Regarding the period of a developing sense of industry, I have referred to *outer and inner hindrances* in the use of new capacities but not to aggravations of new human drives, nor to submerged rages resulting from their frustration. This stage differs from the earlier ones in that it is not a swing from an inner upheaval to a new mastery. Freud calls it the latency stage because violent drives are normally dormant. But it is only a lull before the storm of puberty, when all the earlier drives reemerge in a new combination,

to be brought under the dominance of genitality.

On the other hand, this is socially a most decisive stage: since industry involves doing things beside and with others, a first sense of division of labor and of differential opportunity, that is, a sense of the *technological ethos* of a culture, develops at this time. We have pointed in the last section to the danger threatening individual and society where the schoolchild begins to feel that the color of his skin, the background of his parents, or the fashion of his clothes rather than his wish and his will to learn will decide his worth as an apprentice, and thus his sense of *identity*—to which we must now turn. But there is another, more fundamental danger, namely man's restriction of himself and constriction of his horizons to include only his work to which, so the Book says, he has been sentenced after his expulsion from paradise. If he accepts work as his only obligation, and "what works" as his only criterion of worthwhileness, he may become the conformist and thoughtless slave of his technology and of those who are in a position to exploit it.

Identity vs. Role Confusion

With the establishment of a good initial relationship to the world of skills and tools, and with the advent of puberty, childhood proper comes to an end. Youth begins. But in puberty and adolescence all samenesses and continuities relied on earlier are more or less questioned again, because of a rapidity of body growth which equals that of early childhood and because of the new addition of genital maturity. The growing and developing youths, faced with this physiological revolution within them, and with tangible adult tasks ahead of them are now primarily concerned with what they appear to be in the eyes of others as compared with what they feel they are, and with the question of how to connect the roles and skills cultivated earlier with the occupational prototypes of the day. In their search for a new sense of continuity and sameness, adolescents have to refight many of the battles of earlier years, even though to do so they must artificially appoint perfectly well-meaning people to play the roles of adversaries; and they are ever ready to install lasting idols and ideals as guardians of a final identity.

The integration now taking place in the form of ego identity is, as pointed out, more than the sum of the childhood identifications. It is the accrued experience of the ego's ability to integrate all identifications with the vicissitudes of the libido, with the aptitudes developed out of endowment, and with the opportunities offered in social roles. The sense of ego identity, then, is the accrued confidence that the inner sameness and continuity prepared in the past are matched by the sameness and continuity of one's meaning for others, as evidenced in the tangible promise of a "career."

The danger of this stage is role confusion.* Where this is based on a strong previous doubt as to one's sexual identity, delinquent and outright psychotic episodes are not uncommon. If diagnosed and treated correctly, these incidents do not have the same fatal significance which they have at other ages. In most instances, however, it is the inability to settle on an occupational identity which disturbs individual young people. To keep themselves together they temporarily overidentify, to the point of apparent complete loss of identity, with the heroes of cliques and crowds. This initiates the stage of "falling in love," which is by no means entirely, or even primarily, a sexual matter—except where the mores demand it. To a considerable extent adolescent love is an attempt to arrive at a definition of one's identity by projecting

* See "The Problem of Ego-Identity." *Journal of the American Psychoanalytic Association*, 4(1956), 56–121.

one's diffused ego image on another and by seeing it thus reflected and gradually clarified. This is why so much of young love is conversation.

Young people can also be remarkably clannish, and cruel in their exclusion of all those who are "different," in skin color or cultural background, in tastes and gifts, and often in such petty aspects of dress and gesture as have been temporarily selected as *the* signs of an in-grouper or out-grouper. It is important to understand (which does not mean condone or participate in) such intolerance as a defense against a sense of identity confusion. For adolescents not only help one another temporarily through much discomfort by forming cliques and by stereotyping themselves, their ideals, and their enemies; they also perversely test each other's capacity to pledge fidelity. The readiness for such testing also explains the appeal which simple and cruel totalitarian doctrines have on the minds of the youth of such countries and classes as have lost or are losing their group identities (feudal, agrarian, tribal, national) and face world-wide industrialization, emancipation, and wider communication.

The adolescent mind is essentially a mind of the *moratorium,* a psychosocial stage between childhood and adulthood, and between the morality learned by the child, and the ethics to be developed by the adult. It is an ideological mind—and, indeed, it is the ideological outlook of a society that speaks most clearly to the adolescent who is eager to be affirmed by his peers, and is ready to be confirmed by rituals, creeds, and programs which at the same time define what is evil, uncanny, and inimical. In searching for the social values which guide identity, one therefore confronts the problems of *ideology* and *aristocracy,* both in their widest possible sense which connotes that within a defined world image and a predestined course of history, the best people will come to rule and rule develops the best in people. In order not to become cynically or apathetically lost, young people must somehow be able to convince themselves that those who succeed in their anticipated adult world thereby shoulder the obligation of being the best. We will discuss later the dangers which emanate from human ideals harnessed to the management of super-machines, be they guided by nationalistic or international, communist or capitalist ideologies. In the last part of this book we shall discuss the way in which the revolutions of our day attempt to solve and also to exploit the deep need of youth to redefine its identity in an industrialized world.

Intimacy vs. Isolation

The strength acquired at any stage is tested by the necessity to transcend it in such a way that the individual can take chances in the next stage with what was most vulnerably precious in the previous one. Thus, the young adult, emerging from the search for and the insistence on identity, is eager and willing to fuse his identity with that of others. He is ready for intimacy, that is, the capacity to commit himself to concrete affiliations and partnerships and to develop the ethical strength to abide by such commitments, even though they may call for significant sacrifices and compromises. Body and ego must now be masters of the organ modes and of the nuclear conflicts, in order to be able to face the fear of ego loss in situations which call for self-abandon: in the solidarity of close affiliations, in orgasms and sexual unions, in close friendships and in physical combat, in experiences of inspiration by teachers and of intuition from the recesses of the self. The avoidance of such experiences because of a fear of ego loss may lead to a deep sense of isolation and consequent self-absorption.

The counterpart of intimacy is distantiation: the readiness to isolate and, if

necessary, to destroy those forces and people whose essence seems dangerous to one's own, and whose "territory" seems to encroach on the extent of one's intimate relations. Prejudices thus developed (and utilized and exploited in politics and in war) are a more mature outgrowth of the blinder repudiations which during the struggle for identity differentiate sharply and cruelly between the familiar and the foreign. The danger of this stage is that intimate, competitive, and combative relations are experienced with and against the selfsame people. But as the areas of adult duty are delineated, and as the competitive encounter, and the sexual embrace, are differentiated, they eventually become subject to that *ethical sense* which is the mark of the adult.

Strictly speaking, it is only now that *true genitality* can fully develop; for much of the sex life preceding these commitments is of the identity-searching kind, or is dominated by phallic or vaginal strivings which make of sex-life a kind of genital combat. On the other hand, genitality is all too often described as a permanent state of reciprocal sexual bliss. This then, may be the place to complete our discussion of genitality.

For a basic orientation in the matter I shall quote what has come to me as Freud's shortest saying. It has often been claimed, and bad habits of conversation seem to sustain the claim, that psychoanalysis as a treatment attempts to convince the patient that before God and man he has only one obligation: to have good orgasms, with a fitting "object," and that regularly. This, of course, is not true. Freud was once asked what he thought a normal person should be able to do well. The questioner probably expected a complicated answer. But Freud, in the curt way of his old days, is reported to have said: "Lieben und arbeiten" (to love and to work). It pays to ponder on this simple formula; it gets deeper as you think about it. For when

Freud said "love" he meant *genital* love, and genital *love;* when he said love *and* work, he meant a general work-productiveness which would not preoccupy the individual to the extent that he loses his right or capacity to be a genital and a loving being. Thus we may ponder, but we cannot improve on "the professor's" formula.

Genitality, then, consists in the unobstructed capacity to develop an orgastic potency so free of pregenital interferences that genital libido (not just the sex products discharged in Kinsey's "outlets") is expressed in heterosexual mutuality, with full sensitivity of both penis and vagina, and with a convulsion-like discharge of tension from the whole body. This is a rather concrete way of saying something about a process which we really do not understand. To put it more situationally: the total fact of finding, via the climactic turmoil of the orgasm, a supreme experience of the mutual regulation of two beings in some way takes the edge off the hostilities and potential rages caused by the oppositeness of male and female, of fact and fancy, of love and hate. Satisfactory sex relations thus make sex less obsessive, overcompensation less necessary, sadistic controls superfluous.

Preoccupied as it was with curative aspects, psychoanalysis often failed to formulate the matter of genitality in a way significant for the processes of society in all classes, nations, and levels of culture. The kind of mutuality in orgasm which psychoanalysis has in mind is apparently easily obtained in classes and cultures which happen to make a leisurely institution of it. In more complex societies this mutuality is interfered with by so many factors of health, of tradition, of opportunity, and of temperament, that the proper formulation of sexual health would be rather this: A human being should be potentially able to accomplish mutuality of genital orgasm, but he should also be so constituted as to bear a

certain amount of frustration in the matter without undue regression wherever emotional preference or considerations of duty and loyalty call for it.

While psychoanalysis has on occasion gone too far in its emphasis on genitality as a universal cure for society and has thus provided a new addiction and a new commodity for many who wished to so interpret its teachings, it has not always indicated all the goals that genitality actually should and must imply. In order to be of lasting social significance, the utopia of genitality should include:

1. mutuality of orgasm
2. with a loved partner
3. of the other sex
4. with whom one is able and willing to share a mutual trust
5. and with whom one is able and willing to regulate the cycles of
   a. work
   b. procreation
   c. recreation
6. so as to secure to the offspring, too, all the stages of a satisfactory development.

It is apparent that such utopian accomplishment on a large scale cannot be an individual or, indeed, a therapeutic task. Nor is it a purely sexual matter by any means. It is integral to a culture's style of sexual selection, cooperation, and competition.

The danger of this stage is isolation, that is the avoidance of contacts which commit to intimacy. In psychopathology, this disturbance can lead to severe "character-problems." On the other hand, there are partnerships which amount to an isolation à deux, protecting both partners from the necessity to face the next critical development—that of generativity.

Generativity vs. Stagnation

In this book the emphasis is on the childhood stages, otherwise the section on generativity would of necessity be the central one, for this term encompasses the evolutionary development which has made man the teaching and instituting as well as the learning animal. The fashionable insistence on dramatizing the dependence of children on adults often blinds us to the dependence of the older generation on the younger one. Mature man needs to be needed, and maturity needs guidance as well as encouragement from what has been produced and must be taken care of.

Generativity, then, is primarily the concern in establishing and guiding the next generation, although there are individuals who, through misfortune or because of special and genuine gifts in other directions, do not apply this drive to their own offspring. And indeed, the concept generativity is meant to include such more popular synonyms as *productivity* and *creativity,* which, however, cannot replace it.

It has taken psychoanalysis some time to realize that the ability to lose oneself in the meeting of bodies and minds leads to a gradual expansion of ego-interests and to a libidinal investment in that which is being generated. Generativity thus is an essential stage on the psychosexual as well as on the psychosocial schedule. Where such enrichment fails altogether, regression to an obsessive need for pseudo-intimacy takes place, often with a pervading sense of stagnation and personal impoverishment. Individuals, then, often begin to indulge themselves as if they were their own—or one another's—one and only child; and where conditions favor it, early invalidism, physical or psychological, becomes the vehicle of self-concern. The mere fact of having or even wanting children, however, does not "achieve" generativity. In fact, some young parents suffer, it seems, from the retardation of the ability to develop this stage. The reasons are often to be found in early childhood impressions; in excessive self-love based on

a too strenuously self-made personality; and finally (and here we return to the beginnings) in the lack of some faith, some "belief in the species," which would make a child appear to be a welcome trust of the community.

As to the institutions which safeguard and reinforce generativity, one can only say that all institutions codify the ethics of generative succession. Even where philosophical and spiritual tradition suggests the renunciation of the right to procreate or to produce, such early turn to "ultimate concerns," wherever instituted in monastic movements, strives to settle at the same time the matter of its relationship to the Care for the creatures of this world and to the Charity which is felt to transcend it.

If this were a book on adulthood, it would be indispensable and profitable at this point to compare economic and psychological theories (beginning with the strange convergencies and divergencies of Marx and Freud) and to proceed to a discussion of man's relationship to his production as well as to his progeny.

Ego Integrity vs. Despair

Only in him who in some way has taken care of things and people and has adapted himself to the triumphs and disappointments adherent to being, the originator of others or the generator of products and ideas—only in him may gradually ripen the fruit of these seven stages. I know no better word for it than ego integrity. Lacking a clear definition, I shall point to a few constituents of this state of mind. It is the ego's accrued assurance of its proclivity for order and meaning. It is a post-narcissistic love of the human ego —not of the self—as an experience which conveys some world order and spiritual sense, no matter how dearly paid for. It is the acceptance of one's one and only life cycle as something that had to be and that, by necessity, permitted of no substitutions: it thus means a new, a different love of one's parents. It is a comradeship with the ordering ways of distant times and different pursuits, as expressed in the simple products and sayings of such times and pursuits. Although aware of the relativity of all the various life styles which have given meaning to human striving, the possessor of integrity is ready to defend the dignity of his own life style against all physical and economic threats. For he knows that an individual life is the accidental coincidence of but one life cycle with but one segment of history; and that for him all human integrity stands or falls with the one style of integrity of which he partakes. The style of integrity developed by his culture or civilization thus becomes the "patrimony of his soul," the seal of his moral paternity of himself (". . . pero el honor/Es patrimonio del alma": Calderón). In such final consolidation, death loses its sting.

The lack or loss of this accrued ego integration is signified by fear of death: the one and only life cycle is not accepted as the ultimate of life. Despair expresses the feeling that the time is now short, too short for the attempt to start another life and to try out alternate roads to integrity. Disgust hides despair, if often only in the form of "a thousand little disgusts" which do not add up to one big remorse: *"mille petits dégôuts de soi, dont le total ne fait pas un remords, mais un gêne obscure."* (Rostand)

Each individual, to become a mature adult, must to a sufficient degree develop all the ego qualities mentioned, so that a wise Indian, a true gentleman, and a mature peasant share and recognize in one another the final stage of integrity. But each cultural entity, to develop the particular style of integrity suggested by its historical place, utilizes a particular combination of these conflicts, along with specific provocations and prohibitions of infantile sexuality. Infantile conflicts become creative only if sustained by the

firm support of cultural institutions and of the special leader classes representing them. In order to approach or experience integrity, the individual must know how to be a follower of image bearers in religion and in politics, in the economic order and in technology, in aristocratic living and in the arts and sciences. Ego integrity, therefore, implies an emotional integration which permits participation by followership as well as acceptance of the responsibility of leadership.

Webster's Dictionary is kind enough to help us complete this outline in a circular fashion. Trust (the first of our ego values) is here defined as "the assured reliance on another's integrity," the last of our values. I suspect that Webster had business in mind rather than babies, credit rather than faith. But the formulation stands. And it seems possible to further paraphrase the relation of adult integrity and infantile trust by saying that healthy children will not fear life if their elders have integrity enough not to fear death.

An Epigenetic Chart

In this book the emphasis is on the childhood stages. The foregoing conception of the life cycle, however, awaits systematic treatment. To prepare this, I shall conclude this chapter with a diagram. In this, as in the diagram of pregenital zones and modes, the diagonal represents the normative sequence of psychosocial gains made as at each stage one more nuclear conflict adds a new ego quality, a new criterion of accruing human strength. Below the diagonal there is space for the precursors of each of these solutions, all of which begin with the beginning; above the diagonal there is space for the designation of the derivatives of these gains and their transformations in the maturing and the mature personality.

The underlying assumptions for such charting are (1) that the human personality in principle develops according to steps predetermined in the growing person's readiness to be driven toward, to be aware of, and to interact with, a widening social radius; and (2) that society, in principle, tends to be so constituted as to meet and invite this succession of potentialities for interaction and attempts to safeguard and to encourage the proper rate and the proper sequence of their enfolding. This is the "maintenance of the human world."

But a chart is only a tool to think with, and cannot aspire to be a prescription to abide by, whether in the practice of child-training, in psychotherapy, or in the methodology of child study. In the presentation of the psychosocial stages in the form of an *epigenetic chart* analogous to the one employed in Chapter 2 [in *Childhood and Society*] for an analysis of Freud's psychosexual stages, we have definite and delimited methodological steps in mind. It is one purpose of this work to facilitate the comparison of the stages first discerned by Freud as sexual to other schedules of development (physical, cognitive). But any one chart delimits one schedule only, and it must not be imputed that our outline of the psychosocial schedule is intended to imply obscure generalities concerning other aspects of development—or, indeed, of existence. If the chart, for example, lists a series of conflicts or crises, we do not consider all development a series of crises: we claim only that psychosocial development proceeds by critical steps—"critical" being a characteristic of turning points, of moments of decision between progress and regression, integration and retardation.

It may be useful at this point to spell out the methodological implications of an epigenetic matrix. The more heavily-lined squares of the diagonal signify both a sequence of stages and a gradual development of component parts: in other words, the chart formalizes a progression through time of a differentiation of parts.

This indicates (1) that each critical item of psychosocial strength discussed here is systematically related to all others, and that they all depend on the proper development in the proper sequence of each item; and (2) that each item exists in some form before its critical time normally arrives.

If I say, for example, that a favorable ratio of basic trust over basic mistrust is the first step in psychosocial adaptation, a favorable ratio of autonomous will over shame and doubt, the second, the corresponding diagrammatic statement expresses a number of fundamental relations that exist between the two steps, as well as some facts fundamental to each. Each comes to its ascendance, meets its crisis, and finds its lasting solution during the stage indicated. But they all must exist from the beginning in some form, for every act calls for an integration of all. Also, an infant may show something like "autonomy" from the beginning in the particular way in which he angrily tries to wriggle himself free when tightly held. However, under normal conditions, it is not until the second year that he begins to experience the whole *critical opposition of being an autonomous creature and being a dependent one;* and it is not until then that he is ready for a decisive encounter with his environment, an environment which, in turn, feels called upon to convey to him its particular ideas and concepts of autonomy and coercion in ways decisively contributing to the character and the health of his personality in his culture. It is this encounter, together with the resulting crisis, that we have tentatively described for each stage. As to the progression from one stage to the next, the diagonal indicates the sequence to be followed. However, it also makes room for variations in tempo and intensity. An individual, or a culture, may linger excessively over trust and proceed from I 1 over I 2, to II 2, or an accelerated progression may move from I 1 over II 1 to II 2.

		1	2	3	4	5	6	7	8
I	ORAL SENSORY	TRUST VS. MISTRUST							
II	MUSCULAR-ANAL		AUTONOMY VS. SHAME, DOUBT						
III	LOCOMOTOR-GENITAL			INITIATIVE VS. GUILT					
IV	LATENCY				INDUSTRY VS. INFERIORITY				
V	PUBERTY AND ADOLESCENCE					IDENTITY VS. ROLE DIFFUSION			
VI	YOUNG ADULTHOOD						INTIMACY VS. ISOLATION		
VII	ADULTHOOD							GENERATIVITY VS. STAGNATION	
VIII	MATURITY								INTEGRITY VS. DISGUST, DESPAIR

Each such acceleration or (relative) retardation, however, is assumed to have a modifying influence on all later stages.

An epigenetic diagram thus lists a system of stages dependent on each other; and while individual stages may have been explored more or less thoroughly or named more or less fittingly, the diagram suggests that their study be pursued always with the total configuration of stages in mind. The diagram invites, then, a thinking through of all its empty boxes: if we have entered Basic Trust in I 1 and Integrity in VIII 8, we leave the question open, as to what trust might have become in a stage dominated by the need for integrity even as we have left open what it may look like and, indeed, be called in the stage dominated by a striving for autonomy (II 1). All we mean to emphasize is that trust must have developed in its own right, before it becomes something more in the critical encounter in which autonomy develops—and so on, up the vertical. If, in the last stage (VIII 1), we would expect trust to have developed into the most mature *faith* that an aging person can muster in his cultural setting and historical period, the chart permits the consideration not only of what old age can be, but also what its preparatory stages must have been. All of this should make it clear that a chart of epigenesis suggests a global form of thinking and rethinking which leaves details of methodology and terminology to further study.*

* To leave this matter truly open, certain misuses of the whole conception would have to be avoided. Among them is the assumption that the sense of trust (and all the other "positive" senses postulated) is an *achievement*, secured once and for all at a given state. In fact, some writers are so intent on making an *achievement scale* out of these stages that they blithely omit all the "negative" senses (basic mistrust, etc.) which are and remain the dynamic counterpart of the "positive" ones throughout life. The assumption that on each stage a goodness is achieved which is impervious to new inner conflicts and to changing conditions is, I believe, a projection on child development of that success ideology which can so dangerously pervade our private and public daydreams and can make us inept in a heightened struggle for a meaningful existence in a new, industrial era of history. The personality is engaged with the hazards of existence continuously, even as the body's metabolism copes with decay. As we come to diagnose a state of relative strength and the symptoms of an impaired one, we face only more clearly the paradoxes and tragic potentials of human life.

The stripping of the stages of everything but their "achievements" has its counterpart in attempts to describe or test them as "traits" or "aspirations" without first building a systematic bridge between the conception advanced throughout this book and the favorite concepts of other investigators. If the foregoing sounds somewhat plaintive, it is not intended to gloss over the fact that in giving to these strengths the very designations by which in the past they have acquired countless connotations of superfi-

Maternal Deprivation: Toward an Empirical and Conceptual Re-evaluation*

LEON J. YARROW

FAMILY AND CHILD SERVICES, WASHINGTON, D.C.

The significance of early infantile experience for later development has been reiterated so frequently and so persistently that the general validity of this assertion is now almost unchallenged. An extensive literature on deviating patterns of maternal care, loosely labeled "maternal deprivation," adds up with an impressive consistency in its *general* conclusions: de-

viating conditions of maternal care in early life tend to be associated with later disturbances in intellectual and personal-social functioning. It has been difficult to build on this general premise in formulating more precise research hypotheses relating specific variables of early maternal care to later developmental

Generativity vs. Stagnation: Production and Care

Ego Integrity vs. Despair: Renunciation and *Wisdom*

The italicized words are called *basic* virtues because without them, and their re-emergence from generation to generation, all other and more changeable systems of human values lose their spirit and their relevance. Of this list, I have been able so far to give a more detailed account only for Fidelity (see *Youth, Change and Challenge*, E. H. Erikson, editor, Basic Books, 1963). But here again, the list represents a total conception within which there is much room for a discussion of terminology and methodology.

Reprinted from the *Psychological Bulletin,* 58(1961), 459–490, with the permission of the American Psychological Association and the author.

* Based on invited address, Division on Developmental Psychology, sixty-seventh Annual Convention of the American Psychological Association, Cincinnati, Ohio, September 1959.

This paper was prepared in conjunction with a research project on The Effects of a Change in Mother-Figure during Infancy on Personality Development, conducted under Research Grant 3M-9077 from the National Institute of Mental Health, United States Public Health Service.

---

cial goodness, affected niceness, and all too strenuous virtue, I invited misunderstandings and misuses. However, I believe, that there is an intrinsic relationship between ego and language and that despite passing vicissitudes certain basic words retain essential meanings.

I have since attempted to formulate for Julian Huxley's *Humanist Frame* (Allen and Unwin, 1961; Harper and Brothers, 1962) a blueprint of essential strengths which evolution has built both into the ground plan of the life stages and into that of man's institutions. While I cannot discuss here the methodological problems involved (and aggravated by my use of the term "basic virtues"), I should append the list of these strengths because they are really the lasting outcome of the "favorable ratios" mentioned at every step of the chapter on psychosocial stages. Here they are:

Basic Trust vs. Basic Mistrust: Drive and *Hope*

Autonomy vs. Shame and Doubt: Self-Control and *Willpower*

Initiative vs. Guilt: Direction and *Purpose*

Industry vs. Inferiority: Method and *Competence*

Identity vs. Role Confusion: Devotion and *Fidelity*

Intimacy vs. Isolation: Affiliation and *Love*

320

characteristics. If one attempts to order the empirical data from the many studies and the varied contexts, it becomes apparent that the concept of maternal deprivation is a rather muddied one. Maternal deprivation has been used as a broad descriptive term as well as an overall explanatory concept. As a descriptive term it encompasses a variety of conditions of infant care which are phenotypically as well as dynamically very different. In this review of the research and theoretical literature, our major objective is to clarify the concept of maternal deprivation by identifying the basic variables and concepts which have been indiscriminately combined under this term.

Previous reviews have dealt primarily with the findings (13, 38) or with the methodology of a few studies (66, 67). The chief effort of this review will be directed towards sorting out on an empirical level the varied antecedent conditions of maternal care described in the literature, and relating these empirical conditions to some major theoretical concepts. Through this kind of analysis, it is hoped to facilitate the formulation of more explicit hypotheses on the relationship between specific aspects of early life experiences and later development.

Empirical Analysis of the Research on "Maternal Deprivation"

In the literature on maternal deprivation, four different kinds of deviations from a hypothetical mode of maternal care have been included: institutionalization; separation from a mother or mother-substitute; multiple mothering, in which there is no one continuous person performing the major mothering functions; distortions in the quality of mothering, e.g., rejection, overprotection, ambivalence. In very few studies do we find these "pure conditions." Most often several conditions occur concomitantly or sequentially in complex interaction, e.g., separation

is followed by institutionalization, multiple mothering occurs in an institutional setting.

Tables 1 to 4 present the chief research studies organized in terms of the major conditions of early care: institutionalization, separation, multiple mothering. Studies on distortions in the mother-child relationship, e.g., rejection, overprotection, ambivalence, on which there are many clinical reports, but few research reports, have not been included. The studies presented in the tables are grouped according to their general research designs: retrospective, direct, or contemporaneous. The tables point out the major characteristics of the samples: the population from which the subjects were chosen, the ages at the time of study, and the ages at the time of the experience. Also presented are the major techniques used in data collection or the kinds of data obtained. For the retrospective studies, the presence or absence of data on earlier conditions of maternal care is noted. Finally, overlapping or contaminating conditions are noted where they have been reported.

It is clear from the tables that the major share of studies has been on institutional care. There are many fewer published reports on separation and multiple mothering. In the following section, in considering each of these types of studies, our focus will be on an analysis of the environmental conditions and the impact of these events and conditions on development. Throughout we will attempt to integrate the empirical data in terms of some basic psychological concepts, and to point up some hypotheses amenable to research.

Institutionalization

Most of the generalizations about the effects of "maternal deprivation" are based on retrospective research in which institutionalization has been a major

background condition. The general research designs of the many retrospective
studies reported between 1937 and 1955
are basically similar and tend to suffer
from similar methodological deficiencies.
In all but a few studies there is a sampling bias due to the method of selection
of cases; subjects are chosen from clinic
populations of cases under treatment for
emotional or personality disturbances. (In
delving back into the history of these
patients, it was discovered that many had
spent some part of their earlier life in an
institutional setting.) Perhaps the most
significant deficiency in many of these
studies is the lack of specific data on early
conditions of maternal care. The characteristics of the institutional environment
are unknown or not described, and no
data, or, at the best, very meager data are
given about the circumstances associated
with institutionalization. Such significant
information as age at time of placement,
duration of institutional care, traumatic
conditions preceding or concomitant with
institutional placement is rarely given.
Frequently information about experiences following institutional care is scant
and of uncertain validity. The data on
the personality characteristics of the subjects also vary greatly in depth and adequacy; much data are derived from psychiatric diagnoses based on an unspecified number of interviews or consist of
case history material from unspecified
sources; in a few instances, projective or
other kinds of personality tests have been
used.

THE INSTITUTIONAL ENVIRONMENT

In much of the research on institutions the environment has been dealt with
so grossly that "institutionalization" has
often referred to a setting as broad in
many respects as "the home." Only a few
contemporaneous studies of infants and
young children give sufficiently detailed
descriptions of the institutional setting to
enable one to isolate discrete variables.

Only one study, comparing the institutional and home environments of a small
group of infants, makes a serious attempt
to give an objective description of an institution (74).

The institutional environments in the
direct studies can be ordered in terms of
several theoretically meaningful categories which can be further reduced to
specific research variables.

*The Physical Environment—Quality
and Amount of Sensory Stimulation.*
The importance of sensory stimulation
for development has recently been emphasized by a number of animal experiments. In most of the research, institutional settings are characterized in the extreme as lacking in sensory stimulation;
they are described as colorless and drab
with little visual or auditory stimulation
and with few objects for the child to manipulate.

*The Emotional Environment—Affec-
tive Stimulation.* For research, the emotional environment can be defined in a
restricted sense in terms of formal, measurable aspects of affective stimulation, i.e.,
intensity and variability. Institutions tend
to be characterized by an emotional
blandness and a lack of variation in feeling tone with the result that the infant is
not exposed to strongly negative or
strongly positive affective stimulation.

*The Social Environment—Social
Stimulation.* The amount of mothering,
the quality and consistency of mothering, and the amount and quality of general social stimulation are major aspects
of the animate environment in terms of
which institutional care is defined. Most
of the studies describe a low adult-child
ratio, averaging about one adult to ten
infants in institutional settings. There
are usually many different caretakers,
with the result that the infant has little
opportunity to relate to one person as a
consistent source of gratification. Compared with an infant in his own home,
the research indicates that in institutions
there is much less mothering contact,

less total social stimulation, and less stability in mother-figures.

Learning Conditions. Learning conditions which deviate from those in a "normal" home environment are reported characteristic of institutions: deviations in opportunities for acquiring or practicing new skills, deviations in motivational conditions, and in scheduling. Often infants are confined to the crib or playpen during most of the day, with very limited opportunity to practice emerging motor skills or to make perceptual discriminations. There tends to be little recognition by adults for positive achievements, with no or inconsistent reinforcement for positive learnings or socially desirable responses. Daily routines are sometimes characterized by an element of unpredictability, but more often routines are rigidly scheduled with little variation from day to day, and with little adaptation to individual differences.

It is clear that institutionalization is not a simple variable, and cannot be used as a simple research variable or explanatory concept. Even in the limited sample of institutions found in the direct studies, the environments are not identical. Qualitative as well as quantitative variations are apparent among institutions in the amount of sensory stimulation, in the consistency of mothering, in the consistency of rewards, etc.

INTELLECTUAL, PERSONALITY, AND SOCIAL CHARACTERISTICS ASSOCIATED WITH INSTITUTIONALIZATION

Despite the methodological inadequacies and the great range of antecedent conditions in the research, there is a core of consistency in the findings on the characteristics of children, adolescents, and adults with institutional backgrounds. The major characteristics associated with institutional care are: general intellectual retardation, retardation in language functions, and social and "personality" disturbances, chiefly disturb-

ances centering around the capacity to establish and maintain close personal relationships. Within the overall consistency, however, there is significant variation. Not all children with institutional experience give evidence of intellectual or personality damage, and there is a range in the extent of injury. These variations can sometimes be related to the characteristics of the environment; sometimes significant modifying or interacting variables can be identified.

Intellectual Defects. General intellectual retardation is commonly found in older children and adolescents with a history of institutionalization (7, 44, 60, 62) as well as in infants and young children growing up in institutional environments (25, 30, 31, 36, 85, 86, 91). The data do not, however, permit the simple conclusion that gross intellectual deficiency is a necessary consequence of institutional experience. The incidence and degree of retardation vary considerably from one study to another. In only *some* of the studies do *some* children show severe retardation (25, 36, 44, 45, 85, 86, 91). In others there is only relative retardation; they are functioning on a dull-normal level (27, 30, 31, 33, 58, 73). Several factors seem to be related to the varied outcomes in intellectual functioning:

1. The amount of individualized stimulation provided in these environments seems to be significantly related to the degree of retardation. In the institutions in which attempts were made to provide individualized stimulation, and to foster a relationship between a single caretaker and infant, severe retardation was not found (27, 30, 31, 33, 58, 73).

2. The age of the child at the time of institutionalization varies greatly among the studies; several investigators have concluded that the younger the child at the time of institutionalization, the more likely is subsequent retardation (5, 9, 46). The evidence is meager, consisting of data from two studies. In Gold-

TABLE 1

Research on Institutionalization: Direct Studies of Children in Institutions

Investigator	Subjects	Age at Time of Study	Age when Institutionalized	Techniques or Type of Data	Description of Environment
Brodbeck & Irwin (1946)	Institutional: 94 Controls: 217	Birth to 6 months	Birth to 6 months	Analysis of speech sounds	General—social, emotional
Brown (1937)	Institutional: 200 Controls: 200 from "poor" home environments	9–14 years	Broad range: birth to adolescence	Brown Personality Inventory	No data
Dennis & Najarian (1957)	Institutional: 49 infants; 30 preschool age Controls: 41	2–12 months; 4½–6 years	Birth	Infant tests Goodenough Draw-A-Man Test	Detailed—physical, social, learning conditions
DuPan & Roth (1955)	Institutional: 14	4–30 months	Birth to 3 months	Gesell test	Detailed—physical, social, learning conditions
Fischer (1952)	Institutional: 62	6–7 months	Birth to 3 months	Cattell test Observation	Detailed—physical, social
Flint (1957)	Institutional: 16	2–20 months	Birth to 6 months	Infant security scale Observation	Detailed—physical, social, learning conditions
Freud & Burlingham (1944)	Institutional: approximately 90	Birth to 2 years longitudinal	Early infancy—no specific data	Clinical observation	General—physical, social
Gesell & Amatruda (1941)	Institutional: unspecified number	Birth to 2 years	No data	Gesell test	No data
Goldfarb (1945a)	Institutional: 15 Controls: 15	First test mean: 34 months Follow-up mean: 43 months	Early infancy mean—4½ months	Intelligence tests Language test Test of motor coordination Social maturity scale Rorschach Behavior ratings	General—physical, social
Levy (1947)	Institutional: 101 Foster home controls: 129	122 under 6 months 34: 6 to 12 months, 74 over 12 months	Early infancy	Gesell test Stanford-Binet and other preschool intelligence tests Vineland Social Maturity Scale	Detailed—physical, social

Study	Subjects	Age at test	Period studied	Tests	Data
Rheingold (1956)	Institutional: 16; 8 controls, 8 experimental given special mothering	6–8 months	Early infancy	Cattell test Social responsiveness test	Detailed—physical, social, emotional
Skeels, Updegraff, Wellman & Williams (1938) Wellman & Pegram (1944)	Institutional varying numbers of cases, main group 53 controls; 35 experimental, given preschool experience	1½ to 5½ years	Birth to 2 years	Intelligence test Language test Motor tests General information test Vineland Social Maturity Scale Behavior observations	Detailed—physical, social, emotional
Skeels & Dye (1938) Skeels (1942)	Institutional: 25; 12 controls; 13 experimental given special stimulation	First test controls—12 to 22 months experimental—7 to 36 months Last test controls—5 to 9 years experimental—4½ to 9½ years	Birth to 2 years	Intelligence tests 4 follow-up tests	Detailed—physical, social, emotional
Spitz (1946)	61 infants in foundling home; 69 infants with own mothers in prison; 34 infants in own homes	Early infancy to 2½ years	Birth	Hetzer-Wolf Infant Test Clinical observation	Detailed—physical, social
Spitz & Wolf (1949)	170 infants with own mothers in prison; 61 infants in foundling home; 17 infants in own homes	Birth to 15 months	Birth	Observation Interview Hetzer-Wolf Infant Test Rorschach (mothers)	General—physical, social; detailed personality of mothers

farb's research in which a large percentage of cases showed evidence of retardation, the mean age of admission to the institution was 4.5 months, with only three cases over 1 year of age. Of a group of 37 adolescents and young adults studied by Beres and Obers (9) only four were mentally retarded; all four had entered the institution under 6 months.

3. Constitutional factors. There are no direct data, but the findings that, in seemingly identical environments, some children show retardation and others do not, have been interpreted as evidence of constitutional differences in vulnerability to institutional deprivation.

4. The duration of institutionalization. The data point to a cumulative impact of the institutional environment on intellectual functioning. In most studies, with continued institutional residence, infants show a progressive drop in developmental test quotients (25; 30; 31; 33, no test data; 83; 84; 86; 91). A few studies (27, 73, 75) report no significant cumulative loss in intellectual functioning. Although Dennis and Najarian (24) found a decrease in Cattell test scores in institutionalized infants between 3 and 12 months they discovered no significant retardation on the Goodenough Draw-A-Man Test among a group of older children, 4.5 to 6 years of age, who had been in the same institution for several years. They raise the interesting question as to whether an environment which fails to offer adequate intellectual stimulation to infants is necessarily retarding for preschool children.

The direct association between intellectual retardation and environmental impoverishment is dramatically emphasized by Skeels and Dye's study (84). Retarded institutional children made significant gains in intellectual functions after special environmental stimulation. In another study (85), the intellectual stimulation provided by an experimental nursery school in an institution was found effective in preventing deterioration in intellectual functioning. Whereas a control group showed cumulative losses in IQ scores, children given nursery school experience maintained their IQ level.

Two other studies suggest that intellectual retardation need not be attributed to some elusive, unknown aspect of the institutional environment, but can be directly related to lack of adequate stimulation. Rheingold (72) studying infants in boarding homes found that children who shared the home with several other babies had significantly lower developmental test scores than infants who were "only children" in the boarding homes. Coleman and Provence (21) observed retardation similar to the institutional pattern in children living in very unstimulating home environments.

Analysis of the separate aspects of intellectual functioning indicates that all functions are not equally affected by institutional living. Consistent evidence of retardation is found in language, in time and space concepts, and in capacity for abstract conceptualization.

Language is one function in which severe retardation has been found repeatedly in institutionalized infants and young children (19, 27, 30, 31, 33, 36, 75, 85) as well as in older children and adults with an institutional history (5, 7, 44, 49, 62). There is disagreement in the literature on institutionalization only in the age at which language functions first seem to be affected. Brodbeck and Irwin (19) found evidence of retardation in institutionalized infants in the first few months of life, whereas Freud and Burlingham (33) report no indications of language retardation before 12 months. Brodbeck and Irwin's data were based on careful phonetic analysis of speech sounds, whereas Freud and Burlingham had no systematic language data on infants.

With regard to the etiology of language retardation, Fischer (30, 31) notes that in many institutions there is little reinforcement by adults of the infant's vocalizations, and consequently reduced opportunity for the child to acquire the signal functions and expressive functions of language. Recent data on the conditioning of vocalizations in infants (76) give evidence of the role of reinforcement in young infants' vocalizations. Early studies of language development (22, 96) pointed to a direct relationship between amount of environmental stimulation (e.g., number of hours the child was read to, "extensions of the environment") and vocabulary and sentence length in preschool children. On the simplest level, language retardation, like general intellectual retardation, can be related to inadequate language stimulation. Lack of motivation for imitative behavior may interact with inadequate reinforcement of speech sounds in determining language retardation.

Serious *defects in time and spatial concepts* in older children have been reported in clinical descriptions by Goldfarb (44, 47) and Bender (5, 7). Poor memory for past events is linked by Bender with such character defects as inability to benefit from past mistakes, lack of future goals, and weak motivation to control behavior for future gains. Goldfarb relates social maladjustment to difficulties in time and spatial concepts. As a result of these conceptual difficulties, disregard of school and family rules occurs.

Disturbances in abstract thinking were also found by Bender (7) and Goldfarb (41) in school-aged children and in adolescents with an institutional background. Goldfarb (45) describes as characteristic of these children "an unusually defective level of conceptualization . . . manifested in difficulty in organizing a variety of stimuli meaningfully and in abstracting relationships" (p. 251). On the Rorschach test, adolescents with an institutional background showed "an unusual adherence to a concrete attitude and inadequate conceptualization" (40, p. 222).

Motor Functions. Motor development seems to be less significantly affected than any other aspect of development, although there are markedly discrepant reports. DuPan and Roth (27) and Fischer (31) conclude that there is no significant retardation in motor development during the first year among institutionalized children, Freud and Burlingham (33) report accelerated development during the early part of the second year, while Spitz (86) notes marked retardation in motor functions during the first and second years. Differing opportunities for the exercise of developing motor functions in different institutional settings may be involved (85).

Both extremes in *activity level* are found in institutionalized infants. Hyperactivity is sometimes noted (30) but more common is a lowered activity level, associated with the general passivity noted as part of the pattern of intellectual retardation. There are only vague indications in the data of some factors which may account for these different findings: constitutional differences among infants, the age or developmental level at the time of institutionalization, and the length of institutionalization. For instance, in the initial stages of institutionalization, hyperactivity is often found, with lowered activity level more common after prolonged institutional residence.

Motor disturbances in the form of bizarre stereotyped motor patterns suggestive of neurological damage have been reported by Spitz (86) in infants after a long period of institutional residence; similar but less extreme motor disturbances were noted by Fischer (30, 31). In older children, Bender (7) and Goldfarb (40, 45, 46) found hyperkinetic behavior, a pattern considered part of a syndrome of impulsivity, with psychogenic rather than neurogenic bases.

The findings on deviant motor pat-

TABLE 2

RESEARCH ON INSTITUTIONALIZATION: RETROSPECTIVE STUDIES

Investigator	Subjects	Age at Time of Study	Age When Institutionalized	Duration of Institutionalization	Techniques or Type of Data	Data on Early Experiences	Contaminating Conditions
Bender (1947)	5000 clinic cases	Preadolescence	Birth to middle childhood	Range; not specified	Case history Psychiatric diagnosis	General retrospective	Repeated separations Rejection
Bender & Yarnell (1941)	250 clinic cases	1–6 years	Birth to 6 years	Range; not specified	Intelligence tests Psychiatric diagnosis Case history	General retrospective	
Beres & Obers (1950)	37 clinic cases with institutional background	Adolescence and adulthood	Birth to 12 months	Varying periods up to 4 years Average: 3 years	Case history Psychiatric diagnosis Intelligence test	Detailed case history	Separation and rejection
Bodman et al. (1950)	51 cases with institutional background 52 controls	Early adolescence	16 cases under 2 years Average: 4.4 years	Range from 3 to 15 years Average: 9.6 years	Vineland Social Maturity Scale Case history	General data on variety of institutions	High incidence of mentally defective or disturbed parents Several changes in institutions
Goldfarb (1943b)	20 children with institutional background 20 foster home controls	6–10 years Follow-up	1 to 24 months	3 years	Baruch Preschool Checklist Newell Problem Checklist	General retrospective data	Repeated separations from foster mothers
Goldfarb (1945b)	15 children with institutional background 15 foster home controls	Mean: 12 years	Early infancy	2½ to 3 years	Intelligence tests Concept formation tests—Weigl, Goldstein-Scheerer Clinical assessment of personal-social functioning	Some retrospective data	Repeated separations from foster mothers

Goldfarb (1944)	40 children with institutional background 40 foster home controls	Early infancy	Mean: 7½ years Follow-up	Analysis of problems and reasons for re-placement	Some retrospective data	Repeated separations from foster mothers Maternal rejection
Goldfarb (1947)	15 well-adjusted and 15 poorly adjusted children with institutional background	Poorly adjusted mean: 5.8 months Well-adjusted mean: 10.9 months	Mean: 14½ years	Poorly adjusted: 34 months Well-adjusted: 25 months	Caseworker's ratings on adjustment	Detailed retrospective data	Repeated separations
Goldfarb (1949)	15 institutional 15 schizophrenic 15 foster home	Early infancy mean: 4½ months	Mean: 12 years	Group average: 39 months	Rorschach test Intelligence test	No data	Not reported
Haggerty (1959)	100 social agency cases with institutional background	"First few years of life"	Mean age: 12.7 years	Average: 3½ years	Analysis of language samples	No data	Separation
Lowrey (1940)	28 psychiatric clinic cases with institutional background	Range from 2 weeks to 34 months	Range from 3 to 6 years	Range from 6 to 42 months	Case history Intelligence tests	Variable retrospective history	Repeated separations

terns and the data on defects in conceptual thinking suggest the possibility of central nervous system damage as a result of institutionalization. The evidence is not very strong, however, nor are there clear bases in these data for hypothesizing the conditions under which irreversible neurological damage might occur.

Social and Personality Disturbances. Although the institutional syndrome has most frequently been described in terms of social and personality disturbances, in many respects the data are less clear than are the findings on intellectual development. Personality data are based primarily on clinical impressions, and the characteristics described are usually at the extreme end of the scale, reflecting exaggerated pathology or a complete lack of capacity, rather than a relative deficiency.

Interpersonal Relationships. The major deviations reported in the literature are in the area of interpersonal relationship. Two overtly dissimilar, but dynamically related, types of interpersonal disturbance have been described: social apathy manifested by indifference to social attachments, and "affect hunger" characterized by incessant and insatiable seeking of affection. Several retrospective studies report a syndrome in older children and adolescents described as an inability to establish close, warm personal relationships (7, 8, 40, 45, 47, 62), a personality pattern labeled the "affectionless character" by Bowlby (12), and one which Bender (7) identifies as a psychopathic behavior disorder.

In the contemporaneous studies of infants in institutions, social apathy is described in terms of several specific response patterns:

1. Inadequate social responsiveness, as evidenced by a complete lack of social initiative, by withdrawn or apathetic response to social approaches (3, 30, 31, 33), or in depressed scores on the social sector of developmental tests (27, 30, 31).

2. An indifference to social attachments, manifested by lack of any significant attachments or meaningful relationships with caretakers in the institution (33, 73).

3. Inadequate social discrimination as evidenced by failure to give differentiated responses to strangers and familiar caretakers (33).

4. A lack of normal social sensitivity, indicated by inability to respond discriminatively to different kinds of emotional expression (33).

The specificity of the relationship between social stimulation and social responsiveness in infancy is pointed up by Rheingold's data (73). Infants in an institution who were given intensive social stimulation by one mother-figure, from the sixth to the eighth month of life, showed significantly greater social responsiveness than control subjects cared for by the more usual institutional routine. General developmental progress was not affected, however, by this special type of stimulation. In a follow-up of these children in adoptive homes at 19 months of age, Rheingold and Bayley (75) found no evidence of any lasting impact of this special experience.

The syndrome of "affect hunger" characterized by indiscriminate and insatiable demands for attention and affection is less common than social apathy. It is reported in several retrospective studies (5, 7, 45, 62), but in only one contemporaneous study (33), in which children in an institution are described as "exacting, demanding, apparently passionate, but always disappointed in new attachments" (p. 58). A similar, but less intense pattern of indiscriminate sociability among 6–8 month old infants was observed by Rheingold (73). Freud and Burlingham also noted in infants an associated pattern of exhibitionism, involving indiscriminate display of themselves before strangers.

Behavioral deviations considered symptomatic of disturbances in ego and superego development have been reported in older children (5, 7, 9, 41, 47, 62). Frequently noted is a pattern of diffuse and impulsive behavior suggesting a lack of normal inhibitory controls. In these children overt, antisocial and aggressive behavior is often found. Bender and Goldfarb both note a lack of normal anxiety or guilt about aggression, a low frustration tolerance, a lack of goal-directedness, and low achievement motivation. Goldfarb (40) summarizes the personality pattern as impoverished, meager, and undifferentiated, deficient in inhibition and control. Even as late as adolescence, the institution children show the simple, unrefined, undifferentiated kind of behavior typical of preschool children.

Beres and Obers (9) is the one psychiatrically oriented study which raises some question as to the extent of personality damage resulting from institutionalization. They note a similar underlying pathology in all cases—a distortion in psychic structure, an immature ego, and deficient superego development —but conclude that by late adolescence about half of their 37 cases were making a favorable overt adjustment. They were

. . . functioning well, whether in work situation or at school . . . and presented no evidence of overt disturbance in their behavior or in their relationships within their families or among friends (p. 128).

This study points up the problem for research of making a valid distinction between mental health and pathology. These conclusions illustrate sharply the conflict between a definition of mental health based on overt behavior and a definition derived from a psychodynamic assessment of strengths and liabilities.

In looking to the direct studies for clues to the antecedents of personality deviations in older children, one is disappointed by the limited data on the personality characteristics of infants in institutions. The meager data on infants suggest some precursors of defective ego and superego development such as failure to show imitative behavior at the appropriate developmental period (31, 33). The conflicting findings on autoerotic activity emphasize the lack of agreement as to what constitutes normal behavior in infancy. Freud and Burlingham (33) as well as Fischer (30, 31) describe a high incidence of thumbsucking, rocking, head-banging in young infants, and masturbation in older children. Spitz and Wolf (91), on the other hand, found "practically no autoerotic activities" among the infants in the foundling home. They hypothesize that an emotional relationship between the child and a mother-figure is a prerequisite for the appearance of autoerotic activities.

Few direct studies give information on the age at which personality disturbances first become evident. In most of this research, the youngest children are over six months at the time of study. Where younger children have been studied, frequently no data are given on social or personality characteristics. Only two studies offer data on the age at which personality disturbances are first noted. Freud and Burlingham (33) note that infants in their institution did not show signs of social retardation before five months. Gesell and Amatruda (36) report first signs of "social ineptness" evident at 24 weeks.

The one experimental study on human infants (23) is often cited as evidence that early sensory and social deprivation need have no impact on development. Dennis found no significant retardation in a pair of twins who were given "minimum" social and sensory stimulation during the first seven months of life. Stone (94) on the basis of a careful analysis of a later report (24) suggests that minimum stimulation probably represented minimal adequate stimulation, much more than that provided in many institutional environments. In

Dennis' study the infants were handled for the normal routines, and there was a consistent mother person. The fact that these conditions did not continue much beyond the first half year may also be significant.

Many ad hoc theories have been offered to account for the intellectual and language retardation, the specific defects in abstract thinking, and the varied social and personality disturbances associated with institutionalization. The explanations which offer "maternal deprivation" as the basic etiological entity tend, on the whole, to be vague and generalized, and offer little basis for systematic research. With regard to abstract thought, Bender (6) states:

The earliest identification with the mother and her continuous affectional care is necessary during the period of habit training and the rapid development of language and the formation of concepts within the family unit. Otherwise the higher semantic and social development and the expansion of the educational capacities does not take place (p. 76).

Regarding time concepts, she speculates, "It appears that we develop a concept of time in the passage of time in our early love relationships with our mother" (p. 96). Kardiner (56) suggests that the sense of time develops in relation to the child's activities in looking forward to gratification. Goldfarb (48) hypothesizes that lack of an adult identification model (in institutions) inhibits the development of functions such as language, which are dependent on social forms of imitation and communication. Impairment in abstract thinking is interpreted (48) in terms of Stern's theory (93) which postulates that the development of conceptual thinking is dependent on the growth of a sense of continuity of the self. According to Stern, the grasp of identity, as well as judgments of equality, similarity, and difference are all derived from the sense of continuity of self. At first these judgments are related to concrete

personal events; eventually, they are separated from them and become abstract. Without continuity of mothering in an institution, Goldfarb contends the normal development of the self-concept is impaired, with resulting defects in abstract thought processes. Social and personality disturbances are linked directly to lack of opportunity for close human relationships in infancy in institutional environments. Goldfarb attributes defective ego and superego development to inadequate opportunity for the child to identify with parental figures and to internalize the parental image. Bender (6) describes the etiology of personality disturbances in similar terms:

There is a primary defect in ability to identify in their relationships with other people . . . due to the fact that they never experienced a continuous identification during the infantile period from the early weeks through the period when language and social concepts of right and wrong are normally built up and when psychosexual and personality development are proceeding (p. 76).

She hypothesizes that anxiety and guilt arise in reaction to "threats to object relationship or identification processes" (p. 76). Lack of anxiety and inability to feel guilt are related to the lack of capacity to identify or form object relationships.

Analysis of environmental variables in the research literature points to some more discrete factors than maternal deprivation in the institutional setting. This elusive variable, maternal deprivation, can be analyzed in terms of variables more amenable to research, e.g., amount and quality of tactile, auditory, or visual stimulation; reinforcement schedules; etc. Harlow's (50) research on infant primates has demonstrated the efficacy for research of analyzing mothering in terms of simple stimulus conditions, such as contact stimulation. The discrepancies in the findings of the research on institutionalization suggest the need to consider interacting variables, such as constitutional differences in vulnerability, varying sensitivities at different developmental stages, etc., in formulating hypotheses for more critical research testing.

Maternal Separation

Maternal separation has never been studied under pure conditions. Most often separation has been associated with other traumatic events such as illness and hospitalization or operative procedures, and often with parental rejection or death or disability of a parent. Frequently separation from the parents has been followed by institutional placement with the result that the impact of institutional influences is superimposed on the loss of parental figures. In the literature on separation, the role of such contaminating variables has not been distinguished from the effects of a break in continuity of relationship with the mother. Spitz and Wolf's (91) is the only study in which the physical environment remained unchanged following separation; it is one of the few studies in which the quality of the mother-child relationship prior to separation had been studied.

Most of the research is contemporaneous, reporting on the reactions of children at the time of separation. The long-term effects are almost unknown. Follow-up data more than a year later are given in a few studies (18, 61, 88, 89, 91), but in these studies there are many contaminating conditions, e.g., severely disturbed parental relationships, repeated separations, intermittent institutionalization.

IMMEDIATE REACTIONS TO
SEPARATION

Despite the many different conditions associated with the separation experience, there is some degree of consistency in the findings reported on immediate and short-term reactions of infants and preschool children to separation. In each of the studies some children develop apparently severe reactions, and the behavior sequences in these extreme cases appear to be dynamically similar (15, 78, 80, 91). The characteristic sequence of responses begins with active protest and violent emotional reactions, such as intense and prolonged crying and active reaching out to people, in apparent attempts to bring back the mother or to find a substitute. In time this behavior is followed by active rejection of adults, and finally by apathy and withdrawal of interest in people, accompanied by a decrease in general activity level. Robertson and Bowlby characterize this latter phase as "mourning"; Spitz and Wolf label it "anaclitic depression." Feeding disturbances—refusal of food, sometimes pathological appetite—and regression in motor and other functions are also reported. When the mother is not restored, Spitz found symptoms of progressive deterioration in infants, a complete withdrawal from social interaction, a sharp drop in developmental level on infant tests, and extreme physical debilitation, with loss of weight and increased susceptibility to infections. In older children (over 12 months) marked physical and intellectual deterioration have not been reported, but severe disturbances in interpersonal relationships have been noted (15, 72). The "mourning phase" in infants and young children is followed by behavior described as a "denial of the need for his own mother," which Robertson and Bowlby interpret as an indication of a repression of the mother image. The child shows no apparent recognition of his own mother, but may transfer his attachment to a substitute mother. (There has been some controversy as to whether such behavior can be interpreted as evidence of repression or whether it should be considered more simply as a denial mechanism—14, 54.) If no substitute mother is available, the child may

TABLE 3

RESEARCH ON MATERNAL SEPARATION

Investigator	Subjects	Age at Time of Study	Age at Time of Experience	Techniques or Types of Data	Data on Early Experiences	Contaminating Conditions
Ainsworth & Boston (1952)	One case	Observation: 3 years Follow-up tests: 5 to 6½ years	13 months	Rorschach CAT Stanford-Binet Weigl-Goldstein Sorting Test Goldstein-Scheerer Cube Test	Retrospective report	Hospitalization for tuberculosis
Berg & Cohen (1959)	40 schizophrenic women in mental hospital 40 neurotic women	20–40 years	Birth to adulthood	Case history	Limited retrospective data	Rejection
Bowlby (1944)	44 juvenile thieves	5.7 to 17 years	Birth to adolescence	Case history Psychiatric diagnosis	Variable retrospective data	Institutionalization Rejection
Bowlby (1953b)	49 children in residential nurseries or hospitals	12–48 months	12–24 months	Clinical observation	Direct observation	Institutionalization Rejection Hospitalization for illness
Bowlby, Ainsworth, Boston, & Rosenbluth (1956)	60 children with previous sanitarium experience 57 controls	6–14 years	Range: Birth to 4 years	Intelligence test Clinical evaluation by teacher, psychologist, psychiatrist, social worker	General retrospective data	Rejection Hospitalization for tuberculosis
Edelston (1943)	42 children hospitalized for illness	2½–15 years	Range from early infancy	Clinical observation	Limited retrospective data	Illness Rejection
Heinicke (1956)	Children in residential and day nurseries	15–31 months	12–30 months	Standardized observation and doll play	Direct observation	None reported
Lewis (1954)	500 children in reception center	Under 5 to over 15 years	Birth to adolescence	Clinical assessment	Variable retrospective data	Institutionalization Rejection
Robertson & Bowlby (1952)	Unspecified number of children in hospitals	18–24 months	18–24 months	Clinical observation	Direct observation	Hospitalization
Roundinesco, David, & Nicolas (1952)	20 children placed in institution	12–17 months	12–17 months	Clinical observation	Direct observation	Institutionalization
Schaffer (1958)	76 infants in hospital for illness	3–51 weeks	3–51 weeks	Cattell Infant Test Standardized observation Home follow-up	Direct observation	Illness Hospitalization
Spitz & Wolf (1946)	123 children in a nursery	14 days to 18 months	5–7 months	Clinical observation	Direct observation	None reported

show promiscuously friendly behavior, using adults in an instrumental way, but without establishing meaningful attachments. Such behavior Bowlby considers indicative of a repression of all need for mothering, the prelude to a psychopathic character development. If, however, the child is reunited with his mother before the need for mothering is completely repressed (after some unstated critical time interval) the behavior pattern is believed to be reversible. The child is able on return to his mother to reestablish a relationship with her, although there may be several months of difficult adjustment, with irritability, impulsive expression of feelings, and an exaggeratedly intense attachment.

These descriptions of the reactions of young children to conditions involving loss of a mother-figure have provided the basis for most of the generalizations about the severe effects of maternal separation. The dramatic character of these changes has overshadowed the significant fact that a substantial portion of the children in each study did not show severe reactions to separation. In Spitz's study of 123 infants separated from their mothers between 6 and 8 months of age, severe reactions occurred in only 19 cases. Although in Robertson and Bowlby's (78) research on 45 children ranging in age from 4 months to 4 years, all but three are reported to have shown some reaction; the intensity and duration of the reactions are not clearly specified. Less than half, 20 cases, are reported as showing "acute fretting," a behavior pattern which is not well-defined. The reported duration of the reaction varied from 1 to 17 days. There are no data on the number of children who showed prolonged reactions.

In a careful study of the reactions to hospitalization of 76 infants under 1 year of age (ranging from 3 to 51 weeks) Schaffer (81) found that reactions varied with age. Infants over seven months of age showed overt social and emotional

reactions, such as excessive crying, fear of strangers, clinging and overdependence on the mother. Infants under seven months evidenced more global disturbances, i.e., somatic upsets, blank facial expression, extreme preoccupation with the environment. Schaffer relates the global disturbances to sensory deprivation, whereas the social disturbance at the later age, an age at which more differentiated relationship with the mother exists, are interpreted as reactions to separation from the mother.

Heinicke's research (54) points to less severe effects of simpler, less-complicated separation situations. He found no extreme behavioral disturbances in two groups of children, 15 to 30 months of age, with different separation experiences, one group in a residential nursery, the other in a day nursery. The children in the residential nursery did show more overt and more intense aggression, greater frequency of autoerotic activities, and more frequent lapses in sphincter control. These findings are interpreted as indicating an imbalance between the child's impulses and his power to control and organize these impulses in relation to the external world.

LONG-TERM EFFECTS OF SEPARATION

Conclusions about the long-term effects of separation are very tenuous. They are based on a few studies in which the information about the early history is not well-documented.

In an earlier study of 44 juvenile thieves, Bowlby (12) concluded that separation experiences in childhood resulted in a character disorder distinguished by a "lack of affection or feeling for anyone." The conclusions are based on clinical findings that 12 out of 14 cases diagnosed as "affectionless characters" had been separated from their mothers in infancy or early childhood. Some of these children had been hospitalized for illness without any contact with their mothers

TABLE 4
RESEARCH ON MULTIPLE MOTHERING

Investigators	Subjects	Age at Time of Experience	Techniques	Age at Study	Data on Early Experiences
Rabin (1957)	38 children from kibbutz and 34 controls from neighboring villages	Birth to time of study	Rorschach	9-11 years	General description of environment
Rabin (1958a)	24 infants and 40 children in kibbutz; 20 control infants and 40 control children	Birth to time of study	Rorschach, Vineland Social Maturity, Goodenough Draw-A-Man, Griffiths Infant Scale	9-17 months; 9-11 years	General description of environment

mothers, and some had been institutionalized for long periods during infancy.

In a follow-up study of 60 children between 6 and 13 years of age, who had been in a sanitarium for tuberculosis for varying periods of time before their fourth birthday, Bowlby et al. (18) found less serious long-term effects than in the earlier studies. No statistically significant difference in intelligence was found between the control and the sanitarium group. In personality characteristics, the sanitarium children were judged as showing tendencies towards withdrawal and apathy, as well as greater aggressiveness. On the basis of the psychiatric social worker's interview with the parents, 63 per cent of the children were rated as maladjusted, 13 per cent were considered well-adjusted, and 21 per cent adjusted but with minor problems. Bowlby et al. conclude that "outcome is immensely varied, and of those who are damaged, only a small minority develop those very serious disabilities of personality which first drew attention to the pathogenic nature of the experience" (p. 240). They suggest that the potentially damaging effects of separation should not be minimized, but concede that "some of the workers who first drew attention to the dangers of maternal deprivation resulting from separation have tended on occasion to overstate their case" (p. 242).

The findings of Lewis (61) are sometimes cited as evidence that early separation need not necessarily have lasting harmful effects. Among a group of 500 children who were studied in a reception center shortly after being separated from their parents, only 19 showed "morbid lack of affective responsiveness" (p. 41). Follow-up data were obtained on 240 of these children, 2 to 3.5 years later. Only 100 had a personal follow-up by a psychiatric social worker and a psychiatrist; information on the others was obtained through letters from social workers who had some contact with the children. Of

over a long period of time, others had experienced frequent changes in foster the 100 more intensively studied children, only 3 were diagnosed as having marked personality disorders, 22 were having some difficulties in relationships, and 36 were showing mild neurotic symptoms or mild delinquent behavior. With reference to the timing of separation, Lewis concludes that "separation from the mother before the age of five years was a prognostically adverse feature" (p. 122). Apparently this is a clinically based conclusion, since the data presented in the tables show no significant differences between the children separated before five years of age and those separated after five.

Data from several studies indicate that the impact of separation is modified by the character of the mother-child relationship preceding the separation experience and the adequacy of the substitute mothering following separation. Spitz and Wolf (91) noted that the infants who did not develop severe depressive reactions were those separated from "poor mothers," and conclude that the better the mother-child relationship preceding separation, the more severe the immediate reactions. Lewis (61), on the other hand, found a higher proportion of children who had been separated from normally affectionate mothers in "good" or "fair" condition than those who had not received "adequate" affection. It might be hypothesized that a close relationship with a mother-figure preceding separation will be followed by more severe immediate reaction but will be ultimately more favorable than a poor antecedent relationship. Children who have experienced a close relationship in infancy may be better prepared to form new attachments in later life than children without any experience of close relationships.

The amount, the quality, and the consistency of substitute mothering will presumably influence the intensity of immediate reactions as well as the long-term personality consequences. Spitz and Wolf (91) concluded that infants who were provided with a satisfactory substitute mother did not develop the depressive syndrome. (There were no independent criteria of the adequacy of substitute mothering. The substitute relationship was considered satisfactory in those cases which did not develop depressive symptoms.) Robertson and Bowlby (78) also note that where an adequate substitute mother was provided, there was not a complete withdrawal from social contact.

Multiple Mothering

Serious personality difficulties in later life have been postulated as a consequence of multiple mothering in infancy and early childhood. There has been little research, and in most of the clinical observations multiple mothering has been associated with impersonal or rejecting maternal care. The underlying assumption in much of the literature is that inadequate maternal care is a necessary concomitant of situations in which there is more than one mother-figure. Multiple mothering has never been very precisely defined. In its most general sense, it refers to an environmental setting in which a number of different persons perform the maternal functions for the child, with varying degrees of adequacy and with varying degrees of consistency. From the child's viewpoint, it may mean that there is no single person to whom he can relate as a major source of gratification and on whom his dependency needs can be focused. In some situations the biological mother may share the mothering functions with other chosen women; in other circumstances no biological tie exists between the child and the several mothers. Some current studies in home management houses, a few reports on the Israeli kibbutzim, and a very few anthropological reports provide all the available data on the effects of multiple mothering.

In the anthropological accounts of multiple mothering in different cultural contexts (26, 29, 63, 79) there are variations in the number of people who share mothering functions as well as variations in the role of the natural mother. In cultures in which the extended family is the traditional pattern, the mothering functions may be shared by the mother, grandmother, aunts, and other female relatives of the child; in some groups, male relatives may take over some maternal functions. The biological mother may be clearly identified as the central, most significant person in some cultures; in others she may be assigned a very secondary role.

In Western cultures, grandmothers frequently assume some of the mothering functions, and in some social groups, child nurses play an important role. In the pre-Civil War Southern plantation class group, many mothering functions were taken over by the Negro nurse. The line of demarcation between supplemental maternal care and multiple mothering has never been very clear.

In none of these situations are disturbances in infant functioning associated with multiple mothering practices, nor are later personality characteristics or deviations attributed to this aspect of early maternal care.

The Israeli kibbutzim provide an unique set of conditions of multiple mothering. In this setting, there are two mother-figures, the natural mother and the metapelet, the children's caretaker, each of whom has very distinctive functions. The major share of the daily routine care as well as major training functions, such as toileting and impulse control, are assumed by the caretaker in the communal nurseries. The mother's contacts with the child tend to be limited to scheduled periods during the day, which are free periods and do not involve traditional family routines. The mother seems to function solely as an agent to provide affectional gratification, although obviously the extent of the mother's influence, as well as the specific areas of influence on the child's development, will vary with her concept of her role and with her personality characteristics.

There are several impressionistic reports (39, 55, 71) and a few systematic studies (68, 69) of the development of infants and children in the Israeli kibbutzim. Rabin (69), using the Griffiths Infant Developmental Scale, found slight developmental retardation in infants between 9 and 17 months of age living in a communal nursery. In only one sector of development—the personal-social area —were these infants significantly retarded. Rabin attributes this retardation to less individual stimulation in the kibbutzim as compared to a normal home environment. This study represents the only reported research in a setting in which there may be deprivation in the amount of stimulation without concomitant lack of affectional interchange with the mother.

In an attempt to assess the long-term effects of living under these special conditions of maternal care in the kibbutz, Rabin (69) studied a group of children, between 9 and 11 years of age, who had lived in this environment from infancy. He found no evidences of retardation (using the Goodenough Draw-A-Man Test), nor were there any indications of personality distortions. On the contrary, Rorschach data are interpreted as indicating that the children from the communal settlements showed "better emotional control and greater overall maturity." In ego-strength (using Beck's index) they were judged superior to the control group of children living with their parents. Rabin interprets these findings as evidence of the important role of later experiences in personality development.

In another study, Rabin (70) compared the psychosexual development of 10-year-old kibbutzim reared boys with boys from patriarchal type families. Using the Blacky test, he found significant differences, consistent with theoretical expectations. The kibbutz boys showed less "oedipal intensity," more diffuse positive identification with their fathers, and less intense sibling rivalry. This study also points up the fact that multiple mothering is only one of the significant factors which differentiate the kibbutz from the "normal" family setting. As in the case with other conditions associated with maternal deprivation the kibbutz is atypical in regard to the absence of the father.

Home management houses provide a setting in which multiple mothering occurs without associated deprivation of social stimulation. These houses are set up in university home economics departments to provide practical experience in child care for the students. The infant is separated from his foster mother or removed from a familiar institutional environment and placed in the home management house for a period of several weeks to several months. He is cared for by a number of young women, each of whom assumes primary responsibility for mothering activities for a limited period of time, usually about one week. There is one continuous figure—the instructor in the house—with whom the infant can maintain a relationship; she assumes some of the ordinary child care functions. In the course of his residence in the home management house, the infant may have 15 to 20 different "mothers." In this setting he receives much attention and stimulation from many different "mother-figures." Following his residence in the home management house, the infant is usually placed in a foster or adoptive home. The follow-up studies and the several direct studies of children in home management houses (34, 35) are in agreement in finding no evidence of intellectual retardation and no gross personality disturbances. The long-term effects have not yet been evaluated.

These three settings—the home man-

agement house, the kibbutz, and the extended family—are comparable in only one respect; the mothering functions are distributed among several different persons. They differ in regard to the continuity of the mother-figure, in the role played by the substitute mothers, and in the amount of social stimulation given to the infant. In some situations, because of the high adult-child ratio, it is likely that the infant will receive more sensory as well as more social stimulation than the child in an average family home. For infants, the kibbutz may be similar to an institutional setting in terms of the amount of individual social stimulation provided. It is clear that none of these conditions necessarily involves severe deprivation of mothering, but the mothering experience of children in these settings may differ significantly from that of children in homes with one mother-figure.

None of these studies provides a crucial test of the prevalent hypothesis that multiple mothering results in a diffusion of the mother-image. This theory, developed in the context of institutional care, holds that the child who is cared for by a number of different persons cannot develop a focused image of one significant mother-person in infancy, and consequently, will have difficulties in relationships in later life. On the whole, the few relevant pieces of research suggest that multiple mothering per se is not necessarily damaging to the child.

Distortions in the Mother-Child Relationship

Although distortions in the mother-child relationship have frequently been included in the concept of maternal deprivation, in this report we shall not attempt any comprehensive review of this vast clinical literature. Institutionalization, separation, and multiple mothering represent deviations from a cultural norm of "mothering" primarily on the dimension of amount or consistency of contact with the mother. Under the category of distortions in the mother-child relationship are subsumed all the deviations in maternal relationships which usually have as their antecedents disturbances in the character or personality of the mother. These disturbances in maternal relationships are manifested in overtly or covertly hostile or rejecting behavior, sometimes more subtly in overprotective behavior, and often in unpredictable swings from affection to rejection or in ambivalent behavior. As distinguished from a lack of social stimulation, a lack of responsiveness, and the lack of a mother-figure, this type of deviation in maternal care tends to be characterized by either very strong emotional stimulation, or by stimulation with a preponderance of negative affect. In contrast to institutional care, there may even be very intense intellectual stimulation.

The literature on distorted maternal relationships suggests a somewhat different kind of personality outcome from the psychopathic or affectionless character. The personality distortions tend to be in the schizophrenic, depressive, and neurotic categories. Again there may be rather specific antecedent conditions and organismic vulnerabilities associated with these types of personality deviations (87). A critical review pointed towards a clarification of the variables and an analysis of the many ad hoc theories concerning distorted mother-child relationships is very much needed.

Some Theoretical Issues and Research Implications

The data from the research on institutionalization, maternal separation, and multiple mothering have relevance for a number of fundamental issues in developmental theory: questions concerning the kinds of environmental conditions which facilitate, inhibit, or distort normal developmental progress; the conditions which influence the reversibility of effects of events in infancy and early childhood; and the extent to which the timing of an experience, i.e., the developmental stage at which it occurs, determines its specific impact.

In theories of the effects of early infantile experiences on later development, two concepts have been prominent: deprivation and stress. Although all the intricacies of the mother-child relationship cannot be conceptualized adequately in terms of these concepts, some of the environmental conditions and events found in the research on maternal deprivation can be ordered meaningfully in these terms. Deprivation is a key concept in the analysis of institutional environments. Many of the circumstances associated with maternal separation and multiple mothering can be ordered in terms of the concept of stress.

DEPRIVATION

In institutional settings several types of deprivation, each with potentially different developmental implications, can be distinguished: sensory deprivation, social deprivation, and emotional deprivation. In many settings all three types of deprivation occur and are complexly interrelated, but they do not necessarily vary concomitantly, and they can be independently manipulated in research.

The studies on sensory deprivation in animals indicate that complete restriction of perceptual experience in early life results in permanent impairment in the functions in which deprivation occurs. In the most extreme institutional environments the degree of sensory deprivation is less severe than in the animal studies. Nevertheless, developmental retardation is found, with the extent of retardation corresponding to the degree of sensory deprivation.

Social deprivation probably acts in a similar way as deprivation of sensory stimulation, leading to disturbances in social functioning, such as, social apathy and social hyperresponsiveness. The simplest hypothesis relates social apathy to inadequate social stimulation during a developmental period which is critical for the acquisition of socal responsiveness. If social deprivation occurs after appropriate social responses have been learned, affect hunger or intensified seeking of social response may occur. Although social deprivation is less amenable to experimental manipulation than is sensory deprivation, in natural situations, some simple indices can be used, such as the number of persons with whom the infant has contact during a 24-hour period, the amount of time during which he receives stimulation.

Emotional deprivation has been used popularly and in clinical writings as a catchall term to include deprivation of social, sensory, and affectional stimulation. For research, a more precise usage in terms of deprivation of affective stimulation may be useful. The term, emotional deprivation, can be restricted to characterize an environment with neutral feeling tone or without variation in feeling tone, an environment similar in some respects to the monotonous, bland environment described under sensory deprivation. Emotional apathy, withdrawn behavior, lack of differentiation of affect, and insensitivity to feelings or emotional nuances in others are characteristics which might be related to early emotional deprivation. Within this concept of emotional deprivation, simple objective measures are also possible, e.g., ratings of intensity of positive or negative affect, amount of time during a 24-hour period in which different types and intensities of affective stimulation are provided.

In addition to independent manipulation of each of these types of stimulation —sensory, social, and emotional—in more focused research there might be systematic variation in several dimensions of stimulation: quality of stimulation, e.g., monotonous, varied; intensity; frequency; regularity; cumulative duration of deprivation; sensory modalities in which deprivation occurs.

STRESS CONSEQUENT TO CHANGE

Critical research on maternal separation requires a distinction between the event of separation and later conditions often associated with separation which may be similar to those described under deprivation. The event of separation is associated with significant changes in the physical, and social environments, changes which may be stressful for the young child. In the physical environment, the changes involve the disappearance of familiar objects, sounds, smells, and tactile stimuli; in the social environment, there may be changes in the amount and quality of social stimulation. The new environment may provide more tactile stimulation and less verbal stimulation. There may be modifications in the speed as well as kind of response to the child, e.g., the new caretaker may ignore the child's crying, or she may reward it by tactile stimulation rather than by oral gratification. For the infant or young child, these changes result in a loss of environmental predictability. The degree of stress experienced is likely to vary with the degree of unpredictability.

Change and novelty as stress-inducing agents can be studied through research designs providing for careful measurement or systematic variation in the physical and human environments, i.e., the degree of carryover of familiar objects from the old to the new environment, the degree of similarity between the old and new caretakers in physical and psychological characteristics, variations among the old and new mothers in the modalities in which stimulation is given. The impact of change in the physical environment might be evaluated by holding constant the human environment while systematically varying the physical environment, and conversely, the human environment might be varied, with the physical environment constant. The amount of change necessary to produce a discriminable difference to the child may vary with developmental factors. The significance of a change in the human environment will almost certainly depend on whether a meaningful relationship has developed with the mother-figure. If separation occurs after this point, the stress of change is reinforced by the loss of a significant person.

In the research on multiple mothering the one consistent characteristic of the varied contexts of multiple mothering is environmental unpredictability associated with changing agents of gratification. Unpredictability may be based on differences in technique among the different mother-figures, on variations in speed of response to the child's expression of needs, on inconsistency in the kinds of behavior which are rewarded, punished, or ignored. Unlike separation conditions in which new predictable patterns may soon be established, in multiple mothering unpredictability remains the most characteristic aspect of the environment.

There is not strong research evidence nor very firm theoretical grounds to support the assumption that the presence of several concurrent mother-figures in early life results in a diffusion of the mother-image and later inability to establish meaningful relationships. The variable conditions of reinforcement which characterize some multiple mothering situations provide a special kind of learning situation which may lead to the development of atypical patterns of relationships, but not necessarily shallow ones. It is likely that the presence of several mother-figures will vary in significance at different developmental periods. The lack of a consistent role model is probably

more serious during the early preschool period than in early infancy. In further research, attempts should be made to vary systematically the degree of stress associated with environmental unpredictability, while controlling other variables such as degree of role differentiation among the multiple mothers.

Although deprivation and trauma can be treated as independent concepts, there are conditions under which deprivation can be considered a traumatic stimulus. It is recognized that trauma may result from excessive stimulation, but the conditions under which inadequate stimulation may be traumatic are more obscure. Recent research indicates that extreme sensory deprivation may be stressful for adults (98). We might assume that deprivation becomes a traumatic stimulus after the appropriate motivational conditions have developed. Thus Hebb (53) suggests:

The observed results seem to mean, not that the stimulus of another attentive organism (the mother) is necessary from the first, but that it may become necessary only as psychological dependence on the mother develops (p. 828).

RESEARCH IMPLICATIONS

Analysis of the research on institutionalization, separation, and multiple mothering highlights some theoretically significant questions and points to some specific variables which can be experimentally manipulated or controlled through the opportunistic utilization of natural situations.

Duration of Deprivation or Stress. In much of the research, the subjects have experienced a cumulative series of deprivations or stressful experiences, beginning in infancy and continuing through childhood. Few studies give specific data on the length of time the child has been exposed to these conditions. Goldfarb (45, 46, 48), Bender (5, 7), and Bowlby (2) conclude from retrospective studies that the longer the period of institutional care, the more severe the ultimate damage. These conclusions are based largely on individual case findings. Those cases which did not show the same irreversible patterns as the rest of the population had been in institutions for a shorter period of time. Spitz and Wolf (91) suggest that there may be a critical time interval after which the effects of maternal separation are irreversible. If the infant is reunited with his mother within three months, the process of physical, social, and intellectual deterioration may be arrested, but if the mother-child relationship is not restored within five months, irreparable damage occurs. There are no comparable data on children beyond infancy. One might hypothesize that the critical time interval might be longer with older children.

Research on older children attest to the damaging effects of repeated separations (12, 61). On the whole, no distinction has been made among several different separation experiences: a single instance of separation with reunion, a single separation without reunion, repeated small doses of separation with consistent reunion with the same mother, and cumulative separations with repeated changes in mothers. It can be assumed that each of these experiences provides different learning conditions for the development of meaningful relationships. The most extreme outcome, the "affectionless character," may be the result of the most extreme conditions, i.e., repeated traumatic separations.

Time or Developmental Stage at which Deprivation or Stress Occurs. Psychoanalytic theories regarding the significance of early experience for later development have often been interpreted as postulating that the younger the organism, the more severe and fixed the effects of an environmental impact. Only limited data are available on human subjects. Ribble (77) tends to interpret her data on maternal rejection as support-

ing this point of view. Bender's and Goldfarb's (7) retrospective studies suggest that the younger the child, the more damaging the effects of deprivation and stress. Some animal research supports this hypothesis; other studies do not (4, 57).

The findings on institutionalized infants that intellectual retardation is not apparent before 3 months of age and that personality disturbances are not evident before 5 or 6 months suggest that this type of deprivation has no significant impact in the early weeks of infancy. (Because of the known unreliability of infant tests, and the lack of sensitive measures of personality and intellectual functions in early infancy, some degree of caution is necessary in interpreting these findings.)

A more refined hypothesis regarding the significance of the timing of experiences is the critical phase hypothesis which holds that there are points in the developmental cycle during which the organism may be particularly sensitive to certain kinds of events or most vulnerable to specific types of deprivation or stress. Several animal studies (64, 82, 95) support the general outlines of the critical phase hypothesis. From the assorted data on the intellectual functioning of institutionalized children a testable hypothesis emerges regarding a critical period for institutional deprivation: vulnerability to intellectual damage is greatest during the 3 to 12 month period. Beres and Obers (9) suggest that institutional deprivation will differ in its impact at different developmental periods. The data on which this conclusion is based are limited. Of their four cases showing mental retardation, all were admitted to the institution under six months of age; the four cases developing schizophrenia entered the institution at a later age (specific age not reported).

Although the general consensus in the literature is that maternal separation which occurs before the child is five years of age is likely to be most damaging, the findings are not sufficiently clear to pinpoint any one age as being most vulnerable. Bowlby (12) notes among the affectionless thieves:

. . . in practically all these cases, the separation which appears to have been pathogenic occurred after the age of six months, and in a majority after twelve months. This suggests that there is a lower age limit, before which separations, whilst perhaps having undesirable effects, do not produce the particular results we are concerned with here —the affectionless and delinquent character (p. 41).

On the basis of our knowledge of the developmental characteristics of children, one might postulate differing vulnerabilities at different periods of development. The developmental level of the child is likely to influence the significance of deprivation or the meaning of a separation experience for him. With regard to separation, the period during which the child is in the process of consolidating a relationship with his mother may be an especially vulnerable one. Also significant may be the developmental stage with regard to memory functions. After the point in development at which the child can sustain an image of the mother in her absence and can anticipate her return, the meaning of a brief separation may be less severe than at an earlier developmental period. The degree of autonomy the child has achieved may also affect the extent of trauma experienced. The loss of the mother may represent a greater threat to the completely dependent infant than to the young child who has achieved some locomotion and some manipulatory control over his environment. The advent of language which symbolizes even a greater degree of environmental mastery may mitigate further the severity of trauma.

Similarly, the effects of institutional deprivation may be more severe for the young infant who is completely depend-

ent on outside sources of stimulation than for the older child who is capable of seeking out stimulation. There may also be age linked effects of different types of deprivation. Some animal studies suggest that a minimal level of stimulation may be necessary to produce the biochemical changes necessary for the development of the underlying structures. Deprivation in certain sensory modalities may be more significant at one age than at another. For example, deprivation of tactile stimulation may be most significant during the first weeks of infancy, whereas auditory or visual deprivation may become more significant later. Social deprivation may be most damaging during the earliest period of the development of social responsiveness.

Constitutional Factors. Although the role of constitutional factors in influencing the long-term effects of early trauma has been increasingly stressed, the meager data in support of the significance of constitutional factors have been indirect. Several retrospective studies have found similar deprivation experiences in the history of individuals who in later life made satisfactory life adjustments as in those who made poor adjustments. The different outcomes are accounted for in terms of constitutional factors. In considering the role of constitutional factors a distinction might be made between organismic differences in general vulnerability to deprivation or stress and vulnerabilities in specific sensory modalities. Data from a number of studies attest to individual differences in sensitivities in specific modalities. With regard to research design, it may be important, too, to distinguish between organismic differences which are constitutionally determined and differences in vulnerability which vary with developmental stage. While organismic sensitivities cannot be manipulated experimentally, it may be possible to study constitutional factors by developing research designs in which subjects with known differences in sensitivities are subjected to the same experimental conditions.

The Long-Term Effects: The Issue of Reversibility

It does not seem fruitful to state the question of reversibility in terms of an either-or hypothesis, i.e., whether or not early experiences produce irreversible effects. Rather the question might be: what are the conditions under which an earlier traumatic or depriving experience is likely to produce irreversible effects? The concept of irreversibility implies that an adverse experience results in permanent structural changes in the nervous system such that at some later developmental period a given response sequence is either facilitated or inhibited. A further implication is that subsequent experience plays no role in changing response potentialities or in developing responses which are incompatible with earlier established behavior patterns. Several studies suggest that permanent damage to the central nervous system may result from early sensory deprivation. Increasingly the research points to the resiliency of the organism. Beres and Obers' is one of the few investigations from the psychoanalytic orientation which makes a strong case for the modifiability of the effects of earlier infantile experience. They cite in support a conclusion by Hartmann, Kris, and Lowenstein (51) that

. . . the basic structure of the personality and the basic functional interrelationship of the systems of the ego and superego are fixed to some extent by the age of six, but after this age, the child does not stop growing and developing, and growth and development modify existing structure (p. 34).

Many factors in complex interaction undoubtedly determine the extent to which recovery is possible from early intellectual or personality damage. More pointed research is needed to identify the specific conditions under which irreversible damage to the central nervous system occurs. Also needed are specific research designs on reversibility, designs aimed at reversing intellectual or personality damage.

Toward a Concept of Maternal Deprivation

In focusing on the isolation of simple variables for formulating testable hypotheses on the relationship between early environmental conditions and later development, we have avoided complex concepts centering around the emotional interchange between mother and infant, concepts which have been focal in psychodynamic theories. The mother as a social stimulus provides sensory stimulation to the infant through tactile, visual, and auditory media, i.e., through handling, cuddling, talking and playing with the child, as well as by simply being visually present. The mother also acts as a mediator of environmental stimuli, bringing the infant in contact with the environment and buffering or heightening the intensity of stimuli. The meaning of these mothering activities to the child and the impact of the mother's absence varies with the child's perceptual, cognitive, and motor capacities at different developmental levels. On the simplest level, if the mother is not present, the infant may be deprived of tactile, auditory, and visual stimuli from a social source, as well as of the environmental stimuli which the mother ordinarily makes available to him. At this point, the mother's absence may be experienced by the young infant only as a deprivation of distinctive stimuli offered by a social being. The impact on the infant may be more severe if the mother's absence is accompanied by deviations in need-gratification sequences, such as, failure to have needs anticipated or long delay before gratification is provided, by marked inconsistencies in patterns of gratification, or inadequate gratification. The significance of these kinds of frustration experiences will be modified by the length of time during which they operate, the developmental level of the child, e.g., the degree of autonomy he has achieved.

The usefulness of this reduction of maternal deprivation has been demonstrated in ordering the reported research findings and in suggesting more refined hypotheses for further research. It is likely, however, that not all aspects of the mother-child relationship can be meaningfully reduced to such simple variables. We can only speculate on the process through which the mother comes to acquire special meaning to the child. We assume that the mother-image gradually evolves as a distinctive perceptual entity out of a welter of tactile, visual, auditory, and kinesthetic cues. (There has been some speculation, without definitive data, that in early infancy before these sensory cues are organized into a percept of an object existing outside of himself, the infant may still "recognize" the mother as an assortment of familiar stimuli.) In time through repeated contact these cues become "familiar" or distinctive to the infant, and finally there is a fixation of positive feelings on this perceptual complex. After the point of fixation of positive feelings on the mother, new elements enter into the child's reactions to a loss or a change in mothers. At this point, sensory deprivation and environmental change may be secondary, the loss of a significant person becomes of primary significance. This experience cannot occur until the infant reaches a developmental point at which he is able to conceptualize the existence of an "object" outside of himself. As a matter of conceptual clarity, it might be desirable to limit the concept of maternal deprivation to the conditions associated with the loss of a specific, cathected person, a person who has acquired distinctive signifi-cance for the child, one on whom positive feelings have been fixated.

Conclusions

The wide range of circumstances included under the concept of maternal deprivation stand out when the research is carefully scrutinized. Included are studies of children who have been separated from their parents and placed in institutional settings, other studies deal with children who have been grossly maltreated or rejected by their families, others are concerned with children temporarily separated from their parents because of illness, and in others the maternal functions are assumed by several different persons. These experiences have occurred at different developmental stages in the children's life histories, and there has been considerable variation in the length of exposure to these conditions, and in the circumstances preceding and following the deviating conditions.

It is apparent that the data on maternal deprivation are based on research of varying degrees of methodological rigor. Most of the data consist of descriptive clinical findings arrived at fortuitously rather than through planned research, and frequently the findings are based on retrospective analyses which have been narrowly directed toward verification of clinical hunches.

The areas of knowledge and the areas of uncertainty become more sharply delimited when we break down the complex concept of maternal deprivation into some discrete variables. For instance, in the studies on institutional care in which sensory deprivation emerges as a major variable, we can conclude that severe sensory deprivation before one year of age, if it continues for a sufficiently long period of time, is likely to be associated with severe intellectual damage. Direct observation of children undergoing the experience of maternal separation shows a variety of immediate disturbances in behavior, permitting the simple conclusion that this is a stressful experience for children. There is no clear evidence that multiple mothering, without associated deprivation or stress, results in personality damage.

With regard to the long-term effects of early deprivation or stress associated with institutionalization or maternal separation, no simple conclusions can be drawn. In the retrospective studies, significant interacting variables are usually unknown. Longitudinal studies currently underway may offer data on the reinforcing or attenuating influence of later experiences. We might hope for more pointed longitudinal studies on questions of reversibility, such as, studies of human or animal subjects who have been subjected to experimental deprivation or trauma, or longitudinal studies of special populations chosen because of some known deviation from a cultural norm of mothering, e.g., infants who have experienced separation for adoption (99, 100) and infants in multiple mothering situations (65).

The analysis of the literature points up the need for more definitive research on the role of many "nonmaternal" variables, variables relating to the characteristics of environmental stimulation and variables dealing with organismic sensitivities. After clarification of the influence of such variables, then perhaps systematic research can come to grips with some of the more elusive aspects of the emotional interchange in the intimate dyadic relationship of mother and infant.

References *

1. Ainsworth, Mary D., and Boston, Mary. Psychodiagnostic assessment of a child after prolonged separation in early childhood. *Brit. J. Med. Psychol.*, 25(1952), 169–205.

* Due to space limitations, many relevant references have not been cited. An extensive bibliography of earlier studies can be found in Bowlby (13).

2. ———, and Bowlby, J. Research strategy in the study of mother-child separation. *Courr. Cent. Int. l'Enfance*, 4(1954), 1–47.

3. Bakwin, H. Emotional deprivation in infants. *J. Pediat.*, 35(1949), 512–521.

4. Beach, F. A., and Jaynes, J. Effects of early experience upon the behavior of animals. *Psychol. Bull.*, 51(1954), 239–263.

5. Bender, Lauretta. Infants reared in institutions: Permanently handicapped. *Bull. Child Welf. League Amer.*, 24(1945), 1–4.

6. ———. There's no substitute for family life. *Child Stud.*, 23(1946), 74–76, 96.

7. ———. Psychopathic behavior disorders in children. In R. M. Linder, ed., *Handbook of correctional psychology.* New York: New York Philosophical Library, 1947. Pages 360–377.

8. ———, and Yarnell, H. An observation nursery: A study of 250 children in the psychiatric division of Bellevue Hospital. *Amer. J. Psychiat.*, 97(1941), 1158–1174.

9. Beres, D., and Obers, S. J. The effects of extreme deprivation in infancy on psychic structure in adolescence. *Psychoanal. Stud. Child*, 5(1950), 121–140.

10. Berg, M., and Cohen, B. B. Early separation from mother in schizophrenia. *J. Nerv. Ment. Dis.*, 128(1959), 365–369.

11. Bodman, F., et al. The social adaptation of institution children. *Lancet*, 258(1950), 173–176.

12. Bowlby, J. Forty-four juvenile thieves. *Int. J. Psycho-Anal.*, 25(1944), 1–57.

13. ———. Maternal care and mental health. *WHO Monogr.*, 1951, No. 2.

14. ———. Some pathological processes engendered by early mother-child separation. In M. J. Senn, ed., *Infancy and childhood.* New York: Josiah Macy, Jr. Foundation, 1953, Pages 38–87. (a)

15. ———. Some pathological processes set in train by early mother-child separation. *J. Ment. Sci.*, 99(1953), 265–272. (b)

16. ———. An ethological approach to research in child development. *Brit. J. Med. Psychol.*, 30(1957), 230–240.

17. ———. The nature of the child's tie to the mother. *Int. J. Psycho-Anal.*, 39(1958), 1–24.

18. ———, Ainsworth, Mary, Boston, Mary, and Rosenbluth, Dina. The effects of mother-child separation: A follow-up study. *Brit. J. Med. Psychol.*, 29(1956), 211–247.

19. Brodbeck, A. J., and Irwin, O. C. The speech behavior of infants without families. *Child Develpm.*, 17(1946), 145–156.

20. Brown, F. Neuroticism of institution vs. non-institution children. *J. Appl. Psychol.*, 21(1937), 379–383.

21. Coleman, Ruth W., and Provence.

Sally. Environmental retardation (hospitalism) in infants living in families. *Pediatrics,* **19** (1957), 285–292.

22. Day, Ella J. The development of language in twins: I. A comparison of twins and single children. *Child Develpm.,* **3**(1932), 179–199.

23. Dennis, W. Infant development under conditions of restricted practice and of minimum social stimulation. *Genet. Psychol. Monogr.,* **23**(1941), 143–190.

24. ———, and Dennis, Marsena G. Development under controlled environmental conditions. In W. Dennis, ed., *Readings in child psychology.* New York: Prentice-Hall, 1951. Pages 104–131.

25. Dennis, W., and Najarian, P. Infant development under environmental handicap. *Psychol. Monogr.,* **71**(1957), (7, Whole No. 436).

26. DuBois, Cora. *The people of Alor.* Minneapolis: Univ. Minnesota Press, 1944.

27. DuPan, R. M., and Roth, S. The psychologic development of a group of children brought up in a hospital type residential nursery. *J. Pediat.,* **47**(1955), 124–129.

28. Edelston, H. Separation anxiety in young children: A study of hospital cases. *Genet. Psychol. Monogr.,* **28**(1943), 3–95.

29. Eggan, D. The general problem of Hopi adjustment. *Amer. Anthropologist,* **47** (1945), 516–539.

30. Fischer, Liselotte. Hospitalism in six month old infants. *Amer. J. Orthopsychiat.,* **22**(1952), 522–533.

31. ———. Psychological appraisal of the unattached preschool child. *Amer. J. Orthopsychiat.,* **23**(1953), 803–814.

32. Flint, Betty. Babies who live in institutions. *Bull. Inst. Child Stud., Toronto,* **19**(1957), 1–5.

33. Freud, Anna, and Burlingham, Dorothy T. *Infants without families.* New York: International Univ. Press, 1944.

34. Gardner, D. B., Pease, Damaris, and Hawkes, G. R. Responses of two-year-old adopted children to controlled stress situations. Paper read at Society for Research in Child Development, Washington, D.C., March 1959.

35. Gardner, D. B., and Swiger, M. K. Developmental status of two groups of infants released for adoption. *Child Develpm.,* **29**(1958), 521–530.

36. Gesell, A., and Amatruda, Catherine. *Developmental diagnosis.* New York: Hoeber, 1941.

37. Gewirtz, J. L. Social deprivation and dependency: A learning analysis. Paper read in symposium on Dependency in personality development, American Psychological Association, New York, August 1957.

38. Glaser, K., and Eisenberg, L. Maternal deprivation. *Pediatrics,* **18**(1956), 626–642.

39. Golan, S. Behavior research in collective settlements in Israel: Collective education in the kibbutz. *Amer. J. Orthopsychiat.,* **28**(1958), 549–556.

40. Goldfarb, W. Effects of early institutional care on adolescent personality (graphic Rorschach data). *Child Develpm.,* **14**(1943), 213–223. (a)

41. ———. Infant rearing and problem behavior. *Amer. J. Orthopsychiat.,* **13**(1943), 249–265. (b)

42. ———. Effects of early institutional care on adolescent personality: Rorschach data. *Amer. J. Orthopsychiat.,* **14**(1944), 441–447. (a)

43. ———. Infant rearing as a factor in foster home replacement. *Amer. J. Orthopsychiat.,* **14**(1944), 162–173. (b)

44. ———. Effects of psychological deprivation in infancy and subsequent stimulation. *Amer. J. Psychiat.,* **102**(1945), 18–33. (a)

45. ———. Psychological privation in infancy and subsequent adjustment. *Amer. J. Orthopsychiat.,* **15**(1945), 247–255. (b)

46. ———. Variations in adolescent adjustment of institutionally reared children. *Amer. J. Orthopsychiat.,* **17**(1947), 449–457.

47. ———. Rorschach test differences between family-reared, institution-reared, and schizophrenic children. *Amer. J. Orthopsychiat.,* **19**(1949), 625–633.

48. ———. Emotional and intellectual consequences of psychologic deprivation in infancy: A re-evaluation. In P. H. Hoch and J. Zubin, eds., *Psychopathology of childhood.* New York: Grune & Stratton, 1955. Pages 105–119.

49. Haggerty, A. D. The effects of long-term hospitalization upon the language development of children. *J. Genet. Psychol.,* **94**(1959), 205–209.

50. Harlow, H. The nature of love. *Amer. Psychologist,* **15**(1958), 673–685.

51. Hartmann, H., Kris, E., Lowenstein, R. M. Comments on the formation of psychic structure. *Psychoanal. Stud. Child,* **2**(1946), 11–38.

52. Hebb, D. O. *The organization of behavior: A neuropsychological theory.* New York: Wiley, 1949.

53. ———. The mammal and his environment. *Amer. J. Psychiat.,* **3**(1955), 826–831.

54. Heinicke, C. Some effects of separating two-year-old children from their parents: A comparative study. *Hum. Relat.,* **9**(1956), 105–176.

55. Irvine, Elizabeth. Observations on aims and methods of child rearing in communal settlements in Israel. *Hum. Relat.,* 5(1952), 247–275.

56. Kardiner, A. Social stress and deprivation. In I. Galdston, ed., *Beyond the germ theory.* New York: New York Health Education Council, 1954. Pages 147–170.

57. King, J. A. Parameters relevant to determining the effect of early experience upon the adult behavior of animals. *Psychol. Bull.,* 55(1958), 46–58.

58. Klackenburg, G. Studies in maternal deprivation in infant homes. *Acta Paediat., Stockh.,* 45(1956), 1–12.

59. Levy, D. Primary affect hunger. *Amer. J. Psychiat.,* 94(1937), 643–652.

60. Levy, Ruth. Institutional vs. boarding-home care. *J. Pers.,* 15(1947), 233–241.

61. Lewis, Hilda. *Deprived children.* Toronto: Oxford Univ. Press, 1954.

62. Lowrey, L. G. Personality distortion and early institutional care. *Amer. J. Orthopsychiat.,* 10(1940), 576–585.

63. Mead, Margaret. *Sex and temperament in three primitive societies.* New York: Mentor, 1935.

64. Moltz, H. Imprinting: Empirical basis and theoretical significance. *Psychol. Bull.,* 57(1960), 291–314.

65. Pease, Damaris, and Gardner, D. B. Research on the effects of non-continuous mothering. *Child Develpm.,* 29(1958), 141–148.

66. Pinneau, S. R. A critique on the articles by Margaret Ribble. *Child Develpm.,* 21(1950), 203–228.

67. ———. The infantile disorders of hospitalism and anaclitic depression. *Psychol. Bull.,* 52(1955), 429–462.

68. Rabin, A. I. Personality maturity of kibbutz (Israeli collective settlement) and non-kibbutz children as reflected in Rorschach findings. *J. Proj. Tech.,* 31(1957), 148–153.

69. ———. Behavior research in collective settlements in Israel: Infants and children under conditions of "intermittent" mothering in the kibbutz. *Amer. J. Orthopsychiat.,* 28(1958), 577–586. (a)

70. ———. Some psychosexual differences between kibbutz and non-kibbutz Israeli boys. *J. Proj. Tech.,* 22(1958), 328–332. (b)

71. Rapaport, D. Behavior research in collective settlements in Israel: The study of Kibbutz education and its bearing on the theory of development. *Amer. J. Orthopsychiat.,* 28(1958), 587–597.

72. Rheingold, Harriet L. Mental and social development of infants in relation to the number of other infants in the boarding home. *Amer. J. Orthopsychiat.,* 13(1943), 41–44.

73. ———. The modification of social responsiveness in institutional babies. *Monogr. Soc. Res. Child Develpm.,* 21(1956), No. 63.

74. ———. The measurement of maternal care. *Child Develpm.,* 31(1960), 565–573.

75. ———, and Bayley, N. The later effects of an experimental modification of mothering. *child Develpm.,* 30(1959), 363–372.

76. Rheingold, Harriet L., Gewirtz, J., and Ross, Helen. Social conditioning of vocalizations in the infant. *J. Comp. Physiol. Psychol.,* 52(1959), 58–73.

77. Ribble, Margaret. *Rights of infants.* New York: Columbia Univ. Press, 1943.

78. Robertson, J., and Bowlby, J. Responses of young children to separation from their mothers: II. Observation of sequences of response of children aged 18–24 months during course of separation. *Courr. Cent. Int. l'Enfance,* 2(1952), 131–139.

79. Roscoe, J. Baganda: An account of their native customs and beliefs. In I. T. Sanders, ed., *Societies around the world.* New York: Dryden, 1953. Pages 412–420.

80. Roundinesco, Jenny, David, Miriam, and Nicolas, J. Responses of young children to separation from their mothers: I. Observation of children ages 12 to 17 months recently separated from their families and living in an institution. *Courr. Cent. Int. l'Enfance,* 2(1952), 66–78.

81. Schaffer, H. R. Objective observations of personality development in early infancy. *Brit. J. Med. Psychol.,* 31(1958), 174–183.

82. Scott, J. P., Fredericson, E., and Fuller, J. L. Experimental exploration of the critical period hypothesis. *Personality,* 1(1951), 162–183.

83. Skeels, H. M. A study of the effects of differential stimulation on mentally retarded children: Follow-up report. *Amer. J. Ment. Defic.,* 66(1942), 340–350.

84. ———, and Dye, H. A study of the effects of differential stimulation on mentally retarded children. *Proc. Amer. Ass. Ment. Defic.,* 44(1939), 114–136.

85. ———, Updegraff, Ruth, Wellman, Beth L., and Williams, H. M. A study of environmental stimulation: An orphanage pre-school project. *U. Ia. Stud. Child Welf.,* 15(1938), 7–191.

86. Spitz, R. A. Hospitalism: An inquiry into the genesis of psychiatric conditions in early childhood. *Psychoanal. Stud. Child.,* 1(1945), 53–74; 2(1946), 113–117.

87. ——— The psychogenic diseases in infancy: An attempt at their etiologic classification. *Psychoanal. Stud. Child,* 6(1951), 255–275.

88. ——— Infantile depression and the general adaptation syndrome. In P. H. Hoch and

J. Zubin, eds., *Depression.* New York: Grune & Stratton, 1954. Pages 93–108. (a)

89. —— Unhappy and fatal outcomes of emotional deprivation and stress in infancy. In I. Galdston, ed., *Beyond the germ theory.* New York: New York Health Education Council, 1954. Pages 120–131. (b)

90. —— Reply to Pinneau. *Psychol. Bull.,* **52**(1955), 453–459.

91. —— and Wolf, Katherine. Anaclitic depression. *Psychoanal. Stud. Child,* 2(1946), 313–342.

92. —— Autoerotism. *Psychoanal. Stud. Child,* **3–4**(1949), 85–120.

93. Stern, W. *General psychology from the personalistic standpoint.* New York: Macmillan, 1938.

94. Stone, L. J. A critique of studies of infant isolation. *Child Develpm.,* 25(1954), 9–20.

95. Tinbergen, N. Psychology and ethology as supplementary parts of a science of behavior. In B. Schaffner, ed., *Group processes.* New York: Josiah Macy, Jr. Foundation, 1954.

96. Van Alstyne, D. The environment of three-year-old children: Factors related to intelligence and vocabulary tests., *Teach. Coll. Contr. Educ.,* No. 366, (1929).

97. Wellman, Beth, and Pegram, E. L. Binet IQ changes of orphanage preschool children: A re-analysis. *J. Genet. Psychol.,* 65(1944), 239–263.

98. Wexler, D., Mendelson, J., Liederman, P. H., and Solomon, P. Sensory deprivation. *AMA Arch. Neurol. Psychiat.,* **79**(1958), 225–233.

99. Yarrow, L. J. Research on maternal deprivation. Paper read at symposium on Maternal deprivation, American Association for the Advancement of Science, Section I, Atlanta, Georgia, December 1955.

100. —— The development of object relationships during infancy, and the effects of a disruption of early mother-child relationships. *Amer. Psychologist,* 11(1956), 423. (Abstract.)

Early Infantile Autism, 1943-55

LEON EISENBERG AND LEO KANNER
CHILDREN'S PSYCHIATRIC SERVICE, HARRIET LANE HOME,
JOHNS HOPKINS HOSPITAL

In 1943, under the title "Autistic Disturbances of Affective Contact" (1), eleven children were reported, whose clinical features appeared to constitute a unique syndrome, later termed "early infantile autism" (2). Since this publication of the original paper, more than 120 children so diagnosed with reasonable certainty have been observed at the Children's Psychiatric Service of the Johns Hopkins Hospital. The syndrome is now recognized as having clinical specificity, as is

Reprinted from the *American Journal of Orthopsychiatry,* 26(1956), 556–566, with the permission of the American Orthopsychiatric Association, Inc., and Dr. L. Eisenberg.

attested by numerous case reports and discussions of its theoretical and dynamic aspects. Preliminary data from follow-up studies at this clinic have further verified the uniqueness of the syndrome. It seems appropriate at this point to review briefly the nature of the original conception, to consider the modifications necessitated by greater knowledge, and to evaluate the present status of infantile autism.

In the original paper, the pathognomonic disorder was seen as "the children's inability to relate themselves in the ordinary way to people and to situations from the beginning of life" (1). The extreme nature of their detachment from human relationships separated the appearance and behavior of these children in a fundamental fashion from other known behavioral disturbances. It was noted that the process was not one "of withdrawal from formerly existing participation" with others, as is true of the older schizophrenic child, but rather "from the start an extreme autistic aloneness" (1). This could be discerned from the almost universal report by parents that these children, as infants, had failed to assume an anticipatory posture before being picked up and never displayed the plastic molding which the normal child shows when cradled in his parent's arms. Initially pleased by the child's "goodness"—that is, his ability to occupy himself for long periods without requiring attention—parents later became distressed by the persistence of this self-isolation and by their observation that their coming or going seemed a matter of complete indifference to the child.

A second distinctive feature was noted as the failure to use language for the purpose of communication. In 3 of the 11 cases, speech failed to develop altogether. The remaining 8 rapidly developed a precocity of articulation which, coupled with unusual facility in rote memory, resulted in the ability to repeat endless numbers of rhymes, catechisms, lists of names, and other semantically useless exercises. The parroting of words intellectually incomprehensible to the child brought into sharp relief the gross failure to use speech to convey meaning or feeling to others. The repetition of stored phrases, while failing to recombine words into original and personalized sentences, gave rise to the phenomena of delayed echolalia, pronominal reversal, literalness, and affirmation by repetition.

A third characteristic was described as "an anxiously obsessive desire for the maintenance of sameness" (1), resulting in a marked limitation in the variety of spontaneous activity. Regularly displaying fear of new patterns of activity, these children, once having accepted a new pattern, would incorporate it into the restricted set of rituals which then had to be endlessly iterated. Thus, a walk had always to follow the same prescribed course; bedtime to consist of a particular ritual of words and actions; and repetitive activities like spinning, turning on and off lights and spigots, or flushing toilets could preoccupy the child for long periods. Any attempt to interfere with the pattern would produce bursts of rage or episodes of acute panic.

Fourthly, as distinct from the poor or absent relation to persons, there could be discerned a fascination for objects which were handled with skill in fine motor movements. So intense was this relationship that minor alterations in objects or their arrangement, not ordinarily perceived by the average observer, were at once apparent to these children who might then fly into a rage until the change had been undone, whereupon tranquility was restored.

Finally, it was argued that these children had "good cognitive potentialities" (1). In the speaking group this could be discerned in the extraordinary, if perverted, use of language, manifesting feats of unusual memory. In the mute children, this was concluded, though with less confidence, from their facility with performance tests, particularly the Seguin formboard, at or above their age level.

Thus a syndrome had been delineated which was differentiated from childhood schizophrenia by virtue of detachment present no later than the first year of life, and from oligophrenia by the evidence of good intellectual potentialities. Physical examination failed to reveal any consistence organic abnormality that could be related to the clinical picture. Family background was striking in the universal presence of high intelligence, marked obsessiveness, and coldness. But the extreme aloneness *present from the beginning of life* led to the tentative conclusion that this group of children comprised "pure-culture examples of inborn autistic disturbances of affective contact."

In the light of experience with a tenfold increase in clinical material, we would now isolate these two pathognomonic features, both of which must be present: extreme self-isolation and the obsessive insistence on the preservation of sameness, features that may be regarded as primary, employing the term as Bleuler did in grouping the symptoms of schizophrenia (3). The vicissitudes of language development, often the most striking and challenging of the presenting phenomena, may be seen as derivatives of the basic disturbance in human relatedness. Preoccupation with simple repetitive activities may be seen at times in severely retarded children and may offer a diagnostic problem, but the presence of elaborately conceived rituals together with the characteristic aloneness serves to differentiate the autistic patients. The case material has expanded to include a number of children who reportedly developed normally through the first 18 to 20 months of life, only to undergo at this point a severe withdrawal of affect, manifested by the loss of language function, failure to progress socially, and the gradual giving up of interest in normal activities. These latter cases have invariably been severe and unresponsive. When seen, they could not be differentiated from the children with the more classical account of detachment apparently present in the neonatal period. But even these cases are much earlier in onset and phenomenologically distinct from cases of childhood schizophrenia.

When this conception was set forth 12 years ago, it met with a reception very similar to that which greeted the reports of childhood schizophrenia advanced in the previous decade. Workers in the field, limiting their thinking to the conventional lines prescribed by the then current notions of adult schizophrenia, had had difficulty in accepting as schizo-phrenic a clinical picture in children which necessarily had distinctive differences dictated by the much younger age of these patients. Within the past six years confirmatory reports have appeared with increasing frequency so that now the term infantile autism is rather widely—and often not too accurately—employed. Despert was perhaps the first in a personal communication to note the similarities between this group of children and others she had studied (4, 5). Mahler suggested the useful division between autistic and symbiotic infantile psychoses (6, 7). Rank (8), Weil (9), Sherwin (10), Murphy (11) in this country, Cappon (12) in Canada, Creak (13) in England, Stern (14) and Stern and Schachter (15) in France, and van Krevelen (16, 17) in Holland added significant case reports. Recently, the Dutch Society for Child Psychiatry organized a symposium on infantile autism (Grewel, 44). A number of other workers have discussed the theoretical implications for language and perceptual function of the phenomena shown by the autistic child (18, 19, 20). It therefore seems justified to state that the specificity of early infantile autism is now rather commonly accepted, with, of course, inevitable differences in diagnostic allocation: van Krevelen placing it with oligophrenia, most workers in this country with schizophrenia, Stern and Schachter and Grewel regarding it as a syndrome *sui generis,* and so on.

The preliminary results of our follow-up studies are of interest in that they, too, emphasize the phenomenologic uniqueness of the syndrome. Of the some 50 children followed for a mean period of 8 years, none is reliably known to have exhibited hallucinations. The major pathology remains in the area of inability to relate in the ordinary fashion to other human beings. Even the relatively "successful" children exhibited a lack of social perceptiveness, perhaps best characterized as a lack of *savoir faire.* This can be illustrated by the following incident involving one of our patients who has made considerable progress. Attending a football rally of his junior college and called upon to speak, he shocked the assembly by stating that he thought the team was likely to lose—a prediction that was correct but unthinkable in the setting. The ensuing round of booing dismayed this young man who was totally unable to comprehend why the truth should be unwelcome.

This amazing lack of awareness of the feelings of others, who seem not to be conceived of as persons like the self, runs like a red thread through our case histories. We might cite a four-year-old boy whose mother came to us with the account that on a crowded beach he would walk straight toward his goal irrespective of whether this involved walking over newspapers, hands, feet, or torsos, much to the discomfiture of their owners. The mother was careful to point out that he did not intentionally deviate from his course in order to walk on others—but neither did he make the slightest attempt to avoid them. It was as if he did not distinguish people from things or at least did not concern himself about the distinction. This failure to recognize others as entities separate from oneself was exhibited by the 28-year-old patient retrospectively diagnosed as autistic and reported by Darr and Worden (21). To mention one example of her behavior: "On one occasion she spilled ink on the floor of a dormitory room, dashed out to ask the first person she met to wipe it up, and became angry on being refused." The existence of feelings or wishes in other people that might not accord with the patient's own autistic thoughts and desires seemed beyond recognition.

On clinical grounds, it is now useful to differentiate between the children who have learned to speak by the age of five and those who have no useful language function by that age (3). Of the former

group, about half have made some sort of scholastic adjustment and participate in a limited way in the social life of the community, though we are none too sanguine about their future. Of the latter group—the nonspeakers—only one out of twenty subsequently developed language and is making at least a mediocre adjustment in a protected school setting. The remainder are either in institutions or remain at home, functionally severely retarded. Interestingly, a number of these emotionally isolated children, though confined to institutions for the feebleminded, are still distinguishable from their fellow patients, as is attested by reports of psychological testing that bewilder the observer in the conjunction of social imbecility with the preservation of isolated areas of unusual intellectual performance.

The information obtained from long-term study of these children is beginning to supply us with a natural history of the syndrome, against which therapeutic efforts will have to be evaluated. Thus, it would appear on the basis of current information that, if we consider the cases in aggregate, about one third appear able to achieve at least a minimal social adjustment to school and community. This percentage of improvement without extensive psychiatric treatment is comparable with the data reported on a much larger group of schizophrenic children treated with electric shock by Bender (22), allowing for differences in diagnostic categories and in indices of improvement. It should be stressed that, insofar as our data permit evaluation, psychotherapy seems in general to be of little avail, with few apparent exceptions. If one factor is significantly useful, it is a sympathetic and tolerant reception by the school. Those of our children who have improved have been extended extraordinary consideration by their teachers. They constitute a most trying group of pupils. School acceptance of behavior that elsewhere provokes rejection is undoubtedly a therapeutic experience. Obviously, it is feasible only in the case of the less severely disturbed children.

Etiologic investigations have centered about organic, genetic, and psychodynamic factors. Thorough pediatric examinations of all the children who have passed through our clinic have failed to reveal any more than occasional and apparently unrelated physical abnormalities, unless one considers relevant the consistent preponderance of boys over girls in a ratio of 4 to 1. Careful medical histories of pregnancy, delivery, and development are negative insofar as any consistent pattern of pathological complications is concerned. Electroencephalographic studies have been carried out only sporadically; of the 28 cases on which reports are available, 21 were stated to be negative, 3 definitely abnormal, and 4 equivocal. It must be recognized, however, that neurologic investigations of the integrity of central function remain as yet in their clinical infancy and a negative result with current methods cannot be regarded as a conclusive demonstration of the lack of central nervous system pathology.

If we turn to a study of the families, we learn that, of 200 parents, there are only 6 with clinical psychiatric disorders, only one of whom had a psychotic episode. Among 400 grandparents and among 373 known uncles and aunts, 12 were afflicted with mental illness. This low incidence of psychotic and neurotic relatives, even if we double the figures to allow for the relative youth of these families, contrasts sharply with the high incidence in the families of older childhood schizophrenics reported by Bender (22) and in adult schizophrenics reported by Kallmann (24). Similarly, of 131 known siblings of 100 autistic children, 3 can be regarded as probably autistic on the basis of the information supplied and 7 others as emotionally disturbed. Thus, if one limits his search for genetic factors to overt psychotic and neurotic episodes

in family members, the results would appear to be negative. If one considers the personalities of the parents who have been described as "successfully autistic," the possibility suggests itself that they may represent milder manifestations and that the children show the full emergence of the latent structure. One of the fathers in this group, a physician engaged in research, stressed the mildly schizoid trends in his own grandparents, more strongly evident in his father, fairly marked in himself and to some degree in all of his progeny, and full-blown in his autistic child.

One of the striking features of the clinical histories remains the unusually high percentage of these children who stem from highly intelligent, obsessive, and emotionally frigid backgrounds. Eighty-seven of the fathers and seventy of the mothers had been to college. A large number are professional people who have attained distinction in their fields. A control study of the parents of private patients selected solely by virtue of being next in call number to each of the first 50 autistic cases revealed levels of educational attainment and professional status that were considerably lower. In the control group one does not find the dramatically evident detachment, obsessiveness, and coldness that is almost a universal feature of parents of autistic children. Yet one must admit that some 10 per cent of the parents do not fit the stereotype and that those who do have raised other normal, or in any event, nonpsychotic children. Moreover, similarly frigid parents are seen who do not give rise to autistic progeny.

The emotional frigidity in the typical autistic family suggests a dynamic experiential factor in the genesis of the disorder in the child. The mechanization of care and the almost total absence of emotional warmth in child rearing may be exemplified by the case of Brian, who was one of twins born despite contraceptive efforts, much to the distress of his parents whose plans centered about graduate study and had no room for children. Pregnancy was quite upsetting to the mother and caused the father, who was already immersed in study, to withdraw still further from the family. The mother, a psychology graduate student, decided that the children were to be raised "scientifically"—that is, not to be picked up for crying, except on schedule. Furthermore, an effort was made to "keep them from infections" by minimizing human contact. What little care was dispensed was centered upon Brian's twin who was physically weaker and, according to the mother, more responsive. At five months of age, the twin was found dead after an evening in which both infants had been crying loudly but had not been visited, in accordance with rigid principle. Following this tragedy, the mother withdrew from the remaining child even more completely, spent her days locked in the study reading, and limited her concern almost exclusively to maintaining bacteriological sterility, so that Brian was isolated from children and almost all adults until he was well over two. During this period he was content to be alone and to occupy himself, just how the parents rarely bothered to inquire. It was only when he reached the age of four without the development of speech and began to display temper tantrums when his routines were interrupted that they began to recognize the fact that he was ill. So distant were the members of this family each from the others that the parents failed to be concerned about, if they did not actually prefer, Brian's indifference to them. One might accurately state that this was an environment that rewarded preoccupation with autistic interests and that provided the barest minimum of human contact compatible with the maintenance of physical health. Stimuli that might have fostered attention to or interest in the human environment were almost entirely absent. This case, an extreme instance chosen for em-

phasis, can serve as a paradigm of the "emotional refrigeration" that has been the common lot of autistic children.

Psychiatrists are rather widely agreed that emotional deprivation has profound consequences for psychobiological development (25). Infants subjected to impersonal care in institutions for prolonged periods in the first years of life display both psychomotor retardation and physiological dysfunction, a syndrome that has been termed hospitalism (26, 27). Longer periods of exposure are correlated with depression of intellectual function, as measured by scores on developmental and intelligence tests (28, 29). Analogous data are available from controlled animal experiments, in which poverty of environmental stimulation in the neonatal period produces apparently irreversible loss in adaptive ability (30, 31, 32). Moreover, children exposed to prolonged affective deprivation are likely to display antisocial and psychopathic behavior traits (33, 34, 35). It has been contended that the personality pattern of such children as adolescents is typically "affectionless" (36). The most recent study by Dr. Lewis casts doubt on the concept of a specific personality pattern in the child who has suffered from lack of mothering, but does confirm the significant correlation between disturbed, usually antisocial behavior and early separation from the mother without adequate substitution (37).

Experience in Israel with communally reared children casts cross-cultural light on the nature of the emotional needs of infants and children (38). From six weeks of age, Kibbutz infants live full time in communal nurseries, and though identification with their parents is maintained by frequent visits, the great preponderance of their care is given by permanent nursery workers. They are raised as a group under a common roof until late adolescence. These children grow into mature and capable adults as far as clinical evaluation can determine. Stress should be placed on the fact that the Kibbutz culture is child-oriented, and while the mother is not the main dispenser of care, the children are reared by warm and demonstrative trained people —as it were, in an atmosphere of affectionate interest.

Thus it is evident that affectionate care and a consistent relationship to one or more adults in the mothering role is a prerequisite for normal growth in infancy and childhood.

The case histories of autistic children reveal that in almost all instances they were raised by their own parents. Obvious mistreatment, overt rejection, or abandonment, usual in the life experience of the children who are classified as emotionally deprived, is the exception. But the formal provision of food and shelter and the absence of neglect as defined by statutory law are insufficient criteria for the adequacy of family care. The role of "parent" is not defined merely by the biological task of giving rise to progeny. In the typical autistic family it is as if the Israeli experiment had been repeated in reverse: in having parents, but not a warm, flexible, growth-promoting emotional atmosphere. These children were, in general, conceived less out of a positive desire than out of an acceptance of childbearing as part of the marital contract. Physical needs were attended to mechanically and on schedule according to the rigid precepts of naïve behaviorism applied with a vengeance. One can discern relatively few instances of warmth and affection. The usual parental attitude is cold and formal; less commonly, it is laden with great anxiety. The child's worth seemed to lie in the extent to which he conformed to predetermined parental expectations: "perfect" behavior, cleverness, "self-sufficiency," and so on. Their parents, who were themselves preoccupied with careers and intellectual pursuits to the exclusion of interest in other people, had little more

feeling for their own children. It may be a measure of the intellectual aptitude of some of these children that they were able to parrot long and resonant lists of meaningless words, but it even more clearly bespeaks the emphasis placed at home on such useless activities which were a source of pride to the parents.

It is difficult to escape the conclusion that this emotional configuration in the home plays a dynamic role in the genesis of autism. But it seems to us equally clear that this factor, while important in the development of the syndrome, is not sufficient in itself to result in its appearance. There appears to be some way in which the children are different from the beginning of their extrauterine existence. Indeed, it has been postulated that the aberrant behavior of the children is chiefly responsible for the personality difficulties of their parents who are pictured as reacting to the undoubtedly trying situation of having an unresponsive child (39). While we would agree that this is an important consideration, it cannot explain the social and psychological characteristics of the parents which have a history long anteceding the child.

There is little likelihood that a single etiologic agent is solely responsible for the pathology in behavior. Arguments that counterpose "hereditary" versus "environmental" as antithetical terms are fundamentally in error. Operationally defined, they are interpenetrating concepts. The effects of chromosomal aberrations can be mimicked in the phenotype by environmental pathogens, and genetic factors require for their complete manifestation suitable environmental conditions. It is not possible to distinguish between biochemically mutant microorganisms until we expose them to nutrient media deficient in appropriate metabolites. Conversely, the full effect of environmental agencies cannot be seen unless the genotype is adequate. A culturally rich environment will be little different from a culturally poor one in its influence on the intellectual development of phenylketonuric children.

The dualistic view implicit in a rigid distinction between "organic" and "functional" is no longer tenable. The pharmacologic production of psychosislike states simulating certain features of schizophrenia (40, 41)—and the recent hint that analogue blockade will interfere with chemically induced "model psychoses" (42)—serves to reassert the obvious fact that biochemical change is accompanied by alterations in thought processes. Nevertheless, the disordered thoughts obey the laws governing psychic processes and lend themselves to psychological analysis. It is equally important to recognize that originally psychogenic forces must by their enduring action transform the physiological substrate, as the conditioned reflex so clearly demonstrates (43). The finding of biochemical or psychological abnormalities is only the starting point in a search for etiology.

Early infantile autism is a total psychobiological disorder. What is needed is a comprehensive study of the dysfunction at each level of integration: biological, psychological, and social. The supposition of an innate difference in the autistic child will mean relatively little until we can specify the nature and meaning of that difference. Currently, research sponsored by the League for Emotionally Disturbed Children is attempting to uncover metabolic and electrophysiologic abnormalities, research that complements the psychodynamic investigations at this and other clinics.

In summary, early infantile autism has been fully established as a clinical syndrome. It is characterized by extreme aloneness and preoccupation with the preservation of sameness, and is manifest within the first two years of life. The history, early onset, and clinical course distinguish it from older childhood schizophrenia, to which it is probably related

generically. The degree of aloneness constitutes the important prognostic variable since those children sufficiently related to the human environment to learn to talk have a significantly better outlook for future adjustment. Present knowledge leads to the inference that innate as well as experiential factors conjoin to produce the clinical picture. It remains for future investigation to uncover the precise mode of operation of the pathogenic factors as a basis for rational treatment.

References

1. Kanner, L. Autistic disturbances of affective contact. *Nerv. Child*, 2(1943), 217–250.
2. —— Early infantile autism. *J. Pediat.*, 25(1944), 211–217.
3. —— and Eisenberg, L. Notes on the follow-up studies of Autistic children, in *Psychopathology of childhood*, P. H. Hoch and J. Zubin, eds., pp. 227–239. New York: Grune & Stratton, 1955.
4. Despert, J. L., quoted by Kanner, L. Problems of nosology and psychodynamics of early infantile autism. *Am. J. Orthopsych.*, 19(1949), 416–452.
5. —— Some Considerations relating to the genesis of autistic behavior in children. *Ibid.*, 21(1951), 335–350.
6. Mahler, M. S. On child psychosis and schizophrenia: autistic and symbiotic infantile psychoses, in *The psychoanalytic study of the child*. New York: Internat. Univ. Press, 1952. Volume VII, pages 286–305.
7. Mahler, M. S., Ross, Jr., J. R., and De Fries, Z. Clinical studies in benign and malignant cases of childhood psychosis. *Am. J. Orthopsych.*, 19(1949), 295–305.
8. Rank, B. Adaptation of the psychoanalytic technique for the treatment of young children with atypical development. *Am. J. Orthopsych.*, 19(1949), 130–139.
9. Weil, A. P. Clinical data and dynamic considerations in certain cases of childhood schizophrenia. *Am. J. Orthopsych.*, 23(1953), 518–529.
10. Sherwin, A. C. Reactions to music of autistic (schizophrenic) children. *Am. J. Psychiatry*, 109(1953), 823–831.
11. Murphy, R. C., and Preston, C. E., *Three autistic brothers*. Presented at the 1954 Annual

Meeting of the American Orthopsychiatric Association.

12. Cappon, D. Clinical manifestations of autism and schizophrenia in childhood. *Canad. Med. Ass. J.,* **69**(1953), 44–49.

13. Creak, M. (a) Psychoses in childhood. *Proc. Royal Soc. Med.,* **45**(1953), 797–800. (b) Psychoses in childhood. *J. Ment. Sci.,* **97**(1951), 545–554.

14. Stern, E. À propos d'un cas d'autisme chez un jeune enfant. *Arch. Franç. de Pédiatrie,* **9**(1952).

15. Stern, E., and M. Schachter. Zum problem des frühkindlichen autismus. *Prax. Kinderpsychol. Kinderpsychiat.,* **2**(1953), 113–119.

16. van Krevelen, D. A. Een geval van "early infantile autism." *Ned. Tijdschr. voor Geneeskunde,* **96**(1952), 202–205.

17. ——— Early infantile autism. *Z. für Kinderpsychiatrie,* **19**(1952), 91–97.

18. Arieti, S. Some aspects of the psychopathology of schizophrenia. *Am. J. Psychother.,* **8**(1954), 396–414.

19. Norman, E. Reality relationships of schizophrenic children. *Brit. J. Med. Psychol.,* **27**(1954), 126–141.

20. Ritvo, S., and Provence, S. Form perception and limitation in some autistic children, in *The psychoanalytic study of the child.* New York: Internat. Univ. Press, 1953. Volume VIII, pages 155–161.

21. Darr, G. C., and Worden, F. G. Case report twenty-eight years after an autistic disorder. *Am. J. Orthopsych.,* **21**(1951), 559–570.

22. Bender, L. Childhood schizophrenia. *Psychiatric Quart.,* **27**(1953), 1–19.

23. Kanner, L. To what extent is early infantile autism determined by constitutional inadequacies? *Res. Publ. Ass. Nerv. Ment. Dis.,* **33**(1954), 378–385.

24. Kallman, F. J. *Heredity in health and mental disorder.* New York: Norton, 1953.

25. Bowlby, J. Maternal care and mental health. *WHO Monogr.,* Geneva, 1951.

26. Bakwin, H. Emotional deprivation in infants. *J. Pediat.,* **35**(1949), 512.

27. Spitz, R. A., and K. M. Wolf. Anaclitic depression: an inquiry into the genesis of psychiatric conditions in early childhood, in *The Psychoanalytic Study of the Child.* New York: Internat. Univ. Press, 1946. Volume II, pages 313–342.

28. Steels, H. M., and H. B. Dye. A Study of the effect of differential stimulation on mentally retarded children. *Proc. Amer. Assn. Stud. Ment. Def.,* **44**(1939), 114–136.

29. Gesell, A., and C. Amatruda. *Developmental diagnosis,* 2nd ed., New York: Hoeber, 1947.

30. Thompson, W. R., and W. Heron. Effects of restriction early in life on problem solving in dogs. *Canad. J. Psychol.,* **8**(1954), 17–31.

31. ——— Exploratory behavior in normal and restricted dogs. *J. Comp. Physiol. Psychol.,* **47**(1954), 77–82.

32. Beach, F. A., and J. Jaynes. Effects of early experience on the behavior of animals. *Psychol. Bull.,* **51**(1954), 239–263.

33. Goldfarb, W. Effects of psychological deprivation in infancy and subsequent stimulation. *Am. J. Psychiatry,* **102**(1945), 18–33.

34. ——— Variations in adolescent adjustment of institutionally reared children. *Am. J. Orthopsych.,* **17**(1947), 449–457.

35. Bender, L. Psychopathic Conduct Disorder in Children, in *A handbook of correctional psychiatry,* R. M. Lindner, ed. New York: Philosophical Library, 1947.

36. Bowlby, J. Forty-four juvenile thieves: their characters and home life. *Int. J. Psychoanal.,* **25**(1944), 19–53.

37. Lewis, H. *Deprived children: a social and clinical study.* New York: Oxford Univ. Press, 1954.

38. Caplan, G. Clinical observations on the emotional life of children in the communal settlements in Israel, in *Problems of infancy and childhood: seventh conference,* M. S. E. Senn, ed. New York: Josiah Macy, Jr. Foundation, 1954.

39. Peck, H. B., R. D. Rabinovitch, and J. B. Cramer. A treatment program for parents of schizophrenic children. *Am. J. Orthopsych.,* **19**(1949), 592.

40. Hoch, P. H., J. P. Cattell, and H. H. Pennes. Effects of mescaline and lysergic acid (d. LSD 25). *Am. J. Psychiatry,* **108**(1952), 579–584.

41. Hoch, P. H., H. H. Pennes, and J. P. Cattell. Psychoses produced by the administration of drugs. *Res. Publ. Ass. Nerv. Ment. Dis.,* **32**(1953), 287–296.

42. Fabing, H. D. New blocking agent against the development of LSD-25 psychosis. *Science,* **121**(1955), 208–210.

43. Gantt, W. H. Principles of nervous breakdown—schizokinesis and autokinesis. *Ann. N. Y. Acad. Sci.,* **56**(1953), 143–163.

44. Grewel, F., ed. Infantiel autism. Amsterdam: J. Muusses te Purmerend, 1954.

10. ORGANIC SYNDROMES

T HE ORGANIC SYNDROMES contain those disorders where psychic malfunctioning can be clearly traced to some physical injury, usually to the brain. The symptoms and prognosis differ widely depending on the locus and extent of the injury. However, there are a number of psychological characteristics which seem common to individuals with brain damage, although the profundity of these characteristics differs from person to person and depends only partially on the magnitude of the injury. Goldstein discusses these similarities in his paper, while Doll deals with a particular organic syndrome which has aroused a good deal of recent attention, mental retardation. His paper represents an attempt to promote a clearer social understanding of the retarded.

The Effect of Brain Damage on the Personality[*]

KURT GOLDSTEIN, M.D.

When I was asked to speak before the Psychoanalytic Association about the changes of the personality in brain damage, I was somewhat hesitant because I was not quite sure that I would be able to make myself understood by an audi-

Reprinted from *Psychiatry*, **15**(1952), 245–260, by special permission of The William Alanson White Psychiatric Foundation, Inc., holder of the copyright, and the author.

* This paper was presented, by invitation, at the Annual Meeting of the American Psychoanalytic Association, Atlantic City, May 1952.

ence which thinks mainly in such different categories and speaks in such a different terminology from my own. I finally accepted the invitation, because I thought that members of the Association apparently wanted to hear what I think and because it brought me the opportunity to express an old idea of mine—the idea that it is faulty in principle to try to make a distinction between so-called organic and functional diseases, as far as symptomatology and therapy are

359

concerned (1). In both conditions, one is dealing with abnormal functioning of the same psychophysical apparatus and with the attempts of the organism to come to terms with that. If the disturbances— whether they are due to damage to the brain or to psychological conflicts—do not disappear spontaneously or cannot be eliminated by therapy, the organism has to make a new adjustment to life in spite of them. Our task is to help the patients in this adjustment by physical and psychological means; the procedure and goal of the therapy in both conditions is, in principle, the same.

This was the basic idea which induced a group of neurologists, psychiatrists, and psychotherapists—including myself—many years ago, in 1927, to organize the Internationale Gesellschaft für Psychotherapie in Germany and to invite all physicians interested in psychotherapy to meet at the First Congress of the Society. Psychotherapists of all different schools responded to our invitation, and the result of the discussions was surprisingly fruitful. At the second meeting in 1927, I spoke about the relation between psychoanalysis and biology (2). During the last twenty years, in which I have occupied myself intensively with psychotherapy, I have become more and more aware of the similarity of the phenomena of organic and psychogenic conditions.

It is not my intention to consider the similarities in this paper. I want to restrict myself to the description of the symptomatology and the interpretation of the behavior changes in patients with damage to the brain cortex, particularly in respect to their personality, and would like to leave it to you to make comparisons.

The symptomatology which these patients present is very complex (3). It is the effect of various factors of which the change of personality is only one. Therefore, when we want to characterize the change of personality, we have to separate it from the symptoms due to other factors: (1) from those which are the effect of *disturbance of inborn or learned patterns* of performances in special performance fields—such as motor and sensory patterns; (2) from those which are the *expression of the so-called catastrophic conditions;* and (3) from those which are the *expression of the protective mechanisms* which originate from the attempt of the organism to avoid catastrophes.

In order to avoid terminological misunderstandings, I want to state what I mean by personality: Personality shows itself in behavior. Personality is the mode of behavior of a person in terms of the capacities of human beings in general and in the specific appearance of these capacities in a particular person. Behavior is always an entity and concerns the whole personality. Only abstractively can we separate behavior into parts—as for instance, bodily processes, conscious phenomena, states of feelings, attitudes, and so on (4, pp. 310 ff.).

According to my observation, all the phenomena of behavior become understandable if one assumes that all the behavior of the organism is determined by one trend (5), the *trend to actualize itself*—that is, its nature and all its capacities. This takes place normally in such harmony that the realization of all capacities in the best way possible in the particular environment is permitted. The capacities are experienced by a person as various *needs* which he is driven to fulfill with the cooperation of some parts of the environment and in spite of the hindrance by other parts of it.

Each stimulation brings about some disorder in the organism. But after a certain time—which is determined by the particular performance—the organism comes back, by a process of *equalization,* to its normal condition. This process guarantees the constancy of the organism. A person's specific personality corresponds to this constancy. Because realization has to take place in terms of different needs and different tasks, the behavior of the organism is soon directed more by one than by another need. This does not mean that organismic behavior is determined by separate needs or drives. All such concepts need the assumption of a controlling agency. I have tried to show in my book, *The Organism,* that the different agencies which have been assumed for this purpose have only made for new difficulties in the attempt to understand organismic behavior; they are not necessary if one gives up the concept of separate drives, as my theory of the organism does. All of a person's capacities are always in action in each of his activities. The capacity that is particularly important for the task is in the foreground; the others are in the background. All of these capacities are organized in a way which facilitates the self-realization of the total organism in the particular situation. For each performance there is a definite figure-ground organization of capacities; the change in the behavior of a patient corresponds to the change in the total organism in the form of an alteration of the normal pattern of figure-ground organization (4, p. 109).

Among patients with brain damage we can distinguish between alterations which occur when an area belonging to a special performance field—such as a motor or sensory area—is damaged somewhat isolatedly, and alterations which occur when the personality organization itself is altered. In lesions of these areas—according to a dedifferentiation of the function of the brain cortex (4, p. 131)—qualities and patterns of behavior (both those developing as a result of maturation and those acquired by learning) are disturbed. Indeed, these patterns never occur isolatedly. They are always embedded in that kind of behavior which we call personality. The personality structure is disturbed particularly by lesions of the frontal lobes, the parietal lobes, and the insula Reili; but it is also disturbed by diffuse damage to the cortex —for instance, in paralysis, alcoholism, and trauma, and in metabolic disturbances such as hypoglycemia. The effect of diffuse damage is understandable when we consider that what we call personality structure apparently is not related to a definite locality of the cortex (4, pp. 249 ff.) but to a particular complex function of the brain which is the same for all its parts. This function can be damaged especially by lesions in any of the areas I have mentioned. The damage of the patterns certainly modifies the personality too. Although for full understanding of the personality changes, we should discuss the organization of the patterns and their destruction in damaged patients, that would carry us too far and is not absolutely necessary for our discussion. I shall therefore restrict my presentation to consideration of the symptoms due to damage of the personality structure itself (6).

There would be no better way of getting to the heart of the problem than by demonstrating a patient. Unfortunately I have to substitute for this a description of the behavior of patients with severe damage of the brain cortex. Let us consider a man with an extensive lesion of the frontal lobes (7, 8). His customary way of living does not seem to be very much disturbed. He is a little slow; his face is rather immobile, rather rigid; his attention is directed very strictly to what he is doing at the moment—say, writing a letter, or speaking to someone. Confronted with tasks in various fields, he gives seemingly normal responses under certain conditions; but under other conditions he fails completely in tasks that seem to be very similar to those he has performed quite well.

This change of behavior becomes apparent particularly in the following simple test: We place before him a small wooden stick in a definite position, pointing, for example, diagonally from left to right. He is asked to note the position of the stick carefully. After a half minute's exposure, the stick is removed; then it is handed to the patient, and he is asked to put it back in the position in which it was before. He grasps the stick and tries to replace it, but he fumbles; he is all confusion; he looks at the examiner, shakes his head, tries this way and that, plainly uncertain. The upshot is that he cannot place the stick in the required position. He is likewise unable to imitate other simple figures built of sticks. Next we show the patient a little house made of many sticks—a house with a roof, a door, a window, and a chimney. After we remove it, we ask the patient to reproduce the model. He succeeds very well.

Impairment of Abstract Capacity

If we ask ourselves what is the cause of the difference in his behavior in the two tasks, we can at once exclude defects in the field of perception, action, and memory. For there is no doubt that copying the house with many details demands a much greater capacity in all these faculties, especially in memory, than putting a single stick into a position which the patient has been shown shortly before. A further experiment clarifies the situation. We put before the patient two sticks placed together so as to form an angle with the opening pointing upward (V). The patient is unable to reproduce this model. Then we confront him with the same angle, the opening downward this time (∧), and now he reproduces the figure very well on the first trial. When we ask the patient how it is that he can reproduce the second figure but not the first one, he says, "This one has nothing to do with the other one." Pointing to the second one, he says, "That is a roof"; pointing to the first, "That is nothing."

These two replies lead us to an understanding of the patient's behavior. His first reply makes it clear that, to him, the two objects with which he has to deal are totally different from one another. The second answer shows that he apprehends the angle with the opening downward as a concrete object out of his own experience, and he constructs a concrete thing with the two sticks. The two sticks that formed an angle with the opening upward apparently did not arouse an impression of a concrete thing. He had to regard the sticks as representations indicating directions in abstract space. Furthermore, he had to keep these directions in mind and rearrange the sticks from memory as representatives of these abstract directions. To solve the problem he must give an account to himself of relations in space and must act on the basis of abstract ideas. Thus we may conclude that the failure of the patient in the first test lies in the fact that he is unable to perform a task which can be executed only by means of a grasp of the abstract. The test in which the opening of the angle is downwards does not demand this, since the patient is able to grasp it as a concrete object and therefore to execute it perfectly. It is for the same reason that he is able to copy the little house, which seems to us to be so much more complicated. From the result of his behavior in this and similar tasks we come to the assumption that these *patients are impaired in their abstract capacity.*

The term "abstract attitude," which I shall use in describing this capacity, will be more comprehensible in the light of the following explanation (9). We can distinguish two different kinds of attitudes, the concrete and the abstract. In the concrete attitude we are given over passively and bound to the immediate experience of unique objects or situations. Our thinking and acting are determined by the immediate claims made by the particular aspect of the object or situation. For instance, we act concretely when we enter a room in darkness and push the button for light. If, however, we reflect that by pushing the button we might awaken someone asleep in the room, and desist from pushing the button, then we are acting abstractively. We transcend the immediately given specific aspect of sense impressions; we detach ourselves from these impressions, consider the situation from a conceptual point of view, and react accordingly. Our actions are determined not so much by the objects before us as by the way we think about them: the individual thing becomes a mere accidental representative of a category to which it belongs.

The impairment of the attitude toward the abstract shows in every performance of the brain-damaged patient who is impaired in this capacity. He always fails when the solution of a task presupposes this attitude; he performs well when the appropriate activity is determined directly by the stimuli and when the task can be fulfilled by concrete behavior. He may have no difficulty in using known objects in a situation that requires them; but he is totally at a loss if he is asked to demonstrate the use of such an object outside the concrete situation, and still more so if he is asked to do it without the real object. A few examples will illustrate this:

The patient is asked to blow away a slip of paper. He does this very well. If the paper is taken away and he is asked to think that there is a slip of paper and to blow it away, he is unable to do so. Here the situation is not realistically complete. In order to perform the task the patient would have to imagine the piece of paper there. He is not capable of this.

The patient is asked to throw a ball into open boxes situated respectively at distances of three, nine, and fifteen feet. He does that correctly. When he is asked how far the several boxes are from him, he is not only unable to answer this question but unable even to say which box is nearest to him and which is farthest.

In the first action, the patient has only to deal with objects in a behavioral fashion. It is unnecessary for him to be conscious of this behavior and of objects in a world separated from himself. In the second, however, he must separate himself from objects in the outer world and give himself an account of his actions and of the space relations in the world facing him. Since he is unable to do this, he fails. We could describe this failure also by saying that the patient is unable to deal with a situation which is only possible.

A simple story is read to a patient. He may repeat some single words, but he does not understand their meaning and is unable to grasp the essential point. Now we read him another story, which would seem to a normal person to be more difficult to understand. This time he understands the meaning very well and recounts the chief points. The first story deals with a simple situation, but a situation which has no connection with the actual situation of the patient. The second story recounts a situation he is familiar with. Hence one could say the patient is able to grasp and handle only something which is related to himself.

Such a patient almost always recognizes pictures of single objects, even if the picture contains many details. In pictures which represent a composition of a number of things and persons, he may pick out some details; but he is unable to understand the picture as a whole and is unable to respond to the whole. The patient's real understanding does not depend on the greater or smaller number of components in a picture but on whether the components, whatever their number, hang together concretely and are familiar to him, or whether an understanding of their connection requires a more abstract synthesis on his part. He may lack understanding of a picture even if there are only a few details. If the picture does not reveal its essence directly, by bringing the patient into the situation which it represents, he is not able to understand it. Thus one may characterize the deficiency as an inability to discover the essence of a situation which is not related to his own personality.

MEMORY AND ATTENTION

This change in behavior finds its expression in characteristic changes in memory and attention. Under certain circumstances the faculty for reproduction of facts acquired previously may be about normal. For example, things learned in school may be recalled very well, but only in some situations. The situation must be suited to reawakening old impressions. If the required answer demands an abstract attitude on the part of a patient or if it demands that he give an account of the matter in question, the patient is unable to remember. Therefore he fails in many intelligence tests which may seem very simple for a normal person, and he is amazingly successful in others which appear complicated to us. He is able to learn new facts and to keep them in mind; but he can learn them only in a concrete situation and can reproduce them only in the same situation in which he has learned them. Because the intentional recollection of experiences acquired in infancy requires an abstract attitude toward the situation at that time, the patient is unable to recall infancy experiences in a voluntary way; but we can observe that the aftereffect of such experiences sometimes appears passively in his behavior. Such a patient has the greatest difficulty in associating freely; he cannot assume the attitude of mind to make that possible. He is incapable of recollection when he is asked to recall things which have nothing to do with the given situation. The patient must be able to regard the present situation in such a way that facts from the past belong to it. If this is not the case, he is completely unable to recall facts

which he has recalled very well in another situation. Repeated observation in many different situations demonstrates clearly that such memory failures are not caused by an impairment of memory content. The patient has the material in his memory, but he is unable to use it freely; he can use it only in connection with a definite concrete situation.

We arrive at the same result in testing attention. At one time the patient appears inattentive and distracted; at another time, he is attentive, even abnormally so. The patient's attention is usually weak in special examinations, particularly at the beginning before he has become aware of the real approach to the whole situation. In such a situation he ordinarily seems much distracted. If he is able to enter into the situation, however, his attention may be satisfactory; sometimes his reactions are even abnormally keen. Under these circumstances he may be totally untouched by other stimuli from the environment to which normal persons will unfailingly react. In some tests he will always seem distracted; for example, in those situations which demand a change of approach (a choice), he always seems distracted because he is incapable of making a choice. Consequently, it is not correct to speak of a change of attention in these patients in terms of plus or minus. The state of the patient's attention is but part of his total behavior and is to be understood only in connection with it.

EMOTIONAL RESPONSES

The same holds true if we observe the emotions of the patients. Usually they are considered emotionally dull and often they appear so, but it would not be correct to say simply that they are suffering from a diminution of emotions. The same patients can be dull under some conditions and very excited under others. This can be explained when we consider the patient's emotional behavior in relation to his entire behavior in a given situation. When he does not react emotionally in an adequate way, investigation reveals that he has not grasped the situation in such a way that emotion could arise. In fact, we might experience a similar lack of emotion through failing to grasp a situation. The patient may have grasped only one part of the situation—the part which can be grasped concretely—and this part may not give any reason for an emotional reaction. The lack of emotion appears to us inappropriate because we grasp with the abstract attitude the whole situation to which the emotional character is attached. This connection between the emotions and the total behavior becomes understandable when we consider that emotions are not simply related to particular experiences but are, as I have shown on another occasion (10), inherent aspects of behavior—part and parcel of behavior. No behavior is without emotion and what we call lack of emotion is a deviation from normal emotions corresponding to the deviation of behavior in general. From this point of view, one modification of reactions that is of particular interest in respect to the problem of emotions in general, becomes understandable. Often we see that a patient reacts either not at all or in an *abnormally quick manner*. The latter occurs particularly when the patient believes he has the correct answer to a problem. Although this behavior might seem to be the effect of a change in the time factor of his reactivity, it is rather the *effect of an emotional factor*—that is, it is the modification of his emotional feelings because of the impairment of his ability for abstraction—which in turn modifies the time reaction.

PLEASURE AND JOY

These patients are always somewhat in danger of being in a catastrophic condition—which I shall discuss later—as a result of not being able to find the right solution to a problem put before them. They are often afraid that they may not be able to react correctly, and that they will be in a catastrophic condition. Therefore, when they believe they have the right answer, they answer as quickly as possible. Because of impairment of abstraction, they are not able to deliberate; they try to do what they can do as quickly as possible because every retardation increases the tension which they experience when they are not able to answer. The quick response is an effect of their *strong necessity to release tension;* they are forced to release tension because they cannot handle it any other way. They cannot bear anything that presupposes deliberation, considering the future, and so on, all of which are related to abstraction.

This difference in behavior between these patients and more normal people throws light on the nature of the *trend to release tension*. These patients must, so to speak, follow the "pleasure principle." This phenomenon is one *expression of the abnormal concreteness* which is a counterpart to the impairment of abstraction. The *trend to release tension appears to be an expression of pathology*—the effect of a protective mechanism to prevent catastrophic condition. To normal behavior belong deliberation and retardation; but in addition there is the ability to speed up an activity or a part of it to correspond to the requirements of the task, or at least part of the requirements, so that its performance guarantees self-realization. Sometimes the ability to bear tension and even to enjoy it are also a part of this normal behavior. In contrast, the patients that I am talking about are only able to experience the pleasure of release of tension; they never appear to enjoy anything—a fact which is often clearly revealed by the expression on their faces. This becomes understandable if we consider that immediate reality is transcended in any kind of joy and that joy is a capacity we owe to the abstract attitude, especially that part of it concerned with possibility. Thus brain-injured patients who are impaired in this attitude cannot experience joy. Experience with brain-injured patients teaches us that we have to distinguish between *pleasure by release of tension,* and the active *feeling of enjoyment* and freedom so characteristic of joy. Pleasure through release of tension is the agreeable feeling which we experience on returning to a state of equilibrium after it has been disturbed—the passive feeling of being freed from distress. Pleasure lasts only a short time till a new situation stimulates new activity; we then try to get rid of the tension of the new situation which acts to shorten the span of pleasure. In contrast, we try to extend joy. This explains the different speeds of joy and pleasure. Because of the capacity for joy, we can experience the possibility of the indefinite continuation of a situation. The two emotions of joy and pleasure play essentially different roles in regard to self-realization; they belong to different performances or different parts of a performance; they belong to different moods. Pleasure may be a necessary state of respite. But it is a phenomenon of standstill; it is akin to death. It separates us from the world and the other individuals in it; it is equilibrum, quietness. In joy there is disequilibrium. But it is a productive disequilibrium, leading toward fruitful activity and a particular kind of self-realization. This difference in approach between the normal person and the brain-injured patient is mirrored in the essentially different behavior of the latter and the different world in which he lives. The different significance of the two emotional states in his total behavior is related to their time difference.

Edith Jacobson (11), in the outline of her paper presented to the Psychoanalytic Association, speaks about the speed factor in psychic discharge processes and comes to the conclusion that discharge is not the only process which produces pleasure—that we have to distinguish between different qualities of pleasure in terms of the slow rising and the quick falling of tension. That is very much in accordance with my conclusions derived from experience with brain-injured patients. If one distinguishes two forms of pleasure, one should, for clarity's sake, use different names for them; I think that my use of pleasure and joy fits the two experiences. But I would not like to call them both discharge processes: the one is a discharge process; the other one a very active phenomenon related to the highest form of mental activity—abstraction. From this it becomes clear why they have such an essentially different significance in the totality of performance: the one is an equalization process which prepares the organism for new activity; the other one is an activity of highest value for self-realization. They belong together just as in general equalization process and activity belong together. Therefore they cannot be understood as isolated phenomena.

THE PHENOMENON OF WITTICISM

From this viewpoint of the emotions of brain-injured patients, the phenomenon of witticism appears in a new aspect. We can see that even though a patient makes witty remarks, he is not able to grasp the character of situations which produce humor in an average normal individual. Whether or not some situation appears humorous depends upon whether it can be grasped in a concrete way which is suited to producing the emotion of humor. In accordance with the impairment of his ability for abstraction, such a patient perceives many humorous pictures in a realistic way, which does not evoke the expected humor. But of course any of us who might at a given time perceive a humorous picture in a realistic way would respond similarly. On the other hand a patient may make a witty remark in relation to a situation which is not considered humorous by us, because he has experienced the situation in another way. Thus we should not speak of witticism as a special characteristic of these patients. It is but one expression of the change in their personality structure in the same way that their inability to understand jokes under other conditions expresses this change. Indeed, these patients are in general dull because of their limited experience, and their witticisms are superficial and shallow in comparison with those of normal people.

FRIENDSHIP AND LOVE

The drive towards the release of tension, which I have already mentioned, is one of the causes of the strange behavior of these patients in friendship and love situations. They need close relationships to other people and they try to maintain such relationships at all cost; at the same time such relationships are easily terminated suddenly if the bearing of tension is necessary for the maintenance of the relationship.

The following example is illustrative: A patient of mine, Mr. A, was for years a close friend of another patient, Mr. X. One day Mr. X went to a movie with a third man. Mr. X did not take Mr. A along because Mr. A had seen the picture before and did not want to see it a second time. When Mr. X came back, my patient was in a state of great excitement and refused to speak to him. Mr. A could not be quieted by any explanations; he was told that his friend had not meant to offend him, and that the friendship had not changed, but these explanations made no impression. From that time on, Mr. A was the enemy of his old friend, Mr. X. He was only aware that his friend was the companion of another man, and he felt himself

slighted. This experience produced a great tension in him. He regarded his friend as the cause of this bad condition and reacted to him in a way that is readily understandable in terms of his inability to bear tension and to put himself in the place of somebody else.

Another patient never seemed to be concerned about his family. He never spoke of his wife or children and was unresponsive when we questioned him about them. When we suggested to him that he should write to his family, he was utterly indifferent. He appeared to lack all feeling in this respect. At times he visited his home in another town, according to an established practice, and stayed there several days. We learned that while he was at home, he conducted himself in the same way that any man would in the bosom of his family. He was kind and affectionate to his wife and children and interested in their affairs insofar as his abilities would permit. Upon his return to the hospital from such a visit, he would smile in an embarrassed way and give evasive answers when he was asked about his family; he seemed utterly estranged from his home situation. Unquestionably the peculiar behavior of this man was not really the effect of deterioration of his character on the emotional and moral side; rather, his behavior was the result of the fact that he could not summon up the home situation when he was not actually there.

Lack of imagination, which is so apparent in this example, makes such patients incapable of experiencing any expectation of the future. This lack is apparent, for instance, in the behavior of a male patient toward a woman whom he later married (12). When he was with the girl, he seemed to behave in a friendly, affectionate way and to be very fond of the girl. But when he was separated from her, he did not care about her at all; he would not seek her out and certainly did not desire to have a love relationship with her. When he was questioned, his answers indicated that he did not even understand what sexual desire meant. But in addition he had forgotten about the girl. When he met her again and she spoke to him, he was able immediately to enter into the previous relation. He was as affectionate as before. When she induced him to go to bed with her and embraced him, he performed an apparently normal act of sexual intercourse with satisfaction for both. She had the feeling that he loved her. She became pregnant, and they were married.

CHANGE IN LANGUAGE

Of particular significance in these patients is the change in their language because of their lack of abstract attitude (13, p. 56). Their words lose the character of meaning. Words are not usable in those situations in which they must represent a concept. Therefore the patients are not able to find the proper words in such situations. Thus, for instance, patients are not able to name concrete objects, since as shown by investigation, naming presupposes an abstract attitude and the abstract use of words. These patients have not lost the sound complex; but they cannot use it as a sign for a concept. On other occasions, the sound complex may be uttered; but it is only used at those times as a simple association to a given object, as a property of the object, such as color and form, and not as representative of a concept. If a patient has been particularly gifted in language before his brain is damaged and has retained many such associations or can acquire associations as a substitute for naming something, then he may utter the right word through association, so that an observer is not able to distinguish between his uttering the sound complex and giving a name to something; only through analysis can one make this dis-

tinction (13, p. 61). Thus we can easily overlook the patient's defect by arriving at a conclusion only on the basis of this capacity for a positive effect. In the same way we can be deceived by a negative effect which may only be an expression, for instance, of the patient's fear that he will use the wrong word. I have used the term *fallacy of effect* to describe the uncertain and ambiguous character of a conclusion which is based only upon a patient's effective performance. This term applies not only to language but to all performances of the patients. It is the source of one of the most fatal mistakes which can be made in interpretation of phenomena observed in organic patients; incidentally, it is a mistake which can be made also in functional cases.

FRONTAL LOBOTOMY

In reference to the fallacy of effect, I want to stress how easily one can be deceived about the mental condition of patients who have undergone frontal lobotomy. The results of the usual intelligence test, evaluated statistically, may not reveal any definite deviation from the norm; yet the patient can have an impairment of abstraction that will become obvious through tests which take into consideration the fallacy of effect.* My experience with frontal lobotomy patients and my evaluation of the literature on frontal lobotomy leave no doubt in my mind that at least many of these patients show impairment of abstract capacity, although perhaps not to such a degree as do patients with gross damage

* Thirty years ago we constructed special tests when we were faced with the problem of re-educating brain-injured soldiers. (See K. Goldstein and A. Gelb, "Uber Farbennamen-amnesie," *Psychol. Forsch.* [1924] 6:127.) These tests, which were introduced in America by Scheerer and myself (reference 9), proved to be particularly useful not only for studying the problem of abstraction in patients, but also for the correct organization of treatment.

of the brain. Because of the fallacy of effect, which tends to overlook the defect in abstraction, the reports of the relatives that the lobotomized patient behaves well in everyday life are often evaluated incorrectly by the doctor (14). In the sheltered, simple life that these patients have with their families, the patients are not often confronted with tasks which require abstract reasoning; thus the family is likely to overlook their more subtle deviations from the norm. Sometimes peculiarities of the patient are reported which definitely point to a defect in abstraction, which is more serious than it is often evaluated: for instance, a patient who in general seems to live in a normal way does not have any relationship with even the closest members of his family and manifests no interest in his children; another patient exists in a vacuum so that no friendship is possible with him.

A woman patient after lobotomy still knows how to set a table for guests, and how to act as a perfect hostess. Before lobotomy, she was always a careful housewife, deciding everything down to the last detail; but now she does not care how the house is run, she never enters the kitchen, and the housekeeper does all the managing, even the shopping. She still reads a great number of books, but she does not understand the contents as well as before.

A skilled mechanic, who is still considered an excellent craftsman, is able to work in a routine way; but he has lost the ability to undertake complicated jobs, has stopped studying, and seems to have resigned himself to being a routine worker; apparently all this is an effect of the loss of his capacity for abstraction, which is so necessary for all initiative and for creative endeavor. Thus we see that even when the behavior of the patients appears not to be overtly disturbed, it differs essentially from normal behavior—in the particular way which is characteristic of impairment in abstract

attitude. Freeman (15), who was originally so enthusiastically in favor of the operation, has become more cautious about its damage to the higher mental functions. He writes:

The patients with frontal lobotomy show always some lack of personality depth; impulse, intelligence, temperament are disturbed; the creative capacity undergoes reduction—the spiritual life in general was affected. They are largely indifferent to the opinions and feelings of others.

He apparently discovered the same personality changes in his patients as those which we have described as characteristic of the behavior of patients with impaired capacity for abstraction. Thus we should be very careful in judging personality change following frontal lobotomy. Although I would not deny the usefulness of the operation in some cases, I would like to say, as I have before, that the possibility of an impairment of abstraction should always be taken into consideration before the operation is undertaken.

I would now like to present a survey of the various situations in which the patient is unable to perform. He fails when he has: (1) to assume a mental set voluntarily or to take initiative (for instance, he may even be able to perform well in giving a series of numbers, once someone else has presented the first number, but he cannot begin the activity); (2) to shift voluntarily from one aspect of a situation to another, making a choice; (3) to account to himself for his actions or to verbalize the account; (4) to keep in mind simultaneously various aspects of a situation or to react to two stimuli which do not belong intrinsically together; (5) to grasp the essence of a given whole, or to break up a given whole into parts, isolating the parts voluntarily and combining them into wholes; (6) to abstract common properties, to plan ahead ideationally, to assume an attitude toward a situation which is only possible, and to think or perform symbolically; (7) to do something which necessitates detaching the ego from the outer world or from inner experiences.

All these and other terms which one may use to describe the behavior of the patients basically mean the same. We speak usually, in brief, of an *impairment of abstract attitude.* I hope that it has become clear that the use of this term does not refer to a theoretical interpretation but to the real behavior of the human being and that it is suitable for describing both normal and pathological personality.

In brief, the patients are changed with respect to the most characteristic properties of the human being. They have lost initiative and the capacity to look forward to something and to make plans and decisions; they lack phantasy and inspiration; their perceptions, thoughts, and ideas are reduced; they have lost the capacity for real contact with others, and they are therefore incapable of real friendship, love, and social relations. One could say they have no real ego and no real world. That they behave in an abnormally concrete way and that they are driven to get rid of tensions are only expressions of the same defect. When such patients are able to complete a task in a concrete way, they may—with regard to the effect of their activity—not appear very abnormal. But closer examination shows that they are abnormally rigid, stereotyped, and compulsive, and abnormally bound to stimuli from without and within.

To avoid any misunderstanding, I would like to stress that the defect in patients with brain damage does not always have to manifest itself in the same way—not even in all frontal lobe lesions. To what degree impairment of abstraction appears depends upon the extensiveness, the intensity, and the nature of the lesion. To evaluate the relationship between a patient's behavior and his de-

fect, we have to consider further that personal experience plays a role in determining whether a patient can solve a problem or not. One patient reacts well—at least at face value—when he is given a task, although another patient has failed the same task; to the first patient the task represents a concrete situation; for the second patient it is an abstract situation. But in both cases, the defect will always be revealed by further examination.

Catastrophic Conditions

Impairment of abstraction is not the only factor which produces deviations in the behavior of patients, as I have stated before. Another very important factor is the occurrence of a catastrophic condition (4, pp. 35 ff.). When a patient is not able to fulfill a task set before him, this condition is a frequent occurrence. A patient may look animated, calm, in a good mood, well-poised, collected, and cooperative when he is confronted with tasks he can fulfill; the same patient may appear dazed, become agitated, change color, start to fumble, become unfriendly, evasive, and even aggressive when he is not able to fulfill the task. His overt behavior appears very much the same as a person in a state of anxiety. I have called the state of the patient in the situation of success, *ordered condition;* the state in the situation of failure, *disordered or catastrophic condition.*

In the catastrophic condition the patient not only is incapable of performing a task which exceeds his impaired capacity, but he also fails, for a longer or shorter period, in performances which he is able to carry out in the ordered state. For a varying period of time, the organism's reactions are in great disorder or are impeded altogether. We are able to study this condition particularly well in these patients, since we can produce it experimentally by demanding from the patient something which we know he will not be able to do, because of his defect. Now, as we have said, impairment of abstraction makes it impossible for a patient to account to himself for his acts. He is quite unable to realize his failure and why he fails. Thus we can assume that catastrophic condition is not a reaction of the patient to failure, but rather belongs intrinsically to the situation of the organism in failing. For the normal person, failure in the performance of a nonimportant task would be merely something disagreeable; for the brain-injured person, however, as observation shows, any failure means the impossibility of self-realization and of existence. The occurrence of catastrophic condition is not limited therefore to special tasks; any task can place the patient in this situation, since the patient's self-realization is endangered so easily. Thus the same task produces anxiety at one time, and not at another.

ANXIETY

The conditions under which anxiety occurs in brain-injured patients correspond to the conditions for its occurrence in normal people in that what produces anxiety is not the failure itself, but the resultant danger to the person's existence. I would like to add that the danger need not always be real; it is sufficient if the person imagines that the condition is such that he will not be able to realize himself. For instance, a person may be in distress because he is not able to answer questions in an examination. If the outcome of the examination is not particularly important, then the normal person will take it calmly even though he may feel somewhat upset; because it is not a dangerous situation for him, he will face the situation and try to come to terms with it as well as he can by using his wits, and in this way he will bring it to a more or less successful solution. The situation becomes totally dif-

ferent, however, if passing the examination is of great consequence in the person's life; not passing the examination may, for instance, endanger his professional career or the possibility of marrying the person he loves. When self-realization is seriously in danger, catastrophe may occur together with severe anxiety; when this occurs, it is impossible for the person to answer even those questions which, under other circumstances, he could solve without difficulty.

I would like to clarify one point here —namely, that anxiety represents an emotional state which does not refer to any object. Certainly the occurrence of anxiety is connected with an outer or inner event. The organism, shaken by a catastrophic shock, exists in relation to a definitive reality; and the basic phenomenon of anxiety, which is the occurrence of disordered behavior, is understandable only in terms of this relationship to reality. But anxiety does not originate from the experiencing of this relationship. The brain-injured patient could not experience anxiety, if it were necessary for him to experience this relationship to reality. He is certainly not aware of this objective reality; he experiences only the shock, only anxiety. And this, of course holds true for anxiety in general. Observations of many patients confirm the interpretation of anxiety by philosophers, such as Pascal and Kierkegaard, and by psychologists who have dealt with anxiety—namely, that the source of anxiety is the inner experience of not being confronted with anything or of being confronted with nothingness.

In making such a statement, one must distinguish sharply between *anxiety* and *fear*—another emotional state which is very often confused with anxiety (4, p. 293; 16). Superficially, fear may have many of the characteristics of anxiety, but intrinsically it is different. In the state of fear we have an object before us, we can meet that object, we can attempt to remove it, or we can flee from it. We are conscious of ourselves, as well as of the object; we can deliberate as to how we shall behave toward it, and we can look at the cause of the fear, which actually lies before us. Anxiety, on the other hand, gets at us from the back, so to speak. The only thing we can do is to attempt to flee from it, but without knowing what direction to take, since we experience it as coming from no particular place. We are dealing, as I have shown explicitly elsewhere, with qualitative differences, with different attitudes toward the world. Fear is related, in our experience, to an object; anxiety is not—it is only an inner state.

What is characteristic of the object of fear? Is it something inherent in the object itself, at all times? Of course not. At one time an object may arouse only interest, or be met with indifference; but at another time it may evoke the greatest fear. In other words, fear must be the result of a specific relationship between organism and object. What leads to fear is nothing but the experience of the possibility of the onset of anxiety. What we fear is the impending anxiety, which we experience in relation to some objects. Since a person in a state of fear is not yet in a state of anxiety but only envisions it—that is, he only fears that anxiety may befall him—he is not so disturbed in his judgment of the outer world as the person in a state of anxiety. Rather, driven as he is by the tendency to avoid the onset of anxiety, he attempts to establish special contact with the outer world. He tries to recognize the situation as clearly as possible and to react to it in an appropriate manner. Fear is conditioned by, and directed against, very definite aspects of the environment. These have to be recognized and, if possible, removed. Fear sharpens the senses, whereas anxiety renders them unusable. Fear drives to action; anxiety paralyzes.

From these explanations it is obvious that in order to feel anxiety it is not necessary to be able to give oneself an account of one's acts; to feel fear, however, presupposes that capacity. From this it becomes clear that our patients do not behave like people in a state of fear —that is, they do not intentionally try to avoid situations from which anxiety may arise. They cannot do that because of the defect of abstraction. Also from our observation of the patients we can assume that they do not experience fear and that they only have the experience of anxiety.

Anxiety, a catastrophic condition in which self-realization is not possible, may be produced by a variety of events, all of which have in common the following: There is a discrepancy between the individual's capacities and the demands made on him, and this discrepancy makes self-realization impossible. This may be due to external or internal conditions, physical or psychological. It is this discrepancy to which we are referring when we speak of "conflicts." Thus we can observe anxiety in infants, in whom such a discrepancy must occur frequently, particularly since their abstract attitude is not yet developed, or not fully. We also see anxiety in brain-injured people, in whom impairment of abstraction produces the same discrepancy. In normal people, anxiety appears when the demands of the world are too much above the capacity of the individual, when social and economic situations are too stressful, or when religious conflicts arise. Finally we see anxiety in people with neuroses and psychoses which are based on unsolvable and unbearable inner conflicts.

The Protective Mechanisms

The last group of symptoms to be observed in brain-injured patients are the behavior changes which make it possi-

ble for the patient to get rid of the catastrophic condition—of anxiety (4, pp.
40 ff.). The observation of this phenomenon in these patients is of special
interest since it can teach us how an organism can get rid of anxiety without
being aware of its origin and without
being able to avoid the anxiety voluntarily. After a certain time these patients show a diminution of disorder and
of catastrophic reactions (anxiety) even
though the defect caused by the damage
to the brain still exists. This, of course,
can occur only if the patient is no longer
exposed to tasks he cannot cope with.
This diminution is achieved by definite
changes in the behavior of the patients:
They are withdrawn, so that a number
of stimuli, including dangerous ones, do
not reach them. They usually stay alone;
either they do not like company or
they want to be only with people whom
they know well. They like to be in a
familiar room in which everything is
organized in a definite way. They show
extreme orderliness in every respect;
everything has to be done exactly at an
appointed time—whether it is break-
fast, dinner, or a walk. They show excessive and fanatical orderliness in ar-
ranging their belongings; each item of
their wardrobe must be in a definite
place—that is, in a place where it can be
gotten hold of quickly, without the necessity of a choice, which they are unable to make. Although it is a very primitive order indeed, they stick fanatically
to it; it is the only way to exist. Any
change results in a state of very great
excitement. They themselves cannot voluntarily arrange things in a definite way.
The orderliness is maintained simply because the patients try to stick to those ar-
rangements which they can handle. This
sticking to that which they can cope
with is characteristic for their behavior;
thus any behavior change can be understood only in terms of this characteristic
behavior.

An illustration of this characteristic

behavior is the fact that they always try
to keep themselves busy with things that
they are able to do as a protection
against things that they cannot cope
with. The activities which engross them
need not be of great value in themselves.
Their usefulness consists apparently in
the fact that they protect the patient.
Thus a patient does not like to be interrupted in an activity. For instance,
although a patient may behave well in
a conversation with someone he knows
and likes, he does not like to be suddenly addressed by someone else.

We very often observe that a patient
is totally unaware of his defect—such as
hemiplegia or hemianopsia—and of the
difference between his state prior to the
development of the symptoms and his
present state. This is strikingly illustrated by the fact that the disturbances
of these patients play a very small part
in their complaints. We are not dealing
simply with a subjective lack of awareness, for the defects are effectively excluded from awareness, one might say.
This is shown by the fact that they produce very little disturbance—apparently
as the result of compensation. This exclusion from awareness seems to occur
particularly when the degree of functional defect in performance is extreme.
We can say that defects are shut out
from the life of the organism when they
would seriously impair any of its essential functions and when a defect can be
compensated for by other activities at
least to the extent that self-realization is
not essentially disturbed.

One can easily get the impression
that a patient tries to deny the experience of the functional disturbance because he is afraid that he will get into
a catastrophic condition if he becomes
aware of his defect. As a matter of fact,
a patient may get into a catastrophic
condition when we make him aware
of his defect, or when the particular
situation does not make possible an adequate compensation. Sometimes this hap-

pens—and this is especially interesting —when the underlying pathological condition improves and with that the function.

A patient of mine who became totally blind by a suicidal gunshot through the chiasma opticum behaved as if he were not aware of his blindness; the defect was compensated for very well by his use of his other senses, his motor skill, and his knowledge and intelligence. He was usually in a good mood; he never spoke of his defect, and he resisted all attempts to draw his attention to it. After a certain time, the condition improved; but at the same time he realized that he could not recognize objects through his vision. He was shocked and became deeply depressed. When he was asked why he was depressed, he said, "I cannot see." We might assume that in the beginning the patient denied the defect intentionally because he could not bear it. But why then did he not deny it when he began to see? Or we might assume that in the beginning he did not deny his blindness, but that in total blindness an adjustment occurred in terms of a change of behavior for which vision was not necessary; and because of this it was not necessary for him to realize his blindness. The moment he was able to see, he became aware of his defect and was no longer able to eliminate it. The exclusion of the blindness defect from awareness could thus be considered a secondary effect of the adjustment. But in this patient who was mentally undisturbed a more voluntary denial cannot be overlooked. A voluntary denial is not possible in patients with impairment of abstraction as in brain-injured patients. Here the unawareness of the defect can only be a secondary effect—an effect of the same behavior, which we have described before, by which the brain-injured person is protected against catastrophes which may occur because of his defect. As we have said, the patient, driven by the trend to realize himself as well as possible, sticks to what he is able to do; this shows in his whole behavior. From this point of view, the patient's lack of awareness of his defect, as well as his peculiarities in general, becomes understandable. For instance, in these terms, it is understandable why an aphasic patient utters a word which is only on the normal fringe of the word that he needs; for the word that he needs to use is a word that he cannot say at all or can say only in such a way that he could not be understood and would as a result be in distress (13, p. 226). Thus a patient may repeat "church" instead of "God," "father" instead of "mother," and so on; he considers his reaction correct, at least as long as no one makes him aware of the fact that his reaction is wrong. This same kind of reaction occurs in disturbances of recognition, of feelings, and so on.

One is inclined to consider the use of wrong words or disturbances of recognition, actions, and feelings as due to a special pathology; but that is not their origin. Since these disturbances are reactions which represent all that the individual is able to execute, he recognizes them as fulfillment of the task; in this way, these reactions fulfill this need to such a degree that no catastrophe occurs. Thus the protection appears as a passive effect of an active "correct" procedure and could not be correctly termed denial, which refers to a more intentional activity, "conscious" or "unconscious."

This theory on the origin of the protective behavior in organic patients deserves consideration, particularly because the phenomena observed in organic patients shows such a similarity to that observed in neurotics. One could even use psychoanalytic terms for the different forms of behavior in organic patients. For instance, one might use the same terms that Anna Freud (17) uses to characterize various defense mechanisms against anxiety. Both neurotic and organic patients show a definite similarity in behavior structure and in the purpose served by that structure. In organic patients, however, I prefer to speak of protective mechanisms instead of defense mechanisms; the latter refers to a more voluntary act, which organic patients certainly cannot perform, as we have discussed earlier. In neurotics, the development of defense mechanisms generally does not occur so passively through organismic adjustment, as does the development of protective mechanisms in the organic patients; this is in general the distinction between the two. It seems to me that this distinction is not true in the case of neurotic children, however; some of these children seem to develop protective mechanisms in a passive way, similar to organic patients. Such mechanisms can perhaps be found in other neurotics. Thus, in interpreting these mechanisms, one should take into account the possibility of confusing the neurotic patient with the organic patient.

I would like to add a last word with regard to the restrictions of the personality and of the world of these patients which is brought about by this protective behavior. The restrictions are not as disturbing in the brain-injured patients as is the effect of defense mechanisms in neuroses. In a neurotic, defense mechanisms represent a characteristic part of the disturbances he is suffering from; but the organic patient does not become aware of the restriction since his protective mechanisms allow for some ordered form of behavior and for the experience of some kind of self-realization—which is true, of course, only as long as the environment is so organized by the people around him that no tasks arise that he cannot fulfill and as long as the protecting behavior changes are not hindered. This is the only way the brain-damaged person can exist. The patient cannot bear conflict—

that is, anxiety, restriction, or suffering. In this respect he differs essentially from the neurotic who is more or less able to bear conflict. This is the main difference which demands a different procedure in treatment; in many respects, however, treatment can be set up in much the same way for both (18). In treating these patients, it is more important to deal with the possible occurrence of catastrophe rather than with the impairment of abstraction, for my observations of a great many patients for over ten years indicate that the impairment of abstraction cannot be alleviated unless the brain damage from which it originated is eliminated. There is no functional restitution of this capacity by compensation through other parts of the brain. Improvement of performances can be achieved only by the building up of substitute performances by the use of the part of concrete behavior which is preserved; but this is only possible by a definite arrangement of the environment.

I am well aware that my description of the personality change in brain damage is somewhat sketchy. The immense material and the problems involved, so manifold and complex, make a more satisfactory presentation in such a brief time impossible. I hope that I have been successful in outlining, to the best of my ability, the essential phenomena and problems of these patients. In addition, I trust that I have shown how much we can learn from these observations for our concept of the structure of the personality, both normal and pathological, and for the treatment of brain-damaged patients and also, I hope, of patients with so-called psychogenic disorders.

References

1. Goldstein, K. Ueber die gleichartige functionelle bedingtheit der symptome in organischen

und psychischen krankheiten. *Montschr. f. Psychiat. u. Neurol.,* 57(1924), 191.

2. ——— Die beziehungen der psychoanalyse zue biologie, in *Verhandlungen d. congresses für psychotherapie in nauheim.* Leipzig: Hirzel, 1927.

3. ——— *Aftereffects of brain injuries in war.* New York: Grune & Stratton, 1942.

4. ——— *The organism: a holistic approach to biology.* New York: American Book Co., 1939.

5. ——— *Human nature in the light of psychopathology.* Cambridge: Harvard Univ. Press, 1940. Page 194.

6. ——— *Handbuch der normalen und pathologischen physiologie.* Berlin: J. S. Springer, 1927. Volume 10, pages 600 ff. and 813.

7. ——— The significance of the frontal lobes for mental performances. *J. Neurol. & Psychopathol.,* 17(1936), 27–40.

8. ——— The modifications of behavior consequent to cerebral lesions. *Psychiat. Quart.,* 10(1936), 586.

9. ——— and Scheerer, M. *Abstract and concrete behavior.* Psychol. Monogr. No. 239, 1941.

10. Goldstein, K. On emotions: considerations from the organismic point of view. *J. Psychol.,* 31(1951), 37–49.

11. Jacobson, Edith. The speed pace in psychic discharge processes and its influence on the pleasure-unpleasure qualities of affects. Paper read before the American Psychoanalytic Association, May, 1952.

12. Goldstein, K., and Steinfeld, J. I. The conditioning of sexual behavior by visual agnosia. *Bull. Forest Sanit.,* 1(1942), no. 2, pp. 37–45.

13. Goldstein, K., *Language and language disturbances.* New York: Grune & Stratton, 1948.

14. ——— Frontal lobotomy and impairment of abstract attitude. *J. Nerv. & Ment. Dis.,* 110(1949), 93–111.

15. Freeman, W., and Watts, J. *Psychosurgery,* 2nd ed. Springfield, Ill.: Thomas, 1950.

16. Goldstein, K. Zum problem der angst. *Allg. ärztl. Ztschr. f. Psychotherap. u. psych. Hygiene,* 2(1929), 409–437.

17. Freud, A. *The ego and the mechanisms of defense.* New York: Internat. Univ. Press, 1946.

18. Goldstein, K. The idea of disease and therapy. *Rev. Religion,* 14(1949), 229–240.

Feeble-Mindedness Versus Intellectual Retardation*

EDGAR A. DOLL, PH.D.

DIRECTOR OF RESEARCH, THE TRAINING SCHOOL AT VINELAND, NEW JERSEY

The classification of children for special education with reference to mental handicap has been embarrassed in recent years by the failure to distinguish between feeble-minded and normal. Originally such special education was designed for the clinically feeble-minded. More recently its most effective expansion has been extended to clinically normal but intellectually retarded children. A serious confusion has resulted from the failure to distinguish between these

Reprinted from the *American Journal of Mental Deficiency,* 51(1947), 456–459, with the permission of The American Association on Mental Deficiency and the author.

* Presented as part of a panel discussion on "Education—Selection and Classification" at the 70th Annual Meeting of the American Association on Mental Deficiency, Montreal, October 3, 1946.

two groups. The simple answer achieved by the uncritical use of psychometric measurement, especially when such measurement has been restricted to a particular type of test and to a particular cutting score, has materially reduced the effectiveness of special education for the mentally handicapped. We think that this problem can be resolved by insisting on the distinction between feeble-minded and normal within the psychometric measurement of mental retardation.

The criterion "once feeble-minded, always feeble-minded" is not to be lightly ignored. Consequently the determination of feeble-mindedness merits more than the casual application of a single intelligence test. Feeble-mindedness is a clinical symptom complex whose attributes have repeatedly been formulated. Intellectual retardation without feeble-mindedness is a classification rather than a diagnosis, a position pro tem on a single continuum rather than a syndrome. Hence the distinction calls for clinical rather than merely psychometric evaluation. And certainly the issue of feeble-mindedness is of sufficient importance to warrant the cost of clinical diagnosis.

In the use of psychometric measurement we obtain only the extent of deviation from a norm. The central tendency of this norm is average, but what is average is not necessarily normal. Extreme deviations plus and minus may be designated as high or low, but not as talent or defect.

And the use of other mental tests may yield other degrees of deviation. Thus the degree of deviation from the average revealed by a verbal intelligence test is not necessarily the same as that revealed by a non-verbal test. Likewise the deviation derived from group measurement may not be the same as that obtained from individual measurement.

The Subcommittee on Mental Deficiency of the White House Conference on Child Health and Protection resolved this problem by including both feeble-mindedness and intellectual retardation under the generic term "mental deficiency." That Committee defined feeble-mindedness as mental subnormality coupled with social incompetence, and intellectual retardation as mental subnormality without socal incompetence.

But the term "mental deficiency" has continued to mean feeble-mindedness to most people. And the concept of the essential incurability of feeble-mindedness has been confused by the fact that the mentally deficient who are only intellectually retarded do ultimately attain independent social-economic sufficiency. It is now clear that whereas special education for the feeble-minded accomplishes appreciable improvement in habits and adjustment it does not materially alter the essential nature of the condition. But the intellectually retarded are sufficiently benefited by special education to take their place in society as well-adjusted dull normals.

The educational advantages of insisting on the distinction between feeble-mindedness and intellectual retardation are quite obvious to those who have followed the history of special education for the mentally handicapped during the last two or three decades. What has not yet been achieved is a satisfactory term for the intellectually retarded with clear-cut definition and practical implication for educational philosophy and practise. The continuing use of the term "mental deficiency" has not resulted in a divorce of its traditional implications and has been a serious obstacle to the extension of special education for the intellectually retarded. It seems imperative therefore that the differentiation of these two classes of the mentally handicapped should be made much more realistically than has yet been done.

We repeat that the differentiation is best accomplished by the use of clinical methods. Although the psychometric approach alone is not sufficient, it may if sufficiently elaborated materially minimize the difficulties. To this end we suggest the following propositions:

1. The use of any single mental measurement device in the selection of mentally handicapped children for special education is to be deplored on the ground that no single mental measurement can reveal the full significance of mental subnormality. If group tests are used they should be supplemented by individual tests. If verbal tests are used, they should be supplemented by nonverbal tests. If literate tests are used they should be supplemented by non-literate tests. And the use of such tests should specifically reckon with the consequences of reading disabilities, language handicaps, sensory and motor limitations, test-situational motivation, and other embarrassments to the reliable measurement of native capacity. The use of such tests should further reckon with such psychometric pitfalls as personal equation of the examiner, probable error of the measurement due to various causes, nonequivalence of test scores, variable significance of score deviation, and so on.

2. The multifocal measurement of intelligence should be supplemented by adequate measurement of motor proficiency. The conspicuous difference between the feeble-minded and the intellectually retarded in this respect is of marked vocational and social significance.

3. The possibility of behavioral maladjustment as a hindrance to school success, and as an evidence of emotional conflict which may constitute a serious bar to mental expression should be specifically considered. This includes at least some analysis of the dynamic aspect of personality structure and expression. Such considerations should include evaluation of the social conditioning to which the individual has previously been

subject. Maladjustment should not be confused with feeble-mindedness.

4. The somatic attributes of the individual under consideration should not be overlooked. This should include due regard for the general tendency toward constitutional hypoplasia and neurological deficiency or defect on the part of the feeble-minded, and the usual absence of these on the part of the intellectually retarded.

5. Some analysis of mental pattern should be undertaken, not only because of its relation to the differentiation between feeble-mindedness and intellectual retardation but also because of its direct consequences on the most effective directions and methods of instruction.

6. The measurement of social competence is imperative since this is by definition the crucial first distinction between feeble-mindedness and intellectual retardation. And such measurement should clearly reckon with any influences which limit the effective expression of such competence. This should be the first rather than the last step in seeking the distinction. It has been a grave mistake to assume social incompetence from the measurement of mental incompetence. The direct measurement of both permits an evaluation of their interrelationship.

We have not as yet achieved a satisfactory solution of the problems of concept, definition, and social significance, as related to the distinction between feeble-mindedness and intellectual retardation. Instead we have only confused these issues by using the term "mental deficiency" for both groups. Yet in doing so we have held to the traditional meaning of mental deficiency as feeble-mindedness rather than achieving the desired goal of mental deficiency as intellectual retardation.

Special education has leaned rather too heavily on other authorities to resolve this problem. Perhaps it behooves special education to solve the problem for itself because of its crucial stake in the outcome. The initially great advantage of special education for the mentally handicapped derived from the attempt to educate the whole individual as implied in the concept of feeble-mindedness. That initial advantage has been lost in restricting the purposes of education to the consequences of intellectual retardation alone rather than capitalizing the total individuality of the intellectually retarded but otherwise normal person. If we would adhere to the definition of mental deficiency as feeble-mindedness, and if we would insist on contrasting the attributes of the feeble-minded with those of the intellectually retarded we would materially clarify this problem.

The crucial issue is the serious difference in educational objectives for those who will always be feeble-minded as contrasted with those who will as adults be marginally normal. The former will always require some degree of social assistance and supervision, while the latter will be socially self-sustaining. Education for the former should therefore be directed toward the inculcation of habits and virtues which will minimize the social consequences of social dependency, while encouraging maximum initiative and resourcefulness for those who will be socially self-directing and self-supporting.

Section 3

PSYCHOTHERAPY

ANY STUDY of abnormality would seem incomplete without some mention of the means by which the pathological patterns which have been described may be altered. This is essentially the business of psychotherapy, a procedure having its beginnings in the work of Freud, but one which has come, over the years, to be viewed differently by different theorists. Such diversity has probably stemmed from experiences with varying types of patients and the continued growth of our understanding about the forces which shape the individual's behavior. The chapters which follow deal with samples of approaches to treatment and questions which have been debated in journals in recent years regarding the effectiveness of psychotherapeutic intervention.

11. APPROACHES TO PSYCHOTHERAPY

THE SELECTIONS in this chapter provide a survey of three of the most widely used frameworks within which psychotherapy is carried out. The paper by Knight deals with the many ways a psychoanalytic approach may be utilized. Roger's paper represents one of his more recent statements of the process of change occurring in his own client-centered approach. Shoben's paper was one of the early ones which attempted to conceptualize the process of psychotherapy in terms of principles developed in the laboratory by learning theorists.

A Critique of the Present Status of the Psychotherapies *

ROBERT P. KNIGHT
MEDICAL DIRECTOR OF THE AUSTEN RIGGS FOUNDATION,
STOCKBRIDGE, MASSACHUSETTS

Before one can write a meaningful critical evaluation of the psychotherapies of today, he must attempt to define the types of treatment methods which are commonly assumed to be distinguishable

Reprinted from the *Bulletin of the New York Academy of Medicine,* 25(1949), 100–114, with the permission of The New York Academy of Medicine and the author.

* Read at the Twenty-First Graduate Fortnight of The New York Academy of Medicine, October 6, 1948.

varieties of psychotherapy. This is no easy task, for there exists no such generally accepted classified listing of the psychotherapies. A motley array of adjectives is found to designate brands of psychotherapy which are supposedly different from each other but which actually overlap each other in manifold ways. It will be a necessary preliminary task for us to review the terms commonly used in psychiatric literature and in ordinary professional parlance to designate various types of psychotherapy.

In a survey of usages which probably falls short of being exhaustive, I have noted that the type of psychotherapy may be characterized from any one of a number of frames of reference:

1. With regard to the preponderant attitude taken or influence attempted by the therapist; e.g., suggestion, persuasion, exhortation, intimidation, counselling, interpretation, re-education, retraining, etc.

2. With regard to the general aim of the therapy; e.g., supportive, suppressive, expressive, cathartic, ventilative, etc.

3. With regard to the supposed "depth" of the therapy—superficial psychotherapy and deep psychotherapy.

4. With regard to the duration—brief psychotherapy and prolonged psychotherapy.

5. With regard to its supposed relationship to Freudian psychoanalysis, as, for example, orthodox, standard, classical, or regular psychoanalysis, modified psychoanalysis, wild analysis, direct psychoanalysis, psychoanalytic psychotherapy, psychoanalytically oriented psychotherapy, psychodynamic psychotherapy, psychotherapy using the dynamic approach, and psychotherapy based on psychoanalytic principles.

6. With regard to the ex-Freudian dissident who started a new school of psychotherapy. Thus we have Adler's individual psychology with its Adlerian "analysis," Jung's analytical psychology with its Jungian "analysis," the Rankian analysis, the Stekelian analysis, and the Horney modifications.

7. With regard to whether patients are treated singly or in groups—individual psychotherapy and group psychotherapy.

8. With regard to whether the psychotherapy is "directive" or "non-directive," an issue emphasized strongly by the Rogers group of psychologists.

9. With regard to the adjunctive technique which is coupled with psychotherapy; e.g., narcotherapy (narcoanalysis, narcosynthesis), and hypnotherapy (hypnoanalysis), the first using drugs and the second hypnosis for technical reasons to be discussed later.

It is not surprising that both physicians and the lay public regard this welter of terminology as something less than scientific, and that patients seeking help for emotional distress are often confused as to where to find that help and as to what type of psychotherapy to trust. In defense of the present confusion one can remind himself that although psychotherapy is said to be the oldest form of medical treatment, it is also one of the very latest to achieve a scientific, rational basis, i.e., to rest on a basic science of dynamic psychology. Because of its partial derivation from many unscientific and extra-scientific sources—primitive magical practices of tribal medicine men, religious rites, parental exhortations and commands, mysticism, common-sense advice and intuitive insights of friends, and downright quackery, to mention but a few—psychotherapy has among its practitioners today not only many lay fakirs but also a good many physicians whose training in dynamic psychology is grossly inadequate. Also, even among the best trained psychiatrists there exist some honest differences of opinion regarding principles and techniques of psychotherapy. However, research and experimentation continue to expand, and slowly the phenomena of artful and intuitive psychotherapeutic influence are translated into scientific principles and techniques.

It is impossible to overstate the importance of dynamic psychology as a basic science on which all competent psychotherapy must rest. Without an underlying structure of psychodynamics and psychopathology, in which the psychotherapist must be well trained, all psychotherapy is at best empirical, at the worst the blind leading the blind. No valid critique of the psychotherapies is possible except in relation to the penetrating understanding of human personality and behavior provided by dynamic psychology, the chief contributions to which have been made by psychoanalysis.

It seems necessary, therefore, to review for an essentially nonpsychiatric medical audience the theoretical essentials in modern dynamic psychology. The cornerstone of dynamic psychology is the concept of repression. As the psychic structure of the human personality develops in infancy and childhood, the primitive erotic and aggressive impulses come to be opposed by counter-impulses deriving from the child's training and adaptive experiences. The chief counter-impulse is repression, which banishes from consciousness—but not from continued active existence in the unconscious—those impulses, some native and some stimulated by specific experiences, which the child discovers are condemned and forbidden expression by its upbringers. Both the strength of the alien impulses and the child's capacity to oppose them are partially determined by his native constitution, partly by the nature of his early experiences, and partly by the character and upbringing methods of those adults who rear him. Some condemned impulses are simply repressed, along with their associated fantasies and affects; others are modified in partial expression and partial repression, assisted by other defense mechanisms. Topographically the unconscious is regarded as the repository of repressed impulses and forgotten memories, the preconscious as that part of the mind in which reside the rememberable but currently unattended-to memories, and the conscious mind as the aware, focussing, thinking portion of the psychic structure. Viewed dynamically, the primitive impulses arise out of biological and psychological drives identified collectively as the Id, while the opposing, defensive forces arise from Ego, or organized part of the personality, and the Super-ego—roughly the conscience. The sum total of these dynamic internal and external interactions, plus constitution and native intellectual endowment, equals the developing personality in all of its individual uniqueness. While the major battle between opposing internal forces appears to be settled at about age five or six, thus forming the basic personality structure, there is a continuous internal interaction and a constant external adaptive attempt throughout life, with special crises during adolescence and in reaction to the Protean forms that stressful life experiences can take. Also, each individual, however healthy his adaptation appears to be, has his own particular psychological areas of vulnerability to stress, and he may be precipitated into clinical neurotic or psychotic illness by experiences whose qualitative or quantitative nature exceed his capacity to master them through healthy adaptive methods.

This highly condensed exposition of dynamic psychology with its emphasis on the uniqueness of the individual will, I hope, be sufficient to serve as a background for the following proposition, namely, that competent treatment of a patient by psychotherapeutic means requires of the psychotherapist:

1. That he be thoroughly grounded in the basic science of dynamic psychology.

2. That he be well trained in clinical methods of evaluating the individual patient, not only in terms of general comparison with others presenting similar clinical pictures, but also in terms of the uniquely individual forces and factors in each individual patient.

3. That he then utilize, from among the available psychotherapeutic approaches and techniques, those particular ones which, according to his best clinical judgment, are most appropriate in a given case.

4. A fourth prerequisite does not follow logically from the previous argument but is of an importance at least equal to the other three, namely, that the psychotherapist be a person of integrity, objectivity, and sincere interest in people, and that he be relatively free from personal conflicts, anxieties, biases, emotional blind spots, rigidities of manner, and settled convictions as to how people should properly behave.

This last prerequisite for psychotherapeutic work requires some amplification. Unlike the situation in other fields of medical therapy, the man well grounded in the basic science underlying his therapy, well trained in diagnostic methods, and possessing technical competence to use the indicated therapy may still, in psychotherapy, be a poor practitioner if he is personally anxious, rigid, or full of moral convictions. Other therapies in medicine can be competently performed, with good results on patients, without these personal qualities, largely because a great deal of medical and surgical treatment consists of doing something *to* the patient. To be sure the personal qualities in a physician which cause his patients to love and trust him are exactly the ones which make him a real physician rather than a mechanical artisan; but far greater emotional demands are made on the psychotherapist. The nature of the subject material in psychotherapy, the intense personal give and take in the patient-therapist relationship, the enormously increased possibilities of anti-therapeutic personal involvement, the self knowledge in the therapist required both to understand his patients and to steer a sound therapeutic course with them, all require of the psychotherapist certain personal qualities not essential to other medical specialists. It is not particularly difficult for physicians to acquire protective attitudes of detachment in respect to those bodily elements and products—blood, pus, urine, diseased tissue, mucus, feces, guts—which so upset the squeamish layman, and this detachment serves the physician in good stead as he works coolly and efficiently at his therapeutic task. But this sort of detachment in a psychotherapist is not only no protection against the psychological products of his patients, it actually hampers and distorts his therapeutic work and, if extreme, even disqualifies him from undertaking to deal with psychopathology and psychotherapy. The counterphobic attitude may be sufficient for competent work in physiology, pathology, and surgery; it is a poor and brittle defense for work in psychiatry and psychotherapy.

Such personal considerations with regard to the psychotherapist raise important questions regarding selection of candidates for psychiatric training, and regarding the importance of personal psychoanalysis as a part of psychoanalytic and psychiatric training. Certainly every psychiatrist who wishes to do psychoanalytic therapy should have full psychoanalytic training, including, of course, the personal analysis. It might also be said that every psychiatrist who expects to practice major psychotherapy of any kind should have full psychoanalytic training, just as every physician who plans to do major surgery should have full surgical training.

I have so far attempted to show that the terminology designating supposed varieties of psychotherapy is very confusing because of the many frames of reference in which identifying adjectives were applied, and to indicate that a critique of these psychotherapies is not possible until a valid frame of reference is established. I then tried to show that familiarity with the basic science of dynamic psychology, and the clinical techniques derived from it is necessary to provide a valid frame of reference for a critique. This led to the collateral but vital point of the psychotherapist's personal suitability. It is necessary to establish one more phase of this frame of reference. This has to do with the nature and vicissitudes of the patient-physician relationship in psychotherapy.

Most physicians are not much concerned about the attitudes, emotions, and fantasies their patients have about them as long as the patients are cooperative, don't go to other physicians, and pay their bills for professional services. Occasionally physicians are startled to encounter outbursts of unprovoked hostility or professions of love or jealousy, or suspicion from their patients. I suppose the usual result is that the patient is then discharged by that physician in the event the physician cannot "talk him out of his nonsense." Many psychiatrists of the past (and some in the present) have been more concerned about emotional reactions of patients to them, but have thought of them in terms of "good rapport" or the lack of it, without paying much attention to the exact nature of these reactions, whether friendly or hostile. Sigmund Freud, picking up a cue noted but abandoned by Josef Breuer, had the genius to follow through to a penetrating study of patients' emotional attitudes toward their doctors and to bring this group of phenomena into both the theoretical framework of dynamic psychology and the clinical framework of psychotherapy. He saw that whereas the various emotional reactions of the individual patient appeared at first to be irrational and unprovoked, actually these attitudes could be understood the same as other psychological phenomena in the patient could be understood, such as recovered memories, dreams, fantasies, and so on, and could, instead of being emotionally reacted to by the therapist, provide him with material for fresh insights into his patient. Freud called these reactions "transference" because of his understanding of them as emotions originally felt toward other significant persons in the patient's past experience, and now transferred to the doctor. He discovered that their nature could be interpreted to the patient, and that such interpretations, when correctly timed and accurately expressed, had significant therapeutic effect on the patient. Thus the theoretical understanding and clinical use of transference phenomena became one of the significant contributions of psychoanalysis to the field of psychiatry, and, indeed, to the practice of medicine in general, for transference reactions by patients are by no means limited to those being treated psychotherapeutically.

Freud also had the objectivity to observe and analyze his own reactions to patients, and concluded that all psychotherapists would have their own particular tendencies to react inappropriately (that is, inappropriately from the standpoint of correct therapeutic technique) to the material, or behavior, or persons of their patients. He called such reactions and reaction tendencies "counter-transference," and bade all analysts to be acutely observant of themselves in this regard so that they might analyze and dissipate these counter-transference reactions without letting themselves be unwittingly influenced by them to the detriment of their therapeutic efforts. Again, such counter-transference reactions are not confined to psychiatrists, psychoanalysts, or psychotherapists, but are present in all physicians toward their patients, albeit with considerably less significance, for the most part, in therapy other than psychotherapy. Once more, then, we see the importance for the psychotherapist of those personal qualities of integrity, objectivity, sincerity, and relative freedom from emotional blind spots.

I have now used almost half of my time to develop the background frame of reference in which any psychotherapy may properly be critically evaluated. The following elements have been emphasized:

1. The theoretical understanding of human personality provided by dynamic psychology.

2. The clinical evaluation of each individual patient—the nature and intensity of his internal and external conflicts, the genetic history of those conflicts, his particular defenses against anxiety, his strengths as shown by past adaptations and achievements, his vulnerabilities and weaknesses as shown by the extent of his decompensation, his way of relating initially to the therapist, his intelligence and its possible impairments, the intactness of his concept formation, his loyalty to reality, his capacity for introspection and self-confrontation, and so on.

3. The utilization of psychotherapeutic techniques based on sufficient knowledge of dynamic psychology and applied appropriately to the individual case in the light of the clinical evaluation.

4. The personal qualifications and suitability of the psychotherapist, and, we may now add, his capacity to recognize and deal with transference manifestations in his patients and countertransference tendencies in himself.

If these four criteria provide a valid frame of reference in which to evaluate psychotherapy, it is readily seen that those psychotherapists who have a fixed system of treatment for all patients who come to them are practicing poor psychotherapy. This is true whether it refers to those therapists who treat all patients with such banal exhortations as "Buck up," "Go home and forget it," "Stop worrying about that," "Pull yourself together," "Don't cross bridges until you come to them," and so on; to therapists who treat all patients by assigning reading for subsequent interview discussions in prepared booklets on how to live; to psychoanalysts who put all patients on the couch and tell them to free-

associate; or to therapists who keep the syringe loaded with sodium pentothal for each patient, or who routinely start their hypnotic maneuvers promptly. One may give insulin to every diabetic, or operate every acute appendix, with, of course, some judgment as to dosage, timing, and collateral measures, but psychotherapy is, or should be, a highly individual matter for each patient. Far too often in current practice the type of psychotherapy used with the patient is determined solely by the limited training and ability of the psychotherapist rather than by either the type of illness the patient has or the type of patient that has the illness.

Of the various possible ways of classifying psychotherapeutic attempts, most psychiatrists would agree that two large groups could be identified—those which aim primarily at support of the patient, with suppression of his symptoms and his erupting psychological material, and those which aim primarily at expression. It is actually more appropriate to speak of a group of techniques utilized to accomplish suppression or expression than to speak of sub-groups of psychotherapies under each major heading. Suppressive or supportive psychotherapy, also called superficial psychotherapy, utilizes such devices as inspiration, reassurance, suggestion, persuasion, counselling, re-education, and the like and avoids investigative and exploratory measures. Such measures may be indicated, even though the psychotherapist is well trained and experienced in expressive techniques, where the clinical evaluation of the patient leads to the conclusion that he is too fragile psychologically to be tampered with, or too inflexible to be capable of real personality alteration, or too defensive to be able to achieve insight. Certain recovering schizophrenics or agitated depressions or children might illustrate the fragility; rigid character disorders, certain manics and hypomanics, and elderly patients might illustrate the inflexibility; and some paranoid states might illustrate the defensiveness. The decision to use suppressive measures is made actually because of contraindications to using exploratory devices. One can say, then, that supportive or suppressive psychotherapy, with its variety of techniques and devices for accomplishing support and suppression, is a valid psychotherapy provided it is applied on the basis of sound indications and not indiscriminately to all or most patients simply because the particular psychotherapist does not know how to do anything else with the patient, and provided the psychotherapist realizes that transference and counter-transference manifestations can and do occur, and need to be handled, even in such superficial psychotherapy. Supportive psychotherapy may be brief or prolonged, as indicated, and may be carried out with individuals or with groups.

It is in the group of psychotherapies intended to be expressive that one encounters the various schools of thought, the adjunctive devices, the more frequent conflicts in theory, and the more significant question of personal suitability of the therapist. Expressive psychotherapies utilize such devices as exploratory probing through questioning, free-association, abreaction, confession, relating of dreams, catharsis, interpretation and the like, all with the purpose of uncovering and ventilating preconscious and unconscious pathogenic psychological material. Elements of support, reassurance, suggestion, advice, and direction are not necessarily excluded, and may, in fact, be consciously utilized. Expressive psychotherapy may be brief and intensive or prolonged, depending on the aims of the therapist and the response of the patient. Expressive psychotherapy is major psychotherapy and should not be undertaken without thorough grounding in dynamic psychology, adequate experience in clinical evaluation, practice under supervision, and personal suitability. Lack-

ing this background, the psychotherapist is extremely likely to get into difficulties. He introduces topics for the patient to discuss without being aware that they are irrelevant to the matters pressing for expression within the patient, or that the patient cannot tackle a given topic until certain defenses are first pointed out and removed. He gives long and sententious theoretical explanations which he regards as interpretations, but which are either then learned as intellectual defenses by the patient or their content ignored while the patient basks in this verbal bath at the hands of the therapist. He permits himself unwittingly to be drawn into an active role as an ally in the patient's external interpersonal struggles, while remaining oblivious to the provocative shenanigans of the patient which keep these struggles going on. He pounces on dreams or slips of the tongue with ready and pat interpretations which miss the point. He focusses his attention on symptoms, and tries to treat them by interpretation, or special investigatory questioning. He becomes embroiled in transference-counter-transference jams and does not know how to extricate himself except by discontinuing the interviews for a while. I cite these common errors as illustrations of what may happen if the inadequately trained psychotherapist undertakes expressive psychotherapy. Needless to say such mishandling complicates the patient's illness exceedingly and renders more difficult the task of the inevitable subsequent psychotherapist.

Competent expressive psychotherapy may have goals which vary considerably. In cases where there has been an acute onset of neurotic symptoms in reaction to a discoverable precipitating event, and the patient's history shows a comparatively healthy course, the therapy may properly consist of thorough ventilation of the reaction to the upsetting event, with the therapist pointing out connections, relationships, and hidden motivations in the limited life area of the setting prior to the event, of the event itself, and of the patient's immediate and later reactions to the event. In skillful hands this is a most rewarding type of expressive psychotherapy. Recovery may be achieved in a very few interviews and the patient is restored to his previous good functioning with insights he would not otherwise have achieved. In such instances there is no therapeutic aim of exhaustive investigation, recovery of infantile memories, or altered ego structure. In other cases which may at first seem similar, the early clinical evaluation uncovers more neurotic difficulties than were at first apparent, and it becomes clear that the patient's adjustment prior to the precipitating event was a precarious one at best. The therapeutic aim may now change to one of more thoroughgoing alteration of the neurotic personality structure, and the expressive techniques lead into psychoanalysis. If the psychotherapist is competent to conduct psychoanalysis as well as the shorter expressive therapies with limited aim, he will have so handled the early therapy that the analytic techniques are a logical continuation of his early therapeutic work. If he is not so trained, he should at this point refer the patient to a suitable analyst.

Freudian psychoanalysis—and psychoanalysis actually implies "Freudian" —is a major, time-consuming, and therefore expensive, type of psychotherapy. It is by no means a panacea, and its most competent practitioners would readily concede that as a method of therapy it has limited application in the vast field of human psychological distress. (As a dynamic psychology and as a method of investigation it is, of course, invaluable, and possesses almost unlimited applicability.) Its limitations as a method of therapy do not depend merely on such factors as its duration (twelve to eighteen months as a minimum; four to five years as a maximum), its cost to the patient,

and the availability of analysts (approximately 500 in the United States, with one-fourth of these in New York City). There is also a considerable list of special indications and contraindications, as, for example:

1. The patient should be of at least bright normal intelligence on the Bellevue-Wechsler scale (115 to 120 IQ).
2. The suitable age range for adults is about 20 to 50, with certain exceptions to be made at either end of this range.
3. There must be some capacity for introspection, and some awareness of nuances of feeling in himself and in others.
4. There must be sufficient motivation in terms of initial distress and strong desire to change.
5. The patient must possess sufficient intactness of personality so that this intact portion may become allied with the analyst in the analytic work.
6. In general, patients with unalterable physical handicaps are not suitable subjects for psychoanalysis.
7. The general field for psychoanalytic therapy includes the psychoneuroses, character disorders, some of the perversions, neurotic depressions, anxiety states, and some of the psychoses. Patients in the midst of acute external turmoil should not begin psychoanalysis as such until their life situations are more stable.

With all of its limitations, however, psychoanalytic therapy is, in well-trained hands, a highly effective procedure for achieving in patients a profound alteration in their neurotic personality structure and developing otherwise latent potentialities for achievement and responsible living.

The Freudian school of psychoanalysis is the main stream of the psychoanalytic movement. There have, in the past, been several split-offs from the main stream which resulted in transient and minor developments of non-Freudian schools. The school of the late Alfred Adler took one aspect of psychoanalysis, namely, the methods of the ego in dealing with external forces, and attempted to develop it into a system called individual psychology. The central theme of this psychology was that of inferiority feelings and the drive for power. This psychology and system of therapy died out with its leader. Carl Jung, also an early pupil and associate of Freud, split with him and developed a school of "analytical psychology" which emphasized symbolism and religious beliefs and which explained mental disorders, especially those of middle life and after, in terms of regressions to a collective unconscious, or racial heritage. His school still persists but his incorporation of Nazi racial ideology into his psychological theories has caused him to be severely criticized. The late Otto Rank, also an early pupil of Freud's, developed a system of therapy which emphasized the transference and the uncovering and working through of birth anxiety in a three months' period of treatment. There were many short Rankian analyses in the 1920's, but this system is now also extinct. The late Wilhelm Stekel, a remarkably intuitive man and a prolific writer, attracted a few followers to his technique of rapid and early deep interpretations of symbolic and unconscious meanings. His influence has now become almost nil. Karen Horney, originally a Freudian with many fine contributions to the literature, has led a movement in the last decade to eliminate a number of the fundamental concepts of psychoanalysis and to focus attention on current cultural conflicts as the main source of personality disorders. She rejects the libido theory, the significance of early psychosexual development, and in general takes a stand against genetic psychology in favor of culturalism.

There are other deviations from orthodox psychoanalytic techniques which are not represented by their practitioners nor regarded by others as separate dissident schools of psychoanalysis, but which are modifications of technique to meet the therapeutic problems in patients who are too ill to cooperate in the usual analytic procedure. These modifications are used chiefly with psychotics and involve approaches by the analyst which actively cultivate a treatment relationship, communication with the sick patient being established on whatever level is possible in the individual case. The success of such attempts depends on the resourcefulness of the analyst in coping with the patient's inaccessibility and his capacity for empathy and intuition in understanding what is communicated by the patient's verbalizations, behavior, and attitudes. Long periods of careful therapeutic work are required but the results are often very rewarding. As the patient improves the treatment may merge into a more regular psychoanalytic procedure.

A special type of analytic psychotherapy developed by Rosen, for which the designation "direct psychoanalysis" has been made, deserves some comment. Rosen has reported a striking series of recoveries of severe and chronic schizophrenias. His method consists of repeated, prolonged sessions with the patient in which deep interpretative activity is carried out fearlessly and relentlessly. Interpretations are based on psychoanalytic theory, and sometimes on insights provided by other schizophrenics. The usual cautions and tentative approaches which have characterized others' work with psychotics are abandoned, and direct, deep interpretations are made promptly when the therapist believes he understands. The therapist also, when necessary to make contact, takes the roles of powerful figures in the patient's delusions and shouts denials, reassurances, and interpretations. Remarkable results are reported, and this work is now undergoing study under research conditions. It promises much but is at present difficult to evaluate.

The school of Adolf Meyer, identified as psychobiology, emphasized the
sound concept of all-embracing study of
man in his totality. He developed a new
system of nomenclature which did not
achieve significant acceptance, and
termed his treatment "distributive analysis and synthesis." This psychotherapy
aimed at exhaustive collecting of data
regarding the patient's life, past and present, utilized diagrams to depict life influences, and assigned to the therapist
the role of educator and explainer of the
experiences and reactions in the patient's
life. This procedure may be criticized as
being far too theoretical and intellectual
to influence many patients, and as having
almost totally ignored the elements of
transference and counter-transference in
the relationship between therapist and
patient. As a school of psychotherapy, it
probably has a diminishing number of
adherents.

All of the major psychotherapies—
i.e., those which aim at significant alterations in personality structure rather than
at symptomatic relief—have encountered
the phenomenon discovered by Freud
and termed by him "resistance." This
refers to those partly conscious and partly unconscious tendencies in patients to
resist self-knowledge and change, as
manifested in their inability to remember the past or to capture for therapeutic
use the current unconscious content. Resistance produces a marked slowing
down of progress, often approaching
stalemate, while symptoms continue un-
altered. Technical problems of resistance
are among the most difficult to solve, and
the long duration of major psychotherapy is attributable chiefly to this phenomenon.

In order to shorten the duration of
therapy many attempts have been made
to circumvent resistance. Chief among
these techniques have been the use of
hypnosis and certain sedative drugs. Under hypnosis or narcosis (also mild elation or light anesthesia) some patients are

able to gain access to and to verbalize
with affect otherwise unconscious memories, and to profit from the ventilation
and abreaction and the interpretations of
the therapist associated with this therapeutic experience. During World War II
there was widespread use of intravenous
sodium amytal and sodium pentothal as
well as of hypnosis to produce dissolu-
tion of the resistance barriers against recalling overwhelming traumatic experiences. There often resulted clear recall
and reliving of the traumatic experiences,
with associated assimilation of the over-
stressful event and great diminution or
relief of the symptoms. It was found that
early treatment was essential, delay resulting in the building of stronger barriers against recall and fixing of the
symptomatology, to which was then
added the exploitation of secondary
gains. These psychotherapeutic procedures had enormous significance in military psychiatry, but, as sole treatment
attempts, have proved to be disappointing in civilian psychiatry except with
early traumatic neuroses in civil life.
Such techniques of reducing resistance
through hypnosis or narcosis do not
constitute separate systems of psychotherapy, so that it is incorrect to speak
of narcoanalysis, narcosynthesis, hypnotherapy, and hypnoanalysis as psychotherapies. They are adjuvant techniques
to be used as a preliminary step in overcoming an initial impasse, or as devices
to be introduced during psychotherapy
when strong resistance blocks further
progress.

The attempts to shorten the duration
of psychotherapy have led to other techniques which make use of psychoanalytic principles but which try to achieve
faster results especially through manipulation of the transference, role-taking by
the therapist in order to provide a corrective emotional experience, and inter-
ruptions of treatment to avoid a difficult dependent transference. Alexander,
French, and others who report this work

maintain that their therapy is entitled to be called psychoanalysis—psychoanalysis with more flexible utilization of techniques. Many critics insist that the techniques as reported represent abandonment of fundamental analytic principles and that the goals of such therapy have become relief of symptoms and conventional social adaptation instead of the goals of structural personality alterations of psychoanalysis. Many other studies of short psychotherapy using psychoanalytic principles have been reported in the literature, and it seems well established that the whole field of psychotherapy has been greatly enriched by contributions from psychoanalysis.

In the last analysis there is only one psychotherapy, with many techniques. This one psychotherapy must rest on a basic science of dynamic psychology, and those techniques should be used which are clinically indicated for each individual patient—certain appropriate techniques for the initial stages and others later as the continuous clinical evaluation proceeds pari passu with therapy, and the goals and potentialities for the patient become more clearly delineated through his responses to therapy. And, finally, it is important to recognize that techniques as such are hardly separable from the individual who uses them. Psychotherapy is an enormously complex intercommunication and emotional interaction between two individuals, one of whom seeks help from the other. What is done and said by the one who tries to give help is inevitably his personal version of technique. Beyond all knowledge of dynamic psychology and training in techniques is his own individual personality, with its inevitable variables as to sex, physical appearance, depth of understanding, ability to communicate ideas, tone of voice, set of values, and all of the other highly individual elements which differentiate one therapist from another. The utmost impersonality and analytic incognito cannot exclude the effect of such individual elements. Hence we may say that in addition to a critique of psychotherapy one must also make a critique of the psychotherapist.

A Process Conception of Psychotherapy

CARL R. ROGERS
UNIVERSITY OF WISCONSIN

I would like to take you with me on a journey of exploration. The object of the trip, the goal of the search, is to try to

Reprinted from *The American Psychologist*, 13(1958), 142–150, with the permission of The American Psychological Association and the author.

learn something of the *process* of psychotherapy, or the *process* by which personality change takes place. I would warn you that the goal has not yet been achieved and that it seems as though the expedition has advanced only a few short miles into the jungle. Yet perhaps if I can take you with me, you will be tempted to discover new and profitable avenues of further advance.

The Puzzle of Process

My own reason for engaging in such a search seems simple to me. Just as many psychologists have been interested in the invariant aspects of personality—the unchanging aspects of intelligence, temperament, personality structure—so I have long been interested in the invariant aspects of *change* in personality. Do personality and behavior change? What commonalities exist in such changes? What commonalities exist in the conditions which precede change? Most important of all, what is the process by which such change occurs?

Puzzling over this problem of getting at the process has led me to realize how little objective research deals with process in any field. Objective research slices through the frozen moment to provide us with an exact picture of the interrelationships which exist at that moment. But our understanding of the ongoing movement—whether it be the process of fermentation, or the circulation of the blood, or the process of atomic fission—is generally provided by a theoretical formulation, often supplemented, where feasible, with a clinical observation of the process. I have thus come to realize that perhaps I am hoping for too much to expect that research procedures can shed light directly upon the process of personality change. Perhaps only theory can do that.

A REJECTED METHOD

When I determined, more than a year ago, to make a fresh attempt to understand the manner in which such change takes place, I first considered various ways in which the experience of therapy might be described in terms of some

other theoretical framework. There was much that was appealing in the field of communication theory, with its concepts of feedback, input and output signals and the like. There was the possibility of describing the process of therapy in terms of learning theory or in terms of general systems theory. As I studied these avenues of understanding, I became convinced that it would be possible to translate the process of psychotherapy into any one of these theoretical frameworks. It would, I believe, have certain advantages to do so. But I also became convinced that, in a field so new, this is not what is most needed.

I came to a conclusion which others have reached before: in a new field perhaps what is needed first is to steep oneself in the *events,* to approach the phenomena with as few preconceptions as possible. I take a naturalist's observational, descriptive approach to these events, and to draw forth those low-level inferences which seem most native to the material itself.

THE MODE OF APPROACH

So, for the past year, I have used the method which so many of us use for generating hypotheses, a method which psychologists in this country seem so reluctant to expose or comment on. I used myself as a tool. I have spent many hours listening to recorded therapeutic interviews—trying to listen as naively as possible. I have endeavored to soak up all the clues I could capture as to the process as to what elements are significant in change. Then I have tried to abstract from that sensing the simplest abstractions which would describe them. Here I have been much stimulated and helped by the thinking of many of my colleagues, but I would like to mention my special indebtedness to Eugene Gendlin, William Kirtner, and Fred Zimring, whose demonstrated ability to think in new ways about these matters has been particularly helpful and from whom I have borrowed heavily.

The next step has been to take these observations and low-level abstractions and formulate them in such a way that testable hypotheses can readily be drawn from them. This is the point I have reached. I make no apology for the fact that I am reporting no empirical investigations of these formulations. If past experience is any guide, then I may rest assured that, if the formulations I am about to present check in any way with the subjective experience of other therapists, then a great deal of research will be stimulated, and in a few years there will be ample evidence of the degree of truth and falsity in the statements which follow.

A BASIC CONDITION

If we were studying the process of growth in plants, we would assume certain constant conditions of temperature, moisture, and sunlight in forming our conceptualizations of the process. Likewise in conceptualizing the process of personality change in psychotherapy, I shall assume a constant and optimal set of conditions for facilitating this change. I have recently tried to spell out these conditions in some detail. For our present purpose, I believe I can state this assumed condition in one word. Throughout the discussion which follows, I shall assume that the client experiences himself as being fully *received*. By this I mean that, whatever his feelings—fear, despair, insecurity, anger; whatever his mode of expression—silence, gestures, tears, or words; whatever he finds himself being in this moment, he senses that he is psychologically *received,* just as he is, by the therapist. There is implied in this term the concept of being understood, empathically, and the concept of acceptance. It is also well to point out that it is the client's experience of this condition which makes it optimal, not

merely the fact of its existence in the therapist.

In all that I shall say, then, about the process of change, I shall assume as a constant an optimal and maximum condition of being received.

THE EMERGING CONTINUUM

In trying to grasp and conceptualize the process of change, I was initially looking for elements which would mark or characterize change itself. I was thinking of change as an entity and searching for its specific attributes. What gradually emerged in my understanding as I exposed myself to the raw material of change was a continuum of a different sort than I had conceptualized before.

Individuals move, I began to see, not from a fixity or homeostasis through change to a new fixity, though such a process is indeed possible. But much the more significant continuum is from fixity to changingness, from rigid structure to flow, from stasis to process. I formed the tentative hypothesis that perhaps the qualities of the client's expression at any one point might indicate his position on this continuum, might indicate where he stood in the process of change.

Seven Stages of Process

I gradually developed this concept of a continuum of process, discriminating seven stages in it, with examples from recorded therapeutic interviews illustrating the qualities of the process at each stage. It would be quite impossible to give all of this crude scale here, but I shall try to suggest something of its nature by describing very briefly Stages 1 and 2, to illustrate the lower end of the continuum, and describing more fully Stages 5, 6, and 7, to fill in the upper end of the scale.*

* An amplification of this paper, giving the whole scale with more extended illustrations,

FIRST STAGE

The individual in this stage of fixity and remoteness of experiencing is not likely to come voluntarily for therapy. However, I can to some degree describe the characteristics of this stage:

There is an unwillingness to communicate self. Communication is only about externals.

Feelings and personal meanings are neither recognized as such nor owned.

Personal constructs (to use Kelly's helpful term, 4) *are extremely rigid.*

Close and communicative relationships are construed as dangerous.

No problems are recognized or perceived at this stage.

There is no desire to change.

There is much blockage of internal communication.

Perhaps these brief statements will convey something of the psychological fixity of this end of the continuum. The individual has little or no recognition of the ebb and flow of the feeling life within him. He construes his experience rigidly in terms of the past. He is (to borrow the term of Gendlin and Zimring) structure-bound in his manner of experiencing, reacting to now "by finding it to be like a past experience and then reacting to that past, feeling *it*" (3). The individual at this stage represents stasis, fixity, the opposite of flow or change.

SECOND STAGE OF PROCESS

When the person in the first stage can experience himself as fully received, then the second stage follows. We seem to know very little about how to provide the experience of being received for the person in the first stage, but it is occasionally achieved in play or group ther-

may be obtained from the author by those who are interested in using it for research purposes.

apy where the person can be exposed to a receiving climate, without himself having to take any initiative, for a long enough time to experience himself *as received*. In any event where he does experience this, then a slight loosening and flowing of symbolic expression occurs, which tends to be characterized by the following:

Expression begins to flow in regard to nonself topics.

Ex. I guess that I suspect my father has often felt very insecure in his business relations.*

Problems are perceived as external to self.

Ex. Disorganization keeps cropping up in my life.

There is no sense of personal responsibility in problems.

Ex. This is illustrated in the above excerpt.

Feelings are described as unowned, or sometimes as past objects.

Ex. Counselor: If you want to tell me something of what brought you here. . . . Client: The symptom was—it was—just being very depressed. [This is an excellent example of the way in which internal problems can be perceived and communicated about as entirely external. She is not saying "I am depressed" or even "I was depressed." Her feeling is handled as a remote, unowned object, entirely external to self.]

Feelings may be exhibited, but are not recognized as such or owned.

Experiencing is bound by the structure of the past.

Ex. I suppose the compensation I always make is, rather than trying to com-

* The many examples used as illustrations are taken from recorded interviews, unless otherwise noted. For the most part, they are taken from interviews which have never been published, but a number of them are taken from the report of two cases in a chapter of a forthcoming book.

municate with people or have the right relationship with them, to compensate by, well, shall we say, being on an intellectual level. [Here the client is beginning to recognize the way in which her experiencing is bound by the past. Her statement also illustrates the remoteness of experiencing at this level. It is as though she were holding her experience at arm's length.]

Personal constructs are rigid, and unrecognized as being constructs, but are thought of as facts.

Ex. I can't ever do anything right—can't ever finish it.

Differentiation of personal meanings and feelings is very limited and global.

The preceding example is a good illustration. "I can't *ever*" is one instance of a black and white differentiation, as is also the use of "right" in this absolute sense.

Contradictions may be expressed, but with little recognition of them as contradictions.

Ex. I want to know things, but I look at the same page for an hour.

As a comment on this second stage of the process of change, it might be said that a number of clients who voluntarily come for help are in this stage, but we (and probably therapists in general) have a very minimal degree of success in working with them. This seems, at least, to be a reasonable conclusion from Kirtner's study (5), though his conceptual framework was somewhat different. We seem to know too little about the ways in which a person at this stage may come to experience himself as "received."

THE FIFTH STAGE

I shall omit any description of Stages 3 and 4. Each involves a further loosening of symbolic expression in regard to feelings, constructs, and self. These stages constitute much of psychotherapy. But going beyond these stages, we can

again mark a point on the continuum and call it Stage 5. If the client feels himself received in his expressions, behaviors, and experiences at the third and fourth stage, then this sets in motion still further loosenings, and the freedom of organismic flow is increased. Here I believe we can again delineate crudely the qualities of this phase of the process:

Feelings are expressed freely as in the present.

Ex. I expected kinda to get a severe rejection—this I expect all the time . . . somehow I guess I even feel it with you. . . . It's hard to talk about because I want to be the best I can possibly be with you. [Here feelings regarding the therapist and the client in relationship to the therapist, emotions often most difficult to reveal, are expressed openly.]

Feelings are very close to being fully experienced. They "bubble up," "seep through," in spite of the fear and distrust which the client feels at experiencing them with fullness and immediacy.

Ex. Client is talking about an external event. Suddenly she gets a pained, stricken look. Therapist: What—what's hitting you now? Client: I don't know. [She cries] . . . I must have been getting a little too close to something I didn't want to talk about. [The feeling has almost seeped through into awareness, in spite of her.]

There is a beginning tendency to realize that experiencing a feeling involves a direct referent.

The example just cited illustrates this in part. The client knows she has experienced something, knows she is not clear as to what she has experienced. But there is also the dawning realization that the referent of these vague cognitions lies within her, in an organismic event against which she can check her symbolization and her cognitive formulations. This is often shown by expressions that indicate the closeness or distance the individual feels from this referent. *Ex.* I really don't have my finger on it. I'm just kinda describing it.

There is surprise and fright, rarely pleasure, at the feelings which "bubble through."

Ex. Client, talking about past home relationships: That's not important any more. Hmm. [Pause] That was somehow very meaningful—but I don't have the slightest idea why. . . . Yes, that's it! I can forget about it now and—why, it *isn't* that important. Wow! All that miserableness and stuff!

There is an increasing ownership of self feelings, and a desire to be these, to be the "real me."

Ex. The real truth of the matter is that I'm not the sweet, forbearing guy that I try to make out that I am. I get irritated at things. I feel like snapping at people, and I feel like being selfish at times; and I don't know why I should pretend I'm *not* that way. [This is a clear instance of the greater degree of acceptance of all feelings.]

Experiencing is loosened, no longer remote, and frequently occurs with little postponement.

There is little delay between the organismic event and the full subjective living of it. A beautifully precise account of this is given by a client. *Ex.* I'm still having a little trouble trying to figure out what this sadness—and the weepiness—means. I just know I feel it when I get close to a certain kind of feeling—and usually when I do get weepy, it helps me to kinda break through a wall I've set up because of things that have happened. I feel hurt about something and then automatically this kind of shields things up and then I feel like I can't really touch or feel *anything* very much . . . and if I'd be *able* to feel, or could *let* myself feel the instantaneous feeling when I'm hurt, I'd immediately start being weepy right then, but I can't.

Here we see him regarding his feeling as an inner referent to which he can turn for greater clarity. As he senses his weepiness, he realizes that it is a delayed and partial experiencing of being hurt. He also recognizes that his defenses are such that he can not, at this point, experience the event of hurt when it occurs.

The ways in which experience is construed are much loosened. There are many fresh discoveries of personal constructs as constructs, and a critical examination and questioning of these.

Ex. A man says: This idea of needing to please people—of *having* to do it—that's really been kind of a basic assumption of my life [he weeps quietly]. It's kind of, you know, just one of the very unquestioned axioms that I *have* to please. I have no choice. I just *have* to.

Here he is clear that this assumption has been a construct, and it is evident that its unquestioned status is at an end.

There is a strong and evident tendency toward exactness in differentiation of feelings and meanings.

A client speaks of "Some tension that grows in me, or some hopelessness, or some kind of incompleteness—and my life actually is very incomplete right now. . . . I just don't know. Seems to be, the closest thing it gets to, is *hopelessness*." Obviously he is trying to capture the exact term which for him symbolizes his experience.

There is an increasingly clear facing of contradictions and incongruences in experience.

Ex. My conscious mind tells me I'm worthy. But someplace inside I don't believe it. I think I'm a rat—a no-good. I've no faith in my ability to do anything.

There is an increasing quality of acceptance of self-responsibility for the problems being faced, and a concern as to how he has contributed.

There are increasingly freer dialogues within the self—an improvement in, and reduced blockage of, internal communication.

Sometimes these dialogues are verbalized. *Ex.* Something in me is saying: "What more do I have to give up? You've taken so much from me already." This is *me* talking to *me*—the *me* way back in there who talks to the *me* who runs the show. It's complaining now, saying, "You're getting too close! Go away!"

I trust that the examples I have given of this fifth phase of the process continuum will make several points clear. In the first place, this phase is several hundred psychological miles from the first stage described. Here many aspects of the client are in flow, as against the rigidity of the first stage. He is very much closer to his organic being, which is always in process. He is much closer to being in the flow of his feelings. His constructions of experience are decidedly loosened and repeatedly being tested against referents and evidence within and without. Experience is much more highly differentiated, and thus internal communication, already flowing, can be much more exact.

As a general comment on the description thus far, it would be my observation that a person is never wholly at one or another stage of the process. There is, however, a general consistency in his manner of experiencing and expressing. Thus, a client who is generally at Stage 2 or 3 seems unlikely to exhibit any behaviors characteristic of Stage 5. This is especially true if we limit observations to a single defined area of related personal meanings in the client. Then I would hypothesize that there will be considerable regularity, that Stage 3 would rarely be found before Stage 2, that Stage 4 would rarely follow Stage 2 without Stage 3 intervening. Such tentative hypotheses can, of course, be put to empirical test.

THE SIXTH STAGE

If I have been able to communicate some feeling for the scope and quality of the increased loosening, at each stage, of feeling, experiencing, and construing, then we are ready to look at the next stage, which appears, from observation, to be a very crucial one. Let me see if I can convey what I perceive to be its characteristic qualities.

Assuming that the client continues to be fully received in the therapeutic relationship, then the characteristics of Stage 5 tend to be followed by a very distinctive and often dramatic phase. It is characterized as follows:

A feeling which has previously been "stuck," has been inhibited in its process quality, is experienced with immediacy now.

A feeling flows to its full result.

A present feeling is directly experienced with immediacy and richness.

This immediacy of experiencing, and the feeling which constitutes its content, are accepted. This is something which is, not something to be denied, feared, struggled against.

All the preceding sentences attempt to describe slightly different facets of what is, when it occurs, a clear and definite phenomenon. It would take recorded examples to communicate its full quality, but I shall try to give an illustration without benefit of recording. A somewhat extended excerpt from the eightieth interview with a young man may communicate the way in which a client comes into Stage 6.

Client: I could even conceive of it as a possibility that I could have a kind of tender concern for me. . . . Still, how could *I* be tender, be concerned for *myself,* when they're one and the same thing? But yet I can *feel* it so clearly. . . . You know, like taking care of a child. You want to give it this and give it that. . . . I can kind of clearly see the purposes for somebody else . . . but I can never see them for . . . myself, that I could do this for me, you know. Is it possible that I can really want to take care of myself, and make that a major purpose of my life? That means I'd have to deal with the whole world as if I were guardian of the most cherished and most wanted possession, that this *I* was between this precious *me* that I wanted to take care of and the whole world. . . . It's almost as if I *loved* myself—you know—that's strange —but it's true. Therapist: It seems such a strange concept to realize. Why, it would mean I would face the world as though a part of my primary responsibility was taking care of this precious individual who is me—whom I love. Client: Whom I care for—whom I feel so *close* to. Woof!! That's another *strange* one. Therapist: It just seems *weird*. Client: Yeah. It hits rather close somehow. The idea of my loving me and the taking care of me. [His eyes grow moist] That's a very, very nice one—very nice.

The recording would help to convey the fact that here is a feeling which had never been able to flow in him, which is experienced with immediacy, in this moment. It is a feeling which flows to its full result, without inhibition. It is experienced acceptantly, with no attempt to push it to one side or to deny it.

There is a quality of living subjectively in the experience, not feeling about it.

The client, in his *words,* may withdraw enough from the experience to feel about it, as in the above example, yet the recording makes it clear that his words are peripheral to the experiencing which is going on within him and in which he is living. The best communication of this in his words is "Woof!! That's another *strange* one."

Self as an object tends to disappear.

The self, at this moment, *is* this feeling. This is a being in the moment, with little self-conscious awareness, but with primarily a reflexive awareness, as Sartre terms it. The self *is,* subjectively, in the existential moment. It is not something one perceives.

Experiencing, at this stage, takes on a real process quality.

One client, a man who is approaching this stage, says that he has a frightened feeling about the source of a lot of secret thoughts in himself. He goes on: The butterflies are the thoughts closest to the surface. Underneath there's a deeper flow. I feel very removed from it all. The deeper flow is like a great school of fish moving under the surface. I see the ones that break through the surface of the water—sitting with my fishing line in one hand, with a bent pin on the end of it—trying to find

a better tackle—or better yet, a way of diving in. That's the scary thing. The image I get is that *I* want to be one of the fish myself. Therapist: You want to be down there flowing along, too.

Though this client is not yet fully experiencing in a process manner, and hence does not fully exemplify this sixth point on the continuum, he foresees it so clearly that his description gives a real sense of its meaning.

Another characteristic of this stage of process is the physiological loosening which accompanies it.

Moistness in the eyes, tears, sighs, muscular relaxation are frequently evident. Often there are other physiological concomitants. I would hypothesize that in these moments, had we the measures for it, we would discover improved circulation, improved conductivity of nervous impulses. An example of the "primitive" nature of some of these sensations may be indicated in the following excerpt:

[The client, a young man, has expressed the wish his parents would die or disappear.] It's kind of like wanting to wish them away, and wishing they had never been. . . . And I'm so ashamed of myself because then they call me, and off I go— swish! They're somehow still so strong. I don't know. There's some umbilical—I can almost feel it inside me—swish [and he gestures, plucking himself away by grasping at his navel]. Therapist: They really do have a hold on your umbilical cord. Client: It's funny how real it feels . . . like a burning sensation, kind of, and when they say something which makes me anxious I can feel it right here [pointing]. I never thought of it quite that way. Therapist: As though, if there's a disturbance in the relationship between you, then you do just feel it as though it was a strain on your umbilicus. Client: Yeah, kind of like in my gut here. It's so hard to define the feeling that I feel there.

Here he is living subjectively in the feeling of dependence on his parents. Yet it would be inaccurate to say that he is perceiving it. He is *in* it, experiencing it as a strain on his umbilical cord.

In this stage, internal communication is free and relatively unblocked.

I believe this is quite adequately illustrated in the examples given. Indeed the phrase "internal communication" is no longer quite correct; for, as each of these examples illustrates, the crucial moment is a moment of integration, in which communication between different internal foci is no longer necessary, because they become *one.*

The incongruence between experience and awareness is vividly experienced as it disappears into congruence.

The relevant personal construct is dissolved in this experiencing moment, and the client feels cut loose from his previously stabilized framework.

I trust these two characteristics may acquire more meaning from the following example. A young man has been having difficulty getting close to a certain unknown feeling.

That's almost exactly what the feeling is, too—it was that I was living so much of my life, and seeing so much of my life, in terms of being *scared* of something. [He tells how his professional activities are just to give him a little safety and] a little world where I'll be secure, you know. And for the same reason. [Pause] I was kind of letting it seep through. But I also tied it in with you and with my relationship with you, and one thing I feel about it is fear of its going away. [His tone changes to role-play more accurately his feeling.] Won't you let me have this? I kind of *need* it. I can be so lonely and scared without it. Therapist: M-hmm, m-hmm. "Let me hang on to it because I'd be terribly scared if I didn't!" . . . It's a kind of pleading thing too, isn't it? Client: I get a sense of—it's this kind of pleading little boy. It's this gesture of begging [putting his hands up as if in prayer]. Therapist: You put your hands in kind of a supplication. Client: Yeah, that's right. *"Won't* you do this for me?" kind of. Oh, that's terrible! Who, *me? Beg?* . . . That's an emotion I've never felt clearly at all—something I've never been. . . . [Pause] . . . I've got such a confusing feeling. One is, it's such a won-drous feeling to have these new things come out of me. It amazes me so much each time, and there's that same feeling, being scared that I've so much of this. [Tears] . . . I just don't know myself. Here's suddenly something I never realized, hadn't any inkling of—that it was some *thing* or some *way* I wanted to be.

Here we see a complete experiencing of his pleadingness, and a vivid recognition of the discrepancy between this experiencing and his concept of himself. Yet this experiencing of discrepancy exists in the moment of its disappearance. From now on he *is* a person who feels *pleading,* as well as many other feelings. As this moment dissolves the way he has construed himself, he feels cut loose from his previous world—a sensation which is both wondrous and frightening.

The moment of full experiencing becomes a clear and definite referent.

The examples given should indicate that the client is often not too clearly aware of what has "hit him" in these moments. Yet this does not seem too important because the event is an entity, a referent, which can be returned to, again and again if necessary, to discover more about it. The pleadingness, the feeling of "loving myself" which are present in these examples, may not prove to be exactly as described. They are, however, solid points of reference to which the client can return until he has satisfied himself as to what they are. It is, perhaps, that they constitute a clear-cut physiological event, a substratum of the conscious life, which the client can return to for investigatory purposes. Gendlin has called my attention to this significant quality of experiencing as a referent. He is endeavoring to build an extension of psychological theory on this basis. (2, especially Chap. 7).

Differentiation of experiencing is sharp and basic.

Because each of these moments is a referent, a specific entity, it does not become confused with anything else. The process of sharp differentiation builds on it and about it.

In this stage there are no longer "problems," external or internal. The client is living, subjectively, a phase of his problem. It is not an object.

I trust it is evident that in any of these examples it would be grossly inaccurate to say that the client perceives his problem as internal or is dealing with it as an internal problem. We need some way of indicating that he is further than this and, of course, enormously far in the process sense from perceiving his problem as external. The best description seems to be that he neither perceives his problem nor deals with it. He is simply living some portion of it knowingly and acceptingly.

I have dwelt so long on this sixth definable point on the process continuum because I see it as a highly crucial one. My observation is that these moments of immediate, full, accepted experiencing are in some sense almost irreversible. To put this in terms of the examples, it is my observation and hypothesis that with these clients, whenever a future experiencing of the same quality and characteristics occurs, it will necessarily be recognized in awareness for what it is: a tender caring for self, an umbilical bond which makes him a part of his parents, or a pleading small-boy dependence, as the case may be. And, it might be remarked in passing, once an experience is fully in awareness, fully accepted, then it can be coped with effectively, like any other clear reality.

THE SEVENTH STAGE

In those areas in which the sixth stage has been reached, it is no longer so necessary that the client be fully received by the therapist, though this still seems helpful. However, because of the tendency for the sixth stage to be irreversible, the client often seems to go on into the seventh and final stage without much need of the therapist's help. This stage occurs as much outside of the therapeutic relationship as in it and is

often reported, rather than experienced, in the therapeutic hour. I shall try to describe some of its characteristics as I feel I have observed them:

New feelings are experienced with immediacy and richness of detail, both in the therapeutic relationship and outside.

The experiencing of such feelings is consciously used as a clear referent.

There is a growing and continuing sense of acceptant ownership of these changing feelings, a basic trust in his own process.

This trust is not primarily in the conscious processes which go on, but rather in the total organismic process. One client puts it: I seem to work best when my conscious mind is only concerned with facts and letting the analysis of them go on by itself without paying any attention to it.

Experiencing has lost almost completely its structure-bound aspects and becomes process experiencing—that is, the situation is experienced and interpreted in its newness, not as the past.

An example in a very specific area is given by a client in a follow-up interview as he explains the different quality that has come about in his creative work. It used to be that he tried to be orderly. "You begin at the beginning and you progress regularly through to the end." Now he is aware that the process in himself is different. "When I'm working on an idea, the whole idea develops like the latent image coming out when you develop a photograph. It doesn't start at one edge and fill in over to the other. It comes in *all over*. At first all you see is the hazy outline, and you wonder what it's going to be; and then gradually something fits here and something fits there, and pretty soon it all comes clear—all at once." It is obvious that he has not only come to trust this process, but that he is experiencing it as it *is*, not in terms of some past.

The self becomes increasingly simply the subjective and reflexive awareness of experiencing. The self is much less frequently a perceived object and much more frequently something confidently felt in process.

An example may be taken from the same follow-up interview with the client quoted above. In this interview, because he is reporting his experience since therapy, he again becomes aware of himself as an object; but it is clear that this has not been the quality of his day-by-day experience. After reporting many changes, he says: I hadn't really thought of any of these things in connection with therapy until tonight. . . . [Jokingly] Gee! maybe something *did* happen. Because my life since *has* been different. My productivity has gone up. My confidence has gone up. I've become brash in situations I would have avoided before. And also, I've become less brash in situations where I would have become very obnoxious before.

It is clear that only afterward does he realize what his self as an object has been.

Personal constructs are tentatively reformulated, to be validated against further experience, but even then to be held loosely.

A client describes the way in which such a construct changed, between interviews, toward the end of therapy: I don't know what [changed], but I definitely feel different about looking back at my childhood, and some of the hostility about my mother and father has evaporated. I substituted for a feeling of resentment about them a sort of acceptance of the fact that they did a number of things that were undesirable with me. But I substituted a sort of feeling of interested excitement that— gee—now that I'm finding out what was wrong, *I* can do something about it—correct their mistakes.

Here the way in which he construes his experience with his parents has been sharply altered.

Internal communication is clear, with feelings and symbols well matched, and fresh terms for new feelings.

There is the experiencing of effective choice of new ways of being.

Because all the elements of experience are available to awareness, choice becomes real and effective. Here a client is just coming to this realization: "I'm trying to encompass a way of talking that is a way out of being scared of talking. Perhaps just kind of thinking out loud is the way to do that. But I've got so *many* thoughts I could only do it a little bit. But maybe I could let my talk be an expression of my thoughts, instead of just trying to make the proper noises in each situation." Here he is sensing the possibility of effective choice, perhaps approaching this seventh stage rather than being in it.

By no means all clients move this far on the continuum; but when this seventh stage is reached, it involves us in another dimension. For it will be evident that the client has now incorporated the quality of motion, of flow, of changingness into every aspect of his psychological life. He will therefore continue to be a continually changing person, experiencing with freshness and immediacy in each new situation, responding to its newness with real and accepted feelings, and construing its meaning in terms of what it *is*, not in terms of some past experience.

RECAPITULATION

I have tried to sketch, in a crude and preliminary manner, the flow of a process of change which occurs when a client experiences himself as being received, welcomed, understood as he is. This process involves several threads, separable at first, becoming more of a unity as the process continues.

This process involves a loosening of feelings. From feelings which are unrecognized, unowned, unexpressed, the client moves toward a flow in which ever-changing feelings are experienced in the moment, knowingly and acceptingly, and may be accurately expressed.

The process involves a change in the manner of experiencing. From experiencing which is remote in time from the organic event, which is bound by the structure of experience in the past, the client moves toward a manner of experiencing which is immediate, which interprets meaning in terms of what is, not what was.

The process involves a loosening of the cognitive maps of experience. From construing experience in rigid ways which are perceived as external facts, the client moves toward developing changing, loosely held construings of meaning in experience, constructions which are modifiable by each new experience.

The process involves a change in the self. From being a self which is not congruent with experience, the client moves through the phase of perceiving self as an object, to a self which is synonymous with experience, being the subjective awareness of that experience.

There are other elements, too, involved in the process: movement from ineffective to effective choice, from fear of relationships to freely living in relationship, from inadequate differentiation of feelings and meanings to sharp differentiation.

In general, the process moves from a point of fixity, where all these elements and threads are separately discernible and separately understandable, to the flowing peak moments of therapy in which all these threads become inseparably woven together. In the new experiencing with immediacy which occurs at such mo-

ments, feeling and cognition interpenetrate, self is subjectively present in the experience, volition is simply the subjective following of a harmonious balance of organismic direction. Thus, as the process reaches this point, the person becomes a unity of flow, of motion. He has changed; but, what seems most significant, he has become an integrated process of changingness.

References

1. Bergman, D. V. Counseling method and client responses. *J. Consult. Psychol.*, 15(1951), 216–224.

2. Gendlin, E. The function of experiencing in symbolization. Unpublished doctoral dissertation, Univ. of Chicago, 1958.

3. ———, and Zimring, F. The qualities or dimensions of experiencing and their change. *Counseling Center Discussion Papers*, 1(1955), No. 3. (Univ. of Chicago Counseling Center).

4. Kelly, G. A. *The psychology of personal constructs*. Vol. I. A theory of personality. New York: Norton, 1955.

5. Kirtner, W. L. Success and failure in client-centered therapy as a function of personality variables. Unpublished master's thesis, Univer. of Chicago, 1955.

6. Lewis, M. K., Rogers, C. R., and Shlien, J. M. Two cases of time-limited client-centered psychotherapy. In A. Burton (ed.), *Case studies of counseling and psychotherapy*. New York: Prentice-Hall, 1959.

7. Rogers, C. R. The necessary and sufficient conditions of therapeutic personality change. *J. Consult. Psychol.*, 21(1957), 95–103.

A Theoretical Approach to Psychotherapy as Personality Modification *

EDWARD JOSEPH SHOBEN, JR.
TEACHERS COLLEGE, COLUMBIA UNIVERSITY

There are many possible ways of conceiving of the psychotherapeutic process, and all of them perhaps possess some legitimacy and merit. If an enlarged understanding and a more precise knowledge of therapeutic functioning are to be achieved, however, there is a need to develop some conceptual scheme that will encourage critical research and permit the useful application of research findings to clinical situations.

The first step in the building of such a tentative theoretical approach is the examination of the field of therapeutic activity. Here one is given pause by the welter of divergent practices, each tied more or less loosely to divergent theoretical formulations. Nondirective therapy, insight therapy, release therapy, Gestalt therapy, conditioned reflex therapy, active psychotherapy, hypnotherapy, supportive therapy, and the variety of

Reprinted from the *Harvard Educational Review*, 23(1953), 128–142, with the permission of the Harvard Educational Review and the author.

* This article is slightly modified from a paper read before the Graduate Psychology Club of Vanderbilt University and the George Peabody College for Teachers in Nashville, Tennessee, on February 12, 1953, and before the Personnel Psychology Colloquium at Ohio State University in Columbus, Ohio, on February 25, 1953. Grateful acknowledgment is made for the many suggestions and constructive criticisms offered by these two audiences.

psychoanalytic therapies are some of the terms coined to designate differences in practice and in modes of theorizing about practice. Can order be brought into this seeming chaos of ideas and activities?

Two observations seem relevant. First, as Rosenzweig (30) has pointed out, most therapies can claim successes with very similar degrees of justification. Therapeutic gains, apparently, may be achieved by a wide range of methods. If such a statement is provisionally acceptable, then it follows that a search for commonalities of occurrence among different practices should provide the basis for a comprehensive conceptual approach to the therapeutic process. Such a possibility accords with the suspicion that most existent theories of psychotherapy amount to the ideologies in terms of which particular methods are defended, rationalized, and taught to successive generations of practitioners (31, 34). Such ideological efforts need not be at all deplored; they simply must be recognized as different from a theoretical enterprise aimed at isolating the factors common to all therapeutic endeavor and at accounting for the operation of such factors.

Second, the goals of psychotherapy, regardless of the language in terms of which they are stated, seem always to

405

involve some change in the patient's overt or covert behavior. In perhaps too vague and global terms, a paramount criterion of successful therapeutic outcome is a reportably happier adjustment on the part of the client to his experienced needs and values and to his environment, especially his social environment. Most often, this kind of alteration in the patient's functioning is indexed by verbal changes within the series of therapeutic interviews (3, 27). Far less frequently, it is checked by observations of the client's behavior and his status in the extraclinical world (15, 26). But generally, successful psychotherapy implies some change in the patient's style of life or in that relatively consistent organization of motives, cognitions, and acts that is called personality.*

There are a number of important consequences of such an argument. First, the notions of *disease* and *treatment* as they are applied to the subjects of psychotherapy and to the therapeutic process become instances of concepts developed by analogy only, taken over from organic medicine with little justification beyond the possibility that neither the sick nor the unhappy function at maximum efficiency and that both "feel bad." Second, if psychotherapy is conceived as a process of personality modification, it should be subject to a useful analysis in terms of what is now known about personality formation and development. The laws and hypotheses relating to perception, learning, and motivation, which have shown some utility in accounting for personality *growth,* should shed some light on the therapeutic situation in which personality *change* occurs.

* This statement does not overlook the fact that there are certain therapeutic approaches that do not aim at personality modification. Institutional management procedures and procedures concerned only with the modification of a particular symptom are examples. Attention here is directed only at those therapeutic efforts that claim as goals the enlargement of awareness, the development of insight, or the restructuring of the client's motivations.

Furthermore, such a conception of psychotherapy as a process of modifying personality should make for a more reciprocal and fruitful relationship between clinical and more laboratory-oriented brands of psychology. The clinician should be able to articulate more communicatively the kinds of problems that he faces and to specify more exactly the extent to which current ideas and research findings prove helpful or deficient in the complex interactive situation of psychotherapy. On the other hand, the psychologist more oriented toward investigation and careful theory building should find profit in the insights and hypotheses derived from clinical experience and from the new, challenging, and socially important problems posed from such a context.

Finally, this kind of conception leads to a reformulation of the basic psychotherapeutic question in thoroughly *psychological* terms: How does the therapist interact with his client in such a way as to elicit those reactions which will be significantly correlated with a reported sense of increased security and adequacy and with similar evaluations by the client's "significant others" (36)?

The Nature of Psychotherapy and the Nature of Neurosis

To answer such a question within the conceptual scheme suggested here, it is necessary to give some attention to the problem of defining psychotherapy in terms of what therapists seem to do and to indicating the common characteristics of the people whom psychotherapists serve. The first amounts to an attempt to specify the attributes of the therapeutic *situation;* the second represents an attempt to define the therapeutic *problem.*

THE NATURE OF PSYCHOTHERAPY

If one ignores the special doctrinal flags by which various "schools" identify themselves, one can arrive relatively quickly at a rough, descriptive definition of psychotherapy. It seems to be a kind of social relationship between two people (sometimes one person and a small group) who hold more or less regular conversations in the interest of attaining certain goals—the modification of the client's personality. While many adjuvants and special devices may be employed, all instances of psychotherapy seem at bottom to involve interpersonal relationships and talk, both being manipulated toward the alteration of those characteristics of the client which militate against his long-range comfort and sense of adequacy. For convenience, these two basic aspects of psychotherapeutic interaction may be called *relationship and conversational content.*

With respect to relationship, Fiedler (6, 7) has demonstrated experimentally that experience and "expertness" are more important than is theoretical affiliation as determiners of the way in which therapists conceive of effective therapeutic modes of interaction. Both in describing ideal therapeutic relationships and in evaluating actual therapist-client relationships, there is greater agreement among clinicians of comparable experience and professional reputation than there is among those adhering to the same theory but differing in their judged competence. One feels safe, therefore, in attempting to describe the characteristics of "the" therapeutic relationship without regard to what practitioners say about themselves at the level of ideology.

The first attribute of the relationship side of therapy seems to be that of *concern.** The clinical worker is genuinely interested in his client as a person and is fully committed to the task of being as helpful as possible. There is no neces-

* It seems a little strange that so little systematic attention has been given to this relationship factor that there is not even an agreed-upon terminology in which to describe it. *Concern* as used here, for example, derives more from New Testament philology than from psychological, educational, or psychiatric studies.

sary implication here of "liking" a client; many psychotherapeutic subjects are simply not very likeable people, and their unhappy awareness of this fact is one of the things that bring them to therapy. Likewise, there is certainly no suggestion of erotic overtones or even of a desire for the client's friendship. Both of these attitudes are probably antitherapeutic. All that is meant is that the therapist devotes all his abilities during the time that he is with his client to the business of helping him to achieve those changes that will be associated with a greater sense of comfort and adequacy.

Second, the relationship is marked by a *nonretaliatory permissiveness.* The therapist gives the client full freedom to discuss any topic he chooses, including his reactions to the therapist and to the therapeutic situation. Regardless of the topic chosen, the therapist remains calm and unshocked, and even in the face of attack, his efforts are bent toward understanding rather than toward retribution. In brief, the relationship is a safe one for the client because he is never rejected or subjected to punishment for the behavior he reports or for the attitudes and affects that he verbalizes.

On the other hand, there seems to be a balancing third factor, that of *honesty and understanding.* The therapist appears to be constantly attempting to clarify the interaction between himself and his client and to enlarge his comprehension of the client's actions. Thus, by such types of response as interpretation or clarification or reflection of feeling, the therapist tempers the permissiveness of the relationship by gently insisting on and rewarding increasing degrees of candor and self-exploration. It is as if the clinician were constantly occupied with the questions of what the client is really trying to say and how both to encourage him to think more clearly about himself and to communicate back to him a clarified understanding in both the intellectual and empathic sense of what he has expressed.

If concern, nonretaliatory permissiveness, and honesty and understanding seem appropriate to virtually any desirable human relationship rather than peculiar to the therapeutic situation, such is quite the case. Fiedler (6) found, for example, that clinicians and laymen show little disagreement in describing ideal clinical relationships and the degree to which they are approximated in recorded excerpts from actual case protocols.

But there are some important differences between therapeutic and ordinary social relationships. In the first place, the therapeutic relationship is one-sided in that the therapist does not share his own troubles or pleasures with his clients, nor does he usually permit his own specific values or personal affairs to intrude into the interviews. Second, with the possible exception of child clients, the therapist usually refuses to intervene in the client's extraclinical life, either in terms of environmental manipulations or of interceding with family or work associates. Third, there is much more focus in psychotherapy on the changing qualities of the therapist-patient relationship than is true of interpersonal situations outside the clinic walls. It seems doubtful that in any other type of relationship the interpersonal process is made so explicit. Thus, there are limits on the therapeutic interaction which differentiate it from other forms of personal relationship and which minimize in a very real sense the therapist's own distinctive personality.

Turning from relationship to conversational content, it seems that therapeutic talk is modally concerned with the client's values, motives, and emotions, and his reactions to them and to the situations, both contemporary and historical, to which, as he interprets them, these affects and goal-strivings are relevant. One of these situations, and usually a very important one, seems to be the therapeutic process and the therapeutic relationship themselves.

THE NATURE OF NEUROSIS

The term "neurosis," because of its association with such words as "pathology" and "disease" and because of its etymological connotations of organic dysfunction, may be an unfortunate one by which to refer to the great bulk of people who seek psychotherapeutic services. The rubric of "maladjustment," with its suggestions of conformity, is likewise short of ideal communicative power. Nevertheless, the concept of neurosis is used here with misgivings to apply to those persons who lack the interpersonal skills, including affective and cognitive responses, necessary for the satisfactory performance of the role activities their social contexts demand of them (29). The primary contention is that the subjects of psychotherapy are generally people whose socialization experiences have ill prepared them to live comfortably as members of society and to relate themselves to others in ways that are mutually evaluated as fulfilling. Perhaps the central attribute common to all such persons is the affect of anxiety (9, 11).*

Anxiety may be thought of as possessing a number of properties. It is acquired through punishment, both physical and symbolic, including the threat of loss of love. It is anticipatory in character. It has a very definite motivating value. Subjectively, it is unpleasant and uncomfortable. Finally, it is attached primarily to one's own impulses. One can quite legitimately speak of anxiety as a fear not of external, objective dangers in the environment but of impulses to act in ways that have been interpreted as forbidden and that have met with punishment in the individual's history.

For example, those acts involving sexuality, aggression, dependency, the seeking of achievement and status, and the expression of affection are required

* The next few paragraphs rely heavily upon a previous paper (35).

to take only certain culturally approved forms. Because of their societally defined importance, these areas of human action undergo particularly intensive socialization. If the parents or other agents of socialization, as is common, tend to punish strongly and early all but the sanctioned modes of response in these spheres, there is a large likelihood that *all* impulses to act, say, sexually or in achievement-seeking ways will become cues for anxiety. In this respect, anxiety may be conceived as a kind of fear of one's "self."

This situation is further complicated by the occurrence of repression. Since anxiety functions as a drive,* it tends to initiate variable behavior until some process becomes associated with a reduction in the distressing affect. The number of possible types of response, however, is sharply limited by the fact that the motivating state of affairs, anxiety, is an internal stimulus rather than an external one. Freud (8) suggests that only three techniques are available: (a) flight from the situations provoking the forbidden and punished impulse, (b) "condemnation" or the voluntary suppression of the impulse, and (c) repression. Flight from all the stimuli arousing such impulses as those of sexuality, aggression, and status seeking is virtually impossible if one is to remain in human society, and voluntary suppression requires precisely that niceness of judgment and discrimination among appropriate and inappropriate situations for impulse expression that few children have had an opportunity to develop with limited experience and under punishing methods of socialization. As a result, re-

pression has a high probability of occurrence when anxiety activates the personality.

Repression is here conceived substantially in Freud's (8) own terms. He argues that "the essence of repression lies simply in the function of rejecting and keeping something out of consciousness." By this he means, as he further explains, that ". . . repression denies . . . translation of the idea into words which are to remain attached to the object." Thus, repression consists solely in the excluding from verbalization of the impulse which elicits the painful anxiety. With the stimulating impulse rendered much less identifiable or perceptible by the detachment of its symbolic representation, the intensity of the anxiety is diminished.†

Relief is thus purchased, however, at a twofold cost. First, as is clearly implied in Freud's notions of repression, the individual who meets anxiety with this dynamism loses or is barred from adequately developing his ability to label properly his own impulses, together with their sources and cathexes. He quite literally cannot efficiently interpret his own experience by means of that implicit, intrapersonal communication called thought. It is this emotionally determined defect in the symbolic governance of the neurotic's life that has led Dollard and Miller (2) to speak of neurotic "stupidity."

Second, while repression binds anxiety in some degree through obscuring the impulse which elicits it, repression is apparently almost never complete. Various representations of the tabooed impulse in the form of dreams, incipient motor responses and proprioceptive stimuli, vague but troublesome symbolic

---

* With respect to learning theory, the point of view here followed is essentially Hull's (12, 14) reinforcement theory as modified by Mowrer (23) into a two-factor formulation. While favoring the latter, the position held in this paper is substantially consistent with either. The specific experimental evidence for considering anxiety a drive is given in studies by May (18) and by Miller (22).

† The mechanism operating here is formalized as Hull's (13) postulate relating to the stimulus intensity dynamism. In oversimplified terms, the fundamental contention is that the strength of a response is a function of the strength of its stimulus.

meanings attached to objects or events, and feelings of uneasy restlessness tend to touch off anxiety even though the impulse itself cannot be identified. When such things happen, the discomfort of the anxiety is likely to be complicated by the individual's inability to label its source. He reports himself as experiencing "dread," or a "fear of nothing," or a fear attached without recognizable justification to irrelevant persons, objects, or occurrences.

In short, the anxiety-ridden person is one who feels frequently, sometimes even constantly, stirred up and tense without being able to specify the goals which, if attained, would relieve the discomfort and tension. The issue of this situation is a vicious circle which can be described in a highly condensed form as follows: The neurotic, driven by anxiety and unable to symbolize the source of the stress in his repressed impulses, desperately pursues first one set of goals and then another, giving up each as his strivings fail to bring him satisfaction. Forever dissatisfied, he develops schematizations (19) of himself as inadequate, as unable to cope with the demands of his own existence. These conceptualizations mediate further intolerable anxiety, under the motivation of which he develops various strategies for rationalizing and denying his experience to himself and to others. These devices are at best only partially successful, and he encounters the punishments of both social repudiation and self recrimination. Such punishments set the whole process in motion again in an ever-increasing spiral of neurotic involvement.*

* It may be objected that this brief depiction of the neurotic spiral does not accord with common observations of the obsessive-compulsive way of life. It seems quite possible, however, that any differences are more apparent than real. The so-called obsessive client may not show the kind of flitting from goal to goal or the deficiency in persistence described in these paragraphs, but his desperate ruminations, his clinging to goals of doubtful suitability, his narrow-

Within the context of this neurotic spiral, in his anxiety-motivated pursuit of first this goal and then that, the neurotic becomes stigmatized by others as irresponsible, as lacking in persistence, as unable to bear the ordinary tribulations of living, as childish in his demands for success whether or not he has earned it. Moreover, he comes to conceptualize himself in very similar terms. Here is one of the great sources of guilt as it is nearly universally seen in neurotic clients. Without knowing how it happened, they are forced to the painful realization that they have fallen short of the ideals of responsible adulthood. They conceive of themselves as culpable failures.

But this state of affairs is subject to turbulent compounding. Precisely because of the painfulness of the neurotic sense of inadequacy in relation to the incorporated cultural ideals of adulthood, there is a powerful tendency to deny it, to attribute it to the evil propensities in others or in the "world," or to explain it away somehow. In short, the neurotic becomes deceptive and dishonest with himself and with his fellows, and this kind of dishonesty mediates a number of common symptomatic actions. Examples include the tendency to seek protection from constituted authority figures, the tendency to rebel only as a way of expressing angry aggression against an environment schematized as hostile, unjust, and dangerous rather than as a way of achieving some thoughtfully considered social goal, and the tendency to manipulate or to dominate others sexually or aggressively in order to demonstrate the "untruth" of a strongly felt inadequacy. Thus, deceit becomes an inevitable part of the neurotic course, vio-ing of his life's activities, and his pained adherence to ritualistic behavior all seem to serve the same short-sighted anxiety-reducing function and to lead to similar consequences in the form of self recrimination and social repudiation on the grounds of pedantry, narrow-mindedness, and disregard of others.

lently disrupting opportunities for mutually satisfying interpersonal relationships, calling forth social condemnation, and evoking still further guilt.

Within the framework of the theory of neurosis briefly outlined here, it is held that the neurotic is characterized by a wide range of ways of conceptualizing himself as a failure and his environment as hostile and by an equally wide range of socially incompetent ways of acting. From these inadequacies, both actual and "erroneous," is derived his ubiquitous sense of guilt. The inadequacies and guilt, however, while real and vitally important in the structure of neurosis, are secondary phenomena, dependent upon prior impulse anxiety and repression for their emergence.

Psychotherapy as Personality Modification

Both the depiction here given of psychotherapy and the general conception presented of neurosis emphasize social and interpersonal factors. Psychotherapy represents a special kind of social situation; the phenomena of neurosis are social in their origins and important largely because of their social consequences. How does this social situation operate to modify the client's personality in the direction of greater interpersonal competence?

The central hypothesis to be developed in this section is that psychotherapy provides a kind of microcosm in which the patient has the opportunity to learn new patterns of response which better enable him to function as a social being. In other words, therapy provides the client with a safe world within which the process of socialization may be reconstructed and from which he can generalize his new learning. Magaret (17) has made a similar point in speaking of psychotherapy as a situation in which new "learning sets" (10) are established,

which then are generalized to the patient's extraclinical world.

The chief necessity in this process, as neurosis has been here formulated, is the elimination of anxiety, the basic instigator of the social uneasiness, the distorted perceptions, and the nonintegrative behavioral mechanisms (24) that characterize the neurotic person.* Anxiety is fundamentally a product of experienced punishment, cruelty, rejection, and loss of love. Is it not tenable to suggest that it is eliminated through a process of counter conditioning, based upon the nonpunitive and security-evoking interpersonal situation structured for the client by the clinician (32, 33)? What is meant may be clarified by a schematic outline of events as they occur in therapy.†

When a neurotic presents himself for psychotherapy, he tends to focus on the therapist the same kinds of expectancies of rejection and hostility and the same varieties of deceitful interpersonal strategies that characterize him extraclinically. Typically, he perceives the therapist much as he perceives others: as a feared figure to be dominated and manipulated and to make demands of, but not as one to trust nor from whom real concern might be expected.

The first task of the clinician is primarily that of dealing with these distorted expectancies and nonintegrative social behaviors as they are directed to-

---

* While it is possible that the principles suggested here might apply to *any* person for whom psychotherapy is a suitable form of remediation, the present discussion is limited to those clients who are best described diagnostically as neurotic or "maladjusted." Psychological therapy with psychotics, psychopaths, or those whose behavior pathology is associated with organic disease or damage might require a very different kind of formulation.

† Obviously, the following division of the therapeutic process into stages is intended only for the purpose of conceptual convenience. While they probably have a genuine chronological sequence, they most certainly overlap and blend to a marked degree.

ward the therapeutic situation and the therapist himself. Here he seems to do three things. First, the therapist avoids punishment and moralistic judgments. He attempts to communicate a respect for the client and an understanding of the fact that the client's actions are determined by his discomfort, not by wilfulness or perversity. Second, he labels the distorted perceptions and deceptive social techniques for the patient. Without insisting or arguing and without anger, he merely indicates his knowledge of the client's attempts at evasion, domination, neutralization, or other self-defeating interpersonal devices within the client-clinician relationship, and of the nonveridical nature of the client's perceptions and expectancies regarding that relationship. Finally, he rewards self-revelatory behavior by the client. Such rewards may vary from direct expressions of approval of the patient's efforts to explore his own personality, through overt recognition of the difficulty involved in trying to think straightforwardly about oneself, to a mere heightening of the therapist's degree of participation or the kind of communication suggested by an understanding nod or a denotatively meaningless vocalization.*

These therapist activities may have a number of outcomes. In the first place, the nonjudgmental behavior of the therapist and his concern for his client's increased happiness tends to make available consistent and relatively intense information (1) that is contrary to the neurotic cognitions brought to therapy from previous experience. It is difficult for the therapist to be fitted, neatly under these circumstances, into the client's system of perceptual distortions in which he regularly expects the worst. It seems possible that in successful cases, this dawning recognition that the therapist

is "not like other people," † that he can be trusted to be understanding and non-retaliatory, amounts to a brand of insight that is chronologically first in its occurrence within the sequence of therapeutic events and is basic to all other meliorative procedures.

A second outgrowth of the therapist's early activities may be a decrement in the number of deceptive and evasive "resistances." It should be noted that the procedure of labeling without rancor or argument and with no punishment aside from that implied by the connotative value of the labeling symbols themselves is analogous to such procedures in the learning laboratory as running extinction trials or giving knowledge of the results of actions (20). Where severe punishment apparently has the effect of momentarily depressing the rate of occurrence of a response *without* affecting its strength or its susceptibility to extinction, simple nonreinforcement or very mild punishment tend to yield the steepest extinction curve (4). While the argument is entirely by analogy, it seems quite legitimate to suggest that the deceptive interpersonal stratagems of the neurotic *as they relate to the therapist* are probably extinguished in a very similar fashion through the therapist's noncondemnatory labeling of them.

Third, the client's tendency to talk about himself and those situations in his life which he regards as vital is strengthened through the therapist's various reinforcements. This aspect of the psychotherapeutic process seems important for at least two reasons. Therapy is a painful business at best, and the instigation to

---

* With neither malice nor facetiousness, it is seriously suggested that the primary function of the Rogerian "uh-huh" is this reinforcing of the patient's self-exploratory behavior.

† This point, while arrived at independently, has been much clarified by discussion with Dr. Percival Symonds and by his paper (37) dealing with the same theoretical problem but issuing in quite a different kind of conceptualization. Much of the present discussion has benefited by exposure to Dr. Symonds's thinking, but he must not be charged with any responsibility for any fate with which his ideas may have met in these pages.

quit often threatens to overwhelm the instigation to continue. If some social approval can be won, however, at the same time a hope of relief from anxiety is being held out, therapy may acquire a more positive goal value, and the client is more likely to keep his appointments and to work actively with the therapist. Similarly, this bit of encouragement, along with his other activities described here, facilitates the therapist's becoming a positive if calculatedly vague figure. Because he preserves his relative anonymity, the therapist can hardly be called well known to his clients; but because he behaves as he does, it seems possible that he comes to represent for them the *kind* of person that they would like both to know and to be. The groundwork for possibly very fundamental identification processes may be in preparation during this phase of therapy.* Finally, it may be that it is only the continued self-examination and self-revelatory behavior of the client that can set up the conditions necessary for the counter conditioning of anxiety.

It would seem, then, that in these relatively earlier interviews, the client learns a number of things. First, because he has received a good deal of reinforcement for his self-exploration, he is presumably acquiring more nondeceptive ways of thinking about himself. Second, because another person has reacted to him with a large and consistent concern

---

* An intriguing and probably fruitful conceptualization of the therapeutic process could be built entirely around this concept of identification. Following Mead (21), one could hypothesize that conceptions of the self are basically derived from conceptions of others. Since the therapeutic situation is so structured and the therapist's anonymity so insured that the clinician can appear as almost the prototype of the strong, calm, responsible, and loving adult, it is possible that the outcomes of psychotherapy rest essentially upon the client's taking the perceived therapist as a model, trying to behave as it is thought he would behave and developing ways of conceptualizing himself drawn basically from conceptualizations of the therapist.

and has dealt with him in an understanding, noncondemnatory way, the client's demanding, suspicious, and hostile beliefs and expectancies are challenged and weakened. Third, in his relation to the therapist, the client has developed an affective degree of security and comfort which he probably has seldom experienced before.

But the therapist also clarifies, through interpretation or reflection of feeling, the patient's communications. This process is often spoken of as facilitating insight, conceived as the client's ability to verbalize the connections between his stimulus experiences, the affects they have produced, and his utilization of nonintegrative anxiety-reducing mechanism. Occasionally, it is held that when this type of insight has been achieved, therapy has been successful. This notion seems open to serious challenge. The idea that being able to verbalize correctly the cues for anxiety promotes a lessening in anxiety seems highly rationalistic and is contradicted by the reported experience of psychotherapists for at least the past half century. There are certainly many available examples of clients who can talk at length and probably with great accuracy about their own dynamics but who still are troubled and disturbed by acute anxiety and who still show marked interpersonal incompetence. On the other hand, there are numerous examples of clients who have acquired a decided measure of security, comfort, and increased social efficiency without being able to account in any satisfactory way for the alteration in their personalities. There is no denial here that insight in the present sense occurs or that it may be necessary for the achievement of therapeutic goals. All that is implied is that the equation of insight with success seems quite wrongheaded.

Nevertheless, the clarifying interpretations or reflections of the clinician do seem aimed at the lifting of repression or the facilitation of insight as the ability to symbolize one's affects, their sources, and their consequences. If insight alone occurs, however, if the patient is simply brought to the point where he can accurately label the cues for his anxiety responses, it seems legitimate to predict that he would be rendered more anxious rather than less because of the enhancement of the stimuli (13) through their verbalization. Something else seems necessary to account for the new learning that takes place in successful therapy.

That something else is afforded by the nature of the therapeutic relationship. As a concerned, nonretaliatory, permissive, and honest form of human intercommunication, it presents stimuli which elicit affective responses of comfort and security and hopefulness. It is probable that these responses are mediated and strongly facilitated by the client's altered perceptions of the therapist as a trustworthy and genuinely interested person. If such a state of affairs obtains, there seems to be a high probability that the pairing of the security-eliciting relationship with the symbolically reinstated cues for anxiety results in a new connection, substantially in accordance with the conditioning paradigm, between the historical stimuli for anxiety and the security reactions made to the therapeutic relationship.

Evidence for such a view can be cited from a wide variety of experimental sources: Pavlov's (25) reports of the "unlearning" of fear by dogs through the pairing of food stimuli with the previously established cues for fear, Mary Cover Jones's (16) classical conditioning therapy with the boy Peter, and Razran's (28) modification of attitudes toward various forms of art by his "luncheon technique." It is also well illustrated by Farber's (5) experiment on fixation and its extinction in white rats.

Thus, the argument so far asserts that psychotherapy in its first phases consists fundamentally in the strengthening of the client's self-exploratory skills and the development of perceptions of the therapist that mediate affective security reactions to the therapeutic situation. In its second stage, therapy involves primarily the lifting of repressions, by which is meant chiefly the expression and correct labeling of those impulses which have cued off anxiety. As the repressions are dissipated and the labeling process proceeds, the stimuli for anxiety, thus symbolically introduced through the conversational content, become attached to the security responses elicited to the therapeutic situation. With some accuracy, one could say that when these events have occurred, the client is no longer "afraid of himself."

It should be noted that all that has been said up to now squares with the sometimes heartbreakingly long time that effective therapy seems to require. Repressions cannot be safely removed and therapeutic goals attained until the relationship has acquired a sufficient power to evoke security reactions that are stronger than the anxiety unleashed by the verbalization of the repressed cues. This restriction means that the process of interpretation must be marked with slowness and caution, or the risk is great that the client may develop a kind of intellectualized glibness about himself or discontinue therapy altogether.

But how is this new affective learning implemented outside the clinic's walls? The hypothesis here advanced is that this crucial step is brought about through the generalization of both the affective and the perceptual changes that have occurred during the therapeutic course, resulting in finer discriminations of those social situations in which it is appropriate to express one's impulses and those where it is not. Herein lies a further reason for the personal anonymity upon which most therapists insist.

The central notion here is that the therapeutic relation is essentially a prototype for human relationships generally, not a highly differentiated interaction between the client and the therapist as an individual. Magaret (17), in making a comparable point, says that through therapy the patient:

... learns to know many persons, none of whom is actually the therapist, but each of whom is an organization of behavior— a role or a person—projected upon the therapist. What the patient learns, then, is not to know one person, the therapist. Nor does he learn a repertory of specific reactions which he then employs outside the therapeutic hour . . .

Similarly, it is here asserted that what the patient learns is first to perceive others as potentially capable of mutually fulfilling interpersonal relationships with him, depending primarily on his willingness to behave nondeceptively in relation to them. Second, he learns to react nonanxiously to a wide range of human interactions that have in his neurotic history been associated with punishment. Freed from the distorting effects of anxiety and possessed of perceptual habits that mediate more effective interpersonal actions, the client develops in the final stages of therapy a sharper discrimination of those situations where his impulses may be given expression and those where they must be "condemned," as Freud would say, or voluntarily suppressed in the interest of longer-range gratifications. Thus, he can proceed to acquire a variety of instrumental social responses, including cognitive responses, on the basis of how they are reinforced in the groups in which he gains or holds membership.

The therapist's role in this later phase of the therapeutic process is essentially that of thinking with the client, helping him to anticipate the consequences of his planned actions, to understand the outcomes of his interpersonal trials and errors, and to avoid falling back into his old habits of deceiving himself and projecting his failures onto his environment. His function is *not* that of engrafting his own values onto his client or of directing his client's life. It is primarily at this point that the patient's independence is explicitly reinforced and brought to a level of strength that permits his discharging himself from therapy.

Summary

An attempt has been made here to formulate the psychotherapeutic process as a form of personality modification through manipulation of the psychological variables of learning, perception, and motivation. Therapy is conceived as occurring in an overlapping three-stage sequence. In the first phase, through the therapist's relationship to his client and his manner of dealing with resistances, the client has his distorted perceptual responses weakened and learns to respond to the therapeutic situation with security and comfort. In the second stage, the patient's repressions are lifted and insight in the sense of ability to label the cues for anxiety occurs. Through this symbolic reinstatement of the cues for anxiety within the security-evoking context of the therapeutic situation, counter conditioning occurs and a connection is formed between the previous stimuli for anxiety and the security responses made to the therapeutic relationship. Finally, freed from the distorting effects of anxiety, the client proceeds to form new perceptions and expectancies of his social environment and to discriminate more accurately between those social situations where impulse expression is appropriate and those where it is not.

References

1. Bruner, J. S. Personality dynamics and the process of perceiving. In Blake, R. R., and Ramsey, G., eds. *Perception: an approach to personality.* New York: Ronald, 1951.

2. Dollard, J., and Miller, N. *Personality*

and psychotherapy. New York: McGraw-Hill Book Co., 1950.

3. Dollard, J., and Mowrer, O. H. A method of measuring tension in written documents. *J. Abnorm. Soc. Psychol.,* 42(1947), 3–32.

4. Estes, W. K. An experimental study of punishment. *Psychol. Monog.,* 57(1944), No. 3.

5. Farber, I. E. Response fixation under anxiety and nonanxiety conditions. *J. Exp. Psychol.,* 38(1948), 111–131.

6. Fiedler, F. E. The concept of the ideal therapeutic relationship. *J. Consult. Psychol.,* 14(1950), 239–245.

7. —— A comparison of the therapeutic relationships in psychoanalytic, nondirective, and Adlerian therapy. *J. Consult. Psychol.,* 14(1950), 436–445.

8. Freud, S. Repression. *Collected papers.* London: Hogarth, 1925. Volume IV.

9. —— *The problem of anxiety.* New York: Norton, 1936.

10. Harlow, H. F. The formation of learning sets. *Psychol. Rev.,* 56(1949), 51–65.

11. Hoch, P., and Zubin, J., eds. *Anxiety.* New York: Grune & Stratton, 1950.

12. Hull, C. L. *Principles of behavior.* New York: Appleton-Century-Crofts, 1943.

13. —— Stimulus intensity dynamism (V) and stimulus generalization. *Psychol. Rev.,* 56(1949), 67–76.

14. —— *A behavior system.* New Haven: Yale Univ. Press, 1952.

15. Hunt, J. McV. Measuring movement in casework. *J. Soc. Casework,* 29(1948), 343–351.

16. Jones, M. C. A laboratory study of fear: the case of Peter. *Ped. Sem.,* 31(1924), 308–315.

17. Magaret, A. Generalization in successful psychotherapy. *J. Consult. Psychol.,* 14(1950), 64–70.

18. May, M. A. Experimentally acquired drives. *J. Exp. Psychol.,* 38(1948), 66–77.

19. McClelland, D. *Personality.* New York: William Sloane Associates, 1951.

20. McGeoch, J. A. *The psychology of human learning.* New York: Longmans, Green, 1942.

21. Mead, G. H. *Mind, self, and society.* Chicago: Univ. of Chicago Press, 1934.

22. Miller, N. Studies of fear as an acquir-

able drive: I. Fear as motivation and fear-reduction as reinforcement in the learning of new responses. *J. Exp. Psychol.,* 38(1948), 89–101.

23. Mowrer, O. H. On the dual nature of learning—A reinterpretation of "conditioning" and "problem-solving." *Harvard Educ. Rev.,* 17(1947), 102–148.

24. Mowrer, O. H., and Ullman, A. D. Time as a determinant in integrative learning. *Psychol. Rev.,* 52(1945), 61–90.

25. Pavlov, I. P. *Conditioned reflexes.* London: Oxford Univ. Press, 1927.

26. Pepinsky, H. B., Clyde, R. J., Olesen, B. A., and Vanatta, E. D. The criterion in counseling. I. Individual personality and behavior in a social group. *Educ. Psychol. Measmt.,* 12(1952), 178–193.

27. Raimy, V. C. Self reference in counseling interviews. *J. Consult. Psychol.,* 12(1948), 153–163.

28. Razran, G. H. S. Conditioning away social bias by the luncheon technique. *Psychol. Bull.,* 35(1938), 693 (abst.).

29. Rohrer, J. An evaluation of college personnel work in terms of current research on interpersonal relationships. *Educ. Psychol. Measmt.,* 9(1949), 429–444.

30. Rosenzweig, S. Some implicit common factors in diverse methods of psychotherapy. *Amer. J. Orthopsychiat.,* 6(1936), 412–415.

31. Shaffer, L. F. The problem of psychotherapy. *Amer. Psychologist,* 2(1947), 459–467.

32. Shoben, E. J., Jr. Psychotherapy as a problem in learning theory. *Psychol. Bull.,* 46(1949), 366–392.

33. —— Some observations on psychotherapy and the learning process. In Mowrer, O. H., ed. *Psychotherapy: theory and research.* New York: Ronald, 1953.

34. —— Some problems in establishing criteria of counseling effectiveness. *Personnel and Guid. J.,* 31(1953), 287–291.

35. —— Anxiety vs. immaturity in neurosis and its treatment. *Amer. J. Orthopsychiat.* 25(1955), 71–80.

36. Sullivan, H. S. *Conceptions of modern psychiatry.* Washington, D.C.: William Alanson White Foundation, 1947.

37. Symonds, P. A comprehensive theory of psychotherapy. *Amer. J. Orthopsychiat.* 24(1954), 697–714.

12. THE EFFECTS OF PSYCHOTHERAPY

THE PAPERS which follow are all concerned with the evaluation of the benefits which derive from various psychotherapeutic procedures over and above those changes which may have occurred without psychotherapeutic intervention. The issue is an extremely complex one, as demonstrated by both the theoretical exchange of Eysenck and Rosenzweig and the research review by Zax and Klein. Eysenck's first paper brought forth strong reactions from practitioners and from many who were engaged in psychotherapeutic research insofar as it was interpreted as oversimplifying the problem and drawing unwarranted conclusions. Rosenzweig's response to Eysenck carefully points out the complexities involved in such evaluations and suggests that a well-reasoned approach requires more moderate conclusions than Eysenck drew. Zax and Klein focus on representative criteria used in research evaluating the effects of psychotherapy and direct attention to the intricacies involved in this phase of the research.

The Effects of Psychotherapy: An Evaluation

H. J. EYSENCK
INSTITUTE OF PSYCHIATRY, MAUDSLEY HOSPITAL, UNIVERSITY OF LONDON

The recommendation of the Committee on Training in Clinical Psychology of the American Psychological Association regarding the training of clinical psy-

Reprinted from the *Journal of Consulting Psychology*, 16(1952), 319–324, with the permission of The American Psychological Association and the author.

chologists in the field of psychotherapy has been criticized by the writer in a series of papers (10, 11, 12). Of the arguments presented in favor of the policy advocated by the Committee, the most cogent one is perhaps that which refers to the social need for the skills possessed by the psychotherapist. In view of the

417

importance of the issues involved, it
seemed worth while to examine the evidence relating to the actual effects of psychotherapy, in an attempt to seek clarification on a point of fact.

Base Line and Unit of Measurement

In the only previous attempt to carry
out such an evaluation, Landis has
pointed out that "before any sort of
measurement can be made, it is necessary to establish a base line and a common unit of measure. The only unit of
measure available is the report made by
the physician stating that the patient
has recovered, is much improved, is improved or unimproved. This unit is probably as satisfactory as any type of human
subjective judgment, partaking of both
the good and bad points of such judgments" (26, p. 156). For a unit Landis
suggests "that of expressing therapeutic
results in terms of the number of patients recovered or improved per 100
cases admitted to the hospital." As an
alternative, he suggests "the statement
of therapeutic outcome for some given
group of patients during some stated interval of time."

Landis realized quite clearly that in
order to evaluate the effectiveness of any
form of therapy, data from a control
group of nontreated patients would be
required in order to compare the effects
of therapy with the spontaneous remis-
sion rate. In the absence of anything
better, he used the amelioration rate in
state mental hospitals for patients diagnosed under the heading of "neuroses."
As he points out:

There are several objections to the use
of the consolidated amelioration rate . . .
of the . . . state hospitals . . . as a base
rate for spontaneous recovery. The fact
that psychoneurotic cases are not usually
committed to state hospitals unless in a very
bad condition; the relatively small number
of voluntary patients in the group; the

fact that such patients do get some degree
of psychotherapy especially in the reception hospitals; and the probably quite different economic, educational, and social
status of the State Hospital group compared
to the patients reported from each of the
other hospitals—all argue against the acceptance of [this] figure . . . as a truly
satisfactory base line, but in the absence
of any other better figure this must serve
(26, p. 168).

Actually the various figures quoted
by Landis agree very well. The percentage of neurotic patients discharged annually as recovered or improved from
New York state hospitals is 70 (for the
years 1925–1934); for the United States
as a whole it is 68 (for the years 1926
to 1933). The percentage of neurotics
discharged as recovered or improved
within one year of admission is 66 for
the United States (1933) and 68 for
New York (1914). The consolidated
amelioration rate of New York state
hospitals, 1917–1934, is 72 per cent. As
this is the figure chosen by Landis, we
may accept it in preference to the other
very similar ones quoted. By and large,
we may thus say that of severe neurotics
receiving in the main custodial care,
and very little if any psychotherapy, over
two-thirds recovered or improved to a
considerable extent. "Although this is
not, strictly speaking, a basic figure for
'spontaneous' recovery, still any therapeutic method must show an appreciably
greater size than this to be seriously
considered" (26, p. 160).

Another estimate of the required
"base line" is provided by Denker:

Five hundred consecutive disability
claims due to psychoneurosis, treated by
general practitioners throughout the
country, and not by accredited specialists
or sanatoria, were reviewed. All types of
neurosis were included, and no attempt
made to differentiate the neurasthenic, anxiety, compulsive, hysteric, or other states,
but the greatest care was taken to eliminate
the true psychotic or organic lesions which
in the early stages of illness so often simu-

late neurosis. These cases were taken consecutively from the files of the Equitable Life Assurance Society of the United States, were from all parts of the country, and all had been ill of a neurosis for at least three months before claims were submitted. They, therefore, could be fairly called "severe," since they had been totally disabled for at least a three months' period, and rendered unable to carry on with any "occupation for remuneration or profit" for at least that time (9, p. 2164).

These patients were regularly seen and treated by their own physicians with sedatives, tonics, suggestion, and reassurance, but in no case was any attempt made at anything but this most superficial type of "psychotherapy" which has always been the stock-in-trade of the general practitioner. Repeated statements, every three months or so by their physicians, as well as independent investigations by the insurance company, confirmed the fact that these people actually were not engaged in productive work during the period of their illness. During their disablement, these cases received disability benefits. As Denker points out, "It is appreciated that this fact of disability income may have actually prolonged the total period of disability and acted as a barrier to incentive for recovery. One would, therefore, not expect the therapeutic results in such a group of cases to be as favorable as in other groups where the economic factor might act as an important spur in helping the sick patient adjust to his neurotic conflict and illness" (9, p. 2165).

The cases were all followed up for at least a five-year period, and often as long as ten years after the period of disability had begun. The criteria of "recovery" used by Denker were as follows: (a) return to work, and ability to carry on well in economic adjustments for at least a five-year period; (b) complaint of no further or very slight difficulties; (c) making of successful social

adjustments. Using these criteria, which are very similar to those usually used by psychiatrists, Denker found that 45 per cent of the patients recovered after one year, another 27 per cent after two years, making 72 per cent in all. Another 10 per cent, 5 per cent, and 4 per cent recovered during the third, fourth, and fifth years, respectively, making a total of 90 per cent recoveries after five years.

This sample contrasts in many ways with that used by Landis. The cases on which Denker reports were probably not quite as severe as those summarized by Landis; they were all voluntary, non-hospitalized patients, and came from a much higher socioeconomic stratum. The majority of Denker's patients were clerical workers, executives, teachers, and professional men. In spite of these differences, the recovery figures for the two samples are almost identical. The most suitable figure to choose from those given by Denker is probably that for the two-year recovery rate, as follow-up studies seldom go beyond two years and the higher figures for three-, four-, and five-year follow-up would overestimate the efficiency of this "base line" procedure. Using, therefore, the two-year recovery figure of 72 per cent, we find that Denker's figure agrees exactly with that given by Landis. We may, therefore, conclude with some confidence that our estimate of some two-thirds of severe neurotics showing recovery or considerable improvement without the benefit of systematic psychotherapy is not likely to be very far out.

Effects of Psychotherapy

We may now turn to the effects of psychotherapeutic treatment. The results of nineteen studies reported in the literature, covering over seven thousand cases, and dealing with both psychoanalytic and eclectic types of treatment, are quoted in detail in Table 1. An attempt

TABLE 1

SUMMARY OF REPORTS OF THE RESULTS OF PSYCHOTHERAPY

	N	Cured; Much Improved	Improved	Slightly Improved	Not Improved; Died; Left Treatment	Per Cent Cured; Much Improved; Improved
(A) *Psychoanalytic*						
1. Fenichel (13, pp. 28–40)	484	104	84	99	197	39
2. Kessel and Hyman (24)	34	16	5	4	9	62
3. Jones (22, pp. 12–14)	59	20	8	28	3	47
4. Alexander (1, pp. 30–43)	141	28	42	23	48	50
5. Knight (25)	42	8	20	7	7	67
All cases	760	335			425	44
(B) *Eclectic*						
1. Huddleson (20)	200	19	74	80	27	46
2. Matz (30)	775	10	310	310	145	41
3. Maudsley Hospital Report (1931)	1721	288	900		533	69
4. Maudsley Hospital Report (1935)	1711	371	765		575	64
5. Neustatter (32)	46	9	14	8	15	50
6. Luff and Garrod (27)	500	140	135	26	199	55
7. Luff and Garrod (27)	210	38	84	54	34	68
8. Ross (34)	1089	547	306		236	77
9. Yaskin (40)	100	29	29		42	58
10. Curran (7)	83		51		32	61
11. Masserman and Carmichael (29)	50	7	20	5	18	54
12. Carmichael and Masserman (4)	77	16	25	14	22	53
13. Schilder (35)	35	11	11	6	7	63
14. Hamilton and Wall (16)	100	32	34	17	17	66
15. Hamilton et al. (15)	100	48	5	17	32	51
16. Landis (26)	119	40	47		32	73
17. Institute Med. Psychol. (quoted Neustatter)	270	58	132	55	25	70
18. Wilder (39)	54	3	24	16	11	50
19. Miles et al. (31)	53	13	18	13	9	58
All cases	7293	4661			2632	64

has been made to report results under the four headings: (a) cured, or much improved; (b) improved; (c) slightly improved; (d) not improved, died, discontinued treatment, etc. It was usually easy to reduce additional categories given by some writers to these basic four; some writers give only two or three categories, and in those cases it was, of course, im-

possible to subdivide further, and the figures for combined categories are given.* A slight degree of subjectivity inevitably enters into this procedure, but

* In one or two cases where patients who improved or improved slightly were combined by the original author, the total figure has been divided equally between the two categories.

it is doubtful if it has caused much distortion. A somewhat greater degree of subjectivity is probably implied in the writer's judgment as to which disorders and diagnoses should be considered to fall under the heading of "neurosis." Schizophrenic, manic-depressive, and paranoid states have been excluded; organ neuroses, psychopathic states, and character disturbances have been included. The number of cases where there was genuine doubt is probably too small to make much change in the final figures, regardless of how they are allocated.

A number of studies have been excluded because of such factors as excessive inadequacy of follow-up, partial duplication of cases with others included in our table, failure to indicate type of treatment used, and other reasons which made the results useless from our point of view. Papers thus rejected are those by Thorley and Craske (37), Bennett and Semrad (2), H. I. Harris (19), Hardcastle (17), A. Harris (18), Jacobson and Wright (21), Friess and Nelson (14), Comroe (5), Wenger (38), Orbison (33), Coon and Raymond (6), Denker (8), and Bond and Braceland (3). Their inclusion would not have altered our conclusions to any considerable degree, although, as Miles et al. point out: "When the various studies are compared in terms of thoroughness, careful planning, strictness of criteria and objectivity, there is often an inverse correlation between these factors and the percentage of successful results reported" (31, p. 88).

Certain difficulties have arisen from the inability of some writers to make their column figures agree with their totals, or to calculate percentages accurately. Again, the writer has exercised his judgment as to which figures to accept. In certain cases, writers have given figures of cases where there was a recurrence of the disorder after apparent cure or improvement, without indicating how many patients were affected in these two groups respectively. All recurrences of this kind have been subtracted from the "cured" and "improved" totals, taking half from each. The total number of cases involved in all these adjustments is quite small. Another investigator making all decisions exactly in the opposite direction to the present writer's would hardly alter the final percentage figures by more than 1 or 2 per cent.

We may now turn to the figures as presented. Patients treated by means of psychoanalysis improve to the extent of 44 per cent; patients treated eclectically improve to the extent of 64 per cent; patients treated only custodially or by general practitioners improve to the extent of 72 per cent. There thus appears to be an inverse correlation between recovery and psychotherapy; the more psychotherapy, the smaller the recovery rate. This conclusion requires certain qualifications.

In our tabulation of psychoanalytic results, we have classed those who stopped treatment together with those not improved. This appears to be reasonable; a patient who fails to finish his treatment, and is not improved, is surely a therapeutic failure. The same rule has been followed with the data summarized under "eclectic" treatment, except when the patient who did not finish treatment was definitely classified as "improved" by the therapist. However, in view of the peculiarities of Freudian procedures it may appear to some readers to be more just to class those cases separately, and deal only with the percentage of completed treatments which are successful. Approximately one-third of the psychoanalytic patients listed broke off treatment, so that the percentage of successful treatments of patients who finished their course must be put at approximately 66 per cent. It would appear, then, that when we discount the risk the patient runs of stopping treatment altogether, his chances of improvement under psychoanalysis are approximately equal to his chances of improvement under eclectic treatment, and slightly worse than his chances under a general practitioner or custodial treatment.

Two further points require clarification: (a) Are patients in our "control" groups (Landis and Denker) as seriously ill as those in our "experimental" groups? (b) Are standards of recovery perhaps less stringent in our "control" than in our "experimental" groups? It is difficult to answer these questions definitely, in view of the great divergence of opinion between psychiatrists. From a close scrutiny of the literature it appears that the "control" patients were probably at least as seriously ill as the "experimental" patients, and possibly more so. As regards standards of recovery, those in Denker's study are as stringent as most of those used by psychoanalysts and eclectic psychiatrists, but those used by the State Hospitals whose figures Landis quotes are very probably more lenient. In the absence of agreed standards of severity of illness, or of extent of recovery, it is not possible to go further.

In general, certain conclusions are possible from these data. They fail to prove that psychotherapy, Freudian or otherwise, facilitates the recovery of neurotic patients. They show that roughly two-thirds of a group of neurotic patients will recover or improve to a marked extent within about two years of the onset of their illness, whether they are treated by means of psychotherapy or not. This figure appears to be remarkably stable from one investigation to another, regardless of type of patient treated, standard of recovery employed, or method of therapy used. From the point of view of the neurotic, these figures are encouraging; from the point of view of the psychotherapist, they can hardly be called very favorable to his claims.

The figures quoted do not necessarily disprove the possibility of therapeutic effectiveness. There are obvious shortcomings in any actuarial comparison and these shortcomings are particularly serious when there is so little agreement among psychiatrists relating even to the most fundamental concepts and definitions. Definite proof would require a special investigation, carefully planned and methodologically more adequate than these ad hoc comparisons. But even the much more modest conclusions that the figures fail to show any favorable effects of psychotherapy should give pause to those who would wish to give an important part in the training of clinical psychologists to a skill the existence and effectiveness of which is still unsupported by any scientifically acceptable evidence.

These results and conclusions will no doubt contradict the strong feeling of usefulness and therapeutic success which many psychiatrists and clinical psychologists hold. While it is true that subjective feelings of this type have no place in science, they are likely to prevent an easy acceptance of the general argument presented here. This contradiction between objective fact and subjective certainty has been remarked on in other connections by Kelly and Fiske, who found that:

One aspect of our findings is most disconcerting to us: the inverse relationship between the confidence of staff members at the time of making a prediction and the measured validity of that prediction. Why is it, for example, that our staff members tended to make their best predictions at a time when they subjectively felt relatively unacquainted with the candidate, when they had constructed no systematic picture of his personality structure? Or conversely, why is it that with increasing confidence in clinical judgment . . . we find decreasing validities of predictions? (23, p. 406).

In the absence of agreement between fact and belief, there is urgent need for a decrease in the strength of belief, and for an increase in the number of facts available. Until such facts as may be discovered in a process of rigorous analysis support the prevalent belief in therapeutic effectiveness of psychological treatment, it seems premature to insist on the inclusion of training in such treatment in the curriculum of the clinical psychologist.

Summary

A survey was made of reports on the improvement of neurotic patients after psychotherapy, and the results compared with the best available estimates of recovery without benefit of such therapy. The figures fail to support the hypothesis that psychotherapy facilitates recovery from neurotic disorder. In view of the many difficulties attending such actuarial comparisons, no further conclusions could be derived from the data whose shortcomings highlight the necessity of properly planned and executed experimental studies into this important field.

References

1. Alexander, F. *Five year report of the Chicago Institute for Psychoanalysis. 1932–1937.*

2. Bennett, A. E., and Semrad, E. V. Common errors in diagnosis and treatment of the psychoneurotic patient—a study of 100 case histories. *Nebr. Med. J.,* 21(1936), 90–92.

3. Bond, E. D., and Braceland, F. J. Prognosis in mental disease. *Amer. J. Psychiat.,* 94(1937), 263–274.

4. Carmichael, H. T., and Masserman, T. H. Results of treatment in a psychiatric out-patients' department. J.A.M.A., 113(1939), 2292–2298.

5. Comroe, B. I. Follow-up study of 100 patients diagnosed as "neurosis." *J. Nerv. Ment. Dis.,* 83(1936), 679–684.

6. Coon, G. P., and Raymond, A. A review of the psychoneuroses at Stockbridge. Stockbridge, Mass.: Austen Riggs Foundation, Inc., 1940.

7. Curran, D. The problem of assessing psychiatric treatment. *Lancet,* II(1937), 1005–1009.

8. Denker, P. G. Prognosis and life expectancy in the psychoneuroses. *Proc. Ass. Life Insur. Med. Dir. Amer.,* 24(1937), 179.

9. Denker, R. Results of treatment of psychoneuroses by the general practitioner. A follow-up study of 500 cases. *N. Y. State J. Med.,* 46(1946), 2164–2166.

10. Eysenck, H. J. Training in clinical psychology: an English point of view. *Amer. Psychologist,* 4(1949), 173–176.

11. ———— The relation between medicine and psychology in England. In W. Dennis, ed., *Current trends in the relation of psychology and medicine.* Pittsburgh: Univ. of Pittsburgh Press, 1950.

12. ———— Function and training of the clinical psychologist. *J. Ment. Sci.,* 96(1950), 1–16.

13. Fenichel, O. *Ten years of the Berlin Psychoanalysis Institute. 1920–1930.*

14. Friess, C., and Nelson, M. J. Psychoneurotics five years later. *Amer. J. Ment. Sci.,* 203(1942), 539–558.

15. Hamilton, D. M., Vanney, I. H., and Wall, T. H. Hospital treatment of patients with psychoneurotic disorder. *Amer. J. Psychiat.,* 99(1942), 243–247.

16. Hamilton, D. M., and Wall, T. H. Hospital treatment of patients with psychoneurotic disorder. *Amer. J. Psychiat.,* 98(1941), 551–557.

17. Hardcastle, D. H. A follow-up study of one hundred cases made for the Department of Psychological Medicine, Guy's Hospital. *J. Ment. Sci.,* 90(1934), 536–549.

18. Harris, A. The prognosis of anxiety states. *Brit. Med. J.,* 2(1938), 649–654.

19. Harris, H. I. Efficient psychotherapy for the large out-patient clinic. *New England J. Med.,* 221(1939), 1–5.

20. Huddleson, J. H. Psychotherapy in 200 cases of psychoneurosis. *Mil. Surgeon,* 60(1927), 161–170.

21. Jacobson, J. R., and Wright, K. W. Review of a year of group psychotherapy. *Psychiat. Quart.,* 16(1942), 744–764.

22. Jones, E. *Decennial report of the London Clinic of Psychoanalysis. 1926–1936.*

23. Kelly, E. L., and Fiske, D. W. The prediction of success in the VA training program in clinical psychology. *Amer. Psychologist,* 5(1950), 395–406.

24. Kessel, L., and Hyman, H. T. The value of psychoanalysis as a therapeutic procedure. *J.A.M.A.,* 101(1933), 1612–1615.

25. Knight, R. O. Evaluation of the results of psychoanalytic therapy. *Amer. J. Psychiat.,* 98(1941), 434–446.

26. Landis, C. Statistical evaluation of psychotherapeutic methods. In S. E. Hinsie, ed., *Concepts and problems of psychotherapy.* London: Heineman, 1938. Pages 155–165.

27. Luff, M. C., and Garrod, M. The after-results of psychotherapy in 500 adult cases. *Brit. Med. J.*, 2(1935), 54–59.

28. Mapother, E. Discussion. *Brit. J. Med. Psychol.*, 7(1927), 57.

29. Masserman, T. H., and Carmichael, H. T. Diagnosis and prognosis in psychiatry. *J. Ment. Sci.*, 84(1938), 893–946.

30. Matz, P. B. Outcome of hospital treatment of ex-service patients with nervous and mental disease in the U.S. Veteran's Bureau. *U.S. Vet. Bur. Med. Bull.*, 5(1929), 829–842.

31. Miles, H. H. W., Barrabee, E. L., and Finesinger, J. E. Evaluation of psychotherapy. *Psychosom. Med.*, 13(1951), 83–105.

32. Neustatter, W. L. The results of fifty cases treated by psychotherapy. *Lancet*, I(1935), 796–799.

33. Orbison, T. J. The psychoneuroses: psychasthenia, neurasthenia and hysteria, with special reference to a certain method of treatment. *Calif. West. Med.*, 23(1925), 1132–1136.

34. Ross, T. A. *An enquiry into prognosis in the neuroses.* London: Cambridge Univ. Press, 1936.

35. Schilder, P. Results and problems of group psychotherapy in severe neuroses. *Ment. Hyg., N.Y.*, 23(1939), 87–98.

36. Skottowe, I., and Lockwood, M. R. The fate of 150 psychiatric outpatients. *J. Ment. Sci.*, 81(1935), 502–508.

37. Thorley, A. S., and Craske, N. Comparison and estimate of group and individual method of treatment. *Brit. Med. J.*, 1(1950), 97–100.

38. Wenger, P. Uber weitere Ergebnisse der Psychotherapie in Rahmen einer Medizinischen Poliklinik. *Wien. Med. Wschr.*, 84(1934), 320–325.

39. Wilder, J. Facts and figures on psychotherapy, *J. Clin. Psychopath.*, 7(1945), 311–347.

40. Yaskin, J. C. The psychoneuroses and neuroses. A review of 100 cases with special reference to treatment and results. *Amer. J. Psychiat.*, 93(1936), 107–125.

A Transvaluation of Psychotherapy: A Reply to Hans Eysenck

SAUL ROSENZWEIG

DEPARTMENTS OF PSYCHOLOGY AND NEUROPSYCHIATRY
WASHINGTON UNIVERSITY, ST. LOUIS, MISSOURI

It has been said that men will believe the impossible but not the improbable. The former demand evokes the sense of fancy, of wonder, and of faith; the latter, a set to judge on the basis of everyday, ponderable experience. With this thought in mind we read the actuarial summary of Eysenck's (2, p. 322) recent evaluation of the effects of psychotherapy: "Patients treated by means of psychoanaly-

Reprinted from the *Journal of Abnormal & Social Psychology*, 49(1954), 298–304, with the permission of The American Psychological Association and the author.

sis improve to the extent of 44 per cent; patients treated eclectically improve to the extent of 64 per cent; patients treated only custodially or by general practitioners improve to the extent of 72 per cent. There thus appears to be an inverse correlation between recovery and psychotherapy; the more psychotherapy, the smaller the recovery rate." We are therefore to infer that psychotherapy is less effective than no psychotherapy. Are we expected to believe the improbable—and on the basis of statistics?

One might be content to rest the matter there but for the insightful though militant statement of Isaac Ray (5, p. 67), pioneer of American psychiatry, who seventy-five years ago on a similar issue (the "cult of curability") declared:

Statistics which are not really statistics are worse than useless; and the reason is that they beguile the student with a show of knowledge and thus take away the main inducement to further inquiry. Why should he look further for truth when it already lies before him? Some of the prevalent errors respecting insanity and the insane are fairly attributable to these vicious statistics, for figures make a deeper impression on the mind than the most cogent arguments.

Eysenck's survey could, moreover, be abused by the biased and the uninformed with important ill effects socially: if psychotherapy does more harm than good, why should it be supported financially or by public confidence?

It is therefore the intent of this communication to re-examine critically the data and arguments set forth by Eysenck in his attempt to prove that "the figures fail to support the hypothesis that psychotherapy facilitates recovery from neurotic disorder" (2, p. 323), and briefly to suggest grounds upon which it is possible to undertake a veridical evaluation of the effects of psychotherapy. In view of the strongly supportive role played in Eysenck's analysis by the comparable surveys of Landis (4) and Denker (1), these earlier appraisals will also be incidentally examined.

To be noted at the outset is the difference between Landis and Eysenck in appreciating the difficulties involved in making any appraisal of the effects of psychotherapy. Landis (4, p. 156) summarizes the sources of these difficulties— ignorance of the nature or cause of mental disease, disagreement among experts concerning even such broad differentiations as somatogenic or psychogenic, lack of uniformity with respect to categories of improvement—and concludes: "Be-

cause of these difficulties, it is apparent that statistical figures, rates of recovery, etc., have to be evaluated cautiously, precisely, and with a minimum of generalization." The caution thus advised is in contrast with Eysenck's approach. Not only does Eysenck generalize freely, but in his paper one repeatedly encounters a polite bow of recognition to the sources of difficulty outlined by Landis which are then lightly dismissed. Confronted with the problems involved in assembling data from 24 separate studies, each of which employed its own methods and criteria, Eysenck indicates several reconciliatory devices he adopted, then adds (p. 322): "The total number of cases involved in all these adjustments is quite small. Another investigator making all decisions in exactly the opposite direction to the present writer's would hardly alter the final percentage figures by more than 1 or 2 per cent." Again, considering the definition of neurosis and offering his redefinition, he recognizes (p. 321) that a "degree of subjectivity is probably implied in the writer's judgment as to which disorders and diagnoses should be considered to fall under the heading 'neurosis,'" but, as before, he concludes with facility: "The number of cases where there was genuine doubt is probably too small to make much change in the final figures, regardless of how they are allocated." When he presents his procedure for overcoming the diversity in gradations of improvement as reported in the various studies, he remarks (pp. 320–321): "A slight degree of subjectivity inevitably enters into this procedure, but it is doubtful if it has caused much distortion." In taking up the serious questions as to whether the patients in his control (no treatment) groups were as seriously ill as those in the experimental groups and whether standards of recovery possibly differed in the two divisions, he offers some brief speculations and then concludes (p. 322): "In the absence of agreed standards of severity of illness, or of extent of recovery, it is not possible to go further." The meaning here would seem to be that it is not possible to go beyond speculation but this admission in no wise deters the author from the sweeping conclusions he then proceeds to draw.

The foregoing résumé, largely in the author's own words, will be appraised in the ensuing re-evaluation. The argument will take the following course:

A. What is psychoneurosis? (It should be noted that Eysenck selects the psychoneuroses in making his evaluation.) Is Eysenck's redefinition of neurosis consistent with a true evaluation of the effects of psychotherapy in this type of disorder? Is the severity of illness comparable in his contrasted groups?

B. What is psychotherapy? Did the two control subgroups instanced by the author actually receive no psychotherapy? In other words, does the control group control, and is the so-called base line basic?

C. What is improvement or recovery? Were the criteria for successful outcome as applied in the control and experimental groups identical or even comparable?

What Is Psychoneurosis?

As has already been noted, Eysenck acknowledges a degree of subjectivity in his judgment as to what disorders should fall under this diagnostic category—the critical one for his study. His decision (and redefinition) is as follows (p. 321): "Schizophrenic, manic-depressive, and paranoid states have been excluded; organ neuroses, psychopathic states, and character disturbances have been included." On this basis, which many would question (particularly because of the inclusion of psychopathic states), he then proceeds to redistribute the data in the various reports included in his survey. It is his opinion, as quoted above,

that these reallocations are too unimportant "to make much change in the final figures," but it can be shown by a single example that this sanguinity on his part is not justified. The illustration is afforded by the data of Fenichel's (3) report from the Berlin Psychoanalytic Institute—a report utilized by both Eysenck and Landis. If one compares the number of psychoneurotics treated at that Institute as re-reported by Landis and by Eysenck, one finds that this figure is given by the former author as 312 and by the latter as 484. Since the total number of cases accepted for treatment at the Berlin Institute in the ten years covered by the report was 604, it can be readily appreciated that Eysenck's redefinition has caused a shift in diagnosis of 172 cases or 28 per cent. The effect on the figures for improvement and recovery is even more germane and the difference between the estimates given by Landis and by Eysenck for this same Berlin group is therefore noteworthy: Landis reports 58 per cent improved or recovered, and Eysenck, under this same heading (his Table 1), lists 39 per cent— a difference of 19 per cent. These differences of 28 per cent and 19 per cent are scarcely the negligible quantities that Eysenck has disarmingly led us to expect would be the result of his modified definition.

Of equal significance is the question as to whether the severity of the illness in Eysenck's control and experimental groups can be considered to be comparable. To establish his base line for successful outcome without psychotherapy, Eysenck employed the figure of 72 per cent given by Landis as the consolidated amelioration rate of New York state hospitals (1917–1934), and the identical figure of 72 per cent (for successful treatment within two years) obtained from the report of Denker (1) for a group of 500 psychoneurotic disability claims treated by general practitioners throughout the United States. These control subgroups are compared with 24 experimental groups subdivided by Eysenck, according to the method of psychotherapy, as either *psychoanalytic* or *eclectic*.

If one now returns to the question raised as to the severity of illness in the several groups, the following interpretations seem warranted. The insurance disability cases were, as a whole, in all likelihood less severely ill than any of the others. Denker points out (1, p. 2165) that in these cases where disability income was a factor the illness may have been prolonged by this tangible secondary gain. By the same token the illness may very well have been initiated, or at least partially instigated, by conscious or unconscious prospects of such gains. To compare psychoneuroses of long standing, dating in many instances from early childhood (the typical case treated by psychoanalysis), with such disability neuroses is highly dubious, and the fact that the latter would have cleared up quickly after brief treatment by a general practitioner is thus not surprising. At the other extreme from these disability patients are those cases, cited after Landis, which were institutionalized in the various New York state hospitals. Here one could reasonably expect that the neuroses must have been extraordinarily severe in order for these patients to have become eligible for admission to these crowded institutions. In these instances the outcome of treatment would be expected to be far less favorable than for either the Denker control group or the experimental groups. But at this point a question arises as to the standards of recovery which would apply for discharge from a state hospital as compared with the criteria of recovery utilized by a psychoanalyst or psychiatrist in private practice. To this problem we shall return later. For the present it may be concluded that, in general, the Denker base-line group was probably less seriously ill, the Landis control group more seriously ill than the various

experimental groups instanced by Eysenck. To the degree that this conclusion is sound it may be further inferred that the control and experimental groups fail to meet an essential criterion of comparability—illness severity. When this consideration is added to the previous one, concerning Eysenck's redefinition of neurosis as applied to the various studies, the basis for his generalizations is seriously called into question.

What Is Psychotherapy?

A second point of difference between the control and experimental group in Eysenck's survey concerns treatment: the control groups of Landis and Denker are presented as not having received psychotherapy in contrast to the experimental groups which did. The treatment given the latter groups is merely designated as *psychoanalytic* or *eclectic*. Since Eysenck at no point defines what he means by psychotherapy, it becomes necessary to examine the several specific mentions of psychological treatment or lack of it in his survey, the main problem here being whether his assertion is supported that the control groups did not receive psychotherapy.

If one turns first to the Denker group, it is discovered that in Eysenck's words (p. 320) these patients were "regularly seen and treated by their own physicians with sedatives, tonics, suggestion, and reassurance, but in no case was any attempt made at anything but this most superficial type of 'psychotherapy' which has always been the stock-in-trade of the general practitioner." On the basis of this description it is hardly possible to agree that these patients were not psychotherapeutically treated. The various presumably nonpsychotherapeutic techniques mentioned include suggestion and reassurance—well-known methods of psychotherapy; and psychiatrists regularly use sedatives and tonics as adjuncts to their practice. That one is actually dealing here with psychotherapy—if not, to be sure, with psychoanalysis—becomes eminently clear when it is noted that among the *experimental* groups cited by Eysenck 80 per cent were treated by *eclectic* methods (see Table 1, B). What would these eclectic methods be if they did not include the very techniques attributed to the general practitioner? The only difference between the work of the general practitioner and of the eclectic psychiatrist that could be assumed, in the absence of detailed and specific knowledge, would be a difference in thoroughness or expertness, not a difference in kind. And being aware that some general practitioners working with patient well known to them are excellent eclectic psychotherapists, one would have to make even this qualification very guardedly. A reading of Denker's paper makes it evident that he himself does not regard his 500 disability cases as untreated by psychotherapy; he assumes only that the general practitioner is less expert than the psychotherapeutic specialist.

A similar inference is warranted with respect to the Landis control group. To maintain that neurotic patients admitted to state hospitals receive no psychotherapy is seriously open to doubt. These institutions, despite their notorious shortage of staff, usually make a special effort to treat their neurotic admissions, because these cases have a better prognosis, and because they are far more accessible to treatment. The methods employed would presumably be eclectic, like those of the Denker study and of the various eclectic experimental groups.

It must then be concluded that the control subgroups cited by Eysenck do not sharply differ from the experimental groups in respect to the important variable of having received psychotherapy. As before with regard to illness severity, the necessary contrast between the base line and the experimental groups becomes markedly attenuated.

What Is Recovery?

The crucial question in the present re-evaluation is, finally, whether the degree of improvement or recovery in the control and experimental groups can be regarded as equal. In other words, the control base line for percentage of cases cured can attain true significance only if the degree of improvement for these cases is identical with, or, at least, closely similar to that which the experimental cases may be estimated to have achieved after intensive psychotherapy. To determine, on the available evidence, the answer to the question thus posed is the last step in this re-evaluation.

Needless to say, degree of improvement is extremely difficult to assess and the difficulty is increased when one is dealing at second hand with cases treated by diverse methods and by various therapists. The most significant obstacle to the evaluation of degree of recovery lies, however, in the differences in improvement standards. In the present instance it is this particular difficulty which looms large. In view of the fact that the Denker group has already been shown to represent, in all probability, a less severe degree of illness, this group will not here be further discussed. For the control group, attention will be focused on the far more representative and more generally important base-line figure from Landis, derived from the consolidated amelioration rate of New York state hospitals for 1917–34; for the experimental groups both the eclectic and the psychoanalytic will be considered.

As has been already stated, Eysenck reports that patients treated by psychoanalysis improve to the extent of 44 per cent, those treated eclectically, 64 per cent, and those treated custodially, 72 per cent. It was these figures which at the outset challenged us to believe the improbable. It will be the burden of the present section to show that the improbability resolves itself largely into differences in the presumed standards of improvement invoked in these three treatment pools.

We may begin with two brief statements found in Landis (4). In discussing his Table II, which deals with the percentage of patients discharged from mental hospitals as recovered or improved, he characterizes (p. 159) the presented figures as indicating to what extent "hospitalization of one year or less yields *sufficient improvement for favorable discharge*" (my italics). By contrast, in describing the criterion employed at the Berlin Psychoanalytic Institute for *recovery,* Landis (p. 162) paraphrases Fenichel (3) thus: "Only those cases were classified as recovered in which the success consisted in the disappearance of symptoms, and which also underwent an essential change which was completely explicable from the rational, analytical viewpoint." (A less rigorous standard was, of course, employed by Fenichel for *improvement,* etc.) In other words, while patients residentially treated are generally considered in terms of hospital discharge and return to the community, the criterion of social recovery being highly relevant, patients nonresidentially treated, as by psychoanalysis, live continuously in the community and are worked with in terms of radical therapy which, if successful, permits them to live not only with others but with themselves. This difference in therapeutic goal is so great that percentage figures for residential and nonresident treatment are dubiously commensurable.

The fact that improvement or recovery as defined in relation to hospital discharge may reflect an extremely low standard becomes patent if one notes, for example, that in Table I of Landis, which presents the number of patients discharged annually as recovered or improved per one hundred admitted to state mental hospitals, the figure given for *psychopathic personality* is 75. Anyone having the slightest familiarity with this type of case is aware that such patients are in only the vaguest sense cured or improved at discharge. If 75 per cent of them are returned to the community, this figure can only mean that they have temporarily made a social recovery. The majority of them will doubtless be back again if they do not in the meantime gain admission to some other correctional institution. One is dealing here with a striking illustration of the comparatively low recovery standards inherent in state-hospital discharged.

It would, however, be incorrect to lump together state-hospital discharges and discharges from intensive-treatment institutions like the New York Psychiatric Institute or Maudsley Hospital as if the same standard of recovery prevailed in both. We are here presumably dealing with a gradation not only as between nonresidential and residential improvement standards but as between standards in intensive-treatment hospitals and state hospitals. It must therefore be recognized that residentiality of treatment is only an approximate, and by no means a perfect, criterion of the rigorousness of improvement standards.

The figures for residential and nonresidential treatment in the control and experimental groups cited by Eysenck were accordingly determined and will now be presented as an approximate index of recovery standard. As indicated already, only the Landis control group was considered; it may be stated forthwith that the state-hospital patients included in it were residentially treated. For the experimental groups surveyed by Eysenck, it was found by a study of the available reports included in his survey that approximately 4,040 of 5,262 eclectic cases, or 77 per cent, were residentially treated; of the 760 psychoanalytic cases, none were so treated.*

* The figures here presented were derived from the reports cited by Eysenck in Table 1.

We arrive thus at a resolution of
Eysenck's paradox. If 44 per cent of neurotics treated by psychoanalysis, 64 per
cent of those treated eclectically, and 72
percent of those treated custodially improved or recovered within two years,
this sequence of figures does not prove
the improbability that the more intensive the psychotherapy, the less benefit to
the patient; rather it reflects the probability that the more intensive the therapy, the higher the standard of recovery.
This interpretation is borne out by the
fact that the three patient pools in the
order listed above vary in this same order
with respect to the frequency with which
treatment was given nonresidentially
rather than residentially. The figures 44,
64, and 72 correlate perfectly with the
above-given figures for frequency of residential treatment in the three patient
pools: Psychoanalytic—0 per cent, Eclectic—77 per cent, Custodial—100 per cent.
The implication is: the higher the standard of recovery, the smaller the degree
of reported success.*

(See his list of References.) The following
proved to have been treated *nonresidentially:*
Psychoanalytic—all five groups (total $N = 760$);
Eclectic—Huddleson, Neustatter, Luff and Garrod (two groups), Yaskin, Carmichael and Masserman, Schilder, Wilder (total $N = 1,222$).
The following were treated *residentially:* Psychoanalytic—none; Eclectic—Matz, Maudsley
(1931), Ross, Curran, Hamilton and Wall,
Hamilton, et al., Landis, Miles, et al. (total
$N = 4,040$). Several qualifications should be
noted. The Maudsley reports (Nos. 3 and 4
under B in Eysenck's Table 1) were not available to the writer. However, the survey by
Wilder includes the 1927–1931 Maudsley report, and from this source it is inferred that
these patients were treated residentially. The
later Maudsley group had to be omitted. The
necessary figures for the Institute of Medical
Psychology group (Eysenck's No. B, 17) could
not be found in the source cited by Eysenck. The
50 cases reported by Masserman and Carmichael
are ambiguous as regards residentiality and have
therefore not been included. (Excluded total
$N = 2,031$.)

* Eysenck has made a slip on p. 320 where
he indicates that his survey of treated groups
includes "the results of nineteen studies reported in the literature. . . ." Inspection of Ta-

If this conclusion is thought to depend too much on inference, it is sufficient for the present purpose to rest this
part of the discussion with the more
modest statement that the standards of
improvement and recovery in Eysenck's
various patient groups, control and experimental, bear so little resemblance to
each other that, once again, the basis of
his comparisons has little demonstrable
validity.

The foregoing re-evaluation from the
standpoints of the definition and severity of neurosis, amount of psychotherapy
accorded, and standards of recovery in
the several patient groups thus leads to
the general conclusion that Eysenck's
data and arguments fail to support his
thesis that psychotherapy cannot be
shown to facilitate recovery. The need
for a more circumspect use of statistics
in this highly complex area of evaluation
is underscored. It is not, however, maintained that a conclusion in the opposite
direction is warranted. The only safe
deduction on the basis of currently available data is that, in view of the diversity
of methods and standards in the field of
psychotherapy, broad generalizations as
to the effectiveness of treatment are to
be avoided.

One may seek to evaluate the effects
of psychotherapy either by counting reported outcomes or by considering dynamic change in the process of treatment,
or both. In the former instance each patient serves as a poll, for or against, as
indicated by his subjective report or the
therapist's clinical judgment; in the latter, one examines each treated personality as a system of structures and forces

ble 1 on p. 321 makes it evident that his survey
actually included 24 studies. The total series in
the table is divided in two—subseries (A) including *five* groups who received *psychoanalytic*
therapy, and subseries (B) consisting of *nineteen* groups who received *eclectic* psychotherapy.
Has the author in the error on page 320 tacitly
acknowledged the nineteen eclectic groups and
"repressed" the five psychoanalytic ones?

which, in the course of therapy, is altered in a definable direction. To undertake an evaluation of the effects of psychotherapy by tallying outcomes at second hand, without even introducing the problem of dynamic change in various forms of illness and in differing therapeutic procedures, and, in default of such considerations, to reassign diagnoses and prognoses is to invite the inconsistencies and *non sequiturs* that have been demonstrated in the foregoing reanalysis. But it is not to be concluded that statistical evaluation is totally to be eschewed because such pitfalls exist; the implication is, rather, that the use of statistics in the evaluation of psychotherapy demands special precautions and, in addition, the guarantee of a concurrent or prior dynamic evaluation of each case—an evaluation in which the complexity of the individual patient and of the therapeutic situation has been fully considered. Such a dynamic appraisal must take into account the organization of the patient's personality and life space before, during, and after treatment. It must, for example, even allow for such statistically equivocal outcomes as those in which therapy produces no computable decrease in former symptoms but an increased capacity to accept them and to accept oneself. It must, in other words, reflect an understanding by the therapist and, at least in part by the patient, of the reason or reasons for the alleged outcome of treatment.

In internal medicine and surgery the necessity for empirical adjuncts to any clinical evaluation of therapeutic change has long been recognized—as, for example, when x-rays, blood tests, biological assays, etc. are invoked to determine, quite apart from the patient's subjective report or the physician's clinical judgment, what progress the patient is making in healing a fracture or in overcoming an infection. Psychology and psychiatry may not yet be ready for great precision in the making of such independent evaluations, but the last decade has seen rapid advances toward this goal. One reason for opposing such naive evaluations of the effects of psychotherapy as the one here re-examined is to keep open the intrinsically difficult road which such investigation is destined to follow.

What good is psychotherapy? As good as man's faith in his humanity. Men have always believed in their ability to change for the better and to help each other so to change—through mutual assistance, love, religion, and art. Conceived in the broadest terms psychotherapy derives from the same faith and, employing of necessity some of the same means, attempts to formulate these more precisely. The question is not, then, whether psychotherapy does any good— one might as reasonably ask, "Is life worth living?"; the question is *how* does therapy accomplish its ends in those fortunate instances where, despite the adverse odds, it manages to succeed. It is to the process, not the superficially appraised end result—to the disorganization or organization of forces which may spell illness and partial death or health and growth—that attention should be directed if we are to learn anything about psychotherapy. If, in aiming at this admittedly more difficult kind of assessment, we shall have to postpone rigorous quantification or use it guardedly, to ensure genuine precision, such caution may well constitute a measure of the maturity—the "tolerance for ambiguity" —which keeps us from hasty generalization.

References

1. Denker, P. G. Results of treatment of psychoneuroses by the general practitioner: a follow-up study of 500 cases. *N.Y. State J. Med.,* 46(1946), 2164–2166.

2. Eysenck, H. J. The effects of psychotherapy: an evaluation. *J. Consult. Psychol.,* 16 (1952), 319–324.

3. Fenichel, O. *Ten years of the Berlin Psychoanalytic Institute, 1920–1930.*

4. Landis, C. A statistical evaluation of psychotherapeutic methods. In L. E. Hinsie, ed., *Concepts and problems of psychotherapy*. New York: Columbia Univ. Press, 1937. Chapter V.

5. Ray, I. Statistics of insanity, in *Contributions to mental pathology*. Boston: Little, Brown, 1873.

The Effects of Psychotherapy: A Reply

H. J. Eysenck

INSTITUTE OF PSYCHIATRY, MAUDSLEY HOSPITAL, UNIVERSITY OF LONDON

The title and tone of Dr. Rosenzweig's recent paper in this journal (3) suggest that he does not agree with the main conclusions of my paper entitled "The Effects of Psychotherapy: An Evaluation" (1). It is difficult to argue with him as on all crucial points we seem to be in complete agreement. His criticisms are not directed against what I wrote but against a quite erroneous impression of what my main points were; consequently, a brief restatement of these points should suffice to settle the dispute.

In the first place, Rosenzweig apparently believes that I maintain that psychotherapy does more harm than good. He quotes the actual figures for recovery which I give, showing greatest improvement to follow the least amount of therapy, and least improvement to follow the psychoanalytic type of therapy, and adds "We are therefore to infer that psychotherapy is less effective than no psychotherapy." He does not, unfortunately, quote the sentence which appears at the end of this paragraph dealing with the

Reprinted from the *Journal of Abnormal & Social Psychology*, **50**(1955), 147–148, with the permission of The American Psychological Association and the author.

inverse correlation between recovery and psychotherapy, in which I say: "This conclusion requires certain qualifications." He gives the impression that I am putting forward a dogmatic statement regarding the ineffectiveness of therapy. Nothing could be further from the truth, and in evidence I may perhaps be allowed to quote the qualifications I myself was careful to point out:

The figures quoted do not necessarily disprove the possibility of therapeutic effectiveness. There are obvious shortcomings in any actuarial comparison and these shortcomings are particularly serious when there is so little agreement among psychiatrists relating even to the most fundamental concepts and definitions. Definite proof would require a special investigation, carefully planned and methodologically more adequate than these *ad hoc* comparisons. But even the much more modest conclusion that the figures fail to show any favourable effects of psychotherapy should give pause to those who would wish to give an important part in the training of clinical psychologists to a skill the existence and effectiveness of which is still unsupported by any scientifically acceptable evidence.

Rosenzweig takes me to task for not enumerating the shortcomings mentioned, and contrasts this failure with the procedure of Landis (2), who has discussed them in detail. This does not seem to be a reasonable criticism. Landis was writing a chapter in a book and had ample space for discussion; I was writing a short paper from which the editor would almost certainly have excised any unduly lengthy repetitions of what had already appeared in the literature. After all, it is customary in scientific journals to present new evidence and arguments, not to recapitulate in tiresome detail what had already appeared before and should be presumed to be known to one's colleagues.

I am fully in agreement, therefore, with most of what Rosenzweig says about the difficulties of defining neurosis, of defining psychotherapy, and of defining recovery; these difficulties, as I pointed out in my article, arise from the fact that "there is so little agreement amongst psychiatrists relating even to the most fundamental concepts and definitions." Rosenzweig dots the *i*'s and crosses the *t*'s at some length, but does not, in effect, contradict what I have to say.

All through his article, Rosenzweig seems to criticize me for having attempted to prove that psychotherapy is ineffective. This, however, I never attempted to do. I was not trying to *prove* the null hypothesis, which would be foolish as well as inadmissible; I was simply examining available data to see whether these data *succeeded in disproving* the null hypothesis. For the various reasons which Rosenzweig details, and which I agree with, the available data are not of a kind to inspire much confidence. Nevertheless, *they are the only ones available for the purpose* and, so far as they go, they must be said to fail to disprove the null hypothesis. Hence, I cannot see how it is possible to take issue with my conclusion: "The figures fail to support the hypothesis that psychotherapy facilitates

recovery from neurotic disorder." This statement I take to be, in essence, identical with Rosenzweig's statement that "broad generalizations as to the effectiveness of treatment are to be avoided."

What I cannot understand, however, is Rosenzweig's insistence that I "generalize freely," "lightly dismiss" sources of difficulty, and indulge in "hasty generalization." Perhaps he has failed to read the last sentence of my summary in which, having pointed out that available figures do not disprove the null hypothesis, I go on to say: "In view of the many difficulties attending such actuarial comparisons, no further conclusions could be derived from the data whose shortcomings highlight the necessity of properly planned and executed experimental studies into this important field." I thus only make two claims: (a) that available data have serious shortcomings, and (b) that as far as they go, these data do not support the theory of psychotherapeutic effectiveness. As Rosenzweig himself explicitly agrees with both these statements, it is difficult to see precisely what it is that he is criticizing.

The only possibility left is that he disagrees with some of the subjective judgments which, as I explicitly pointed out in my paper, I had to make in order to summarize the data. It would be fruitless to discuss points of disagreement in detail; I can only suggest to anyone interested in the issue that he should go through all the papers quoted, making his own subjective judgments as to what is or is not to be included in the terms "neurosis," "psychotherapy," and "improvement." I think it will be found that no possible combination of criteria will yield results showing psychotherapy to be therapeutically effective. When it is realized that these data, poor as they are, are all the evidence available regarding a method of therapy which has been practiced for more than 50 years on hundreds of thousands of patients, then it will, I think, be agreed that the failure of the data to show any degree of therapeutic effectiveness should act as a spur to ensure the initiation of large-scale, properly planned, rigidly controlled, and thoroughly analyzed experimental studies in this important field. I feel that on this point, just as much as on the others, Rosenzweig and I are in complete agreement.

References

1. Eysenck, H. J. The effects of psychotherapy: an evaluation. *J. Consult. Psychol.,* **16** (1952), 319–324.
2. Landis, C. A statistical evaluation of psychotherapeutic methods. In L. E. Hinsie, ed., *Concepts and problems of psychotherapy.* New York: Columbia Univ. Press, 1937.
3. Rosenzweig, S. A transvaluation of psychotherapy—a reply to Hans Eysenck. *J. Abnorm. Soc. Psychol.,* **49**(1954), 298–304.

Calumet

SAUL ROSENZWEIG
DEPARTMENTS OF PSYCHOLOGY AND NEUROPSYCHIATRY
WASHINGTON UNIVERSITY, ST. LOUIS, MISSOURI

If I had "a quite erroneous impression" of Eysenck's main conclusions, it is my further impression that I was not alone in this reaction to his paper. The implicit tone as well as the explicit statement work together in the process of communication. But it is good to see that Eysenck has troubled to correct the false impression his paper created. It is particularly gratifying that he reiterates the subjective basis of the judgments he found it necessary to make in summarizing the literature. Since he insists that we are in agreement—calumet!

Reprinted from the *Journal of Abnormal & Social Psychology,* **50**(1955), 148, with the permission of The American Psychological Association and the author.

Measurement of Personality and Behavior Changes Following Psychotherapy*

MELVIN ZAX AND ARMIN KLEIN

UNIVERSITY OF ROCHESTER AND RESIDENTIAL TREATMENT CENTER AND
UNIVERSITY OF ROCHESTER, RESPECTIVELY

In his general review of the area of psychotherapy in 1946, Snyder (51) expressed optimism and foresaw that this field was at least in the early stages of becoming a science. He saw as a "commendable trend" the fact that the scientific approach was being more widely used in the study of all methods of therapy and pointed out that the measurement of outcome was undergoing objectification. Since the time of that paper at least 400 studies have been published in which some effort was made to evaluate the effects of psychotherapy. Despite this extensive research activity, there are some (15) who have questioned whether anyone has adequately demonstrated that psychotherapy is effective.

Evaluatory research in psychotherapy is a most complex activity but an extremely important one if we are to understand more about the nature of what can bring about personality change. The practical and theoretical problems involved in acquiring Ss, developing meaningful controls, and making measure-

ments are enormous. Add to these the question of what one should measure, that is, what criterion should be used, and the complexity is increased many times over.

It is the purpose of this paper to summarize and evaluate some of the approaches which have been used to deal with the problem of the criterion. This is based largely on an exhaustive survey of the many experiments, proposals for experiments, theoretical papers, and some reports of case studies involving the evaluation of individual or group psychotherapy which have appeared in the major American psychological and psychiatric journals between 1946 and 1959 (60). In this context Snyder's (51) definition of psychotherapy has been adopted which rules out studies devoted to educational procedures and guidance activities emphasizing the giving of information, as well as social activities, occupational therapy, shock therapy, chemotherapy, etc.

The present review is divided into two major sections devoted to (a) criteria based on client behavior in the therapy situation or his personal report and (b) criteria based on the client's behavior outside of the therapy situation. The studies cited in this paper are selected as being illustrative of these two

Reprinted from the *Psychological Bulletin,* **57** (1960), 435–448, with the permission of The American Psychological Association and the authors.

* The authors are grateful to E. L. Cowen of the University of Rochester for reading the manuscript and offering many pertinent criticisms and suggestions.

435

approaches. Phenomenological measures and indices of client behavior within the therapy situation have been used in some of the major systematic programs for evaluating psychotherapy (44, 52). Measures of extratherapeutic behavior represent logically a most important yardstick. In addition to these two major approaches, psychological tests have also found frequent use as criteria, but, because of space limitations, it was felt that they might better be reviewed separately.

Intratherapeutic Behavior and Phenomenological Criteria

Criteria based on *S*'s self-experience and his behavior within the therapy situation have stemmed largely from the work of the client-centered group who have actively studied their treatment approach. In their research program, they have developed a few instruments which were directly intended to serve as outcome criteria and several indices which have important implications for outcome.

Seeman (47) constructed a measure which has found considerable use both as a criterion of therapeutic outcome and as a validating instrument for other indices (44). It consists of 10 nine-point scales, several of which required the counselor to evaluate some aspect of the client's experience. This instrument was applied to 23 therapy cases, and it was found that for all items but one there was significant change in the direction of improvement from the beginning to the end of treatment. Also, correlations between ratings on individual items and an item which referred simply to success of outcome revealed that when a client was judged to be successfully treated he was rated highly on scales measuring the extent to which he used therapy as an emotional experience, used it for personal rather than situational exploration, liked and respected his therapist, moved in the direction of both personal integra-

tion and situational adjustment, and was satisfied with the outcome of therapy. While this appears as a validation of the instrument it seems likely that the changes measured by many of these individual scales are implicit dimensions of the global judgment of success to which it was compared.

The other instrument which has been used as a criterion in a number of studies (52) was developed by Tucker (56) who termed it the "multiple criterion." This involved a Client Post Therapy Scale which was essentially a self-assessment device in which the client was asked to rate his feelings toward such things as the possibility of having problems in the future, the status of the problem which brought him to treatment, relationship with immediate family, sexual adjustment, relationship to others, etc. Another measure as part of the criterion was the Counselor Post Therapy Check List which involved 29 items referring to the client's behavior during therapy and was based on a careful review of therapy notes and interview recordings. This check list was filled out by both the therapist and in each case by one other of a group of trained raters who also used transcribed interview material. Finally, the first and last interviews in each case were analyzed as to the number of positive and negative emotional statements made by the client and an index derived by dividing number of negative statements by the sum of negative and positive ones.

The client's self-report which was an integral part of Tucker's "multiple criterion" has been used as the sole criterion at times and represents the most direct phenomenological measure of therapy outcome. Investigations using such measures have ranged from those employing elaborate rating devices, with some effort at standardizing the procedure, to ratings based on relatively unstandardized interviews in which the *S* is asked to describe his present state or changes which may have occurred as the result of therapy. Fiedler's study (16) serves as an example of the former. He had Ss fill out a 10-item self-rating scale with each item scaled from 0 to 12. The items referred to emotional tensions related to the stress of taking academic examinations and to changes as the result of psychotherapy.

In studies using less systematic self-evaluative techniques, like that of Lipkin (30), general questions have been asked such as, "What seemed to go on during your visits here?" "How do things look to you now?" Responses were evaluated subjectively and the clients' descriptions of their experience in therapy and its effect on them were seen to confirm the expectations of Rogerian theory.

Cowen and Combs (9) used a third approach for eliciting the clients' evaluation of therapeutic progress. They conducted open-ended follow-up interviews which were recorded and evaluated by three judges as being "successful, progress, or failure" cases.

Other instruments have been developed which elicit self-descriptions from the client. While such descriptions have not been a direct evaluation of the therapy experience itself, they have implications for the effects of therapy and have been used as outcome measures. In one study, Butler and Haigh (3) used a Q sort involving 100 self-referent statements which had been randomly selected from available therapy protocols. Ss were required to sort these to describe themselves as they were at the time on a "like-me" to "unlike-me" continuum. They were further asked to make sortings which would describe their own ideal on a "like-ideal" to "unlike-ideal" continuum. The investigators reported significant increases in the correlation between self and ideal sorts of clients who underwent therapy despite the fact that the same clients failed to show such changes on the same sorts made before

and after a waiting period prior to the beginning of therapy. A no-therapy control group also failed to demonstrate such changes. Cartwright (4) found a significant relationship between success in treatment as rated by the therapist and an increased consistency in the sorting of the Butler-Haigh items when three self-sorts were made each using different people as interacting reference points.

Rosenthal (45) constructed a Morals Value Q-Sort comprising 100 statements which the S sorted into two piles as being relatively more or less descriptive of himself. This was administered to the patients in his sample before and after treatment and the therapists involved also made the sort. His findings were that patients judged as improved tended to revise more values in the direction of those of the therapist than the unimproved.

Dymond (11) selected 74 of the Butler and Haigh items which two non-client-centered psychologists had sorted into two equal piles as being characteristic of the well adjusted on the one hand and of the poorly adjusted on the other. These in turn were given to four other judges who sorted them independently in a similar fashion and a high degree of agreement was found. Ss were then given an adjustment score based on how many of either kind of statement appeared on the "like-me" or "unlike-me" sides of their sortings. She found scores on this Q-adjustment scale, as it was termed, to move toward good adjustment following therapy (11, 12). Cartwright and Roth (5) found the correlation of a client's self and ideal sorts to be related to the Q-adjustment sort and the client's self-rating on the Willoughby Emotional Maturity scale. Although Dymond (11) had not found differences in the Q-adjustment scores after a two-month interval during which her Ss were waiting to enter therapy and ultimately did, Grummon (21) did find significant changes in this type of score among Ss who requested treatment but then decided against it when it was available. In this case a two-month interval had also elapsed between tests. Dymond (13) reexamined the Q sorts of Grummon's Ss and concluded that

. . . although positive adjustment changes appear to take place in maladjusted persons in the absence of psychotherapy, these are not identical with the changes which occur in equally maladjusted persons who complete therapy (p. 107).

She denied that any "deep" reorganization takes place and saw the improvement as characterized by "a strengthening of neurotic defenses and a denial of the need for help."

A number of studies of personality change as seen in the therapeutic interaction have implications for criteria, especially insofar as these changes have often been related to direct evaluations of outcome. Snyder (50), following a pioneer investigation of the therapy process by Porter (38), made the earliest of such studies. He classified client statements into four major categories along the dimension of content significance: descriptions of problems, simple responses asking for advice or accepting or rejecting clarification of feeling, responses showing insight into remedies for a problem, and responses which were unrelated to the principal problem of the client. A second dimension for clients' statements was identified as expressions of feeling and nine categories were set up to classify them. These described attitudes expressed in clients' statements as being positive, negative, or ambivalent with reference to the self, the counselor, or other persons or situations. As a result of his analysis of nearly 10,000 client responses in the 48 interviews he used, Snyder concluded that there was a marked tendency for the client's feelings to change in affective tone from negative to positive. Further he noted that in his attitude toward the counselor the pa-

tient was slightly rejecting at first, and indifferent during most of the treatment; but in the last interview or so, there was a marked increase in positive attitudes. He also interpreted his findings as indicating that "clients approaching the end of treatment show an excellent amount of insight into the nature of their problem."

In another of the early studies of personality change with psychotherapy, Raimy (39) was concerned with changes in self-concept. He analyzed client responses in a set of 14 cases by classifying statements into six categories. These involved self-references which were positive, negative, ambivalent, and ambiguous; statements which did not involve self-references; and nonrhetorical questions. He found that in cases considered successfully treated on the basis of the judgments of the counselor, the supervisor of most of the cases, and Raimy himself, the client went from a preponderance of negative and ambivalent self-references to a preponderance of positive self-references. This was taken to support the hypothesis that in successful therapy a positive change in self-concept took place.

Several measures of client experience were developed in a series of studies of the process of psychotherapy in a single sample of 10 cases at the University of Chicago. Changes in the clients' experience reflected by these measures were found by Raskin (40) to be associated with success in therapy as judged by the counselor. Thus, in the more successful cases clients showed an increase in acceptance of, and respect for, self as measured by a scale developed by Sheerer (49); an increase in positive and objective attitudes directed toward the self as measured by a scale developed by Stock (53); a tendency toward more mature behavior as judged from the client's own verbalizations in therapy (24); and a decrease in defensiveness as measured by Haigh (22).

In a later study of his own, Raskin developed a four-step scale, illustrated at each point by three examples of client statements, on the basis of which judges estimated whether the client, in what he said, was being governed largely by the expectations of others or by his own values and standards. Ratings on this "locus of evaluation" scale were found to correlate significantly with therapists' ratings as to the success of treatment and with the five parallel interview measures described in the previous study, but not with rated change on the Rorschach.

In a later study of the changes in personality in successful psychotherapy, seen phenomenologically, Vargas (57) measured self-awareness in three ways and related increase on his measures to a number of criteria of outcome. He summarized his findings by saying:

The conclusion which seems to follow from these observations is that the hypothesis—increasing self-awareness during therapy correlated with success in therapy—is confirmed when success is measured by instruments which rate highly those changes and states deducible from client centered theory (p. 165).

It should be noted that nearly all of these studies relating personality change in psychotherapy to judgments of the general outcome of treatment involve a certain circularity. In nearly all cases the judgment as to outcome was made by people holding theoretical viewpoints similar to those of the researchers who developed the scales for measuring change. It is, therefore, likely that the two measures were not completely independent.

A few measures of changes in clients' verbal behavior within the therapy interaction have been developed outside of the client-centered framework. One of these was the Discomfort Relief Quotient (henceforth referred to as DRQ) which was first proposed by Dollard and Mowrer (10). This measure classifies words, clauses, or sentences as to whether they signify discomfort, relief from discomfort, or a neutrality of emotion. To arrive at the quotient the number of discomfort words, clauses, or sentences are divided by this same number plus the number of relief words, phrases or clauses. Thus, the quotient may vary from zero to one, with scores nearer zero representing a preponderance of expressions of relief and those approaching one indicating considerable expression of discomfort. Dollard and Mowrer made no claim that the DRQ measured "success" in treatment. To do this they felt that it must first be related to a reliable measure of "real life success."

Several attempts have been made to validate the DRQ as a measure of success in therapy. Hunt (25, 26) applied it in a social casework setting and found that changes in DRQ failed to correlate significantly with judgments of improvement made by case workers. Other studies (1, 6, 36) reported analyses of the published protocols of cases presented by the therapist as successful, with two finding the predicted change and the third finding no relationship.

Kauffman and Raimy (29) derived a related measure from Raimy's self-concept categories (described above). It consisted of the number of negative self-references plus the number of ambivalent self-references divided by the number of negative self-references plus the number of ambivalent self-references plus the number of positive self-references (more conveniently termed the PNAvQ). Using this quotient, they analyzed 17 verbatim interviews and compared their analysis with an analysis of the same protocols using the DRQ. They concluded that both methods traced changes from maladjustment to adjustment in a similar fashion. They also noted that PNAvQ judgments were obtained in about one-third the time required for DRQ judgments.

Another study of the nature of personality change was recently reported by

Berg (2). He analyzed an eight-interview protocol of a case published by Rogers as successful and proposed that early in treatment, clients are preoccupied with self and move in the direction of a more empathic concern for others. He made a frequency count of "ego" words (I, me, my, myself, mine), "empathic" words (we, our, they, us, you, your), "negative" words and "expletive-bombastic sounds" at various points in treatment. It was found that empathic words did indeed increase while ego, negative, and expletive-bombastic expressions decreased with succeeding interviews.

Most recently, Rogers (43) has developed and given a preliminary report on a scale of process levels in psychotherapy which bears considerable significance for the measurement of the effects of successful psychotherapy. Again, his goal was a further understanding of the nature of change in personality from a theoretical framework rather than measurement of outcome. He conceived that clients move "not from fixity or homeostasis through change to a new fixity . . . but much the more significant continuum is from fixity to changingness. . . ." He hypothesized that the nature of clients' immediate relationship to their feelings at any point in the therapeutic interaction might indicate their position on a seven-stage continuum.

Behavioral Criteria

In many instances, studies of the results of psychotherapy have used criteria which depend on an evaluation of the way the patient actually behaves without inference as to its personal meaning for him. Such indices were generally developed directly as criteria for use in a given situation and were not related to a theoretical framework about personality change.

Of the many studies which have used behavioral criteria, certain ones have been particularly noteworthy in that they dealt with crucial aspects of behavior which can be objectively established. The simplest of such criteria focused on relatively circumscribed individual behaviors which were seen to be central to the person's difficulty in living. The more complex criteria attempted to assess wide, more representative areas of functioning through the use of elaborate rating scales.

A study by Friedman (18) is typical of those employing criteria emphasizing delimited behaviors which are central to the person's difficulty in living. His Ss were 50 patients complaining of a "phobia of travel," which can be objectively measured. Evaluation was based on their ability to travel after treatment and it was found that 12 patients were unimproved, 15 showed some improvement, and 23 were completely recovered. Another example of a study utilizing a single symptom which bore implications for a much wider range of behavior was that of Teuber and Powers (54). They simply totaled the number of court appearances among a large group of potential juvenile delinquents who had received treatment and made comparisons with a matched control group which had received no treatment. No significant differences were found between groups on this measure.

A variation in the use of an important individual behavior as a criterion was introduced by Thetford (55) who derived an autonomic measure of frustration tolerance. This study stands out in that the behavior which was measured was not a specific complaint but depended on the theoretical consideration that therapy should reduce anxiety and tension so that the manner in which one responds to stress as reflected in the autonomic nervous system should be altered. He developed a "Recovery Quotient" based on various Galvanic Skin Response measures and found significant changes as the result of psychotherapy which indicated the development of a higher frustration threshold.

The criterion used by Pascal and Zax (37) likewise involved objective behavioral measures, but these varied with the individual patient, reflecting presenting complaints. These complaints were evaluated for 30 cases which had undergone various types of treatment. In 28 of these, changes in the predicted direction were found.

Institutional settings have made it possible to study wider samples of behavior objectively. In such settings Cowden, Zax, Hague and Finney (7); Fox (17); and Ludwig and Ranson (32) have used multiple but individually significant behaviors as their criteria. Cowden et al. (7) considered the number of times hospitalized patients required neutral wet packs, electroconvulsive maintenance shock, or engaged in fights, in addition to such indications of improvement as transfer to a ward requiring a higher level of integration or discharge from the hospital. They concluded that patients who received group psychotherapy in addition to tranquillizing drugs showed more improvement than various control groups. To evaluate the effects of counseling programs in a prison, Fox (17) used such behavioral criteria as work stability, school stability, financial budgeting, reports from chaplain, block officers, and work supervisors, successful discharge from parole, and return to prison as a parole violator; he found counseled groups had significantly higher adjustment scores on such indices than similar uncounseled groups. In a report of results of psychiatric treatment among soldiers, Ludwig and Ranson (32) reported that relatively high percentages of treated patients were able to return to duty stations and that ratings of commanding officers indicated that most of them were able to perform their services adequately.

Many studies have made use of longer and more elaborate rating scales which attempted to assess the extratherapy functioning of the individual on the basis of diverse behavioral observations. One of the older instruments of this type which was used in the evaluation of treatment with children (20, 34) is the Haggerty-Olson-Wickman Behavior Rating Schedules (28). This consists of two separate schedules (A and B) the first of which (A) lists 15 problems such as cheating, lying, defiance of discipline, speech difficulties, sex offenses, obscene notes, talk, or pictures, etc. Raters checked in one of four columns according to the frequency of occurrence of each for a given individual. Standardized weights were assigned according to the frequency and seriousness of a given problem. The other schedule (B) comprised a series of 35 graphic five-point rating scales covering traits which may be classified according to intellectual, physical, social, and emotional traits. On the basis of ratings made before and after group therapy with juvenile delinquents, Gersten (20) reported progress in emotional security and social maturity among his subjects. Mehlman (34), who used the scale to rate mentally retarded children before and after group therapy, found significant increases in adjustment at the time of the second rating.

Of the many devices which have been used to evaluate change in hospitalized patients, perhaps the most promising and certainly the most searching are the Palo Alto Hospital Adjustment Scale (33) and the Lorr Multidimensional Scale (31). The Palo Alto scale consists of 90 descriptive statements applicable to psychiatric patients. Examples of these statements are, "the patient ignores the activities around him" or "the patient's talk is mostly not sensible." Each one is marked as true, not true, or does not apply, for a particular patient and is keyed in such a manner that a general hospital adjustment score can be obtained. The scale was designed to be filled out at intervals by ward personnel who are familiar with the patient's behavior. On this measure, schizophrenics were seen to improve with group psychotherapy (48). In another study (58) items from this scale were combined with others suggested by personnel in an institution for defective children, and by this index group therapy was found to be effective.

The Lorr scale consists of 62 brief rating scales which are directed toward observable or inferable patient behavior. Many of the items refer to relatively objective behaviors concerning which judgments should be quite reliable, such as bizarre postures, speech peculiarities, orientation, eating, sleeping, assaultiveness. On the other hand many other items refer to aspects of behavior which are probably less reliably rated such as emotional responsiveness, attitude toward himself, suspiciousness, recurrence of useless thoughts, etc. The use of this scale was reported in a study with long-term schizophrenic patients who were seen by this measure to have improved significantly more than a control group (19).

The scales used to evaluate out-patients have as a rule been more difficult to apply and often have been more complex. This is due to the obvious fact that the behavior of the nonhospitalized patient is less limited by the structured aspects of institutional life so that he functions in a much wider range. Observation is thereby also made more difficult. Hunt (25, 26) has attempted to measure "movement" in social casework by developing a criterion to evaluate the DRQ. Movement was defined as "the change which appears in an individual client and/or his environmental situation between the opening and closing of his case" (26, p. 76). His scale was set up in seven steps ranging from minus two, through zero, to plus four with anchoring illustrations at each of

these three points. It was found that experienced workers could use the scale reliably, but no relationship was found between movement and DRQ changes in the course of therapy.

The Willoughby Emotional Maturity Scale (59) has been used by Rogers (42) to evaluate changes in psychotherapy. It consists of 60 statements descriptive of varying levels of maturity of functioning. The levels had been determined by 100 clinicians who sorted a large number of statements along a nine-step continuum. The 60 items selected for the scale were representative of the nine levels of maturity and were ones on which there was high agreement among judges. In Rogers' study, each client was rated by himself and two personal friends whom he designated. Although intra-rater reliability was high, interrater reliabilities were all low. Conceivably, this scale might have higher reliability in the hands of trained observers although this might limit its use to a somewhat standardized setting such as a dormitory or school setting.

Miles, Barrabee, and Finesinger (35) developed a series of five-point scales covering the general areas of (a) symptoms; (b) social adjustment including functioning in the areas of occupation, marriage, interpersonal relations, and sex; (c) insight; and (d) life situation since hospitalization. As a group, the scales were comprehensive and individual steps were well described. On the basis of these instruments, overall evaluations were made of patients and summarized in the categories "apparently recovered, much improved, improved, slightly improved, unimproved, and worse." In using this measure to assess a group of 62 cases two years after treatment, they found that 58 per cent had improved in varying degrees while 42 per cent were unchanged. Imber, Frank, Nash, Stone, and Gliedman (27) derived a Social Ineffectiveness score on the basis of a series of six-point scales which applied to each of 15 behavioral categories concerning the patient's relationships with the significant individuals in his life (spouse, sibs, children, parents, boss, etc.). Some of the categories were overly independent, withdrawn, superficially sociable, extrapunitive, officious, impulsive, etc. Using this scale they investigated the relationship between improvement and amount of therapeutic contact, and they found less improvement for patients with restricted therapy contacts than for those with more frequent ones.

Raush, Dittman, and Taylor (41) have made a recent contribution to the methodology of making observations and developing behavioral criteria to assess change with treatment. Working in a residential treatment setting for children, they standardized their observations of six male *S*s and systematically studied samples of their behavior in a variety of settings including mealtimes, play periods, and an arts-and-crafts period. One set of observations was made early in the children's stay at the center and another 18 months later focusing on interpersonal behavior at these two points in time. Objective observations were recorded and later rated on a scale based on two polar coordinates: love (affiliate, act friendly) to hate (attack, act unfriendly) and dominate (command, high status action) to submit (obey, low status action). More striking changes were found in the relationships of these children to adults than in their relationships to their peers.

Discussion

As is the case with any measure of personality, a criterion for evaluating the effects of psychotherapy must satisfy the requirements of reliability and validity. The latter usually poses the more serious problem in that no absolute state of complete validity exists as a standard. In dealing with this problem we generally conclude that a given measure is valid for certain specified purposes and not necessarily valid for others. Therefore, we may have a variety of "valid" measures of the outcome of psychotherapy. The judgment of whether these are useful measures, however, must be based upon our evaluation of the purposes for which they are valid. The criteria which have been reviewed will be considered in the light of such issues.

Perhaps the simplest and most direct means of assessing a client's progress in treatment is to ask him to evaluate his own status. Such a phenomenological approach has often been used. Unfortunately, on close analysis, this deceptively simple procedure is seen to be fraught with serious pitfalls. Standards for such assessments will vary both among clients and between client and researcher; clients will vary in the extent to which they can report what they feel; the reports of many clients will be subject to various unconscious distortions; finally, the client's evaluation of his condition may be affected by conscious or semiconscious motives. In positing the "hello-goodbye" effect, Hathaway (23) has warned of the subtle social influences which limit the reliability of many of the phenomenological measures which have been made. On entering treatment the client is under the conventional pressure to justify his appeal for help so that problems are discussed freely. When seeking to terminate, however, he feels an obligation, out of courtesy toward one who has attempted to help, to express gratitude and satisfaction. A fundamental weakness of the phenomenological approach would, therefore, seem to reside in the difficulty in obtaining reliable assessments. It seems likely that the content of such assessments depends greatly upon who asks for it and the circumstances under which it is requested.

Intratherapy behavior, usually verbal behavior, lends itself to measurement and has been used often as a criterion. In many of the studies reporting the use of such criteria a single theoretical system, that of Rogers, has guided the expectations of researchers. As a result many of these studies relate to each other in a more systematic fashion than is usually the case with outcome studies. The aspects of verbal behavior which have been studied by the client-centered group have usually been carefully defined and found to be reliably measured. Designed to explore personality changes during psychotherapy rather than to be evaluators of psychotherapy, their significance for outcome measures is mostly by implication for they remain unvalidated, not yet having been compared to an independent criterion. Used for the purpose of exploring changes, they were compared in the published studies only to a judgmental criterion of the therapist who shared the same theoretical point of view as the researcher and whose global judgment could have included the concept under study.

Those intratherapy criteria which have not stemmed from the work of the client-centered group have found relatively infrequent use and the one attempt to relate change in DRQ to an independent, external criterion (25, 26) resulted in an insignificant correlation.

The most serious failing at this time in the use of phenomenological measures and measures of intratherapy behavior as criteria of outcome is that neither has yet been related to everyday, externally observable behaviors in the life space of the Ss. Unless phenomenological changes and changes in verbal behavior in therapy can be related to concomitant behavioral changes in the family and the community their significance remains unclear.

External measures of clients' behavior stand out as potential criteria having validity for purposes which are extremely important. However, when one attempts

to use such criteria he is beset by a host of measurement problems which are much more difficult to resolve than is the case with phenomenological and intratherapy indices. The central problem here is the development of criteria of sufficient breadth that they are meaningful and representative of a wide range of functioning and yet, at the same time, circumscribed enough to be measured with reliability.

The present review would seem to indicate that the development of such criteria is in the stage of infancy. Many workers have been able to reliably observe narrow aspects of functioning which had implications for a wider range of behavior. In such cases, however, the possibility remains that one circumscribed symptom was abandoned in favor of another which was equally or even more disabling. The assessment of broader areas of functioning has been carried on primarily within the confines of institutional settings where the patients' range of functioning is limited. Perhaps the most glaring weakness in the way such criteria have been developed and applied is that there has been no unifying set of principles to guide observations. Consequently, the results which have been reported are fragmented. We are told of a variety of behavioral changes which take place as the result of therapy but very few of these appear in any one study and even fewer are observed in more than one study. It would seem that the present need is for the development of a theory or even a set of loose hypothetical notions about "normal" behavior to guide our observations and systematize our thinking.

It seems likely that one of the obstacles to the development of such a theory has been the reluctance of many psychologists to become embroiled in the philosophical issues of the desirability of different behaviors. Actually, the problem of making value judgments when one conducts research cannot be avoided. The very selection of the phenomena which will be observed and measured is in itself a judgment depending upon the values one holds. Indeed then, the further development of criteria for evaluating the effects of psychotherapy awaits the clarification, resolving, and communication of the values we hold.

One approach to the development of a systematic set of values which may clarify our thinking about what behavior is generally considered "psychologically desirable" would be to formalize the notion of the client's relationship to social norms which was discussed by Pascal and Zax (37). Their concern was with the behaviors on the part of the person presenting himself for treatment which were notably deviant from expected social norms (i.e., overt homosexual acts, frequent crying spells, few friends) and the extent to which such behaviors were changed. Other writers have suggested that the clinician does generally function with a concern for such social norms. As the result of his work in the area of personality assessment, Edwards (14) has suggested that the notions of the clinician about what constitutes disturbance in patients may correspond essentially to an operational definition of what is socially undesirable. Cowen (8) who was investigating the social desirability variable in personality assessment actually provided data which lend support to this idea. He found a correlation of $-.917$ between the published ratings of a group of clinicians on 77-trait descriptive terms scaled for abnormality and the social desirability ratings of the same terms by 67 undergraduate students of psychology.

This approach suggests that the person considered most psychologically handicapped is the one who is unable to function in the way in which it is expected that he should in his social group. Furthermore, it suggests that

phenomenological reports of how one feels are characteristically considered in the light of such evidence about how he functions in the same way that the felt experience of physical comfort or discomfort is evaluated on the basis of various measures of bodily function.

While this approach, which is probably implicit in the thinking and functioning of most clinicians, may provide a useful beginning to the development of criteria of what therapy should accomplish, it is unlikely that any single set of norms would apply to all. In essence, we are proposing that there are, contentwise, many "normal" or "healthy" personalities. That which is common to each is the ability to function in relation to the norms of his particular social setting. The uniqueness of each individual's social setting makes this a complex area of study and is undoubtedly discouraging. It may well develop, however, that what people have in common is important enough to permit the development of a relatively limited number of norms reflecting basic interpersonal environments which can be useful. At any rate, it would seem that what is now needed is a series of broad normative studies of a personal-social psychological nature. In addition to providing norms which can be used as a foundation for behavioral criteria of "normality," they would provide a basis for determining just which dimensions of social group membership have significance for actual functioning. The availability of a criterion based on such indices would also provide a context in which to evaluate the significance of changes in the experiencing of Ss, either reported directly or reflected in their intratherapy verbal behavior. Ultimately, a combined measure of related changes in observed behavior and experiencing might facilitate a common, communicative frame of reference among workers of different orientations and be a basis for delineation of dimensions of personality change.

References

1. Assum, A. L., and Levy, S. J. Analysis of a nondirective case with followup interview. *J. Abnorm. Soc. Psychol.,* 43(1948), 78–89.

2. Berg, I. A. Word choice in the interview and personal adjustment. *J. Counsel. Psychol.,* 5(1958), 130–135.

3. Butler, J. M., and Haigh, G. V. Changes in the relation between self concepts and ideal concepts consequent upon client-centered counseling. In C. R. Rogers and R. F. Dymond, eds., *Psychotherapy and personality change.* Chicago, Ill.: Univ. Chicago Press, 1954.

4. Cartwright, D. S., and Roth, I. Success and satisfaction in psychotherapy. *J. Clin. Psychol.,* 13(1957), 20–26.

5. Cartwright, Rosalind D. Effects of psychotherapy on self consistency. *J. Counsel. Psychol.,* 4(1957), 15–22.

6. Cofer, C. N., and Chance, June. The discomfort-relief quotient in published cases of counseling and psychotherapy. *J. Psychol.,* 29 (1950), 219–224.

7. Cowden, R. C., Zax, M., Hague, J. R., and Finney, R. C. Chlorpromazine: Alone and as an adjunct to group psychotherapy in the treatment of psychiatric patients. *Amer. J. Psychiat.,* 112(1956), 898–902.

8. Cowen, E. L. The social desirability of trait descriptive terms: Preliminary norms and sex differences. *J. Soc. Psychol.,* 53(1961), 225–233.

9. ——— and Combs, A. W. Follow-up study of 32 cases treated by nondirective psychotherapy. *J. Abnorm. Soc. Psychol.,* 45(1950), 232–258.

10. Dollard, J., and Mowrer, O. H. A method of measuring tension in written documents. In O. H. Mowrer, ed., *Psychotherapy theory and research.* New York: Ronald, 1953.

11. Dymond, Rosalind F. An adjustment score for Q sorts. *J. Consult. Psychol.,* 17(1953), 339–342.

12. ——— Adjustment changes over therapy from self-sorts. In C. R. Rogers and R. F. Dymond, eds., *Psychotherapy and personality change.* Chicago, Ill.: Univ. Chicago Press, 1954.

13. ——— Adjustment changes in the absence of psychotherapy. *J. Consult. Psychol.,* 19 (1955), 103–107.

14. Edwards, A. E. *The social desirability variable in personality assessment and research.* New York: Dryden, 1957.

15. Eysenck, H. J. The effects of psychotherapy: An evaluation. *J. Consult. Psychol.,* 16 (1952), 319–324.

16. Fiedler, F. E. An experimental approach to preventive psychotherapy. *J. Abnorm. Soc. Psychol.,* 44(1949), 386–393.

17. Fox, V. The effects of counseling on adjustment in prison. *Soc. Forces,* 32(1954), 285–289.

18. Friedman, J. H. Short-term psychotherapy of "phobia of travel." *Amer. J. Psychother.,* 4(1950), 259–278.

19. Funk, I. C., Shatin, L., Freed, E. X., and Rockmore, L. Somato-psychotherapeutic approach to long-term schizophrenic patients. *J. Nerv. Ment. Dis.,* 121(1955), 423–437.

20. Gersten, C. An experimental evaluation of group therapy with juvenile delinquents. *Int. J. Group Psychother.,* 1(1951), 311–318.

21. Grummon, D. L. Personality change as a function of time in persons motivated for therapy. In C. R. Rogers and Rosalind F. Dymond, eds., *Psychotherapy and personality change.* Chicago, Ill.: Univ. Chicago Press, 1954.

22. Haigh, G. Defensive behavior in client-centered therapy. *J. Consult. Psychol.,* 13(1949), 181–189.

23. Hathaway, S. R. Some considerations relative to nondirective psychotherapy as counseling. *J. Clin. Psychol.,* 4(1948), 226–231.

24. Hoffman, A. E. A study of reported behavioral changes in counseling. *J. Consult. Psychol.,* 13(1949), 190–195.

25. Hunt, J. McV. The problem of measuring the results of psychotherapy. *Psychol. Serv. Cent. J.,* 1(1949), 122–135. (a)

26. ——— A social agency as the setting for research. *J. Consult. Psychol.,* 13(1949), 68–91. (b)

27. Imber, S. D., Frank, J. D., Nash, E. H., Stone, A. R., and Gliedman, K. H. Improvement and amount of therapeutic contact: An alternative to the use of no-treatment controls in psychotherapy. *J. Consult. Psychol.,* 21(1957), 309–315.

28. Jones, H. E. Haggerty-Olson-Wickman Behavior Rating Schedules. In O. K. Buros, ed., *The 1940 mental measurements yearbook.* Highland Park, N.J.: Mental Measurements Yearbook, 1941. Pages 1222–1223.

29. Kauffman, P. E., and Raimy, V. C. Two methods of assessing therapeutic progress. *J. Abnorm. Soc. Psychol.,* 44(1949), 379–385.

30. Lipkin, S. The client evaluates nondirective psychotherapy. *J. Consult. Psychol.,* 12 (1948), 137–146.

31. Lorr, M. Multidimensional scale for rating psychiatric patients. *VA Tech. Bull.,* TB 10-507 (1953), 1–44.

32. Ludwig, A. O., and Ranson, S. W. A statistical follow-up of effectiveness of treatment of combat-induced psychiatric casualties: I. Returns to full combat duty. *Milit. Surg.,* 100 (1947), 51–62.

33. McReynolds, P., and Ferguson, J. T.

Clinical manual for the Hospital Adjustment Scale. Stanford, Calif.: Stanford Univ. Press, 1953.

34. Mehlman, B. Group therapy with mentally retarded children. *J. Abnorm. Soc. Psychol.,* 48(1953), 53–60.

35. Miles, H. W., Barrabee, Edna L., and Finesinger, J. E. Evaluation of psychotherapy. *Psychosom. Med.,* 13(1951), 83–105.

36. Murray, E. J., Auld, F., Jr., and White, Alice M. A psychotherapy case showing progress but no decrease in the discomfort-relief quotient. *J. Consult. Psychol.,* 18(1954), 349–353.

37. Pascal, G. R., and Zax, M. Psychotherapeutics: Success or failure. *J. Consult. Psychol.,* 20(1956), 325–331.

38. Porter, E. H., Jr. The development and evaluation of a measure of counseling interview procedures: II. The evaluation. *Educ. Psychol. Measmt.,* 3(1943), 215–238.

39. Raimy, V. C. Self reference in counseling interviews. *J. Consult. Psychol.,* 12(1948), 153–163.

40. Raskin, N. J. An analysis of six parallel studies of the therapeutic process. *J. Consult. Psychol.,* 13(1949), 206–221.

41. Raush, H. L., Dittman, A. T., and Taylor, T. J. The interpersonal behavior of children in residential treatment. *J. Abnorm. Soc. Psychol.,* 58(1959), 9–26.

42. Rogers, C. R. Changes in the maturity of behavior as related to therapy. In C. R. Rogers and Rosalind F. Dymond, eds., *Psychotherapy and personality change.* Chicago, Ill.: Univ. Chicago Press, 1954.

43. ——— A process conception of psychotherapy. *Amer. Psychologist,* 4(1958), 142–149.

44. ——— and Dymond, Rosalind F., eds. *Psychotherapy and personality change.* Chicago, Ill.: Univ. Chicago Press, 1954.

45. Rosenthal, D. Changes in some moral values following psychotherapy. *J. Consult. Psychol.,* 19(1955), 431–436.

46. Seeman, J. A study of the process of nondirective therapy. *J. Consult. Psychol.,* 13(1949), 157–169.

47. ——— Counselor judgments of therapeutic process and outcome. In C. R. Rogers and R. F. Dymond, eds., *Psychotherapy and personality change.* Chicago, Ill.: Univ. Chicago Press, 1954.

48. Semon, R. G., and Goldstein, N. The effectiveness of group psychotherapy with chronic schizophrenic patients and an evaluation of different therapeutic methods. *J. Consult. Psychol.,* 21(1957), 317–322.

49. Sheerer, Elizabeth T. The relationship between acceptance of self and acceptance of others. *J. Consult. Psychol.,* 13(1949), 169–175.

50. Snyder, W. U. An investigation of the nature of nondirective psychotherapy. *J. Gen. Psychol.,* 33(1945), 193–223.

51. ——— The present status of psychotherapeutic counseling. *Psychol. Bull.,* 44(1947), 297–386.

52. ——— *Group report of a program of research in psychotherapy.* State College, Pa.: Pennsylvania State Coll., 1953.

53. Stock, Dorothy. The self concept and feeling toward others. *J. Consult. Psychol.,* 13 (1949), 176–180.

54. Teuber, H. L., and Powers, E. Evaluating therapy in a delinquency prevention program. *Res. Publ. Ass. Nerv. Ment. Dis.,* 31 (1951), 138–147.

55. Thetford, W. N. An objective measurement of frustration tolerance in evaluating psychotherapy. In W. Wolff and J. A. Precker, eds., *Success in psychotherapy.* New York: Grune & Stratton, 1952.

56. Tucker, J. E. Measuring client progress in client-centered therapy. In W. U. Snyder, chmn., *Group report of a program of research in psychotherapy.* State College, Pa.: Pennsylvania State Coll., 1953.

57. Vargas, M. J. Changes in self-awareness during client-centered therapy. In C. R. Rogers and Rosalind F. Dymond, eds., *Psychotherapy and personality change.* Chicago, Ill.: Univ. Chicago Press, 1954.

58. Wilcox, G., and Guthrie, G. Changes in adjustment of institutionalized female defectives following group psychotherapy. *J. Clin. Psychol.,* 13(1957), 9–13.

59. Willoughby, R. R. A scale of emotional maturity. *J. Soc. Psychol.,* 3(1931), 131–136.

60. Zax, M., and Klein, A. The criterion in evaluation studies of psychotherapy. Unpublished manuscript, Univ. of Rochester, 1958.